Fifty Years at the US Environmental Protection Agency

Fifty Years at the US Environmental Protection Agency

Progress, Retrenchment, and Opportunities

Editors
A. James Barnes
John D. Graham
David M. Konisky

ROWMAN & LITTLEFIELD
Lanham • Boulder • New York • London

Published by Rowman & Littlefield
A wholly owned subsidiary of The Rowman & Littlefield Publishing Group, Inc.
4501 Forbes Boulevard, Suite 200, Lanham, Maryland 20706
www.rowman.com

6 Tinworth Street, London SE11 5AL, United Kingdom

British Library Cataloguing in Publication Information Available

Library of Congress Cataloging-in-Publication Data

Names: Barnes, A. James, editor. | Graham, John D. (John David), 1956– editor. | Konisky, David M., editor. | Rowman and Littlefield, Inc.
Title: Fifty years at the U.S. Environmental Protection Agency : progress, retrenchment, and opportunities / edited by A. James Barnes, John D. Graham, and David M. Konisky
Other titles: 50 years at the United States Environmental Protection Agency
Description: Lanham : Rowman & Littlefield Publishers, 2020. | Includes bibliographical references and index. | Summary: "In conjunction with the 50th anniversary of the creation of the Environmental Protection Agency, this book brings together leading scholars and EPA veterans to provide a comprehensive assessment of the agency's key decisions and actions in the various areas of its responsibility. Themes across all chapters include the role of rulemaking, negotiation/compromise, partisan polarization, judicial impacts, relations with the White House and Congress, public opinion, interest group pressures, environmental enforcement, environmental justice, risk assessment, and interagency conflict. As no other book on the market currently discusses EPA with this focus or scope, the authors have set out to provide a comprehensive analysis of the agency's rich 50-year history for academics, students, professional, and the environmental community"— Provided by publisher.
Identifiers: LCCN 2020031162 (print) | LCCN 2020031163 (ebook) | ISBN 9781538147146 (Cloth : acid-free paper) | ISBN 9781538147139 (ePub)
Subjects: LCSH: United States. Environmental Protection Agency. | Environmental protection—United States—History.
Classification: LCC TD171 .F54 2020 (print) | LCC TD171 (ebook) | DDC 363.700973—dc23
LC record available at https://lccn.loc.gov/2020031162
LC ebook record available at https://lccn.loc.gov/2020031163

∞™ The paper used in this publication meets the minimum requirements of American National Standard for Information Sciences—Permanence of Paper for Printed Library Materials, ANSI/NISO Z39.48-1992.

Contents

Preface

The US Environmental Protection Agency (EPA) was established on December 2, 1970, through an executive order signed by President Richard Nixon. Over the course of its fifty years, the agency has both contributed to landmark achievements in environmental protection and suffered many setbacks. The objective of this book is to tell this story, both to celebrate the successes and to identify the unmet challenges.

One of us (John), initially conceived of this book as an opportunity to reflect on the EPA at its 50th anniversary. John invited Jim, his long-time colleague and former dean of the Paul H. O'Neill School of Public and Environmental Affairs at Indiana University, Bloomington, and his colleague David to work as an editorial team to put the book together. We eagerly agreed.

The EPA is a cherished institution for us at "SPEA," as the O'Neill School is commonly known. The "E" in SPEA has been at the heart of the school's mission since its establishment in 1972, and we take great pride in our national and global reputation as a leader in research and training in environmental science and policy. Indeed, SPEA is one of the few public affairs schools that combines education in environmental science with environmental policy. The EPA is also one of the largest employers of SPEA graduate students: seventy of the school's master's degree graduates currently work at the agency and more than fifty other alums have been employed at EPA at some point in their career.

The three of us come to the EPA from different vantage points. Jim first worked at EPA at the time of its creation. Jim served as the chief of staff to EPA's first administrator, Bill Ruckelshaus, and later returned to the agency as its general counsel and deputy administrator. John worked closely with EPA during his time as administrator of the Office of Information and Regulatory Affairs in the Office of Management and Budget during the George

W. Bush administration. David is a political scientist with two decades of experience analyzing EPA policy and programs, in areas ranging from air and water pollution to Superfund and environmental justice. Collectively we share a belief in both the historical and future role of the EPA in leading US efforts to provide environmental protection.

A book of this scope requires making many difficult decisions, including the topics for the chapters. After many conversations, and input from diverse EPA experts and scholars, we decided to organize the book around the agency's primary programmatic responsibilities: air pollution, water pollution, drinking water, solid and hazardous waste, contaminated site remediation, and pesticides and chemicals; as well as key cross-cutting issues: science, economics, politics, and agenda-setting. Although other topics (e.g., international activities, federalism, environmental justice) would have made excellent chapters as well, we did our best to be sure that they were effectively integrated throughout the book.

Our approach in putting together this book was to recruit leading scholars and practitioners of environmental policy, many of whom held positions at the EPA at some point during their careers. We are grateful to Jon Cannon, Penny Fenner-Crisp, Jody Freeman, Bernie Goldstein, Gene Lucero, Dick Morgenstern, Megan Mullin, Bill Pedersen, Jim Salzman, Jonathan Wiener, Marcia Williams, and Terry Yosie for their contributions.

The project also benefitted from the insights, expertise, and guidance of a large number of people who participated in workshops, peer-review sessions, and other conversations over the past three years as this book came together. The list is long, and we are thankful to them all: Pete Andrews, Phil Angell, John Applegate, Kat Bagley, Bill Becker, Karl Bourdeau, Bill Buzbee, Leslie Carothers, Dan Costa, Terry Davies, Devra Lee Davis, David Doniger, Chuck Elkins, Don Elliott, Dan Fiorino, Linda Fisher, Art Fraas, C. Boyden Gray, Lynn Goldman, Jeff Holmstead, Bob Huggett, Tom Jorling, Michael Livermore, Al McGartland, Margo Oge, Bob O'Keefe, Bob Perciasepe, Bob Percival, Kate Probst, Alan Roberson, Sam Sankar, Phil Sharp, Betsy Southerland, and Bob Sussman.

We are also indebted to our Indiana University colleagues and friends who have supported the project both intellectually and administratively. Sarah Mincey was instrumental in helping us design the project, especially in the early stages as our ideas were still coming together. Elizabeth Benson made sure we stayed organized, and did a masterful job copyediting the manuscript, with the able assistance of Susie Van Doren. Nikki Rolf Boyd, Lora New, and Maggie Pearson also provided enormous support for the many meetings we held with authors, peer-reviewers, and other contributors to the project.

At Rowman & Littlefield, we are grateful to Jon Sisk who was an enthusiastic supporter of the project from the start. We would also like to thank Dina Gulak, Benjamin Knapp, and Jessica McCleary for the administrative and editorial support they provided during production.

Finally, we want to note our personal appreciation and gratitude to the more than fourteen thousand people who work at the EPA, and the many more thousands that have served at the agency over its fifty years. Political appointees garner the most attention, but it is the countless employees of the agency—ranging from scientists and engineers to attorneys and economists to financial managers and support staff—that are the most critical for the agency's success. EPA employees are dedicated public servants, and one of the main lessons from this project is that they deserve much of the credit for what the agency has accomplished. We are all indebted to their service.

Editors' Note

As this book was being conceived, we knew that Bill Ruckelshaus, as EPA's first administrator, would be an integral part of the story of the agency's formation in 1970. We also knew that Ruckelshaus had been a continuing influence on the agency, both because of his return as the fifth administrator in 1983 and in his role as an informal advisor to the EPA administrators who succeeded him.

We saw Ruckelshaus as uniquely positioned to write the final chapter of the book, to reflect on the history of EPA from its exhilarating first years to its complicated and contentious present—and to provide a perspective on the challenges of the future and how this EPA might meet them. His untimely death in November 2019 changed all of that.

We asked Philip Angell, who was Ruckelshaus' chief of staff at EPA, and who was working with him to write the final chapter, to provide us a short reflection on Bill Ruckelshaus and EPA.

We dedicate this book to the memory of Bill Ruckelshaus.

—A. James Barnes, John D. Graham, David M. Konisky

The former administrators of the Environmental Protection Agency are, by and large, a collegial group. Each, in his or her administration, has come to quickly realize just how encompassing and difficult the job is—how critical the decisions are that each has to make, and the sweeping impact they can have on the life of the American people and its economy.

Bill Ruckelshaus has been called the "father of EPA." But he was also the agency's constant supporter and an advisor to every single administrator, save the last two appointed by the Trump administration. Each new administrator, most soon after taking office, would reach out to Bill Ruckelshaus.

They wanted his advice and his perspective, which he willingly gave; he was generous with his time to help the agency because he cared deeply about it and its people, of whom he said there were "no finer public servants anywhere in the world."

He was not blind to the problems at EPA; he knew the need to review and reauthorize the landmark statutes that defined EPA's mission, to make them more efficient and effective. What troubled him was the growing politicization of the issue that rendered such reforms unattainable. When EPA took an action required by law that seemed to defy common sense, EPA was hurt, its influence diminished.

Bill Ruckelshaus understood from his first days at EPA the absolute importance of the agency's credibility. In its early days, it meant that EPA would enforce the laws entrusted to it by Congress, that the agency meant business, that the environment was not a passing fad, that government had listened and responded.

He also knew that the true mission of the agency was to protect public health, and that raised the stakes for him and every subsequent administrator. If EPA was charged by law to protect the health of Americans from pollutants in the environment, then the American people had to trust the agency—that the air was safe to breathe, that water was safe to drink, that food was safe to eat. Without that trust, the agency was lost.

The loss of trust in government, Bill believed, was the greatest threat to democracy. And he conducted himself at EPA in ways to show that government could work, that it could be trusted. Late in life, reflecting on where EPA stood and what the future held, he remarked that the future of EPA rested on the strength of our democracy. "Could a free society," he wondered, "meet the existential challenges the environment presents us?" It was, to him, an open question.

Ruckelshaus lamented the fact that fewer and fewer Americans have any memory of the threats to our environment and our health fifty years ago and how much has been accomplished in response to public demand for action. A sense of that history would better prepare us, he thought, for future environmental problems, ones that would be more complex and international in scope.

Several years ago, Ruckelshaus was asked about what was most important to him in a job. He named four criteria: interest, excitement, challenge, and fulfillment. "I've never worked anywhere," he said, "where I could find all four to quite the same extent as at EPA." He said he never found the same level of fulfillment in other jobs as he did in the government. "At EPA, you work for a cause that is beyond self-interest and larger than the goals people normally pursue. You're not there for the money; you're there for something beyond yourself."

Bill Ruckelshaus, EPA's first and fifth administrator, died on November 27, 2019. He believed in the good of government, in the power of information, and in the wisdom of an informed people. The decisions he made fifty years ago, and the manner in which he conducted himself, still help to define EPA today.

—Philip Angell

Chapter One

The Establishment of EPA

A. James Barnes[1]

THE ESTABLISHMENT OF THE EPA

The environment barely registered as an issue in the presidential election of 1968. Civil rights and the war in Vietnam dominated political discourse during the 1960s. But as the decade came to an end and we entered the 1970s, America experienced a rising tide of public concern—in many cases, outrage—about environmental problems.

Newspaper headlines and stories chronicled the problems: Lake Erie was dying, choking to death on algae fed by excessive nutrients reaching its waters; the Cuyahoga River that runs through Cleveland caught fire again (for the thirteenth time), damaging two railroad bridges; an oil well erupted in the Santa Barbara channel, coating prized beaches with oil; the national bird, the bald eagle, was in danger of becoming extinct, the shells of its eggs fatally thinned by the birds' exposure to the pesticide DDT; emissions from steel plants blackened the skies and made breathing the outdoor air dangerous when atmospheric inversions trapped the pollution; and a thick haze of photochemical smog regularly settled over Los Angeles, burning the eyes and aggravating the lungs.

This was not the first time America had experienced widespread concerns about pollution adversely affecting public health and the environment. Indeed, from colonial times forward those living in towns and cities, in particular, faced problems with human and animal wastes, garbage and other refuse, and the need to obtain water safe for domestic purposes. The sanitation movement of the mid-1800s saw urban reformers, physicians, engineers, and others focused on controlling the disposal of sewage and other wastes, providing clean water, and cleaning up pollution in the cities. Later in that century, primarily in cities, reforms in waste management were introduced and various civic movements, often led by women, urged—and were successful in getting—cities to adopt smoke control ordinances. The early 1900s saw federal efforts to address conditions in the meatpacking industry and in 1913 the Public Health Service began regulating the quality of drinking water on interstate carriers.[2]

There also had long been a sub-current of national concern about the natural environment. The early environmentalists—Henry David Thoreau, John Muir, Gifford Pinchot, Theodore Roosevelt, and Aldo Leopold—were conservationists, alarmed over the exploitation of natural resources and the preservation of wildlife and natural areas of significance.

But in the late 1960s and early 1970s, the public's attention was directed at pollution affecting health, on assaults on the environment, about problems that they could see, smell, or taste. People saw rivers and streams where they no longer found fish, or where the only fish caught were trash fish, with huge sores on their bodies, that were unsafe to eat. Water bodies were posted with "no swimming signs," and unhealthy air made breathing difficult. And, if Rachel Carson's *Silent Spring*[3] in 1962 was a siren call for action, the growing public outcry reached a crescendo on April 22, 1970, with the first Earth Day, a series of public gatherings across the nation where millions of citizens expressed their deep concern about the state of the nation's environment.

The prologue to a biography of Senator Gaylord Nelson of Wisconsin—often credited as the founder of Earth Day—succinctly captures the essence of that day:

> On a remarkable spring day in 1970, environmental activism entered the mainstream of American life and politics, stirring ripples worldwide. It was Earth Day, and the American environmental movement was forever changed. Twenty-million people—10 per cent of the United States population—mobilized to show their support for a clean environment. They attended marches, rallies, concerts, and teach-ins. They planted trees and picked up tons of trash. They confronted polluters and held classes on environmental issues. They signed petitions and wrote letters to politicians. They gathered in parks, on city streets, in campus auditoriums, in small towns and major cities.[4]

Politicians soon took notice of the growing chorus of voices—amplified by increased media attention—demanding that something be done. In late 1969 Congress made its first significant response to the public demand for action by passing the National Environmental Policy Act (NEPA).[5] At its core was what was considered at the time a radical idea, one first advanced by a professor at Indiana University, Lynton Caldwell, that before acting, the government should consider the environmental consequences of the planned action.

The concept was embodied in a requirement that before the government takes a "major federal action" with the potential to "significantly affect the human environment," it should prepare an "environmental impact statement" (or EIS) in which it assesses the potential environmental impacts, considers possible alternatives, and identifies possible steps to mitigate the adverse effects.

Though it was ready for his signature the last week of December 1969, President Richard Nixon briefly delayed signing the bill so he could proclaim on January 1, 1970, that "the 1970s absolutely must be the years when America pays its debt to the past by reclaiming the purity of the air, its waters, and our living environment. It is literally now or never."[6]

NEPA established a new entity, the Council on Environmental Quality (CEQ), as part of the Executive Office of the President. The president named Russell Train, a pioneering conservationist then serving as the deputy secretary of the Department of the Interior, to head the council. (Train later became the second administrator of EPA.) The council was given a variety of responsibilities, including implementing the environmental impact statement process, issuing an annual report on the state of the environment, and coordinating and developing legislative and other environmental policy initiatives. Over the next several years CEQ, despite its small staff (thirty to forty people), produced a series of initiatives that set the environmental legislative agenda for the next decade. The initiatives included comprehensive rewrites of the air pollution, water pollution, and pesticide laws, and the development of whole new areas, such as toxic substances control. Other CEQ proposals that focused on noise control and on national land use policy proved to be more than Congress or the American public were willing to accept.

On February 10, 1970, Nixon delivered his historic President's Message on the Environment to Congress,[7] setting out a comprehensive thirty-seven-point program, including twenty-three major legislative proposals and fourteen measures being taken by administrative action or Executive Order in five categories: water pollution control; air pollution control; solid waste management; parklands and public recreation; and "Organizing for Action." The statement was followed over the next several years by the submission to Congress of detailed proposals for legislation developed by the CEQ. In today's political climate it is difficult to imagine a president sending Congress similar proposals on any subject, much less the environment.

On July 9, 1970, President Nixon took another action that not only responded to public concern about the environment, but also better positioned himself to neutralize the issue that Senator Edmund Muskie (D-MN), Nixon's presumed Democratic challenger in the 1972 election, would be looking to ride to the presidency. Nixon notified Congress that he was proposing to use his authority as president under the Reorganization Act to reorganize certain parts of the executive branch to create what would be known as the Environmental Protection Agency.[8] Earlier in January, Muskie had suggested the establishment of an independent environmental agency and in April introduced a bill to do so, which had broad bipartisan support.

The formal reorganization plan establishing EPA grew out of work by the President's Advisory Council on Executive Organization (named the Ash Council for its Chairman, Roy L. Ash).[9] Nixon established the council shortly after he assumed office and charged it with analyzing the structure of the executive branch and making recommendations for reorganization. At the time, Ash was the CEO of Litton Industries, one of the early corporate conglomerates. The council was composed primarily of corporate executives; only two members had any governmental experience, and the council's proposals often reflected contemporary corporate organizational practices.

The initial reorganization plan developed by the Ash Council did not include a separate environmental regulatory agency.[10] Rather it envisioned four "super" departments, including a department of natural resources. This department was to comprise the current Department of the Interior (DOI) along with some major programs in the Department of Agriculture (such as the Forest Service and the Soil and Water Conservation Service), the Department of Commerce's Weather Service, and the US Army Corps of Engineers. The resulting department would have presented significant management challenges—and the proposal faced opposition not only from the constituents of the affected units and some cabinet officers who would lose parts of their departments, but also from chairmen of committees in the House and Senate who would lose some of their committees' jurisdiction.

Nixon then asked the Ash Council to assess the effectiveness of combining all federal environmental regulatory responsibilities in one agency. At the time, the Federal Water Quality Administration in the Department of the Interior (DOI) was focused on pollution of surface waters. The Department of Health Education and Welfare (HEW) managed the National Air Pollution Control Administration, the Bureau of Water Hygiene (which dealt with drinking water), the Bureau of Solid Waste Management, and the Bureau of Radiological Health. Federal responsibilities for regulating pesticides were split among three different departments: The Department of Agriculture was in charge of pesticide registration; HEW was responsible for regulating pesticide residues on food; and DOI focused on the possible effects of pesticides on fish and wildlife. Some radiation-related responsibilities were vested in the Atomic Energy Commission (AEC) and in the Executive Office of the President.

Although Ash initially favored a single cabinet department with responsibilities for both environmental protection and natural resource management, on April 29, 1970, he formally recommended the creation of an "Environmental Protection Administration" as a regulatory agency within the executive branch reporting to the president.[11] The Ash Council and the Office of Management and Budget (OMB) then collaborated to prepare the formal reorganization plan for what was to be called the Environmental Protection Agency.

There were several advantages to going the regulatory agency route. Formation of a subcabinet level agency could be accomplished much faster and without the need for affirmative congressional approval that would be required for the creation of a new department. And, a department with developmental as well as environmental regulatory responsibilities would be in the difficult position of having to regulate the environmental aspects of its own activities as well as the activities of other departments. Moreover, creation of a new agency specifically focused on environmental protection would give the president a highly visible basis for claiming he was actively responding to the public's concern about environmental conditions.

The document sent to Congress carried the dry and unrevealing title, "Message of the President Relative to Reorganization Plans Nos. 3 and 4 of 1970."[12] Plan No. 3 created the Environmental Protection Agency while Plan No. 4 created the National Oceanic and Atmospheric Administration (NOAA) within the Department of Commerce with responsibilities for weather, climate, oceans, and fisheries. Under the law at that time, presidents could propose reorganization plans; if Congress took no action within sixty legislative days, the plans went into effect. Congress could not modify reorganization plans; Congress could only express disapproval by voting to kill the plan.

The reactions in the Senate to the proposed reorganization were generally favorable and Senator Muskie, the Chair of the Air and Water Subcommittee, was a strong advocate for it. Hearings were held in the Senate on July 28, 29, and September 1, 1970, before the Subcommittee on Executive Reorganization and Government Research of the Committee on Government Operations.[13] Hearings were held in the House of Representatives on July 22, 23, and August 4 before the Executive and Legislative Reorganization Subcommittee of the Committee on Government Operations,[14] where several committee chairmen opposed the transfer of programs over which they had jurisdiction: William Poage (Agriculture); Jamie Whitten (Agriculture Appropriations Subcommittee), who was concerned about transfer of the pesticide program at USDA; John Blatnik (Public Works), the father of the sewage treatment plant construction program; and Chester Holifield (Government Operations), who was concerned about transfer of some radiation authority from AEC. Notwithstanding that opposition, both subcommittees issued reports approving the president's proposal, and in late September 1970, the House, by voice vote, defeated a resolution that would have formally disapproved of the reorganization plan.[15]

THE FIRST ADMINISTRATOR

On November 6, 1970, President Nixon announced that he would nominate William D. Ruckelshaus of Indiana to be the first administrator of EPA.[16] The nomination came as a surprise to many people. Although Ruckelshaus' name had been included as a possibility in a *Newsweek* gossip column during the prior summer, no one gave it much credence. In fact, there was very little public attention given to the plan to create this new agency, to say nothing about whom the president would select to lead it.

Individuals who had both environmental experience and the personal qualities to take on the immense challenge of putting together a new agency and establishing its credibility with the public were not in plentiful supply. Ruckelshaus was nominated on the recommendation of Attorney General John Mitchell, Nixon's former law partner and close advisor, clearly with the belief that he had the requisite personal qualities and managerial skill to do the job—and enough environmental experience to be credible.

At the time of his nomination, Ruckelshaus was serving as the assistant attorney general for the Civil Division in the Department of Justice, a job that entailed managing hundreds of attorneys and supervising thousands of cases brought by—and against—the United States. He previously had been a

Figure 1.1. William Ruckelshaus being sworn in as the first EPA administrator on December 4, 1970. https://www.sos.wa.gov/legacy/who-are-we/exhibit/bill-ruckelshaus/ Associated Press/Charles Tasnadi

deputy attorney general in Indiana where he represented the Indiana Board of Health and the Stream Pollution Control Board, drafted the state's air pollution law, and prosecuted violators of the state's air and water pollution laws. Before coming to Washington in 1969 to join the Nixon administration, he had served as the majority leader in his first term in the Indiana House and had run, unsuccessfully, for the US Senate. Thus, he brought both federal and state law enforcement experience as well as legislative experience at the state level to his new position as EPA administrator.

Two others were believed to have been offered the position before Ruckelshaus but turned it down. One was a businessman, Arjay Miller, the president of Ford Motor Company, and the other was John Whitaker, a geologist with a PhD and former presidential advance man, who was the environmental point person on the president's domestic policy staff. Viewed through the rearview mirror of the challenges the new agency faced—and how it addressed them—it is easy to imagine a much different evolution for the agency if a businessman or a scientist, rather than an enforcement-minded lawyer, had become its first administrator.

ORGANIZATION OF THE AGENCY

The first decision the new administrator had to make was how to organize the Washington, DC headquarters of the agency and its field operations. On day one, EPA was comprised of some 5,743 employees. Some were transferred as whole units from two cabinet departments while others came through the transfer of bits and pieces of fifteen departments, agencies, and offices. The employees were located in offices all across the Washington metropolitan area and, indeed, all across the country (one hundred and fifty different locations). On paper they were part of a new agency, but on December 2, 1970, they were sitting in the same offices they had been in before the agency was created, waiting for direction from a new leader who most knew only from what they read in the newspaper.

The formal documents that created the Environmental Protection Agency did not provide the new administrator with a pre-set plan for organizing the new agency; they simply provided transfers of money, people, positions, and legal authority to the agency.[17] It would be up to Ruckelshaus to decide how to organize and deploy those resources.

Government organization charts and delegations of authority are normally of little interest except to the most serious students of management science—and to those whose positions and responsibilities are implicated. However, a number of the initial decisions made by Ruckelshaus have had long-lasting effects on the agency's ability to perform its mission, both providing some inherent strengths and, concomitantly, carrying with them some limitations.

Once the Reorganization Plan was sent to Congress, a task force from the Office of Management and Budget (OMB) under the leadership of Doug Costle (who had been in charge of the Ash Council's study of environmental programs and later became EPA's third administrator) was established to identify the issues and decisions the new administrator would have to make so that the new agency could be operational when it opened December 2. After Ruckelshaus was nominated on November 6, he and the OMB staff focused on two basic models for organizing the headquarters' offices.

The first option—and the one recommended by the Ash Council—was for a "functional organization" with separate offices for monitoring, research, standards setting, enforcement, and assistance. The Council noted that:

> Many agency missions are designed along media lines—air, water, and land. Yet the sources of air, water, and land pollution are interrelated and often interchangeable. A single source may pollute the air with smoke and chemicals, the land with solid wastes, and a river or lake with chemical and other wastes. Control of the air pollution may convert the smoke to solid wastes that then pollute land or water. Control of the water-polluting effluent may convert it into solid wastes which then must be disposed of on land. Similarly, some pollutants—chemicals, radiation, pesticides—appear in all media.[18]

It argued that "a more effective approach to pollution control would: (1) identify contaminants; (2) trace them through the entire ecological chain, observing and recording changes in form as they occur; (3) determine the total exposure of man and his environment; (4) examine interactions among forms of pollution; and (5) identify where in the ecological chain interdiction would be most effective."

A second option was to set up offices based on media or subject matter—for example, air pollution, water pollution, protection of drinking water, pesticide registration, and land pollution—with each office having responsibilities for research, standards setting, and compliance/enforcement related to that media or subject matter. This would largely maintain the approach reflected in the units being transferred to EPA and consistent with the current legislation that focused on a single media.

President Nixon gave EPA seven presidential appointee positions (PAS) that were subject to Senate confirmation: an administrator, a deputy administrator, and five assistant administrators. In addition, the agency had the authority to create a number of lower level management positions that could be used for the heads of a Congressional Affairs office, a Public Affairs office, an International Affairs office, and for various other office directors reporting to the assistant administrators.

One important decision, then, was how to deploy the five assistant administrator positions. Ruckelshaus recognized that, among other things, adopting a completely functional approach would require disaggregating the units coming to EPA and then reassembling the pieces in a new organizational structure which would render EPA unable to act for a considerable period of time while the new organization took shape—a politically unacceptable result. Ruckelshaus knew that the agency would have to make its mark early, establish its credibility publicly, and at the same time send a signal to the staff that this would be an aggressive, action-oriented agency. Accordingly, he opted for a hybrid approach that, after a brief transitional period, created three "functional" offices headed by an assistant administrator: (1) research; (2) enforcement/general counsel; and (3) planning and management, including contracting, budget, financial administration, and personnel. A fourth assistant administrator was assigned the responsibility for two media programs (air pollution control and water pollution control), and the fifth assistant administrator was assigned responsibility for what were designated categorical programs (solid waste, pesticides, and radiation). Figure 1.2 shows the EPA organization chart as of April 30, 1971.

Over time, the number of assistant administrator positions has significantly increased. While the number has varied from time to time, and there have

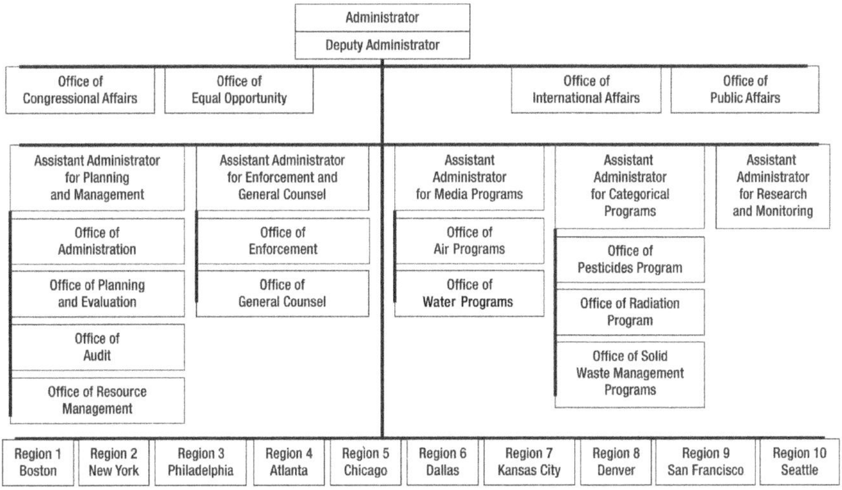

Figure 1.2. EPA organization chart as of April 30, 1971.

been some changes in how they have been utilized and how they are titled, for the purposes of this book it may be helpful to think of EPA as having the following major offices/responsibilities: (1) air pollution; (2) water pollution and drinking water; (3) pesticides and toxic substances; (4) solid and hazardous waste; (5) research and development; (6) enforcement and compliance; (7) policy planning and evaluation; (8) general counsel; (9) international and Indian affairs: (10) management/financial administration; and (11) inspector general.

The decision provided program coherence for the media programs from the start, particularly for air and water which remained in separate program offices, albeit initially under a single assistant administrator. Each had their own program operation, standard-setting and compliance functions, but this ultimately produced a silo effect as separate program offices administered media-focused statutes (e.g., the Clean Air Act, the Clean Water Act, and the Resource Conservation and Recovery Act) that were developed by similarly media-focused congressional subcommittees and closely tracked by similarly focused stakeholder and interest groups.

There is a strong argument that such focus is necessary because of the complexity of dealing with problems in a particular media. Nonetheless, this almost inevitably leads to inconsistent demands on regulated entities and results in a concerted effort to remove pollutants from a particular media with sometimes inadequate attention to where the pollutants are going and whether that is, in fact, the best place for them to end up.

Consistent with Nixon's "New Federalism," Ruckelshaus also opted to create a strong regional component for the agency and followed the ten-region concept (modeled on the Roman pro consuls) that Nixon had put in place for some of the domestic agencies such as, then, Health Education and Welfare (HEW), Housing and Urban Development (HUD), and the Department of Labor (DOL).[19] The plan created ten groups of states which each had a set of regional federal offices conveniently co-located in a major city (Boston, New York, Philadelphia, Atlanta, Chicago, Dallas, Kansas City, Denver, San Francisco, and Seattle) within the region and theoretically, at least, closer to the states and the people in them who would be affected by EPA's programs and decisions. Ruckelshaus aggressively sought permission from the Civil Service Commission and OMB to have the EPA regional offices headed by appointees at higher pay grades (then-called "Supergrades," now known as SES or Senior Executive Service positions) than was the case for other agencies' regional office heads, sending a strong signal to the agency and to the states of the importance he placed on the regional operations.

The conceptual framework for the agency's structure and the regulatory approaches that Ruckelshaus was putting in place—embodied in many of the major pieces of legislation that Congress was to enact during the 1970s—was that the federal government would establish minimum standards and elements of pollution control programs which would then be delegated to the states to administer, with the federal government providing support and backup enforcement when/if the states fell short. Ruckelshaus envisioned that EPA headquarters would delegate to the EPA regional offices much of the authority to provide technical support to, and maintain oversight over, the states as well as to provide backup enforcement where states failed to act. This structure was intended to facilitate sensitivity to regional/local considerations and differences. However, in some instances the headquarters offices were reluctant to cede authority to the regional offices, and the states in turn often clashed with regional offices, sometimes with good reason where the regional offices overreached; in other instances the states wanted freedom to ignore federal statutory mandates and/or to shield/excuse violations of the law by important local economic interests.

The organization of the field activities and operations presented a different set of challenges and political considerations than did the headquarters operations. Although the number of research and support laboratories inherited by EPA was significant (thirty-one labs in nineteen states), dealing with them was fairly straightforward. A number of them came to be located where they were by congressional sponsors—for example, a water lab in Ada, Oklahoma, was in the district represented by the then Speaker of the House of Representatives, Carl Albert. They could simply be left in place so as to not ruffle any feathers or dislocate the ongoing work and the responsibilities of the labs; later their roles would be rationalized and adjusted.

AGENCY STAFFING AND BUDGET

Significant increases in both budget[20] and staffing were necessary as the agency took on additional responsibilities. Ruckelshaus obtained a commitment from the president to support relatively large increases in both—and also a commitment for the agency to get a headquarters building in Washington, DC, that would allow the personnel there to be consolidated at a single location and serve as a visible public presence of the newly established agency.

Staffing was a challenge as EPA was not inheriting the cohort of managers it would need to manage the anticipated structure, and the profiles of the inherited employees were not necessarily a good match with the range of expertise and skills needed in a regulatory agency. There were intense negotiations with the departments and agencies giving up employees as to which employees would be transferred. At the same time, EPA received a flood of resumes as there was a lot of interest and excitement about working in the new agency. For many years, the EPA attracted—and kept—a workforce that was particularly attached to its mission.

A concomitant challenge for the administrator, and the leadership team he assembled, was posed by the fact that the inherited employees came from a varied mix of bureaucracies, each with their own culture, *modus operandi*, constituencies, and relationships (not only within the departments from which they were drawn but also externally with Congress and the states). On paper they were now all part of what was to be a highly visible new agency created and charged with addressing significant public concerns; however, establishing a culture and identity for the EPA would not spring quickly and automatically from the act of creating it and would require considerable effective leadership over a number of years. As Ruckelshaus later observed:

> From a management point of view, the task was daunting: how to form a cohesive, integrated functioning entity out of 15 different agencies and parts of agencies from throughout the federal government, two of which, in the case of pesticides, had conflicting missions.[21]

EPA'S LEGAL AUTHORITY

Unlike most federal agencies, EPA was created, and continues to exist, without benefit of organic authorizing legislation establishing an overall framework for the agency and a coherent set of legal authorities for it to address a legislatively designated mission. As noted, EPA came into existence, without affirmative congressional action, through the presidentially directed Reorganization Plan that transferred a hodge-podge of statutory responsibilities to the agency.

Over the decade of the 1970s, Congress established the comprehensive regulatory schemes known as the Clean Air Act (1970),[22] the Clean Water Act (1972),[23] the Federal Insecticide, Fungicide, and Rodenticide Act (FIFRA) (1972),[24] the Safe Drinking Water Act (SDWA) (1974),[25] the Resource Recovery and Conservation Act (RCRA) (1976),[26] the Toxic Substances Control Act (TSCA) (1976),[27] and the Comprehensive Environmental Response, Compensation and Liability Act (CERCLA or "Superfund") (1980).[28] They largely were the product of different congressional subcommittees and incorporated varying criteria and approaches to deal with specific aspects of the agency's overall mission—to protect public health and the environment—though they were far from a coherent whole. Moreover, in a number of important respects, they represented a marked departure from earlier federal legislation dealing with environmental and public health problems.

Despite their different perspectives, the authors of the environmental statutes of the 1970s believed that existing regulatory programs had been too slow and inactive—and that legislative changes were needed to enable action on the required scale. Accordingly, the new laws supplemented or replaced general grants of authority with detailed lists of tasks to be accomplished on set deadlines, a tendency that only grew over time. Moreover, Congress made these deadlines enforceable by private litigation. Such "deadline suits" to compel agency action have shaped EPA's history ever since.

As noted above, the new laws also reshaped relations between the states and the federal government. Before the environmental era, the federal government itself almost always administered federal regulatory programs. This was true for regulation of trucks and railroads by the Interstate Commerce Commission, of electricity and gas by the Federal Power Commission, for securities and holding company regulation by the Securities and Exchange Commission (SEC), for the setting of pure food and drug standards by the Food and Drug Administration (FDA), and for the protection of workers' organizing rights by the National Labor Relations Board.

By contrast, the 1970s enactments often called on states to adopt plans subject to EPA approval to achieve goals set by the federal government. The Constitution does not generally allow Congress to legally direct states to regulate their citizens to achieve federal goals. Accordingly, Congress did not require states to adopt such plans. Instead, it required EPA to adopt and implement a plan in any state that declined to adopt one. Congress also authorized federal support for state environmental programs—support that would be withheld for unsatisfactory state performance.

States almost never want EPA to run their environmental programs because EPA generally lacks the local knowledge, political sensitivity, and administrative resources that a state agency would command. Nor does EPA want the expense and controversy of running a state program. Accordingly, the structure of the law gives states incentives to come up with the desired plans and gives EPA incentives to be generous in approving them. In practice, state plans generally do not fall below a certain level of stringency. But there are limits to what EPA will accept, and the courts can strike down the approval of a plainly inadequate submission.

The purpose, structure, key provisions, implementation, and evolution of each of the acts noted above, as well as an assessment of their effectiveness over the past five decades, are detailed in subsequent chapters. However, to understand the challenges faced by the first administrator and the new agency, it is useful to briefly outline the limited nature of some of the tools that they had on day one to address the kind of problems that prompted the agency's creation.

Water Pollution

The first water pollution control legislation enacted by Congress in the modern era was the 1965 Water Quality Act.[29] It looked to the states to improve water quality within their jurisdiction, requiring them to designate the intended uses (such as swimming or drinking water) for interstate waters located within the state and to adopt water quality standards that would ensure the waters could be used for the intended purpose. The states also had the lead in producing plans to implement the standards. The federal role was limited to convening conferences to cajole states to adopt standards and to promulgate plans to implement the standards. While the federal government could adopt its own standards where the state did not—and could impose an implementation plan where the state did not produce one—it had to go through a very long and cumbersome process and, even then, there was no mechanism for it to impose limits on individual dischargers, much less to enforce them. The most significant federal authority to address water pollution was to make grants to assist cities in building treatment plants to handle municipal sewage.

The states commonly lacked the expertise and the political will to achieve the act's objectives. Municipal and industrial wastewater was rarely adequately treated before it was discharged into the nation's waters, and it would be an understatement that in 1970 the country faced very serious water quality problems.

Air Pollution

While there had been some earlier embryonic federal legislation dealing with air pollution, the Air Quality Act of 1967[30] represented the first comprehensive federal approach. It authorized the secretary of [then] HEW to regulate stationary and mobile sources and to seek court-ordered abatement of air pollution presenting a "clear and substantial danger." It also required the secretary to designate "air quality control regions" within states and/or interstate regions. Within those regions, the states were required to set standards to limit the levels of pollutants set out in documents (denoted as "criteria documents") prepared by the federal government that detailed the risks to health from exposure to those pollutants. Enforcement of those standards was left to the states.

As EPA was being created in 1970, and as Ruckelshaus was being confirmed as the first administrator, Congress was finalizing the legislation entitled the Clean Air Amendments of 1970, now commonly referred to as the Clean Air Act. The Act passed unanimously in the Senate and by voice vote in the House of Representatives and was signed by President Nixon on December 31, 1970. A significant portion of the confirmation hearing held earlier in December involved senators pressing Ruckelshaus on his views on the pending legislation and how he would anticipate administering it.[31]

Solid Waste

The authorities transferred to EPA for dealing with solid waste were (1) the Solid Waste Disposal Act of 1965[32] that, in essence, confirmed the view that waste management was the responsibility of the states and encouraged them to develop their own waste management programs, and (2) the Resource Recovery Act of 1970[33] that authorized federal funding for waste recovery and recycling programs. At the time, very little attention was paid to distinguishing between hazardous and non-hazardous solid waste. However, the discovery of "Love Canal" in New York (where chemical wastes deposited in an abandoned canal started oozing into the basements of homes and schools built on the former landfill), and the "Valley of the Drums" in Kentucky (where thousands of drums of waste had been abandoned on a farm), provided poster children for the nation's hazardous waste problems and brought waste onto the national legislative agenda. RCRA,[34] which established a cradle-to-grave management scheme for hazardous waste, was enacted in 1976 and CERCLA ("Superfund"),[35] which dealt primarily with the cleanup of past releases of hazardous substances, was enacted in 1980.

EPA's first initiative for solid waste was to promote the closing of open dumps and to encourage the use of sanitary landfills. EPA's June 1971 "Mission 5,000" was to close 5,000 of the estimated 14,000 open dumps in the country—or convert them to sanitary landfills requiring a six-inch soil cover at the end of each day.

Pesticides

The responsibilities transferred to EPA relating to pesticides were those set out in the Federal Insecticide, Fungicide and Rodenticide Act of 1947 (FIFRA)[36] that provided for regulation of the interstate marketing of pesticide products. Essentially, it provided for registration of pesticides by the Department of Agriculture as well as the removal of products from the market that were found to be "misbranded."

EARLY ACTIONS THAT SHAPED THE PUBLIC PERCEPTION OF THE AGENCY

Ruckelshaus often described the challenge he faced as EPA's first administrator as being like "performing an appendectomy on yourself while running a 100-yard dash." If anything, he understated the challenge. He had to keep the personnel and bits of authority he inherited functioning as he shaped the new agency's structure and mission and obtained additional resources and legal authority. As importantly, he had to take high profile actions to show the public that the agency was moving swiftly and credibly to deal with the problems it had been created to address.

The following actions, taken in the first eighteen months after EPA was established, served to assure the public that the new agency did indeed mean business: (1) enforcement actions against three cities and numerous industrial dischargers; (2) a ban on most uses of DDT in the United States; and (3) an aggressive stance to implement technology-forcing automobile emission standards in the 1970 Clean Air Act.

These actions also serve to illustrate three important operational elements that have come to characterize EPA: (1) a strong enforcement mentality; (2) the importance of sound science in identifying public health and environmental problems warranting attention, assessing the risks and then acting to sensibly manage those risks; and (3) the capacity to evaluate, and then determine, the appropriate technologies to meet standards mandated by statute, and to see that those standards are implemented.

Enforcement Actions against Detroit, Cleveland, Atlanta, and Industrial Polluters

On December 10, 1970, eight days after EPA came into existence, Ruckelshaus traveled to Atlanta to speak to a gathering of mayors and other city officials at the Annual Congress of Cities and provided the public with its first insight into how he and the new agency were approaching the challenge and the responsibility entrusted to them.[37]

He began with some general remarks, noting: "It will be our job in the Environmental Protection Agency to be an advocate for the environment wherever decisions about our common future are made—whether it be in the councils of government, in the boardrooms of industry, or the living rooms of our citizens."

Moments later the audience sat in stunned silence as he moved into the heart of his remarks:

> The responsibilities which are entrusted to this new agency I must meet head-on today. A gross pollution problem exists in Atlanta, Georgia, and clearly something must be done about it now. The Chattahoochee River flows clean and clear above Atlanta. But when it reaches this great city, 32 million gallons of untreated effluents are dumped into it daily, along with another 40 million gallons

> with only primary treatment. Beneath the city of Atlanta, the Chattahoochee River, an interstate stream, flows into Alabama. It is virtually an open sewer.

Ruckelshaus announced he was giving the city 180 days to halt its violation of water quality standards or EPA would ask the Department of Justice to file a court action against the city.

He followed quickly with indictments of Detroit and Cleveland for their massive contributions of inadequately treated sewage to Lake Erie—and announced that they, too, were being served with 180-day notices. As the audience reacted in shock, it is not clear how many focused on the words that followed:

> By serving these 180-day notices we are not saying that the Chattahoochee River or Lake Erie can be restored tomorrow. What we are saying is that we have not done enough, fast enough—at any level of government—to meet the needs that exist and to implement the corrective action necessary. It is not our intent to vindicate our policies in the courtroom. It is our hope, rather, to act as a catalyst—to encourage all of us in Washington, in the State House and in the City Halls of this country to address ourselves to the hard decisions which must be made if the environment is to be protected. . . . The logjam of inertia must be broken somewhere, and we propose to do it at the federal level.

Ruckelshaus moved on to the press room jam-packed with reporters and cameramen where pandemonium broke loose. Cleveland Mayor Carl Stokes stormed in, looking for Ruckelshaus. "This is a politically motivated cheap shot," he shouted. Stokes went on to suggest that it was not a mere coincidence that a Republican administration had singled out three cities led by Democratic mayors. The mayor also pointed the finger at the federal government which, he alleged, had not come through with the money it had promised the cities to improve their sewage treatment facilities, a refrain about "unfulfilled promises" that EPA also heard from other cities. Ruckelshaus responded that the lack of a grant from EPA was not a valid excuse for polluting the nation's waters in violation of the law.

Support for the action against the cities came from some interesting quarters. A January 16, 1971 *Business Week* editorial praised the action, stating:

> The crackdown on municipalities fills an important spot in the record of anti-pollution efforts. Industry, lashed by stinging criticism, no longer assumes it can dump its wastes into the air and water as a matter of right. But too many city officials are inclined to take the position that pollution control is no problem of theirs. . . . Pollutants of the air, water and land are just as toxic and just as objectionable when they come from a municipal sewer or a city incinerator as when they come from an industrial plant. . . . Nor can the program stop with

> municipal government alone. The federal government is a major polluter and a stubborn one about cleaning up. . . . If the U.S. really means to clean up its air and water, it must go after all sources of pollution. It cannot act on the assumption that public pollution is harmless while private pollution is intolerable.

Contemporaneously, the Department of Justice, acting at the request of EPA, filed suit against Armco Steel, charging it with polluting the Houston Ship Channel with cyanide.[38] The following week, on December 18, Attorney General John Mitchell held a press conference to announce, among other things, that the department that day had filed suit against Jones and Laughlin Steel Corporation for discharging substantial quantities of cyanide into the Cuyahoga River in Cleveland. He also announced that the Department of Justice had established a new Pollution Control Section to handle all litigation in the environmental field, including criminal litigation, "with the prospect of many more cases to come."[39]

In January, and in the succeeding months, numerous other water pollution cases—as well as a number of air pollution cases—were filed by the Department at EPA's request. And, in November 1971, when an inversion trapped emissions from the steel plants in Birmingham, Alabama, resulting in a public health emergency, EPA sought and obtained an order from a federal district court judge in the middle of the night ordering the shutdown of twenty-three major industries in the city until the threat to public health had passed.[40] It was the first time the emergency provisions of the Clean Air Act had been invoked and demonstrated that EPA was prepared to take aggressive action when warranted.

The enforcement actions garnered headlines across the country. However, to assess their impact, it is useful to separate out the practical impact from the perspective the public gained from the press attention these actions received.

In reality, they showed how limited and weak any federal authority was to deal with water pollution at the time. Where interstate pollution was involved, EPA could convene a conference of contributors and affected parties and try to cajole action. In the case of industrial wastewater discharges, EPA and the Department of Justice pulled out an old 1899 law known as the "Refuse Act"—enacted, as Ruckelshaus used to say tongue in cheek, "under the last great Republican environmentalist president, William McKinley."

The Refuse Act[41] prohibited the disposal of "refuse" into navigable waters without a permit from the US Army Corps of Engineers; it was designed to keep piers and floating debris from being placed in navigable waters that might obstruct passage through the waterway or damage vessels. There was one small problem: The Corps of Engineers had never put in place a system for issuing such permits—a "minor difficulty" that the firms sued by EPA and the Department of Justice for violating the act brought to their attention.

That did not deter the government from continuing to pursue violations of the act, and it hurried to put such a system in place; on December 23, 1970, President Nixon signed an Executive Order creating the Refuse Act Permit Program.[42] The permit system, in modified form, then found its way into the comprehensive water pollution law (now known as the Clean Water Act) that Congress enacted in late 1972.

At the request of EPA, the Department of Justice brought more than one thousand enforcement actions in the first two years.[43] The major impact of these actions was the widespread publicity they received that sent a clear signal to polluters in both the private and public sector. The impact on improved water quality came slowly as the details of what the regulated entities were required to do to reduce their pollution had to be worked out on a case by case basis until the implementation of nationally applicable requirements in the Clean Water Act of 1972. The message that the public did get was—to use the vernacular—there was "a new sheriff in town who was prepared to take names and kick ass." And, with the perception established that EPA would be aggressive in pursuing polluters, Ruckelshaus had bought some critical time to put rules and procedures in place so the agency could have real muscle behind its actions.

Ban on DDT

In October 1969, several major environmental groups petitioned the secretary of agriculture to begin the proceedings that would lead to cancellation of the right to make interstate sales of DDT in the United States. At the time, the Department of Agriculture (USDA) had the legal authority under FIFRA[44] to register and thus authorize the sale and shipment of "economic poisons" such as DDT. When those responsibilities were transferred to EPA, the matter almost immediately was put on the desk of the new administrator when, in January 1971, the US Court of Appeals ordered him to commence cancellation proceedings for all remaining uses of DDT and consider immediately suspending all sales and shipments of it in the United States.[45]

At the time, DDT was the world's leading insecticide, used extensively worldwide for mosquito eradication and in the US to deal with boll weevils, cabbage worms, and gypsy moths. It was considered essential to the livelihoods of cotton, peanut, and soybean farmers. While the annual usage in the US had declined to about thirteen million pounds (a sixth of the volume in its peak year), much of what had been used in the past remained in the environment. That was the downside of DDT: it was a persistent chemical that did not readily break down in the environment; rather it moved up the food chain and bioaccumulated as larger organisms ate smaller ones that had ingested DDT.

Evidence began to accumulate that the use of DDT resulted in high mortality among robins and other birds—as well as fish kills—in areas where it had been used to deal with tree disease. Rachel Carson noticed these phenomena on the Michigan State University campus where she was then working; she also learned that DDT residues were being found in polar regions where DDT had never been sprayed. Her 1962 book, *Silent Spring*, became a siren call to action. Other scientists were calling attention to the decreasing thickness of the eggshells of some species like the bald eagle and the peregrine falcon, resulting in high infant mortality and risk of potential extinction. The perceived threat to the national bird—the bald eagle—provided the proverbial poster child for demands that something be done about the continued widespread use of DDT.

The regulatory scheme (FIFRA)—within which the administrator had to address the order of the court as well as the public calls for action on DDT—was, to put it mildly, cumbersome and imperfect. Largely a registration process for pesticides, it had been run by the Department of Agriculture whose mission was to promote agriculture and saw agricultural chemicals as critical to the success of that mission. At the core of FIFRA and its registration process is a *risk-benefit balancing principle*, which means that a product, no matter how dangerous to man or nontarget species, can be allowed on the market as long as the benefits of its use are determined to exceed the risks/dangers of its use. When there is reason to believe a product that has already been registered no longer meets this standard—i.e., the risks may outweigh the benefits—the secretary (now the administrator) could initiate a "cancellation proceeding" and indicate his intention to cancel the registration unless the registrant could make the case that the product continued to pass the risk-benefit balancing test.[46] At the registrant's discretion, it could invoke the right to have a scientific advisory board appointed to look at the question as well as to make its case before an administrative law judge at EPA and, if it was unsuccessful, to appeal the ruling to the administrator himself/herself and ultimately to a federal court. These proceedings could easily consume years before reaching a final verdict on the continued registration of the product. The hearing process accommodated participation by registrants, users, and the agency—but not the public or other interest groups concerned about the continued use of the product.

In response to the order from the DC Circuit, the administrator initiated cancellation proceedings, and the registrant, in turn, invoked all of its rights by requesting the appointment of a scientific advisory board and a public hearing. In September 1971, the scientific advisory board recommended accelerated reductions in the use of DDT "with the goal of virtual elimination of any significant additions to the environment." Then, after a seven-month hearing and 8,500 pages of testimony, a hearing officer released his decision. He concluded that, in his judgment, the benefits of DDT outweighed the risks and recommended reversal of the proposed cancellation.[47]

The administrator personally reviewed the record and evidence concerning the risks and benefits of DDT. As is true in almost every major decision made at EPA, the scientific evidence is rarely unequivocal and there are competing considerations, some of which may not be among those the law permits the administrator to consider. Ruckelshaus could not help but be aware that while there would be substitutes for DDT where it was used in the US on cotton, soybeans, and peanuts, that option might not be economically feasible in underdeveloped countries or that adequate substitutes might, in fact, not be available. Thus, while his decision would directly affect only its use in the United States, other countries, looking to the US for leadership, might be under pressure to ban DDT domestically before finding satisfactory alternatives, resulting in crop losses and increases in insect-borne diseases like malaria.

On June 14, 1972, Ruckelshaus announced his decision to cancel almost all uses of DDT in the United States—but delayed the effective date to December 31, 1972.[48] He had concluded that continued use of DDT posed "an unacceptable risk." In making the announcement he noted:

> I am convinced by a preponderance of the evidence that, once used, DDT is an uncontrollable, durable chemical that persists in the aquatic and terrestrial environments. The evidence of record showing storage in man and magnification in the food chain is a warning to the prudent that man may be exposing himself to a substance that may ultimately have a serious effect on his health.
>
> The risks to the environment from continued use of DDT in massive quantities are more clearly established.

Ruckelshaus delayed the effective date because the chief substitute that would replace DDT for most crop uses, methyl parathion, was a highly toxic chemical that posed a short-term danger to untrained applicants. He wanted the Department of Agriculture, the states, and the industry to have time to institute training programs for those who would be applying methyl parathion. If such training programs were in place, the advantage of using methyl parathion was that it degraded rapidly after use and did not bioaccumulate, thus not presenting the kind of long-term risk to the environment that DDT did. Shipments of DDT to other countries for public health purposes were not affected by the ban on sale of DDT for most uses in the United States.

In the press release announcing the decision and order, Ruckelshaus urged Congress to quickly enact the pesticide legislation which had been submitted as part of President Nixon's 1971 Environmental Message. The legislation would, he noted, give him much more flexibility in controlling pesticides so as to maintain their benefit to the public while minimizing or eliminating their environmental hazard. The law also would allow pesticides to be designed only for restricted use and applied only by a certified applicator. Before the year was out, Congress enacted a major rewrite of FIFRA and adopted many of the measures recommended by the administration.

Reaction to the decision was swift. Within minutes, the registrants filed an appeal with the Court of Appeals challenging the ban, and the Environmental Defense Fund filed as well, asking that the ban be made effective immediately and that even the remaining minor uses also be banned.[49] The press carried interviews with farmers and other users of DDT, particularly in the South, who were bitter about the decision and its possible implications for their cotton, peanut, and soybean crops. Other concerns included the cost, efficacy, and toxicity of the substitute.

The *New York Times* editorial page[50] offered a different take:

> Ten years after Rachel Carson sounded the alarm against the threat of DDT to animal and human life, a slow-moving Federal bureaucracy has finally banned the persistent pesticide for nearly all domestic uses.
>
> Frightening amounts of this "elixir of death" have passed into the rivers and streams of America, the oceans of the world, and into the universal life cycle while manufacturers, farmers, lawmakers and the Department of Agriculture, among others, were stubbornly resisting Miss Carson's eloquently reasoned warning. But the mute evidence of "silent springs" across the land ultimately spoke louder than their prejudiced protests.
>
> Overruling the exceptionally misinformed report of a trial examiner, Environmental Protection Administrator William D. Ruckelshaus decided, as Miss Carson had done a decade ago, that DDT poses "an unacceptable risk to man and his environment." His ruling is a landmark in the national struggle to preserve and restore the country's natural heritage.

Ruckelshaus signed the order as he prepared to leave for Stockholm for the United Nations Conference on the Human Environment. It was released in Washington as he arrived in Sweden where he would be seen either as a hero or as a pariah for his DDT decision.

First Showdown with Detroit over Automobile Emission Standards

In the environmental legislation enacted by Congress in the 1970s, Congress commonly directed EPA to establish limits on the discharge of various pollutants to the air or water based on its assessment of what existing, demonstrated technology could achieve in practice. However, in the Clean Air Act of 1970, Congress took a very aggressive, *stringent* approach toward controlling tailpipe emissions from automobiles. Knowing that dramatic reductions in those emissions would be necessary for the nation to achieve healthy air and that the automobile companies had resisted designing and manufacturing less polluting vehicles, Congress directed that EPA establish tailpipe emission standards for hydrocarbons and carbon monoxide that would require a ninety percent reduction by 1975 from the levels allowed from 1970 models. These were not only ambitious standards, they were "technology-forcing"—that is, at the time they were enacted in the legislation, there was no known and demonstrated technology for meeting them. The rationale for adopting this approach—and an assessment of how it played out during the 1970s—is detailed in Chapter 3.

Congress knew that the legislation carried some real risks as to whether the automobile companies could meet the goal; equally, if not more, important was the awareness that one in every seven jobs in the country was tied to the production and sale of automobiles. Consequently, the law provided what Senator Howard Baker described as a "realistic escape hatch." The automobile manufacturers could petition the administrator of EPA for a one-year suspension of the requirement. For a suspension to be granted, the administrator would have to find, among other things, that (1) the suspension was essential to public interest or public health or welfare; (2) all good faith efforts had been made to meet the standards; and (3) the companies established that effective control technologies were not available, or would not be available with sufficient lead time, to be utilized in the 1975 model year.

During his confirmation hearing, Ruckelshaus was pressed by Senator Muskie as to how he would approach making a decision if the automobile companies sought a suspension. He advised the senator:

> As Administrator, in the event I am confirmed, I would intend to look with a very jaundiced eye at any claim that everything had been done—with a very jaundiced eye that they could not comply with the standards as set by the Congress and that I would hold the automobile industry to the strictest possible proof to show and convince me that they had done everything in their power to comply with those standards and that they had not been able to achieve a device that would do that.[51]

Once the legislation was signed into law, the automobile companies wasted little time or effort trying to convince official Washington—as well as the public—that they had been asked to do the impossible and the public would be the loser. The act provided that an application for a suspension could be filed any time after January 1, 1972, and that the administrator was required to make a decision within sixty days thereafter. On March 13, 1972, a small foreign manufacturer, Volvo, formally filed for a suspension thereby triggering the sixty-day period for a decision. Not until April 5 did the large domestic manufacturers—Ford, GM, and Chrysler—come forward to file as well. At that point, the administrator had five weeks to make his decision.[52]

The agency held public hearings from April 10-27, 1972. Representatives of most of the major automobile manufacturers, suppliers of emission control devices, and various public interest groups and public bodies testified and submitted data. The automobile manufacturers were adamant that suitable technology would not be available with sufficient lead time to use with any confidence in the 1975 model-year cars; the manufacturers of the add-on device, the "catalyst"—that could largely eliminate the targeted emissions after they left the engine—were much more optimistic that with the time available before the tooling for those 1975-model cars would have to be in place, technology that would meet the standards would be available to the manufacturers.

After reviewing the hearing record, the industry submissions, and the EPA analyses, Ruckelshaus concluded that the industry had not met their burden of proof and that he had to deny the suspension request at this time (the industry would have the option of applying again the following year).[53] Further buttressing his decision was his conviction that it was very important, given the intense public pressure directed at him by the industry, that the first time the public saw EPA go eyeball to eyeball with the industry, the agency not blink.

In retrospect, the press conference announcing the decision only marked the end of what was act one, scene one in what has proved to be a long-running, multiple-act drama involving EPA and the auto industry. The subsequent history is detailed in Chapter 3.

Just as the DDT matter illustrated the key role science and risk assessment would play in EPA decision-making, the congressional mandate that EPA set stringent automobile emission standards carried with it the unspoken requirement that EPA develop the capacity to independently assess the technologies available to meet those standards.

THE EARLY EPA/WHITE HOUSE RELATIONSHIP

One recurring theme throughout the fifty years since EPA was established is the tension between the agency and the White House, often in the form of the Office of Management and Budget (OMB) in the Executive Office of the President, over environmental decision-making. Commonly intertwined with that tension is another one between the protection of human health and the environment and the benefits thereof, and the costs/impact on the economy and jobs of achieving that protection. These tensions became apparent soon after EPA came into existence and have continued since. In addition, they often resulted in considerable friction with other executive branch entities that perceived EPA was unreasonably interfering with their ability to perform their assigned missions. Regulations adopted by EPA pursuant to statutory mandates often apply to activities of other departments and agencies—or to their constituencies—and, pursuant to NEPA, EPA provides comments on the environmental impacts of actions other agencies are planning to take.

At the heart of the EPA/White House tension are two sets of factors: one legal in nature and the other grounded in practical political realities. The legal factors are straightforward. Most of the legislation under which EPA operates assigns the decision-making to the administrator. In a number of instances, Congress mandates that the administrator perform certain actions pursuant to very specific dictates in the legislation and does not contemplate that the decisions would be made elsewhere in the executive branch. At the same time, the Constitution provides that the president holds the executive power; he is given the power to appoint officials in the executive branch (some subject to the advice and consent of the Senate), as well as to require opinions in writing from the principal officer in each of the executive departments. His oath of office requires him to swear [or affirm] that he will faithfully execute the Office of President of the United States and "preserve, protect and defend the Constitution," which is seen as an affirmation that he will see that the laws are "faithfully executed." Presidents see this as the responsibility, as well as the authority, for them to dictate decisions being made by their subordinates.

The second factor—political realities—reflects the fact that EPA really does not have a core constituency apart from the general public interest, whereas the White House, which nominally should be focused as well on broad public interest, in fact pays particular attention to what it considers to be important constituencies such as the business community, which tends to get more attention than Non-Governmental Organizations (NGOs) like environmental groups. While at the time EPA was created environmental groups thought they would be EPA's core constituency, some rather quickly became disaffected and critical of the agency when they realized that EPA's decision-making authority—and the decisions it reached in particular cases—were not necessarily synonymous with their positions on issues.

With the debate in Congress over the Clean Air Act of 1970 and the early efforts of EPA to address problems of air and water pollution, industry began a drumbeat in the trade and popular press about the amounts of money that would be required to comply with the emerging environmental standards. Within the administration, that argument was carried by the Secretary of Commerce, Maurice Stans, who complained privately as well as publicly that EPA was getting carried away with enforcement. In September 1971, President Nixon traveled to Detroit to address the Detroit Economic Club where he sought to reassure automobile executives that "we are not going to allow the environmental issue to be used, sometimes falsely and sometimes in a demagogic way, basically to destroy the system—the industrial system that made this great country what it is." Later, Ruckelshaus would joke that when he was introduced for a speech at that same Economic Club, he was described as the "greatest friend of American industry since Karl Marx."

At Stans' urging, in April 1970 Nixon created the National Industrial Pollution Control Council (NIPCC)[54] which was composed of top corporate executives from more than fifty of the nation's largest industrial firms, including General Motors, Ford, DuPont, Exxon, and US Steel. Operating out of the Department of Commerce, NIPCC and its thirty sub-councils produced technical reports and case studies of industry efforts that focused increased attention on the prospective costs of environmental regulation. It argued to have its voice heard early in the development of regulations dealing with the environment and consumer protection.

At the time, the White House was actively involved in EPA decision-making—and in providing other agencies an opportunity to provide input into an agency's decisions—on an ad hoc, uncoordinated basis. For example, the White House Office of Science and Technology policy looked at the proposed standards for automobiles; the Domestic Policy Council, headed by Presidential Assistant John Ehrlichman, reviewed regulations EPA was proposing to remove phosphates from detergents (to protect lakes against eutrophication); and the Office of Management and Budget reviewed EPA's proposed guidelines for the states to develop plans to implement the provisions of the recently enacted Clean Air Act.

On October 5, 1971, George Shultz, then the Director of the Office of Management and Budget (OMB,) signed a memorandum to all federal agencies which required that all "agency standards, regulations and guidelines pertaining to environmental quality, consumer protection, and occupational and public health and safety" would have to be submitted to OMB at least thirty days prior to adoption whenever they might be expected to "(1) have a significant impact on the policies, programs or procedures of other agencies; or (2) impose significant costs on, or negative benefits to, non-federal sectors; or (3) increase the demand for Federal funds . . . for programs . . . beyond those in . . . the current budget requests submitted to Congress."[55] Known as the Quality of Life review process, it was criticized by environmentalists for taking place out of public view, providing OMB an opportunity to weaken proposed EPA standards, and for being so time-consuming that it caused EPA to miss statutorily established deadlines for actions. As will be seen in Chapter 11 and Chapter 13, every president who followed Nixon adopted some form of review process, often with similar objections being raised. The review process became the focal point where the tensions between protecting public health and the environment and the costs of those efforts—as well as the tensions between the agency and the White House—played out.

Recognizing that EPA would need to bring sound and supportable analyses of the benefits of proposed regulations and actions—as well as the economic impacts of adopting them—into the discussions with OMB, Ruckelshaus created an office of planning and evaluation to provide policy analysis and recruited a Rhodes Scholar and top-ranking graduate of the Air Force Academy, Robert Sansom, to head it.

Congress quickly became aware of the role that OMB was playing as EPA carried out its responsibilities under authorizing legislation. It made its position clear on the Quality of Life review process in the conference report that accompanied the 1972 Clean Water Act.[56]

> The Conferees clearly contemplate that the decision-making responsibility, as in the Clean Air Act, on guidelines and regulations to be published under this Act rests, unless otherwise specified, with the Administrator of EPA and not such other agencies as the Office of Management and Budget and the National Industrial Control Council. EPA regulations and guidelines are not to be reviewed by these and other agencies prior to their publication except as on the same basis as review and comment by members of the public. OMB comment and review should thus come in the form of comments available to the public, made during the period for public comment.

Needless to say, Nixon, and all of his successors, have taken a different view of the authority they have under the Constitution for carrying out the responsibilities of the executive branch—and how that authority can and should be exercised. Despite what Congress said in the conference report, every president since Nixon has pursued some measure of oversight or review of actions taken by EPA, as well as other executive branch agencies and departments.

Ruckelshaus thus found himself operating in a sometimes uncomfortable position between the president who had appointed him and a Democratic Congress suspicious that sinister forces within, and external pressure on, the Executive Branch would produce actions and decisions inconsistent with the clear language and intent of the congressional enactments. On several occasions while announcing major decisions, Ruckelshaus took pains to indicate that while he had informed the White House of his decision, he had made the decision himself without direction or concurrence from the White House—and consistent with the charge he had in the authorizing legislation.

RELATIONSHIP WITH CONGRESS

The first insights into the relationship that would evolve between EPA and Congress came from the congressional deliberations over whether to exercise its authority to formally disapprove the Reorganization Plan creating the Environmental Protection Agency. As noted earlier, in the House the objections to the proposed creation of EPA came primarily from committee chairmen who were concerned that moving entities such as the Federal Water Pollution Control Agency from DOI—or the National Air Pollution Control Administration from HEW—to the new agency would take away some of their authority.

On the Senate side, the hearings to consider Nixon's nomination of Ruckelshaus to be the first administrator also offered some insights. Formally, the hearing was held in the Senate Committee on Public Works chaired by Senator Jennings Randolph. However, three other committee chairmen, Henry (Scoop) Jackson of Interior, George Aiken of Agriculture and Forestry, and James Pearson of Commerce, were invited to have visible roles, reflecting the interest their respective committees had in the new agency.

Consequently, at the outset, EPA found that some fourteen congressional committees and subcommittees claimed some authority over the agency; the norm for most agencies would be that they only had to be concerned with an authorizing committee and an appropriations subcommittee in the House as well as in the Senate. In the House, the Chairman of the House Appropriations Committee, George Mahon (D-TX), did consolidate the authority for EPA appropriations in the Agriculture, Environment and Consumer Protection Subcommittee chaired by Congressman Jamie Whitten (D-MS). However, despite entreaties to Congress to consolidate the authorizing authority in a single committee in each body, the authority remained divided among a number of committees/subcommittees in both chambers.

In his classic study, *The Making of Environmental Law*,[57] Richard Lazarus succinctly describes the reality EPA faced:

> The environmental laws that Congress passed during the 1970s changed tenor as the decade progressed to reflect increasing skepticism and distrust of the executive branch. The statutes imposed hundreds of stringent deadlines on . . . EPA, and increasingly reduced that agency's discretion in meeting those deadlines. One-third of the deadlines in those early years were for six months or less; 60

> percent were for one year or less. . . . The comprehensive amendments Congress passed in 1977 to both the Clean Air Act and the Clean Water Act were far longer and more detailed than the original acts passed in 1970 and 1972, with Congress eliminating much of the discretion contained in the short, broadly worded provisions of the prior enactments.
>
> The federal statutes were, however, only the most prominent strands in a detailed web of congressional efforts to oversee the EPA's work. Congress oversaw the executive branch through the budgetary process, mandatory reports to Congress, confirmation hearings on presidential nominations, and general oversight hearings. Congressional oversight of the EPA was remarkably intense because of the extraordinarily large number of congressional committees and subcommittees that could validly claim that the agency's work fell within their jurisdiction. Whether the subject of a given congressional committee was agriculture, marine fisheries, public works, transportation, commerce, small business, energy, science or foreign affairs, the relationship to environmental protection policy was likely to be direct and substantial. The vast and crosscutting implications of both ecological injury and pollution control virtually guaranteed that the EPA would not lack legislative oversight.

FEDERALISM: THE RELATIONSHIP WITH THE STATES

Ruckelshaus brought to the new agency a view that the states could be important laboratories for trying different approaches to problems and for many decisions to be keyed, where appropriate, to local conditions that often differ widely across the country. He also brought personal knowledge of how industry in Indiana had intervened with the governor to derail actions to halt discharges of pollution to waters in the state. He understood the need to have a strong federal presence to support state actions to address pollution problems.

As of 1970, states generally had legislation on the books dealing with sanitation and discharges of industrial wastewater, smoke pollution, and drinking water, with the authority often vested in a public health agency. But, as was evident from the environmental conditions around the country with a few exceptions, environmental protection was not a high priority. And, with states competing to attract industry and jobs, there were many signs of a race to the bottom.

The response of Congress was to enact comprehensive federal regulatory schemes that (1) established minimum standards that had to be met everywhere in the country, but allowed states to be more protective if they wished; (2) set out programs that states could seek to have delegated to them so they had the primary responsibility for issuing permits and enforcement; (3) gave EPA the responsibility for providing technical support to states; (4) provided federal financial support for state programs, serving as an impetus for states to develop expertise and capacity; and (5) gave EPA the authority to act to enforce the laws where the states failed to do so.

The laws made the feds the hammer of last resort and thus built in a level of tension between EPA and the various state agencies that could not be ignored. Progressive states used that "threat" to their advantage in moving forward to address pollution. Other states saw it as unwarranted interference and acted accordingly. Those tensions remain to this day.

EPA ENGAGEMENT WITH THE PUBLIC AND STAKEHOLDERS WITH AN INTEREST IN AGENCY ACTIONS

From the outset, Ruckelshaus realized that broad and aggressive communication, both internal and external, would be an essential element in how he managed the early years of the agency. EPA was formed in response to public demand for action against pollution and the general public needed to know what the new agency could and would do.

He also realized he had to reach the other important external audience, namely those entities that were or were about to be regulated by EPA. They needed to hear that EPA meant business, that the environment was not a passing fad. And he understood that his internal audience, the 5000+ men and women now part of a new, highly visible government agency also needed to hear from him.

Those disparate communication needs created significant demands on the administrator, given the state of communication technologies in the 1970s. Travel was a given; every trip he took, whether it be to make a speech or to visit a regional office, required press events to draw attention to EPA: press conferences, editorial board meetings, meetings with state and local officials, and tours of major facilities (press in tow). Where feasible, he did TV and radio talk shows, morning news shows, late night news shows—any opportunity to explain what this new agency was all about and, more importantly, to demonstrate that government was listening and acting.

In the first six months, he visited every one of the ten regional offices of EPA and every major research facility. He held all staff meetings, met with environmental reporters, and held open-house public meetings at night in each city where he would explain EPA and its new mandate and take any and all questions from the audience. Those meetings were also a chance for EPA staff to take a measure of how Ruckelshaus would operate as administrator.

Finally, to facilitate communication with groups of stakeholders particularly impacted by EPA actions, he established liaison positions for outreach to industry, agriculture, labor organizations, and national environmental groups; he also created a youth environmental council to respond to the enthusiasm that young people had about protecting the environment.

Ruckelshaus spoke about his public approach in 1993 as part of EPA's Oral History Project, drawing on his two stints as EPA administrator:

> I think the administrator must view himself not only as responsible to the president who appointed him; but also to the Congress, which confirmed him, and in a broader sense, to the public which he ultimately serves. He must let the public know what he is doing and convince them he is doing the best he can to act in their interest.
>
> This is very, very important because in the environmental field you are dealing with things that are so intimate to people, so important to them in terms of public health, their own health, and the health of the planet we all share. If they do not think you are doing the best you can to act in their interest, and you lose their trust and support, I think you will have real trouble in succeeding. Not just the administrator himself, but the agency itself gets into trouble. It is much tougher for EPA to do the right thing if that bond of trust is ever broken.[58]

EPA'S INTERNATIONAL ROLE

At the time Ruckelshaus was nominated by Nixon to be administrator, he met with Russell Train, the Chairman of the Council on Environmental Quality, and agreed that he would focus on the organization and management of EPA while Train would, among other things, take the lead in international activities related to the environment. Train had a diplomat's persona and social skills, and in his position as head of CEQ he was involved in crafting administration policies and initiatives across a broad range of environmental-related issues, many beyond the purview of EPA. Moreover, he had more time for such involvement internationally. However, it quickly became apparent that in many cases, the primary interest of other countries was in interacting directly with EPA to learn how it was organizing and how it was dealing with the environmental problems in the United States. EPA, with its much larger staff than CEQ (thirty- to forty-person staff), was in a better position to be able to share technical and scientific expertise with other countries.

Ruckelshaus created an Office of International Affairs at EPA whose function was to serve as a contact point between the agency and agencies in other countries, as well as to coordinate the various international activities of the agency. The initial emphasis of the office was on developing bilateral relationships and agreements with other countries. At the top of the priority list was an agreement with Canada concerning the Great Lakes. Culminating two years of negotiation, the Great Lakes Water Quality Agreement was signed in Ottawa, Canada, on April 15, 1972, by President Nixon and Prime Minister Pierre Trudeau of Canada. Viewed retrospectively, it represented an early effort to identify some common goals and objectives concerning the two countries' shared interests in the largest reservoir of fresh water in the world, as well as to create some joint mechanisms to help them achieve their mutual interests. The agreement established basin-wide water quality objectives and included commitments to design, implement, and monitor programs to control municipal and industrial pollution.

As the agreement was being negotiated, it became apparent that both countries had different mechanisms for addressing water pollution domestically and that both were in the process of trying to get their act together to do a more effective job of addressing pollution in the Great Lakes. Both Russell Train and Bill Ruckelshaus, along with Jack Davis, Minister of the Environment for Canada, spoke at the press conference that was held under the auspices of the White House Press Office and Press Secretary. In his opening remarks, Train noted:

> So many of the difficult environmental problems facing the countries of the world tend to be regional in nature and can best be dealt with on a bilateral, or otherwise regional basis, rather than by some very broad, multinational undertaking. So, we see this Great Lakes Agreement between Canada and the United States as pointing the way to comparable agreements among the countries bordering the Mediterranean, the Baltic, the rivers of Europe, and other regional problems around the world.[59]

In May 1972, Ruckelshaus made an official visit to Mexico where, among other things, he met with several senior environmental officials and later with the president, Luis Echeverria.[60] At the time, Mexico was one of the few countries in the world (along with the US, Canada, and the United Kingdom) to have an environmental agency and Mexico's was headed by the president's brother who was an MD. The parties exchanged information about their respective pollution abatement programs, as well as their mutual interests in addressing automobile pollution, the use of pesticides, and control of municipal sewage. As the meeting ended, they agreed on the need to continue to share information. It was readily apparent that the environmental program in Mexico was at a very early stage and that even though there were border issues such as the salinity of the Colorado River as it flowed into Mexico, the conditions were not yet ripe for the kind of formal agreement between the United States and Mexico that had just been signed between the United States and Canada.

The meeting with President Echeverria gave Ruckelshaus a preview of the tensions that soon would be apparent at the forthcoming UN Conference in Stockholm between the already developed countries (like the United States and Canada) and the developing world (like Mexico) that had some concerns about pollution, but first wanted their share of the kind of industrial prosperity that had created pollution problems in the developed countries.

While the focus of this chapter is on public concern about the environment in the United States and establishment of EPA in 1970, it can be useful to also have a sense of how the issue was viewed at the time in the international community.

The United Nations Conference on the Human Environment

If Earth Day 1970 can be seen as marking the beginning of an era of environmental consciousness in the United States, then the UN Conference on the Human Environment can be seen as marking the beginning of an era of global environmental consciousness. From June 5-16, 1972, in what local officials had anticipated would be the "biggest peaceable invasion in the city's 720-year history," some "1,500 delegates and observers, 350 UN officials, 1,000 reporters and more than 10,000 students, campers, and other ecology enthusiasts" descended on Stockholm.[61] It was not your normal meeting of diplomats speaking quietly in measured tones. Indeed, at times the various events pushed the boundaries of what one would consider peaceful discourse.

A June 12, 1972 *Newsweek*[62] dispatch, projecting even larger numbers of participants, painted a graphic picture of the scene:

> Stockholm had never seen anything quite like it. At the railroad and airline terminals last week, motley groups of hippies, radicals, and ecofreaks were mingling with scientists, diplomats, politicians, and newsmen from 109 nations. The 3,000-man Stockholm police force, braced for the onslaught by the addition of 2,000 provincial policemen, was nervously eyeing the antics of fully 30,000 visitors to the Swedish capital. The whole scene suggested a complex cross between a scientific convention, a summit conference, and a rock festival—and in effect, that is exactly what this week's UN Conference on the Human Environment will amount to.
>
> Wags were calling the gathering "Woodstockholm," but if the optimists were right, the conference might achieve lasting gains for the environmental cause—raising global consciousness of the planet's problems and providing at least the beginning of a common search for solutions. Those aims are symbolized by the conference insignia—a man in a circle surrounded by olive leaves, with the legend: "Only One Earth."

The initiative for the conference came from a proposal made by Sweden in 1968 that the UN address the international problems caused by rapid industrialization and population growth. While the resolution was quickly adopted, the central questions inevitably were going to reveal very different perspectives between the developed and the developing worlds, the East versus the West, and the free world versus the communist world. A twenty-seven-member committee was established to determine the issues to be discussed at the conference itself, a process that took more than two years.

More than one-hundred countries sent official delegations and, on what were glorious blue-skied days, the streets of Stockholm were filled with men and women wearing a wide array of native dress and speaking a multitude of different languages. It was a true snapshot of the diverse global community. Several EPA staffers attending the conference found themselves sharing the elevators in their hotel with a delegation wearing Mao suits as the People's Republic of China emerged from behind the Bamboo Curtain (for the first time in many years) to participate. The most conspicuous no-shows were Russia and several of its eastern European allies who were upset that Russia's satellite, East Germany, had been invited to attend only as a nonvoting participant. Yakow A. Malik, Russia's chief delegate to the UN complained, "This is like inviting a guest to your house for dinner and then telling him he can sit at your table but not eat."[63]

The official US delegation was led by CEQ Chairman Russell Train and Christian Herter, Jr., an assistant secretary of state for environment and population affairs. Members included twelve members of Congress, among them Senator Howard Baker, as well as cabinet officers, Presidential Assistant John Ehrlichman, and former child actress Shirley Temple Black. Ruckelshaus was a member of the delegation and found himself being sought out by delegates from other countries interested in hearing first-hand about his experiences setting up EPA and the approach the US was taking to deal with pollution problems—and to register their reactions to his DDT decision.

In addition to the formal conference sessions for the official delegations, other forums took place. The UN sponsored an environmental forum that was supposed to be a high-level scientific seminar on environmental issues. A number of prominent scientists and authors were there and made presentations at open meetings: economist Lady Barbara Ward, Stanford biologist Paul Ehrlich (*The Population Bomb*), Cleveland toxicologist Samuel Epstein, and biologist Rene Dubos (who is often credited with originating the phrase "think globally, act locally").

Some insight into the conflicting tensions and viewpoints outside the conference hall can be gleaned from an item in a column entitled "A Stockholm Notebook," in the June 26 edition of *Time* magazine:[64]

> Motherhood was almost a dirty word here—but it had its defenders. At the Scientists' Environmental Forum, Stanford biologist Paul Ehrlich blamed half the world's environmental problems on increases in population. A woman biologist from Nigeria, aided by four burly colleagues, startled the audience by seizing Ehrlich's microphone and declaring that birth control was merely a way for the industrial powers to remain rich by preserving the status quo. Peace was restored only after Ehrlich conceded that the US should curb its own consumption of natural resources before urging pollution controls on developing countries. Brazilian Economist Josue de Castro fumes at the very mention of birth control. "Genocide of the unborn!" he charges.

The question of whether there are, or should be, limits to technology or growth was a central issue at the conference. The *Time* article went on to note that "talk of slowing industrialization was anathema to the developing nations. The Chinese delegation, led by Tang Ke, minister of fuel, had an answer. The world's resources are 'inexhaustible,' he said, provided all nations follow the teachings of Mao Tse-tung."

The highlight of the formal conference, indeed of the entire happening in Stockholm, was an eloquent address by Indian Prime Minister Indira Gandhi, who spoke to the north-south divide on the environmental issues the world was confronting:

> On the one hand the rich look askance at our continuing poverty—on the other they warn us against their own methods. We do not wish to impoverish the environment any further and yet for a moment forget the grim poverty of large numbers of people. Are not poverty and need the greatest polluters? For instance, unless we are in a position to provide employment and purchasing power for the daily necessities of the tribal people and those who live in and around our jungles, we cannot prevent them from combing the forest for food and livelihood; from poaching and despoiling the vegetation. When they themselves feel deprived, how can we urge the preservation of animals? How can we speak to those who live in villages and in slums about keeping the oceans, the rivers, and the air clean, when their own lives are contaminated at the source? The environment cannot be improved in conditions of poverty. Nor can poverty be eradicated without the use of science and technology.[65]

The conference discussed—and then adopted—a wide range of often watered-down resolutions dealing with such topics as stopping the killing of whales and getting France and China to stop testing nuclear weapons. In that the UN had no real way to enforce the resolutions, they had no force, but the conference had put the issues on the world's radar screen and signaled they were a matter of global concern. The Stockholm conference raised awareness of the interconnectedness of many environmental and health issues—and that had to be considered a success. It was the harbinger of many conferences to come that dealt with biodiversity, ocean pollution, and climate change, with varying degrees of success. One of those efforts to deal with stratospheric ozone depletion, the Montreal Protocol, and the EPA role in it is discussed in Chapters 4 and 13.

More significantly, the conferees urged creation of a new UN office to coordinate international activities and maintain a global system to monitor the spread of pollutants. That office was ultimately established in Nairobi, Kenya.

THE END OF THE BEGINNING

Ruckelshaus carried on an extensive speaking schedule during 1972 (a presidential election year), addressing a broad range of groups and editorial boards about the agency's accomplishments to date. At the same time, rumors were rife that the president's chief fundraiser, Maurice Stans, was indicating to donors that the president intended to replace Ruckelshaus after the election. Immediately after Nixon was reelected, all presidential appointees were requested to submit their resignations so that decisions could be made as to who would be retained and who would be replaced.

When no decision relative to EPA administrator had been announced by the third week in December, while almost all other major decisions had been announced, and amid rumors from reporters that he was about to receive reappointment, Ruckelshaus requested a meeting with the president before any announcement was made. He subsequently reported that he had sought—and received—assurance from the president that he would continue to have "the authority to exercise the decision-making power given to the administrator of this agency by law."

On Friday afternoon, April 27, 1973, as the Watergate saga continued to grow in Washington, Ruckelshaus received an urgent summons to come to the White House. Meeting alone with Nixon in the Oval Office, he was told that the president wanted to nominate him to be the next director of the FBI. The current director, Patrick Gray, had just resigned, having admitted to destroying documents related to the Watergate investigation. The president also confided that on the following Sunday, he was going to fire his chief of staff, Robert Haldeman, Presidential Assistant John Ehrlichman, Attorney General Richard Kleindienst, and White House Counsel John Dean.

Ruckelshaus resisted the offer—noting that he had never aspired to that position—but, ultimately driven by a sense of public service, reached a compromise with the president that he would report to the FBI the following Monday and serve as the acting director of the FBI until a new permanent director could be recruited. Subsequently, in the summer of 1973, Nixon nominated Russell Train, then serving as the chairman of CEQ, to succeed Ruckelshaus as administrator of EPA, and nominated Ruckelshaus to be deputy attorney general. On Saturday, October 20th, Ruckelshaus, along with Attorney General Elliot Richardson, resigned their positions in what became known as the "Saturday Night Massacre" rather than follow President Nixon's order to fire the Watergate special prosecutor, Archibald Cox.

And so, as EPA's first administrator left EPA that Monday morning in April 1973 and reported to the FBI, it marked the end of the beginning of EPA. But that was not to be the end of Ruckelshaus's role and influence at EPA. Though he moved to Seattle in 1976, he kept in close contact with the Agency, providing advice and support to two succeeding Administrators, Russ Train and Doug Costle.

In the spring of 1983 President Ronald Reagan's EPA was in turmoil. Daily revelations in the press, along with Congressional oversight hearings, detailed failed leadership, mismanagement, and worse: political appointees hostile to EPA's mission and the career staff, cozy relationships with industry, the secrecy of decision-making, and the lack of enforcement, all of which contributed to the forced resignation of EPA head Anne Gorsuch and the firing or resignation of other political appointees.

Reagan asked Ruckelshaus, by then known as "Mr. Clean," to return to Washington and take the helm at EPA again, to right the agency. He accepted and was given a free hand to pick his staff, with no political interference. Ten years away gave Ruckelshaus a valuable perspective on the agency. On his first day back he issued what has come to be called "the fish-bowl memo" to all agency employees, encouraging them to be open and accessible to the public and the press, and requiring that senior political appointees publicly post their daily schedules. The "gorilla in the closet" memo reiterated that EPA was an enforcement agency, ready to back up the states and see the laws enforced. He opened key decision-making meetings to staff who wanted to be heard on an issue. Leaks from the agency—once a flood—became a trickle, if that. After what the agency had been through, Ruckelshaus knew that being forthcoming about EPA's actions and decisions was necessary to restore agency morale and public trust.

His assignment to right the agency accomplished, Ruckelshaus resigned as Administrator in January of 1985. For the next thirty years, EPA remained on a relatively even keel generally consistent with principles Ruckelshaus had articulated during his tenure—despite switching between Republican and Democratic administrations, increasing polarization of Congress that impeded new needed legislation, and significantly increasing lobbying activity by special interests, many of which opposed regulation. But in the Trump administration, many of the problems that characterized the Anne Gorsuch era have resurfaced and, as this book goes to press, the agency's future is again uncertain. The balance of this book details many facets of EPA's history from its inception in 1970 through 2020.

NOTES

1. The perspective in this chapter is based on the unique opportunity I had to observe and participate in the formation of EPA as an assistant to the first Administrator, William Ruckelshaus. The content is drawn from contemporaneous personal observations, conversations with other individuals who were at EPA at this time or who were interacting with it, notes and documents retained at the time, including some that are not in publicly available form. Endnotes are provided for the references to statutes, formal administrative actions, judicial decisions, and quotations drawn from published works or reported by the media.

2. This paragraph is drawn from Richard N. L. Andrews, *Managing the Environment, Managing Ourselves: A History of American Environmental Policy,* 2nd ed. (New Haven, CT: Yale University Press, 2006).

3. Rachel Carson, *Silent Spring* (Boston: Houghton Mifflin, 1962).

4. Bill Christofferson, *The Man from Clear Lake: Earth Day Founder Senator Gaylord Nelson* (Madison, WI: University of Wisconsin Press, 2004).

5. 42 U.S.C. 4321–4370, Pub. L. 91–90. 83 Stat. 852 (January 1, 1970).

6. Richard M. Nixon, "Statement About the National Environmental Policy Act of 1969," *The American Presidency Project,* https://www.presidency.ucsb.edu/node/239921.

7. Richard M. Nixon, "Special Message to the Congress on Environmental Quality, February 10, 1970," *The American Presidency Project*, http://www.presidency.ucsb.edu/ws/?pid=2757.

8. Richard M. Nixon, "Special Message to the Congress About Reorganization Plans To Establish the Environmental Protection Agency and the National Oceanic and Atmospheric Administration," *The American Presidency Project,* https://www.presidency.ucsb.edu/node/240055.

9. President's Advisory Council on Executive Reorganization, memoranda from April 1969 to November 1970, https://www.nixonlibrary.gov/finding-aids/presidents-advisory-council-executive-organization-white-house-central-files-staff.

10. See also John C. Whitaker, *Striking a Balance: Environment and Natural Resources Policy in the Nixon-Ford Years* (Washington, DC: American Enterprise Institute for Public Policy Research, 1977), 53–66.

11. President's Advisory Council on Executive Organization, Memorandum re: Federal Organization for Environmental Protection, April 29, 1970, hereafter Ash Council Memo.

12. Nixon, "Reorganization Plans," 578–86; Reorganization Plans nos. 3 and 4 of 1970, H. Doc. 91-366. 91st Cong., 2nd sess.

13. US Congress, Senate, Hearings before the Subcommittee on Executive Reorganization and Government Research, Committee on Government Operations, Reorganization Plans nos. 3 and 4 of 1970, 91st Cong., 2nd sess., July 28–29, 1970, and September 1, 1970.

14. US Congress, House, Hearings before the Subcommittee on Executive Reorganization and Government Research, Committee on Government Operations, Reorganization Plan no. 3 of 1970, 91st Cong., 2nd sess., July 28–29, 1970, and September 1, 1970.

15. Disapproving Reorganization Plan No. 3 of 1970—To Establish an Environmental Protection Agency as an Independent Entity of Government, HR 1209, 91st Cong., 2nd sess., 116 Cong. Rec. 33871.

16. Carroll Kilpatrick, "Nixon Selects Environmental Administrator," *Washington Post*, November 7, 1970, A6.

17. Richard Corrigan, "Success of New Agency Depends Upon Ruckelshaus' Direction," *National Journal* 2, no. 47 (November 28, 1970): 2591.

18. Ash Council Memo.

19. Nixon intended to devolve federal power to local/regional offices of the domestic federal agencies. EPA offered the chance to do that at the beginning. The result was that EPA regional administrators have more authority and discretion than their domestic agency counterparts.

20. The EPA Budget for FY1971 was approximately $1.4 billion. US Environmental Protection Agency, "EPA's Budget and Spending," *EPA.gov,* https://www.epa.gov/planandbudget/budget.

21. William D. Ruckelshaus, "Environmental Regulation: The Early Days at EPA" *EPA Journal* (March 1988): 5-6.

22. Pub. L. No. 91-604, 84 Stat. 1676 (1970); 42 U.S.C. §§7401–7431.

23. Pub. L. No. 92-500, 86 Stat. 816 (1972); 33 U.S.C. §§1251–1387.

24. Pub. L. No. 92-516, 86 Stat. 973 (October 21, 1972).

25. Pub. L. No.93-523, 88 Stat. 1660 (1974).

26. Pub. L. No. 94-500, 90 Stat. 2796 (1976)

27. Pub. L. No. 94-469, 90 Stat. 2003 (1976).

28. Pub. L. No. 96-510, 94 Stat. 2796 (1980).

29. Pub. L. No. 92-500, 86 Stat. 816 (1972).

30. Pub. L. No. 90-148, 81 Stat. 485 (1967).

31. US Congress, Senate, Hearing Before the Committee on Public Works, Nomination of William D. Ruckelshaus, 91st Cong., 2nd sess., December 1–2, 1970.

32. Pub. L. No. 89–271, 79 Stat. 992 (1965).

33. Pub. L. No. 91–512, 84 Stat. 1227 (1970).

34. Pub. L. No. 94-500, 90 Stat. 2796 (1976).

35. Pub. L. No. 96-500, 94 Stat. 2796 (1980).

36. Pub. L. No. 80–104, 61 Stat. 163 (1947).

37. William D. Ruckelshaus, "The City Must be the Teacher of Man" (address to the Annual Congress of Cities, Atlanta, GA, December 10, 1970).

38. John N. Mitchell, "Cyanide Pollution," *Department of Justice*, December 9, 1970.

39. Ruckelshaus, "The City Must be the Teacher of Man."

40. John Quarles, *Cleaning Up America: An Insider's View of the Environmental Protection Agency* (Boston: Houghton Mifflin, 1976), 53–57.

41. Rivers and Harbors Act of 1899, 33 U.S.C. 403, 30 Stat. 1152 (1899).

42. Executive Order 11574 of December 23, 1970, Administration of Refuse Act Permit Program, 35 Fed. Reg. 19627 (December 25, 1970), https://www.govinfo.gov/content/pkg/FR-1970-12-25/pdf/FR-1970-12-25.pdf#page=1.

43. Quarles, *Cleaning Up America*, 53.

44. Pub. L. No. 80-104, 61 Stat. 163 (1947).

45. Environmental Defense Fund v. Ruckelshaus, 439 F.2d 564 (D.C. Cir. 1971).

46. The version of FIFRA (1947) extant when Administrator Ruckelshaus made his decision did not explicitly call for the balancing of risks and benefits, but the courts and administrative practice had interpreted the act to provide for it. Congress made it explicit when it amended FIFRA later in 1972.

47. US Environmental Protection Agency, Consolidated DDT Hearings, Opinion and Order of the Administrator, 37 Fed. Reg. 13370 (July 7, 1972).

48. Ibid.; US Environmental Protection Agency, "EPA Bans General Use of DDT," *EPA Press Release*, June 14, 1972.

49. "Environment: Verdict on DDT," *Time*, June 26, 1972, 41.

50. "Unacceptable Risk," *New York Times*, June 26, 1972.

51. US Congress, Senate, *Committee Report: Hearings on the Nomination of William D. Ruckelshaus* (Washington, DC: Senate Committee on Public Works, December 1–2, 1970).

52. These facts are drawn from International Harvester Co. v. Ruckelshaus, 478 F.2d 615 (D.C. Cir. 1973) and the Decision of the Administrator (see endnote 53).

53. Decision of the Administrator re: Application for Suspension of 1975 Motor Vehicle Exhaust Emission Standards, May 12, 1972.

54. Executive Order 11523 of April 9, 1970, Establishing the National Industrial Pollution Control Council, 35 Fed. Reg. 55985, 5993-5994 (April 11, 1970), https://www.govinfo.gov/content/pkg/FR-1970-04-11/pdf/FR-1970-04-11.pdf#page=1.

55. George P. Shultz, *Official memorandum: Agency Regulations, Standards, and Guidelines Pertaining to Environmental Quality, Consumer Protection, and Occupational and Public Health and Safety* (Washington, DC: OMB, October 5, 1971), https://thecre.com/ombpapers/QualityofLife1.htm.

56. Amendment of Federal Water Pollution Control Act, HR 11896, 92nd Cong., 118 Cong. Rec. 33572, 33697 (1972).

57. Richard Lazarus, *The Making of Environmental Law* (Chicago: University of Chicago Press, 2004), 79-80.

58. US Environmental Protection Agency, "William D. Ruckelshaus: Oral History Interview," EPA 202-K-92-0003, *epa.gov,* January 1993, https://archive.epa.gov/epa/aboutepa/william-d-ruckelshaus-oral-history-interview.html.

59. *Transcript of April 15, 1972, Press Conference* (Washington, DC: Office of the White House Press Secretary, 1972).

60. Philip Angell, Memorandum: WDR Visit to Mexico—May 17-19, 1972. Assistant to the Administrator Philip Angell accompanied Ruckelshaus on the trip.

61. "Whole Earth Conference," *Time*, May 22, 1972, 73.

62. "The Big Cleanup: The Environmental Crisis '72," *Newsweek*, June 12, 1972, 38.

63. *Time*, "Whole Earth Conference."

64. Friedel Ungeheuer, "A Stockholm Notebook," *Time*, June 26, 1972, 40.

65. Indira Gandhi, "Speech at the United Nations Conference on the Human Environment," (Stockholm, June 14, 1972), full text available at https://lasulawsenvironmental.blogspot.com/2012/07/indira-gandhis-speech-at-stockholm.html.

Chapter Two

Clean Air: Regulation of Stationary Sources

William F. Pedersen

HISTORICAL DEVELOPMENTS BEFORE 1970

Air pollution from cooking and heating fires has damaged human health since the stone age. In many countries today, it still does. With the development of urban living, pollution became a collective problem, one that got worse as cities grew bigger and more industrial during the 19th century, especially as coal use increased. However, the extent of the damage was uncertain since mortality rates were high and the statistical techniques of the time could not pick out the specific air pollution contribution.

Legal and political reaction to rising pollution levels took the form of urban "smoke control" ordinances of questionable effectiveness, and of more targeted efforts directed at more isolated problems.[1] For example, in the early 1900s pollution from a copper smelter in Tennessee damaged forests, crops, and orchards both in Tennessee and in neighboring Georgia. The smelter, in response, shifted from roasting the ore in open piles to roasting it in a furnace with a tall smokestack. But the state of Georgia claimed that the result caused "the poisonous gases to be carried to greater distances than ever before, [so] that the evil has not been helped."[2]

The Supreme Court allowed Georgia to sue for relief in an opinion that expressed concerns still timely today about pollution damage, pollution dispersion, and the responsibilities of states to each other. The Court said that:

> It is a fair and reasonable demand on the part of a sovereign that the air over its territory should not be polluted on a great scale by sulphurous acid gas, that the forests on its mountains, be they better or worse, and whatever domestic destruction they have suffered, should not be further destroyed or threatened by the act of persons beyond its control.[3]

Fifty years after that decision, events placed a renewed—and quantitative—focus on urban air pollution. In 1948, a five-day weather inversion trapped emissions from steel and zinc production in the Monongahela River valley at ground level in and around the town of Donora, Pennsylvania. The mix of pollutants included sulfur oxides, particulates, nitrogen dioxide, fluorine, and other poisonous gases. Before wind and rain cleared the pollution naturally, some twenty people had died and a third to a half of the total affected population of fourteen thousand had sickened. Many required hospitalization.

Even more dramatically, in 1952 a similar inversion over London trapped particles and sulfur oxides from the soft coal the city used for heating at ground level for a week. Hospitals were overwhelmed with respiratory patients. Contemporary accounts blamed an estimated four thousand deaths on the smog. The episode has been much analyzed since, and current studies estimate the death toll at about twelve thousand.

Although Los Angeles has never burned much coal, starting in the 1940s the city began to experience continuing episodes of "smog" on days when atmospheric inversions trapped emissions inside the natural bowl of mountains within which the city grew. In 1952 scientists discovered an unexpected cause for this pollution, finding that nitrogen oxides and unburned hydrocarbons from gasoline engine exhaust were reacting together in the atmosphere with sunlight to cause the smog.[4]

All this set the stage for dramatic political action in the 1970s. In this chapter we examine both that action and its successors. We also examine the progress the nation—and EPA—have made in the fifty years since 1970 in reducing air pollution from stationary pollution sources such as power plants. Chapter 3 will then examine the parallel efforts to control emissions from motor vehicles and their fuels.

THE PATH TO FEDERAL LEGISLATION

Congress enacted its first air pollution law in 1955. However, the law simply authorized research and training and had no regulatory content.[5] In 1963 a new law authorized the Secretary of Health and Welfare to develop and publish "criteria" outlining the impact of selected air pollutants on human health. It also authorized federal legal action against damaging pollution, but only after a long and convoluted process.[6] Meanwhile, California had addressed its smog problem by adopting controls on organic evaporative emissions from motor vehicles in 1961 and setting tailpipe standards in 1966.[7] In 1965

Congress followed that lead and directed the establishment of national mobile source emission standards.[8] They took effect in 1968.

In 1967, Congress addressed clean air again, strengthening the powers of the federal government to address damaging local air pollution, to issue "criteria" defining damaging levels of air pollution, and to set auto emission standards.[9] The 1967 law also prohibited most state and local auto emissions standards, thus almost granting the desire of the automobile industry for a single national set of emission rules. However, it maintained California's right to set its own emission standards after every California member of Congress, regardless of party, supported such a measure.

Despite this increased activity, before 1970 federal air pollution law was still far from aggressive, lacking in clear goals or regulatory mechanisms and short on enforcement authority.

THE 1970 AMENDMENTS

All of that changed with the Clean Air Act Amendments of 1970, the first modern environmental regulatory statute, a path-breaking piece of legislation often referred to simply as "the Clean Air Act" (CAA).[10] This law was not simply a statement of aspirations; it included programs to address and reduce each major type of air pollution, together with detailed requirements and timetables for federal and state regulatory action toward those goals. These new control programs adopted and relied on new approaches to regulatory decision-making that would become patterns for all of environmental and administrative law. We will discuss both the substantive control programs and the new control toolbox.

The New Air Pollution Control Programs

Congress in 1970 commanded EPA to establish comprehensive control regimes in five separate areas which, taken together, covered all the major types and sources of man-made air pollution.

National Ambient Air Quality Standards (NAAQS)

Congress required EPA to set national ambient air quality standards (NAAQS)—maximum permissible concentrations of a pollutant in the air—to serve as the foundation of most other CAA control efforts. EPA had to set NAAQS for any pollutant that might be thought to endanger public health or welfare, "the presence of which in the ambient air results from numerous or diverse mobile or stationary sources." Congress directed that EPA propose, within thirty days of CAA enactment, such standards for six pollutants for which the government had already issued criteria documents under the 1967 legislation. They were particulate matter, ozone (then called "photochemical oxidants"), sulfur oxides, nitrogen oxides, carbon monoxide, and hydrocarbons. Because standards for these pollutants are based on criteria documents, they are called "criteria pollutants."[11]

These six pollutants have been the focus of the national air pollution control effort ever since although, as discussed below, EPA has extensively redefined the exact type of particulate regulated in response to advancing scientific knowledge. "Primary" NAAQS had to be "requisite" to protect the public health "with an adequate margin of safety," while "secondary" standards had to be "requisite" to protect against welfare effects such as soiling, damage to plants and materials, and visibility impairment.

State Implementation Plans (SIPS)

Once the NAAQS had been set, the law directed states to come up with plans ("state implementation plans" or SIPs) to reduce air pollution permanently below NAAQS levels. These plans required EPA approval. If EPA did not approve a plan within two years of the specified deadline, it would have to develop and issue a plan of its own.[12] EPA had power to enforce any approved SIP provision whether it had been promulgated by the state or by EPA.[13]

Congress initially set the attainment deadline for primary standards at three to five years. This would prove dramatically too short a period to achieve that goal. Secondary standards would have to be achieved in a "reasonable" time.

Almost without exception the CAA allowed a state to adopt any SIP measures it chose as long as they were predicted to achieve the NAAQS on schedule. That gave states considerable flexibility to write their standards after considering cost and technical feasibility without requiring them to do either. States also had to prevent their own emissions from interfering with NAAQS attainment and maintenance in neighboring states.[14]

The law clearly required the use of any means necessary for primary NAAQS attainment by the deadline, including restrictions on the use of automobiles ("transportation controls") as a last resort.[15]

New Source Performance Standards (NSPS)

In addition to requiring NAAQS attainment, Congress, in what might be termed a "belt and suspenders" approach to ensuring healthy air, directed EPA to list all major categories of stationary sources of air pollution, such as steel mills and power plants (also known as electric generating units or

EGUs), and then set emission standards for new and modified sources in these categories. Those standards would be based on what the technology of the day could achieve rather than on what was needed to protect air quality.[16] This, Congress thought, would both assist NAAQS attainment and make sure that pollution would continue to decline as the industrial stock turned over even after the NAAQS had been achieved. Congress' expectation that older sources would close down and be replaced by better controlled new ones proved far from universally true, particularly for EGUs, as we discuss below.

One detailed provision of the law stated that if EPA established an NSPS for a pollutant for which no NAAQS—and therefore no SIP requirement—existed, states would be called on to enact SIP-like plans to control existing sources of that pollutant.[17] With the exception of a so-far failed effort to use this section to control greenhouse gas (GHG) emissions as discussed in Chapter 4, and a failed attempt by the George W. Bush administration to apply it to EGU mercury emissions, EPA has only used this authority for a few relatively localized pollutants like fluorides, reduced sulfur, and sulfuric acid mist.[18]

Hazardous Air Pollutant Standards (HAPS)

Congress in 1970 dealt with widespread pollutants through NAAQS. However, Congress also believed that many other local sources emitted non-criteria but highly dangerous air pollutants. Congress therefore called on EPA to issue standards for both new and existing sources of such "hazardous air pollutants" (HAPs).[19]

These standards had to be set as emissions limits prescribing maximum out-of-stack pollution levels rather than as measures of atmospheric pollutant concentrations like NAAQS. They had to be tight enough to protect the "public health" with an "ample" margin of safety—the same language that governed the primary NAAQS, with "ample" substituted for "adequate." Congress broke with its deadline-heavy approach to other air pollution issues and left EPA almost complete discretion whether to issue HAP regulations.

Emergency Authority

Congress also granted EPA very broad power to seek judicial relief to abate air pollution of any type that might pose an "imminent and substantial endangerment" to public health.[20] Within months of CAA enactment, EPA used this authority against steel mill pollution in Alabama. EPA has never used it since.

Mobile Sources and Fuels

The 1970 statute expanded and strengthened EPA's authority to set emissions standards for trucks and automobiles. In the most dramatic single move of the 1970 legislation, Congress commanded EPA to set such standards for passenger automobiles at a ninety percent reduction from prior levels, unless the companies could demonstrate in a special proceeding that these levels were infeasible.[21]

Congress also gave EPA authority to regulate motor fuel additives, both to remove ingredients—lead was the main target—that might damage the emissions controls needed to achieve the new automobile standards, and to remove ingredients—lead, once again—that might harm human health directly.[22] Chapter 3 describes in detail the dramatic early history of EPA's implementation of these provisions.

The New Control Toolbox

As Chapter 1 explained, the environmental laws of the 1970s were the first federal statutes that relied systematically on a "cooperative federalism" approach that enlisted state regulatory power to pursue federal goals. Those laws also introduced "action forcing" mechanisms to compel agencies to actually address the problems they were established to correct. Deadlines for issuing control standards enforceable by private lawsuits (now universally called "citizen suits") were the most notable of these.[23]

The 1970 Clean Air Act, as the first major environmental regulatory statute, served as a proving ground for both these new departures. Several other features of the new law have had continuing importance and are worth discussion.

Use of Command and Control Regulation to Achieve Results

For the CAA, command and control regulation means directing specific pollution sources to reduce specified emissions to a specified degree. The CAA does not generally tell sources *how* to achieve such reductions.

This approach is so familiar that it may seem strange to count it among the 1970 innovations. But before 1970, pollution control efforts tended to rely on generating research, seeking consensus, and disseminating information, or on enforcement actions under vague standards for localized pollution caused by individual sources. Against that background the CAA's multitude of direct commands did indeed represent a new departure.

A Mix of Results-Based and Technology-Based Standards

Authors of environmental statutes must always decide whether to (1) direct regulators to set rules based on achieving a specific environmental result, or (2) simply command a certain level of pollution control, which is generally based on what the technology of the day can accomplish.

Examples of the first approach would include requirements to reach ambient pollution levels low enough to protect public health, plant life, or visibility. It would also cover directives to avoid pollution levels that pose an "unreasonable risk" to such values—a formulation that allows balancing of factors such as cost and economic impact. Commands to reduce emissions to levels achievable by the "best available control technology" or the "maximum achievable control technology" or to reach the "lowest achievable emissions rate"—the different formulations are legion—would be examples of the second.

The 1970 legislation adopted both approaches, enacting a number of technology-based programs to supplement a central focus on ambient results. This mix has characterized the CAA ever since. The two approaches are related in that ambient standards can show where new technology is needed, while technology-based standards can help develop and put into use new control methods that can then be used to achieve ambient standards.

Technology Forcing

In framing technology-based standards, the 1970 legislation sometimes decreed that industry should not simply put current knowledge into use, but should invent and install technology with performance beyond the existing state of the art. This was particularly true of auto emissions as discussed in the next chapter.

Most formulas for technology-based standards are not this ambitious. But even where they are not, the new idea of technology forcing has often created space for an aggressive EPA approach to standard setting when the data and the bureaucratic will were there.[24]

THE NEXT TWENTY YEARS: 1970-1990

As EPA began to implement the new CAA, it was very conscious of the need to establish both its political (small "p") credibility and its authority as a regulator over essentially all of American heavy industry. To do this, it had to come as close as possible to actually putting Congress' numerous and detailed commands into effect on schedule. At the same time, the agency was almost totally unfamiliar with administrative regulatory practice or how to develop and present to the public, the courts, and the political system the extensive detail that would often be needed to justify a regulation.[25]

Lobbying by industry, states, and Congress pressed on the agency in those years as it always does. However, the urgent need to establish the agency's foundations tended to reduce its influence somewhat. Environmental groups, by contrast, had a major impact despite being a relatively new addition to the Washington scene. EPA staff viewed them as allies with advice worth hearing on how to achieve common goals. These groups hired extraordinarily talented staff, particularly in their early days. Finally, the environmental groups took full advantage of the deadline suits authorized by the 1970 law to force the agency to act.

Toward the 1977 Amendments

NAAQS

EPA's two most important achievements in the early CAA years were to establish NAAQS and the SIPs to achieve them, and to set up and defend the mobile source and fuel control requirements discussed in Chapter 3.

EPA established the six statutorily required NAAQS in 1971, proposing rules in January and issuing final standards ninety days later in April.[26] The proposal addressed all six pollutants in less than twenty pages and contained literally no discussion of the scientific conclusions involved or how EPA had reasoned from those conclusions to the standards. The final version was equally summary.

The abbreviated promulgation schedule allowed little time for internal deliberation. Indeed, even a thirty-year veteran of EPA's air quality standards process was unable to reconstruct the decision-making process for a history of the NAAQS program.[27] All this reflected the times and the novelty of the issues far more than any specific EPA failings. In another reflection of those times and novelty, EPA received no detailed comments on its proposal and very few comments at all, despite the foundational importance of the NAAQS. Even more surprising, in that distant era nobody challenged the NAAQS in court within the legally prescribed filing deadline. (The law required (and requires) challenges to CAA regulations to be brought very soon after their promulgation).

This freedom from litigation did not last long. In 1972 Kennecott Copper Company succeeded in challenging the scientific basis for EPA's 1971 secondary sulfur oxides standards even though it had missed the filing deadline.

In that litigation, the United States Court of Appeals for the D.C. Circuit (the "D.C. Circuit")—which has exclusive power to review most CAA rules subject to potential Supreme Court appeal—asked for a more complete explanation of the basis for the standard.[28] As EPA worked on its response, it realized that its justification was flawed and accordingly withdrew the rule. EPA's chief air attorney wrote the Deputy Administrator that "[t]here appears to be no doubt that the standard was incorrectly established."[29]

Reflecting on this embarrassment, EPA air staff decided that the agency needed a more formal and structured process for setting NAAQS and proceeded to establish one. It called for detailed review of any standards by other offices within EPA and by outside scientific advisors, as well as the public. Somewhat later the agency set up a separate office dedicated entirely to assuring the quality of criteria documents on which NAAQS are based. During this time, at the recommendation of an outside scientific advisory panel, EPA also set in place a plan for the periodic review and updating of NAAQS and the information behind them.[30]

These efforts at process reform survived their baptism of fire when EPA relied on them to set a NAAQS for lead—a standard it had never wanted to set in the first place. In 1975 environmentalists used the new action-forcing litigation provisions to contend that EPA had a "nondiscretionary duty" to set a lead NAAQS, since it had admitted the truth of the key factual predicates for such a standard. At the beginning of 1976, the United States Court of Appeals for the Second Circuit agreed, rejecting agency arguments that other approaches would be less burdensome and just as effective.[31]

This made lead the proving ground for EPA's new NAAQS-writing procedures. After some initial missteps, EPA produced a far more sophisticated analysis and justification than it had in 1971. For example, it used detailed scientific surveys to define a blood lead level that if achieved would protect 99.5 percent of children against defined adverse effects and then calculated an air lead level to attain that goal. In 1980 the D.C. Circuit upheld EPA's standards in all respects.[32]

SIPS

The 1970 SIP requirements called on EPA to oversee the establishment of comprehensive air pollution control programs for every state in the union within two years. This was an assignment of the type that had led William Ruckelshaus to describe the agency's early years as "Running a 100-yard dash while having your appendix removed."

States in 1970 already had air pollution control systems of widely varying degrees of sophistication embodied in laws, regulations, policy guidance, or simply the practices of the relevant regulatory agencies. To submit a SIP, a state would gather a set of these documents into a single package and send it off to EPA. No particular form or format was required. Over time, the agency's professional stationary source control staff, mostly located in Durham, North Carolina, established guidelines and procedures to structure this process. Nevertheless, even today SIPs have no single defined format or context.

Court opinions, however, did begin to refine the process and the standards for approving these submissions. A mixed record in court led EPA to reverse its earlier position and give public notice and invite public comment before approving a SIP.[33] The courts also held that the law barred EPA from considering the economic or technical feasibility of state SIPs in deciding whether to approve them, since the CAA left that decision to the states alone.[34]

In these years EPA also made decisions of generic importance to the future structure of the SIP program in five separate areas, generally but not always in response to environmentalist lawsuits. We will discuss them in turn.

Offsets

The 1970 CAA required SIPs as a matter of bedrock principle to provide for attaining the NAAQS on schedule. But as the 1975 attainment deadline approached, many areas still had persistent NAAQS violations, and many did not have a credible plan to correct them.

It was not clear how EPA could allow the construction of new pollution sources in those areas since they would contribute new emissions to the already excessive existing levels. Yet it would be politically unacceptable to bar all new industry. The answer was suggested by Paul DeFalco, a long-time civil servant and the head of the agency's California office.[35] His suggestion, eventually embodied in a 1976 "Emissions Offset Interpretive Ruling," was to allow construction if the source (1) could obtain enough new emissions reductions from other sources to "offset" its own new emissions and (2) if it installed strict controls itself.[36]

This was the first significant EPA use of "emissions trading," in which greater emission reductions at one source are allowed to substitute for lesser emissions reductions at another. It was an idea with a great future before it. It was also the first of many steps to supplement controls based on air quality factors with requirements for strict controls regardless of air quality computations.

Prevention of Significant Deterioration

In its initial SIP approvals, EPA followed the pretty clear language of the law in approving SIPS that would allow air quality cleaner than the NAAQS to become dirtier as long as NAAQS compliance was preserved. Environmental groups challenged this decision in court. They relied on both the basic purpose of the law and some favorable language in congressional debates.

A federal judge sided with the environmentalists. He ruled, in a short, handwritten emergency order, that SIPs for these areas had to "prevent significant deterioration" (PSD) of the quality of such cleaner-than-NAAQS air. The appeals court and an equally divided Supreme Court upheld his decision without issuing any opinions.[37] No court addressed what PSD might actually mean in program design terms.

EPA considered two different ways to fill this blank slate. The one favored by the air pollution control staff would have limited total emissions increases in any given area. However, this could be said not to directly limit deterioration in air *quality*, and so the agency chose an approach that would directly address increases in ambient pollution levels.

EPA had originally opposed the PSD ruling but in writing the regulations to implement it, the agency became convinced that they would be workable and could fill a gap in the control system. That in turn led the agency to successfully oppose efforts by the White House and energy agencies to reverse the court decisions.[38]

Construction Permits

EPA's new nonattainment and PSD policies worked together to establish detailed construction permit requirements for new pollution sources, including a requirement to install high-performing controls. Congress had not required any of this by law, but once these requirements were established, they grew in importance through the years.

Transportation Controls

In 1973 and 1974 EPA lost environmentalist lawsuits arguing that the agency was required to issue SIPs that would restrict traffic enough to attain the NAAQS by the tight deadlines in the 1970 act if states failed to do this.[39] That was legally correct. Many EPA staff drew back from working on these controls because they doubted the political acceptability of measures like forced carpooling, parking taxes, and gasoline rationing. However, the Administrator and Deputy Administrator supported the effort, young enthusiasts were eager to work on it, and the rules came out.

This triggered a political firestorm, which led EPA to quickly withdraw the offending regulations, stating abjectly that it had received "firm congressional guidance" to do so.[40] Walter Cronkite, America's leading newscaster, repeated this language to begin his evening broadcast. Legislation to remove EPA's authority to restrict traffic or land use quickly followed.[41] The experience gave EPA a so far permanent reluctance to even consider any pollution control measures that might directly affect the private choices of individuals.

Tall Stacks

EPA originally approved the efforts of some states to allow coal fired EGUs to achieve the NAAQS, not by reducing emissions, but by building "tall stacks" to disperse those emissions over a much broader area, thus diluting their impact at any one spot and greatly reducing control costs. Indeed, after the enactment of the 1970 CAA, sources nationwide built about 175 stacks over 500 feet tall.[42] This, was the same approach used by the Tennessee Copper Company at the beginning of the century. EPA approved it without much detailed thought as part of the general rush to get SIPs in place.

Environmental groups challenged this policy in court and won, invoking the slogan that "Dilution is not the solution to pollution." Thus forced to consider the issues, the agency concluded that reliance on dispersion should indeed be limited. The environmentalist litigation then provided very useful support to agency efforts to fend off attempts by energy interests inside and outside the government to allow continued use of dispersion.

In the end, EPA issued a policy that allowed the use of tall stacks to achieve NAAQS only after all feasible emission controls had been applied. This approach was faring well in the courts until it was superseded by legislation as discussed below.[43]

NSPS and Technocratic Decision-Making

Between 1970 and 1977 EPA issued nineteen CAA NSPS, with five of them coming in 1971.[44] These standards did not affect broad sectors of American life like some of the SIP programs or the NAAQS that lay behind them, since they simply prescribed the degree of emission reduction that specified new sources would have to achieve.

However, since the law required these standards to be economically and technically feasible, it also required EPA to analyze large amounts of data in order to determine feasibility. The inevitability of judicial review likewise required the agency to document its reasoning in a form acceptable to a reviewing court—and the courts were not reluctant to specify what that form might be. Making and reviewing such decisions without first having a courtroom type hearing to structure the record was a new task both for agencies and for courts, and both were still grappling with that challenge at the time of the 1977 amendments.[45]

The 1977 Amendments

Congress began to consider Clean Air Act amendments seriously in the mid-1970s. President Carter signed final legislation in 1977.[46] Although Congress almost tripled the length of the law, it very largely reacted to, adapted, and built on the administrative decisions that EPA had made in the previous seven years, adding few entirely new thoughts of its own. Congress authorized a new generation of auto emissions standards as discussed in Chapter 3, allowed other states to adopt the stricter California vehicle emissions standards, and made clear that EPA should err on the side of public health when regulating fuels and fuel additives. On the stationary source side, Congress (1) required periodic review of NAAQS, (2) extended the SIP attainment deadlines and tightened SIP requirements for the preattainment period, (3) added a PSD requirement adapted from EPA's regulations, (4) reformed the NSPS provisions to provide regulatory protection for high-sulfur coal, a move EPA had already begun to consider, and (5) established new rulemaking procedures. We will discuss each in turn.

NAAQS Review

The 1970 CAA allowed EPA to revise NAAQS when and if it chose. EPA, as part of its own post-1970 reform of the NAAQS process, had decided to do this systematically at regular intervals. In 1977 Congress codified and strengthened this approach, legally requiring EPA to review NAAQS every five years and to involve non-government scientific advisors in the review.[47] This made NAAQS revision a duty that could be enforced by citizen suits, which in turn allowed environmental groups to force the agency to take account of new research results as they developed. As NAAQS changed in response to this new knowledge, many other EPA programs also would have to change as a consequence.

Revising the SIP Process

Controlling emissions to achieve a NAAQS requires detailed understanding of the exact emissions responsible and the sources that emit them, together with scientific evaluation of the effect of different controls on air quality. After all that, regulations must be adopted after a full legal process and possible litigation, and the required emission controls must be installed and operated. All these steps must be based on predictions of future effects, which makes them subject to uncertainty and debate. The law gives both states and EPA every incentive to view those uncertainties optimistically so as to avoid any need to write painfully strict SIPs.

To develop a SIP, a state would have to determine when and where its air exceeded NAAQS levels, make an inventory (often broken down by region) of the emissions sources that contributed to these violations, calculate the impact of the emissions from these sources on the level of NAAQS pollutants in the air, and finally devise a set of emission-reducing measures that could be projected to meet the standards by the statutory deadline.[48]

Beyond these timetable and incentive issues, the understanding of air pollution causes on which the 1970 SIP provisions were built has proved inaccurate in significant ways. For all these reasons, nonattainment areas still exist today, fifty years after the 1970 CAA. EPA lists about one hundred areas with a total population of 130 million people as not attaining one or more of the federal NAAQS.[49]

Congress in 1977 took the first steps toward more realistic planning requirements. Most basically, it extended attainment deadlines to as late as 1987. It also added both "best technology" requirements and interim planning requirements to the 1970 approach based solely on air quality. Specifically, Congress required every nonattainment SIP to provide for the use of "reasonably available control measures" and to provide not just for attainment, but for constant increments of "reasonable further progress" toward attainment.[50] Congress adopted and codified EPA's requirement that new sources in nonattainment areas get preconstruction permits, offset their emissions, and install state-of-the-art controls.[51]

On a smaller scale, Congress forbade the use of "tall stacks" to meet air quality standards unless all reasonable emission reduction measures had been employed first, and such stacks were needed to avoid excessive local pollutant concentrations due to downwash.[52] This codified a somewhat tightened version of pre-existing EPA policy. Congress also required all new federally permitted or funded activities in nonattainment areas, including highway projects, to show their "conformity" with the nonattainment strategy before construction could begin.[53]

Finally, Congress acted to give EPA powers short of the "nuclear option" of taking over the SIP itself to induce reluctant states to write and enforce their own SIPs. Congress authorized EPA to direct the withholding of certain non-EPA money, like highway funds, from nonperforming states, and to restrict the issuance of new source construction permits in areas without a proper plan.[54]

Prevention of Significant Deterioration

Congress agreed with the courts that the CAA should protect clean air areas through a "prevention of significant deterioration" program. Congress modeled its approach on EPA's regulations, but tightened the requirements. It allowed only limited increases in particulate or sulfur oxide levels in clean air areas but gave states the authority to allow greater deterioration if they affirmatively so chose through a difficult process. No state has ever tried to make this choice. Congress required unalterable strict protection levels for the air over specifically designated national parks and wilderness areas.[55]

Congress also added an elaborate preconstruction permit program aimed at "major sources"—very roughly, those that emitted more than one hundred tons of pollution a year. Such sources had to show that they would not cause violations of the permissible degradation levels ("increments) or otherwise damage the "air quality related values" of national parks—for example, by impairing visibility. They also had to commit to install the "best available control technology" for all pollutants they emitted in "significant" amounts whether or not the PSD increments applied to those pollutants.[56]

The PSD permit requirements, together with requirements for permits and offsets in nonattainment areas, are known collectively as "NSR" for "new source review." They have become the statutory feature of most recurrent concern to regulated industries. NSR applies to all major sources in the country, since every area is either a PSD area or a nonattainment area, and often both. For emitting industries, the preconstruction permit requirement therefore inserts permit issues into every new plant project nationwide.

In addition, Congress required permits not just for completely new "greenfield" sources but also for any "physical change or change in the method of operation" of an existing source that would "increase" its emissions (The courts later interpreted this phrase to mean that only a "significant" pollution increase (which EPA could and did define) would trigger the permit requirements).[57] Computing an emissions increase can get complicated, since past emissions will differ with the choice of the baseline period over which they are measured, while future emissions must be predicted since they have not occurred yet. For many years EPA's regulations did almost nothing to clarify the resulting uncertainties.

Coal Protection

Economists and policy analysts have long contended that government regulations should set goals for the regulated to achieve, but should not tell them how to achieve it. That allows private initiative to figure out better ways of attaining a specified result.

Accepting that logic, the 1970 legislation directed EPA, whenever possible, to set NSPS as numerical emissions limits and allowed sources to meet them either by the technical controls of their choice, or by burning cleaner fuels. That in turn gave EGUs a strong incentive to meet their NSPS requirements by switching from high-polluting eastern coal to lower-polluting fuel from western mines. That created political concern about job losses at eastern mines. Moreover, switching plants might be able to meet the NSPS requirements without installing any sulfur controls at all, a prospect environmentalists did not like.

In the mid-1970s environmentalists petitioned EPA to revise its power plant NSPS to require all new EGUs to scrub their coal even if they did not need to scrub it to meet the standards. EPA granted that petition and agreed to consider the issue.[58] Given that running start, Congress adopted the environmentalist/eastern coal position and expressly required the NSPS for coal fired EGUs—and that NSPS alone—to make regulated new sources reduce their emissions by a given percentage as well as meeting an absolute control level.[59] That reduced any incentive to switch fuels, since installation of control technology would still be required.

Rulemaking Procedures

The 1977 amendments required EPA to base major CAA rules on a clearly defined "administrative record" that would be made available for public comment, but not for challenge by courtroom-like procedures like cross-examination.[60] This followed the suggestions of the courts and of a law review article by an EPA lawyer that built on those opinions.[61] This approach has worked well and has provided a model for administrative law generally.

From 1977 to 1990

For EPA, the next thirteen years saw dramatic political changes with the 1980 election of Ronald Reagan, his 1981 appointment of Administrator Anne M. Gorsuch (who was basically hostile to many EPA programs), her failure and replacement by William Ruckelshaus (the agency's original head), and the agency's 1983 return to its traditional path under Ruckelshaus and his like-minded successors.

In addition, there were more gradual developments that prepared the ground for dramatic changes in agency direction beginning in 1990. First, experience during these years demonstrated that the HAP control program could not be expected to actually regulate many HAP sources under its existing design. Second, evidence developed that sulfur emissions from large areas of the Midwest were acidifying rainfall in downwind areas and damaging eastern forests and lakes even in the absence of any NAAQS violation. That suggested that the NAAQS-SIP approach could not readily target and control all damages from air pollution.

Third, experience proved once again that the congressionally mandated deadlines for attaining certain NAAQS—ozone in particular—were too optimistic, and that many SIPS lacked enforcement measures adequate to attain them.

Finally, during these years some of the forces that motivated EPA began to change. In the agency's early years, the most central drive had been an all-consuming effort to implement the law, and to deal with the problems arising from that effort. But as the agency and indeed the entire environmental protection field matured, scientific and policy analysis in academe, in think tanks, and within EPA itself began to address environmental regulatory issues.

These studies led over time to a greater understanding of which pollutants were more damaging and which were less, and thus to changes in agency priorities. They also led to a far more refined understanding of the benefits and costs of regulation and thus eventually to the development and implementation of more cost-effective pollution control efforts. We will discuss the first three points in turn.

HAP Control

By the early 1980s EPA had only issued seven HAP control regulations, in dramatic contrast to its activity in other fields.[62] The legal requirement that such regulations protect public health "with an ample margin of safety" proved a major obstacle. EPA had to decide in each case what "public health" was, what "protecting" it would require, how to determine the "margin of safety," and whether economic or technical feasibility should play a role at any stage. Moreover, HAP controls had to be set as emission requirements for individual sources. Yet the effect on health of any given emissions level will vary with the local terrain, weather, and population density. Generating the medical, epidemiological, toxicological, and economic data to even analyze these questions proved a significant task in addition to the conceptual issues.

These difficulties were increased by the statutory focus on controlling *pollutants* rather than *sources*. The structure of the law did not acknowledge that whenever a source emitted more than one HAP, no single HAP could be regulated without a full assessment of the significance of those controls for control of all the other HAPs that the source might emit. In addition, the agency's analysis of potential target chemicals persistently failed to demonstrate that HAPs were causing significant numbers of deaths or other major health events.

Expected deaths are not the only way to measure health concerns. One can also believe that no person should be exposed to more than a certain level of individual risk from hazardous pollutant sources. Environmentalists increasingly emphasized this "acceptable individual risk" perspective in arguing for HAP controls. Switching from an events-based to a risk-based approach almost by definition made it vastly easier to justify strict controls.

Many of these concerns came together in the 1983 case of the Tacoma copper smelter, which was located in a residential suburb of Seattle and processed ore high in arsenic. The plume from the smelter fell on the surrounding community, where the smelter also provided many jobs. Moreover, the smelter was struggling economically and could not afford major new pollution controls.

Health effects modeling revealed projected cancer risks from arsenic exposure greater than one in one hundred—an almost unprecedented number for environmental regulation. But when the Administrator himself questioned the briefers in detail, the numbers lost some solidity. Moreover, the calculations were theoretical at best and almost impossible to verify. As EPA's Assistant Administrator for Research, a public health physician with an international reputation, said in a sidebar conversation: "If we believed these numbers, we'd shut the place down tomorrow. But we don't."[63]

Instead, Administrator Ruckelshaus commissioned a series of meetings in the local community to discover what the residents themselves thought should be done. The *New York Times* criticized him for this, comparing him to a Roman emperor asking the crowd in the arena for advice on whether or not to spare a gladiator, and arguing that he should just make the decision himself instead.[64]

The final result had a certain irony. EPA decided, in accordance with pretty clear local sentiment, to require only a relatively moderate level of pollution control that would allow the smelter to stay open. But even so, the smelter elected to close—thus creating the benefits of a decision for strict controls without anyone actually having to make it.[65]

On the broader HAP control front, EPA's inability to issue HAP control regulations became a political issue. This issue gathered more force in the late 1980s when enterprising congressional staffers brought about the enactment of a freestanding non-CAA requirement for most of American industry to disclose its releases of toxic chemicals. Those disclosures in turn revealed very high levels of air releases of many such substances.[66]

William Ruckelshaus had promised to reinvigorate the HAP control program, but had no more success than his predecessors. In fact, he encountered some trouble with the courts for declining to regulate in cases where it seemed clear to him that the benefits to be gained did not justify action.

In the mid-1980s EPA attempted to move the air toxics program toward the "best technology" approach. In a proposal to regulate vinyl chloride, a carcinogen, EPA rejected the view that since the best science could not identify any risk-free level of exposure to carcinogens, only a zero emissions regulation would conform to the statute.

Instead, EPA chose a more practical result—namely, that when setting emission standards for sources of non-threshold pollutants where there was no actual evidence of human harm at a given emission level, where a no-emissions standard would result in widespread plant closures, and where the costs of such closure would be grossly disproportionate to the benefits of moving beyond strict controls to closure, EPA could simply require use of such strict controls and leave it at that.

The D.C. Circuit, sitting *en banc* with all eleven judges participating, rejected this approach as without statutory foundation. Judge Robert Bork wrote a unanimous opinion for the court that could be read as highly results-oriented or as statesmanlike and creative or both. The court broadly construed the statutory mandate to "protect public health with an ample margin of safety" so as to give EPA a way forward.[67]

To do this, it first ruled that the requirement to achieve "safety" in regulation was absolute. The court stated that EPA had great discretion to decide the exact meaning of this phrase, particularly given the uncertainties of the underlying science. The court stressed that "safe" did not mean "risk free." It suggested that driving a car or breathing city air might be considered "safe." The court then upheld EPA's ability to consider cost and technical feasibility in setting a "margin of safety" once "safety" itself had been assured.

This opinion gave EPA a lot to work with, as Judge Bork and his colleagues doubtless understood. Indeed, its conclusion that breathing city air could be considered "safe" probably went beyond what any prudent EPA lawyer would have thought the courts would accept, since many EPA programs were aimed precisely at reducing pollution levels in such air, which would hardly be necessary if the air were "safe" to begin with.

EPA then developed and proposed a HAP standard for benzene based on the principles of Judge Bork's decision.[68] It adopted the "maximum individual risk" approach for which environmentalists had contended. Under it, risks greater than one in ten thousand would trigger automatic regulation regardless of cost. Risks between one in ten thousand and one in a million would trigger an analysis of whether regulation was justified considering all the factors, and risks less than one in a million would be considered acceptable.

Acid Rain

In the early 1980s research demonstrated that emissions from midwestern coal-fired EGUs were acidifying rainfall in New England and other eastern regions. The resulting "acid rain" was causing vegetation damage. Since the Clean Air Act lacked regulatory tools adapted to this problem, the acid rain issue led to demands for legislation.

After heated debates in which Administrator Ruckelshaus took a leading role, the Reagan administration decided not to support such legislation, both because of its expense and because its demonstrable benefits—measured by avoided vegetation damage—seemed quite small. In his frustration, Ruckelshaus said to a staff member, " If it wasn't so damned expensive, the science would be a lot clearer."[69]

Other benefits that were deliberately not considered much at the time would prove more important in the future. Acid rain controls would clearly reduce atmospheric haze and improve visibility, creating welfare improvements that could fairly be quantified at a large value. The Administrator and others, however, considered these improvements to be too subjective and aesthetic to persuade a skeptical White House to support a multi-billion-dollar program.

In these years EPA analysts also encountered the first faint indications that "fine particulates" caused by the same emissions that cause acid rain could have health effects far beyond any previous consensus.

THE 1990 AMENDMENTS

George H.W. Bush campaigned on a promise to be the "environmental president." His administration began work on Clean Air Act amendments as soon as it took office and Congress enacted them twenty-two months later. Following a general trend toward greater legislative complexity, they were more than twice as long as the 1977 amendments, which in turn had been more than twice as long as the 1970 act.[70]

Like the 1977 amendments, the 1990 amendments extensively rewrote some existing EPA programs. Unlike 1970, Congress also added some new programs without much foundation in earlier EPA regulations. In rough order of significance, the 1990 amendments:

1. Added a completely new "acid rain" control program covering all coal fired EGUs in the country outside of Alaska and Hawaii.
2. Removed the requirement that HAP regulations protect "public health with an ample margin of safety" and replaced it with technology-based control requirements for all "major sources" of specifically listed HAPs, reserving risk analysis to a second regulatory stage.
3. Required the pollutant-reducing "reformulation" of gasoline sold in areas that did not meet NAAQS.
4. Extended once again the deadlines for attaining NAAQS and set up a graduated level of control efforts tied to nonattainment severity to move toward attainment.
5. Extensively revised the CAA authority to control substances that deplete the stratospheric ozone layer.

6. Required all "major sources" of air pollution to get operating permits that would record in one place all their applicable air pollution control requirements.

We will discuss, in turn, each of the four changes (1, 2, 4, and 6) that will not be discussed in other chapters.

Acid Rain Control

Congress decisively resolved the acid rain dispute by requiring all EGUs in the continental United States to reduce their collective emissions of sulfur dioxides by ten million tons (about forty percent) within ten years.[71]

For the first time, Congress built a major CAA program on the market principles long favored by economists. It did this by first imposing emissions limits on covered EGUs, but then generally allowing any individual EGU to reduce its emissions less to the extent that it could induce another EGU to reduce its emissions more. Congress thought that this would allow sources with high control costs to pay low-cost sources to reduce emissions instead, thus causing emissions reductions to take place increasingly at low-cost sources and reducing the overall cost of the program.

To accomplish this, Congress directed EPA to require all EGUs to cover their annual emissions with EPA-issued "allowances." The allowances for each year would add up to that year's permissible source emissions and would be issued without payment to EGUs in proportion to their heat input in a baseline year, with an adjustment that disfavored high-emitting plants. Only the most limited exemptions from this reduction requirement were allowed.

To provide the exact quantification of emissions that enforcing an annual aggregated limit on emissions from many sources requires, Congress required each regulated source to install continuous emission monitors. Though these devices are expensive, the regulated units were so big that monitoring expense was a relatively trivial part of their operating budget.

At the end of each compliance period EPA would compare the number of allowances a source held to its total emissions. Any source that did not hold enough allowances to cover its emissions would be in violation. Congress allowed the transfer of allowances between sources to make trading possible.

Congress in 1990 also repealed the 1977 requirements that an EGU NSPS require not just an emission limit, but also a percentage reduction in emissions. This requirement, adopted to protect high-sulfur eastern coal, had come under withering academic criticism[72] and was traded away to get the support of western senators for the acid rain program.

In addition, Congress broadened and tightened 1977 requirements aimed at eliminating all humanly caused impairment of visibility in national parks and wilderness areas. The law called for SIP revisions to make "reasonable" progress toward this goal, but did not set any deadline for achieving it.[73] EPA regulations set 2064 as the target date for achieving unimpaired natural visibility.[74]

HAP Regulation

For all HAPs except those emitted by fossil fuel fired EGUs, Congress established a completely new system of technology-based control.[75] It listed 189 specific HAPs, and then required EPA to set "maximum achievable control technology" (MACT) standards for all "major sources" of each of them. MACT standards for existing sources had to be set without regard to cost and had to reflect the performance of the best twelve percent of existing sources in the industrial category being regulated. This "MACT floor" could be made more stringent upon consideration of a variety of factors including cost. Standards for new sources at a minimum had to reflect the performance of the best controlled similar source, and could also be made more stringent on the same terms as MACT for existing sources. EPA had to re-examine established MACT standards every eight years. Congress also provided a second stage at which EPA would apply the prior standard of protecting public health to any residual risk remaining after the MACT requirements had been applied.

Congress applied this same system to EGU emissions, but added a crucial preliminary requirement that EPA find that regulation would be "appropriate and necessary" after considering studies of the hazards of EGU mercury and other HAP emissions.[76]

Finally, Congress reacted to mass releases of acutely toxic chemicals in Bhopal, India, and Institute, West Virginia, by requiring EPA to prescribe regulations for the prevention and detection of releases of acutely toxic chemicals, and calling on the agency to respond to any releases of such chemicals that did occur.[77]

Nonattainment Provisions

By 1990 it was clear that despite much progress, attainment of at least the ozone NAAQS was years away in many areas. Indeed, a significant number of nonattainment areas still exist today.[78] In particular, the state of California had proved unable to devise an attainment plan for Los Angeles and several other areas, even though California is more experienced in air pollution control than any other state and probably more willing than any other state to regulate air pollution strictly.

Congress responded by establishing five categories of ozone nonattainment areas—Marginal, Moderate, Serious, Severe, and Extreme—with successively longer attainment deadlines—up to twenty years—and successively tighter control requirements. Congress called for progressively tighter technology-based standards for existing sources and progressively more restrictive NSR rules applicable to progressively smaller sources as the nonattainment severity increased.[79] Congress set up less elaborate versions of this system for carbon monoxide and particulate nonattainment areas, and a still less elaborate version for the remaining criteria pollutants.[80] Ozone is not emitted by sources directly, but is created by complex atmospheric reactions powered by sunlight. Until about the time of the 1990 amendments, EPA's efforts to attain the ozone NAAQs had focused mostly on reducing emissions of "volatile organic compounds."

However, around that same time new scientific research sponsored by EPA, industry, and outside scientific advisors began to suggest that emissions of nitrogen oxides were actually more important. This new perspective had the potential to reorient the control effort away from sources of organic chemicals like oil refining and painting toward combustion sources like power plants.[81]

Evidence of the interstate and regional nature of ozone nonattainment also got stronger. In response, in the 1990 amendments Congress directed a study of this issue, called on thirteen eastern states to work together in an Ozone Transport Commission on recommendations to address it, and called for SIPs for ozone nonattainment areas to include nitrogen oxides controls unless EPA found they would not be beneficial.[82]

Congress also gave EPA new authority to set standards for consumer products like household cleaners and waxes that emit "volatile organic compounds."[83]

Title V Permits

In 1972 Congress had required every major source of water pollution to get an operating permit that would specify all its applicable pollution control requirements, a provision with no counterpart in either the 1970 or 1977 CAAs.[84] In 1990 Congress required such permits for all "major sources" of air pollution—very roughly, all sources that emitted more than one hundred tons a year of criteria pollutants or were subject to HAP control requirements.[85] (EPA estimated that in 2014 there were about fifteen thousand Title V sources in the country).[86]

FROM 1990 TO THE PRESENT

EPA's post-1990 efforts to implement the new law went remarkably smoothly, considering the size of the task. Indeed, the most dramatic developments concerned new issues that the language of the CAA did not address in much detail.

The first, of course, was global warming. Chapter 4 describes EPA's extensive and creative efforts to use the CAA to deal with GHG emissions, or, more than once, to avoid dealing with them. The second development involved efforts to create regional emissions control programs beyond the state-by-state basis reflected in SIPS. Advances in scientific understanding had provided increasingly strong evidence that non-GHG air pollution was markedly more dangerous than previously realized. These dangerous emissions spread over large areas and travelled long distances and required correspondingly broad-based control efforts to be effectively addressed. These years were also the first in which enforcement actions led to pressure for change in the regulatory system.

We will discuss in turn the 1990 amendments, the emerging new issues, and enforcement, and conclude with a few words on the Trump administration.

Implementing the 1990 Amendments

Acid Rain and Visibility

The acid rain program proved easy to implement, considering its scope and impact. The regulations the agency had to promulgate were largely procedural and did not require detailed analysis of scientific or technical issues. Rather they addressed issues like how to issue and trade allowances. In addition, the required controls were universally regarded as technically feasible and affordable.

The program achieved its required reductions at less cost than EPA had projected and far less cost than industry had foreseen, even though many states adopted measures to require the use of local coal that reduced compliance flexibility and cost savings. It operated with only a fifty-person EPA oversight staff. It generated very few legal challenges to its implementing rules and had a negligible noncompliance rate. An EPA review of its first ten years of operation showed that it had achieved reductions of twenty to fifty percent in levels of sulfur-related pollutants in eastern states, that its benefits exceeded its costs by over thirty to one ($3 billion costs versus over $100 billion in benefits) and that acidified lakes were slowly beginning to recover.[87]

Acid rain control may well be the most successful single EPA program ever, apart from absolute or almost absolute bans on products like leaded gasoline, DDT, or CFCs, which are inherently easy to enforce. The visibility program, meanwhile, proved to be an important foundation for controls on EGU emissions, particularly in western states that were not covered by the EPA-developed and NAAQS-based regional trading programs that succeeded the acid rain program.

HAP Control

By 1990 EPA had a generation of experience in writing technology-based standards under the CAA and other statutes. Though of course individual errors were not always avoided, the agency knew how to gather the relevant data (generally through contractors), analyze it, document the analysis in a form suitable for public comment, confer with its various constituency groups, and issue a final rule that responded to the comments received. That, in turn, enabled the agency to issue over 100 MACT regulations between 1990 and 2010 to implement the new MACT requirements.[88] The agency lost a number of lawsuits challenging these standards for failing to implement the provisions of the new law strictly enough, but in the end these losses did not derail the program.[89]

Industry has long complained about uncoordinated or even conflicting regulations set by EPA for the same source under different EPA statutes or sometimes even under the same law. The wave of new MACT standards that the new law commanded led to efforts, in EPA's "cluster" rule, to coordinate new air and water pollution control requirements for sources in the pulp and paper industry.[90] However, despite much interest, the potential for such integrated approaches for other industries turned out to be limited.

At the end, the first and most demanding stage of the statutory MACT requirement had been fulfilled, and the agency moved on to set "residual risk" standards. EPA has combined this review with the required periodic review of MACT technology. EPA's residual risk review applies the same acceptable risk framework articulated thirty years ago in the benzene NESHAP. To date this effort has not led to significant health-based tightening of standards.[91]

Utility regulation took a different course, shaped by the twin facts that (1) EGU HAP emissions would unquestionably qualify for MACT regulation if they came from any other source category, while (2) the specific benefits of very tight HAP control seemed far less than the costs, even though power plant mercury emissions certainly presented appreciable risks. As this issue unfolded over thirty years, two other environmental benefits of mercury standards became apparent, namely (3) that HAP controls would probably cause many coal fired EGUs to close, thus reducing GHG emissions and (4) that both mercury controls and coal plant closures would lead to dramatic health benefits from reduced particulate emissions.

After balancing these factors, the Clinton administration listed EGUs for HAP regulation but did not actually regulate them.[92] The George W. Bush administration tried instead to regulate EGUs under the far less demanding provisions of CAA §111(d). The courts disapproved that effort.[93] The Obama administration returned to the Clinton approach and issued a MACT regulation. After the compliance deadline had passed and essentially all regulated plants had complied with their HAP limit either by installing controls or shutting down, the Supreme Court, in an opinion by Justice Scalia, disapproved the rule for failure to specifically find that regulation was "appropriate and necessary" in a broad sense.[94] The Obama administration then made that finding and reissued the rule.[95] The Trump administration has proposed to withdraw it, arguing that only HAP control benefits can be considered and that these do not justify the expense.[96]

The 1990 amendments set off a new round of SIP development. In eastern and midwestern states, this effort was overshadowed by EPA's move to regional controls since these controls apply almost entirely to EGUs and are administered by the federal government. In California, however, SIP development required a comprehensive effort to restrict emissions of organic compounds and nitrogen oxides from all sources, which at the outer limit might require efforts to limit motor vehicle traffic.

The development of SIPS is always characterized by interchange and bargaining between states and EPA, and that has characterized California SIP development as well, even though no one can seriously question California's commitment to aggressive air pollution control.

EPA also implemented the Title V program without major controversy. At first the agency's permit application requirements were widely viewed as notably expensive and overreaching, and led to pointed congressional inquiries. However, EPA quickly moderated its approach by issuing "guidance" documents that greatly reduced the required information.[97]

EPA also reduced administrative burdens by letting sources of little air quality importance sign up for "general permits" that do not require a detailed application. After that, the major controversies concerned the extent to which permitted sources should be allowed to change their operations without going through a permit amendment process.

Moving Toward Regional Controls

The New Fine Particulate Data

The original particulate NAAQS had regulated atmospheric concentrations of all particles below about twenty to fifty microns in diameter as measured by a somewhat undiscriminating test. Researchers had recognized since 1972 that this aggregate could be divided into small and large particles, and that the small particles were of more health concern. EPA commissioned research into this issue. After some years of active deliberation, EPA in 1987 issued new standards changing the focus of the program to particles with a diameter of ten microns or less (PM10).[98]

This was only a prelude. In the early 1990s academic studies indicated that low levels of exposure to particulate matter with a diameter of 2.5 microns or less (PM 2.5) caused widespread premature mortality and might present risks at any level of exposure.[99] Research in the ensuing almost thirty years has repeatedly reconfirmed that conclusion. These findings were not lost on the environmental community, which brought deadline suits to compel EPA to update the particulate NAAQS.

EPA reacted in 1997 by adding a new "indicator"—PM2.5—to the PM NAAQS, and creating a standard for this indicator separate and apart from that for PM10.[100] Industry litigation resulted in a decisive (and unanimous) EPA victory in the Supreme Court, which emphatically confirmed a long-standing lower court view that NAAQS must be set to protect public health without considering costs or implementation practicalities in any way.[101]

EPA's new NAAQS was highly controversial since it could require much tighter air pollution controls. Opponents of the standard said it could lead to bans on lawnmowers and backyard barbecues. To blunt that controversy, EPA worked with the White House—including President Clinton personally—to issue a guidance memorandum from the president to EPA. EPA drafted it.[102] This document directed that the new standards be implemented in a "common sense, flexible, and cost effective" manner. It postponed the implementation of any drastic control measures until after the next review of the data behind the NAAQS.

This gambit worked as well as its authors could have hoped. New data did indeed confirm the health damage due to PM2.5, leading to a modest tightening of the standard in 2007.[103] It also became apparent over time that a well-designed control program would focus on EGUs and other large sources and not on lawnmowers and barbecues, a development that greatly reduced political opposition.

Nevertheless, the new information put significant pressure on the NAAQS system by emphasizing a characteristic of air pollution that agency staff and other professionals had long recognized. Specifically, the new analysis suggested there was *no* safe level of PM2.5, much less a level that contained a margin of safety. That in turn raised the question exactly how to determine the proper NAAQS level.

EPA's protocols for setting NAAQS address this problem by setting stringent requirements for when studies that show health harm from a given level of pollution will be considered solid enough to support a NAAQS decision. In addition, court decisions have held that NAAQS need not be set at "risk free" levels, and have granted EPA major discretion to set the exact level. Yet at the same time, and in some contradiction to this approach, in making the benefits computations that OMB has long required for all major rules, EPA, with very strong scientific support, has computed massive health benefits for PM2.5 reductions even below the NAAQS levels.

The NOX SIP Call

EPA had long recognized that ozone once formed could persist in the atmosphere and move from one state to another. That, by its nature, challenged the assumptions of the SIP control system that NAAQS exceedances are generally caused by specific local sources and are best addressed state by state. If aggregate emissions in one state are the major cause of ozone violations in another, a state will often be unable to attain the ozone standard by its own efforts. It will also become hard—perhaps impossible—to say that any one source alone is the "cause" of that violation. By 1994 the Ozone Transport Commission established by the 1990 amendments had recommended a nitrogen oxides emission budget for each of the thirteen states it included. Twelve of them had accepted it.

In 1995, the Environmental Council of the States, a relatively new organization that reflected the increased sophistication of state environmental programs, called for the creation of a broad-based working group (the Ozone Transport Assessment Group (OTAG)) to consider the ozone transport problem. The group would be composed of EPA, industry, environmentalists, and thirty-seven states; EPA accepted the suggestion. This step was partly brokered by the Natural Resources Defense Council (NRDC), an environmental group that had sued EPA to compel it to issue the ozone control plans that the state had failed to devise. NRDC offered to settle the case if EPA agreed to work with the states on a broad-based control program, and EPA agreed.[104]

These efforts combined developing scientific knowledge, environmental group litigation, interstate cooperation and lobbying, and EPA willingness to consider new approaches into what eventually became one of the most creative initiatives in the agency's history. Remarkably, it was not propelled by any clear legal deadline for action. Nevertheless, it would lead to three major rulemakings over four presidential administrations. Collectively, they would produce more emission reductions at more reasonable cost than any other single EPA program.

EPA based this effort on CAA provisions that expressly require SIPs to control interstate pollution. Although the CAA had included such provisions since 1970, and a number of court cases had considered them, EPA had never before used them as the foundation for a regulatory program.

Now, however, EPA invoked these provisions to justify a regional "cap and trade" limit called the NOx SIP Call.[105] This effort would restrict NOx emissions during the times of year— the warmer months—when ozone violations occur. Its requirements would apply to EGUs and a few other source types in twenty-nine eastern and midwestern states. The levels would be set as aggregate limits for each state and sources would be allowed to comply, as with the acid rain program, by trading reduction obligations with each other and with sources in other states.

EPA faced two major challenges in framing its program. First, though the agency had pretty clear legal authority to require one state to reduce its emissions by a specified amount if it could show that step was necessary to prevent air quality damage in another state, EPA could not require reductions beyond what this goal required. It therefore had to show that its reduction requirements met a precise target, being both strict enough to remove the undue interstate impact, and no stricter than was necessary to accomplish this. Meeting this condition required addressing some disputable legal questions and detailed documentation and analysis of economic, technical, and air quality factors.

Second, for a cap and trade program to work, each state in the regulated area would have to adopt the same procedures for documenting, quantifying, and trading allowances. Yet the CAA gave EPA no power to compel this uniformity. States would have to adopt it voluntarily.

In the end, EPA overcame all these obstacles. The courts upheld its emissions reduction assignments with minor changes (and one dissent), and all states adopted the trading system voluntarily.[106] They were encouraged to do so by EPA regulations that complied with the letter of the law, but ingeniously made the EPA matrix an easy-to-accept "default option" and made clear that any attempt to do something else would require states to get EPA approval through a long and complex process.

The Clean Air Interstate Rule and its Successors

Like ozone, PM2.5 in general is not emitted by sources directly, but is created by atmospheric reactions among several "precursor" pollutants. The CAA SIP provisions simply call on states to regulate all sources without discrimination to the extent needed to attain the NAAQS. But the data made clear that EGUs were the overwhelming source of PM 2.5 among stationary sources, with a small number of industrial fuel burners responsible for the balance. That made much of the planning and updating complexity of the SIP process irrelevant for effective PM 2.5 control. The cap and trade approach already applied to EGUs by the acid rain program and the NOx SIP Call seemed much more on target.

For these reasons, the George W. Bush EPA adopted a Clean Air Interstate Rule (CAIR) that extended the NOx SIP call model to PM2.5 and added sulfur oxides to the pollutants controlled.[107] The overall structure of the program was very similar to that of the SIP call, except that since PM2.5 violations are not sensitive to the time of year, the particulate control requirements applied year-round.

The new particulate-based sulfur oxide control requirements were tighter than the acid rain limits and thus largely superseded them. Indeed, the price of an acid rain program "allowance" to emit sulfur oxides dropped to almost nothing once the CAIR rule took effect.[108]

By now the massive benefits of PM2.5 control were generally accepted, and the CAIR rule found general acceptance even in a basically anti-regulatory administration. Indeed, EPA's Assistant Administrator for Water complained that his air counterpart breezed his regulations through OMB review by showing an actual body count while he was reduced to talking about fish.[109]

The D.C. Circuit was not as friendly even though very few of the litigants before it challenged the core of EPA's decision. The court disapproved the CAIR rule in a notably aggressive opinion modeled on the dissent in the NOx SIP Call case.[110] This did not reduce EPA's commitment to the regional approach. The Obama administration revised the rule to attempt to meet the court's objections. It also conducted a new air quality analysis that led to tighter requirements and an increase in the number of states covered. Finally, EPA renamed the program the Cross State Air Pollution Rule (CSAPR).[111]

The D.C. Circuit disapproved the rule once again in another aggressive opinion[112] but the Supreme Court reversed this second decision.[113] With that, the trading approach took full effect—indeed, unchallenged effect since the Trump administration has endorsed it and the D.C. Circuit in 2019 rejected all remaining significant legal objections.[114]

According to the EPA's most recent report, these programs collectively have reduced sulfur emissions by ninety percent from the sources they cover. They have reduced nitrogen oxides emissions by about seventy-five to eighty percent. They have led to further reductions in acid rain emissions and further improvements in water quality.[115]

Enforcement at Center Stage

Congress conferred major new enforcement authority on EPA in the 1970 CAA and expanded it in 1977 and 1990. That new authority included the right to impose fines after an agency hearing without having to go to court, and an innovative program to require enforcement penalties to reflect the full value of compliance costs avoided by violators.[116]

Since 1970 the Clean Air Act has given private citizens the right to sue emitting sources directly for emission standards violations.[117] However, this has been of little generic importance to the evolution of CAA controls. EPA has always had an active CAA enforcement program. But, in general, enforcement actions were not driven by efforts to change the basic rules or practices of EPA control programs. Though EPA and the steel industry in the 1970s extensively discussed the impact of enforcement on the industry and how to mitigate the compliance burden, this did not lead to any significant policy modifications.

That changed in the 1990s as EPA turned to enforcement to achieve extensive reductions in emissions from existing major pollution sources.

Congress had believed in 1970 and 1977 that air pollution would naturally decline quite apart from NAAQS requirements as old plants closed down and were replaced by new plants subject to NSPS and NSR. Instead, operators of older coal fired EGUs in particular found ways to extend their operating lives far beyond originally projected limits by maintenance and updating. In 1991 a federal court, following the pretty clear language of the law, ruled that such changes did not trigger NSR as long as they did not increase plant emissions beyond historical levels.[118] Even where such increases might plausibly have been thought to occur, and involved major projects costing tens of millions of dollars, plants often claimed that the changes were "routine maintenance, repair and replacement," which did not trigger NSR.[119]

In response, EPA during the 1990s brought coordinated NSR enforcement actions against the power industry and against industrial sectors such as pulp and paper and oil refining. The agency promoted aggressive approaches to measuring an NSR-triggering emissions increase. These approaches, if universally applied, would have raised questions whether a plant could do anything at all to a major emitting unit without triggering NSR.[120]

These enforcement actions led both to major emissions reductions and to calls for NSR reform to reduce the number of changes in a plant that could trigger it. After extensive discussions between EPA and industry spanning ten years, the George W. Bush administration granted most of industry's requests, making the test for determining an NSR-triggering "emissions increase" clearer and less demanding, and defining and codifying a very broad definition of "routine maintenance, repair and replacement."[121] The courts struck down the second initiative, but the change in the NSR accounting system survived and, by itself, has greatly moderated demands for regulatory change.[122]

Trump

The 2016 election of Donald Trump brought to EPA—for the second time in the agency's history—a management team unsympathetic to the agency's mission and constituencies. But, as of this writing, the impact on control programs for non-GHG stationary source pollutants has been limited, in marked contrast to the frontal attack on mobile source and GHG programs. What might explain this? Almost all stationary source controls programs are many years old. Most of their costs are sunk, and they do not remotely generate the same controversy as GHG controls.

EPA is currently reviewing the PM2.5 NAAQS, the foundation of the most ambitious CAA control programs. There are preliminary signs that the agency may decline to accept the scientific consensus on the dangers of PM2.5. If that proves true, it will represent the single most dramatic step that any administration could take to change the course of the nation's air pollution control effort.

A BALANCE SHEET

The Successes

Widely accepted EPA studies concluded that total CAA benefits from 1970 to 1990, compared to a world without air pollution controls, were about $25 trillion, while the costs were about $500 billion—a favorable ratio of fifty to one.[123] A parallel study for the years from 1990 to 2020 found a favorable ratio of thirty to one and similar overall benefits and costs. Conventional pollutant emissions declined seventy-three percent between 1970 and 2017.[124]

Several CAA innovations in regulatory process have also proved notably successful. Cooperative federalism has worked pretty much as its framers intended and has proved absolutely crucial whenever numerous and varied local pollution sources must be controlled. Similarly, any major future environmental protection law would undoubtedly include numerous deadlines for action enforceable by citizen suits.

The requirement to build the core CAA control programs around NAAQS that must be updated periodically has also worked as intended. It has required the agency to adjust to new knowledge indicating new problems. Other environmental statutes without clearly defined goals or a mechanism for updating them have adjusted much less well to advances in scientific understanding.

The Debatable

Technology-based controls have proved easy to set and enforce. EPA has regularly relied on them to address difficult control problems. Congress has endorsed and expanded the technology-based approach in all three sets of CAA amendments. Technology-based standards can have clear political benefits. In the HAP control field, the MACT approach essentially defused twenty years of controversy over perceived agency inaction. It may be that technology-based controls, regardless of their analytic defensibility, can respond more effectively than other approaches to popular demands that something be done about an issue.

On the other hand, economists have long criticized technology-based standards as unlikely to target the real problem, too expensive for the results they achieve, and justified by flawed arguments about the need to avoid a "race to the bottom" as states compete to set lenient standards to attract industry.[125]

Reliance on technology-based standards, at least in the air pollution field, may be entering a natural decline. EPA's NSPS program to address pollutants has been essentially dormant for many years except for its use to support GHG controls. Similarly, all the required MACT standards have been issued and the required periodic reviews have so far led only to modest changes. Though there is certainly a case for additional air pollution reduction, any future control efforts seem likely to rely more on emission trading than on technology-based source by source controls.

The Problematic

Almost from the beginning, scholars have criticized the CAA's reliance on "command and control" regulation as intrusive, slow, expensive to implement, and unlikely to provide least-cost solutions. Even "technology forcing" by regulation has been considered inferior to approaches that put a price on pollution and thus motivate sources to achieve reductions simply to reduce their costs.

These criticisms have had their impact. In particular, the most frequently suggested alternative—setting aggregate limits for a number of polluters and letting them trade the right to emit among themselves—has been adopted in the acid rain program, the NOx SIP Call, and the Cross-State rule. It seems poised for an even bigger future role.

WHAT NEXT

Possible Future Amendments

In these days of political stalemate combined with increasing focus on global warming, the question how to best revise the CAA has not drawn broad attention. However, those few and perhaps unrepresentative commenters who have written on CAA reform have come to strikingly similar conclusions.[126] In broad outline, they think that:

1. The existing "cap and trade" program for power plants and other sources of regional pollutants should be tightened, broadened, and simplified. Increased emission reductions should be required over time, but the rate and extent of the decrease should be set and adjusted by considering costs and benefits. The reduction obligations should not be tied to detailed calculations of NAAQS attainment.
2. In return, many other CAA programs to control criteria pollutants should be scaled back or even eliminated since the cap and trade program would achieve their goals more effectively. Candidates would include SIPS, NSR, PSD, and visibility protection requirements.
3. Other programs, such as those for NSPS or HAP control, would be retained in order to protect gains already achieved, but not much future activity would be expected of them absent clear evidence of unaddressed problems.

Open Questions

Adding details to this easily articulated consensus would raise difficult issues. How tight should the cap and trade limits be? How fast should they decline? Exactly which existing programs should be "scaled back" and how? And what programs should be completely eliminated?

More fundamental issues would also arise.

Relation to GHG Control

Almost without exception, big sources of conventional air pollutants are also big GHG sources. Any measures to reduce GHG emissions from these sources would unquestionably reduce conventional air pollutants as well. Separating these two control efforts would make no sense. Indeed, one might reasonably speculate that Congress' inability to address GHG control has prevented any motion on the much less divisive issue of conventional pollutant controls. But if there were to be comprehensive GHG legislation—and that is probably a precondition to CAA reform—what problems would be left for air pollution control specifically to address?

Rethinking the Role of the States

A national cap and trade system for large fuel burning sources might well eliminate most to all of the multi-state problems from air pollution, such as health damage from regionally distributed PM2.5 or large-scale visibility impairment. Since most of the remaining problems would be confined within a single state, what justification would remain for the pressure that the CAA puts on states to conform to federal directives? Should the statute allow states more freedom than at present to decide how to deal with such problems?

This would not necessarily mean federal abdication. Even if the responsibility for actual regulatory decisions rested with states, it would be easy to defend calling on the federal government both to provide technical information relevant to those decisions and to evaluate the actual results of state programs to provide a quality control check.

Where pollution comes from many small sources, a primary reliance on state initiative seems inevitable since the federal government is not well adapted to control them. In such cases a federal program of reporting comprehensively on the state of air pollution control and the remaining dangers might induce states to regulate in appropriate cases even if they were not required to regulate. A somewhat similar program of release disclosure called the "toxics release inventory" seems to have had such an effect, and legal commenters have extensively addressed the ways in which more focused data disclosure could be used to achieve environmental goals.[127]

NOTES

1. See generally John Bachman, "Will the Circle be Unbroken: A History of the U.S. National Ambient Air Quality Standards," *Journal of the Air and Waste Management Association* 57, no. 6 (2007): 655–58 (henceforth "Bachman").
2. Georgia v. Tennessee Copper, 206 U.S. 230 (1907), 230, 240.

3. Ibid., 239.

4. Bachman, 659-60. For a book-length discussion of Donora and its consequences, see Devra Davis, *When Smoke Ran Like Water* (New York: Basic Books, 2002).

5. Act of July 14, 1955, Pub. L. 84–159, 69 Stat. 322. This "one-and-a-half-page law authorized the Secretary of [the Department of Health, Education and Welfare] to fund federal research and to assist states and educational institutions in training personnel and carrying out research," Bachman, 660.

6. Clean Air Act of 1963, Pub. L. 88–206, 77 Stat. 392.

7. California Air Resources Board, "History," accessed March 15, 2020, https://ww2.arb.ca.gov/about/history.

8. Motor Vehicle Air Pollution Control Act of 1965, Pub. L. 89–272, 79 Stat. 992.

9. Air Quality Act of 1967, Pub. L. 90–148, 80 Stat. 485.

10. Clean Air Act Amendments of 1970, Pub. L. 91–604, 84 Stat. 1676.

11. For the exact legal language, see Clean Air Act ("CAA") §§108 and 109. The relevant language has remained essentially unchanged since 1970. (Henceforth, unqualified citations to CAA sections mean that the provision discussed has survived without fundamental change to the present day.)

12. CAA §110 (1970 version).

13. CAA §113 (1970 version).

14. CAA §110(a)(2).

15. Not only was the duty to attain expressed in unconditional terms, the Senate Report on the legislation expressly stated that reductions of up to seventy-five percent in vehicle traffic might be needed to attain on schedule. S. Rep. No. 91–1196, 91st Cong. 2d. Sess., 2, 12–13.

16. CAA §111.

17. CAA §111(f).

18. See 40 C.F.R. Part 60, subpart C.

19. CAA §112 (1970 version). As discussed below, Congress fundamentally changed this provision in 1990.

20. CAA §303.

21. See Chapter 3.

22. Ibid.

23. Since 1970 CAA §304(a)(2) has authorized "any person" to sue EPA in federal district court to compel the performance of any duty that is "not discretionary with the Administrator." Since the Administrator has no discretion to refuse to issue regulations subject to a statutory deadline for issuance, this provision allows suits to enforce every such deadline in the CAA. Indeed, EPA has never in its history won such a deadline suit.

24. For further discussion, see John Bonine, "The Evolution of Technology Forcing in the Clean Air Act," *Environmental Reporter*, Monograph 21 (1975).

25. For an illustration of the learning curve, see the discussion in Portland Cement Association v. Ruckelshaus, 486 F.2d. 375 (D.C. Cir. 1973) (Leventhal, J.).

26. 36 Fed. Reg. 1514 (January 30, 1971) (proposal); 36 Fed. Reg. 8186 (April 30, 1971) (final.)

27. Bachman, 672 ("Even more elusive is the decision-making process itself.").

28. Kennecott Copper v. EPA, 462 F.2d. 846 (D.C. Cir. 1976).

29. R. Shep Melnick, *Regulation and the Courts: The Case of the Clean Air Act* (Washington DC: Brookings Institution Press, 1983), 241.

30. For further discussion of the reforms, see Bachman, 673–78.

31. NRDC v. Train, 545 F.2d. 320 (2d. Cir. 1976).

32. Lead Industries Association v. EPA, 647 F.2d. 1130 (D.C. Cir. 1980).

33. See William F. Pedersen, "Why the Clean Air Act Works Badly," *University of Pennsylvania Law Review* 129, no. 5 (1981): 1078.

34. Union Electric Co. v. EPA, 427 U.S. 246 (1976).

35. Elliott "Fifty Years of EPA: Chapter III," unpublished manuscript, (2019), 21.

36. 41 Fed. Reg. 55524 (1976).

37. Sierra Club v. Ruckelshaus, 344 F.Supp. 253 (D.D.C.), *aff'd mem.* 4 E.R.C. 1815 (D.C. Cir. 1972), *aff'd by an equally divided court sub nom.* Fri. v. Sierra Club, 412 U.S. 541 (1973).

38. For further discussion, see Melnick, *Regulation and the Courts.*

39. See, e.g., NRDC v. EPA, 475 F.2d. 968 (D.C. Cir. 1973); City of Riverside v. Ruckelshaus, 4 E.R.C. 1728 (C.D. Calif. 1972).

40. 39 Fed. Reg. 1848 (January 15, 1974).

41. The repeal was made in the Energy Supply and Environmental Coordination Act, Pub. L. 91-190, enacted in June 1974.

42. US Environmental Protection Agency, *Identifying and Assessing Technical Bases for Stack Height for EPA Regulatory Analysis,* Preliminary Report, EPA-69-02-3323 (Washington, DC: EPA, September 1979), 13.

43. For further discussion, see Melnick, *Regulation and the Courts.*

44. Compiled from Dale Pahl, "EPA's Program for Establishing Standards of Performance for New Stationary Sources of Air Pollution," *Journal of the Air Pollution Control Association* 33, no. 5 (1983): 468.

45. For an illustrative discussion of these problems, see Portland Cement Association v. Ruckelshaus.

46. Clean Air Act Amendments of 1977, Pub. L. 95–95, 69 Stat. 322 (1977).

47. CAA §109(d).

48. For further discussion, see Pedersen "Why the Clean Air Act Works Badly," 1063–67.

49. US Environmental Protection Agency, "Nonattainment Areas for Criteria Pollutants (Green Book)," *epa.gov,* accessed April 13, 2020, https://www.epa.gov/green-book.

50. CAA §§171 & 172.

51. CAA §§172(b)(6); 173.

52. CAA §123.

53. CAA §176(c).

54. CAA §176(a).

55. CAA §§160-169.

56. CAA §165.

57. CAA §§165(c)(2) and 172(a)(1) and 171(4). The D.C. Circuit authorized the exclusion of "insignificant" emissions increases in Alabama Power v. Costle, 636 F.2d. 323, (1980). EPA's exclusion levels are set out in 40 C.F.R. 52.21(b)(23) (definition of "significant emissions increase").

58. "Use of Scrubbers with Coal Boilers Pushed by Carter," *New York Times,* May 31, 1977, 15.

59. CAA §111(a)(1) (definition of "standard of performance") (1977 version).

60. CAA §307(d).

61. Portland Cement Association v. Ruckelshaus; William F. Pedersen, "Formal Records and Informal Rulemaking," *Yale Law Journal* 85 (1975): 38-89.

62. See Robert J. Martineau, Jr. and Ben Snowden, "Hazardous Air Pollutants," In *The Clean Air Act Handbook*, eds. Julie R. Domike and Alec C. Zacaroli (Chicago: American Bar Association, 2011), 232. Henceforth "Martineau and Snowden."

63. Personal recollection of author.

64. "Mr. Ruckelshaus as Caesar," *New York Times,* July 16, 1983.

65. "Smelter Putting Arsenic in the Air is Set to Close," *New York Times*, June 30, 1984, 14.

66. The statute was the Emergency Planning and Community Right to Know Act, Pub. L. 99-499, 100 Stat. 1613 (1986), codified at 42 U.S.C. §§11001–11050. "The initial . . . report [under the statute] indicated that in 1987 toxic releases to the air from major manufacturing facilities were approximately 2.7 billion pounds. The report brought renewed public attention to the fact that substantial amounts of [hazardous air pollutants] were being emitted into the atmosphere, particularly in industrial centers and where chemical manufacturing facilities were located, such as in Louisiana, Ohio, Texas, Tennessee, and Virginia," Martineau and Snowden, 233.

67. Natural Resources Defense Council v. EPA, 824 F.2d 1146 (D.C. Cir. 1987). Since so many cases have this title, the decision is generally known as the "Vinyl Chloride case."

68. 53 Fed. Reg. 28496 (July 28, 1988).

69. Personal recollection of author.

70. Clean Air Act Amendments of 1990, Pub. L. 101-549, 104 Stat. 2399.

71. CAA §§401–16.

72. Especially in Bruce A. Ackerman and William T. Hassler, *Clean Coal/Dirty Air: or How the Clean Air Act Became a Multibillion-Dollar Bail-Out for High-Sulfur Coal Producers* (New Haven: Yale University Press, 1979).

73. CAA §§169A& 169B.

74. See 40 C.F.R. 51.308(d)(1)(B).

75. CAA §§112.

76. CAA §112(n)(1).

77. CAA §112(r).

78. See note 49.

79. CAA §§181-5.

80. CAA §§186-7, 188-90.

81. Bachman, 686.

82. CAA §§182(f), 184-5.

83. CAA §183(e).

84. Clean Water Act §§301 and 401, 33 U.S.C. §§1311, 1342.

85. CAA §§501-507.

86. See Utility Air Regulatory Group v. EPA, 572 U.S. 302 (2014).

87. US Environmental Protection Agency, *Acid Rain Program: 2004 Progress Report*, EPA-430-R-05-012 (Washington, DC: EPA, October 2005).

88. Martineau and Snowden in Appendix 1 to their article list the §112 regulations issued as of the beginning of 2011.

89. See, e.g., NRDC v. EPA, 489 F.3d 1364 (D.C. Cir. 2007); Sierra Club v. EPA, 479 F.3d 875 (D.C. Cir. 2007).

90. Wayne B. Gray and Ronald J. Shadbegian, "Multimedia Pollution Regulation and Environmental Performance: EPA's Cluster Rule," working paper DP 15-26 (Washington, DC: Resources for the Future, 2015).

91. EPA lists its residual risk reviews at https://www.epa.gov/stationary-sources-air-pollution/risk-and-technology-review-national-emissions-standards-hazardous#status. A review of over fifty completed actions showed only two modest tightenings based on risk factors, involving the standards for petroleum refining and chromium electroplating. See National Association for Surface Finishing v. EPA, 795 F.3d. 1 (D.C. Cir. 2015) (upholding risk-based tightening of chromium electroplating standards).

92. 65 Fed. Reg. 71825 (December 20, 2000).

93. New Jersey v. EPA, 517 F.2d. 574 (D.C. Cir. 2008).

94. Michigan v. EPA, 576 U.S. (2015).

95. 81 Fed. Reg. 24420 (April 25, 2016).

96. 84 Fed. Reg. 2670 (February 7, 2019).

97. See US Environmental Protection Agency, *White Paper for Streamlined Development of Part 70 Permit Applications* (Washington, DC: EPA, July 10, 1995), https://www.epa.gov/title-v-operating-permits/white-paper-streamlined-development-part-70-permit-applications.

98. 52 Fed. Reg. 24634 (July 1, 1987).

99. The most prominent of these was known as the "Six Cities study." Douglas W. Dockery et al., "An Association between Air Pollution and Mortality in Six U.S. Cities," *New England Journal of Medicine* 329, no. 24 (1993): 1753.

100. 62 Fed. Reg. 38652 (July 18, 1997).

101. Whitman v. American Trucking, 531 U.S. 457 (2001).

102. Bachman, 688. The memorandum is reprinted at 62 Fed. Reg. 38421 (July 18, 1997).

103. 71 Fed. Reg. 61144 (October 17, 2006).

104. For further discussion, see Philip E. Karmel, "Interstate Transport and Regional Implementation Plans," In *The Clean Air Act Handbook*, eds. Julie R. Domike and Alec C. Zacaroli (Chicago: American Bar Association, 2011), 114-16.

105. 63 Fed. Reg. 57356 (October 27, 1998).

106. Michigan v. EPA, 213 F.3d 663 (D.C. Cir. 2000).

107. 70 Fed. Reg. 25162 (May 12, 2005).

108. "By 2012, allowances cleared at auction prices less than $1 per ton, well below the $1,000 per ton allowance prices of the mid 2000s," Joseph E. Aldy et al., "Looking Back at 50 Years of the Clean Air Act," working paper 20-01 (Washington DC: Resources for the Future, 2020), 12.

109. G. Tracy Mehan, former EPA assistant administrator for water, personal conversation with William F. Pedersen.

110. North Carolina v. EPA, 531 F.3d. 896, modified 550 F.3d. 1176 (D.C. Cir. 2008).

111. 76 Fed. Reg. 48208 (D.C. Cir. 2012).

112. EPA v. EME Homer City Generation, 696 F.3d. 7 (D.C. Cir. 2012).

113. EPA v. EME Homer City Generation, 572 U.S. 489 (2014).

114. Wisconsin v. EPA, 938 F.3d. 303 (D.C. Cir. 2019).

115. US Environmental Protection Agency, *Power Sector Programs Progress Report* (Washington, DC: EPA, 2018), https://www3.epa.gov/airmarkets/progress/reports/.

116. CAA §§113(d), 120.

117. CAA §304(a)(2), (a)(3).

118. Wisconsin Electric Power Company v. EPA, 893 F.2d. 901 (7th Cir. 1990).

119. For examples, see EPA's Environmental Appeals Board discussion of the enforcement order issued to TVA, "In re Tennessee Valley Authority," No. CAA-2000-04-008, EPA App. Lexis 25 (September 25, 2000).

120. Specifically, EPA argued for determining whether an NSR-triggering emissions increase had occurred at a source by subtracting the source's past *actual* annual emissions from what it would emit in the future if it ran at full capacity every hour of the year. Since in fact no plant ever operates that intensively, this apples-to-oranges approach computed emissions increases—often quite major emissions increases—even when there was no reason to believe that they would actually occur.

121. 67 Fed. Reg. 80186 (December 31, 2002); 68 Fed. Reg. 61248 (October 27, 2003).

122. New York v. EPA, 413 F.3d 3 (D.C. Cir. 2005).

123. US Environmental Protection Agency, *The Benefits and Costs of the Clean Air Act 1970-1990* (Washington, DC: EPA, 1997), https://www.epa.gov/environmental-economics/benefits-and-costs-clean-air-act-1970-1990-1997.

124. US Environmental Protection Agency, *The Benefits and Costs of the Clean Air Act 1990-2020* (Washington, DC: EPA, March 2011), https://www.epa.gov/clean-air-act-overview/benefits-and-costs-clean-air-act-1990-2020-report-documents-and-graphics.

125. See, e.g., Bruce A. Ackerman and Richard B. Stewart, "Reforming Environmental Law," *Stanford Law Review* 37 (1985); Richard L. Revesz, "Rehabilitating Interstate Competition: Re-thinking the 'Race to the Bottom' Rationale for Federal Environmental Regulation," *NYU Law R*eview 67 (1992):1210-54.

126. Robert Nordhaus, "Modernizing the Clean Air Act: Is there Life After 40?" *Energy Law Journal* 33, no. 2 (2012); William F. Pedersen and David Schoenbrod, "The Overwhelming Case for Clean Air Act Reform," *Environmental Law Reporter* 43, no. 10971 (2013).

127. See, e.g., William F. Pedersen "Regulation and Information Disclosure: Parallel Universes and Beyond," *Harvard Environmental Law Review* 25, no. 151 (2001).

Chapter Three

Clean Air: Controls on Cars, Trucks, and Fuels

John D. Graham[1]

INTRODUCTION

With post-World War II prosperity and construction of the Interstate Highway System came dramatic increases in the number of automobiles and vehicle miles traveled. Household mobility was enhanced, but it came with a pernicious downside: a growing air pollution problem in the country. By 1970, emissions from automobiles contributed an estimated sixty percent of some air pollutants and eighty percent of some air pollutants in many urban areas.[2]

The poster child for air pollution from automobiles was Los Angeles, often referred to as the most polluted major city in the US.[3] Throughout the 1960s, the number of days per year when air pollution in LA reached unhealthy levels was increasing each year.

Part of the problem is southern California's distinctive topography. When ocean breezes draw cool marine air onshore beneath a mass of warm air above, an inversion layer forms. The same dirty air can be held in place by the mountains that surround LA on the north and east. On average, an inversion ceiling hovers over LA approximately 260 days per year. Even worse, the warm, sunny climate of southern California facilitates the formation of smog. When unburned hydrocarbons and nitrogen oxides are emitted from cars and industrial facilities, they interact in the presence of sunlight to produce ozone, also called photochemical smog. Breathing elevated levels of ozone is known to impair health, particularly among susceptible subpopulations such as children, asthmatics, senior citizens, and people with cardio-pulmonary problems.[4]

To help combat these problems, California and EPA became pioneers of "technology-forcing" regulation that reduced the rate of tailpipe emissions from cars by more than 99% over the agency's fifty-year history. By "technology forcing," I mean a regulation that stimulates the development and commercialization of innovative pollution-control technologies, some that are not even discovered at the time a regulation is imposed. In the 1960s this was a radical idea, one that many leaders of the automotive and oil industries were not prepared to accept.

A key to EPA's success was recognizing that strict regulations of the design of both fuels and engines are necessary. The amount of pollution produced by the internal combustion engine is related to three factors: the characteristics of the fuel that is combusted, the design of the engine, and the design of the post-combustion treatment systems that clean the exhaust stream.[5] For regulators, it became especially crucial to understand how the three factors interact to produce the pollution, and how those factors change over the lifetime of the vehicle, which can be as long as thirty years or more.

As EPA entered the arena of technology-forcing regulation, the agency repeatedly encountered strong resistance from the segments of industry that were impacted.[6] In hindsight, EPA's success seems remarkable given that this modestly sized regulatory agency was pitted against two of the largest and politically most potent industries in America, who in turn were often pitted against each other as the required innovations entailed changes to both engines and fuels. The automotive industry includes not just the auto manufacturers and their suppliers located throughout the heartland of the country but the network of car dealers who are present in every congressional district. The oil industry is also an immense sector that includes employees engaged in exploration and production, refining, distribution, and retail sales at the 170,000 refueling stations around the country.

Many factors contributed to this success story, but several are highlighted in this chapter. First, EPA had the opportunity to learn from—and collaborate with—the California Air Resources Board, which Congress allowed to set its own regulations, as long as they were stricter than EPA's regulations. Second, EPA was blessed with an underappreciated technical resource, an engineering laboratory in Ann Arbor, Michigan, that could test vehicles and fuels, engage in research and development (R&D), and help enforcement officials expose corporate cheaters in the auto and fuels industries. Finally, at numerous points in its history, EPA was backed by elected officials from both parties—members of Congress and presidents—who had the political courage to take on the industries within EPA's purview.

In this chapter, I examine the lessons learned from technology-forcing regulation with four illustrations that span the agency's fifty-year history: invention and commercialization of the catalytic converter; removal of lead and sulfur from gasoline; the growing use of ethanol as an additive to gasoline;

and measures to curb exhaust from diesel engines. I also highlight the role EPA plays in ensuring that companies comply with regulations and how EPA made creative use of its enforcement authority to boost the development of the nascent electric-vehicle sector. I do not address the carbon dioxide emissions from vehicles since they are addressed in Chapter 4.

I begin with the origins of California's role and the mandate Congress gave to EPA in 1970; then I proceed to the four illustrations and the enforcement issues. In the conclusion of the chapter, I comment on EPA's success as a technology-forcing regulator and what lessons from the previous fifty years are crucial to appreciate as the agency moves forward.

CALIFORNIA LEADS IN ADDRESSING AUTOMOBILE EMISSIONS

The story of how dramatic reductions in automobile emissions have been achieved really begins in California—and that state deserves considerable credit for its contributions.[7] In the 1950s, a Dutch scientist, Dr. Arie J. Haagen-Smit of the California Institute of Technology, determined the atmospheric processes that lead to formation of ozone. Studies from his research team pinpointed the key role of automobiles in Los Angeles's smog problem.[8]

In 1959 the California legislature responded by directing the State Department of Public Health to establish necessary controls on motor vehicles.[9] A board was established to test vehicles for emissions and certify whether emissions were adequately controlled. The first regulation on automakers was adopted in 1961 (for model year 1963), followed by tailpipe emissions limitations on hydrocarbons (HC) and carbon monoxide (CO) in 1964 (for model year 1966). California regulators went beyond tailpipe emissions control. They were concerned about the gasoline vapors that escape into the atmosphere from the fuel tank and fuel system before the gasoline is burned. A California standard to control these "evaporative emissions" began with model year 1970. In 1971, during EPA's first full year of operation, the newly branded California Air Resources Board (CARB) also added a tailpipe standard for nitrogen oxides (NOx) for model year 1974, as NOx was also increasingly seen as smog precursor.

Prior to enactment of these standards, auto engineers had focused primarily on design issues salient to consumers such as performance, interior volume, comfort, air conditioning, and style. Pollution control was largely ignored.[10] The early California standards triggered a number of changes to the design of the internal combustion engine, which had not been refined significantly during the 20th century. The changes included leaner carburetors, air pumps, timing controls on engine operation, small carbon canisters to capture gasoline vapors, and systems of exhaust gas recirculation. California's regulatory pressure also induced GM to devote several years of R&D effort to the catalytic converter, though GM initially opposed regulations that would force the technology's implementation.[11]

The federal government was aware of the progress being made in California, and Congress in 1965 authorized the Department of Health, Education, and Welfare (HEW) to set national standards for automobile emissions based on a test of technical and economic feasibility. HEW responded by applying the 1961 and 1964 California regulations nationally, starting with model year 1968 vehicles. National evaporative-emissions standards took effect in model year 1971. This pattern—California acting first and then the federal government—would be repeated numerous times throughout the fifty-year history of EPA.[12]

The US Congress recognized the unique challenges of pollution control in southern California—as well as the leadership the state had shown in addressing emissions from automobiles. In 1967 and again in 1970, Congress added legislative language recognizing CARB's expertise and role in regulating automotive emissions. The other forty-nine states and the territories were treated differently. Automakers and dealers feared that other states would begin adopting standards different from CARB's standards, creating a proliferation of conflicting state regulations for a product intended to be sold across state lines.[13]

Congress responded by preempting the field for federal regulation, forbidding any state other than California from regulating motor vehicle emissions. California was permitted to request a waiver from EPA to establish stricter auto standards than those promulgated by EPA. Congress subsequently authorized other states to adopt California standards as long as they were precisely the same as California.[14]

CONGRESS ADOPTS A TECHNOLOGY-FORCING APPROACH TO CONTROLLING AUTOMOBILE EMISSIONS

In 1970, as Congress took stock of the air pollution problem the country faced, legislators were concerned that simply continuing on the current trajectory of encouraging small improvements in the internal combustion engine was not going to result in healthy air across the country in the foreseeable future. The Secretary of HEW, John Gardner, testified in 1967, "the state of the art has tended to meander along until some sort of regulation took it by the hand and gave it a good pull. . . . There has been a long period of waiting for it, and it hasn't worked very well."[15]

The automobile companies were seen as dragging their feet to reduce emissions from their vehicles. In fact, in January 1969 the Department of Justice brought suit against General Motors, Ford, Chrysler, and American Motors, alleging they had conspired, through a joint research venture, to suppress the development and diffusion of pollution control technologies. The suit was settled through a consent agreement that led to termination of the joint venture.[16]

Reducing emissions from vehicles was going to be very important to states, as they could take account of the anticipated reductions when crafting their state implementation plans to show attainment with EPA's national air-quality standards. Consequently, less pollution from vehicles would take some of the pressure off state and local officials to reduce emissions from job-producing stationary sources. It would take time before decreases in emissions from the new automobiles entering the market would result in a significant change in the overall level of emissions because the automobile fleet turned over slowly. Moreover, it was important to try to achieve significant emissions reductions from new cars as rapidly as possible, as vehicle miles traveled were increasing and would offset some of the reductions in emissions per mile traveled.

Origins of the 90% Reduction Requirements

In the 1970 Clean Air Act, Congress went well beyond the pioneering CARB standards and required that EPA set standards to reduce the emissions of HC and CO emitted from 1975 model vehicles by 90% from the levels of those pollutants emitted from 1970 model-year vehicles. A similar reduction of 90% in the emission of NOx in 1976 model-year cars compared to their 1971 levels was also mandated. The standards would have to be met by every new car, and compliance had to be maintained for at least five years of the vehicle's life or fifty thousand miles.

These were not only ambitious standards, they were technology-forcing—that is, at the time they were enacted in the legislation, there was no known and demonstrated technology for meeting them.[17] Congressional staff selected the 90% figure because it was a research goal established by the Nixon administration.[18] Up until then, emission standards were based on what was seen as reasonably achievable; these standards in the 1970 Act were based on what Congress perceived to be the necessary reduction in pollution from automobiles to meet the goal of healthy air. Prescribing the standards in the statute itself reflected a concern on the part of some authors of the legislation that industry pressure would "crumple" an administrative agency which attempted to set its own standards.[19]

In this way, Congress deviated from the approach used elsewhere in the Clean Air Act, as well as in the Clean Water Act, where technology-based based requirements are generally based on existing, demonstrated technology. By adopting technology-forcing standards, Congress created a strong incentive for innovation in engine design and/or development of add-on emission control technology.[20]

Technology-forcing regulations can provide a potential new market for suppliers of pollution-control equipment.[21] The firm that is successful in developing technology that can meet ambitious standards will generate large revenue flows, especially if the firm can obtain and enforce patent protection for those innovations. A huge source of revenue can be created for innovators if the new technology is ultimately installed on all new cars sold around the world. A large automaker might also favor a technology-forcing regulation if it perceives that it is better positioned with its suppliers than other automakers to comply with the regulation. Thus, the regulator looks for ways to harness competition within the industry to spur innovation.

The legislative history indicates that Congress expected the 1970 mandate to force the industry to explore new types of engines and treatment systems for reducing emissions. Domestic automakers had shown little interest in moving beyond reciprocating internal combustion ("piston") engines, but some foreign manufacturers were looking at different engine designs such as the rotary (Mazda) and stratified charge (Honda) engines which generate far fewer emissions in the engine combustion chamber. Those engines were highly effective in reducing CO and HC emissions but tended to exacerbate NOx emissions.[22] There were also some promising exhaust treatment technologies under development—namely, noble metal catalysts (which burn unwanted pollutants outside the engine), reactors, and catalyst/reactor combinations with the potential to achieve very significant reductions in tailpipe emissions.

But the idea of legislating a 90% reduction in emissions raised some important, practical questions. What if there were reliability issues with the new technologies, or the cars had drivability issues, and consumers shied away from buying them? What if there were not sufficient compliant cars (or even any) able to meet the market demand for new automobiles in 1975? What if some domestic manufacturers were not able to meet the standards—or could meet them with only some of their models—while other manufacturers were able? Would a significant part of the industry have to shut down production? Insofar as foreign manufacturers were the only ones able to meet the standards, was the US prepared to turn over the domestic market to them? EPA was compelled to face these issues.

Congress knew that the standards were "drastic medicine" and that the legislation carried some real risks as to whether the automobile companies could meet the goal. Congress also recognized that one in every seven jobs in the country was tied to the production and sale of automobiles.[23] As Republican Senator Howard Baker of Tennessee noted, "this may be the biggest industrial judgment that has been made in the United States in this century." His colleague from Michigan, where a large segment of the auto industry was located, Republican Senator Robert Griffin described it as a "dangerous game of economic roulette."[24]

Consequently, the law provided what Senator Baker described as a "realistic escape hatch": automobile manufacturers could petition the EPA Administrator for a one-year suspension of the requirement. The law also provided for the National Academy of Sciences to undertake a study of the feasibility of meeting the standards. For the one-year extension to be granted, the EPA Administrator would have to find, among other things, (1) that the suspension was essential to the public interest or the public health or welfare, (2) all good faith efforts had been made to meet the standards, and (3) that the companies had established that effective control technologies were not available, or would not be available with sufficient lead time, to be utilized in the 1975 model year.

As Congress was considering these technology-forcing provisions—and after they were enacted—the auto industry vigorously contested them, arguing that not only was there no currently known technology to meet the standards but, even if such technologies were developed, the long lead time involved in producing cars would make it impossible to get them in place for the 1975 model-year. The industry also argued that the 1975 EPA HC/CO standards would be unduly costly, would cause a fuel economy penalty, might cause vehicles to be underpowered, and would hit the Big Three harder than the Japanese vehicle manufacturers. The industry persuaded the United Auto Workers of America to support their efforts to convince Congress to relax the requirements, arguing that they would lead to job loss.

At the time, the auto industry was also under considerable pressure from another federal agency, the National Highway Traffic Safety Administration (NHTSA), with respect to automobile safety. Many industry leaders held the view that the federal government had no business trying to tell companies how to design and market automobiles.[25]

Ruckelshaus's 1972 Decision

Under the Clean Air Act, an application for a suspension could be filed any time after January 1, 1972, and the Administrator was required to make a decision within sixty days thereafter. On March 13, 1972, a small foreign manufacturer, Volvo, formally filed for a suspension, thereby triggering the sixty-day period for a decision. Not until April 5 did the Big Three (Ford, GM, and Chrysler) come forward to file as well. At that point, the Administrator had five weeks to make his decision.

The agency held public hearings from April 10-27. Representatives of most of the major automobile manufacturers, a number of suppliers of emission control devices, and various public interest groups and public bodies testified and submitted data. EPA had data concerning 384 test vehicles run by those who had applied for suspension and eight other manufacturers plus another 116 vehicles run by catalyst and reactor manufacturers. The 500 hundred vehicles were used to test five types of control systems, including the noble metal oxidizing catalyst that was viewed as the most promising technology in the near term. Only one of the cars tested had actually met the standard and none had been driven for the fifty thousand mile "useful life" for which the standard was required to be met. In many cases the test protocols used and the reasons for the numerous failures were not apparent from the test records.

EPA also had a study conducted by the City of New York on a fleet of police cars equipped with platinum monolith catalysts that showed no safety hazards, no increased fuel consumption, and no performance deficiencies. The study, based on five 1971 Plymouth police cars equipped with Englehard exhaust catalysts, came close to meeting the 1975 standards—without engine adjustments. But the small size of the study did not permit meaningful statistical conclusions.

A key issue was how long a catalyst would continue to work effectively in the harsh environment of an internal combustion engine. Auto engineers were worried that the lead in gasoline would gradually degrade the performance of the catalysts. EPA's engineers in Ann Arbor did important work showing that, while there would be some degradation, the engines with catalysts would remain compliant with EPA's limits for at least forty thousand miles, given current technology. And that technology was improving due to the R&D at suppliers such as Engelhard Industries of Murray Hill, New Jersey. It could improve even more if lead were taken out of gasoline, which EPA was trying to do with separate regulations of the oil industry (see next major section below).

EPA was encouraged that Ford moved forward first, among the Big Three, and contracted Engelhard to build two plants to make platinum-coated catalytic purifiers to remove the HC and CO. Those plants could make catalysts for about half of Ford's projected 1975 fleet. But Chrysler simply cancelled their relationship with Engelhard, raising questions about whether Chrysler was punishing the supplier for its optimistic public testimony to EPA about the promise of catalytic converters.[26]

Overall, the two thousand pages of data in the rulemaking record fell short of the quantity and quality of data EPA ideally prefers when making an important policy decision with significant ramifications for both public health and for the economy. But it was all the agency had available in the timeframe dictated by Congress.

The automobile manufacturers had their reasons to seek delay; each year the standards were delayed saved the industry about five billion dollars in equipment costs alone.[27] The industry was adamant that suitable technology would not be available with sufficient lead time to use with any confidence in all 1975 model-year cars; the catalyst manufacturers were much more optimistic that the technology would be available in time for manufacturers to meet the standards. But EPA knew that each year of delay also deprived the public of the substantial public health benefits of cleaner air in cities throughout the country.[28]

After reviewing the hearing record, industry submissions, and EPA analyses, Administrator Ruckelshaus acknowledged that it was a "close question."[29] Nonetheless, he determined that the industry had not met their burden of proof, and he denied the suspension request at that time (the industry had the option of applying again the following year).[30] In making the decision, the Administrator stated:

> On the record before me, I do not believe it is in the public interest to grant these applications, where compliance with the 1975 standards by application of present technology can probably be achieved and where ample additional time is available to manufacturers to apply existing technology to 1975 vehicles.[31]

Reactions to the Ruckelshaus decision were polarized. Industry was annoyed. A few days before EPA released its decision, Chairman Henry Ford II told Ford stockholders: "If the standards are not suspended, the result so far as we can see would be to force suspension of most US automotive manufacturing operations in 1975."[32] Robert Rauch of the environmental group Friends of the Earth praised EPA's decision: "It shows Ruckelshaus won't buckle to industry."[33] Consumer advocate Ralph Nader described the action as "surprisingly encouraging" but added skeptically "I just hope it isn't going to find any reversal after the election."[34]

Judicial Setback

The automobile industry quickly appealed the Administrator's decision to the United States Court of Appeals for the D.C. Circuit. That was par for the course; in fact, most major EPA decisions are challenged in court, often by both industry and environmental groups.

As the court was deliberating, President Nixon won a landslide re-election in November 1972 against Democratic challenger George McGovern. The industry decided the time was ripe to undertake a "massive campaign" to amend the Clean Air Act. A coalition was formed that included not only the automakers but the American Petroleum Institute, the National Automobile Dealers Association, and the United Auto Workers of America. Chrysler Corporation Chairman Lynn Townsend went directly to John Ehrlichman, President Nixon's domestic-policy advisor, to make the case that the Clean Air Act needed to be changed.[35]

In Congress, the Republicans gained twelve seats in the House in the 1972 elections, but the Democratic Party retained a large majority. The Republicans lost two seats in the Senate, thereby enlarging the Democratic majority. The Senate's architect of the 1970 Clean Air Act, Democrat Edmund Muskie of Maine, made it clear that the industry would face some very tough questions in the Senate before any legislative changes would be considered.

Meanwhile, the court sent the case back to EPA to supplement the record of decision to incorporate a January 1972 report from the National Academy of Sciences and explain how the Administrator's decision comported with its findings. The complex NAS Report made several determinations, some supporting the agency's decision and some supporting the industry's position.

NAS expressed concerns about long lead times and potential drivability/performance issues with catalysts, concluding that "the technology necessary to meet the requirements of the Clean Air Act Amendments for 1975 model light-duty motor vehicles is not available at this time."[36] However, the NAS also found that the costs of meeting the standards would be much less than what the industry contended ($800 to $1400 per car) and closer to what EPA estimated ($200 per car).[37] NAS went on to state:

> The status and rate of progress make it possible that the larger manufacturers will be able to produce vehicles that will qualify, provided that provisions are made for catalyst replacement and other maintenance, for averaging emissions of production vehicles, and for the general availability of fuel containing suitably low levels of catalyst poisons [e.g., lead].[38]

After considering EPA's response to the NAS report, the Court vacated the standards and remanded the case back to the agency. It reasoned that the risks to the economy and to the environment of an erroneous denial were greater than those of an erroneous grant of a suspension; the court then shifted the burden of proof to EPA and concluded that the Administrator had not adequately supported his conclusion that the standards could be met. Specifically, EPA had not considered whether the available technology, catalysts, would be available for a sufficient variety of model lines or in sufficient quantities to meet the market demand in 1975.[39]

Ruckelshaus's Response to the Court

In response to the court's decision, EPA re-opened the rulemaking and sponsored another round of public hearings, which provided a stunning moment: representatives of two Japanese manufacturers, Honda and Toyo Kogyo (Mazda), testified that their 1975 model-year vehicles would be able to meet the standards.[40] This raised a nightmare scenario in which foreign manufacturers might meet the standards and take over the US market, sidelining domestic manufacturers if their cars were unable to meet the standards. Even if they tried to meet the standards, domestic manufacturers might end up marketing poorly performing cars. Another NAS report concluded that the Honda engine (a dual carbureted, stratified-charge engine) not only met the 1975 HC and CO standards for over fifty thousand miles, but was simpler and cheaper to make and maintain than a catalyst, and had no fuel-consumption penalty.[41]

Ruckelshaus was well aware of such innovative alternatives; indeed, EPA was supporting their development through grants to engineers inside and outside of government.[42] Detroit's unwillingness to consider alternative engine designs, along with the very tight 1975 deadline, essentially foreclosed that route and left the catalyst as the only viable method for meeting the 1975 standards.

Internal agency analysis indicated that GM could meet the standards with 93% of its production, Ford with 55%, American Motors with 26%, and Chrysler with none. The overall industry percentage would be 66%. Ruckelshaus concluded that this was not sufficient to meet the basic demand for cars and that it was too risky to try.[43]

In the 1970 Act, Congress had authorized the Administrator to establish interim emission standards in the event he granted a suspension of the 1975 deadline. The interim standards were to reflect the "greatest degree of emission control which is achievable" by available technology, considering the cost of applying it.

Industry requested standards with deadlines applicable only in California in model year 1975 and later nationally. Ruckelshaus rejected that request, preferring a more stringent option. On April 11, 1973, EPA granted the one-year suspension, set interim standards for 1975 requiring 50% reduction from 1974 levels for cars sold in 49 states, and with somewhat higher standards for California. EPA essentially required that catalysts be used on all new cars sold in California during 1975 and that industry make progress toward catalysts being phased in the following year for the rest of the country.[44]

Much, but not all, of the reaction to the 1973 decision was negative. Ralph Nader charged that "once again the concessionaires within the Nixon administration have sold out the environment to industry polluters."[45] The

Sierra Club charged that the decision would permit the auto industry to use the delay for a "massive public relations campaign" to get the Clean Air Act changed and weakened.[46] Democratic Senator John V. Tunney of California objected on the grounds that EPA was forcing California residents "to be the guinea pigs for pollution systems that Detroit concedes are costly and troublesome."[47] Tunney argued that EPA should have given more consideration to completely new types of engine designs.

Industry, led by GM Chairman Richard C. Gerstenberg, complained that the interim standards were too strict and that it was unwise to require the utilization of catalysts.[48] Chrysler issued a statement saying that the Clean Air Act provisions go "far beyond the need for protection of health and will encourage the American people to pay a great deal for little if any additional benefit."[49] Honda executives offered a different view, noting that US manufacturers were too rigid in their approach and that the Japanese had been more successful because they are more flexible in trying new techniques.[50]

Not all the commentary was negative. Democratic congressman Paul Rogers of Florida called the decision "a realistic one aimed at meeting our goal in the shortest amount of time."[51] House Minority Leader Gerald Ford said the decision was "in the best interests of the consumer."[52] Democratic Senator Edmund Muskie of Maine, the chief author of the Clean Air Act, approved Ruckelshaus's decision as "most nearly consistent" with the act's objectives, considering "the inadequate response" of the industry to the act's "challenge."[53]

Shortly after EPA granted the suspension, GM announced that it would put catalysts on its 1975 model-year automobiles, the warranty would be for a fifty-thousand-mile useful life, and the catalysts would also improve fuel economy. This was a complete reversal in the position that GM Chairman Richard C. Gerstenberg had expressed previously.[54]

Documents later revealed that GM sensed that it had a competitive advantage over Toyota and some other manufacturers on catalyst development. The company licensed its catalyst technology to Nissan in 1975 and later sued Toyota (unsuccessfully) for allegedly copying GM's catalyst technology.[55] The rest of the industry followed GM's lead and moved rapidly toward widespread installation of two-way catalytic converters across their national vehicle fleets.

Some Legislated Delays

With respect to the 1976 NOx standard mandated by Congress, there was a consensus that it was unworkable; moreover, trying to address it at the same time as the HC/CO standards was the cause of many of the drivability concerns. Neither the engineers within EPA's Ann Arbor office nor the industry believed that the legislated NOx value could be achieved by model year 1976. Consequently, the Administrator recommended that Congress modify both the standard and the deadline.

In 1974 Congress used energy-related legislation to delay the NOx standard to model year 1978 and to extend the interim HC and CO standards an additional year. Then, as part of the 1977 amendments to the Clean Air Act, Congress further extended the interim HC and CO standards to model year 1980 and delayed the NOx standard to 1981, while at the same time resetting it at a more permissive 1.0 grams per mile instead of 0.4 grams per mile.

This suite of tailpipe standards came to be known as the Tier 0 standards, as additional Tiers would follow in the decades ahead. But the innovation due to Tier 0 did not stop with the two-way catalytic converter.

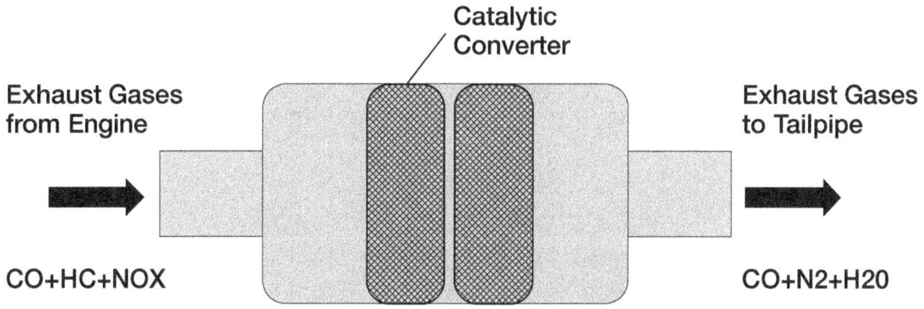

Figure 3.1. Schematic of Three-Way Catalytic Converter. ***Author-generated***

While the NOx standards were delayed, they ultimately stimulated the invention and commercialization of the three-way catalyst. The original two-way catalyst performs two simultaneous tasks: it oxidizes the pollutant CO into harmless carbon dioxide; and it oxidizes HC into carbon dioxide and water. The three-way catalyst has the additional advantage of controlling NOx by breaking it down into harmless nitrogen and oxygen. The control of NOx was a major innovation because NOx, once emitted into the atmosphere, contributes to the formation of smog (ozone) and particulate matter.

In summary, EPA's initial experience with technology-forcing regulation—the 90% reduction standards mandated by Congress—was technically complex and highly controversial. But the decisions made by Ruckelshaus helped establish the credibility of the young agency. Although not on the original schedule envisioned by Congress, the agency's efforts did eventually lead to dramatic reductions in air pollution from cars without the draconian consequences alleged by some in the industry. There were some delays in the US, but the exhaust streams were cleansed much faster in the US than in

Europe.[56] There were also unexpected side benefits from the innovation in engines induced by the Tier 0 standards: enhancements to both vehicle fuel economy and performance.[57]

CONGRESS AUTHORIZES EPA TO REGULATE FUELS

Congress recognized that the amount of pollution from the tailpipe is a function of three factors: the design of the engine, the composition of the fuel combusted in the engine, and the post-combustion treatment systems added to the engine. In 1970, 1977, and 1990, Congress gave EPA increasing authority to regulate the fuels used in gasoline- and diesel-powered vehicles. Some of the most significant successes in EPA's history relate to technology-forcing regulations that modified the composition of the fuels. In this sense, fuel is a "technology" subject to modification in chemical composition. Here I consider four innovations: unleaded gasoline, low-sulfur gasoline, ethanol blending, and low-sulfur diesel.

Unleaded Gasoline

Fuel must have adequate octane content in order to prevent engine knocking, which annoys motorists and, in extreme cases, can damage the engine. Oil refineries began adding lead to gasoline in the 1920s to boost octane because lead was less expensive than alternative octane additives. Today, a typical gasoline pump will offer three levels of octane: 87 (regular), 89 (mid-grade), and 91-93 (premium). The higher octane levels allow the engine to operate at higher compression ratios, which enhances engine performance. By the early 1970s, more than two hundred thousand tons of lead were added to gasoline each year in the US, and the practice rapidly spread worldwide.[58]

In the 1970s, Congress and EPA demanded removal of lead from gasoline. By attaching to the metals on the surface of the catalytic converter, lead degrades the ability of catalysts to control HC, CO, and other tailpipe pollutants. Moreover, when added to gasoline, lead is not controlled but emitted from the tailpipe as a pollutant. Decades of public health research linked even low levels of lead exposure to neurotoxic effects among children and elevated blood pressure levels among adults.[59] The move to lead-free gasoline was not without scientific and legal controversy, as discussed in Chapters 2 and 10.[60]

The 1970 Clean Air Act provided EPA the necessary authority to order a phase out of lead in gasoline. During the Nixon administration, EPA ordered the phase out beginning with model year 1975 new cars, the year when catalytic converters became widely used. The phase out was accelerated by

EPA early in the Reagan administration due to public health concerns about children's health and blood pressure levels in adults. As a result, from 1970 to 1987 the number of children in the US with toxic levels of lead in their blood was reduced by two million. From an international perspective, EPA's restrictions on leaded gasoline were far more aggressive than the rules in European countries, where both lead-free gasoline and catalytic converters were delayed for more than a decade.[61]

Unleaded gasoline does have some drawbacks. Alternative sources of octane are necessary to prevent engine knocking, and two are commonly used: the BTEX complex (a mixture of aromatic compounds including benzene, toluene, xylene, and ethyl benzene) and oxygenates (such as alcohol, ethanol, and the chemical MTBE). Each source of octane poses significant environmental health concerns that have been major challenges for EPA since the 1990s.

Some amount of the BTEX mixture is native to gasoline, but more is typically added by refiners to achieve the desired octane rating.[62] The BTEX complex in the engine leads to both fine particle pollution and formation of polycyclic aromatic hydrocarbons (PAHs), both of which are hazardous to humans. In addition, some of the individual aromatics are neurotoxins and carcinogens (most notably benzene, which is a known cause of leukemia among highly exposed workers). EPA and CARB ultimately developed regulations limiting the amount of aromatics in gasoline, especially benzene.[63] But BTEX remains an issue today for both CARB and EPA.

Ethanol, also called grain alcohol, is a volatile, flammable, colorless liquid with a distinctive odor. When gasoline is blended with 10% ethanol (so called E10), the fuel's octane rating is typically large enough to meet commercial requirements. Moreover, the toxicity of ethanol is generally considered to be low compared to the BTEX complex. But blending ethanol with gasoline as a motor fuel raises a host of other issues, as I explore below, such as greenhouse gas emissions from the energy-consuming processes of growing corn and refining ethanol from corn.

Low-Sulfur Gasoline

A decade-long logjam in Congress was broken in 1989 when, after pledging to be "the environmental president" in the 1988 election campaign, President George H. W. Bush worked with Congress on ambitious amendments to the Clean Air Act. With assistance from Bush's EPA administrator William K Reilly and EPA staff, the administration negotiated with key Democrats in Congress such as representatives John Dingell of Michigan, Henry Waxman of California, and Senator Max Baucus of Montana.

The final 1990 amendments to the Clean Air Act are considered a watershed event in the history of the agency because they contained vast new responsibilities and tools for EPA to curb mobile source emissions: mandatory Tier 1 standards related to engines for passenger vehicles; EPA authorization for additional tiers of standards, if necessary; new authority for a national reformulated gasoline program; special rules to limit toxic air emissions (e.g., benzene) from vehicles; new authority for EPA to regulate heavy-truck pollution more stringently than in the past; and new authority for EPA to regulate a wide variety of non-road engines ranging from snowmobiles to construction equipment and ocean-going vessels.

Under Reilly's leadership, EPA finalized new Tier 1 standards in 1991 that took effect during model years 1994 to 1997. The Tier 1 program compelled even lower rates of NOx and VOC emissions than Congress mandated in 1970. The focus was reducing emissions from the engine itself, without changes in fuels or post-combustion treatment. The program offered somewhat smaller emissions-control effectiveness than CARB's Low-Emission Vehicle (LEV I) program because EPA's tailpipe standards were somewhat less stringent, and CARB's LEV I program covered some larger vehicles that were not covered by EPA's Tier 1 program. However, Tier 1 covered the entire country.

From 1989 to 1993 fourteen oil companies and the Big Three launched the "Auto/Oil Air Quality Improvement Research Program" (AQIRP) to provide legislators and regulators technical information on how the design of fuels and engines affects pollution from motor vehicles. AQIRP generated extensive vehicle emissions measurements with different fuels, air quality modeling to link vehicle emissions to ozone formation in the atmosphere, and economic analysis of alternative fuel/vehicle systems.[64] The importance of reducing the sulfur content of fuel was underscored by industry R&D.

Unlike lead, sulfur is a natural component of crude oil that is present in gasoline and diesel fuel unless it is removed through specialized processing. Sulfur is a challenge for engine designers because—like lead—it impairs the functioning of the catalytic converter. Specifically, the presence of sulfur in the exhaust gas mixture reduces the reduction activity of the three-way catalyst, leading to greater CO, HC, and NOx emissions. To produce low-sulfur fuel, refiners need to make capital investments in a high-temperature, catalytic process called hydrodesulfurization.[65] But the US refining industry was not a highly profitable sector and thus the resistance to low-sulfur gasoline requirements was intense and sustained. Indeed, the refining sector argued that the auto industry could solve the problem with innovation in engines and catalytic converters.

California led the country with low-sulfur gasoline requirements in the 1990s. Once again, EPA followed suit.

An impetus for EPA action were findings from new epidemiological studies indicating that EPA's air-quality standards needed to be tightened, especially the ambient standards, to protect public health from inhalation of particulate matter and ozone.[66] Under Administrator Carol Browner's leadership during the Clinton administration, EPA overcame determined industry opposition and established the agency's first standards for fine particles (PM2.5) and tightened the prevailing standard for ozone. The states soon realized that their future SIPs would need to be even more stringent than they had planned. Thus, many states were pleased when CARB and EPA announced plans for another round of vehicle and fuel standards—the LEV II/Tier 2 standards—which states could take credit for in their SIPs.

Automakers did not protest EPA's decision to move forward with Tier 2 standards as long as they included large reductions in the sulfur content of fuel. EPA encountered but overcame sustained opposition from the petroleum and refining industries. In 1999 EPA, again under Administrator Carol Browner, phased in a nationwide requirement for low-sulfur gasoline, similar to what CARB had already adopted for fuels sold in California. Under the rule, the average sulfur content of gasoline was slashed by 90%.

For the targeted pollutants linked to smog and soot, Tier 2 standards were generally as stringent or almost as stringent as CARB's LEV II standards. The notable exception was NOx where, due to flexibility provisions in Tier 2, EPA's standards were more permissive for automakers and engine suppliers than CARB's NOx requirements. However, both agencies decided against continuation of a less stringent NOx standard for diesel-powered cars, preferring "fuel-neutral" standards. In this respect, both EPA and CARB departed from the European and Japanese standards for NOx, which were less stringent for diesel-powered cars than gasoline-powered cars. For German automakers, the pioneers of advanced diesel technology, the US and California standards became a formidable compliance challenge.

Compared to the Tier 1 standards, the economic case for Tier 2 was powerful. Based on EPA information, the Office of Management and Budget reported that the Tier 2 standards would produce approximately five dollars in benefits (mostly public health benefits) for every one dollar in cost (mostly cost to the consumer for higher gasoline and vehicle prices). By investment standards, that is an impressive rate of return.

Blending Ethanol with Gasoline

Technology-forcing regulation does not always work since it is not feasible to schedule R&D breakthroughs. When new technology is unavailable or developing too slowly, EPA is left with the dilemma of when to compromise on a technology-forcing deadline and when to hold firm. This is what happened from 2008 to 2020 as EPA implemented an ambitious, mandatory expansion of the use of ethanol as an additive to motor fuel.

With support from the George W. Bush administration, Congress passed several laws that boosted use of ethanol as a blender with gasoline.[67] Meanwhile, the commercial future of a cheaper octane booster—MTBE—dimmed when it was detected as a contaminant of surface water and groundwater in numerous locations. EPA had supported widespread use of MTBE in its reformulated gasoline regulations but, in light of new evidence of MTBE carcinogenicity and water contamination, was considering a prohibition of MTBE under the Toxic Substances Control Act of 1976.

To secure the votes of Midwestern Democratic Senators for his 2005 energy plan, Bush (43) agreed to a pro-ethanol provision that banned MTBE as a fuel additive and included a requirement for "renewable oxygenates."[68] Since the federal government was enforcing a tariff on imported ethanol, the new law created a nationwide market for corn-based ethanol produced in the US. Mandated ethanol blending increased from 1.1 billion gallons in 2002 to 4 billion gallons in 2006 and 7.5 billion gallons by 2012. At the end of Bush's second term, Congress compelled a dramatic expansion of the ethanol-blending mandate to 36 billion gallons by 2022. During this period, total US gasoline use was hovering around 150 billion gallons per year.

The Bush (43) administration did not see ethanol blending as an environmental policy; it was an energy policy designed to reduce US dependence on foreign oil. It also boosted land values and economic development in the Midwest where corn is grown and ethanol refineries are located. Some environmentalists also favored ethanol blending because it is a renewable fuel that reduces tailpipe emissions of some aromatics and PM-related pollutants, leading to significant public health benefits.[69]

But the rapid expansion of ethanol blending also raised environmental concerns such as expansion in land use, water consumption, and fertilizer use for corn production. Adverse effects on water quality near farms were a concern.[70] Even air pollution was a major concern because energy is consumed throughout the ethanol supply chain, and energy consumption triggers air pollution. The ethanol supply chain is a long one: clearing land for corn fields, planting seeds, harvesting the corn, transporting the corn to ethanol refineries, making ethanol from corn, and transporting ethanol to blending facilities and refueling stations. Some of the ethanol refineries in the Midwest obtain electricity from coal-fired power plants, which are a major source of air pollution linked to smog and soot as well as the greenhouse gas emissions implicated in climate change. The lifecycle air emissions from the entire process of producing corn and ethanol are so large (relative to the lifecycle of petroleum fuels) that the air-quality case for corn ethanol is not decisive and depends on numerous variables that are uncertain and site specific.[71]

As Congress recognized the environmental concerns about a massive expansion in the use of corn-based ethanol, EPA was put in charge of the program to ensure those concerns were addressed. Congress did not require that all 36 billion gallons of fuel in 2022 be made from corn; instead, the law stipulates that at least 22 of the 36 billion gallons must be an advanced form of renewable fuel, largely "cellulosic" ethanol (cellulose is the stringy fiber of a plant). One of the most promising ways to make cellulosic ethanol is to make it from the corn "stover" (the leaves, the stalk, and the cobs) that remains after the field is harvested. By making ethanol from agricultural waste rather than food, the environmental profile of ethanol is enhanced while upward pressure on land, corn, and food prices is attenuated.

Congress also gave EPA new technology-forcing responsibilities. To ensure a market for the innovative biofuels, EPA was directed to require refiners to blend at least 250 million gallons of cellulosic ethanol by 2013, with amounts progressively increasing thereafter. Congress did give EPA authority to waive the cellulosic ethanol requirement each year, based on feasibility analysis.

When EPA was given this responsibility in 2007, no large-scale commercial production of cellulosic ethanol was underway in the US. The Department of Energy made some efforts in the 1990s to start pilot plants, but they were not successful. Congress and the Bush (43) administration were determined to push forward, which caused the DOE and the USDA to pour hundreds of millions of dollars of federal money into cellulosic ethanol research, development, and demonstration.[72]

By the time the presidential election campaign of 2008 was underway, the future of ethanol was a contested issue. A large 2007-08 rise in corn and food prices led to hardship among low-income populations in the US and abroad. Riots in Mexico and other poor countries were triggered by higher food prices. There was much debate about which factors were responsible for the rise of food prices: the US ethanol mandate, growth in global demand for food, crop failures in other countries, decline in the value of the US dollar (which increases foreign demand for US grain), and even speculative activity in the global marketplace. A growing chorus of criticism in Congress argued that it was unwise for the US to make motor fuel from agricultural products.

In the 2008 presidential election campaign, ethanol was a salient issue. Among the Democratic candidates, then Illinois Senator Barack Obama was the only one to speak on behalf of ethanol with unqualified enthusiasm. (Obama won the Iowa caucuses, but it is unclear how important his ethanol stance was, though it surely did not hurt his candidacy). In the general election,

Obama faced Republican John McCain of Arizona, a longtime opponent of ethanol subsidies and mandates. The American Corn Growers Association endorsed Barack Obama for president, only the second time in the organization's twenty-two-year history that an endorsement was made.

Once in office, President Obama took some key steps that facilitated the continued commercialization of corn-based ethanol. Those steps put EPA in an awkward position, as some EPA scientists shared many of the concerns about the environmental impacts of corn ethanol.

First, in response to a legislative requirement, EPA devised a regulation that compelled corn ethanol to be produced in a manner that would reduce the greenhouse gas intensity of corn ethanol by 20% by 2022. This rule was stimulated by a disturbing study showing that the large amounts of land cleared for corn production would trigger a substantial near-term increase in greenhouse gas emissions.[73] Yet, EPA's final rule in 2010 made a technical determination that corn-based ethanol would reduce lifecycle greenhouse gas emissions by close to the 20% figure that Congress required in 2007.[74] There was some research from USDA scientists that supported EPA's determination, but environmental critics of ethanol insist that the greenhouse-gas footprint of corn ethanol in 2022 is quite uncertain and could be much larger than what EPA found.[75]

Second, the Obama EPA expanded the permission for ethanol blending. The issue was whether ethanol blends could rise above E10 as excessive ethanol can damage the fuel systems of older-model cars. Based on supportive data from the DOE, EPA issued a regulation allowing use of E15 in recent model cars in certain months of the year.

Third, the Obama administration protected the ethanol mandate from legislative reversal. The politics of ethanol are not for the faint hearted. EPA and the Obama White House were confronted by a bipartisan coalition of ethanol opponents: fiscal hawks, many environmentalists, free-market conservatives, oil producers and refiners, and hog and poultry farmers who depend on low-priced corn feed for their animals. Supporters of ethanol included landowners in the Midwest, the corn farmers, ethanol producers, and transport companies that work in the ethanol supply chain, and companies that supply to the ethanol refineries.

When the federal tax credits for ethanol and tariffs on imported ethanol were scheduled to expire at the end of 2011, the Obama White House feared that any effort to save them in Congress could lead to a repeal or weakening of EPA's ethanol-blending mandate. So, a decision was made to let the credits and tariffs expire; as planned, EPA ethanol-blending mandate survived.

Finally, the Obama EPA did not press hard for cellulosic ethanol. It was a tough dilemma. Environmentally, cellulosic ethanol is much more compelling than corn ethanol, but the technology was not progressing fast enough to be economically competitive at a commercial scale. The costs to farmers and ethanol refineries of collecting and transporting food waste are so high that cellulosic ethanol is not economically attractive. Many farmers distrusted the whole idea since some of their food waste needs to stay on the fields to enrich the soil for the next season's crop.

In 2013, due to the tiny volumes of cellulosic ethanol in the market, EPA waived much of the requirement for cellulosic ethanol, a decision that EPA has had to reaffirm each year since 2013. Much litigation has centered on whether EPA has properly exercised its technology-forcing authority in the RFS program.[76] By the end of the Obama administration, several demonstration plants for cellulosic ethanol were shut down and repurposed; only one, in Iowa, continued to operate.

In 2014 the Obama EPA shifted directions and revised the ethanol mandate to allow use of renewable natural gas to qualify as "cellulosic." This is a potentially promising development that could breathe life into the future of cellulosic ethanol.

The Donald Trump administration struggled to deliver on candidate Trump's pro-ethanol promises. The administration's first EPA administrator, Scott Pruitt of Oklahoma, was a well-known ally of the oil industry and an opponent of the ethanol mandate. He devoted more effort to giving "hardship" waivers to small oil refineries than to making the renewable-fuel standard work more effectively. The Trump EPA did approve another modest increase in the cellulosic blending requirement.

After Pruitt's abrupt resignation in 2018, President Trump—looking forward to a re-election effort in 2020—instructed EPA to remove the prohibition on E15 in summer months, thereby creating more commercial opportunity for corn-based ethanol. Soon after this pledge, EPA released a long-delayed scientific report to Congress that documented many environmental problems with corn-based ethanol.[77] The US Department of Agriculture countered with a new report suggesting that greater use of ethanol will reduce greenhouse gas emissions from a lifecycle perspective.[78] The oil industry and national environmental groups publicly shared their determination to defeat the E15 rule change in litigation, but the Trump EPA decided to take the legal risk and proceed. The struggle continues.

Low-Sulfur Diesel Fuel

During the Bill Clinton and George W. Bush administrations, EPA used discretionary authority under the 1990 Clean Air Act amendments to issue ambitious technology-forcing regulations aimed at reducing pollution from the diesel engines that are used throughout the US economy. These engines became a priority at EPA for multiple reasons: they are a significant source of smog and soot in urban communities, they emit cancer-causing toxic emissions, and, in some cities, diesel engines became an environmental justice issue, since low-income and minority people often reside near highways with truck traffic or near special facilities that received cargo from diesel-powered trucks or ships.[79]

EPA's first regulation of diesel exhaust actually occurred in 1986 under the Reagan administration when performance standards were established for both NOx and PM emissions. EPA anticipated that heavy trucks would be equipped with particulate traps, but innovation in engine design reduced engine-out emissions so effectively that engine suppliers could meet the PM standard without installing particulate traps. However, in the decade after the 1986 standards were implemented, it became apparent that much greater progress in diesel-exhaust control was required to protect public health. Low-sulfur diesel fuel was needed to increase the effectiveness and longevity of diesel catalysts.

The politics of low-sulfur diesel fuel led to some unusual alliances. The oil and refining sectors effectively resisted a national low-sulfur diesel rule through most of the 1990s but ultimately confronted a formidable coalition: the auto industry, environmental groups, and public health associations. At EPA's public hearings in Los Angeles in 2000, the "unlikely pairing" of interest groups stood "shoulder to shoulder" to argue for an EPA rule that would slash the sulfur content of diesel fuel.[80]

Under Carol Browner's leadership in the Clinton administration, EPA's "on-road diesel rule" further reduced pollution from new diesel engines used in heavy-duty trucks. Starting model year 2007, all diesel trucks were equipped with a diesel particulate filter to reduce soot, and at least fifty percent were equipped with advanced NOx control technology. By model year 2010, all trucks were required to have the advanced NOx controls. EPA originally expected that engine suppliers would comply with NOx adsorbers but instead suppliers found it necessary to adopt a more complex control system called selective catalytic reduction (SCR). This system is not simply a technical change to the engine; it requires that the truck operator maintain required levels of a fluid called urea to support SCR operation. A notable feature of this rulemaking was extensive collaboration between EPA, CARB, and all stakeholders with an interest in the issue, leading to EPA recognition by the Council for Excellence in Government.[81]

Critical to the success of the on-road diesel rule is a mandatory ninety-seven percent reduction in the sulfur content of diesel fuel, a requirement that EPA imposed on refiners. The regulation is not cheap, as it is projected to cost the refining sector billions of dollars in capital expenditures. The rule, though, is projected to accomplish large public health benefits. Based on information from EPA, the US Office of Management and Budget estimates that the rule will generate up to thirty dollars in public benefits for every one dollar in cost.

When George W. Bush entered the White House in 2001, some elements of the petroleum industry tried to persuade the administration to relax or repeal EPA's on-road diesel rule. EPA Administrator Christie Todd Whitman, with support from OMB, rejected this idea and instead decided to extend the exhaust-control requirements to off-road diesel engines used in construction, agriculture, and mining.[82] Later, the Bush (43) EPA—again in collaboration with CARB—further extended the low-sulfur diesel requirements to locomotive and marine engines, and played a global leadership role in diesel-exhaust controls on ocean-going vessels. Table 3.1 displays the impressive public health benefits of the suite of clean-air standards beginning with the Tier 2 passenger-vehicle standards and extending through the ocean-vessel standards.

Table 3.1. Public Health Benefits of Selected EPA Clean Air Standards in 2030

Clean Air Standard	*Lives Saved*	*Fewer Hospital Admissions*	*Avoided Lost Workdays*
Tier 2 Light-Duty Passenger Vehicle Standards	4,300	3,000	700,000
Highway Diesel Truck Standards	8,300	7,100	1.5 million
Nonroad Diesel Engine Standards	12,000	8,900	1.0 million
Locomotive/Marine Diesel Standards	1,400	870	120,000
Ocean Vessel Standards	13,000	12,400	1.4 million

Source: US Environmental Protection Agency, "Benefits and Costs of Five Important Clean Air Rules in 2030," *Epa.org*, accessed April 29, 2020.

Under the Trump administration, EPA has announced another round of regulation to curtail residual pollution from new heavy-duty trucks used on the highway. As a result, EPA is seen around the world as a pioneer on this issue, certainly much further along than Europe where regulators have been slower to crack down on diesel-engine exhaust.

THE ENFORCEMENT CHALLENGE

EPA's air-quality assignment does not stop after emissions standards are established for motor vehicles, engines, and fuels. EPA, in coordination with

CARB, must oversee industry compliance with the standards and make sure that any non-complying firms are discovered and punished.

EPA's lead for this activity is the National Vehicle and Fuel Emissions Laboratory (NVFEL) in Ann Arbor, Michigan. NVFEL benchmarks vehicle and engine technology, develops advanced technologies, provides emissions testing to inform rulemakings, develops new test procedures, and supports enforcement actions. Specifically, the Laboratory certifies that new vehicles and engines meet federal emissions and fuel-economy standards. It also tests engines for in-use performance and compliance. Given the complexity of fuels, NVFEL performs specialized analyses of fuel composition, fuel additives, and the chemical composition of exhausts. The technical staff of NVFEL also hold over 60 patents on advanced technologies related to emissions control and fuel economy.

EPA and CARB do not inspect or test every engine and vehicle. The compliance process relies on a process whereby companies certify themselves: self-certification. EPA and CARB decide, on a case-by-case basis, how intensively to review a company's self-certification case. As we shall see, this self-certification process has some significant limitations that have created setbacks for the credibility of both EPA and CARB.

When EPA was created, the US auto industry was an oligopoly dominated by the Big Three. It has since evolved into a more competitive industry, as Japanese, European, and Korean producers are big players in the US market and around the world. When any global company produces a new engine or vehicle, the company looks as hard as possible for cost savings to improve the company's competitive position in US and global markets. As a result, cheating on compliance with EPA and CARB emissions standards is a persistent temptation.

I consider two important cases where corporate cheating on EPA/CARB emissions standards was alleged and/or documented, and how EPA handled the issues. Both cases involve exhaust-control systems for diesel engines: the first case concerns engines used in heavy trucks, the second concerns cars.

The appeal of diesel engines, compared to gasoline engines, is rooted in their superior fuel economy, minimal CO and HC emissions, ability to deliver additional acceleration and torque, and greater engine durability and longevity.[83] The major downside is that a diesel engine is more expensive to produce than a gasoline engine, especially since advanced technologies are necessary to control NOx and particulate emissions under EPA and CARB standards.[84]

Early efforts to control diesel exhaust relied on in-cylinder techniques such as combustion chamber design, improvements in fuel-injection systems (e.g., pressure, timing, and rate shaping), and application of exhaust-gas recirculation. As EPA and CARB tightened standards for particulate matter and NOx, in-cylinder techniques proved to be inadequate and after-treatment technologies were necessary.

Engineers discovered several effective ways to control NOx and PM through treatment of the exhaust stream. A specialized catalytic converter for diesel engines was devised to control particles at low exhaust temperatures. A particulate trap was also invented to capture PM before it is emitted into the atmosphere. The converter must be selective enough to control targeted pollutants but not oxidize sulfur dioxide into sulfuric acid. Thus, diesel exhaust control requires a combination of pre-combustion and post-combustion technologies and can add hundreds to thousands of dollars to the cost of producing a vehicle, depending on the size of the vehicle.[85]

Computerized Defeat Devices

A major dispute within the engine sector erupted over EPA enforcement activities concerning 1.3 million pre-1998 engines used in heavy-duty trucks. EPA alleged that several diesel-engine producers used computerized "defeat devices" on trucks to shut off pollution controls during specific stages of highway operation.

The controls were known to hurt a truck's fuel economy and the defeat devices would allow the driver (or owner of the truck) to have more control over the vehicle's fuel consumption and associated expenditures. EPA alleged that the presence of the defeat devices was a violation of law since the devices were not adequately disclosed to EPA during the engine certification process. Such devices, depending on how they are programmed, can lead to large increases in NOx pollution from trucks during real-world operation.

The defendants in the case—Caterpillar Inc., Cummins Engine Company, Detroit Diesel Corporation, Mack Trucks Inc., Navistar International Transportation Corporation, Renault Vehicles Industrials, and Volvo Truck Corporation—did not confess guilt but agreed to pay $83.4 million in civil fines, the largest in environmental enforcement history at the time. During the Clinton administration, the companies also agreed in the July 1999 consent decrees to subject their new heavy-duty diesel engines to a tighter standard two years earlier than the deadline in EPA's prevailing standard. This "pull-ahead" provision of the settlement was intended to accelerate the development and commercialization of advanced emissions-control technology.

Once the consent decrees were signed, the seven diesel-engine suppliers engaged in an R&D race to determine which companies could certify a new engine technology to the stricter, pull-ahead emissions test. Companies failing to certify would lose the privilege to sell new engines in the United States or be forced to pay a non-compliance financial penalty.

The first company to receive EPA certification of a new on-road diesel engine was Cummins Engine of Columbus, Indiana. In April of 2002 Cummins announced EPA certification of the new ISX engine, disclosed results from some real-world testing performed on the engine, and challenged other engine suppliers to match the new engine's performance and fuel economy.[86]

When George W. Bush was elected president in 2001, other engine suppliers saw a possible opportunity to delay or remove the pull-ahead requirement. They formed an informal coalition to persuade key members of Congress and the Bush administration to either provide additional time for compliance or to set a small noncompliance penalty.

The Bush (43) EPA, under the leadership of Christie Todd Whitman (the former governor of New Jersey), was not impressed with the case for delay or small noncompliance penalties. In June 2001, EPA sent a letter to all seven suppliers confirming the 1998 settlement and stating that the agency would not agree to a delay in the schedule for a new engine.[87]

Several House members convened a meeting of senior EPA and OMB officials, urging that relief be provided from this allegedly onerous regulation and enforcement settlement. On the other hand, representatives of Cummins Engine Company reached out to both EPA and OMB and cautioned against additional relief. They advocated a sufficiently large non-compliance penalty to prevent Cummins from being put at a competitive disadvantage for its decision to satisfy its obligations under the consent decree.

EPA and OMB officials met, discussed the dispute, and ultimately agreed with the position taken by Cummins.[88] In 2004 EPA finalized a stiff noncompliance penalty rule.[89] It was based on a detailed accounting of all of the tangible cost savings that a non-compliant company would enjoy by refusing to comply with the pull-ahead provision in the 1999 consent agreement.

Thus, EPA's enforcement strategy became another avenue for technology-forcing innovation. This enforcement case is especially interesting because major investments in innovation were made by the engine suppliers, on top of paying fines, without any company admitting to illegal behavior.

The next case concerns a better-known company, Volkswagen (the largest auto company in the world), that cheated for almost a decade, was discovered, confessed guilt to EPA and CARB, and agreed to a huge, wide-ranging settlement that could change the future of the global automotive industry.

Keeping It Secret

Engineers in the German auto industry, especially Volkswagen, have been arguing for at least thirty years that diesel-powered cars should be encouraged in North America like they are in Europe. Starting in the 1970s, European countries favored the diesel engine by taxing diesel fuel at a lower rate than gasoline. More importantly, European countries used fuel taxes (rather than fuel-economy standards) to conserve petroleum fuels. The average European consumer pays $5 to $8 per gallon at the pump compared to less than $3 per gallon in the US, with most of the difference due to fuel taxes. Since diesel engines are typically 20–30% more fuel efficient than a gasoline engine, diesel-powered cars are favored by consumers in a high fuel-tax environment. As diesel engines were refined to become cleaner, quieter, and more powerful, diesel-powered cars became popular in Europe, capturing—at their peak—more than 50% of the new car market.[90]

When climate change emerged as a major issue in the early 1990s, diesel advocates revamped their pro-diesel arguments from a climate-policy perspective. A diesel-powered car emits 10-20% fewer grams of CO2 per mile of travel than a comparably sized gasoline-power car, even considering the higher carbon content of diesel fuel compared to gasoline.[91] Thus, the Germans argued, climate-change concerns only underscore the virtues of diesel-powered cars.

From an environmental perspective, the Achilles heel of the diesel engine is pollution in the exhaust stream, particularly NOx and carbon-containing particles. As mentioned earlier in this chapter, the European NOx and PM standards have always been designed carefully to accommodate a vibrant diesel sector in Europe. In contrast, CARB and EPA decided to eliminate the special consideration given to diesel-powered passenger vehicles. US regulators were reacting to two new pieces of evidence: atmospheric chemistry data revealed that NOx-emissions control was crucial to reducing smog levels in many US cities, and new epidemiological studies showed that inhalation of seemingly low levels of smog and soot (PM) were associated with elevated rates of heart attacks, hospital admissions, and premature deaths.[92] This latter body of evidence was slow to penetrate thinking among European regulators, since most of the key studies were performed on US populations and some European scientists were skeptical of the validity of the findings.[93] Over time, an independent organization funded by EPA and automakers, the Health Effects Institute in Boston, played a significant role in building more global scientific consensus on diesel-related health issues.[94] In any event, European regulators were more concerned about greenhouse gas emissions than adverse health effects from inhalation of diesel exhaust.[95]

When CARB and EPA moved to require low-sulfur diesel fuel, German vehicle manufacturers began to consider offering more diesel cars in the US, as significant improvements in the performance of diesel engines were achieved through turbocharging and other innovations. The Big Three and the major Japanese and Korean manufacturers did not have strong commercial interests in diesel-powered cars in the US. The German car manufacturers ultimately realized that they would have to advocate for diesel cars on their own.

The German government suspected, rightly or wrongly, that the US diesel-emission standards were nontariff barriers to trade that complicated German efforts to introduce diesel-powered cars into the US market.[96] When differences in standards, test cycles, and enforcement regimes are taken into account, the European NOx limits were much less stringent than US standards.

Absent major innovations in NOx control, the CARB standard was seen as a de facto prohibition on diesel powered cars and light trucks in California and the other states aligned with California. EPA's standard was also seen as unduly harsh by German industry experts.

Mercedes Benz was the first German company to make enough progress on NOx emissions to consider marketing diesel-powered cars in the US. Volkswagen developed an ambitious US plan to sell affordable small cars (VW) and premium luxury sedans (Audi) powered by diesel as well as gasoline engines but VW did not have a solution to the NOx-control problem.

In 2005 the management of VW explored whether the company should purchase the rights to the Mercedes Blue Tec system for reducing NOx pollution. This system starts with a specialized catalytic converter but adds two additional components: selective catalytic reduction (SCR) via a diesel exhaust additive (a combination of water and the chemical urea) and NOx adsorbers. The NOx adsorbers are incorporated into the coat of the catalytic converter and serve to chemically bind with NOx during lean engine operation. When adsorber capacity is saturated, the system is regenerated during periods of rich engine operation. Captured NOx is catalytically reduced to harmless nitrogen. Whenever necessary, urea is injected into the exhaust stream to help convert more NOx into nitrogen. A separate particulate trap controls carbon-containing particulates.

In 2007 VW decided against the BlueTech system, preferring to develop their own system. VW halted sales of diesel-powered cars temporarily in the US until the company could solve the NOx challenge. In 2008 VW made a flashy public announcement that they had invented new "clean diesel" technology that could comply with CARB as well as EPA NOx standards. VW used NOx adsorber catalysts on most of their models. In model year 2009 VW began shifting its turbocharged direct injection (TDI) engines to a common-rail fuel-injection system. Some models also were equipped with a urea-based exhaust treatment system. In reality, the VW systems did not achieve both good fuel economy and CARB-compliant NOx emissions as VW claimed in public communications.

In a grossly disturbing case of corporate cheating, VW engineers used computer software to shift the engine back and forth from high fuel economy/high NOx emissions and low fuel economy/low NOx emissions, the latter employed only when the software detected that an emissions-certification test was to take place. VW was saving money on NOx control technology and knew that owners cared more about fuel economy than NOx emissions, which were not observable to the owner. The cheating went undetected for almost a decade.[97]

Meanwhile, the German auto industry continued its efforts to persuade CARB and EPA to respect the advantages of diesel technology. Prime Minister Angela Merkel of Germany was a proponent of the pro-diesel case. In 2010 she agreed to travel to California and make the case personally to California's Republican Governor Arnold Schwarzenegger, as CARB was considering even more stringent NOx requirements in its LEV III program. CARB is led by a full-time chair that serves at the pleasure of the Governor; the other members of the CARB Board are part-time appointees of the Governor. If Merkel could persuade Schwarzenegger to instruct CARB to be more reasonable, then Germany might also be able to persuade EPA to be more reasonable.

In the meeting with the California Governor, Merkel pressed the CO2-control advantages of the diesel engine, since California was becoming increasingly concerned about climate change. Without some regulatory flexibility on NOx control, Merkel argued, German companies might not be able to access the California market, and the CO2-control advantages of the diesel engine would be foregone.

California was not persuaded by Merkel's position and no change was made in CARB's plan to introduce a new, more stringent NOx standard. Indeed, in 2012 CARB tightened controls on NOx with its LEV III standards and EPA followed in 2014 with its similar Tier 3 standards. Merkel, Schwarzenegger, CARB, and EPA did not realize that VW was already cheating on emissions control in California's lucrative new-car market.

In 2014 the nonprofit International Council on Clean Transportation (ICCT), with foundation funding and a history of CARB collaboration, asked a team of researchers at West Virginia University (WVU) to look into the emissions-control performance of diesel engines sold in the US.[98] ICCT was planning an effort to persuade EU regulators that the EU needed to tighten enforcement of exhaust standards for diesel-powered cars, since EU enforcement was seen as lax and without adequate penalties for noncompliance. The WVU team was surprised to find poor on-road emissions-control performance for VW vehicles sold in the US. The team presented the data at public meetings and published the results.

Once alerted to these data, EPA's Ann Arbor Laboratory repeated the tests on VW's vehicles and contacted VW for an explanation. In December 2014 VW ordered a recall but EPA and CARB were not satisfied with VW's explanation. EPA threatened to deny certification of VW's model year 2016 diesel-powered vehicles.

On September 3, 2015, Volkswagen admitted to EPA that the software was programmed to cheat during certification testing. Two weeks later VW management admitted the deception and extended a public apology. A few days later, the CEO of VW, Martin Winterkorn, resigned, followed by several other executives. Ultimately criminal convictions occurred due to the scandal.

VW Shifts to Electric Cars

Massive civil litigation against VW ensued in courts around the world, some initiated by governments and some by private citizens and companies. The aftermath of the scandal led to an intriguing possibility: a regime shift at VW away from the internal combustion engine to electric propulsion based on lithium ion batteries. Several aspects of the VW settlement with EPA and the Department of Justice (DOJ) played an influential role in the regime shift.

VW—once a staunch skeptic of electric vehicle technology—flip-flopped as part of the legal settlement and pledged to bring more than twenty electric-vehicle models to global markets by 2022. VW arranged fifty-six billion dollars in contracts with battery suppliers to purchase enough batteries to power fifty million vehicles worldwide. As part of the "dieselgate" settlement with EPA and DOJ, VW also agreed to spend two billion dollars in the US promoting electric vehicles through a new company called Electrify America. The company will build recharging stations around the US and engage in public information and education about the promise of electric vehicles.

Within the European Union, the credibility of VW and the German government were tarnished by dieselgate. The European Commission, over Germany's objections, enacted highly stringent CO2 controls on new cars, so stringent that European companies may be compelled to switch much of their fleets to electric propulsion. And the Commission enacted new rules that ensure the industry compliance will be monitored and that non-compliant companies will be punished.

The VW settlement is certainly not the only factor boosting the commercial future of electric vehicles. A big factor has been the large drop of lithium-ion battery prices, which has reduced the cost disadvantage of the electric car. The US Congress in 2009 also authorized a $7,500 federal tax credit for consumers who purchase fully battery-operated vehicles.[99] This credit has boosted the sales of plug-in electric vehicles offered by Tesla, Nissan, and General Motors. CARB has also played a key role with its zero-emission vehicle (ZEV) regulations that are expected to sharply increase the market share of electric vehicles by 2025 in both California and another dozen states that have aligned with California.[100] The 2015 Paris agreement on climate change made it clear to automakers that some degree of electrification would likely be required in countries around the world; the European CO2 standards are now so stringent that a substantial amount of electrification will be required. China's government embraced electric vehicles as industrial policy and required all automakers doing business in China to offer a growing percentage of electrified vehicles. The Chinese auto market is so large that virtually all global automakers are now planning to offer electric cars in China. Moreover, many governments around the world have adopted generous financial and nonfinancial incentives that favor purchase and use of electric vehicles.[101] In Norway the incentives are so generous that more than half of new car sales are electric.[102]

Tesla's new products, especially the all-electric Model 3, have attracted a large number of early adopters but, given VW's new corporate strategy as well as electrification decisions by GM and Nissan, Tesla will not necessarily dominate the global electric-car market in 2025 as Tesla did in 2018. Forecasts vary widely about how fast the transition to electric vehicles will occur, but there is no question that EPA's handling of the VW scandal has accelerated the pace of the transition, yet another consequence of EPA's technology-forcing strategy.

CONCLUSION

The progress the United States has made in reducing air pollution from cars and trucks is one of the great success stories of American government, whether measured in public health terms or economic terms.[103] Several factors contributed to EPA's successes.

Congress gave EPA legal authority to impose technology-forcing regulations that stimulated the invention of cleaner engines and fuels. EPA overcame opposition from the auto and oil industries, in part because the two sectors were rarely united in opposition to EPA. EPA was successful working simultaneously with both sectors—technically and policy-wise—to achieve successes in pollution control.

It should not be forgotten that EPA had a unique resource—an engineering laboratory in Ann Arbor, Michigan—that provided independent technical information without interference by industrial experts in the auto and oil industries. No other program office within EPA is blessed with this kind of technical support laboratory.

There was also political will in some presidential administrations (Republican and Democrat) to impose near-term burdens on the automotive, engine, and fuels sectors of the economy in exchange for long-term public-health and environmental benefits. Likewise, the agency exhibited a strong will to enforce against non-complying companies and seek creative enforcement settlements.

Finally, EPA could discuss issues, exchange data, and collaborate on policy with California's experts. The EPA-CARB relationship was competitive and not always harmonious, but both EPA and CARB became smarter and more effective because of the special and unusual relationship established for the two agencies in the Clean Air Act.

Technology-forcing regulation was successful in bringing the catalytic converter to the marketplace, an innovation that was enhanced by lead-free and low-sulfur fuel. But technological forcing did not work well in the case of ethanol blending; the country remains dependent on corn-based ethanol, which is associated with a variety of environmental problems. EPA's quest for cellulosic ethanol as a sustainable replacement for corn-based ethanol has yet to achieve large-scale commercialization. Thus, EPA's track record with technology-forcing regulation has some blemishes as well as successes.

NOTES

1. The author gratefully acknowledges comments and assistance from faculty colleague Professor A. James Barnes, especially in drafting the description of EPA Administrator Bill Ruckelshaus's decisions related to the installation of catalytic converters under the 1970 Clean Air Act.

2. National Research Council, *State and Federal Standards for Mobile Source Emissions* (Washington, DC: The National Academies Press, 2006), 35–37 (especially Figures 2–10).

3. Despite dramatic progress since the 1960s, LA remains the worst US city based on smog measurements. Doyle Rice, "LA Languishes in Same Spot as Most Polluted US City," *USA Today*, April 25, 2019, 3A.

4. World Health Organization, "Ambient Air Pollution: Health Impacts," *Who.int*, accessed February 9, 2020, https://www.who.int/airpollution/ambient/health-impacts/en/.

5. J. Robert Mondt, *Cleaner Cars: The History and Technology of Emission Control Since the 1960s* (Warrendale, PA: Society of Automotive Engineers, 2000).

6. Devra Davis, *When Smoke Ran Like Water: Tales of Environmental Deception and the Battle Against Pollution* (New York: Basic Books, 2002), 55–122.

7. David Vogel, *California Greenin': How the Golden State Became an Environmental Leader* (Princeton: Princeton University Press, 2018); Davis, *When Smoke Ran Like Water*, 85–88.

8. A. J. Haagen-Smit and M. M. Fox, "Photochemical Ozone Formation with Hydrocarbons and Automobile Exhaust," *Journal of Air Pollution Control Association* 4 (1954): 105–9.

9. California Air Resources Board, "History," accessed May 27, 2019, https://ww2.arb.ca.gov/about/history.

10. John C. Esposito and Larry G. Silverman, *Ralph Nader's Study Group on Air Pollution—Vanishing Air* (New York: Grossman Publishers, 1970).

11. Michael Weisskopf, "Auto-Pollution Debate Has Ring of the Past," *Washington Post*, March 26, 1990; Harry Stoffer, "GM Fought Safety, Emissions Rules, But Then Invented Ways to Comply," *Automotive News*, September 14, 2008.

12. Ann Carlson, "Iterative Federalism and Climate Change," *Northwestern University Law Review* 103, no. 3 (2009): 1097–161.

13. Fear of conflicting state standards ultimately caused the auto industry to favor national EPA standards. See E. Donald Elliott, Bruce A. Ackerman, and John C. Miller, "Toward a Theory of Statutory Evolution: The Federalization of Environmental Law," *Journal of Law, Economics, and Organizations* 1, no. 2 (1985): 313, 326.

14. Barry G. Rabe, "Leveraged Federalism and the Clean Air Act: The Case of Vehicle Emissions Control," In *Lessons from the Clean Air Act: Building Durability and Adaptability into US Climate and Energy Policy*, eds. Ann Carlson and Dallas Burtraw (Cambridge: Cambridge University Press, 2019), 113, 121–28.

15. US Congress, Senate, Subcommittee on Air and Water Pollution, Senate Committee on Public Works, *Hearings on Air Pollution—1967*, 90th Cong., 1st Sess., 766-67.

16. David Gerard and Lester Lave, "Implementing Technology-Forcing Policies: The 1970 Clean Air Act Amendments and the Introduction of Advanced Automotive Emissions Controls in the United States," *Technological Forecasting and Social Change* 72, no. 7 (September 2005): 762, 766; Steven C. Hackett, "Pollution-Controlling Innovation in Oligopolistic Industries: Some Comparisons Between Patent Races and Research Joint Ventures," *Journal of Environmental Economics and Management* 29, no. 3 (1995): 339–56.

17. Thomas McGarity, "Radical Technology-Forcing in Environmental Regulation," *Loyola University Law Review* 27, no. 3 (1994).

18. Gerard and Lave, "Implementing Technology-Forcing Policies," 762, 766–67.

19. This was a view expressed by Senate staff member Leon Billings. See Gerard and Lave, "Implementing Technology-Forcing Policies," 761, 767; Jack Doyle, *Taken for a Ride: Detroit's Big Three and the Politics of Pollution* (New York: Four Walls Eight Windows, 2000).

20. Gerard and Lave, "Implementing Technology-Forcing Policies," 761–78.

21. Jaegul Lee et al., "Forcing Technological Change: A Case of Automobile Technology Development in the United States," *Technovation* (2010): 249–64.

22. Gerard and Lave, "Implementing Technology-Forcing Policies," 761, 771.

23. International Harvester Co. v. Ruckelshaus, 478 F.2d 615 (D.C. Cir. 1973).

24. The Baker and Griffin quotes can be found in International Harvester Co. v. Ruckelshaus.

25. Davis, *When Smoke Ran Like Water*, 92–94.

26. "Auto Emissions Rules Delayed to '76: Relatively Strict Interim Curbs Set," *Wall Street Journal*, News Roundup, April 12, 1973.

27. Gerard and Lave, "Implementing Technology-Forcing Policies," 761, 768.

28. At the time, it was not clear whether the public health benefits of the standards, expressed in dollars, were greater than the costs. Alfred Marcus, "Environmental Protection Agency," In *The Politics of Regulation*, ed. James Q. Wilson (New York, NY: Basic Books, 1980), 279.

29. Dana Bullen, "Auto Firms, Denied Delay on Emissions, Weigh Action," *Washington Star*, May 13, 1972.

30. E. W. Kenworthy, "US Agency Bars Delay on Cutting Auto Pollutants," *New York Times*, May 13, 1972.

31. William D. Ruckelshaus, *Decision of the Administrator In re: Applications for Suspension of 1975 Motor Vehicle Exhaust Emission Standards* (Washington, DC: EPA, May 12, 1972).

32. "A Costly Order to Auto Makers: Clean Up Car Exhausts by 1975," *US News and World Report*, May 22, 1972; Bullen, "Auto Firms, Denied Delay on Emissions, Weigh Action."

33. "Why Detroit Failed to Sway EPA," *Business Week*, May 20, 1972, 29–30.

34. Bullen, "Auto Firms, Denied Delay on Emissions, Weigh Action."

35. Seth Lipsky, "The Automakers Are Given Delay in Exhaust Rules, But Major Battles Loom," *Wall Street Journal*, April 12, 1973.

36. National Research Council, *Semi-Annual Report by the Committee on Motor Vehicle Emissions, Division of Engineering* (Washington, DC: National Academy of Sciences, 1972).

37. Kenworthy, "US Agency Bars Delay on Cutting Auto Pollutants."

38. Cited by Judge Leventhal in International Harvester Co. v. Ruckelshaus, 478 F.2d. 615 (D.C. Circ. 1973).

39. International Harvester Co. v. Ruckelshaus.

40. "Auto Emissions Rules Delayed to '76."

41. National Research Council, *Report by the Committee on Motor Vehicle Emissions, Division of Engineering* (Washington, DC: The National Academies Press, 1973).

42. William D. Ruckelshaus, "Transportation and Environmental Protection," *Traffic Quarterly* (April 1973): 173–81.

43. E. W. Kenworthy, "Ruckelshaus: Center Lane on Pollution," *New York Times*, April 12, 1973.

44. William D. Ruckelshaus, *Decision of the Administrator In re: Applications for Suspension of 1975 Motor Vehicle Exhaust Emission Standards* (Washington, DC: EPA, April 11, 1973).

45. "Ecology Leader Charges Sellout," *New York Times*, April 12, 1973.

46. "EPA Media Summary," *ABC Radio*, April 11, 1973.

47. "Ecology Leader Charges Sellout."

48. Agis Salpukas, "Detroit Unhappy with EPA Action," *New York Times*, April 11, 1973.

49. United Press International, *Company Statement*, April 11, 1973.

50. Walter Cronkite, CBS Evening News, New York: CBS, April 11, 1973.
51. "Ecology Leader Charges Sellout."
52. Ibid.
53. "Auto Emissions Rules Delayed to '76."
54. David Smith, "1975 GM Cars May Have Catalytic Converters," *Washington Post*, May 25, 1973.
55. General Motors Corp. v. Toyota Motor Co., 467 F.Supp. 1142 (S.D. Ohio 1979); Douglas Williams, "Catalytic Converter Suit Pits Toyota Against GM," *Washington Post*, December 4, 1977.
56. Michael P. Walsh, "Automobile Emissions," In *The Reality of Precaution: Comparing Risk Regulation in the United States and Europe*, eds. Jonathan B. Wiener et al. (Washington, DC: Resources for the Future Press, 2011): 146–48.
57. Timothy Bresnahan and Dennis Yao, "The Nonpecuniary Costs of Automobile Emissions Standards," *RAND Journal of Economics* 16, no. 4 (1985): 437–55.
58. Jessie Stolark, "A Brief History of Octane in Gasoline: From Lead to Ethanol," *EESI*, March 2016, https://www.eesi.org/papers/view/fact-sheet-a-brief-history-of-octane.
59. George M. Gray, Laury Saligman, and John D. Graham, "The Demise of Lead in Gasoline," In *The Greening of Industry: A Risk-Management Approach*, eds. John D. Graham and Jennifer Kassalow Hartwell (Boston: Harvard University Press, 1997), 17, 19–21.
60. Albert L. Nichols, "Lead in Gasoline," In *Economic Analyses at EPA: Assessing Regulatory Impact*, ed. Richard D. Morgenstern (Washington, DC: Resources for the Future Press, 1997), 49–86.
61. United Nations Environment Programme/Organisation for Economic Co-Operation and Development, *Phasing Lead Out of Gasoline: An Examination of Policy Approaches in Different Countries* (Paris: UNEP/OECD, 1999).
62. Stolark, "A Brief History of Octane in Gasoline."
63. US Environmental Protection Agency, *Control of Hazardous Air Pollutants from Mobile Sources: Final Rule to Reduce Mobile Source Air Toxics,* EPA 420-F-07-017 (Washington, DC: EPA, February 2007).
64. John K. Pearson, *Improving Air Quality: Progress and Challenges for the Auto Industry* (Warrendale, PA: Society for Automotive Engineers, 2001), Chapter 5.
65. J. R. Minkel, "Pinching Out Sulfur: Refining Ways to Turn Heavy Oil into Sweet Crude," *Scientific American* (February 1, 2006).
66. Douglas W. Dockery et al., "An Association between Air Pollution and Mortality in Six U.S. Cities," *New England Journal of Medicine* 329, no. 24 (1993): 1753–59; C.A. Pope, III et al., "Particulate Air Pollution as a Predictor of Mortality in a Prospective Study of US Adults," *American Journal of Respiratory and Critical Care Medicine* 151, no. 3 (1995): 669-74; US Environmental Protection Agency, *Regulatory Impact Analyses for the Particulate Matter and Ozone National Ambient Air Quality Standards and Proposed Regional Haze Rule* (Research Triangle Park, NC: EPA, 1997).
67. Sanya Carley, Natalie Messer Betts, and John D. Graham, "Innovation in the Auto Industry: The Role of the US Environmental Protection Agency," *Duke Environmental Law and Policy Forum* 21, no. 2 (Spring 2011): 367–99.

68. John D. Graham, *Bush on the Home Front: Domestic Policy Triumphs and Setbacks* (Bloomington, IN: Indiana University Press, 2010), 149–60.

69. Katherine Von Stackleberg et al., "Public Health Impacts of Secondary Particle Formation from Aromatic Hydrocarbons in Gasoline," *Environmental Health* 12 (2013): 19.

70. National Research Council, *Renewable Fuel Standard: Potential Economic and Environmental Effects of US Biofuel Policy* (Washington, DC: The National Academies Press, 2011).

71. Ibid.

72. John D. Graham, *Obama on the Home Front: Domestic Policy Triumphs and Setbacks* (Bloomington, IN: Indiana University Press, 2016), 261–64.

73. Tim Searchinger et al., "Use of US Croplands for Biofuels Increases Greenhouse Gases through Emissions from Land-Use Changes," *Science* 319, no. 5867 (February 29, 2008): 1238–40.

74. US Environmental Protection Agency, *Renewal Fuel Standard Program (RFS2) Regulatory Impact Analysis*, EPA-420-R-10-006 (Washington, DC: EPA, February 2010).

75. In support of EPA's official view, see M. J. Flugge et al., *A Life-Cycle Analysis of the Greenhouse Gas Emissions of Corn-Based Ethanol* (Washington, DC: ICF, January 30, 2017); for a skeptical perspective, see Chris Malins, "Navigating the Maize: A Critical Review of the Report 'A Life-Cycle Analysis of the Greenhouse Gas Emissions of Corn-Based Ethanol,'" *Cerulogy, CATF and NWF* (July 2017).

76. Jonathan Coppess, "Upon Further Review: The Decision on EPA's RFS Waiver Authority," *farmdoc daily* 7, no. 151 (August 18, 2017).

77. US Environmental Protection Agency, *Biofuels and the Environment: Second Triennial Report to Congress*, EPA-600-R-18-195 (Washington, DC: EPA, 2018).

78. Jan Lewandrowski et al., "The Greenhouse Gas Benefits of Corn Ethanol–Assessing Recent Evidence," *Biofuels* 11, no. 3 (March 25, 2019).

79. Charisse Jones, "Activists Use Research to Win Pollution Battle," *USA Today*, December 6, 2006, 13A.

80. John O'Dell, "Auto Industry Teams with Clean-Air Groups to Cut Sulphur in Diesel," *Los Angeles Times*, June 26, 2000.

81. Margo T. Oge, *Driving the Future: Combating Climate Change with Cleaner, Smarter Cars* (New York: Arcade Publishing, 2015), 295–99.

82. John D. Graham, "Saving Lives through Administrative Law and Economics," *University of Pennsylvania Law Review* 157, no. 2 (2008): 466–69.

83. National Research Council, *Review of the 21st Century Truck Partnership, Second Report* (Washington, DC: The National Academies Press, 2012).

84. National Research Council, *Cost, Effectiveness, and Deployment of Fuel-Economy Technologies for Light-Duty Vehicles* (Washington, DC: The National Academies Press, 2015), 97–128.

85. Ibid., 106-7.

86. Cummins Inc., "Cummins First to Receive EPA Certification: ISX Engine Certified to October 2002 On-Highway Standard," *investor.cummins.com*, April 2, 2002.

87. DieselNet, "US EPA Upholds the Consent Decree Schedule," *dieselnet.com*, June 8, 2001.

88. Graham, *Bush on the Home Front*, 206–7.

89. US Environmental Protection Agency, *Final Technical Support Document: Nonconformance Penalties for 2004 Highway Heavy Duty Diesel Engines*, EPA-420-R-02-021 (Washington, DC: EPA, August 2002).

90. Eugenio J. Miravete, Maria J. Moral, and Jeff Thurk, "Fuel Taxation, Emissions Policy, and Competitive Disadvantage in the Diffusion of European Diesel Automobiles," *RAND Journal of Economics* 49, no. 3 (2018): 504–40.

91. J. L. Sullivan et al., "CO2 Emission Benefit of Diesel (Versus Gasoline) Powered Vehicles," *Environmental Science and Technology* 38, no. 12 (2004): 3217–23.

92. National Research Council, *Rethinking the Ozone Problem in Urban and Regional Air Pollution* (Washington, DC: The National Academies Press, 1991).

93. Paolo Boffeta, Carlo La Vecchia, and Suresh Moolgavkar, "Chronic Effects of Air Pollution Are Probably Overestimated," *Risk Analysis* 35, no. 5 (2015): 766–69.

94. Health Effects Institute, "Diesel Exhaust," *Healtheffects.org*, accessed May 28, 2019.

95. David Vogel, *The Politics of Precaution: Regulating Health, Safety and Environmental Risks in Europe and the United States* (Princeton: Princeton University Press, 2012), 115–20. Walsh, "Automobile Emissions," 146.

96. Miravete et al., "Fuel Taxation, Emissions Policy," 524–27.

97. Patrick McGee, "How VW's Cheating on Emissions Was Exposed," *Financial Times*, January 11, 2017.

98. Jack Ewing, "Researchers Who Exposed VW Gain Little Reward from Success," *New York Times*, July 24, 2016.

99. Transportation Research Board and National Research Council, *Overcoming Barriers to the Deployment of Plug-In Electric Vehicles* (Washington, DC: The National Academies Press, 2015).

100. California Air Resources Board, *Staff Report: Initial Statement of Reasons, Advanced Clean Cars, 2012 Proposed Amendments to California Zero Emission Vehicle Program Regulations* (Sacramento, CA: CARB, December 7, 2011); California Air Resources Board, *Advanced Clean Cars Midterm Review* (Sacramento, CA: CARB, 2015).

101. Transportation Research Board, *Overcoming Barriers*.

102. International Energy Agency, "Global EV Outlook 2018," *iea.org*, 2018.

103. US Environmental Protection Agency, *The Benefits and Costs of the Clean Air Act, 1970 to 1990*, 410-R-97-002 (Washington, DC: EPA, 1991); US Environmental Protection Agency, *The Benefits and Costs of the Clean Air Act, 1990 to 2010: First Prospective Study*, 410-R-99-001 (Washington, DC: EPA, November 1999); A. Myrick Freeman, III, "Environmental Policy Since Earth Day I: What Have We Gained?" *Journal of Economic Perspectives* 16, no. 1 (Winter 2002): 125–46; John Bachman, David Calkins, and Margo T. Oge, *Cleaning the Air We Breathe: A Half Century of Progress* (Washington, DC: EPA Alumni Association, September 2017).

Chapter Four

EPA and Climate Change

Jody Freeman[1]

INTRODUCTION

In 1983, the little-known Strategic Studies Staff, within the somewhat obscure Office of Policy Analysis in the United States Environmental Protection Agency (EPA), released—at no one's request—a report entitled *Can We Delay a Greenhouse Warming?* The report summarized the results of the then most current atmospheric temperature and carbon cycle models, drawing on James Hansen's work at NASA's Goddard Institute, among other sources.[2] Those models showed that due to rising atmospheric concentrations of carbon dioxide, global average temperatures could increase by two degrees Celsius by the middle of the twenty-first century, and that this temperature rise "likely" would be accompanied by "dramatic changes in precipitation and storm patterns and a rise in global average sea levels," significantly altering agriculture, disrupting environmental and economic conditions, and stressing political institutions.

The study went on to explore the potential for various strategies to slow or limit warming, including some policies that, in retrospect, seem eye-popping even for EPA to have considered internally, let alone discuss in a public report, including a 300% tax on fossil fuels, and a ban on both coal and shale oil. When *Can We Delay* appeared on the front page of the *New York Times*, it caused a firestorm in the Reagan White House. The president's science advisor disavowed it, calling it "unwarranted and unnecessarily alarmist."[3]

But it wasn't.

This chapter recounts EPA's role in US climate policy over the last fifty years. It tells the story of how climate change evolved at EPA from a long-term research project—of interest to a handful of staff—into the agency's top priority, on which it trained the full measure of its regulatory might. An important turning point in the story is the Supreme Court's ruling in

Massachusetts v. EPA. Eventually, EPA would rely on that decision to fully embrace its legal authority, and the Clean Air Act would, for a time, serve as the US government's most potent instrument for tackling climate change. In the roughly twenty years leading up to that point, EPA staff contributed to climate policy in a variety of important ways: by conducting research, modeling, and analysis of climate impacts and mitigation strategies, and beginning to explore adaptation; by testifying and building awareness across the government, in Congress, in the media, and among the public; by engaging in the government's interagency process to educate, persuade, and sometimes confront other agencies, and the White House, on the need to do more; by developing a suite of non-regulatory programs to reduce greenhouse gases (GHGs); and by participating in major international meetings, and helping to negotiate international agreements.

EPA is charged by Congress with protecting public health and the environment, but it had no grand plan on climate change for the majority of its history. To understand the agency's handling of the issue, one must appreciate the delicate context in which the agency operates day-to-day: subject to presidential supervision, congressional oversight, judicial review, and buffeted by the whirlwind of domestic politics. It would have been hard, if not unimaginable, for EPA to prioritize climate change throughout the 1980s and 1990s with Congress so assiduously opposed, and without powerful White House support. Eventually, a series of legal and political developments, some of which the agency itself helped to engineer, put EPA in position to act, and during the Obama administration the agency began to regulate GHG emissions in the US economy for the first time.

EPA's legacy on climate change is still unfolding, however. At the time of writing, Joe Biden has won the 2020 presidential election, promising to restore the climate regulations that Donald J. Trump spent four years rescinding or weakening. In the absence of congressional leadership on climate change, however, EPA will remain in a frustrating posture—adapting its approach to climate regulation with each new president's agenda, within the constraints afforded by aging statutory authorities, as interpreted by an increasingly conservative Supreme Court.

THE 1970s AND 1980s: EPA AND THE SCIENCE OF CLIMATE CHANGE

A Long-Term Research Project

The basic science of the greenhouse effect has long been known and is well-documented. Every president since Lyndon Johnson was briefed on global warming.[4] In 1965, President Johnson's "Special Message" to Congress on the need for conservation, which addressed pollution broadly, included a specific reference to "a steady increase in carbon dioxide from the burning of fossil fuels," which the president had learned from a report conducted by his science advisory committee.[5] By 1970, the US had four climate modeling centers, including the nation's premier lab—the National Oceanic and Atmospheric Administration's Geophysical Research Dynamics Laboratory at Princeton University. President Nixon's Domestic Policy Council organized a United States Climate Program to coordinate federal government research on climate change. The National Academy of Sciences produced the first of several reports on atmospheric carbon dioxide concentrations in 1975,[6] and the first congressional hearing on the topic was held in 1976. That year, a House subcommittee held several days of hearings on climate change.[7] By then, various scientific agencies across the US government had established robust climate research programs, as had several leading universities and international research institutes. In 1978, Congress passed the National Climate Program Act, which directed the president to establish a National Climate Program Office, and oversee a coordinated program of research to be led by the Department of Commerce.[8] By the end of the decade, the international scientific community was coordinating climate research.[9]

Indeed, that is how EPA viewed climate change throughout the 1970s: as a topic for long-term scientific research. Bill Ruckelshaus, the agency's first administrator, was pre-occupied with organizing EPA, defining its mission, and implementing new landmark statutes, including the new Clean Air and Clean Water Acts.[10] His successor, Russell Train, managed the next phase of implementing these laws into the Gerald Ford administration, focusing on auto emissions standards, pesticides and toxics, among other things.[11] President Jimmy Carter's EPA head, Doug Costle, had his hands full implementing backlogged regulations, fending off litigation, preparing for reauthorizations, and advocating for the agency on Capitol Hill.[12]

During both the Ford and Carter administrations, EPA staff fought many internal battles over energy policy, in the wake of the OPEC oil embargo against the United States. By the Carter years, EPA had established four "policy evaluation" offices that specialized in particular topics like regulatory reform, economics, and energy. The energy group represented EPA in inter-agency debates over administration energy policy, and its staff would go toe-to-toe with other agencies—chiefly, DOE—in discussions with the White House over issues like sulfur standards for coal plants, or the synthetic fuels program (which would *increase* pollution by liquefying and gasifying coal), which President Carter eventually included in his energy plan.[13] Members of the energy group were focused on public health, but also "well aware of climate change," and raised it "regularly" as a consideration.[14] Carter himself understood the climate issue. He had been briefed on climate change by his science advisor, Frank Press, and by Gus Speth, who chaired his Council on Environmental Quality.[15] But Carter's highest energy priority was the synfuels program.[16] He was grappling with high oil prices, inflation, and a recession, which would help to doom his chances for re-election.

As the Reagan administration began, a small group of entrepreneurial EPA career staff launched their own research project on climate change. The self-named "Strategic Studies Staff" was located within the agency's Office of Policy Planning and Evaluation, and would come to include people whose names are on the earliest EPA climate studies, including Stephen Seidel, Jim Titus, and Dennis Tirpak.[17] The team was led by John Hoffman, a career staffer who had worked on early emissions trading concepts, like the "bubble," which sought to reduce pollution more efficiently.[18] Hoffman had developed a reputation for being innovative and was given considerable leeway to follow his own research agenda; he reportedly took up the greenhouse effect because he thought it was "interesting."[19]

It was an unlikely time to launch a climate change research program at the agency. President Reagan's new EPA Administrator, Anne M. Gorsuch was cutting the agency's budget, pulling back on enforcement, and reducing staff levels to such a significant extent that one former assistant administrator complained that she had "demolish[ed] the nation's environmental management capacity."[20] Yet because climate change was still viewed as relatively obscure, and nowhere near ripe for regulation, it apparently escaped the attention of Gorsuch and the top political appointees at the agency. The OPPE group—"a couple of guys in the bowels of EPA"—could operate under the radar without garnering attention.[21]

That anonymity would not last long, however. Hoffman's staff produced the 1983 *Can We Delay* report, which reviewed the climate science to date, discussed the implications for society, and explored policy options for slowing the projected warming.[22] It concluded by calling for research into climate adaptation and additional study to reduce remaining scientific uncertainties (about GHG sources, sinks, and thermal sensitivities among other things) as soon as possible. No one in the White House or at the top of the agency appears to have requested the study, it was not subject to an internal review process, and there is no evidence the administrator saw it before its release.[23]

Although EPA had not called for regulation, the report's tone was substantially more alarming than the latest National Academies of Science report, conducted at the request of Congress, released just three days later. The NAS panel had examined the same studies as EPA and concluded much the same thing, that warming was human-induced and largely caused by fossil fuel consumption, and echoed EPA's prediction that if atmospheric CO_2 concentrations continued to rise there would be significant average global temperature and sea level rise with serious consequences. Yet despite the fairly dire findings, the *synthesis* of the NAS Report, which most people would read, stated that, "Our stance is conservative. We believe there is reason for caution, not panic."[24] When *Can We Delay* was leaked to the *New York Times*, it seemed to contradict this calming tone. The President's science advisor, George Keyworth, promptly repudiated the EPA report and endorsed the NAS study, emphasizing that "no actions are recommended other than additional research at this time."[25] Then, a few days later, Hoffman's group at EPA issued another report, this one called *Projecting Future Sea Level Rise*.[26] Citing the National Academies' own conclusion of near-certain global warming, it estimated likely sea level rise based on scenarios ranging from "the very conservative to the less restrictive." Like *Can We Delay*, it called for additional research on a faster timeline to help coastal planners mitigate the adverse impacts.

It is hard to precisely measure the impact of these reports, but given the prominent media attention they received, and the consternation they caused, it seems fair to say that they helped to raise public awareness about climate change and provided fodder for activists and those in Congress pushing for additional hearings.[27] It bears noting, though, that no one, including the Hoffman group, was suggesting that EPA embark on a regulatory program to control greenhouse gases. Climate change was still regarded as a longer-term research issue, not ripe for "policy."

EPA was soon in transition. Administrator Gorsuch had been forced to resign, and Bill Ruckelshaus returned to the agency at the president's request.[28] Ruckelshaus recalled that climate change was still somewhat abstract—a "question being studied."[29] He discussed climate change with President Reagan, whom he described as "a skeptic but with an open mind and willing to listen; genuinely curious about it."[30] But Ruckelshaus focused on repairing the damage done during Gorsuch's tenure by rebuilding the agency's relationship with Congress and restoring morale.[31]

When Ruckelshaus resigned at the end of Reagan's first term, Lee Thomas took over as administrator.[32] Thomas had come to EPA from the Federal Emergency Management Administration, and had briefly run EPA's solid waste office. He had little experience with air pollution, had "never dealt with ozone depletion or climate change," and "knew nothing about either."[33] But after briefings from the OPPE staff, he came to understand the importance of both problems, and that they were connected.[34]

The two issues were percolating at EPA simultaneously, but ozone depletion gained traction first. Scientists had determined by the mid-1970s that the atmospheric ozone layer was thinning and suspected the cause was chlorofluorocarbons, a set of gases commonly used in refrigeration, air conditioning, and a range of consumer products.[35] A thinner ozone layer would mean higher rates of skin cancer and cataracts, along with damage to plants, animals, and agriculture.[36] Congress had called for more research and cooperation on ozone in the 1977 Clean Air Act Amendments but also included a provision with bite, requiring the EPA administrator to propose rules for ozone-depleting substances that could "reasonably be anticipated to pose an endangerment for the public health and welfare."[37] Under this authority, the agency had issued an endangerment finding for chlorofluorocarbons and banned their use in certain aerosol spray cans.[38] But momentum on further regulation had stalled in the Reagan administration, and environmental groups sued the agency in 1984 to force next steps. EPA settled the litigation by promising to conduct a study on a timeline to issue rules in 1987.[39] That study was underway, with John Hoffman as the lead, when Lee Thomas became administrator.[40]

At the same time, the Vienna Convention for the Protection of the Ozone Layer—the international framework agreement calling for "appropriate actions to protect the ozone layer"—was before the United States Senate, awaiting consent to ratification. EPA staff had been working with the US State Department to support international negotiations over ozone controls, which had been launched by the United Nations Environment Programme in 1981.[41] In 1985, scientists published a paper confirming that a giant hole had appeared in the ozone layer over Antarctica, allowing dangerous levels of UV radiation to reach the earth's surface,[42] and vividly demonstrating that the impact of CFCs was not small and mostly in the future but significant and happening already.[43] By the end of the year, twenty-one industrialized nations, including the United States, had joined the Vienna Convention.[44]

Having been briefed by EPA staff, Thomas understood the ozone threat. But he also knew that, politically, he could not just restrict US companies; an international agreement would be necessary. He supported ratification of the Convention,[45] and spent the next two years lobbying the Reagan cabinet and urging the president to sign the follow-on Montreal Protocol, which would cut global CFC production by fifty percent over ten years.[46]

During the period between the Vienna Convention and the Montreal Protocol, EPA became deeply engaged in the interagency process to develop the US position on ozone controls. As regulation looked increasingly politically feasible, Hoffman and Seidel, who had worked together on early climate research, moved to EPA's air office to work under Eileen Claussen, whom Thomas had chosen to manage the regulatory effort.[47] Hoffman produced a comprehensive risk assessment focused on skin cancer impacts, which was instrumental in convincing the Reagan administration that the benefits of regulating CFCs outweighed the cost. The analysis also noted the significant contribution CFCs make to climate change.[48]

Dennis Tirpak, meanwhile, had stayed at OPPE. Tirpak was well connected to the international scientific community working on climate change research, and he knew climate would be "the next big thing."[49] He and a small group of remaining OPPE staff[50] working under Dick Morgenstern continued to conduct modeling and analysis, building and expanding on the work Hoffman had begun.[51] Yet, despite several new international studies pointing to dire consequences, climate change would not follow the path of ozone. Thomas had backed OPPE's research on climate change and publicly spoken and testified about the greenhouse effect.[52] But the Reagan White House did not support an international climate accord, feeling that the science was still too uncertain. At the urging of EPA and the State Department, however, the administration agreed to propose that an intergovernmental body be established to conduct a comprehensive scientific assessment of the issue,[53] which led to the creation of the Intergovernmental Panel on Climate Change.[54] That strategy accomplished two things the administration wanted: it delayed the need for negotiating a climate convention, and it put governments, rather than scientists, firmly in control of the international research program. But it also took a necessary next step toward building consensus for an international agreement, just as had happened with the ozone agreement.

Congressional interest in climate change grew steadily, if less urgently than its interest in ozone depletion.[55] In 1986, Congress held two days of hearings on both issues, with testimony from Lee Thomas, NASA's Goddard Space Institute's James Hansen, and then Senator Al Gore. Gore argued that there was no significant disagreement in the scientific community about whether the greenhouse effect was real.[56] After the hearing, a group of senators requested two studies from EPA: one on the effects of climate change, and the other on possible policy responses.[57] In 1987, Congress passed the Global Climate Protection Act, calling for more research and asking EPA and the State Department to develop policy options.[58] And in 1988, Senator Tim Wirth presided over the dramatic hearing where NASA scientist James Hansen, in a packed hearing room on a sweltering June day, testified to being "99% certain" that global warming was the result of a buildup of carbon dioxide in the atmosphere rather than natural variation, and warned that "it is already happening now."[59]

Yet, regulation was still far off. While many staffers at EPA increasingly recognized the importance of the climate issue,[60] some regarded it as a distraction and a drain on scarce resources. In addition, it was still not clear what statute might be used to move forward, or which program office would take the lead.[61] The policy office was focused on research and analysis, and the Air office had its plate full with other things.[62]

The analogy between ozone and climate change, it turned out, was deeply flawed.[63] Among other things, there were no ready substitutes for fossil energy, as there had been for the CFCs responsible for deteriorating the ozone layer, let alone substitutes that would disproportionately benefit American companies.[64] And the harms from climate change remained remote. The ozone process had galvanized industry opposition, too, and a powerful coalition of energy, chemical, and auto sector companies joined forces, determined not to let what happened in Montreal happen to them on climate change.[65] Congressional hearings and press coverage of climate change did increase throughout the 1980s, and some members of Congress introduced far-reaching bills.[66] But the notion that Congress was on the precipice of passing legislation to regulate greenhouse gas emissions seems overly optimistic.[67] And EPA was not about to get ahead of Congress.

GEORGE H. W. BUSH: THE RIO TREATY AND VOLUNTARY PROGRAMS

The 1990 Clean Air Act Amendments

When running for president in 1989, George H. W. Bush sought to distinguish himself from Reagan by promising to be "the environmental president." He pledged to support reauthorizing the Clean Air Act, which was then stalemated in Congress. Among other measures, the amendments included a new market-based program to address acid rain. In the end, the 1990 Clean Air Act Amendments were to be the first and last major environmental legislative initiative of the first Bush administration.

While the update to the CAA was far-reaching, Congress did not add new provisions on climate change. The bill was already complex, costly, and controversial. The acid rain program was a signature achievement, but adding a greenhouse gas plan to the package would have been a bridge too far.[68] The amendments did, however, include several provisions that would *indirectly* reduce GHGs, including the acid rain program itself, the clean fuels requirements for the transportation sector, and the mandatory phase out of CFCs to address stratospheric ozone. There was, however, one new provision directly related to greenhouse gases: sources would be required to monitor CO2 emissions and report emissions data to EPA, which the agency would be required to make public. This was a seed planted with future GHG regulation in mind—monitoring emissions is, of course, a first step to creating an emissions inventory, which provides a baseline for regulation.[69]

Administration Divisions Over the Rio Treaty

Internationally, with the IPCC's first assessment due, momentum was building for a framework convention on climate change.[70] As a presidential candidate, Bush had invoked "the White House effect" to combat "the greenhouse effect."[71] He had said that climate change would require an international solution, pledging to hold a global conference on the environment during his first year in office.[72] And Bush had appointed Bill Reilly, the former president of the World Wildlife Fund, as his EPA administrator. Reilly argued that the US should support a framework climate treaty "to define the problem and its remedies."[73] But John Sununu, Bush's chief of staff, squelched action on climate, believing the science too uncertain to justify the economic cost.[74] Only when the press questioned Bush's commitment to the issue did he agree to attend the first IPCC plenary in early 1990[75] and host the first session of UN negotiations.[76]

Early on, Reilly appeared to have an ally in James Baker, the Secretary of State. In his first official speech, Baker had gone surprisingly far in urging action on climate change,[77] encouraging nations to act now rather than waiting "until all the uncertainties have been resolved."[78] Yet those remarks would be Baker's lone intervention on the issue—he subsequently recused himself from deliberations about global warming, citing his investments in the oil industry. The real reason was apparent in a message Baker sent Reilly: "Remember Bill, you never beat the White House,"[79] which alluded to Sununu and other members of Bush's senior staff, who adamantly opposed an international climate agreement. He was telling Reilly he would be on his own.

Baker was right. With the US now committed to participating in international negotiations, Sununu centralized control. He handpicked Robert Reinstein, a trade expert opposed to binding emission reduction targets, as the lead negotiator. At Sununu's direction, the United States would accept only voluntary programs that could be defended on their own terms—the "no regrets" policy—and oppose transferring funds to the developing world. As Reinstein put it, there were two no-nos: "no targets, no money."[80]

In the run-up to Rio, EPA staff were deeply involved in climate-related research, analysis, and modelling. They had produced the two congressionally mandated reports from the 1986 hearings: The first, published in 1989, described potential impacts by region and sector, done purposely to get the attention of members of Congress whose constituencies might be affected.[81] The second, on potential stabilization strategies, was released in 1990, after intense inter-agency scrutiny.[82] EPA staff testified in Congress on these reports and related topics, and participated in inter-agency discussions in which they tried to persuade largely skeptical DOE, DOI, and White House officials about the seriousness of the climate risk.[83]

After the Montreal Protocol, John Hoffman had turned his attention back to climate change. He began developing "voluntary" climate programs which could be advertised as good for both business and the environment.[84] The first two to launch were "Green Lights" and "Energy Star;"[85] they later blossomed into dozens of programs.[86] At the time, EPA's posture toward polluters was largely adversarial, and it was innovative to think in terms of *incentives* for industry, rather than just regulation.[87] Hoffman was searching for measures to reduce GHG reductions that might attract Bush administration support, and he knew that regulatory standards were off the table. Voluntary programs fit under the administration's "no regrets" banner and philosophically aligned with market-based approaches, like the acid rain trading regime. Hoffman would send Cathy Zoi to pitch the programs to the White House as a way to stabilize GHGs with a profit to the US economy.[88]

From February 1991 to the Rio Summit in June 1992, the US delegation, at the direction of Sununu, worked diligently to ensure that the agreement would not commit the US to specific emission targets. In the end, the Rio Treaty set as a goal the "stabilization of greenhouse gas concentrations in the atmosphere at a level that would prevent dangerous anthropogenic interference with the climate system."[89] Rather than agreeing to cap emissions at 1990 levels by 2000, as the Europeans had proposed, the US agreed only to "action plans" requiring industrialized nations to submit reports "with the aim" of returning emissions to 1990 levels.[90] Bill Reilly, the most powerful voice for environmental protection in the Bush cabinet, had been rebuffed very publicly during the Rio conference,[91] and the treaty itself created no mandate for domestic action. President Bush had sided with the climate naysayers on his staff.[92]

THE 1990s—KYOTO PROTOCOL AND EPA'S EVOLVING UNDERSTANDING OF THE CAA

When Bill Clinton won the 1992 presidential election, the prospects for meaningful US action on climate change seemed to brighten. His running mate, Al Gore, was closely identified with environmental issues, especially climate change, from his days in Congress, and had written *Earth in the Balance: Ecology and the Human Spirit*, which was published in the summer of 1992, around the time Clinton picked him.[93] Gore's people filled the administration's key environmental posts: Clinton nominated Carol Browner, Gore's thirty-seven-year-old former Senate legislative director, as EPA administrator, while another young Gore staffer, Katie McGinty, would become a deputy assistant to the president, and go on to chair the Council on Environmental Quality. At EPA, after twelve years of Republican control, a backlog of issues needed urgent attention: the Superfund program, food quality protection, pesticide regulation, national ambient air quality standards, and more.[94] These were immediate action items linked to clear statutory mandates, court deadlines, and congressional demands.[95] Browner herself was interested in strengthening what she viewed as weak and overdue pollution rules. She was less internationally and more domestically focused than her predecessor, Bill Reilly. Climate change was not at the top of her list.

The BTU Debacle and the Return to Voluntary Programs

The White House, meanwhile, had included a climate measure in the president's economic plan: a British Thermal Unit tax, based on an energy source's heat content. While not exclusively designed to address climate change, the tax would raise the cost of fossil fuel energy and reduce greenhouse gas emissions substantially. EPA's OPPE staff had done the underlying analytic work, modeling the tax's impact on emissions and the economy. Had it passed, the BTU tax would have been the most important climate policy adopted in the United States to date.[96] But it failed spectacularly. By summer, Democratic leaders told Clinton that its prospects were "extremely gloomy," with key Senate Democrats emphatically opposed.[97] The administration tried to salvage it with a scattershot of exemptions, but couldn't. Congress imposed a modest gasoline tax of 4.3 cents per gallon and moved on.[98]

The lesson of this experience could not have been lost on Browner: even with a Democratic Congress, the administration could not pass a broad-based energy tax. Browner would focus on strengthening the nation's pollution rules. That would be hard enough—key Democrats in Congress, and influential members of Clinton's own team, were concerned about the cost of regulations. But after the 1994 mid-term elections, when the Republicans seized control of Congress, EPA went fully on defense, trying to preserve the agency's budget and defending its rulemakings as necessary for public health and required by science and law.[99]

Still, EPA staff would play a prominent role in what would become the administration's default domestic climate policy: voluntary programs. On Earth Day in April 1993, Clinton pledged to reduce greenhouse gas emissions voluntarily to 1990 levels by 2000, consistent with the Rio Treaty's goal of stabilizing emissions. The BTU tax would have produced a significant share of the required emissions cuts, but once it failed, the administration combined over fifty voluntary initiatives into a "Climate Change Action Plan."[100] The programs targeted emissions from the electricity, building, and transportation sectors, and ran the gamut from specific agreements with particular companies to industry- and sector-wide programs. They were designed to demonstrate the emissions reductions potential and economic benefits of energy efficiency, and unlock promising technological innovation.[101] A disproportionate share of these programs already were underway at EPA, or were now being proposed by the agency, the groundwork having been laid by John Hoffman and his team.[102]

The Kyoto Protocol

From the mid-1990s on, senior EPA staff were also active in the White House-led inter-agency process to develop the US position in international climate negotiations, aimed at implementing the 1992 UN Framework Convention. EPA had a track record of working well with the State Department on the Montreal Protocol and brought substantive expertise to the Kyoto discussions that no other agency possessed. The US negotiating position for Kyoto was that any binding commitment to reduce emissions should rely on flexible market mechanisms, such as cap-and-trade, exactly the kind of approach that EPA already was successfully implementing for acid rain.[103] EPA staff provided valuable input into the design of the Kyoto agreement—modelling emissions reductions, technology penetration rates, and cost; helping to address concerns from Treasury and other agencies over economic impacts; and dueling with the Department of Energy modelers, who were less optimistic than EPA about what technology could accomplish.[104] They were among the most technically capable, thoughtful, and determined contributors to the inter-agency process.[105]

At the first Conference of the Parties meeting in Berlin in April 1995, Undersecretary of State for Global Affairs, former Senator Tim Wirth, agreed on behalf of the administration to the so-called "Berlin Mandate," which called for emissions targets for developed but not developing countries.[106] The US later announced, in follow-on negotiations, that it would support making those targets legally binding.[107] That decision prompted a strong reaction in Congress: in July 1997, five months before the Kyoto negotiations, the US Senate adopted a "sense of the Senate" resolution, 95-0, stipulating that the United States should not sign any agreement imposing mandatory emission reductions on the developed world without also requiring commitments from developing countries in the same time period, or do "serious harm" to the US economy.[108] Parties to the Convention, including the US, adopted the Kyoto Protocol in 1997. It committed the US to a seven percent reduction in emissions by 2012, and, as expected, failed to impose mandatory emission limits on developing countries. Recognizing that it could not succeed, the president would never submit it to the Senate for advice and consent to ratification.

EPA's Thinking Evolves

Meanwhile, EPA's thinking about its authority to address climate change was evolving. In 1994, when developing ideas for the Climate Action Plan, a handful of EPA staff had drafted a series of one-page proposals on ideas such as tightening fuel efficiency standards, adopting an energy tax, and capping utility greenhouse gas emissions, among other things.[109] Many of the ideas would require new legislation or depend on other agencies, but some suggested steps EPA might take with the existing Clean Air Act, such as regulating carbon dioxide as a hazardous air pollutant.[110] These proposals were exploratory, preliminary, and tentative—a thought experiment driven by the hunt for "more tons" to include in the president's climate plan. Each one-pager briefly identified political pros and cons and implementation obstacles, but nothing approaching detailed legal analysis. (On a scale of 1 to 10, the proposal to regulate carbon dioxide as a hazardous air pollutant received the lowest possible preference ranking at 10: "Such aggressive use of Clean Air Act Authority may create a backlash in Congress.")[111] The thought of embarking on a regulatory program at this stage was premature. Browner was occupied with other things, and the White House was developing its strategy for international climate negotiations. That process would or would not produce an agreement, which EPA would or would not have a role in implementing. The impetus for action would come from the international arena. No one was proposing that EPA regulate CO_2.

After the 1996 presidential election, Mary Nichols, the assistant administrator for the Office of Air and Radiation, persuaded Browner to consolidate the agency's climate work in the air office.[112] Nichols deputized David Doniger as her representative to the administration's inter-agency process on all things related to climate change.[113] During interagency meetings on the Department of Energy's plan to restructure the electricity sector in 1998, Doniger wrote a memo stating formally for the first time that EPA possessed the authority to regulate CO_2 under the Clean Air Act.[114] DOE had advocated deregulation to lower electricity costs, and EPA had argued for addressing the power sector's air pollution emissions, including CO_2, at the same time, in one package.[115] When DOE officials balked at including air pollution provisions in the bill—especially CO_2, which they viewed as beyond EPA's authority—Doniger set out to write a memo to persuade them, in which he explained that CO_2 was a pollutant subject to regulation under various provisions of the Clean Air Act *if* EPA made an endangerment finding that it posed a threat to public health or welfare.[116] The memo artfully acknowledged that existing authorities did not "easily lend themselves" to EPA regulating CO_2 using a cap-and-trade approach, and argued that the electricity restructuring legislation DOE was seeking should clarify EPA's authority to implement a cap-and-trade system.[117]

The memo leaked.[118] At a 1998 appropriations subcommittee hearing, Congressman Tom Delay (R-TX) surprised Carol Browner by brandishing a copy of the memo, and asking if she agreed that EPA possessed the authority to regulate CO_2.[119] (This was 1998 and Delay, along with many other members of Congress, was concerned that the Clinton administration would try to implement the Kyoto Protocol through executive action, even though it had not been submitted for ratification.) Browner had not seen the memo,[120] but answered without hesitation: "That is a general summary statement about authorities provided in the Clean Air Act which I would agree with. There are broad authorities granted to EPA to address certain pollutants, including those listed, and many others."[121] Delay asked for a formal legal opinion on the matter, and—with Jon Cannon, EPA's general counsel, sitting behind her—Browner replied, "certainly."[122]

Delay's request thus produced what came to be known as the Cannon Memo, the EPA general counsel's opinion published in 1998 which defends the legal position that greenhouse gases are pollutants under the Clean Air Act.[123] Cannon picked up on the theme from Doniger's earlier analysis that a market-based approach would be preferable: "[A] number of specific provisions of the [Clean Air Act] are potentially applicable to control [greenhouse gases] from electric power generation. However . . . these potentially applicable provisions do not easily lend themselves to establishing market-based national or regional cap-and-trade programs, which the Administration favors for addressing these kinds of pollution problems."[124] The memo adeptly walks the line between *claiming* legal authority, and *exercising* it—a step, EPA explicitly said, it was not prepared to take.

The Seeds of *Massachusetts v. EPA*

The Cannon Memo formally established the agency's legal position, which sent a message both internally and externally. It also inadvertently helped a group of petitioners who were seeking to force EPA to regulate GHGs.[125] In a bid that many in the environmental movement initially questioned as a less than ideal test case,[126] the little-known International Center for Technology Assessment (ICTA) petitioned EPA to determine whether emissions of greenhouse gases from new motor vehicles "cause or contribute to air pollution, which may reasonably be anticipated to endanger public health or welfare."[127] Under Section 202 of the Clean Air Act, an affirmative "endangerment finding" would require EPA to set mandatory emission standards for CO_2 from new cars and trucks.[128] The petition launched the litigation that would lead, eventually, to the Supreme Court's decision in *Massachusetts v. EPA*.[129] And it certainly helped that the agency had already claimed to have the authority to regulate CO_2 in a formal opinion by the general counsel.[130]

Arriving in the waning days of the Clinton administration, the ICTA petition presented a conundrum, however. Granting it risked provoking a backlash in the Republican-controlled Congress in the form of an appropriations rider, or worse, and denying it would require the administration to take a position on endangerment, which it was not prepared to do.[131] And the agency had deliberately preserved the option of regulating greenhouse gases. So, EPA chose to let the petition sit. The thinking was, in part, that if Vice President Gore won the 2000 presidential election, EPA would have plenty of time to decide whether and how to regulate greenhouse gases.[132] When George W. Bush was declared the winner, EPA changed course and put the petition out for public comment, a tactic designed to pressure the incoming administration to grant or deny it.[133] On the chessboard of climate strategy, this move would wind up being very shrewd.

THE 2000s: THE GEORGE W. BUSH ADMINISTRATION

The Kyoto Protocol had catalyzed industry opposition to climate policy, and by the end of the 1990s climate change had become increasingly partisan, even as the scientific consensus about its causes had grown stronger.[134] During the 2000 presidential election, Al Gore did not highlight the issue and often found himself on the defensive about his environmental record.[135] George W. Bush, the former oil man from Texas, while critical of the Kyoto Protocol, did say that he favored mandatory limits on carbon dioxide emissions and would support a "four-pollutant" bill to comprehensively address air pollution from the electricity sector.[136] It was a clever maneuver to try to outflank Gore on an environmental issue he should have owned.

After the election, Bush stoked hopes that he would support climate policy by appointing Christine Todd Whitman, a moderate New Jersey Republican with a strong record on conservation, to lead EPA. Based on what Bush had said on the campaign trail, Whitman took the job planning to work on new legislation to control carbon emissions from power plants, and use that step to re-engage the US in international climate negotiations. Although she had not expressly discussed carbon regulation with Bush, the four-pollutant bill had appeared in the transition books summarizing the president's campaign commitments, which were handed to incoming political appointees.[137] The White House also convened a cabinet-level committee under the aegis of the National Security Council to discuss climate policy. Chaired by Condoleezza Rice, the president's national security advisor, the group, which included Whitman, reportedly held over a dozen meetings in which they received briefings from scientists, and, among other things, reviewed modeling of the economic, energy, and environmental impacts of a four-pollutant bill.[138]

This White House committee would be eclipsed by another one, however. In his second week in office, President Bush created the National Energy Policy Development Group (NEPDG), otherwise known as the Energy Task Force, led by Vice President Dick Cheney. Its purpose was to devise a national energy plan to address perceived shortfalls in domestic supply and reduce what was seen as excessive US dependence on foreign oil.[139] Whitman was a member of this group too, and was amazed at its disdain for environmental regulation.[140] She believed that the electricity sector could deliver reliable and affordable energy while at the same time curbing pollution, including greenhouse gas pollution, which she saw as a serious problem.[141] And she thought Bush thought so too.[142] But many of the Republican party's core constituencies, which had fought against climate policy in the Clinton years, were disgruntled over the president's campaign commitments. They thought his support for carbon regulation had been a mistake in the first place, and now wanted it undone.[143]

Reversing Commitments to Act on Climate Change

The opponents of carbon regulation ultimately prevailed. The President renounced his campaign position almost immediately after Whitman returned from a G8 Ministerial meeting in Italy where she had given a well-received speech reiterating support for climate regulation.[144] Whitman was not freelancing: she had cleared her remarks in advance with the White House. But the speech had stirred opposition among those who thought she had gone too far, and it provided an opportunity to reconsider Bush's position. Shortly after her return,[145] Senators Chuck Hagel, Jesse Helms, Pat Roberts, and Larry Craig delivered a letter to the White House, citing Whitman's various remarks on carbon regulation, and asking the president for a "clear understanding" of administration policy.

It has been widely reported that the letter from the Senators was solicited, if not largely drafted, by the vice president's office in a setup to allow the president to reverse himself.[146] Without consulting Whitman, the president signed a letter in response announcing that he was abandoning his pledge to regulate CO_2 from power plants and formally rejecting the Kyoto protocol.[147] The letter cited the California "energy crisis," uncertainty over climate science, and potential harm to the US economy. It also declared that carbon dioxide is not a pollutant,[148] a decision clearly aimed at preempting EPA from regulating greenhouse gases under the Clean Air Act. The president's abrupt policy reversal blindsided and embarrassed Whitman after her debut in Trieste and led Secretary of State Colin Powell to dub her the administration's "wind dummy" on climate policy. "It's a military term for when you are over the landing zone and you don't know what the winds are," Whitman explained. "You push the dummy out the door and see what happens to it."[149]

The Cheney Energy Task Force report came out in May, a couple of months after Bush reversed himself on carbon regulation. The report included many proposals to support nuclear power, invoked the need for energy conservation and energy efficiency, and advocated tax incentives to promote investment in renewable energy, but it also underscored that renewable energy sources were a fraction of supply, and could not come close to meeting the nation's energy needs. Its main thrust was to advocate for more domestic fossil energy exploration and production, which would require new energy infrastructure and relaxed regulation to eliminate what the report deemed market and regulatory barriers to greater supply.[150] The unmistakable message from the cumulative actions of the first few months of the Bush administration was that fossil energy production would be preeminent, and there would be no regulation of greenhouse gas emissions. The Rice task force on climate had been run over by the Cheney Energy Task Force. Whitman, and EPA, retreated to focus on other things.

Bush was increasingly disdainful of climate change. He openly dismissed scientific reports[151] and allowed White House officials to rewrite agency documents to downplay the risks and emphasize the uncertainties of climate change.[152] Whitman and her staff at EPA did their best to defend against this kind of meddling. She once opted to delete an entire section on global warming from an EPA report rather than accept major revisions that would have misstated the science.[153] Whitman remained at EPA for two-and-a-half years, overseeing the agency's response to the events of September 11, 2001, supporting and building on EPA's voluntary GHG reduction programs, and pushing back against administration efforts to weaken pollution rules for power plants.[154] Her credibility and stature within the administration had been badly diminished, however, by the events surrounding the president's about-face on climate policy. She left in mid-2003 to spend more time with her family.[155]

Renouncing Legal Authority over CO_2 and *Massachusetts v. EPA*

Soon after Whitman's departure, the new acting EPA administrator renounced the Cannon memo from the Clinton era, officially rejecting the view that greenhouse gases are "pollutants" under the Clean Air Act and aligning EPA with Bush's stated position.[156] In addition, after letting it languish for nearly three years, EPA finally denied the ICTA petition to make an endangerment determination for greenhouse gases from new vehicles.[157]

In retrospect, denying the petition was a tactical mistake. It converted agency "inaction"— typically difficult to challenge in court, even in cases of lengthy delays—into agency "action," which courts routinely review.[158]

EPA easily could have reversed the Cannon memo by eschewing legal authority and left it at that. But Jeff Holmstead, the assistant administrator for the Office of Air and Radiation, argued that the agency ought to "make its position clear that EPA did not have this authority."[159] The denial spurred a wide variety of plaintiffs, including several states, cities, and environmental and public health organizations, to join the original petitioners in the case that would become *Massachusetts v. EPA*.[160]

The history of this litigation has been comprehensively and compellingly recounted by others, and there is no space to do it justice here.[161] But it was a somewhat risky case to bring to the Supreme Court for a variety of reasons, including the high bar plaintiffs must satisfy to show they have "standing" to sue.[162] In addition, long-established principles of deference to agency discretion seemed to support EPA's preference *not* to make a threshold judgment of endangerment.[163] Another problem: the Supreme Court had ruled a few years earlier that an agency could not assert new, expansive regulatory authority over matters of high political and economic salience without express congressional authorization.[164]

For these and other reasons, the result in *Massachusetts v. EPA* was far from a foregone conclusion, and its importance is hard to overstate. By a narrow 5-4 margin, the Supreme Court granted standing to a state petitioner complaining that a federal agency's failure to act on climate change was unlawful; confirmed that greenhouse gases are pollutants under the Clean Air Act; and rejected all of the Bush administration's reasons for refusing to decide on endangerment.[165] Justice John Paul Stevens' opinion for the Court also helped to legitimize the scientific consensus on climate change at a time when the Bush administration had undermined it. Symbolically, the Court's decision was the biggest win for the environmental movement, ever. And practically, it would put pressure on the Bush administration to act on greenhouse gases.

Responding to the Court

While *Massachusetts v. EPA* was pending, agency lawyers were "working on a Plan B" in case they lost, including the possibility of adding carbon dioxide to the administration's pending proposal to regulate mercury using a cap-and-trade approach. But that possibility evaporated when the DC Circuit Court of Appeals struck down the administration's mercury plan.[166]

The White House was split over how to respond. Jim Connaughton, the CEQ chair, argued for turning lemons into lemonade by issuing the endangerment finding and taking credit for moving forward on climate change. After debating the matter, the White House authorized only the most preliminary step: Stephen Johnson, then EPA administrator, was instructed to prepare an Advanced Notice of Proposed Rulemaking (ANPRM) on the endangerment finding, soliciting comments on how to respond to the Supreme Court decision in *Massachusetts v. EPA*.[167]

Alas, Johnson would become the second EPA wind dummy of the Bush administration. After months of painstaking work by EPA staff on the massive rulemaking package—which included a thorough assessment of the science and a judgment that EPA unequivocally supported a finding that greenhouse gases endanger human health and welfare—the White House abruptly pulled the plug. When Johnson sent the draft document over for regulatory review, the Office of Information and Regulatory Affairs, which conducts the White House's regulatory review process, initially refused to open it, then accepted it only to turn around and ask EPA to withdraw it. Susan Dudley, the OIRA director, returned the package to EPA with a letter waiving the normal review process, declaring that "the staff draft cannot be considered administration policy or representative of the views of the administration."[168] Jason Burnett, the young associate deputy administrator who had overseen the ANPRM, resigned in protest.[169]

Johnson had the legal power to issue the ANPRM as written, but he bent to the White House and reworked the draft. The revised version no longer said that lingering doubts about climate change were irrelevant in the face of the overwhelming evidence, and no longer proposed to make the endangerment finding. The package now began, awkwardly, with the EPA administrator disavowing his own agency's work,[170] followed by several letters from the director of OMB, the chairs of the National Economic Council and the Council on Environmental Quality, and the heads of the Departments of Agriculture, Commerce, Energy, and Transportation saying that regardless of the science and despite the Supreme Court's decision in *Massachusetts v. EPA*, the Clean Air Act was "a deeply flawed and unsuitable vehicle for reducing greenhouse gases."[171] The press declared this turn of events "the low-water mark of a tumultuous era that has left the EPA badly wounded, largely demoralized and, in many ways, emasculated."[172] Johnson, the only career scientist ever to lead EPA, reportedly was "upset and disgusted" to have been put in this position.[173]

Bush's remark in his 2006 State of the Union speech that America must "break its addiction" to oil,[174] could have been a transformational moment for American climate policy. But it was not to be. While he signed a bill to improve energy efficiency and raise CAFE standards,[175] his administration disparaged climate science and firmly rejected greenhouse gas regulation. His time in office was bookended by two consequential decisions to block EPA: early on, by withdrawing his support regulating electricity sector emissions of carbon dioxide, and at the end of his tenure by repudiating the endangerment finding for greenhouse gases, which would have unleashed the regulatory power of the existing Clean Air Act.

THE OBAMA ADMINISTRATION: EPA UNLEASHED

Hope and Change

By the time Barack Obama clinched the Democratic nomination for president in 2008, a handful of leading states had become the driving force of US climate policy. In 2002, California directed its Air Resources Board to set greenhouse gas emission standards for new cars and trucks—the nation's first.[176] Seven states signed a memorandum of understanding in 2005 to reduce CO_2 emissions in the northeast and mid-Atlantic region, an agreement that would evolve into the Regional Greenhouse Gas Initiative. In 2006, California set an ambitious target to reduce greenhouse gas emissions by eighty percent by 2050.[177] Other states experimented with a variety of renewable energy, energy efficiency, and emissions reduction policies.[178] Climate change by this time had also entered the courts. States, cities, and other plaintiffs were suing the major power plants, oil companies, and auto manufacturers for their contributions to the harms caused by global warming.[179]

During the campaign, Obama pledged to put the federal government back in the game: his EPA would reconsider the endangerment finding for greenhouse gases and revisit California's request for a federal waiver to set its own CO_2 standards for cars and trucks,[180] which Bush's EPA had denied.[181] Obama spoke of climate change with a sense of urgency and obligation to future generations.[182] In addition to Lisa Jackson as EPA administrator, Obama named Carol Browner, Clinton's former EPA chief, to lead a new White House Office of Energy and Climate Change.[183] It seemed that, along with health care and a stimulus plan to boost the battered economy, climate change would be a top legislative priority.

In the end, climate legislation never materialized, even though the Democrats controlled both chambers. While the House of Representatives narrowly passed the American Clean Energy and Security Act in June 2009,[184] the bill stalled in the Senate and was dead by spring of 2010. There was plenty of blame to go around, and the White House got the lion's share: the president spent too much political capital on health care, and that bill had taken too long;[185] the White House failed to send a draft climate bill, or even draft principles, to the Hill;[186] the administration inexplicably gave away a number of concessions, like opening up offshore drilling and providing loan guarantees for nuclear power, without linking them to a legislative deal;[187] Carol Browner "lacked influence" and was outmaneuvered by aides more concerned about the bill's cost and less sure of its political payoffs;[188] and so on. Others blamed Democratic leaders in the Senate for fumbling the process by never settling on a single bill. Perhaps it was never realistic to expect Congress to raise energy prices in the wake of the financial crisis, or to ask

Democrats to take another hard vote after the health care bill. The end result, however, was no legislation.

Leveraging the Clean Air Act

Even before Waxman-Markey failed, the administration was working on another track, using executive power to make progress on climate change. This strategy would put EPA at the center of climate policy, since it possessed the most potent regulatory tool: the Clean Air Act. In the first months of 2009, the White House Office of Energy and Climate quietly led a process to set the first federal greenhouse gas standards for new cars and trucks, essentially delivering on the promise of *Massachusetts v. EPA*. The deal was designed to harmonize EPA's new standards (aimed at GHG pollution from vehicles) with fuel efficiency standards set by the National Highway Traffic Safety Administration (NHTSA) (aimed at vehicle fuel economy), *and* bring California into the fold by persuading the state that an ambitious and uniform national regime could accomplish more than California could on its own.[189] In exchange for the simplicity and predictability of a single national standard, and a phased-in approach to compliance, the auto industry agreed not to challenge the new rules, which improved fuel efficiency about five percent per year to 2016.[190] The administration later used the same approach to negotiate a second round of standards, extending the deal to 2025.[191] All told, the standards were projected to double fuel efficiency by 2025 to an estimated 54.5 miles per gallon, save the country billions of barrels of imported oil, and spare consumers trillions of dollars at the pump. In the process, EPA had repaired the damage to the ANPRM on endangerment wrought by the Bush administration, which was important to rank-and-file staff. After an intense effort by the agency to rebuild the record, Lisa Jackson signed a powerful statement that the endangerment finding for greenhouse gases was warranted on the basis of the overwhelming scientific consensus.[192]

EPA's role in the car deal was extremely impressive. Agency career staff in the Office of Transportation and Air Quality, including experts from the agency's state-of-the-art "car lab" in Michigan,[193] worked ferociously under huge pressure to model the impacts of the new standards; reconcile their numbers with NHTSA's; present their projections of technology penetration, cost, and other impacts to various White House officials; and respond to countless demands for more data.[194] It was a potent demonstration of the expertise housed within the agency and the eagerness of the career staff to act on climate change.

Within the first year, the administration had shown that it could successfully use the Clean Air Act to regulate greenhouse gas emissions from the transportation sector—the fastest growing share of emissions in the US economy. This achievement did two things: signal to Congress that EPA would act if the climate bill failed; and signal to the international community, in advance of the 2009 United Nations Climate Change Conference in Copenhagen, that the US would regulate domestically.[195]

Next Step: the Clean Power Plan

By late 2010, however, the White House's appetite for bold regulatory action on greenhouse gases seemed to wane. The midterm elections had flipped control of the House of Representatives to Republicans, who also gained seats in the Senate, in an electoral result the president himself deemed a "shellacking."[196] Even before the midterms, climate and energy politics were becoming more, not less, fraught. The Deepwater Horizon rig had exploded in the Gulf of Mexico, causing the worst environmental disaster in US history,[197] prompting the president to impose a highly unpopular moratorium on offshore drilling. After the mid-terms, the constituencies needed to support comprehensive clean energy and climate legislation were pulling farther apart. The White House was turning its attention to re-election, and would rather EPA not push aggressive pollution rules, especially greenhouse gas rules.[198]

In the spring of 2012, however, EPA finally planned to propose New Source Performance Standards for greenhouse gas emissions from power plants, fulfilling a commitment the agency had made in a settlement agreement.[199] Within a few months, however, the agency recognized that developing standards for *existing* power plants raised a number of hard issues which would require considerable agency time and invite fierce controversy. To succeed, EPA would need to convene a stakeholder process and do extensive outreach, which realistically could not happen before the 2016 election. And a proposal of this importance would require express White House backing. So, EPA officials issued the proposal for new power plants only, and "hibernated" until after the election.[200]

Following his re-election, President Obama re-engaged on climate change. He told Gina McCarthy that climate was the reason he wanted her to lead the agency,[201] and appointed Denis McDonough, a known climate hawk, as chief of staff.[202] Obama viewed climate change as part of his legacy, and his 2013 State of the Union speech made clear that if Congress would not act, he would use executive power.[203] By June, the White House had announced a comprehensive Climate Action Plan as a roadmap for the second term.[204] In another signal of the president's commitment to the issue, the White House climate and energy brief would belong to former Clinton chief of staff John Podesta, a deeply experienced political operator with unquestioned stature, who would become counselor to the president. Upon his departure in 2015, to lead Hillary Clinton's presidential campaign, the role went to Brian Deese, a young

White House star, who had already proved himself to be highly influential and effective in earlier White House posts. Together, Podesta, McDonough, and then Deese, would provide crucial support for EPA.[205]

EPA's most important climate initiative of the second term was the rulemaking to limit carbon dioxide from the nation's power plants, known as the "Clean Power Plan," which the president now directed the agency to finalize by 2015.[206] As EPA had anticipated before the election, this would be a hugely controversial rulemaking, consuming countless hours of painstaking work by senior career staff and political appointees, including the EPA administrator herself.[207]

Section 111 of the Clean Air Act defines performance standards as the level of emission control achievable by applying the "best system of emission reduction" that the administrator determines has been "adequately demonstrated."[208] EPA first proposed the standard for *new* power plants under Clean Air Act section 111(b), based on the successful operation of carbon capture and sequestration technology at sites in the US and Canada.[209] That first rule was most significant, however, because it would trigger regulation of *existing* power plants[210]—the far more important regulatory target, since the oldest and dirtiest power plants produce the largest share of electricity sector GHG emissions.[211]

In the Clean Power Plan, EPA adopted a broad interpretation of "best system," which conceived of power plants as interconnected, as if they were a single giant machine.[212] The agency asked: What CO_2 reductions would be achievable if electric utilities took advantage of the same broad set of opportunities they already use, on the regionally interconnected electricity grids, to meet pollution limits for sulfur dioxide and nitrogen oxides? Following this approach, EPA set separate emission limits for coal- and gas-fired plants, calculated by applying three factors: (1) the potential emission reductions achievable by improving the efficiency of the units themselves; (2) additional emission reductions achievable by substituting natural-gas fired electricity for coal-fired electricity; and (3) reductions achievable by displacing both coal- and gas-fired units with more renewable energy.

The agency's approach to "best system" was controversial. Broadening emission reduction opportunities beyond the so-called fenceline of the power plant, to include the possibility of fuel substitution through grid management strategies, inevitably would produce stricter standards than taking a narrower view that looks only at efficiency improvements made locally at the source. But EPA reasoned that its approach reflected how the grid already worked in practice.[213] In any event, ambition was the point: EPA wanted to build on the shift from coal- to natural gas-fired power already underway in the electricity sector due to the fracking revolution and the trend toward renewable energy spurred by state renewable portfolio standards, and other policies. A federal rule would send a strong market signal, cement that shift, and drive emissions reductions deeper over time.[214]

Finalizing the Clean Power Plan was a massive undertaking. EPA staff conducted innumerable meetings with stakeholders in an unprecedented outreach effort, and received hundreds of thousands of comments on its proposal. Administrator McCarthy pushed her staff hard to complete the rulemaking on the schedule the president had laid out, ahead of the international climate meeting in Paris, knowing the US would rely on it for negotiating leverage to achieve an international agreement.[215] The agency had adopted a legal interpretation of "best system" that it thought reasonable and appropriate, but knew that it would be sued.

The Paris Agreement

At the Paris climate talks in 2015, nearly two hundred nations pledged to mitigate their greenhouse gas emissions.[216] Along with the vehicle emission standards set in the first term, the Obama administration relied on projected reductions from the Clean Power Plan to set US targets. These two policies were key pillars of the US commitment to reduce greenhouse gas emissions between twenty-six and twenty-eight percent by 2025, compared to 2005 levels.[217]

The Paris Agreement was a signature achievement of the Obama administration. The accord had overcome the structural limitations of the Kyoto Protocol by committing all of the world's major economies, for the first time, to take steps to reduce their greenhouse gas emissions, lower the carbon intensity of their economies, and shift to cleaner energy.[218] The agreement was voluntary—each state would decide what it could achieve domestically, as the basis for its pledge. This "pledge and review" design was meant to ensure that, unlike the Kyoto Protocol, the agreement would accommodate distinctions in national circumstances, and thus be more durable and effective over time.

The agreement was also a victory for EPA. The agency had given the State Department the leverage it needed to negotiate with China and India by demonstrating that the US was prepared to translate its pledge into domestic action. Throughout the 1980s and 1990s, most observers, including many career staff and political appointees at EPA, believed that an international agreement would drive domestic regulation—meaning that a climate agreement, once ratified, would lead Congress to pass implementing legislation, which would lead to domestic regulation. But that order had reversed itself. In the years after Kyoto, through Copenhagen, and leading to the Paris Agreement, the question became, what could be done *domestically* to provide the basis for an international pledge? This switch, from a top-down to a bottom-up process, made EPA crucial. Now that the agency could harness the power of the Clean

Air Act, it had the regulatory power to deliver significant emissions reductions as the basis for the US pledge.

When Obama left office, he had done more on climate change than any of his predecessors, and the success was largely due to the career staff and political appointees at EPA. The president's Climate Action Plan had included many measures led by other agencies—but its two signature domestic policies, the vehicle greenhouse gas and efficiency standards, and the Clean Power Plan, relied on EPA.[219] The administration had taken a sector-by-sector approach, rather than the economy-wide plan envisioned by the Waxman-Markey bill, and brought nearly two-thirds of the nation's emissions under a regulatory framework. EPA had adopted, in addition, rules to control methane leaks from oil and gas facilities and to replace, at least incrementally, hydrofluorocarbons.[220] It had adopted other air pollution rules, like the Mercury and Air Toxics Standards, and the Cross-State Pollution Rule, which would have collateral climate benefits.[221] Without question, at the end of Obama's tenure, EPA was firmly ensconced as the lead federal agency for US climate policy.

All of this would change drastically after the 2016 presidential election.

DONALD J. TRUMP

Soon after taking office, President Trump began dismantling the Obama climate legacy. He revoked the Climate Action Plan[222] and announced that the US would withdraw from the Paris Agreement.[223] Under Administrator Scott Pruitt, and later Andrew Wheeler, the Trump EPA took steps to revoke, replace, and weaken every greenhouse gas rule adopted in the Obama years. The agency has rescinded the Clean Power Plan,[224] substituting a far more modest proposal requiring on-site efficiency upgrades only (achieving, by their own estimates, at best a 1.5% emission reduction),[225] and delegating discretion to the states over whether and to what extent to limit power plant carbon dioxide emissions;[226] proposed a policy allowing coal plants to update their equipment and increase their run-time without installing modern pollution controls;[227] rescinded the rules to control methane emissions from oil and gas operations on public and private land;[228] weakened the greenhouse gas and fuel efficiency standards for light duty vehicles, requiring only 1.5% annual fuel economy improvement, down from 5% in the rescinded rule (and, by their own estimates, increasing costs for consumers and premature deaths);[229] revoked California's waiver allowing the state to set its own vehicle greenhouse gas standards and warned state leaders that its standards are unlawful because they are preempted by the Energy Policy Conservation Act;[230] and launched a preliminary antitrust investigation into four auto companies that had voluntarily agreed to ignore the federal rollback and meet California's vehicle standards.[231] The Department of Justice under President Trump also filed a lawsuit seeking to block California's agreement with Quebec to jointly implement an emissions trading regime to reduce greenhouse gases.[232] The administration also has sought to weaken EPA's capacity to regulate by excluding many academic scientists from scientific advisory panels, shifting expert personnel to different posts, restricting access to public records, and imposing hurdles to accountability.[233] These initiatives, and more, are underway at the time of writing;[234] all of them either have been already, or will be, challenged in court by coalitions of plaintiffs including states, cities, and environmental and public health groups, among others.

In its first three years, the Trump administration did not fare well defending its environmental rollbacks in court. EPA lost virtually every case challenging its decisions to suspend or delay regulations, mostly for skirting required legal procedures. But the agency also lost cases on the merits for arbitrary decision making.[235] Still, the most important policy reversals, in which the government has rescinded major climate rules, in some cases advancing untested legal interpretations, have yet to be decided. To the extent that much of this litigation is still pending in January 2021, President Biden will almost certainly reverse course and re-institute a more ambitious regulatory agenda, with the most significant constraint being a more conservative Supreme Court. Biden could also immediately, and unilaterally, set events in motion to rejoin the Paris Agreement.

CONCLUSION

EPA's evolution on climate change can be divided into roughly four stages: conducting research and analysis in the 1970s and 1980s into what was then viewed as a long-term problem; developing, in the 1990s and 2000s, a suite of voluntary initiatives to reduce greenhouse gases; turning to regulation from 2009 to 2016 and setting ambitious greenhouse standards; and sharp regulatory reversals since then.

To a person, the EPA administrators from the 1970s, 80s, and 90s whom I interviewed for this chapter—without in any way diminishing the importance of climate change—said that they had other pressing issues to manage when taking over the agency, and that existing statutory mandates, court deadlines, budget imperatives, and other near-term crises dominated their tenures.[237] Climate change seemed abstract and theoretical compared to many other concrete and compelling environmental problems, such as chemical soups seeping into people's basements, pesticides poisoning the food supply, deadly local air pollution, and highly polluted rivers catching on fire. Stratospheric ozone depletion and acid deposition had more immediate and visible consequences, and commanded more urgent attention.

These administrators might be faulted for not doing more, but they were constrained by the political contexts of their time. It is a lesson: executive branch agencies in the United States constitutional system are creatures of statute, answerable to their congressional overseers, their chief executive, and the courts. They cannot afford to stick their necks out too far, for fear of losing their heads. But when they are given the remit by a president who is also willing to stake his own political capital on the issue, they are able to wield a formidable array of tools to create significant policies.

Many EPA administrators who led the agency in these decades, both Republican and Democrat, deserve credit for the things they *did* do, which directly or indirectly helped to lay the foundation for EPA to take a leadership role on climate. Lee Thomas courageously advocated within President Reagan's cabinet for the Montreal Protocol, which set a precedent for international environmental cooperation, and in doing so helped to cultivate expertise in the agency that would later prove critical on climate policy. While climate change is a very different and much harder problem to solve, the experience on ozone depletion was instructive, and built crucial relationships with the State Department that would bear fruit in later international negotiations. Bill Reilly, a natural globalist and big thinker, pressed hard for a stronger US commitment to the Rio Convention, despite concerted efforts by senior White House aides to torpedo his efforts. That agreement launched the international process that would ultimately lead, after twists and turns, to the 2015 Paris Agreement.

In the Clinton administration, a fast-thinking Carol Browner put on the spot in a hostile congressional hearing answered yes to the surprise question whether EPA had authority over carbon dioxide—even before she had a legal opinion to that effect. Although Browner herself had prioritized regulating conventional pollutants during her tenure, her instinctive reaction to Delay's provocation was a crucial first step toward EPA ultimately issuing the first federal rules to regulate greenhouse gases, though no one, including Browner, at the time imagined how that process might unfold.

Christine Todd Whitman advocated for a "four pollutant bill" to regulate CO_2 from the power sector, and fought to restore US leadership in international climate negotiations, but was blocked by the White House. Lisa Jackson repaired the all-important "endangerment finding" and presided over the first federal greenhouse gas rules in the United States. Her successor, Gina McCarthy, built on that beginning, with the support of the White House, to fully leverage the power of the Clean Air Act.

Throughout this history there has been one constant: the dogged, professional work by many EPA career staff and political appointees who have cared deeply about climate change. They have worked from administration to administration, under considerable political constraints, and mindful of the limits of their legal authority, to maintain momentum and propel policy forward.

There have been many moments of serendipity, too. Had John Hoffman and his merry band of staffers not been so interested in the greenhouse effect in the 1980s, perhaps the first EPA research projects would never have been launched; and had the Office of Policy, Planning, and Evaluation never been created to house such work, or had it been run by less supportive leaders, perhaps those early studies would have been sidelined. Many other moments of chance changed the course of events. Had Texas Representative Tom Delay not gotten hold of a leaked memo claiming EPA could regulate carbon dioxide, he might never have confronted the EPA administrator, setting off the chain of events that forced EPA to carefully consider and formally declare its legal authority for the first time. Had the Bush EPA opted to let the ICTA petition lie unanswered, there would not have been agency "action" to challenge in court—at least not yet. And in perhaps the greatest stroke of luck of all, had a single Supreme Court Justice, John Paul Stevens, not deftly nudged Justice Anthony Kennedy's fifth vote into his column in the Court's seminal decision granting the state of Massachusetts standing, and holding that greenhouse gases are air pollutants under the Clean Air Act, EPA would have lacked the power to regulate greenhouse gases at all, absent new congressional authority.

Congress may eventually adopt a carbon tax, an economy-wide cap-and-trade program, a collection of sectoral approaches, or other climate policies, in which EPA may or may not have a role. EPA became such an important player in climate change because Congress was not ready to confront the issue. That is a key lesson from this fifty-year review: that in the absence of congressional action, policy will be made by the executive branch, together with the courts. Yet the flexibility EPA has to manage greenhouse gases may be shrinking because the Court's composition has changed. The majority of Justices on the Court now appear to adhere to a brand of textualism that requires agencies to root every exertion of regulatory authority in clear and explicit statutory text. The Court has increasingly portrayed agencies as dangerous behemoths, with vast regulatory powers, which must be checked to a greater extent by the courts. It will be harder, going forward, for a president wanting to act on climate change to use executive power in bold ways, by interpreting existing statutes like the Clean Air Act expansively. In the absence of congressional action, the Supreme Court will have the last say on federal climate policy. As a result, perhaps the strongest blow President Trump will have dealt to climate policy, is his appointment of three conservative Justices who are skeptical of the administrative state.[238]

NOTES

1. I am grateful to the following people for consenting to interviews and being so generous with their time: Roger Ballentine, Jim Barnes, Sue Biniaz, Carol Browner, Rob Brenner, William Clark, James Connaughton, Eileen Claussen, David Doniger, Bill Drayton, Linda Fisher, Dirk Forrister, Jessica Furey, Gary Guzy, David Gardiner, Thomas Gibson, Joe Goffman, Lisa Heinzerling, Tom Jorling, Jeff Holmstead, Lisa Jackson, Dan Lashof, Michael Leavitt, Andrew Lundquist, Janet McCabe, Gina McCarthy, Katie McGinty, Dick Morgenstern, Mary Nichols, Michael Oppenheimer, Bob Perciasepe, Rafe Pomerance, Bill Reilly, Bill Ruckelshaus, Stephen Seidel, Gus Speth, Bob Sussman, Sue Tierney, Lee Thomas, Dennis Tirpak, Karen Wayland, Cathy Zoi, and other former senior officials, who wished to remain anonymous. To the extent that this account relies on the recollections of people directly involved in events, it should be acknowledged that memories can be flawed, and perspectives can be partial. My hope is that the account here resonates sufficiently with those most closely involved in these events that they regard it as, on balance, a fair telling. I have confirmed with interviewees all quotes and attributions made to them personally. Any factual mistakes are mine alone. This chapter is more lightly footnoted than a typical law review article. A longer version, with detailed supporting material, is forthcoming in Jody Freeman, "The EPA and Climate Change," *Duke Law and Policy Forum*, Fall 2020.

2. Stephen Seidel and Dale Keyes, *Can We Delay A Greenhouse Warming?: The Effectiveness and Feasibility of Options to Slow a Build-up of Carbon Dioxide in the Atmosphere* (Washington, DC: EPA OPPE, 1983).

3. Philip Shabecoff, "Haste on Global Warming Trend Opposed," *New York Times,* October 21, 1983, https://perma.cc/K6B7-KK6E.

4. For an in-depth account of what each presidential administration has known about climate change, see James Gustave ("Gus") Speth, Corrected Expert Report, Juliana v. United States, 217 F.Supp.3d 1224 (D. Or. 2016) (No. 6:15-cv-01517-TC), hereafter Speth Report.

5. Lyndon B. Johnson, "Special Message to the Congress on Conservation and Restoration of Natural Beauty, February 8, 1965," In *Public Papers of the Presidents of the United States: Lyndon B. Johnson, 1965*, vol. I (Washington, DC: Government Printing Office, 1966), 155–65. See also President's Science Advisory Committee, *Restoring the Quality of Our Environment: Report of the Environmental Pollution Panel* (Washington, DC: Government Printing Office, November 1965), including an analysis from Roger Revelle, director of the Scripps Institution of Oceanography, on the status of atmospheric concentrations of carbon dioxide.

6. See US Committee for the Global Atmospheric Research Program, *Understanding Climatic Change: A Program for Action* (Washington, DC: National Academy of Sciences, 1975). See also National Research Council, *Carbon Dioxide and Climate: A Scientific Assessment Report* (Washington, DC: National Academies Press, 1979).

7. See US Congress, House, The National Climate Program Act: Hearings before the Subcommittee on the Environment and the Atmosphere, Committee on Science and Technology, 94th Cong. (1976), 1.

8. National Climate Program Act of 1978, Pub. L. 95–367, 92 Stat. 601 (1978) (as amended at 15 U.S.C. §§2901–2908 (2012)).

9. See Speth Report, 6. In 1979, the World Meteorological Organization and the International Council of Scientific Unions had combined forces to create the Global Atmospheric Research Program.

10. Clean Air Act Amendments of 1970, Pub. L. No. 91–604, 84 Stat. 1676 (1970); Federal Water Pollution Control Act Amendments of 1972, Pub. L. No. 92-500, 82 Stat. 844 (1972). Ruckelshaus focused on highly visible pollution problems like pesticides and auto emissions, he said, to show that the agency would enforce the new statutes. See William D. Ruckelshaus, former EPA administrator, interview with Jody Freeman, May 2, 2019, hereafter Ruckelshaus Interview. See also Dennis C. Williams, *The Guardian: EPA's Formative Years, 1970-1973*, EPA 202-K-93-002 (Washington, DC: EPA, 1993).

11. US Environmental Protection Agency, "Russell E. Train: Oral History Interview," EPA 202-K-93-001, *epa.gov,* July 1993, https://perma.cc/8VLJ-XCJ2 (excerpting interview of Russell E. Train by Michael Gorn, May 5, 1992).

12. US Environmental Protection Agency, "Douglas M. Costle: Oral History Interview," EPA 202-K-01-002, *epa.gov,* January 2001, https://perma.cc/C96R-6URG (excerpting interview of Douglas M. Costle by Dennis Williams, August 4–5, 1996, mentioning climate change only once to note scientific uncertainty).

13. See Jimmy Carter, "Energy and the National Goals: A Crisis of Confidence," (televised speech, July 15, 1979), *American Rhetoric,* https://www.americanrhetoric.com/speeches/jimmycartercrisisofconfidence.htm.

14. William Drayton, former assistant administrator for Planning and Management, interview with Jody Freeman, May 9, 2019.

15. See Frank Press, "Release of Fossil CO2 and the Possibility of a Catastrophic Climate Change," memo to the president, July 7, 1977. See also generally, Speth Report, 7–12, explaining that President Carter appreciated climate change, referred to it in speeches, and proposed a broad energy plan that included alternatives to fossil energy. Speth was prevailed upon by Rafe Pomerance and Gordon McDonald to advance the climate issue within the administration. The pair also briefed Frank Press, prompting him to request a National Academies study on the latest science. Gus Speth, former chair of the Council on Environmental Quality, interview with Jody Freeman, March 19, 2019; Rafe Pomerance, former deputy assistant secretary of state for Environment and Development, interview with Jody Freeman, March 12, 2019, hereafter Pomerance Interview. The 1979 NAS panel, chaired by MIT professor Jule Charney, concluded that, "the equilibrium surface global warming due to doubled CO_2 will be in the range 1.5° to 4.5° C with the most probable value near 3° C." NRC, *Carbon Dioxide and Climate*.

16. Gus Speth, email communication with Jody Freeman, November 9, 2019 (on file with author).

17. Dennis Tirpak, former director of EPA Global Climate Change Policy Division, interview with Jody Freeman, March 12, 2019, hereafter Tirpak Interview.

18. David Doniger, "Remembering John Hoffman, Ozone Defender and Climate Protector," *NRDC Expert Blog*, October 1, 2012, https://perma.cc/3NHB-ZH88. See

also William Drayton, "Getting Smarter About Regulation," *Harvard Business Review* 59, no. 4 (1981): https://perma.cc/BUN7-WPGH.

19. Stephen Seidel, former director of EPA's Stratospheric Protection Division, interview with Jody Freeman, April 3, 2019, hereafter Seidel Interview.

20. Joanna Brenner, "Neil Gorsuch's Late Mother Almost Annihilated the EPA. Is History Repeating Itself?" *Newsweek,* February 1, 2017, https://perma.cc/CJ22-ZY97 (quoting former EPA Assistant Administrator Bill Drayton). See also Philip Shabecoff, "US Environmental Agency Making Deep Staffing Cuts," *New York Times*, January 3, 1982, https://perma.cc/7KMU-TQGL.

21. Seidel Interview.

22. See Seidel and Keyes, *Can We Delay.*

23. Seidel Interview.

24. National Research Council, *Changing Climate: Report of the Carbon Dioxide Assessment Committee* (Washington, DC: National Academies Press, 1983), xiii. See Naomi Oreskes and Erik M. Conway, *Merchants of Doubt: How a Handful of Scientists Obscured the Truth on Issues from Tobacco Smoke to Global Warming* (New York: Bloomsbury Publishing, 2011), chapter 6 (recounting the relevant history). See also Michael Oppenheimer, "To Delay Global Warming," *New York Times*, Opinion, November 9, 1983, https://perma.cc/UMN4-QMJB (comparing the two assessments).

25. Philip Shabecoff, "Haste on Global Warming." Joe Cannon, the assistant administrator of OPPE overseeing Hoffman's group, was believed to have leaked the report.

26. John S. Hoffman, Dale Keyes, and James G. Titus, *Projecting Future Sea Level Rise: Methodology, Estimates to the Year 2100, and Research Needs*, EPA 230-09-007 (Washington, DC: EPA OPPE, 1983).

27. See, e.g., US Congress, Senate, Ozone Depletion, the Greenhouse Effect, and Climate Change: Hearings Before the Subcommittee on Environmental Pollution, Committee on Environment and Public Works, 99th Cong. (1986), 1, 43, 98, 106, 143, 147 (discussing the 1983 reports).

28. See Steven R. Weisman, "President Names Ruckelshaus Head of Troubled EPA," *New York Times*, March 22, 1983, https://perma.cc/7BRR-48BC.

29. See Steven R. Weisman, "President Names Ruckelshaus Head of Troubled EPA," *New York Times*, March 22, 1983, https://perma.cc/7BRR-48BC. Ruckelshaus recalled that during his second time leading the agency, acid rain was a much more salient topic of discussion than climate change, which was somewhat more abstract; a "question being studied." Ruckelshaus Interview.

30. Ibid.

31. Gorsuch's impact on EPA career staff morale was satirized famously in a series of Doonesbury cartoons in January 1983, which featured an agency employee sitting out on a ledge and threatening to jump unless the administrator "publicly admits that the purpose of the Environmental Protection Agency is to protect the environment." Gary Trudeau, "Morale at EPA," *Doonesbury*, cartoon, January 28, 1982, https://perma.cc/E9UE-M7EG.

32. See Philip Shabecoff, "President Names Toxic Waste Chief to Head the EPA," *New York Times*, November 30, 1984, https://perma.cc/RB6N-LBH2.

33. Lee Thomas, former EPA administrator, interview with Jody Freeman, March 28, 2019, hereafter Thomas Interview.

34. Ibid.

35. See e.g., Mario J. Molina and F. Sherwood Rowland, "Stratospheric Sink for Chlorofluoromethanes: Chlorine Atom-Catalysed Destruction Of Ozone," *Nature* 249, no. 5460 (1974): 810.

36. See Stephen Leahy, "Without the Ozone Treaty You'd Get Sunburned in 5 Minutes," *National Geographic*, September 25, 2017, https://perma.cc/D8YP-SX8E.

37. See Clean Air Act Amendments of 1977, Pub. L. 95–95, 91 Stat. 685, 725–31 (1977) (establishing policies for "Ozone Protection").

38. See US Environmental Protection Agency, Consumer Product Safety Commission & US Food and Drug Administration, Certain Fluorocarbons As Propellants In Self-pressurized Containers: Prohibition On Use, 43 Fed. Reg. 11301 (March 17, 1978).

39. It was Hoffman who persuaded the plaintiffs to stand down, advising them bluntly that they would lose, and urging them to give EPA time to conduct the necessary research and build a broad consensus for regulation. See Doniger, "Remembering John Hoffman."

40. Hoffman became engaged on ozone after EPA's Toxic Substances Office circulated a draft notice stating that CFCs posed no further risk to the environment. He took over management of the issue internally. See Stephen Seidel, email communication with Jody Freeman, November 11, 2019 (on file with author).

41. The alliance between EPA and the State Department forged over the ozone issue would later prove important to establishing the Intergovernmental Panel on Climate Change (IPCC), and to negotiating subsequent international climate agreements. See notes 51–52, and accompanying text.

42. See Joseph C. Farman, Brian G. Gardiner, and Jonathan D. Shanklin, "Large Losses of Total Ozone in Antarctica Reveal Seasonal ClO_x/NO_x Interaction," *Nature* 315, no. 6016 (1985): 207–10.

43. See ibid. (describing study results including data over the five years previous); British Antarctic Survey, "The Ozone Hole," *bas.ac.uk*, April 1, 2017, https://perma.cc/YY6F-NTQN.

44. Vienna Convention for the Protection of the Ozone Layer, opened for signature March 22, 1985, T.I.A.S. No. 11, 097, 26 I.L.M. 1529 (1987).

45. Testimony of Lee Thomas, EPA administrator, describing all of the measures the EPA was taking to conduct research on ozone depletion, and declaring the administration's support for the Vienna Convention for the Protection of the Ozone Layer. US Senate, Ozone Depletion, the Greenhouse Effect, and Climate Change, 199–202.

46. The agreement required developed countries to achieve a twenty percent reduction relative to 1986 consumption levels by 1994 and a fifty percent reduction by 1999. See Montreal Protocol on Substances that Deplete the Ozone Layer, opened for signature September 16, 1987, S. Treaty Doc. No. 100–10 (1987). See Thomas Interview. The Reagan cabinet was split over mandatory CFC targets. The president's science advisor remained skeptical, and the Secretary of the Interior, Don Hodel, dismissively suggested that Americans should wear hats and sunscreen instead. See

Robert Gillete, "Suggests Wearing Hats, Sunscreen, Instead of Saving Ozone Layer: Hodel Proposal Irks Environmentalists," *Los Angeles Times,* May 30, 1987, https://perma.cc/K9KC-KA49. But President Reagan, urged by Secretary of State George Schultz, ultimately directed Thomas to negotiate a phase-out in Montreal. Reagan, who had had skin cancer, reportedly said, "If it happens, it's a catastrophe, so let's take out an insurance policy." See Jamie Lochhead, *Ozone Hole: How We Saved the Planet*, documentary, PBS, 2019.

47. Richard Morgenstern, email communication with Jody Freeman, December 5, 2019 (on file with author), hereafter Morgenstern Email.

48. John S. Hoffman, ed., *Assessing the Risks of Trace Gases that Can Modify the Stratosphere,* EPA 400/1-87/001C (Washington, DC: EPA OAR, 1987); US Environmental Protection Agency, Office of Air and Radiation, *Regulatory Impact Analysis: Protection of Stratospheric Ozone* (Washington, DC: EPA OAR, 1987). EPA's Science Advisory Board, which had created a subcommittee to review the ozone risk assessment, was now on record, saying climate change "is real and important." Seidel Interview. See also US Environmental Protection, Science Advisory Board, Stratospheric Ozone Subcommittee, *Review of EPA's Assessment of the Risks of Stratospheric Modification,* SAB-EC-87-025 (Washington, DC: EPA SAB, March 1987).

49. Tirpak Interview.

50. The staff included Dan Lashoff and Joel Smith, among others.

51. Morgenstern Email.

52. See e.g., Lee M. Thomas, "Global Challenges at EPA," *EPA Journal* 12, no. 10 (December 1986): 2–3. "The burning of coal, oil, and natural gas today adds about five gigatons of carbon dioxide to the atmosphere each year. . . . Many scientists believe that these chemicals are causing important changes in the chemical composition of our atmosphere."

53. See Robert Reinstein and Stephanie Kinney, interview by Charles Stuart Kennedy, October 5, 2010, https://perma.cc/6P7K-X8J7.

54. Michael Oppenheimer, former senior scientist at the Environmental Defense Fund and head of its Climate Program, interview with Jody Freeman, June 20, 2019. See Alan D. Hecht and Dennis Tirpak, "Framework Agreement on Climate Change: A Scientific and Policy History," *Climatic Change* 29 (1995): 381.

55. See generally Nathaniel Rich, "Losing Earth: The Decade We Almost Stopped Climate Change," *New York Times Magazine*, August 1, 2018, https://perma.cc/6URT-VSPP (describing lobbying efforts by environmental activists to spur congressional interest in climate change).

56. See US Senate, Ozone Depletion, The Greenhouse Effect, and Climate Change, 8–11; see also Hecht and Tirpak, "Framework Agreement on Climate Change," 381.

57. See Pomerance Interview (describing cooperation between environmental activists, EPA, and congressional staffers to arrange the hearings and request the reports).

58. Global Climate Protection Act of 1987, Pub. L. 100-204, 101 Stat. 1408, 1408–09 (1987) (establishing a policy to conduct more research on climate change).

59. See Philip Shabecoff, "Global Warming Has Begun, Expert Tells Senate," *New York Times,* June 24, 1988, https://perma.cc/4GEX-3C8G.

60. See generally US Environmental Protection Agency, *Unfinished Business: A Comparative Assessment of Environmental Problems,* 000R87901 (Washington, DC: EPA OP, 1987) for ranking climate change as the top ecological challenge facing EPA.

61. See Tirpak Interview; Morgenstern Email.

62. The air office was busy implementing the Montreal Protocol and working on the Clean Air Act re-authorization. See Eileen Claussen, former director of EPA's Office of Atmospheric Programs, interview with Jody Freeman, March 28, 2019. See also Morgenstern Email explaining that the matter was not ripe for regulation.

63. See Michael A. Toman, Richard D. Morgenstern, and John W. Anderson, *The Economics of "When" Flexibility in the Design of Greenhouse Gas Abatement Policies,* discussion paper 99-38-REV (Washington, DC: Resources for the Future, 1999), https://perma.cc/6A9G-3SC3, select "view the live page" to download.

64. See James Maxwell and Forrest Briscoe, "There's Money in the Air: The CFC Ban and DuPont's Regulatory Strategy," *Business Strategy and the Environment* 6, no. 5 (1988): 276–85.

65. The Global Climate Coalition spread disinformation about climate science and worked to defeat both international and domestic regulation of greenhouse gases. See generally Dianne Rahm, *Climate Change Policy in the United States: The Science, the Politics and Prospects for Change* (Jefferson, NC: McFarland, 2009); Kathy Mulvey and Seth Shulman, *The Climate Deception Dossiers* (Cambridge, MA: Union of Concerned Scientists, June 29, 2015); Neela Banerjee, Lisa Song, and David Hasemyer, "Exxon: The Road Not Taken," *Inside Climate News,* September 16, 2015, https://perma.cc/2GUK-AXRP.

66. See, e.g., National Energy Policy Act of 1988, S. 2667, 100th Cong. (1998).

67. See Rich, "Losing Earth," 53.

68. William K. Reilly, former EPA administrator, interview with Jody Freeman, March 14, 2019 (recalling the significant challenges of passing the bill). Hereafter Reilly Interview.

69. The monitoring proposal was developed by the Environmental Defense Fund and adopted during legislative negotiations. Joseph Goffman, email communication with Jody Freeman, November 7, 2019 (on file with author).

70. In 1989 the UN General Assembly adopted a resolution calling upon the Conference to promote and further develop international environmental law, and to "examine . . . the feasibility of elaborating general rights and obligations of States, as appropriate, in the field of the environment." UN Conference on Environment and Development, G.A. Res. 44/228, U.N. GAOR, 44th Sess., Supp. No. 49. U.N. Doc. A/43/49 (1989).

71. George H. W. Bush, "Address on the Environment" (speech, Erie Metropark, MI, August 31, 1988).

72. Ibid.

73. See, e.g., Michael Weisskopf, "Bush was Aloof in Warming Debate," *Washington Post*, October 31, 1992, https://perma.cc/H483-UPA7.

74. Reilly Interview, 66.

75. Reinstein and Kinney, 11.

76. Ibid., 21. In April 1990, the White House also hosted the Conference on Science and Economics Research Related to Global Change, co-chaired by the presi-

dent's science advisor, the chair of the Council of Economic Advisors, and the chair of the Council on Environmental Quality.

77. Baker called for reducing CFC emissions, improving energy efficiency, and limiting deforestation, going beyond anything President Bush himself had said while campaigning. See John M. Goshko, "Baker Urges Steps on Global Warming," *Washington Post,* January 31, 1989, https://perma.cc/G4JU-MQ7G.

78. Ibid.

79. Reilly Interview.

80. Reinstein and Kinney.

81. See US Environmental Protection Agency, *The Potential Effects of Global Climate Change on the United States: Report to Congress*, EPA-230-05-89-050 (Washington, DC: EPA OPPE, 1989); see also William Yardley, "John Hoffman, a Force in Energy Efficiency, Dies at 62," *New York Times*, October 16, 2012, https://perma.cc/HFR3-6LSR.

82. See US Environmental Protection Agency, *Policy Options for Stabilizing Global Climate: Report to Congress*, 21P-2003.1 (Washington, DC: EPA OPPE, 1990); see also Hecht and Tirpak, "Framework Agreement on Climate Change," 382. Richard Morgenstern calls these reports "highly influential." See Morgenstern Email.

83. See Morgenstern Email.

84. Hoffman had begun this work while at OPPE but developed it now at the Air Office. Ibid.

85. See US Environmental Protection Agency, *Green Lights Program: The First Year*, EPA/400/1-92/003 (Washington, DC: EPA, February 1992); US Environmental Protection Agency, *Introducing. . . . The Green Lights Program*, EPA 430-F-93-050 (Washington, DC: EPA, December 1993), announcing the growth of the Energy Star program out of the Green Lights Program.

86. Ibid. Energy Star later expanded into the comprehensive program for rating consumer appliances run by EPA and DOE, which still exists today.

87. The programs were controversial among economists at EPA, who worried about overstating their effectiveness. Critics said the programs were unenforceable, and gave firms credit for doing what they were going to do anyway. And they rankled Department of Energy officials, who thought they were in charge of efficiency.

88. Cathy Zoi, former assistant secretary for Energy Efficiency and Renewable Energy, US Department of Energy, interview with Jody Freeman, September 30, 2019 (on file with author). "We would be in these meetings with OMB and CEA and say, here is where we can get all these tons—from lighting and air conditioning, and office management, etc., etc., and they would push back on our assumptions or our math, and we'd come back with more programs and more tons. We outlasted them."

89. UN Conference on Environment and Development, Framework Convention on Climate Change, May 9, 1992, in Report of the Intergovernmental Negotiating Committee for a Framework Convention on Climate Change on the Work of the Second Part of Its Fifth Session, INC/FCCC, 5th Sess., 2d Part, at Annex I, U.N. Doe. A/AC.237/18 (Part II)/Add.1, reprinted in 31 I.L.M. 851.

90. The US delegation also made it clear that the president would not sign the related biodiversity convention out of concern for US biotechnology patents, among other issues.

91. Keith Schneider, "White House Snubs US Envoy's Plea to Sign Rio Treaty," *New York Times*, June 5, 1992, https://perma.cc/PY45-XSLP.

92. Reilly subsequently criticized the US position in a memorandum to EPA staff. See William K. Reilly, *Memorandum to All EPA Employees: Reflections on the Earth Day Summit* (Washington, DC: EPA, July 15, 1992), 4.

93. Albert Gore, Jr., *Earth in the Balance: Ecology and the Human Spirit* (Boston: Houghton Mifflin, 1992).

94. Carol Browner, EPA administrator, interview with Jody Freeman, March 26, 2019. Hereafter, Browner Interview.

95. "Climate was still seen as more of a scientific issue, and the mechanisms of action were longer-term." Gary Guzy, former counselor to the administrator and EPA general counsel, interview with Jody Freeman, March 20, 2019. Hereafter, Guzy Interview.

96. Roger C. Dower and Richard D. Morgenstern, "Energy Taxation in the United States: A Case Study of the BTU Tax Proposal," *International Journal of Global Energy Issues* 10, no. 2 (1998): 181, showing tax would achieve up to twenty-five percent of US greenhouse gas reductions called for by the UNFCCC.

97. See Steven Greenhouse, "Clinton Backs Off Plan for New Tax on Heat in Fuels," *New York Times*, June 9, 1993, https://perma.cc/HR76-8KG7.

98. See Eric Pianin and David Hilzenrath, "Hill Agrees to Raise Gas Tax 4.3 Cents," *Washington Post,* July 30, 1993, https://perma.cc/HA5M-ZZAU.

99. Browner Interview.

100. William J. Clinton and Albert Gore, Jr., *The Climate Change Action Plan* (Washington, DC: Executive Office of the President, 1993). From the White House, Katie McGinty led the inter-agency effort to coordinate the plan. Katie McGinty, former deputy assistant to the president and chair of the Council of Environmental Quality, interview with Jody Freeman, June 10, 2019, hereafter McGinty Interview.

101. See, e.g., Janice Mazurek, *The Use of Voluntary Agreements in the United States: An Initial Survey* (Paris: OECD ENV/EPOC/GEEI, 1998) evaluating these and other voluntary programs implemented by the US government.

102. US Government Accountability Office, *Global Warming: Information on the Results of Four of EPA's Voluntary Climate Change Programs,* GAO/RCED-97-163 (Washington DC: GAO, 1997), 3.

103. McGinty Interview, describing the White House preference for a market-based approach, and the need to persuade the Europeans of its merits.

104. Sue Biniaz, Former Deputy Legal Adviser and lead climate lawyer, US State Department, interview with Jody Freeman, April 14, 2019, hereafter Biniaz Interview; McGinty Interview, 98.

105. Biniaz Interview.

106. See UN Framework Convention on Climate Change, Rep. of the Conference of the Parties on its First Session, 2, U.N. Doc. FCCC/CP/1995/7/Add.1, June 6, 1995, https://perma.cc/5U4W-FWFH. The UNFCCC itself had referred to "common but differentiated responsibilities" in light of different capacities, and called for the developed world to take the lead in reducing emissions. See United Nations Framework Convention on Climate Change Article 3.1., May 9, 1992, 1771 U.N.T.S. 107. Wirth made this commitment after direction from the White House.

107. UN Framework Convention on Climate Change, Report of the Conference of the Parties on its Second Session, Held in Geneva from July 8–9, 1996, Action Taken by the Conference of the Parties, U.N. Doc. FCCC/CP/1996/15/Add.1, Annex, October 29, 1996, para. 8, https://perma.cc/5XTY-FUZV.

108. Susan Biniaz, *What Happened to Byrd-Hagel? Its Curious Absence from Evaluations of the Paris Agreement* (New York: Columbia University, Sabin Center for Climate Change Law, January 2018), https://perma.cc/2AB5-HMEL.

109. Michael Shelby, Memorandum on "'More Tons' One Pagers" to Karl Hausker, David Doniger and Dick Morgenstern (Washington, DC: EPA OPPE, May 31, 1994).

110. Ibid.

111. Ibid.

112. For some time, there had been tension between the air and policy offices over who would lead on climate change. Reilly had favored the research-oriented policy shop, which was dominated by economists, but Browner favored the regulators in air.

113. Mary Nichols, former assistant administrator for the Office of Air and Radiation, interview with Jody Freeman, March 15, 2019. In the interagency process, "Doniger was omnipresent." Roger Ballentine, former deputy assistant to the president for Environmental Initiatives, and chairman, White House Climate Change Task Force, interview with Jody Freeman, April 16, 2019.

114. See Jonathan Z. Cannon, EPA general counsel, memorandum to Carol M. Browner, EPA administrator, April 10, 1998 (hereafter Cannon Memo), discussing the memo, "Electricity Restructuring and the Environment: What Authority Does EPA Have and What Does it Need"; see also Margo T. Oge, *Driving the Future: Combating Climate Change with Cleaner, Smarter Cars* (New York: Arcade Publishing, 2015) chapter 5, describing the memo.

115. David Doniger, former counsel to the assistant administrator for Air and Radiation, interview with Jody Freeman, April 29, 2019, hereafter Doniger Interview.

116. See Cannon Memo.

117. David Doniger, email communication with Jody Freeman, November 1, 2019 (on file with author).

118. See "GOP Climate Treaty Critics Step Up Oversight of Administration Strategy," *Inside EPA*, March 6, 1998, 7–8 (referring to anticipated Republican oversight hearings: "In particular, congressional critics are becoming increasingly concerned that the administration may seek to control greenhouse gas emissions through regulation without winning Senate ratification of the accord, citing a recent EPA memorandum which suggests that the agency has the authority to set pollution control requirements for carbon dioxide under the Clean Air Act." The memo referred to was Doniger's. See Doniger Interview.)

119. See United States Congress, House, Appropriations for 1999: Hearings Before the Subcommittee on VA, HUD, and Independent Agencies, Committee on Appropriations, 105th Cong. 199–200 (1998).

120. Browner Interview, "I was shocked at the question. Shocked."

121. Ibid.

122. Ibid.

123. Cannon Memo, describing EPA authority to regulate CO_2 under the CAA.

124. Ibid., 2.

125. International Center for Technology Assessment, et al., Petition for Rulemaking and Collateral Relief Seeking the Regulation of Greenhouse Gas Emissions from New Motor Vehicles under §202 of the Clean Air Act (October 20, 1999), https://perma.cc/JZ64-GBQL.

126. Lisa Heinzerling, "Climate Change in the Supreme Court," *Environmental Law* 38 (2008): 4-5, referring to the original groups filing the petition as "rather obscure" and explaining that the environmental community disagreed about the best legal strategy for prompting action on climate change. The litigation could put the Clinton administration in a difficult position. David Doniger worried that it would provoke the Republican-controlled Congress. Doniger Interview.

127. 42 U.S.C. §7521 (2012). This section of the Clean Air Act provides that the administrator of EPA "shall by regulation prescribe . . . standards applicable to the emission of any air pollutant" from any class of motor vehicles "which in his judgment cause, or contribute to, air pollution which may reasonably be anticipated to endanger public health or welfare."

128. Ibid.

129. Massachusetts v. EPA, 549 US 497 (2007). Eventually the mainstream environmental movement, along with several states and local governments, coalesced around ICTA's strategy. They filed comments when EPA, at the end of the Clinton administration, put the petition out for comment, and ultimately joined the litigation challenging EPA's decision, in the George W. Bush administration, to deny it. For a complete history of the litigation, see Richard J. Lazarus, *The Rule of Five: Making Climate History at the Supreme Court* (Cambridge, MA: Belknap Press, 2020).

130. "Absolutely mattered that Cannon memo was out there. We would have gone forward anyway, but no question, that it paralleled our position made it helpful." Joe Mendelson, former legal director, International Center for Technology Institute, interview with Jody Freeman, November 21, 2019, hereafter Mendelson Interview.

131. Jonathan Z. Cannon, former EPA general counsel, interview with Jody Freeman, March 5, 2019, noting that the agency had no process in place to make the endangerment finding.

132. Guzy Interview.

133. US Environmental Protection Agency, Control of Emissions From New and In-use Highway Vehicles and Engines, 66 Fed. Reg. 7486 (January 23, 2001). See also Guzy Interview; Browner Interview.

134. Powerful firms and trade associations had opposed mandatory limits on CO_2, including Exxon, the American Petroleum Institute, and the National Coal Association. See generally Oreskes and Conway, *Merchants of Doubt*.

135. John F. Harris and Ellen Nakashima, "Gore's Greenness Fades," *Washington Post*, February 28, 2000, https://perma.cc/2MS9-BEFV.

136. George W. Bush (speech on Energy Issues at Saginaw, MI, September 29, 2000).

137. See Christine Todd Whitman, *It's My Party Too: The Battle for the Heart of the GOP and America* (London: Penguin Books, 2005), 170.

138. James Connaughton, former chairman of the White House Council on Environmental Quality and former director of the White House Office of Environmental Policy, interview with Jody Freeman, June 13, 2019, hereafter Connaughton Interview.

139. "At the time, the president was facing blackouts in California with electricity and natural gas prices spiking; we thought there would be natural gas shortages, and oil prices were viewed as getting high. This was the number one issue until 9/11." Andrew Lundquist, former executive director, National Energy Policy Group, interview with Jody Freeman, April 29, 2019.

140. Whitman's committee service was an "eye-opening encounter with just how obsessed so many of those in the energy industry, and in the Republican Party, have become with doing away with environmental regulation," Whitman, *It's My Party Too,* 182.

141. See "Interview with Christine Todd Whitman," *Frontline Politics*, April 24, 2007, https://perma.cc/EAM6-88BC.

142. Ibid. "As a governor, [Bush] had imposed carbon caps in Texas, so I noticed."

143. "There was just massive incoming against carbon regulation." Connaughton Interview. See also "Interview with Christine Todd Whitman," recounting industry opposition to carbon caps.

144. See EPA Administrator Christine Todd Whitman, "Address at the G8 Environmental Ministerial Meeting with Representatives of International Nongovernmental Organizations" (speech, Trieste, Italy, March 2, 2001), https://perma.cc/E83S-H59A; Edmund L. Andrews, "Bush Angers Europe by Eroding Pact on Warming," *New York Times*, April 1, 2001, https://perma.cc/P97Z-7XT3.

145. On the same day, Whitman had sent Bush a frank private letter about the Trieste meeting, in which she urged US leadership in international climate negotiations, which she called "a credibility issue for the administration." See Christine Todd Whitman, Memorandum to the President of the United States on G-8 Meeting in Trieste, March 6, 2001, https://perma.cc/YCX3-32PQ.

146. See, e.g., Ron Suskind, *The Price of Loyalty: George W. Bush, the White House, and the Education of Paul O'Neill* (New York: Simon & Schuster, 2004), 124–25.

147. See *President Bush Discusses Global Climate Change* (Washington, DC: Office of the White House Press Secretary, June 11, 2001), https://perma.cc/TC7Q-YFTX. See also Peter Baker, *Days of Fire: Bush and Cheney in the White House* (New York: Anchor, 2013), 589, referring to "a letter Cheney had him sign" to reverse the president's campaign position on climate change and withdraw from Kyoto.

148. See *President Bush Discusses Global Climate Change*.

149. "That's what Colin Powell has been calling me at cabinet meetings, the wind dummy." See Gregg Easterbook, "Hostile Environment," *New York Times Magazine*, August 19, 2001, https://perma.cc/XS9C-E28G.

150. National Energy Policy Development Group, *Reliable, Affordable, and Environmentally Sound Energy for America's Future* (Washington, DC: Government Printing Office, 2001), https://perma.cc/M64V-UBMV.

151. Lloyd Bries, "Bush Disses Global Warming Report," *CBS News*, June 3, 2002, https://perma.cc/H3UM-LYE3.

152. See e.g., Andrew C. Revkin, "Bush Aide Softened Greenhouse Gas Links to Global Warming," *New York Times*, June 8, 2005, https://perma.cc/AF3F-K4BT; Jeremy Symons, "How Bush and Co. Obscure the Science," *Washington Post,* July 13, 2003, https://perma.cc/K36X-JLNS. See also "Interview with Christine Todd Whitman," recounting Council on Environmental Quality demands to alter the wording of reports.

153. Andrew C. Revkin and Katharine Q. Seeyle, "Report by EPA Leaves out Data on Climate Change," *New York Times,* June 19, 2003, https://perma.cc/5EEA-XATK. White House officials objected to the report linking a significant rise in global temperatures to human activity, and wanted to delete a reference to a National Academy of Sciences report. EPA staff concluded that to accept the changes would expose the agency to "severe criticism from the science and environmental communities for poorly representing the science." Whitman dropped it entirely. See US Environmental Protection Agency, "Issue Paper: White House Edits to Climate Change Section of EPA's Report on the Environment," April 29, 2003, published in Union of Concerned Scientists, *Scientific Integrity in Policymaking: An Investigation into the Bush Administration's Misuse of Science* (Cambridge, MA: UCS, 2004), 34–38.

154. See Gregg Easterbrook, "Christie Todd Whitman May Have the Most Thankless Job in Washington," *New York Times,* August 23, 2001, https://perma.cc/X6G2-WXER.

155. David Stout, "EPA Chief Whitman Resigns," *New York Times,* May 21, 2003, https://perma.cc/32A8-P9BW.

156. See Robert E. Fabricant, "EPA's Authority to Impose Mandatory Controls to Address Global Climate Change under the Clean Air Act," memorandum to Marianne L. Horinko, EPA acting administrator, August 28, 2003, determining that the EPA does not possess authority to regulate "for global climate change purposes" under the Clean Air Act.

157. See ibid.

158. See Ronald A. Cass et al., *Administrative Law: Cases and Materials*, 7th ed. (Philadelphia: Wolters Kluwer, 2015), 248–49, discussing the difference between inaction and action for purposes of judicial review.

159. Jeff Holmstead, former EPA assistant administrator for the Office of Air and Radiation, interview with Jody Freeman, April 23, 2019, hereafter Holmstead Interview.

160. Massachusetts v. EPA, 415 F.3d 50, 52 (D.C. Cir. 2005). The Petition for Review was first filed on October 23, 2003, little more than a month after EPA denied the rulemaking petition. See Petition for Review Cases Docketed, Massachusetts v. EPA, 415 F.3d 50 (D.C. Cir. 2005) (Case Nos. 03-1361 to 03-1368). "The plan was to let the states appeal first, and then everyone joined," Mendelson Interview.

161. See generally Lazarus, *The Rule of Five*.

162. See Heinzerling, "Climate Change in the Supreme Court," 5–6, describing the risks; see also Jody Freeman and Adrian Vermeule, "Massachusetts v. EPA: From Politics to Expertise," *Supreme Court Review* 2007, no. 1 (2007): 51–60. Each element of the standing test (that the injury be actual or imminent, not speculative; "fairly traceable" to the challenged government action; and likely to be redressed if

the plaintiff wins) is hard to demonstrate with an incremental, cumulative, and global phenomenon like climate change.

163. See Freeman and Vermeule, "Massachusetts v. EPA."

164. See FDA v. Brown & Williamson Tobacco Corp., 529 US 120 (2000).

165. See Freeman and Vermeule, "Massachusetts v. EPA," explaining the significance of the decision.

166. New Jersey v. EPA, 517 F.3d 574, 577, 582 (D.C. Cir. 2008), striking down EPA's proposal to delist mercury as a hazardous air pollutant under CAA §112 and regulate it using a voluntary cap-and-trade approach under CAA §111.

167. Connaughton Interview.

168. See Susan Dudley, OIRA administrator, "Regulating Greenhouse Gas Emissions Under the Clean Air Act," letter to EPA Administrator Stephen L. Johnson on Draft ANPRM submitted to OMB, July 10, 2008, https://perma.cc/28TH-JUBW.

169. See Felicity Barringer, "A New (and Unlikely) Tell-All," *New York Times*, July 22, 2008, https://perma.cc/HVV3-Z7DG.

170. The "Preface from the Administrator" said that the Clean Air Act is ill-suited for regulating GHGs and that none of the views in the notice represented agency decisions or recommendations. Regulating Greenhouse Gas Emissions Under the Clean Air Act, 73 Fed. Reg. 44354–55 (July 30, 2008). Johnson had "brought the program offices together and said we would do an ANPRM, maybe we can use the Clean Air Act to regulate GHGs. And the staff believed him. He gave them six months and they worked so hard to think through all the elements of the act. People could not go on vacation, worked around the clock. When he brought them to his office to tell them what he did, they thought it was the most depressing thing he could have done. They were all disgusted. Especially as a former career person, he dishonored the agency and his people. He should have resigned." Margo Oge, former office director of Office of Transportation and Air Quality, interview with Jody Freeman, November 20, 2019.

171. See Dudley, "Regulating Greenhouse Gas Emissions."

172. John Shiffman and John Sullivan, "An Eroding Mission at EPA," *Philadelphia Inquirer,* December 2, 2008, https://perma.cc/Y2ZM-TLU8.

173. "What happened to Johnson was what happened to Whitman—he was sent on an errand by people in the White House that hadn't anticipated the pressure they'd come under. The rug got pulled out from under him." Holmstead Interview.

174. President George W. Bush, "The State of the Union Address by the President of the United States" (speech, Washington, DC, January 31, 2006).

175. Energy Independence and Security Act of 2007, Pub. L. 110–140, 121 Stat. 1492 (2007), codified as amended in scattered sections of the US Code.

176. A.B. 1493, 2001–2002 Leg., Reg. Sess., 2002 Cal. Stat. ch. 200, codified as amended at Cal. Health & Safety Code §43018.5(a).

177. See The California Global Warming Solutions Act of 2006, Cal. Health & Safety Code §38501 *et seq*., establishing a state-wide CO_2 cap-and-trade system and setting targets based on 2010 levels.

178. See J. R. DeShazo and Jody Freeman, "Timing and Form of Federal Regulation: The Case of Climate Change," *University of Pennsylvania Law Review* 155, no. 6 (June 2007): 1525, describing state initiatives to regulate GHGs.

179. See, e.g., Connecticut v. American Electric Power, 406 F.Supp.2d 265 (S.D.N.Y. 2005); Comer v. Murphy Oil USA, Inc., 2007 WL 6942285 (S.D. Miss. August 30, 2007); People of State of California v. Gen. Motors Corp., 2007 WL 2726871 (N.D. Cal. September 17, 2007).

180. Andrew C. Revkin, "On Global Warming, McCain and Obama Agree: Urgent Action Is Needed," *New York Times,* October 19, 2008, https://perma.cc/67W2-D9N8.

181. See Stephen L. Johnson, letter to California Governor Arnold Schwarzenegger on California's Request for a Clean Air Act Preemption Waiver, December 19, 2007, https://perma.cc/2VRU-3W9U.

182. See, e.g., Barack H. Obama (speech, St. Paul, MN, June 3, 2008), upon winning the Democratic Party primary; Barack H. Obama, "Inaugural Presidential Address" (speech, Washington, DC, January 21, 2009).

183. This was not entirely positive. Jackson hadn't known about Browner's appointment when she accepted the EPA job, and it limited her influence to have climate policy led from the White House.

184. American Clean Energy and Security Act of 2009, H.R. 2454, 111th Cong. (2009), passing the US House of Representatives on a vote of 219–212.

185. See, e.g., Randy Rieland, "The Blame Obama Game," *Grist*, July 27, 2010, https://perma.cc/4TRU-7SMM, collecting a variety of articles that blamed President Obama; Tim Dickinson, "Climate Bill, R.I.P.," *Rolling Stone,* July 21, 2010, https://perma.cc/4ZN9-3C44.

186. See, e.g., Ryan Lizza, "As the World Burns," *The New Yorker,* October 11, 2010, https://perma.cc/79D4-AQMN; Editorial Board, "With a Whimper," *New York Times*, July 22, 2010, https://perma.cc/8SU6-W4UE.

187. See, e.g., David Robert, "Why Did the Climate Bill Fail?" *Grist,* July 27, 2010, https://perma.cc/8FW7-P8YL; Lee Wasserman, "Four Ways to Kill a Climate Bill," *New York Times,* July 25, 2010, https://perma.cc/HZ5K-Y64M.

188. See Lizza, "As the World Burns." Insiders have noted that neither Rahm Emanuel, Obama's first chief of staff, nor David Axelrod, Obama's counselor, seemed to have the fire in the belly for climate change the way they did for health care.

189. The standards initially covered the 2012-2016 model years, with an average annual improvement in efficiency of five percent. See Jody Freeman, "The Obama Administration's National Auto Policy: Lessons from the 'Car Deal,'" *Harvard Environmental Law Review* 35 (2011): 344-46, describing the negotiations as "six-dimensional chess." California officially received its preemption waiver, preserving its legal right to set its own standards, but it "stood down," treating compliance with federal standards as the functional equivalent of meeting its own.

190. The auto companies also agreed to withdraw litigation challenging California's authority to set its own standards, which the state would formally retain. See ibid.

191. See *Obama Administration Finalizes Historic 54.5 MPG Fuel Efficiency Standards* (Washington, DC: White House Office of the Press Secretary, August 28, 2012), https://perma.cc/E9CE-JJN2; 2017 and Later Model Year Light-Duty Vehicle Greenhouse Gas Emissions and Corporate Average Fuel Economy Standards, 77 Fed. Reg. 62624 (October 15, 2012), finalizing the announced rule.

192. Endangerment and Cause or Contribute Findings for Greenhouse Gases Under Section 202(a) of the Clean Air Act, 74 Fed. Reg. 66496 (December 15, 2009), "The Administrator finds that six greenhouse gases taken in combination endanger both the public health and the public welfare of current and future generations."

193. See US Environmental Protection Agency, "About the National Vehicle and Fuel Emissions Laboratory (NVFEL)," *epa.gov*, last updated August 7, 2019, https://perma.cc/26VQ-VJXM, describing the lab.

194. See Freeman, "Lessons from the 'Car Deal.'"

195. The Copenhagen meeting was the Fifteenth Conference of the Parties to the United Nations Framework Convention on Climate Change, opened for signature May 9, 1992, S. Treaty Doc. No. 102–38, 1771 U.N.T.S. 164. President Obama attended the Copenhagen meeting, and pledged the US to achieve greenhouse gas emissions reductions "in the range of 17%" below 2005 levels by 2020, based on what the Waxman-Markey bill was projected to achieve. See generally *Support for President's Copenhagen Announcement Receives Immediate Support* (Washington, DC: White House Office of the Press Secretary, November 25, 2009), https://perma.cc/63SX-DSWS.

196. William Branigin, "Obama Reflects on 'shellacking' in Midterm Elections," *Washington Post*, November 3, 2010, https://perma.cc/ECX9-RBTU.

197. See David Barstow, David Rohde, and Stephanie Saul, "Deepwater Horizon's Final Hours," *New York Times*, December 25, 2010, https://perma.cc/WSU5-2UMT.

198. Joseph Goffman, former associate assistant administrator for climate and senior counsel in the EPA Office of Air and Radiation, interview with Jody Freeman, July 2, 2019, hereafter Goffman Interview; Gina McCarthy, former EPA administrator, interview with Jody Freeman, June 18, 2019, hereafter McCarthy Interview; Robert Sussman, former EPA deputy administrator, email communication with Jody Freeman, May 5, 2019 (on file with author).

199. See Settlement Agreement, New York v. EPA, No. 06-1322 (D.C. Cir. Dec. 23, 2010); Settlement Agreement, Am. Petrol. Inst. v. EPA, No. 08-1277 (D.C. Cir. Dec. 23, 2010).

200. See Proposed Standards of Performance for Greenhouse Gas Emissions for New Stationary Sources: Electric Utility Generating Units, 77 Fed. Reg. 22,392 (Apr. 13, 2012) (to be codified at 40 C.F.R. 60); Goffman Interview.

201. McCarthy Interview.

202. See Carol Davenport, "The Man Who Could Put Climate Change on the Agenda," *National Journal*, April 4, 2013, https://perma.cc/9U3L-6UZA.

203. "I urge this Congress to get together, pursue a bipartisan, market-based solution to climate change . . . [b]ut if Congress won't act soon to protect future generations, I will." See Barack H. Obama, "Second Inaugural Presidential Address" (speech, Washington, DC, January 21, 2013); President Barack H. Obama, "The State of the Union Address by the President of the United States" (speech, Washington, DC, February 12, 2013).

204. *Fact Sheet: President Obama's Climate Action Plan* (Washington, DC: White House Office of the Press Secretary, June 25, 2013), https://perma.cc/3KBD-JCV3, hereafter Fact Sheet.

205. McCarthy Interview.

206. Standards of Performance for Greenhouse Gas Emissions from New, Modified, and Reconstructed Stationary Sources: Electric Generating Units, 80 Fed. Reg. 64510 (October 23, 2015); Carbon Pollution Emission Guidelines for Existing Stationary Sources: Electric Utility Generating Units, Final Rule, 80 Fed. Reg. 64662 (October 23, 2015). The President's Climate Action Plan had included a separate Presidential Memorandum directing EPA to set carbon standards for power plants using its Clean Air Act Authority, specifying deadlines, and instructing the agency to conduct broad stakeholder outreach. See Fact Sheet.

207. The effort was organized and managed by Assistant Administrator Janet McCabe. The key architects were a team of core staff from the Office of Air Quality Planning and Standards, the Office of Atmospheric Programs, and the Office of General Counsel, coordinated by Associate Assistant Administrator for Climate and Senior Counsel, Joe Goffman.. Goffman Interview.

208. See CAA §111(a), 42 U.S.C. §7411(a)(1), defining "standard of performance."

209. EPA had initiated the rule for new sources in 2012, but now withdrew it and re-proposed standards for both new and existing sources. Standards of Performance for Greenhouse Gas Emissions from New, Modified, and Reconstructed Stationary Sources: Electric Generating Units, 80 Fed. Reg. 64,510 (Oct. 23, 2015); See Carbon Pollution Emission Guidelines for Existing Stationary Sources: Electric Utility Generating Units, Final Rule, 80 Fed. Reg. 64662 (October 23, 2015), hereafter CPP Final Rule.

210. See CAA §111(d), 42 U.S.C. §7411(d) (2012).

211. CPP Final Rule.

212. See Steven Mufson, "Vintage US Coal-Fired Power Plants Now an 'Aging Fleet of Clunkers,'" *Washington Post*, June 13, 2014, https://perma.cc/BM59-98AD. See also CAA §111(d), 42 U.S.C. §7411(d) (2012).

213. In EPA's view, there was no logical reason why performance standards in Section 111 must be limited to engineering solutions that can be installed to units on-site if off-site measures might reduce emissions from such units cost-effectively. See CPP Final Rule, 64,717–811, describing EPA's approach to Best System of Emission Reduction and its "building block" methodology.

214. "The CPP was a market signal that said this will be the least that will happen. That's what you do with regulations—signal where you need to head. The utilities are smart and can figure it out. It also gave them an excuse to make politically controversial decisions in states where they operate, to shut down old units, and blame us," McCarthy Interview.

215. Ibid.

216. Paris Agreement to the United Nations Framework Convention on Climate Change, December 12, 2015, T.I.A.S. No. 16-1104, https://perma.cc/4UWL-2DVA, hereafter Paris Agreement.

217. See United States, Intended Nationally Determined Contribution Submitted in Accordance with Art. 4, Para. 12 of Paris Agreement (March 9, 2016), https://perma.cc/UF89-AR4A. While the US had no obligation to achieve its pledge through these two policies, it was widely expected that they would be implemented.

218. For an overview and assessment of the Paris Agreement, see Susan Biniaz, "The Paris Agreement—Au Revoir?" *Columbia Law School Climate Law Blog*, May 24, 2019, https://perma.cc/F7X4-AX8Q, describing and responding to common criticisms of the accord; Susan Biniaz, "The Paris Agreement at Three Years Old, The Doctor's Report," *Harvard Law School Environmental & Energy Law Program*, December 17, 2018, https://perma.cc/XG35-37RU, reviewing the history of the Paris Agreement and assessing its performance to date.

219. See, *The President's Climate Action Plan* (Washington, DC: Executive Office of the President, June 2013), https://perma.cc/JH8K-583F.

220. In the fall of 2016, the US delegation, led by EPA Administrator McCarthy, negotiated the Kigali Amendment to the Montreal Protocol, creating a global framework to comprehensively phase-out hydrofluorocarbons. See UN Environmental Programme, *Report of the Twenty-Eighth Meeting of the Parties to the Montreal Protocol on Substances that Deplete the Ozone Layer*, UNEP/OzL.Pro.28/12, Annex I (Geneva: UNEP, November 15, 2016); Coral Davenport, "Nations, Fighting Powerful Refrigerant That Warms Planet, Reach Landmark Deal," *New York Times,* October 15, 2016, https://perma.cc/P8JT-463R.

221. See, e.g., Regulatory Finding on the Emissions of Hazardous Air Pollutants from Electric Utility Steam Generating Units, 65 Fed. Reg. 79,826 (December 20, 2000); Federal Implementation Plans: Interstate Transport of Fine Particulate Matter and Ozone and Correction of SIP Approvals, 76 Fed. Reg. 48208 (August 8, 2011); National Emission Standards for Hazardous Air Pollutants From Coal and Oil-Fired Electric Utility Steam Generating Units and Standards of Performance for Fossil-Fuel-Fired Electric Utility, Industrial-Commercial Institutional, and Small Industrial Commercial-Institutional Steam Generating Units, 77 Fed. Reg. 9304 (February 16, 2012); Oil and Natural Gas Sector: New Source Performance Standards and National Emission Standards for Hazardous Air Pollutants Reviews, 77 Fed. Reg. 49490 (August 16, 2012).

222. Exec. Order No. 13,783, 82 Fed. Reg. 16093 (March 31, 2017) ("Promoting Energy Independence and Economic Growth").

223. Nikki Haley, US Representative to the United Nations, letter to the Secretary-General of the United Nations, August 4, 2017, https://perma.cc/RZC8-3RBF.

224. Repeal of the Clean Power Plan, hereafter CPP Repeal. Emission Guidelines for Greenhouse Gas Emissions from Existing Electric Utility Generating Units; Revisions to Emission Guidelines Implementing Regulations, 84 Fed. Reg. 32520 (July 8, 2019).

225. CPP Repeal, at 32,561 (Table 3) (showing projected Electricity Sector Emission Impacts).

226. See Joseph Goffman and Caitlin McCoy, "EPA's House of Cards, The Affordable Clean Energy Rule," *Harvard Law School Environmental & Energy Law Program*, October 23, 2019, https://perma.cc/6RTP-ARKU.

227. Although this New Source Review policy was a component of the proposed ACE Rule, it has not been finalized as of this writing. For an analysis of the proposal, see Environmental & Energy Law Program, "Review of New Source Review Changes in Affordable Clean Energy (ACE) Proposal," *Harvard Law School Environmental & Energy Law Program*, October 29, 2018, https://perma.cc/QGS2-YV6J.

228. See Oil and Natural Gas Sector: Emission Standards for New, Reconstructed, and Modified, Sources Review, 85 Fed. Reg. 57,018 (Sep. 14, 2020); Waste Prevention, Production Subject to Royalties, and Resource Conservation; Rescission or Revision of Certain Requirements, 83 Fed. Reg. 49,184 (Sep. 28, 2018). The Bureau of Land Management's Revised Rule was vacated in federal district court and was on appeal in the Ninth Circuit Court of Appeals at the time of writing. *See* California v. Bernhardt, No. 4:18-cv-05712-YGR, 2020 WL 4001480 (N.D. Cal. July 15, 2020), *sub. nom.* Cal. Air Res. Bd. v. Am. Petrol. Inst., No. 20-16801 (9th Cir. Sep. 17, 2020).

229. See The Safer Affordable Fuel-Efficient (SAFE) Vehicles Rule for Model Years 2021–2026 Passenger Cars and Light Trucks, 85 Fed. Reg. 24174 (April 30, 2020).

230. Stephen G. Bradbury, general counsel, US Department of Transportation, and Matthew Z. Leopold, general counsel, Environmental Protection Agency, letter to Mary Nichols, chair, California Air Resources Board, September 6, 2019, https://perma.cc/X2WY-RPW7.

231. Timothy Puko and Ben Foldy, "Justice Department Launches Antitrust Probe into Four Auto Makers," *Wall Street Journal,* September 6, 2019, https://perma.cc/8CQ9-QK2V.

232. Rebecca Beitsch, "DOJ Sues California to Stifle Cap and Trade Program With Quebec," *The Hill*, October 23, 2019, https://perma.cc/L795-WGPM.

233. For a list of initiatives intended to undermine EPA capacity, see Harvard Law School Environmental & Energy Law Program, "EPA Mission Tracker," https://perma.cc/GHW6-F9ZY, select "View the live page" at the top of the perma link for a live view.

234. For a running list of these initiatives, see Harvard Law School Environmental & Energy Law Program, "Regulatory Rollback Tracker," https://perma.cc/E27V-SP7R, select "View the live page" at the top of the perma link for a live view.

235. See, e.g., Physicians for Social Responsibility v. Wheeler, 2020 WL 1921539 (D.C. Cir. 2020), striking down an EPA directive prohibiting scientists in receipt of certain EPA grants from serving on EPA's federal advisory committees. See also Fred Barbash and Deanna Paul, "The Real Reason the Trump Administration is Constantly Losing in Court," *Washington Post*, March 19, 2019, https://perma.cc/LQB5-7KLB, describing administration losses and highlighting environmental cases.

236. A new administration could ask reviewing courts to hold pending matters in abeyance during the development of new regulations. Only in rare circumstances would a rule rescission be irreversible by a new administration—for example, where the Supreme Court has ruled that there is only one lawful way to read a statute. See National Cable & Telecommunications Association v. Brand X Internet Services, 545 US 967 (2005).

237. In virtually every administration, EPA administrators took over the agency only to encounter some crisis. This includes Love Canal, the Bhopal disaster, the Exxon Valdez oil spill, the 9/11 terrorist attacks, the BP Deepwater Horizon Oil Spill, and more.

238. Freeman, "What Amy Coney Barrett's Confirmation Will Mean for Environmental Law and Joe Biden's Climate Plan," Vox, October 21, 2020, https://perma.cc/4BJP-BQN2.

Chapter Five

EPA and the Clean Water Act

Jonathan Z. Cannon

Despite earlier state and federal laws to limit water pollution, there were graphic signs in the late 1960s that many of the nation's waters were not healthy. Researchers found that fishermen in the Chesapeake Bay were losing $3 million per year to pollution. The Hudson River registered bacteria levels well over a hundred times the safe level. Record fish kills were reported around the country, many attributable to industrial discharges.[1] One of the most vivid abuses—and one that would become the banner for clean water legislative reform—was a fire on Ohio's Cuyahoga River. Floating oil and debris under a railroad bridge in Cleveland ignited on June 22, 1969, and burned for twenty minutes before firefighters extinguished it.[2] Widely covered in national media, the fire had a galvanizing effect.[3]

The 1969 Cuyahoga fire was not the first time the river had burst into flames. Lined with chemical plants, paper and steel mills, and oil refineries that used it as a conduit for their wastes, the river had caught fire more than half a dozen times before, and several of those blazes lasted longer and posed greater risks to the public than the 1969 conflagration.[4] What was different now was the nascent environmental movement, which interpreted the fire through the lens of human abuse of environmental resources. An article about the fire in *Time* magazine was damning: "Some river! Chocolate-brown, oily, bubbling with subsurface gases, it oozes rather than flows."[5] That image resonated with the public's growing environmental concern; a river so fouled that it burned became a persistent and powerful symbol of the need to address water quality more aggressively.

Three years after the Cuyahoga fire the modern Clean Water Act (CWA) came into being with the Federal Water Pollution Control Amendments of 1972. Although amended several times since, the 1972 legislation created the core regulatory armature that still operates today. The act was among a cascade of federal environmental laws adopted at the height of the environmental movement and is among the movement's most significant monuments. It has proved remarkably durable and effective. Since its enactment, we have seen dramatic reductions in industrial and municipal pollution of the nation's surface waters and in the destruction of its wetlands. We have also seen the fruits of efforts to restore and protect local and regional watersheds, such as the Chesapeake Bay and the Great Lakes.

First enacted in 1948, the Federal Water Pollution Control Act had been amended five times before 1972 but had failed to establish an effective federal presence. Prior to the 1972 amendments, the legislation required states to adopt water quality standards only for their interstate waters, and only half the states adopted those required standards. States were also tasked to adopt implementation plans that set requirements for dischargers necessary to meet the standards. But the federal government had no authority to impose a plan if a state did not, and states' compliance with the implementation-plan mandate was spotty. "As a result," concludes Professor Robert Percival, "even when water quality standards were adopted, there was no effective mechanism to translate them into workable requirements on individual dischargers, and the federal government had no meaningful enforcement authority."[6] The modern Clean Water Act that emerged in 1972 was Congress' bid to transcend the lackluster performance of the prior legislation and meet the growing public demand for environmental stewardship.[7]

AN OVERVIEW OF THE CWA: ORIGINS AND TERMS

The CWA announced a bold new national policy for water quality and provided a suite of regulatory tools to advance that policy. It broadened the scope of federal authority and increased the stringency and enforceability of pollution controls. I trace below the key features of this visionary and powerful law.

Goal-Setting and Policy

The act's overall objective, stated in the opening words, is "to restore and maintain the chemical, physical, and biological integrity of the nation's water." This emphasis on ecological integrity makes the CWA unusual among federal pollution control statutes. To achieve this objective, the act set a national goal of eliminating the discharge of pollutants into the waters of the US by 1985.[8] The act also set an interim goal: by July 1, 1983, "wherever attainable," attain water quality that "provides for the protection and propagation of fish, shellfish, and wildlife and provides for recreation in and on the water."[9] This goal is often shorthanded as "fishable/swimmable." EPA has made "fishable/swimmable" the touchstone for water quality standards under the act, giving it particular influence over discharges into water bodies with marginal water quality.

Jurisdictional Scope

Federal regulatory authority under the Water Quality Act of 1965 was restricted to interstate waters. The Clean Water Act expanded federal jurisdiction to "navigable waters," which it defined as "waters of the United States and the territorial seas." Navigable waters had a traditional meaning as waters that had been, were now, or could be used in interstate commerce. The 1972 act pointedly omitted navigable from the statute's definition of navigable waters, indicating a reach beyond the traditional meaning. The conference committee report that accompanied the legislation stated Congress' intent "that the term 'navigable waters' be given the broadest possible constitutional interpretation, unencumbered by agency determinations which have been made or may be made for administrative purposes."[10] While proving crucial to the protection of wetlands and smaller lakes and tributaries, the new definition has also stoked continuing legal and policy debates, to which I return later in this chapter.

Prohibition on Discharges Except in Compliance with the Act

To overcome the lack of enforceable requirements for individual dischargers in the pre-1972 legislation, Section 301(a) of the act prohibits "the discharge of any pollutant" except in compliance with enumerated requirements, including discharge-authorizing permits.[11] Section 402 establishes the National Pollutant Discharge Elimination System (NPDES) applicable to discharges of most pollutants. Pollutants for which NPDES permits were required included everything from chemical wastes and sewage to rock and sand. Under Section 404, a different kind of permit is required for discharges of a specific class of pollutants—"dredged or fill material." Dischargers are liable for civil and criminal penalties for failure to obtain required permits or comply with them.[12]

Technology-Based Standards

The Clean Water Act aimed to correct the shortcomings of the pre-1970s legislation by shifting its primary reliance from water quality standards to technology-based limitations. By July 1977 it required that all existing industrial dischargers meet effluent limitations based on "best practicable technology" for each category of discharger; by July 1983 the same dischargers faced still more demanding limitations, reflecting "best available technology economically achievable" (BATEA).[13] (A less demanding alternative standard—"best conventional pollutant control"—was later created for a handful of common pollutants.)[14] New industrial sources were subject to an even stricter "standard of control" keyed to "the greatest degree of effluent reduction . . . achievable" and "including, where practicable . . . a standard permitting no discharge of pollutants."[15] Separate standards applied to publicly owned sewage treatment plants (POTWs) and to industrial and commercial sources that discharged into POTWs rather than directly into the nation's waters.[16] The act gave EPA the demanding job of converting this array of general standards into limitations specific to each class or category of discharger, and writers of NPDES permits were tasked with making sure that the appropriate technology-based limitations appeared in a permit for every discharger.

This technology emphasis was in sharp contrast to the primary reliance on ambient air quality standards in the 1970 Clean Air Act.

Water Quality Standards

The act also tasked NPDES permit writers with including any more stringent effluent limitations necessary to meet water quality standards. That is, permittees might be called upon to do better than the "best," if protecting the integrity of the receiving water demanded it. Under Section 404, a discharge of dredge and fill materials will not be permitted if it will violate water quality standards. The act required states to set water quality standards for *all* their "navigable waters," not just interstate waters as under the pre-1972 legislation. It also gave EPA authority to disapprove state standards, and any revisions that failed to meet the act's requirements, and to substitute federally adopted standards if a state failed to make adequate revisions. The agency measured the adequacy of water quality standards against the act's goal of preserving and protecting the nation's waters.

Section 402 Permits and State and Federal Roles

NPDES permits may be issued by EPA or by states with programs approved by EPA. A state applying to administer the program must show EPA it has "adequate authority" to issue permits and carry out enforcement in accordance with federal requirements.[17] Upon EPA approval of its program, the state takes over the issuance of permits, although EPA retains the authority to object to state-issued permits and, if a state fails to meet its objection, to issue a permit that comports with its view of the act's requirements.[18] EPA has approved forty-six states to implement the NPDES program.[19] Because the majority of NPDES permits are issued by states, the majority of enforcement actions fall under that system.[20] EPA retains a veto over NPDES permits issued by states with approved programs and may file its own enforcement actions in those states. It may also withdraw its approval of a state program, in whole or in part, on finding that the state is not administering the program in accordance with the act. Such withdrawals are rare.

Section 404 and Wetlands Protection

Reserved for discharges of dredged or fill material, Section 404 permits are issued by the US Army Corps of Engineers (Corps), not by EPA, although EPA may veto a Corps-issued Section 404 permit that it concludes does not meet the requirements of the act. The Section 402 and 404 permitting regimes are mutually exclusive: a discharge covered by a 404 permit does not require a 402 permit and vice versa.[21] Section 404 is associated with protection of wetlands, but it covers discharges of dredged and fill materials into *all* "waters of the US"—open waters as well as jurisdictional wetlands. Also, because it is limited to control of discharges, it does not protect wetlands from other sources of degradation, such as channelization, that do not involve discharges, as discussed later in the chapter. Like Section 402, Section 404 authorizes states and tribes to assume permitting authority if they show they will meet federal requirements, but unlike Section 402, it limits the scope of state authority to waters that do not fall within the traditional definition of navigable waters.[22] Only two states, New Jersey and Michigan, have taken on the administration of the Section 404 program.

Government Enforcement

The CWA provides EPA (and its litigating arm, the Department of Justice) with a robust set of enforcement tools. The agency can sue alleged violators in federal court for civil penalties and injunctive relief to bring them into compliance; as of January 2019, civil penalties for most violations can range up to $54,833 per day of violation, with potential penalties reaching into many millions of dollars for extended violations.[23] For less serious violations, EPA has the option of obtaining penalties and compliance orders through administrative actions. Civil liability for CWA violations is strict. The fact of a violation is enough; no showing is required that the discharger was careless, knowing, or willful. The act also establishes criminal penalties (including fines and incarceration) for "knowing" (felony) or "negligent" (misdemeanor) violations.

Citizen Suits

In a distinctive innovation characteristic of the generation of environmental statutes to which it belongs, the CWA enables "any citizen" to bring a civil action in federal court against a violator of the act or against the EPA itself for failure to carry out actions mandated by Congress. In suits against violators, citizens are entitled to the same relief—in penalties and court injunctions—that would be awarded in a government action.[24] As the Supreme Court has written, the main purpose of allowing citizens to sue violators is "to abate pollution when the government cannot or will not command compliance."[25] In line with this purpose, the act requires that an individual or group give sixty days' notice to the EPA, the state, and the violator before filing suit and precludes the suit if at the time of filing the EPA or the state has "commenced and is diligently prosecuting" a judicial enforcement action of its own. Contrary to the general rule in the United States that each side bears its own litigation costs, the court in such suits may award attorneys' fees and other costs to the "prevailing or substantially prevailing party."[26] The prospect of recouping costs removes a barrier for thinly funded local or regional environmental groups contemplating action.

POTW Construction Grants

Upgrading the treatment capacity of the nation's Publicly Owned Treatment Works (POTWs) was essential to improving water quality. Sensitive to the fiscal constraints on the local governments that maintained and operated these facilities, Congress first authorized federal grants for the construction of waste treatment works in 1956. It vastly increased their size and scope in the 1972 amendments. It increased the federal share to seventy-five percent of construction costs, extended eligibility for federal funds beyond the treatment plant itself to sewage collection and related systems, and authorized $18 billion over five years to fund the program.[27] Calling the program "budget-wrecking," then President Richard Nixon vetoed the legislation.[28] After Congress overrode his veto by overwhelming margins, Nixon moved to sequester the funds, drawing a final rebuke from the Supreme Court.[29] At its height, the construction grants program administered by EPA was the nation's largest public works program. In 1987, however, Congress replaced it with the Clean Water State Revolving Fund,[30] under which federal dollars go to capitalize loan funds that are replenished with repayments by municipal recipients.

Oil and Hazardous Waste Spills

In 1970, a year after an oil rig off Santa Barbara suffered a blowout that spawned a city-size oil slick and killed thousands of seabirds, Congress amended the Federal Water Pollution Control Act to create statutory liability for oil spills. In the 1972 amendments, it strengthened those requirements and extended them to releases of hazardous substances in Section 311 of the CWA.[31] Section 311 prohibits discharges of oil or hazardous substances into the nation's waters "in such quantities as may be harmful."[32] For the owners or operators of the source of the spill, whether a vessel or onshore facility, it authorizes imposition of administrative or civil penalties.[33] Owners and operators can also be fined for failing to immediately notify the government of spills covered by the act. Finally, the act assigns liability to the owners and operators for cleaning up the spill and reimbursing the government for its removal costs.[34] In the wake of the disastrous Exxon Valdez oil spill in Alaska, Congress in 1990 enacted the Oil Pollution Act, expanding the scope of owners' and operators' liability for oil spills.

IMPLEMENTATION CHALLENGES: PAST AND PRESENT

EPA came into being by executive order signed by President Nixon in 1970. It brought together an amalgam of offices and programs from across the federal government, including the Federal Water Quality Administration from the Department of Interior, which had administered the early versions of federal clean water legislation. The first administrator of EPA, William D. Ruckelshaus, faced the complex task of bringing together these diverse units into a single functioning enterprise, implementing the new environmental mandates that were streaming out of Congress, and establishing the credibility of his new agency with a range of external stakeholders. By his account, Ruckelshaus' goal in that moment of origin was "to demonstrate that the government was capable of being responsive to [the public's] expressed concerns; namely that we would do something about the environment. Therefore it was important for us . . . to actually show that we were willing to take on the large institutions in society which hadn't been paying much attention to the environment."[35]

The implementation challenges posed by the new Clean Water Act when it came across Ruckelshaus' desk in 1972 were formidable: defining the basic terms of the act, such as the jurisdictional scope of "navigable waters"; crafting technology-based effluent limitations for each category and class of industrial discharger; creating an NPDES permit system; working with the Corps of Engineers to establish the separate program under Section 404 for discharges of dredged and fill material; managing an expanded public works program for POTWs; and deploying the act's new enforcement tools—just to name a few. These challenges were not EPA's alone; they were shared with the White House, other federal agencies, states and tribes, citizen groups and regulated entities, and the federal courts. As the stories of implementation that follow will show, progress under the act, or lack thereof, has been a product of the actions of all these parties.

NPDES Permits and Technology-Based Effluent Limitations

EPA faced two monumental tasks under its new CWA authorities: issuing permits to dischargers that incorporated the act's pollution reduction requirements, and defining effluent limits for the technology levels specified in the act. EPA and the states were given two years to issue NPDES permits, after which time dischargers without permits could be held in violation of the act.[36] The act gave EPA even less time—one year—to adopt guidelines that implemented the technology-based requirements. Robert Percival and his colleagues vividly capture EPA's predicament:

> By mid-1974 EPA had received 65,000 applications [for NPDES permits], but only 15 states had taken over responsibility for permit issuance. It soon became apparent that EPA would have to write more than 50,000 permits and define the range of technologically possible effluent limits for dozens of different industries, an enormous technical and administrative burden.[37]

Managing the Permit Burden

One early strategy by EPA was to reduce the number of dischargers subject to NPDES permitting. The CWA's Section 301 prohibits "the discharge of any pollutant" without a permit under Section 402 or 404 or in violation of other requirements.[38] A "discharge of a pollutant" means "any addition of a pollutant to navigable waters from a point source."[39] And point source is "any discernible, confined and discrete conveyance, including . . . any pipe, ditch, . . . conduit, well, [or] discrete fissure, . . . from which pollutants are or may be discharged."[40] EPA believed that a literal interpretation of point source would sweep hundreds of thousands of sources into the NPDES net. For example, the agency estimated there were over three hundred thousand silvicultural point sources and another one hundred thousand municipal storm sewers that channeled stormwater runoff into the navigable waters. Concluding that these numbers would overwhelm its capacity to process applications and also doubting its ability to write effluent limitations for stormwater, EPA exempted these and similar sources from the NPDES permit requirement.

These permit exemptions were overturned by the US Court of Appeals for the DC Circuit in *NRDC v. Costle*.[41] It was "Congress' clear mandate that all point sources have permits," the court ruled, and EPA had interpretative options consistent with that mandate to shape a workable program. First, if numerical effluent limitations were unfeasible, EPA could issue permits with other conditions to achieve acceptable levels. Second, EPA could reduce its administrative burden by issuing general permits to classes of point source dischargers defined by a geographic area or type of discharge.

EPA and the states used the general permit authority recognized by the court to streamline their NPDES programs. In the 1987 amendments to the act, Congress also helped reduce the number of permits by exempting "agricultural stormwater discharges and return flows from irrigated agriculture."[42] Still, EPA estimates have put the number of NPDES permits issued as high as five hundred thousand, including for industrial and municipal stormwater discharges identified in the 1987 amendments.[43] And the act requires the permits to be renewed every five years. Given these high numbers, limited state and federal resources, and the complexity of writing permits for major sources, the program has faced a nagging backlog of expired permits.[44] The agency addressed the backlog as a "material weakness" from 1998-2002 and reduced the percentage of expired NPDES permits. In 2003, EPA's Office of Inspector General found that the backlog for major permits was still close to twenty percent but down from earlier years.[45] Despite these challenges, the regulatory benefits of the CWA's permit programs led Congress to add Title V to the Clean Air Amendments of 1990, requiring comparable permits for all major stationary sources of air emissions.

Technology-Based Effluent Limitations

Mind-numbingly complex, the CWA's alphabet soup of technology-based requirements sought to cover the whole range of industrial and municipal dischargers. In 1972, EPA faced two threshold questions in applying these requirements. First, it was not clear from the statute what form the agency's implementation should take. Section 304 of the act ordered EPA to write "guidelines for effluent limitations" (within one year of enactment); Section 301 required compliance with "effluent limitations" in regulations "issued by the administrator" or "as defined by the administrator." Was EPA required to issue "guidelines" separate from "regulations"? Were its regulations meant to be binding on permit writers, producing uniform limitations on all dischargers in each category? Second was the closely related question of whether and how NPDES permits should incorporate technology-based effluent limitations before national guidelines or regulations for the relevant source category had been adopted. Read literally, the statute required all NPDES permittees to comply with the technology-based levels of treatment on the schedule outlined in the statute, but what was the authority of permit writers to interpret those levels on a case-by-case basis?[46] Industry advocates argued "that effluent limits should be determined in individual permit proceedings and that issuance of the guidelines was a prerequisite to issuance of individual permits."[47]

EPA's answers to these questions reflected the enormity of the tasks it faced. National effluent limitations (in whatever form) could not be established in the time necessary to issue NPDES permits and indeed would take long past the one-year statutory deadline to develop. To manage the delay, EPA authorized state and federal permit writers to interpret the act's technology-based requirements on a case-by-case basis. In *NRDC v. Train*, the DC Circuit upheld that approach, making way for determinations based on the permit writer's best professional judgment.[48] But with so many federal and state permit writers exercising broad discretion, the results were grossly uneven. As one EPA official put it, "You get some real good permits, and you get some trash," describing permits written so loosely as to allow sources "never to have to worry about [their] permit limits."[49]

To speed implementation, EPA telescoped the process of setting national effluent limitations by issuing "effluent limitations guidelines" as regulations without first issuing separate guidelines and by making those regulations binding on permit writers. In *DuPont v. Train*, the Supreme Court sanctioned this approach. Noting that the "deadlines imposed upon the Administrator were too ambitious for him to meet," the Court upheld the agency's resort to a procedure that "is somewhat different from that apparently contemplated by the statute."[50]

The agency issued permits and proceeded with its massive effluent limitations guidelines enterprise. Oliver Hauk celebrates the latter as:

> . . . the most Herculean task ever imposed on an environmental agency. EPA had literally to manage the economics, engineering, and technology of every industrial process in the most industrialized and fastest growing economy in world history. It had to learn state-of-the- art and potential alternative technologies for each process. It had to be able to defend its technology-forcing conclusions against the most experienced engineers, economists, and lawyers money could buy.[51]

As of 2019, EPA had issued effluent guidelines for almost sixty industrial categories, the most recent for airport deicing in 2012.[52] The agency had also issued revisions of its original guidelines for the great majority of these industries.[53] The guidelines process, as it turns out, is an unending work in progress.

Flannery Decree

In addition to the CWA's technology-based limitations, Section 307 of the 1972 amendments provided for risk-based effluent standards for toxic pollutants. In contrast to the technology-based approach, these effluent standards took environmental risk into account: they were to be set at levels that protected potentially affected organisms with an "ample margin of safety."[54] Also, unlike Section 301 and 304, Section 307 seemed to preclude consideration of economic impacts and technological feasibility. EPA struggled to implement it. The toxicity science was uncertain and the "prospects of requiring a technology that did not exist, or forcing an entire industry . . . to close was unthinkable."[55]

When EPA failed to execute, environmental groups took it to court in *NRDC v. Train* (see above). Lengthy negotiations among the government, environmental groups, and industry led to a settlement entered by the court and popularly known as the Flannery Decree after the district judge who signed it.[56] For its part, EPA agreed to evaluate sixty-five classes of toxins for inclusion in BAT guidelines for twenty-one industrial categories, effectively shifting the regulation of toxic pollutants from a risk-based to a technology-based regime. EPA also agreed to develop criteria for toxic pollutants in reviewing and enforcing water quality standards.

Amendments to the Clean Water Act in 1977 incorporated the Flannery Decree. Although Congress retained the risk-based standards as an option for EPA, they have not been used since 1976.[57]

Water Quality Standards

Demoted from their central role in pre-1972 legislation, water quality standards took up much less of the agency's attention and resources under the CWA than the new technology-based regime. Unlike the promulgation of effluent limitations guidelines, for which the agency bore the full burden, the states had primary responsibility for producing water quality standards, and EPA sat in a review role. Also, because of the act's emphasis on technology-based limitations as the frontline regulatory tool, there was less attention to water-quality-based limitations in NPDES permits. This was so despite Section 301's mandate that existing discharger's meet "any more stringent limitation . . . necessary to meet water quality standards" by the same date—July 1, 1977—as BPT limitations.[58] As the CWA has matured, however, and water quality problems remain, water quality standards and limitations based on them have taken on new importance.

Setting and Reviewing Water Quality Standards

EPA adopted regulations for setting and reviewing water quality standards in 1975 and made modest revisions to them in 1983. Under these rules, "water quality standards should, wherever attainable, provide water quality for the protection and propagation of fish, shellfish and wildlife and for recreation in and on the water."[59] This fishable/swimmable standard derives from the act's Section 101(a)(2) goals. The policy signaled the agency's strong commitment to restoring and protecting the ecological integrity of aquatic ecosystems. As Robert Adler has recounted, for congressional proponents of the act in 1972, "integrity" connoted an ideal of stability and consistency over time.[60] The regulations amplified this signal by incorporating an antidegradation policy which required states to maintain existing uses of its waters and also to maintain existing water quality—even where it exceeded fishable/swimmable standards—unless lowering water quality "is necessary to accommodate important economic or social development in the area."[61]

The regulations identify two components of water quality standards: criteria and use. The designated use or uses for a water body represent the activity set to be protected by the standard: for example, water supply, irrigation, fish and wildlife protection and propagation, and contact recreation. EPA interprets its regulations to require a fishable/swimmable use designation unless a state can demonstrate that this use cannot be attained without "substantial and widespread economic and social impact."[62] Under Administrator Anne Gorsuch, EPA proposed an alternative test, under which the agency would have balanced the costs of achieving Section 101(a)(2) goals against the water quality benefits in determining whether a fishable/swimmable use classification was appropriate—an approach that would have given much greater weight to costs than the existing attainability formula.[63] However, in the final 1983 rule revisions, made after Gorsuch stepped down and William Ruckelshaus returned for his second term as administrator, EPA rejected this approach, citing the "inherent difficulties" in a cost-benefit balancing.[64]

Criteria establish the conditions (e.g., maximum pollutant concentrations) necessary to sustain a designated use. The 1972 Act gave EPA one year to develop and publish criteria for water quality standards reflecting "the latest scientific knowledge" on the effects of pollutants on "health and welfare," including "biological community diversity, productivity, and stability."[65] These federal criteria were offered as guidance to the states as they reviewed and selected the criteria for their water quality standards. A state's designation of uses for each of its waterbodies, and the criteria the state set for each use, together constituted its water quality standards. The criteria were essential to define acceptable levels of water quality for the uses designated and to supply the basis for enforceable limitations on dischargers.

Although EPA's water quality criteria have a presumptive force, and the agency retains the authority to reject divergent state criteria as not meeting the "requirements of the Act," the federal criteria are not legally binding on the states. This was starkly evident in Virginia's and Maryland's 1989 adoption of dioxin criteria for uses that included human consumption (water supply, fish). EPA's criteria guidance set a maximum concentration for this toxic chemcial of .0013 parts per quadrillion; the states set a criterion of 1.2 parts per quadrillion, less stringent than EPA's by almost three orders of magnitude.[66] After EPA reviewed and approved the state standards, environmental groups sued in federal court to overturn them. In *NRDC v. EPA*, the Fourth Circuit Court of Appeals upheld EPA's approval.[67] The court emphasized (repeating twice) that under the CWA states have the "primary responsibility" for establishing appropriate water quality standards.[68] With this as a premise, it defended the deference that EPA had given the state standards against NRDC's claim that EPA "should have exerted a more dominant role in the review process."[69] Rejecting a series of scientific and technical objections to the states' dioxin criteria, the court concluded that EPA's decision was rationally supported and in accordance with the CWA.[70]

Implementation Challenges

The nation saw steady improvement in water quality in the first decades of the CWA's technology-focused regime. As experience under the act matured, however, there was a growing sense that technology-based limitations were reaching the limits of their effectiveness. A significant portion of the nation's waters were still not meeting water quality standards or the act's goals. Dissolved oxygen deficits—an important measure of "fishability" —had decreased almost every year through 1990 but leveled out after that.[71] Toxic hotspots continued to plague stretches of rivers and bays notwithstanding the new BAT requirements that flowed from the Flannery Decree. Reacting to what they viewed as weak implementation by EPA and the states of the act's failsafe mechanism, environmentalists pushed for stricter water quality standards and for more aggressive application of those standards.

In the Flannery Decree, EPA had agreed to develop water quality criteria for the toxic "priority pollutants" for incorporation into state water quality standards and ultimately into permit terms for individual dischargers. That requirement of the decree restated, with specific respect to toxics, an obligation that EPA and the states already had under the act. But as Oliver Houck observes, it "had as little effect after the *NRDC v. Train* settlement as before."[72] In the 1987 amendments, Congress took steps to sharpen the effectiveness of water quality standards to address toxic pollution. To facilitate translation of water quality standards into enforceable limitations, it required states to adopt "numerical criteria" for toxic pollutants in lieu of unquantified narrative criteria (e.g., "no toxic pollutants in toxic amounts").[73] It also required states to list waters that could not be expected to meet water quality standards after the application of technology-based standards due to toxic pollutants; to identify the dischargers responsible; and to set more stringent permit limitations for these dischargers to meet the standards.[74] EPA and states targeted 879 dischargers for action under these provisions.[75]

A more comprehensive tool for addressing water quality problems, however, turned out to have been waiting to be discovered in the act since 1972. That tool was the Total Maximum Daily Load (TMDL) provision—as Robert Percival has dubbed it, "the true 'sleeping giant' of the Clean Water Act."[76] Section 303 of the act requires states to identify their "impaired waters" —waters failing to meet water quality standards after application of technology-based requirements to point source dischargers—and prepare TMDLs for each of those impaired waters. The TMDL establishes the total amount of a pollutant that can be discharged into an impaired water body by all sources consistent with achieving and maintaining water quality standards. This translation of water quality standards into loadings for particular water bodies is a crucial step in computing the limitations on sources necessary to achieve the desired ambient conditions.

Under EPA regulations, that total loading is apportioned between point sources ("waste load allocation") and non-point sources ("load allocation").[77] The waste load allocation becomes the basis for more stringent effluent limitations in NPDES permits for point sources. The load allocation provides a means of addressing non-point sources, which are not directly regulated under the CWA, as discussed in the next section.

EPA and the states were not brought willingly at first into a robust embrace of TMDLs. Section 303(d) puts the burden of compliance with its requirements on the states. The states are to submit their lists of impaired waters and their TMDLs to EPA for approval; if the EPA disapproves, it "shall" impose its own list or TMDL. The statute, by its terms, gives EPA no authority to compel the state to submit a TMDL.

Until an onslaught of lawsuits by environmentalists beginning in the 1980s, state compliance with these provisions was desultory at best: some states had submitted no TMDLs in over a decade and others only a few, despite lengthy lists of impaired waters. EPA did not view itself as having a mandatory duty to act in the face of state inaction. But courts in bellwether cases agreed that state inaction over long periods amounts to a "constructive submission" of no TMDLs, triggering the agency's obligation to promulgate its own.[78] Facing the prospect of cascading adverse court rulings, EPA agreed to consent orders to promulgate TMDLs in dozens of states.[79] This forced march generated concern within EPA that hastily prepared TMDLs would lack the quality to make them effective, but the TMDL litigation greatly accelerated the shift of EPA resources and management focus to the challenges and potential of water quality standards, with lasting effects on the agency's clean water program.

Non-Point Source Pollution

The CWA's regulatory focus on point source discharges has led to mixed results for the quality of the nation's waters. On one hand, under universal technology-based standards, point sources have substantially cut their pollutant loadings, and they have made even further reductions toward meeting water quality standards. On the other, Congress' choice not to regulate non-point source pollution may have put the act's fishable-swimmable goal out of reach. Uncontrolled non-point source pollution is by far the largest contributor to the nation's continuing water quality deficits.

The legislative record of the Clean Air Act Amendments of 1972 shows Congress understood that unchecked non-point source pollution would prevent achieving water quality standards in many cases.[80] There are several explanations for the act's exclusion of non-point sources from regulation notwithstanding this understanding. First, Congress believed that diffuse runoff would be difficult to monitor and control.[81] Second, Congress may also have believed that regulation of non-point source discharges—particularly surface flows across farms or forestlands—would intrude on the states' customary prerogatives in land use control. Mandated non-point source management practices, such as vegetative cover or terracing, look more like land use controls than the pollution control technologies typically applied to point sources.[82] Finally, the political clout of the farm and timber lobbies, which have strongly resisted environmental regulation, particularly by federal authorities, may have been a factor in the exclusion.

While not regulating non-point sources, the act does not ignore them. An "areawide waste treatment management planning process" provided for in Section 208 requires identification of "agriculturally and silviculturally related nonpoint sources of pollution" and methods to control them.[83] Section 304(f) of the act requires EPA to develop guidelines for evaluating "nonpoint sources of pollutants" and information for controlling them.[84] More consequentially, Section 319 requires states to submit to EPA reports and programs describing and implementing best management practices and other measures for controlling nonpoint source pollution. The act authorizes federal grants to the states to help carry out their non-point source programs as approved by EPA. State non-point source programs under 319 may include regulation of non-point sources, but regulatory approaches are not required. In 2011, a national evaluation of the Section 319 program by EPA found that only a few states used "broad-based regulatory authorities" to address non-point sources. Other states used regulatory approaches limited to discrete segments of non-point sources, such as concentrated animal feeding operations, or nonregulatory techniques, such as promoting "broad use of nutrient management."[85]

EPA's 2011 national assessment reconfirmed the crucial role of non-point sources in the nation's failure to reach the CWA's goals. The assessment concluded that non-point source pollution was the principal cause of failure to meet water quality standards in more than thirty thousand impaired waterbodies in the US—the great majority of all impaired waters.[86] Over the previous six years, state efforts under Section 319 had been successful in bringing 354 impaired waterbodies into compliance with water quality standards. As the agency wrote candidly, however, "the successful remediation of 354 waterbodies during the past 6 years has only addressed less than 1% of all primarily NPS-impaired waters. This indicates that at the current pace of waterbody remediation, it will take about 700 years to achieve full restoration of currently impaired waterbodies."[87]

Total Maximum Daily Loads (TMDLs) give additional leverage for addressing non-point sources. Courts have held that this requirement extends to water bodies whose quality is affected only by non-point sources as well as in whole or part by point sources. The load allocation does not impose a federal regulatory requirement on non-point sources or require an enforceable implementation plan for achieving the allocation. In 2000, in the waning days of the Clinton administration, EPA adopted revisions to its TMDL regulations to require states to provide "reasonable assurance" that TMDL load allocations would be met.[88] But Congress withheld funds to implement the regulations, and the George W. Bush administration later withdrew them.[89] Nevertheless, the load allocation serves an important purpose by quantifying the ceiling for non-point source pollution to be met through best management practices or other state measures.

EPA's 2003 Water Quality Trading Policy sought to facilitate trading to reduce compliance costs for point source dischargers and incentivize reductions in non-point source pollution.[90] The policy recognizes water quality trades between point sources and non-point sources as well as between point sources. Point and non-point sources create water quality credits by reducing pollution below a "baseline" level. For point sources the baseline under the 2003 policy is the discharge permitted by technology-based limitations: they may trade only to offset more stringent requirements imposed to meet water quality standards. For non-point sources, baseline is historical discharge levels adjusted for any BMPs that would apply in the absence of trading.[91] Because non-point source reductions are typically cheaper than the costs to point sources of treating beyond technology-based requirements, purchases of credits from non-point sources can be attractive to point sources. Such trades can offer incentives for further reductions by non-point sources and a more cost-effective compliance option to point sources, while achieving water quality objectives.

But trading has been limited. Commentators have offered a host of reasons for the disappointing lack of growth in water quality markets generally and non-point source trading in particular. Problems include the relatively small geographical scope of most water quality trading areas. Trading regimes benefit from a large number of potential buyers and sellers and low transaction costs. For water quality markets, the potential market may be confined to a single water body or a discrete portion of that water body affected by an impairment. The small scope can reduce the number of traders and increase transaction costs, undercutting market efficiency and effectiveness.[92] Other problems have included uncertainty about the number and reliability of credits generated by non-point source control measures and concerns among farmers and other non-regulated dischargers that participating in a credit trading system is a step toward mandatory controls.[93]

In February 2019, David Ross, EPA assistant administrator for water in the Trump administration, attempted to breathe new life into water quality trading by increasing flexibility and reliance-adaptive management.[94] His memorandum "updating" the 2003 policy sought "to accelerate the adoption of market-based programs." To that end, it encouraged parties to implement trading at larger geographic scales; to permit trading in the face of uncertainties about the effectiveness and performance of non-point strategies, using adaptive management to make "refinement[s] over time without sacrificing regulatory certainty for existing market participants"; and to simplify (and relax) baseline requirements and allow credits to be banked for future use.[95] While not withdrawing the 2003 guidance, the Ross memo made clear the current EPA's willingness to take increased regulatory risks in order to create a more hospitable environment for trading.

Major Watersheds

Much of the public concern about the health of the nation's waters coalesces around major national watersheds, such as the Mississippi River-Gulf of Mexico system, the Great Lakes, and the Chesapeake Bay. The threats to these iconic interstate systems come from a range of sources: industries and POTWs, municipal storm sewers, animal feedlots, and non-point source agricultural run-off. As with the nation's waters generally, however, non-point source pollution has proved the most persistent threat to these waters.

Nutrient runoff into the Mississippi River causes the occurrence annually of a "dead zone" in the upper Gulf of Mexico—a large area of low dissolved oxygen that can kill marine life and threatens "to inexorably change the biology of the region."[96] In 2017, scientists determined this dead zone occupied 8,776 square miles, roughly the size of New Jersey—"the largest measured since dead zone mapping began there in 1985."[97] The Chesapeake Bay has experienced similar dead zones from similar causes. These dead zones and other chronic effects of non-point source pollution on major aquatic systems have attracted national concern, but solutions are still very much works-in-progress.

Unlike the Clean Air Act, the CWA does not have a well-developed structure for addressing interstate water pollution.[98] It was not clear in the early days of the act, for example, that downstream states could protect themselves from violations of their water quality standards caused by discharges from upstream states. That issue was resolved by the Supreme Court in *Arkansas v. Oklahoma*, which upheld EPA's authority to require compliance by upstream sources with downstream state's water quality standards.[99] Despite this ruling, water quality management in interstate watersheds heavily affected by nutrient runoff has proved challenging, due not only to the unregulated status of non-point source contributors, but also to the diversity of interests and goals among the states sharing the watershed. For decades commentators have encouraged "watershed" approaches in implementing the CWA, emphasizing ecological integrity, adaptive responses, and systemic thinking within the natural unit of the watershed. But the art of watershed management remains elusive.[100]

Congress and EPA have sponsored a number of geographically targeted programs to restore and protect large watersheds. These efforts take a variety of approaches, from a relatively informal, largely bottom-up effort in the Mississippi River-Gulf of Mexico watershed to a more elaborately institutionalized and centralized arrangement in the Great Lakes, which operates under a formal interstate compact adopted with the consent of Congress and an international agreement with Canada.[101] The Chesapeake Bay initiative occupies a middle ground between these models but recently, with the assent of the basin states, has come to rely more on centralized direction and oversight.[102] On a smaller scale, EPA's National Estuary Program applies a place-based approach to twenty-eight estuaries "of national significance" and their watersheds.[103]

A brief account of the Chesapeake Bay Program illustrates both the promise and perils of large watershed management under the CWA and state authorities. The Chesapeake Bay is the largest estuary in the United States.[104] Its drainage is shallow and large, covering about sixty-four thousand square miles in six states—Maryland, Virginia, Pennsylvania, New York, West Virginia, and Delaware—and in the District of Columbia. Parts of it are heavily urbanized; other portions are in farms and forestland. About eighteen million people live in the watershed of the bay.[105] Running through Pennsylvania, the Susquehanna River provides about half of the flow of freshwater to the bay. The shore of the bay proper is divided between Maryland (upper) and Virginia (lower).

The primary cause of the bay's water quality problems is nutrient and sediment pollution entering from the bay's tributaries—most of it from non-point sources, although sewage treatment plants and industrial dischargers also contribute.[106] A 1983 EPA study documented the role of excessive nutrient loadings in the bay's decline. Upon completion of that study, EPA, Virginia, Maryland, Pennsylvania, and the District entered into a landmark agreement to reduce the nutrient loadings and restore the bay.

Federal funds sponsored scientific research including modeling of the sources and effects of nutrients on the bay's water quality. A Chesapeake Bay Program Office coordinated efforts among the states and other stakeholders. Committees of experts and citizens provided broad input into the workings of the program. The parties attempted to adapt as they received new information about the state of the bay and the success of their restoration efforts. The original 1983 agreement among EPA and the bay states was amended in 1987, 1992, and 2000 with increasing specification of goals and strategies for progress.

Despite the sophistication and high political salience of this cooperative effort, the water quality of the bay declined. While publicly committed to cleaning up the bay, the states faced the collective action problems that threaten any effort to protect a common resource from overuse: in this case, excessive pollution. States might be tempted to free ride, for example, seeking to shift burdens of reducing nutrients onto other states while hoping still to enjoy the benefit of a cleaner bay. Divergent interests among the bay states also meant that some states had a smaller stake in the bay's restoration than others. For example, those with expansive stretches of shoreline on the bay—Maryland and Virginia—would benefit directly from water quality improvements in a way Pennsylvania would not. Although it is a major contributor of pollutant loadings to the bay via the Susquehanna River, Pennsylvania has no shoreline on the bay and, therefore, would have less to gain for its citizens from nutrient reductions.

As a federal regulatory agency whose jurisdiction encompassed all the waters of the bay and its tributaries, EPA would be the obvious candidate among the parties to the cleanup agreement to impose the collective discipline necessary to achieve the mutually agreed upon goals. But out of deference to the initiative taken by the states and perhaps also sensitive to the limits of its authority to deal with non-point sources of nutrient pollution, EPA kept a modest profile for decades, acting primarily as convener and facilitator of state-led efforts. In 2000, however, EPA took on a more assertive role with the issuance of a bay-wide TMDL.

The bay-wide TMDL was to give structure and accountability to the restoration effort that the parties had come to believe was essential for success. It was keyed to dissolved oxygen criteria that EPA identified as necessary to protect the bay's "important species and biological communities"; the bay states incorporated these criteria into their water quality standards.[107] Acting on commitments in the 2000 amendments to the Chesapeake Bay Agreement, states submitted initial Watershed Improvement Plans (WIPs) containing pollution targets and "reasonable assurances" that the targets would be met, and they agreed to strengthen the WIPS in later submittals.[108] EPA used the state-submitted WIPS to fashion a comprehensive TMDL for nitrogen, phosphorous, and sediment—the "largest, most spatially explicit TMDL ever developed."[109]

Covering the bay and its tributaries, the TMDL combined ninety-two separate sub-basin TMDLs. Although the state-submitted WIPs were not "an approvable part" of the TMDL, the agency stated its intent to use them as part of an "accountability framework" to ensure the TMDL's implementation.[110] It made clear that a state's failure to carry out a WIP could subject its point source dischargers to more stringent standards to compensate for the shortfall, thereby maintaining pressure on the states to meet the reductions promised by the WIPs, including reductions by non-point sources.[111] The bay TMDL expressly authorized pollution offsets and water quality trading among point and non-point sources.

The Farm Bureau and other associations of farmers and builders took EPA to court over the TMDL. On review by the Third Circuit Court of Appeals, twenty states *outside* the bay watershed joined in an amicus brief questioning EPA's authority to integrate the WIPs with its TMDL. The bay states, along with environmental groups and an assortment of municipal and other interests, supported EPA's rule. The Third Circuit Court of Appeals upheld the TMDL as within EPA's CWA authority.[112]

The restoration of fishable-swimmable water quality in the bay is far from complete. Monitoring indicates, however, that the health of the bay is at last trending in a positive direction.[113] This turnaround suggests that the recent institutional adjustments have brought us closer to the right mix of bottom-up and top-down approaches and accountable decision-making necessary for success, but uncertainties over robust federal support and Pennsylvania's commitment persist.[114]

Wetlands and Section 404

Complementing NPDES permits issued under Section 402 for the broad range of point source discharges, Section 404 of the act reserves a second type of permit specifically for discharges of dredged or fill material. These permits are issued by the US Army Corps of Engineers, not by EPA, although EPA, "in conjunction with" the Corps, developed the Section 404(b)(1) guidelines for review of permit applications. EPA may veto a Corps-issued Section 404 permit that it concludes does not meet the requirements of the act.

The Section 402 and 404 permitting regimes are mutually exclusive: a discharge covered by a 404 permit does not require a 402 permit and vice versa.[115] But uncertainty over exactly where the line between the two programs should be drawn has demanded attention by the agencies and the courts. Section 404 is associated with protection of wetlands, but it covers discharges of dredged and fill materials into *all* "waters of the US," open waters as well as wetlands. Also, because it is limited to control of "discharges," it does not protect wetlands from other sources of degradation, such as channelization, that do not involve discharges, as discussed further below.

The requirements for Section 404 permits differ from those for Section 402 permits. National technology-based effluent limitations are not required for 404 discharges. Instead, under the Section 404(b)(1) guidelines, the Corps subjects individual permit applications to a localized, case-specific examination of the necessity for the project and its environmental effects. (For categories of projects having minimal impacts, the Corps may issue general or national permits that set the conditions under which those projects may go forward.)[116]

The premise of the guidelines is that no Section 404 permit should be issued if there is "a practicable alternative to the proposed discharge which would have less adverse impact on the aquatic ecosystem, so long as the alternative does not have other significant adverse environmental consequences."[117] Although this creates a seemingly high bar for projects that do not require access to the water, permit applicants can often define the purpose of their projects to qualify them as "water-dependent."[118] The guidelines also do not allow permits for discharges that will violate water quality standards or significantly degrade the waters of the US.[119] Despite these apparently demanding requirements, the overwhelming majority of Section 404 permit applications are granted.[120]

The Section 404(b)(1) guidelines require permittees to take practicable steps to minimize their environmental impacts and to mitigate impacts that cannot be eliminated.[121] The mitigation requirement offers hope that the amount and functionality of a watershed's aquatic habitat can be maintained despite discharges permitted under Section 404. But that hope is qualified by concerns that replacement habitats may fail or fall short of fully replicating the functions of the disturbed habitat.[122] The guidelines address the risk of project failure by requiring, for example, that mitigation be undertaken before or during the permitted activity, rather than after, and that financial assurances be provided to ensure that the "mitigation project will be successfully completed."[123] To help guarantee equivalent functionality, the rules direct that mitigation should "be located within the same watershed as the impact site, and . . . where it is most likely to successfully replace lost functions and services."[124]

Like Section 402, the scope of Section 404 depends on the definition of "waters of the United States." It also depends on the definition of "dredged or fill material"—to the discharge of which Section 404 uniquely applies. In the absence of statutory definitions, agency regulations separately define "dredged material" as "material that is excavated or dredged from waters of the United States" and "fill material" as "material placed in the waters of the United States" that has the effect of replacing any of those waters with dry land or "changing the bottom elevation" of any of those waters.[125] A prior version of the "fill material" definition required that the material be placed in waters with the *intent* of changing the bottom elevation. By removing the "intent" requirement, regulators enabled the application of Section 404 to extractive industries, such as mountaintop mining, that would otherwise be subject to potentially more demanding requirements under Section 402.

The consequences of the division between Sections 402 and 404 were striking in the Supreme Court's decision in *Coeur Alaska v. Southeast Alaska Corp.*[126] In that case, the Corps of Engineers successfully defended the permitting of a gold mining operation under Section 404 rather than 402. The operation included the processing of the crushed ore in tanks of frothing water ("froth flotation process"). The mine owner, Coeur Alaska, proposed to dispose of the waste from this process—a mixture of water and crushed rock—by piping it to Lower Slate Lake, a natural, forested lake that all parties agreed met the definition of "waters of the United States." Disposal of the process waste in the lake would destroy existing fish populations, double the lake's surface area, reduce its depth from fifty-one feet (maximum) to one foot, and require extensive damning to contain the lake within its wider, shallower configuration. New Source Performance Standards (NSPS) promulgated by EPA for froth flotation operations would have precluded any discharge of process wastewater into the lake. Because the NSPS only applied to discharges subject to Section 402, however, the Court sanctioned disposal in Lower Slate Lake as approved in the Corps' Section 404 permit.

EPA does not exercise its Section 404 veto authority often. In most cases, any differences with the Corps over permits are worked out in informal negotiations. In several high visibility cases, however, these differences have spilled over into a formal veto. One of these involved a mammoth mountaintop coal mining venture in the Cumberland Plateau of West Virginia. Mingo Logan Coal's Spruce No. 1 project was one of the largest mountaintop mines in a state noted for them.[127] Decapitating ridgetops to get at the underlying coal, Spruce No. 1 would have deposited the overburden in six valley fills along Song Camp Creek, Pigeonroost Branch, and Oldhouse Creek, all tributaries of the Coal River. The project would have disturbed 2,278 acres of land (mostly in forest) and filled 7.48 miles of streams. Studies documented impacts on macroinvertebrates, salamanders, fish, and water birds. The Corps granted a Section 404 permit notwithstanding these residual impacts.

Four years after initially acquiescing in the Corps' action (and after a change in administrations from George W. Bush to Barack Obama), EPA did an about-face and issued a veto, withdrawing about eighty-eight percent of the stream area that the Corps had permitted for disposal sites. Reasons for the withdrawal were unacceptable impacts on wildlife and habitat resulting from "the direct burial of 6.6 miles of high quality stream habitat" and from water contamination and salinity downstream of the fills.[128] The agency justified its reversal based on new post-permit information. On review, the DC Circuit upheld the veto as "the product of reasoned decision-making supported by evidence in the record and based upon the EPA's technical expertise."[129]

Although Section 404 is commonly identified with wetlands protection, it does not offer a comprehensive wetlands program due to limitations on its scope. As discussed later in this chapter, only some wetlands are covered as "waters of the United States." That leaves many wetlands, including many of significant ecological value, without protection under Section 404. In addition, even in jurisdictional wetlands, not all land clearing, ditching, draining, or excavation is subject to regulation—only activities that result in the "addition" of dredged or fill material to the waters.[130] As a consequence, activities destructive of wetlands are not regulable under the act, to the extent that any redeposit of material excavated from the wetland qualifies as "incidental fallback." More generally, nothing in the CWA protects wetlands against other threats: for example, changes in flooding patterns or temperature regimes due to climate change.

Section 404 is among the most controversial of the CWA's programs. The statute and the regulations provide a host of exemptions from Section 404 permits for common agricultural and forestal activities and even for some construction and mining activities. National permits provide ready-made coverage for some construction, mining, and other development activities. Yet the requirements of Section 404 reach potentially into sensitive areas of private property rights and local land use practices. It should be no surprise that key judicial cases testing the scope of the Clean Water Act and the procedural protections available to citizens subject to it have arisen from the application of Section 404 to local wetlands.[131] As long as the rules of application remain unsettled, we can expect the roil of disputes under this crucial section of the act to continue.

Waters of the United States: The Jurisdictional Linchpin

"Waters of the United States, including the territorial seas" was the new definition of "navigable waters" that came in 1972 to define the CWA's scope. "Navigable waters" had been installed as the jurisdictional linchpin in early drafts of the 1972 amendments. On the eve of the enactment of the amendments, however, the legislative staffers removed the qualifier "navigable" from the definition of that term, leaving "navigable waters" defined more broadly as "waters of the United States," and the new definition survived in the text enacted by Congress. This change was instigated by three congressional staffers—Tom Jorling, Leon Billings, and Lester Edelman—who concluded that the traditional definition would not give federal agencies the jurisdictional latitude to protect the integrity of the nation's aquatic systems, as the legislation proposed. As Jorling would put it later, they wanted to make the regulatory program match the hydrologic cycle.[132]

Whatever the drafters' intent, the new definition required further elaboration to serve as a workable guide for implementation. Prior to 2015, the official definition in regulations of both the Corps and EPA included not only traditionally navigable waters and all interstate waters, but also "all other waters," including intermittent streams and wetlands, "the use, degradation or destruction" of which "could affect interstate or foreign commerce" and wetlands "adjacent to" other jurisdictional waters.[133] While in effect for decades, this definition was qualified in its application by a remarkable series of Supreme Court decisions; the Corps and EPA gamely tailored their interpretations of their regulations to accommodate these decisions. In response to the last of them, however, the Obama administration undertook a comprehensive revision, issued jointly by the Corps and EPA in June 2015. During the Trump administration, the same agencies undertook first to rescind the Obama-era rule, returning the jurisdictional playing field to the *status quo ante*, and then to replace that rule with a much more constrained version of agency jurisdiction, as described more fully below.

The Supreme Court's Close Encounters with "Waters" and Consequences Thereof

In a series of three Supreme Court decisions and regulatory responses thereto, the judicial and executive branches have groped toward a functional and judicially acceptable definition of "waters of the United States."[134] This has occurred against a backdrop of federalism concerns, in which the permissible scope of federal authority is measured against the residual powers of states to determine their environmental policies and the limits of federal power under the Commerce Clause. Because they rest on the constitutional footing of the Commerce Clause, the CWA's regulatory provisions cannot exceed these limits. Although the Supreme Court has never directly addressed the act's consistency with the Commerce Clause, concerns that the scope of its application may be pressing the bounds of the commerce power have colored its interpretations of "waters of the United States."

The first of the "waters of the US" triad was *United States v. Riverside Bayview Homes*, decided in 1985.[135] In that case, the Army Corps of Engineers asserted Section 404 jurisdiction over wetlands "adjacent" to open waters. The open waters were "navigable" in the traditional sense as waters that "are currently used, or were used in the past, or may be susceptible to use in interstate or foreign commerce."[136] But the wetlands were certainly not. The question was whether the statute's definition of "navigable waters"—as "waters of the United States"—was broad enough to encompass these connected aquatic environments. Citing the act's objective to protect and restore the "integrity" of the nation's waters, the Court ruled unanimously that it was.

By the time of its next encounter with "waters" in 2001, however, the Court had taken on a half dozen new justices and the "federalism revolution" under Chief Justice William Rehnquist was well underway. In this altered jurisprudential environment, the Court decided *Solid Waste Agency of Northern Cook County (SWANCC) v. US Army Corps of Engineers*, the second of the "waters" triad.[137] The "waters" in *SWANCC* were "a scattering of permanent and seasonal ponds of varying size and depth" located on an old mining site. The Corps claimed jurisdiction over the ponds and denied a Section 404 permit to construct and operate a solid waste disposal facility at the site. The Corps based its jurisdictional claim on its Migratory Bird Rule, an interpretative statement that extended CWA jurisdiction to waters that were or could be used as migratory bird habitat.[138] In a closely divided decision, the Court held that the Migratory Bird Rule was in excess of the Corps' authority under the act as applied to the ponds, which the Court observed, were "isolated, . . . some only seasonal" and lacked a "significant nexus" to traditionally navigable waters. The Court cited statutory language recognizing the primary responsibilities and rights of states in protecting the integrity of the nation's waters and invoked judicial canons favoring interpretations that protect state prerogatives and avoid constitutional questions (here, the limits of the Commerce Clause).[139]

The final decision in the CWA federalism triad—*Rapanos v. United States*[140]—continued the Court's effort begun in *SWANCC* to cut federal jurisdiction down to size. Having dealt with "isolated waters" in *SWANCC*, the Court turned its attention to two important remaining categories—non-navigable tributaries of traditionally navigable waters and wetlands adjacent to those tributaries. The wetlands in *Rapanos* were on or near ditches, drains, or streams that fed ultimately into traditionally navigable waters. The Corps had claimed jurisdiction over them, and its claims had been upheld by two federal appeals courts.

In rejecting the Corps' claims, a plurality opinion by Justice Antonin Scalia laid down new rules for what could qualify as "the waters" regulable under the act. To be jurisdictional, tributaries had to be physically defined bodies of water with "continuous" (not intermittent or ephemeral) flows. And wetlands had to have a continuous surface connection to a traditionally navigable water or qualifying tributary (not mere proximity). These rulings promised a jurisdictional footprint considerably smaller than had been established under the Corps' and EPA's prior interpretations and applications. As in *SWANCC*, the plurality opinion emphasized the act's nod to "the primary rights and responsibilities of the states" as qualifying the act's "integrity" objective, and deployed the same avoidance and federalism canons to bolster its figure-slimming construction of the act.

Justice Anthony Kennedy wrote a separate opinion agreeing that the cases should be sent back, but offering a rationale for that result that differed from Justice Scalia's. He believed that waters, including adjacent wetlands, could be jurisdictional by having a "significant nexus" to traditional navigable waters. For wetlands this meant "significantly affect[ing] the chemical, physical, and biological integrity of other covered waters more readily understood as navigable."[141] Kennedy's test could extend jurisdiction to wetlands and other waters that would not be included under the plurality's tests. The four remaining justices joined a dissenting opinion by Justice John Paul Stevens, who would have upheld jurisdiction based on existing EPA and Corps' criteria. These divisions among the justices—with only four agreeing with Scalia's rationale for reversal and four others disagreeing with the result—gave Kennedy's lone concurrence status as a separate basis for finding jurisdiction under the act.[142]

The aftermath of *Rapanos* was widespread confusion. The Sixth Circuit Court of Appeals wrote that *Rapanos* "satisfied any 'bafflement' requirement."[143] In 2015 the Obama administration adopted a rule that narrowed the decades old definition of "waters of the United States" in an effort to codify the Court's pronouncements.[144] The rule included six categories of "jurisdictional by rule waters," based on factors from both the plurality and concurring opinions in *Rapanos*. It also included two categories of waters subject to a case-by-case jurisdictional determination based on the "significant nexus" theory.

The 2015 rule was controversial, condemned as "regulatory overreach" by some states and interest groups, but supported by others. In 2017 the Trump administration moved quickly to rescind it—a move that met with mixed reception from the courts in litigation that followed.[145] In September 2019, in an effort to perfect the rescission, the Corps and EPA issued a final rule repealing the 2015 rule and purporting to reinstate the pre-2015 regulations and guidance nation-wide.[146] This rule went into effect on December 23, 2019.

Meanwhile the Trump administration proposed a replacement rule, which substantially cut back on the jurisdictional scope claimed by the 2015 regulation.[147] With some modifications, that proposal became final in January 2020 as the Navigable Waters Protection Rule (NWPR).[148] Favoring Justice Scalia's bright-line definitions in *Rapanos*, the regulation narrowly interprets Justice Kennedy's "significant nexus" standard. For example, under the 2015 rule ephemeral (episodic) streams feeding into other jurisdictional waters, as well as wetlands adjacent to those streams, could qualify as "waters of the US" if they demonstrated a "significant nexus." Under the NWPR, those streams and wetlands do not qualify. The rule also cuts back on numerous other aspects of the 2015 regulation, including coverage of canals, lakes, and ponds.

Citing data limitations, the Corps and EPA refused to estimate the geographical extent of the NWPR's impact. They also refused to compare the NWPR's coverage to that of the 2015 regulation on the theory that that rule had been repealed a month earlier. They did acknowledge that the NWPR "will reduce the scope of waters subject to CWA permitting compared with" the pre-2015 rule and case interpretations but did not say by how much. In its own study, Trout Unlimited found that "six million miles of streams—half the total in the United States" and "[m]ore than 42 million acres of wetlands—again about half the country's total" will lose federal protection under the new rule.[149]

Groundwater

Another CWA issue with federalism connotations arises where discharges from "point sources" reach "waters of the US" through groundwater. As rehearsed earlier, the act regulates "any addition of any pollutant to navigable waters from any point source."[150] "Navigable waters," as waters of the United States, are limited to surface waters. The discharge of pollutants to groundwater would not itself be regulable, even if effected through a "point source." A question arises, however, when pollutants discharged into groundwater find their way into nearby surface waters. And as with the definition of "waters of the US," the question has immediate implications for the balance of authority between EPA and the states, although on a much smaller scale.

In a variety of rulemakings over more than two decades, EPA's position on this question was that although the CWA's permitting requirements did not generally cover discharges to groundwater, they did extend to discharges that reached "jurisdictional surface waters via groundwater or other subsurface flow that has a direct hydrological connection" to the surface waters.[151] Because pollutants reaching surface waters through a direct subsurface hydrological connection could have the same or similar water quality impacts as if they had been discharged directly into the surface waters, the agency believed regulation was important to advance the act's goals. That position changed, however, in 2019 when the Trump EPA issued a new interpretation excluding "all releases of pollutants from a point source to groundwater . . . , regardless of a hydrologic connection between the groundwater and jurisdictional surface water" from NPDES program coverage.[152] Initial contact with subsurface waters was decisive on the jurisdictional question; a discharge to groundwater could never be a discharge to waters of the United States. The immediate occasion for this change was to allow the administration to shift its position on groundwater discharges in a case before the Supreme Court, as more fully described below. Over forty environmental groups opposed the change, contending that it "undercut bedrock protections for our rivers, lakes, and bays for the benefit of polluting industries."[153]

In the years leading up to the 2019 reinterpretation, lower federal courts split on whether and under what circumstances groundwater discharges come within the scope of the CWA's regulatory authority.[154] The US Sixth Circuit Court of Appeals decided two cases rejecting the theory that pollutants discharged by point sources into groundwater become regulable by reaching surface water through the groundwater. Only point source discharges directly into surface water are covered, it held. In both decisions, the court framed its inquiry as balancing the environmental goals of the act with Congress' concern to preserve "the primary responsibilities of the States" over the control of pollution and "the development and use . . . of land and water resources."[155]

These rulings diverged sharply from decisions by Ninth and Fourth Circuit Courts of Appeals that gave determinative weight to the protective goals of the act over the federalism concerns expressed by the Sixth Circuit. In *Upstate Forever v. Kinder Morgan Energy Partners, L.P.*, the Fourth Circuit held a "direct hydrological connection" between groundwater and surface waters brought pollution from an underground pipeline break within the scope of the act.[156] Similarly, in *Hawai'i Wildlife Fund v. County of Maui*, the Ninth Circuit relied on a hydrological connection theory to uphold CWA jurisdiction over groundwater-facilitated pollution of the Pacific Ocean. In that case, a county sewage treatment plant discharged effluent into an injection well. It was "undeniable" in the court's view that pollutants from the injection well made their way via groundwater flow to the ocean in significant amounts. Based on its further observation that the pollutants from the sewage plant emerged at "discrete points" in the ocean, the court was confident that the requisite jurisdictional nexus was established, leaving to another day "the task of determining when, if ever, the connection between a point source and a navigable water is too tenuous to support liability under the CWA."[157] Consistent with long-settled agency views on this issue, the Justice Department had filed an amicus brief in the case, urging that the Ninth Circuit find CWA jurisdiction over the injection well discharges.[158]

Aggrieved by the Ninth Circuit's decision, the County of Maui sought review by the Supreme Court, which was granted in February 2019 on the question of whether the act "requires a permit when pollutants originate from a point source but are conveyed to navigable waters by a nonpoint source, such as groundwater."[159] Based on the EPA's brand-new interpretive statement, published just a month earlier, the government abandoned the position it had taken in the Ninth Circuit and argued for reversal of that court's finding of CWA jurisdiction. In its ruling in April 2020, the Supreme Court rejected both the Ninth Circuit's interpretation (too broad) and EPA's newly minted gloss (too narrow).[160] Balancing concern for state autonomy against the need to plug a "loophole" that could undercut the CWA's goal of protecting surface waters from direct discharges, the Court offered its own test. Discharges to groundwater that reached jurisdictional waters would be covered if they were "the functional equivalent of a direct discharge." Acknowledging that this general standard left much to be worked out in practice, the Court passed that task to states, EPA, and the lower courts.

Oil and Hazardous Waste Spills

In January 1969, six months before the Cuyahoga River fire, an oil rig a few miles off the California Coast near Santa Barbara suffered a blowout that roiled the ocean with escaping natural gas, spawned a city-sized oil slick, and killed thousands of seabirds.[161] The worst oil spill up to that time, Santa Barbara added fuel to the growing environmental movement and focused specific attention on sudden and unanticipated releases of oil and hazardous substances. These emergency releases were different from predictable events—recurring discharges under Section 402 or planned dredge or fill operations under Section 404—and demanded separate legal treatment. In Section 311 of the 1972 Act, Congress imposed liability on facility owners and operators for spills of oil and hazardous substances.

The liability provisions of Section 311 provided a model for the 1980 Comprehensive Environmental Response Compensation and Liability Act (CERCLA or Superfund), which applied to releases of hazardous substances into the environment. CERCLA expressly exempted petroleum from its coverage. After the disastrous Exxon Valdez spill in 1989, in which an Exxon tanker ruptured on a reef in Alaska's Prince William Sound and emptied almost eleven million gallons of crude oil into the aquatic ecosystem, Congress enacted the Oil Pollution Act of 1990 (OPA), which granted additional authority to EPA and the Coast Guard to prevent and respond to catastrophic oil spills.[162]

Although catastrophic spills are rare and, therefore, do not figure prominently in EPA's routine operations, the agency's response role is critical during high visibility spill events. Occurring just five weeks into his term as EPA administrator, the Exxon Valdez disaster quickly propelled William Reilly—the administration's point person on the disaster—into national prominence, sparking resentment among conservative colleagues in the White House who dubbed him an environmental "rock star."[163] As part of the Obama administration's Unified Command, EPA officials were also prominent in efforts to monitor and clean up the Deepwater Horizon blowout, which in 2010 eclipsed Exxon Valdez as the largest oil spill in US history.[164]

Government Enforcement

The great bulk of CWA enforcement is done by states authorized to administer the act, but EPA enforcement actions provide an important deterrence element. As William Ruckelshaus described the agency's role from the beginning, the federal agency was to be "this 'gorilla in the closet' . . . which could assume control if the state authorities proved too weak or inept to curb local polluters."[165] Not infrequently, the EPA gorilla comes out of the closet. In 2018, EPA conducted over 10,000 inspections and evaluations, initiated and concluded more than 1,800 administrative and civil judicial enforcement cases, and obtained almost $70 million in fines in these cases.[166] The amount of civil fines has been much greater in other years: in 2016, for instance, EPA garnered over $6 billion in fines, reflecting a record settlement with British Petroleum for the Gulf spill. The value of compliance actions resulting from administrative and civil judicial enforcement actions in 2018 was almost $4 billion.[167] Also in 2018, the agency opened over one hundred new criminal cases and obtained sentences amounting to seventy-three years of incarceration.[168]

The primary goal of the agency's enforcement program has been to correct existing violations and deter future ones. Deterrence requires that the agency make it more costly for dischargers to violate than to comply. To achieve this, discounting for the probability that dischargers in some cases will avoid detection and enforcement entirely, the agency presses for fines in civil judicial and administrative actions that are greater than the benefits to the discharger of noncompliance. For example, in settling these cases under the CWA, EPA will seek the economic benefit of noncompliance, to put the discharger on the same footing as it would have been in the absence of its violation, and an additional "gravity component," "'to ensure that the violator is economically worse off than if [he] had obeyed the law.'"[169] The agency calculates the gravity component based on the significance of the violation and the seriousness of the environmental harm, among other factors. It may also take litigation risks and the discharger's ability to pay into account.

These fines are not only designed to deter future violations by the immediate target of enforcement but also by "other members of the regulated community."[170] Typically, on the occasion of settling a large civil judicial enforcement case, EPA and the Department of Justice make a prominent public announcement to remind the regulated community that the EPA enforcement cop is on the beat. The attorney general and the EPA administrator followed this tradition by appearing at a press conference to announce the record settlement with BP for the Gulf oil spill, including over $5 billion in civil fines under the CWA.[171]

EPA has also created incentives to encourage violators to voluntarily undertake environmentally beneficial projects and to install internal audit programs to guard against future violations. Supplemental Environmental Projects (SEPs) are environmental improvements "that have a close nexus to the violations and that a defendant agrees to undertake voluntarily as part of the settlement." EPA can take them into account in reducing its demand for civil penalties. In 2018 the agency agreed to SEPs worth $28 million. In its Audit Policy, EPA offers penalty relief in return for a discharger's voluntary self-reporting and correction of violations detected through the discharger's internal audit or compliance management system.[172] In 2018 the agency notched voluntary disclosures by 532 entities at 1,500 facilities under this policy.

Citizen Suits

Citizen suits have come to play an outsized role in CWA enforcement. Although slow to gain momentum, a recent study showed that the number of CWA citizen enforcement suits from 2010 to 2016 was more than double the number of civil judicial enforcement actions under the act during that same period. This discrepancy may be less dramatic than it seems at first glance, as EPA reserves judicial enforcement for its most serious cases and most of its enforcement actions are administrative, an option not available to citizen groups. But, as the author of the study, Mark Ryan, observes, "the large number of citizen suits filed—and the relative high success rate of those suits—indicates that the suits are serving their intended purpose of enforcing the law where the government has either failed or opted not to enforce."[173]

Although the initiation of citizen suits against violators is—by design—outside of its control, EPA has generally been sympathetic to them as supplementing its own enforcement efforts. Acting through the Department of Justice, the agency has filed numerous *amicus curiae* ("friend of the court") briefs in citizen suits, supporting legal interpretations that ease the maintenance of these actions. In *North and South Rivers Watershed Association, Inc. v. Town of Scituate*, for example, the Department of Justice told the court on behalf of EPA:

> The United States has a direct interest in the development of the law regarding citizen enforcement of the Act since citizen suits serve as a valuable supplement to government enforcement. Citizens are very important to the enforcement of the Act since the government has only limited resources with which to bring its own enforcement actions.[174]

In these cases, the agency has qualified its support by characterizing citizen suits as *supplemental* to government enforcement. In other cases, it has registered concerns that, without proper limits, citizens could undermine effective enforcement by state and federal officials. For example, in *Environmental Conservation Organization v. Dallas*, EPA's justice department lawyers argued against the continuation of a citizen suit where the alleged violations had been addressed in a court-approved consent decree between EPA and the city-defendant. In that case, EPA told the court no "supplementary role" for the citizen plaintiffs remained.[175]

After finding and documenting violations, citizen plaintiffs face several hurdles in bringing violators to task. The statute imposes several of these hurdles. It requires a citizen plaintiff to give prior written notice of its intent to file suit to EPA, the state, and the alleged violator(s) and to wait to bring suit until sixty days after that notice has been given.[176] This requirement gives the prospective defendant an opportunity to escape suit entirely by correcting the violation during the sixty days the plaintiff must wait to file its case in court: the Supreme Court has read the act to allow citizen suits only if there are ongoing violations at the time of filing.[177] The statute also precludes citizen suits if, at the time of the complaint, the state has "commenced and is diligently prosecuting" its own judicial enforcement action for the same violations.[178]

Perhaps the most prominent hurdle to citizen enforcement actions, however, has its basis not in the statute but in constitutional standing doctrine. Standing requirements derive from the Constitution's limitation of the judicial power to "cases" and "controversies."[179] Although its understanding of the meaning of these terms has meandered over time, the Court now reads them to require that parties bringing claims before a federal court show a concrete injury caused by the unlawfulness complained of and capable of being rectified by judicial action. Although the CWA authorizes "any citizen" to bring suit, as a constitutional matter that suit cannot go forward without a showing by the plaintiff on these three elements of standing, often shorthanded as injury, causation, and redressability.

In recent decades, the Court has frequently used environmental cases to expound its standing doctrine. One of its canonical standing cases is a CWA citizen suit, *Friends of the Earth v. Laidlaw.*[180] The key standing question in *Laidlaw*, as in many citizen suits under the CWA, was whether the plaintiffs—Friends of the Earth and individual members of that group who lived near the North Tyger River—had suffered the requisite injury.[181] The trial court found that the defendant, Laidlaw, had discharged pollutants into the river in violation of its permit. It also found that those discharges had not caused discernable harm to the environment. The Supreme Court concluded that individuals living near the river or desiring to recreate on the river had suffered harm, even in the absence of proof that the river itself was harmed. Concerns about whether it was safe to go near the river were reasonable considering Laidlaw's serious and persistent illegal discharges. Plaintiffs in CWA citizen suits must still be careful to identify and document injuries to individual members from the violations alleged, but *Laidlaw,* as well as rulings by lower federal courts, have created the space for standing to be successfully pleaded and defended in these cases.

CONCLUSION

Under the Clean Water Act, the nation has seen marked reductions in pollution by industrial and municipal sources. It has also seen marked improvements in the water quality and ecological health of streams, lakes, and estuaries primarily affected by these sources. Although we cannot run a counterfactual to determine exactly how many of these improvements, if any, would have materialized in the absence of a strengthened CWA, common sense tells us that the act has been of enormous influence—both directly through application of its regulatory and other programs and indirectly in setting national goals to orient and motivate diverse actors.

Despite its signal success, however, challenges and questions remain, including:

- The country has yet to achieve the act's interim fishable-swimmable goal, set for 1985, and its no-discharge goal seems impossibly remote. In a comprehensive 2008-2009 study assessing the health of the nation's rivers and streams, EPA found that only twenty-eight percent of the nation's river and stream length was in good biological condition. Twenty-five percent was in fair condition and forty-six percent in poor condition.[182] This shortfall, after decades of implementation, raises questions about the feasibility of the act's goals.
- EPA still searches for an effective response to polluted runoff from non-point sources, the predominant cause of the nation's remaining water quality problems.
- Economists question the efficiency of the act's goals and tools, such as uniform BAT requirements. They argue that cost-benefit balancing should temper the setting of water quality standards and technology-based limitations.

Against these challenges and questions are hopeful signs and possibilities:

- Successes in large watersheds such as the Great Lakes and the Chesapeake Bay suggest that, with commitments from local and regional stakeholders and steady support from EPA, the CWA can achieve its ultimate aim of restoring and maintaining the integrity of the nation's waters. The Mississippi-Gulf of Mexico Basin should be next.
- Cost-effective reductions in non-point source pollution are available to advance the act's stated policy goals if ways can be found to incentivize them. Technologies and management techniques, such as no till farming and variable rate fertilizer application, can save money for farmers while yielding water quality and other environmental benefits.[183]
- Public opinion polls show water pollution consistently ranked high among environmental concerns.[184] Public concerns about water quality reflect a smaller partisan divide than other environmental issues such as species protection and climate change.[185] There seems no weakening of support for the act's ambitious goals.

Uncertainty in the interpretation of important terms of the legislation fuels conflict and increases implementation costs, both social and economic. This is most unfortunately true for the act's core jurisdictional term, "waters of the United States," which remains in flux almost fifty years after the 1972 amendments. The cycling of politically motivated rule changes and the lack of clear judicial guidance threaten continuation of this uncertainty. We may hope, however, that these swings will dampen as courts clear up outstanding questions and agency policies mature.

The dynamic tension between federal and state authorities remains a dominant theme in CWA implementation. Federalism has figured importantly in judicial interpretations of the act and is likely to in the future, particularly on questions of its jurisdictional scope. Federal-state relations also shape countless day-to-day decisions in the act's administration. The "cooperative federalism" hardwired into the act has proved manageable over time, but requires adequate resourcing of both state and federal agencies for its continued success.

Aided by citizen suits, enforcement of the CWA has been generally robust since the 1972 amendments, helping to secure compliance, deter future violations, and protect the collective bargain. But enforcement pressure has varied with the political tides, ebbing or flowing in rough synchrony with an administration's views on regulation. Enforcement numbers have shown some declines recently, but the persistence of these declines and their effect on the integrity and effectiveness of the CWA and other environmental statutes remain to be seen.[186]

NOTES

1. James L. Oberstar, *The Clean Water Act: 30 Years of Success in Peril* (Washington, DC: US Congress, House, Committee on Transportation and Infrastructure, October 18, 2002), 2–3.
2. Jonathan Adler, "Fables of the Cuyahoga: Reconstructing a History of Environmental Protection," *Fordham Environmental Law Journal* (2002): 89, 90.
3. Carol M. Browner, "Vice President's Clean Water Action Announcement," *epa.gov*, March 9, 1991, https://archive.epa.gov/epapages/newsroom_archive/speeches/0679ee19816044458525701a0052e319.html.
4. Adler, "Fables of the Cuyahoga," 101–04.
5. "The Cities: The Price of Optimism," *Time*, August 1, 1969, 41.
6. Robert V. Percival et al., *Environmental Regulation: Law, Science and Policy*, 6th ed. (Philadelphia: Aspen Publishers, 2009): 644.
7. In response to the disappointing performance of the pre-1972 legislation, environmental advocates seized on an obscure provision of the Rivers and Harbors Act of 1899 (RHA) to serve as a water quality enforcement tool. Section 13 of that act prohibits the deposit of "refuse matter" into the navigable waters of the United States without a permit from the Secretary of the Army, 33 U.S.C.A. §407. In two decisions in the 1960s, the Supreme Court blessed the use of this provision to prohibit

unpermitted discharges of "industrial solids" and gasoline. United States v. Republic Steel Corp., 362 U.S. 482, 491 (1960); United States v. Standard Oil Co., 384 U.S. 224 (1966).

Although a federal permitting program under §13 was never operationalized, the RHA's discharge permit model helped shape the CWA as it emerged in 1972. Percival et al., *Environmental Regulation*, 644–45.

8. 33 U.S.C. §1251(a)(1).
9. 33 U.S.C. §1251(a)(2).
10. H.R. Rep. No. 92-911, (1972), 131.
11. 33 U.S.C. §1251(a).
12. 33 U.S. C. §1319.
13. 33 U.S.C. §1311(b)(1)(A), (b)(2)(A).
14. 33 U.S.C. §1311(b)(2)(E).
15. 33 U.S.C. §1316.
16. 33 U.S.C. §1317((b).
17. 33 U.S.C. §1342(b).
18. 33 U.S.C. §1342 (c).
19. "NPDES State Program Information," *epa.gov,* last updated December 2, 2019, https://www.epa.gov/npdes/npdes-state-program-information.
20. " . . . Massachusetts, New Hampshire, New Mexico, District of Columbia, U.S. territories, and on federal and tribal lands. Other states have been delegated by EPA to issue their own permits," US Environmental Protection Agency, "NPDES Permits Around the Nation," *epa.gov*, last updated December 30, 2019, https://www.epa.gov/npdes-permits.
21. See 33 U.S.C. §1342(a)(1), authorizing issuance of Section 402 permits "[e] xcept as provided in . . . [section 404]."
22. 33 U.S.C. §1344(g).
23. The Federal Civil Penalties Adjustment Act of 1990 requires annual adjustment of statutory civil penalties to reflect inflation. See 84 Fed. Reg. 2056, 2058 (February 6, 2019).
24. 33 U.S.C. §1365(a).
25. Gwaltney of Smithfield v. Chesapeake Bay Foundation, 484 U.S. 49, 62 (1987).
26. 33 U.S.C. §1365(d).
27. US Environmental Protection Agency, *Handbook of Procedures: Construction Grant Program for Municipal Treatment Works* (Washington, DC: EPA, 1984), 111.
28. Annie Snider, "Clean Water Act: Vetoes by Eisenhower and Nixon Presaged Today's Partisan Divide," *E&E News*, October 18, 2012, https://www.eenews.net/stories/1059971457.
29. Train v. City of New York, 420 U.S. 35 (1975).
30. 33 U.S.C. §1383.
31. Theodore L. Garrett, "Federal Liability for Spills of Oil and Hazardous Substances under the Clean Water Act," *Natural Resources Lawyer* 12, no. 4 (1979): 693.
32. 33 U.S.C. §1321(b)(3).
33. 33 U.S.C. §1321(b)(6)–(7).

34. 33 U.S.C. §1321(f).

35. US Environmental Protection Agency, "William D. Ruckelshaus: Oral History Interview," EPA 202-K-92-0003, *epa.gov*, January 1993, https://archive.epa.gov/epa/aboutepa/william-d-ruckelshaus-oral-history-interview.html.

36. Percival et al., *Environmental Regulation*, 698.

37. Ibid., 698–99.

38. 33 U.S.C. §1331(a).

39. 33 U.S.C. §1362(12).

40. 33 U.S.C. §1362(14).

41. NRDC v. Costle, 568 F.2d 1369 (D.C. Cir. 1977).

42. Percival et al., *Environmental Regulation*, 689.

43. Ibid.

44. Ibid.

45. Backlog for major permits in 1999 estimated at twenty-eight percent. US Environmental Protection Agency, Office of Inspector General, *Efforts to Manage NPDES Permit Backlog Need to be Accompanied by Greater Program Integration*, 2005-P-00018 (Washington, DC: EPA OIG, June 13, 2005); Percival et al., *Environmental Regulation*, 689.

46. 33 U.S.C. §§1311(a)-(b), 1342(a)(1).

47. Percival et al., *Environmental Regulation*, 699.

48. NRDC v. Train, 510 F.2d 692, 709 (1975).

49. Barry Boyer and Errol Meidinger, "Privatizing Regulatory Enforcement: A Preliminary Assessment of Citizen Suits Under Federal Environmental Laws," *Buffalo Law Review* 34 (1985): 886.

50. E. I. du Pont de Nemours & Co. v. Train, 430 U.S. 112, 122 (1977).

51. Oliver A. Houck, "The Regulation of Toxic Pollutants under the Clean Water Act," *Environmental Law Reporter* 21 (1991): 10537.

52. US Environmental Protection Agency, "Industrial Effluent Guidelines," *epa.gov*, last updated April 17, 2020, https://www.epa.gov/eg/industrial-effluent-guidelines.

53. Requiring review and where appropriate revision of guidelines every year. See 33 U.S.C. §1314(b)

54. Houck, "The Regulation of Toxic Pollutants," 10533.

55. Ibid., 10534.

56. Percival et al., *Environmental Regulation*, 701.

57. Houck, "The Regulation of Toxic Pollutants,"10535.

58. 33 U.S.C. §1311(b)(1)(C).

59. 40 C.F.R. §131.2.

60. Robert W. Adler, "Resilience, Restoration, and Sustainability: Revisiting the Fundamental Principles of the Clean Water Act," *Washington University Journal of Law & Policy* 32 (2010): 142–50.

61. 40 C.F.R. §131.12(a)(2).

62. 40 C.F.R. §§131.10(g), (j).

63. Jeffry M. Gaba, "Federal Supervision of State Water Quality Standards under the Clean Water Act," *Vanderbilt Law Review* 36 (1983): 1168–69, 1194n.135.

64. 48 Fed. Reg. 51, 400-01 (November 8, 1983).

65. 33 U.S.C. §1314(a).

66. Percival et al., *Environmental Regulation*, 717.

67. Natural Resources Defense Council, Inc. v. EPA, 16 F.3d 1395 (1993).

68. Ibid., 1399, 1401.

69. Ibid., 1401.

70. Ibid., 1405–6.

71. David A. Keiser and Joseph S. Shapiro, "Consequences of the Clean Water Act and the Demand for Water Quality," *The Quarterly Journal of Economics* 134, no. 1 (2019).

72. Houck, "The Regulation of Toxic Pollutants."

73. 33 U.S.C. §1313(c)(2); Percival et al., *Environmental Regulation*, 739.

74. 33 U.S.C. §1314(*l*).

75. Percival et al., *Environmental Regulation*, 728.

76. 33 U.S.C. §1313(d); Percival, et al. Environmental Regulation, 739.

77. 40 C.F.R. §130.2(f)-(h), 130.7.

78. Scott v. City of Hammond, 741 F.2d 992 (7th Cir. 1984); Alaska Center for the Environment v. Reilly, 762 F.Supp. 1422 (W.D. Wash. 1991), *aff'd* 20 F.3d 981 (9th Cir. 1994).

79. Percival et al., *Environmental Regulation*, 739.

80. See Robert L. Glicksman and Matthew R. Batzel, "Science, Politics, Law, and the Arc of the Clean Water Act: The Role of Assumptions in the Adoption of a Pollution Control Landmark," *Washington University Journal of Law & Policy* 32 (2010): 115.

81. "Many nonpoint sources of pollution are beyond present technology of control." See S. Rep. No. 92-414 (1972), reprinted in 1972 U.S.C.C.A.N. 3668, 3706.

82. Glicksman and Batzel, "Science, Politics, Law," 116.

83. 33 U.S.C. §1288(b)(2)(F).

84. 33 U.S.C. §1314(f).

85. US Environmental Protection Agency, *A National Evaluation of the Clean Water Act Section 319 Program* (Washington, DC: EPA, November 2011), 2.

86. Ibid.

87. Ibid., 13.

88. 65 Fed. Reg. 43586 (2000).

89. 68 Fed. Reg. 13607 (2003); Jonathan Z. Cannon, "A Bargain for Clean Water," *NYU Environmental Law Journal* 17, no. 1 (2008): 623.

90. US Environmental Protection Agency, *Water Quality Trading Policy* (Washington, DC: EPA, January 13, 2003).

91. US Environmental Protection Agency, *Water Quality Trading Toolkit for Permit Writers* (Washington, DC: EPA, August 2007, updated June 2009), 28.

92. Cannon, "Bargain for Clean Water," 632–33; Marc O. Ribaudo and Jessica Gottlieb, "Non-Point Trading—Can it Work?" *Journal of the American Water Resources Association* 47, no. 1 (2011): 10.

93. Ribaudo and Gottlieb, "Non-Point Trading," 8–10.

94. David P. Ross, *Memo: Updating the Environmental Protection Agency's (EPA) Water Quality Trading Policy to Promote Market-Based Mechanisms for Improving Water Quality* (Washington, DC: EPA, February 6, 2019).

95. Ibid.

96. Mississippi River/Gulf of Mexico Watershed Nutrient Task Force, *Gulf Hypoxia Action Plan 2008*, 842K09001 (Washington, DC: EPA, 2008).

97. National Atmospheric and Oceanic Administration, "Gulf of Mexico 'Dead Zone' is the Largest Ever Measured," *noaa.gov*, August 2, 2017, https://www.noaa.gov/media-release/gulf-of-mexico-dead-zone-is-largest-ever-measured.

98. Federal common law that had developed for addressing interstate pollution disputes was ruled by the Supreme Court to be preempted by the CWA. See Robert V. Percival, "The Clean Water Act and the Demise of the Federal Common Law of Interstate Nuisance," *Alabama Law Review* 55 (2004).

99. 503 U.S. 91 (1992).

100. See, e.g., A. Dan Tarlock, "Putting Rivers Back in the Landscape: The Revival of Watershed Management in the United States," *Hastings Environmental Law Journal* 6, no. 2 (2000); Adler, "Resilience, Restoration, and Sustainability."

101. 33 U.S.C. §1268 (establishing a Great Lakes National Program Office); Great Lakes-St. Lawrence River Basin Water Resources Compact, *45 I.L.C.S. 147* (2008).

102. 33 U.S.C. §1267 (establishing a Chesapeake Bay Program); *Chesapeake Watershed Agreement* (revised 2014), www.epa.gov/sites/production/files/2016-01/documents/attachment1chesapeakebaywatershedagreement.pdf.

103. US Environmental Protection Agency, "Overview of National Estuary Program," *epa.gov,* last updated October 26, 2018, https://www.epa.gov/nep/overview-national-estuary-program.

104. US Environmental Protection Agency, "Addressing Nutrient Pollution in the Chesapeake Bay," *epa.gov,* last updated July 18, 2019, https://www.epa.gov/nutrient-policy-data/addressing-nutrient-pollution-chesapeake-bay.

105. Chesapeake Bay Program, "Population Growth," *Chesapeakebay.net*, 2020, https://www.chesapeakebay.net/issues/population_growth.

106. Agriculture and forests account for the bulk of nitrogen, phosphorous, and sediment delivered to the bay. US Environmental Protection Agency, *Chesapeake Bay Total Maximum Daily Load for Nitrogen, Phosphorus, and Sediment* (Washington, DC: EPA, December 29, 2010), 4–29, 4–36 https://www.epa.gov/chesapeake-bay-tmdl/chesapeake-bay-tmdl-document, hereafter *Chesapeake Bay TMDL.*

107. EPA, *Chesapeake Bay TMDL*, 3–1; Richard Batiuk et al., "Derivation of Habitat-Specific Dissolved Oxygen Criteria for Chesapeake Bay and Its Tidal Tributaries," *Journal of Experimental Marine Biology and Ecology* 381, Supplement (2009): S213.

108. EPA, *Chesapeake Bay TMDL*, 8–1 to 8–2; American Farm Bureau Federation v. U.S. EPA, 792 F.3d 281 (3rd Cir. 2015), *cert. denied*, 136 S. Ct. 1246 (2016).

109. Jamison E. Colburn, "Coercing Collaboration: The Chesapeake Bay Experience," *William & Mary Environmental Law and Policy Review* 40, no. 3 (2016): 702.

110. EPA, *Chesapeake Bay TMDL*, 7-5.

111. Ibid., ES-8; Colburn, "Coercing Collaboration," 709–11.

112. American Farm Bureau Federation v. U.S. EPA, 792 F.3d 281 (3rd Cir. 2015), *cert. denied*, 136 S. Ct. 1246 (2016).

113. E.g., University of Maryland Center for Environmental Science, "Overall Chesapeake Bay Health Improving for the First Time," *umcs.edu*, June 15, 2018, https://www.umces.edu/news/overall-chesapeake-bay-health-improving-first-time; "Chesapeake Bay Water Quality Continues to Improve," *Water and Waste Digest*, December 19, 2017, https://www.wwdmag.com/pollution-control/chesapeake-bay-water-quality-continues-improve.

114. See Gina McCarthy and William Reilly, "Pa. Efforts to Curb Chesapeake Pollution Have Stalled, Leaving the Bay at Risk," opinion, *Philadelphia Inquirer*, September 3, 2019, https://www.inquirer.com/opinion/commentary/chesapeake-bay-pollution-susquehanna-river-pennsylvania-20190903.html.

115. See 33 U.S.C. §1342(a)(1), authorizing issuance of Section 402 permits "[e] xcept as provided in . . . [section 404]."

116. 33 U.S.C. §1344(e).

117. 40 C.F.R. §230.10(d).

118. See National Wildlife Federation v. Whistler, 27 F.3d 1341 (8th Cir. 1994). Upholding issuance of a Section 404 permit for construction of a channel for boat access to an upland development which the court found would have been built without the permit, thus allowing the boat channel to stand on its own as a water-dependent project.

119. 40 C.F.R. ch. 1, subch. H, pt. 230, subpts. H & J.

120. Data from Florida showing one hundred percent of permit requests granted. Alyson Flournoy, "Supply, Demand and Consequences: The Impact of Information Flow on Individual Permitting Decisions under Section 404 of the Clean Water Act," *Indiana Law Journal* 83 (2008): 557.

121. 40 C.F.R. §§230.10 (d), 230.93.

122. Sylvia Quast, "Regulation of Wetlands: Section 404," in *Clean Water Handbook*, ed. Mark A. Ryan, 3rd ed. (Chicago: American Bar Association, 2011).

123. 33 C.F.R. §332.3(m), (n).

124. 33 C.F.R. §332.3(b).

125. 40 C.F.R. §232.2

126. 557 U.S. 261 (2009).

127. US Environmental Protection Agency, Proposed Determination to Prohibit, Restrict, or Deny the Specification or the Use for Specification of an Area as a Disposal Site, 84 Fed. Reg. 45749 (August 30, 2019); Spruce No. 1 Surface Mine, Logan County, WV, 75 Fed. Reg. 16788, 16691 (April 2, 2010).

128. 76 Fed. Reg. 3126 (January 19, 2011) (Final rescission).

129. Mingo Logan Coal Co. v. EPA, 829 F.3d 710, 724 (o.c. Cir2016).

130. National Mining Association v. U.S. Army Corps of Engineers, 145 F.3d 1399 (1998).

131. Rapanos v. United States, 547 U.S. 715 (2006) (scope of "waters of the United States"); United States Army Corps of Engineers v. Hawkes Co., Inc., 136 S. Ct. 1807 (2016) (judicial reviewability of Corps' wetland jurisdiction); Sackett

v. EPA, 132 S. Ct. 1367 (2012) (judicial reviewability of EPA wetlands compliance order).

132. Ariel Wittenberg, "What Does 'Waters of the US' Mean? We Asked the Authors," *E&E News*, June 29, 2017, https://www.eenews.net/stories/1060056818.

133. 33 C.F.R. §328.3(a) (Corps) (as previously in effect); 40 C.F.R. §230.3(s)(3) (EPA) (as previously in effect).

134. For treatments of the Supreme Court's Clean Water Act federalism cases, see Jonathan Z. Cannon, *Environment in the Balance: The Green Movement and the Supreme Court* (Cambridge, MA: Harvard University Press, 2015), 177-97; Robin Kundis Craig, *The Clean Water Act and the Constitution: Legal Structure and the Public's Right to a Clean and Healthy Environment* (Washington, DC: Environmental Law Institute, 2004), 94–117.

135. 474 U.S. 121.

136. 33 C.F.R. §328.3.

137. 531 U.S. 159 (2001).

138. 51 Fed. Reg. 41217 (1986).

139. 531 U.S. at 174.

140. 547 U.S. 715 (2006).

141. Ibid., 780.

142. See Wade Foster, "Parsing Rapanos," *Environmental Law Review Syndicate,* April 7, 2018, http://www.velj.org/elrs/parsing-rapanos.

143. See ibid., citing United States v. Cundiff, 555 F.3d 200, 208 (6th Cir. 2009).

144. 80 Fed. Reg. 37053 (June 29, 2015).

145. US Environmental Protection Agency, "Definition of 'Waters of the United States': Rule Status and Litigation Update," *epa.gov*, last updated December 23, 2019, https://www.epa.gov/wotus-rule/definition-waters-united-states-rule-status-and-litigation-update.

146. 84 Fed. Reg. 56626 (October 22, 2019).

147. 84 Fed. Reg. 4154 (February 14, 2019).

148. 85 Fed. Reg. 22250 (April 21, 2020), https://www.epa.gov/sites/production/files/2020-01/documents/navigable_waters_protection_rule_prepublication.pdf.

149. Chris Wood, Collin O'Mara, and Dale Hall, "Trump Weakens the Nation's Clean Water Efforts," *New York Times,* op. ed., February 10, 2020, https://www.nytimes.com/2020/02/10/opinion/clean-water-act-trump.html.

150. 33 U.S.C. §1362(12).

151. US Environmental Protection Agency, Request for Comment, Clean Water Act Coverage of "Discharges of Pollutants" via a Direct Hydrological Connection to Surface Water, 83 Fed. Reg. 7126, 7127 (February 20, 2018).

152. US Environmental Protection Agency, Interpretive Statement on Application of the Clean Water Act National Pollution Discharge Elimination System Program to Releases of Pollutants From a Point Source to Groundwater, 84 Fed. Reg. 16810 (April 23, 2019).

153. "40+ Groups Oppose Attacks on Vital Clean Water Act Safeguard," *Clean Water Action,* April 17, 2018, https://www.cleanwateraction.org/publications/40-groups-oppose-attacks-vital-clean-water-act-safeguard.

154. Compare Upstate Forever v. Kinder Morgan Energy Partners, 887 F.3d 637 (4th Cir.) (discharge from broken pipeline through groundwater) and Hawai'i Wildlife Fund v. County of Maui, 886 F.3d 737 (9th Cir. 2018) (discharges from disposal wells) with Kentucky Waterways Alliance v. Kentucky Utilities Co., 905 F.3d 925 (6th Cir. 2018) (seepage from coal ash pond through karst formation) and Tenn. Clean Water Network v. TVA, 905 F.3d 436 (6th Cir. 2018) (seepage from coal ash pond through groundwater).

155. Kentucky Waterways Alliance, 905 F.3d at 928; Tennessee Clean Water Network, 905 F.3d at 439.

156. Upstate Forever, 887 F.3d at 651–52.

157. Hawai'i Wildlife Fund v. County of Maui, 886 F.3d at 749.

158. Hawai'i Wildlife Fund v. County of Maui (Brief for the United States as Amicus Curiae in Support of Plaintiffs-Appellees (May 31, 2016).

159. www.supremecourt.gov/docket/docketfiles/html/public/18-260.html.

160. County of Maui v. Hawai'i Wildlife Fund, 140 S. Ct. 1462 (2020).

161. Jon Hamilton, "How California's Worst Oil Spill Turned Beaches Black and the Nation Green," *Morning Edition*, National Public Radio, Washington, DC: NPR, January 28, 2019, https://www.npr.org/2019/01/28/688219307/how-californias-worst-oil-spill-turned-beaches-black-and-the-nation-green.

162. 33 U.S.C. §2701 et seq.; US Environmental Protection Agency, "Summary of the Oil Pollution Act," *epa.gov*, last updated February 13, 2020, https://www.epa.gov/laws-regulations/summary-oil-pollution-act.

163. Gregg Easterbrook, "William Reilly: Rebuilding the EPA From the Ashes Into a Political Force to Reckon With," *Los Angeles Times*, June 2, 1991, https://www.latimes.com/archives/la-xpm-1991-06-02-op-183-story.html; William K. Reilly, "Panel Chief on the Gulf Spill: Complacency Led to Disaster," interview by John McQuaid, January 27, 2011, https://e360.yale.edu/features/panel_chief_on_the_gulf_spill_complacency_led_to_disaster.

164. US Environmental Protection Agency, "Questions and Answers about the BP Oil Spill in the Gulf Coast," *epa.gov,* last updated February 20, 2016, https://archive.epa.gov/emergency/bpspill/web/html/qanda.html#role.

165. EPA, "William D. Ruckelshaus: Oral History Interview," 10.

166. US Environmental Protection Agency, *EPA Enforcement Annual Results 2018* (Washington, DC: EPA, 2018), https://epa.maps.arcgis.com/apps/Cascade/index.html?appid=0b9d73f351d648698f63bba3f3b15114.

167. Ibid.

168. Ibid.

169. US Environmental Protection Agency, *Interim Clean Water Act Settlement Penalty Policy* (Washington, DC: EPA, 1985), 6.

170. Ibid., 2.

171. US Department of Justice, "Loretta E. Lynch Delivers Remarks at Press Conference Announcing Settlement with BP to Resolve Civil Claims Over Deepwater Horizon Oil Spill" October 5, 2015, https://www.justice.gov/opa/speech/attorney-general-loretta-e-lynch-delivers-remarks-press-conference-announcing-settlement.

172. US Environmental Protection Agency, Incentives for Self-Policing: Discovery, Disclosure, Correction and Prevention of Violations, 65 Fed. Reg. 19618 (April 11, 2000), https://www.epa.gov/compliance/epas-audit-policy.

173. Mark A. Ryan, "Clean Water Act Citizen Suits: What the Numbers Tell Us," *Natural Resources & Environment* 32 (Fall 2017): 22.

174. North and South Rivers Watershed Association, Inc. v. Town of Scituate, 949 F.2d 552 (1st Cir. 1991) (Brief for the United States as Amicus Curiae in Support of Plaintiff-Appellant); also see Citizens for a Better Environment v. Union Oil Co. of California, 83 F.3d 1111 (9th Cir. 1996) (Brief for the United States as Amicus Curiae in Support of Plaintiffs-Appellees), "The United States values citizen suits as a supplement to government enforcement and believes that, when responsibly invoked, these suits provide a strong incentive to comply with the Act."

175. 529 F.3d 519 (5th Cir. 2008) (Brief of the United States as Amicus Curiae).

176. 33 U.S.C. §1365(b)(1)(A).

177. *See* Gwaltney of Smithfield v. Chesapeake Bay Foundation, 484 U.S. 49 (1987).

178. 33 U.S.C. §1365((b)(1)(B).

179. United States Constitution, Art. III.

180. 528 U.S. 167 (2000).

181. The Court in *Laidlaw* also upheld the redressability of Friends of the Earth's claims even though Laidlaw had closed the offending facility after the suit began, making injunctive relief moot. The Court ruled that monetary penalties available against Laidlaw could provide redress by "abating present violations and preventing future ones."

182. US Environmental Protection Agency, *National Rivers and Streams Assessment 2008-2009,* EPA-841-R-16-007 (Washington, DC: EPA, March 2016), viii, http://www.epa.gov/national-aquatic-resource-surveys/nrsa.

183. Elizabeth Creech, "Saving Money, Time and Soil: The Economics of No-Till Farming," *USDA blog*, November 30, 2017, https://www.usda.gov/media/blog/2017/11/30/saving-money-time-and-soil-economics-no-till-farming.

184. In 2016 fifty-six percent of those polled expressed "a great deal of concern" about pollution of lakes, rivers, and reservoirs. Justin McCarthy, "American's Concerns about Water Pollution Edge Up," *Gallup,* March 2016, https://news.gallup.com/poll/190034/americans-concerns-water-pollution-edge.aspx.

185. Ibid.; Mitch Tobin, "6 Things I Learned Studying the Polls on Water," *Waterpolls.org,* March 24, 2017, https://waterpolls.org/public-opinion-on-water/.

186. Environmental Integrity Project, "New Report: EPA Enforcement at Record Low in 2018," *EnvironmentalIntegrity.org,* February 26, 2019, http://www.environmentalintegrity.org/news/new-report-epa-enforcement-at-record-low-in-2018/; Ellen M. Gilmer and Steven Lee, "Some EPA Enforcement Stats Stronger While Others Lag in 2019," *Bloomberg Law: Environment and Energy Report*, February 13, 2020, https://news.bloomberglaw.com/environment-and-energy/epa-civil-enforcement-drops-other-metrics-up-in-2019?context=article-related.

Chapter Six

Safe Drinking Water

James Salzman

The history of environmental policy can well be told by place names. Love Canal—hazardous waste. Los Angeles—air quality. The Cuyahoga River—water quality. And, most recently, Flint—drinking water. The tragedy in Flint, Michigan, entered the 24/7 national news cycle in 2015, led President Barack Obama to visit the city, and resulted in over a dozen criminal indictments. Flint is undoubtedly the most publicized drinking water story in US history and continues to influence funding and policy decisions.

The origins of the Flint crisis lay in poverty. Located sixty-six miles northwest of Detroit, Flint was a major auto manufacturing city after World War II, with a population of 100,000 in 1960. As the car jobs went away, Flint followed the sad pattern of other Rust-Belt cities with a declining population and standard of living. By 2015, the city's population had fallen by half. White flight had led to a majority-black city with a forty-two percent poverty rate and one of the worst murder and crime rates in the country. With such a small tax base, the city could not balance its budget. Making use of his executive authority, Michigan governor Rick Snyder appointed an emergency manager in 2011 to supervise the city's operations. The mayor and city council could vote to show their support or displeasure, but they had no authority. In addition to ensuring provision of basic services, the manager was charged with getting the city's books back in order, and that meant cutting costs.

Prior to the 1960s, the city had drawn its drinking water from the local Flint River and the city's treatment plant. Starting in 1967, Flint bought water from Detroit's utility, piped from Lake Huron seventy miles away. An analysis by the state Department of Treasury persuaded the emergency manager that a large cost saving opportunity, up to $200 million over twenty-five years, would come from switching sources to the closer Karegnondi Water Authority (KWA), which also drew from Lake Huron. The problem was that a pipeline from the KWA to Flint would take two years to complete. Supported by the city council and mayor, the emergency manager notified the Detroit utility that Flint would switch to the KWA, but Detroit made clear that Flint either needed to sign a thirty-year contract or lose its water supply in a year.

Looking for an interim source of water, the city made plans to use its original source and turn back to the Flint River for the interim. The Flint water treatment plant had been retired, but the city spent money to bring it quickly back in operation. It was soon apparent that the plant was not immediately up to the task. In late summer of 2014, officials detected the presence of coliform bacteria in the water and issued boil-water advisories. The plant responded with the traditional treatment technique of increasing levels of chlorine. This also increased the water's corrosiveness. The classic treatment to counter the acidity is the addition of corrosion inhibiting chemicals, usually with the inexpensive compound, orthophosphate. Over time, a protective layer of the compound can build up, completely blocking the pipe from contact with water. For reasons that remain unclear, however, the water treatment plant failed to add the orthophosphate.

This was particularly harmful in Flint which, like many other cities, contains lead water pipes. Indeed, a Flint city ordinance from 1897 actually required that all connections with water mains must be lead pipe. Known as lead service lines, these run water from the large water mains running underneath streets into individual homes. Lead pipe was banned by the Safe Drinking Water Act (SDWA) in 1986 (though even then, "lead-free" pipe was defined at no more than eight-percent content). Special rules for managing lead and copper were added in 1991. No one knew how many lead service lines were in Flint or where they were located, but the number was clearly in the thousands. Absent adequate corrosion control, the water in the mains leached lead from the aged service lines, leading to elevated lead levels in the drinking water provided to much of the community.

Lead is a potent neurotoxin. Children are particularly vulnerable because of their rapidly developing brains and nervous systems. As a result of lead's clear dangers, no blood level is considered safe. It is highly regulated across the breadth of environmental law, from the Clean Air Act to hazardous waste laws. SDWA's lead and copper rule was adopted in 1991. The rule proved difficult to draft because, unlike most other contaminants, lead in drinking water does not come from the treatment plant but instead from each home's lead service lines. Thus, the lead and copper rule mandates that water be tested at the household tap rather than just when water leaves the treatment plant. The standard methodology requires that utilities collect samples from household taps that have not been used for six hours. If more than ten percent of the samples exceed the action level (15 ppb for lead), certain water treatment steps become mandatory for the water provider. One of the first consequences of the rule was shutting off the drinking fountains at the EPA headquarters in Washington, DC.

It later emerged that lead sampling was not done properly in Flint. The state agency responsible for implementation of SDWA in Michigan, the Department of Environmental Quality (MDEQ), had cherry-picked data, leaving out high samples that would have triggered the action level.[1]

Throughout the period that citizens and scientists were raising concerns about elevated lead levels in Flint, MDEQ not only insisted the water was safe to drink but publicly attacked anyone suggesting otherwise. Marc Edwards, the Virginia Tech professor whose fieldwork confirmed the prevalence of high lead levels in drinking water, was denounced by the MDEQ spokesman for "offering broad dire public health advice based on some quick testing [that] could be seen as fanning political flames irresponsibly."[2] The pediatrician Mona Hanna-Attisha, who documented elevated lead blood levels in children, was criticized by MDEQ as contributing a climate of hysteria.

EPA failed to act, as well. A regional EPA staffer wrote a memo raising concerns over the dangers posed by elevated lead levels in the water and shared it with the local resident who had raised concerns about the problem. She shared the memo with the local ACLU office, which published it. The EPA staffer was denounced by MDEQ as "a rogue employee" and reprimanded by the EPA regional office for sharing his memo with a member of the public. It took nearly a year after concerns had first been raised about the quality of Flint's water for a state of emergency to be declared and meaningful actions taken to secure the public health.

The Flint crisis did not happen simply because it had lead service lines. Many cities have lead service lines and provide safe water (though there are some, such as Newark, who do not). The SDWA relies on a federalist structure, so the system depends on the federal, state, and local governments acting well together. It is assumed that information will be shared, that officials will act in good faith, and that they have the capacity to act. None of this happened. Indeed, Flint represents a massive failure of governance at every level.

Local water plant officials did not add the orthophosphate. They subverted the testing standard. While they claimed to have tested the water in homes with lead service lines and found lead levels acceptable, it later turned out that they did not even know which houses contained lead service lines. In telling residents to run their water a few minutes before taking samples, the officials ensured lead particles would have been flushed out. Monitoring samples that would have triggered the action level were excluded. It seems the local and state officials did everything they could to avoid finding high lead levels in their city's water. And the EPA's regional office came under severe criticism for showing too much deference to MDEQ, refusing to step in and take over out of concerns that the agency would be seen as too aggressive and intrusive.

At its very core, though, Flint represents a disturbing example of environmental injustice. A Freedom of Information Act (FOIA) request later uncovered an internal EPA email stating, "I am not so sure Flint is a community we want to go out on a limb for."[3] Imagine that the early events in this story had occurred not in Flint but, instead, in Grosse Point, a wealthy suburb outside of Detroit. Would water supply have proceeded if plant engineers had protested that they were not yet ready? Would widespread reports of rashes, loss of hair, and other ailments from the new drinking water source be dismissed by officials? Would independent reports over high levels of lead in the water be vehemently denied? And would EPA refuse to take a closer look? Or would each of these red flags, and many others, have been addressed and fixed? The resulting mistrust of public officials will take years to restore. Indeed, "How many Flints are out there?" has now become a common query in public drinking water meetings.

The saga of Flint lays bare the difficult challenges of providing safe drinking water—from treatment of the water, maintenance of the distribution system, setting safe contaminant levels, monitoring and enforcing the standards, and ensuring the local-state-federal partnership protects all Americans, not just the wealthy.

DRINKING WATER PROTECTION PRIOR TO SDWA

Drinking water is one of the few essential requirements for life. Throughout history, human settlements have been built with ready access to sources of safe drinking water. Without this, no population can long remain in place, and it has always been so. The basic task of providing safe water comprises three distinct challenges. A safe source must be identified, the source must be free from contamination (whether through source protection or treatment), and the water must be moved safely to the final point of consumption. To protect the population from waterborne diseases, every one of these tasks must be effectively managed, and each presents its own set of quite difficult technical, policy, and legal challenges. Largely taken for granted, the ubiquity of safe drinking water has not been the case for most of human history. The high levels of cholera, typhoid, dysentery, and other waterborne diseases that were commonplace in times past have thankfully become rare, if not nonexistent, today. Consider that in 1900, an American had a 1 in 20 chance of dying from a gastrointestinal infection before the age of seventy. In 1940, this had been reduced to a 1 in 3,333 chance, and in 1990 to a 1 in 2,000,000 chance.[4] This is a staggering achievement—a 100,000-fold public health improvement in less than a century. SDWA is the latest development in a much longer story.

The newly created Public Health Service (PHS) established the nation's first drinking water standards in 1914.[5] There was a good deal of local suspicion and often outright opposition to these PHS standards. While they were binding only on common carriers involved in interstate commerce (such as trains, buses, and ferries), the standards had a widespread and immediate impact. Since water was taken on at local depots along the rail lines, for example, national standards indirectly forced all communities providing water to common carriers to chlorinate their water, as well. By 1941, eighty-five percent of the country's more than five thousand public water systems (PWS) chlorinated their drinking water.[6] It has been claimed that chlorination of drinking water saved more lives than any other technological advance in the history of public health.[7]

The PHS standards were revised in 1925, 1946, and 1962, at which point they covered twenty-eight substances but were purely focused on bacteria and microorganisms. They did nothing to address the recent scientific discoveries highlighting threats posed by chemicals, pesticides, and viruses. Moreover, implementation was surprisingly poor. By 1970, only 650 of the nation's 35,000 PWS had enforcement authority over the standards and only fourteen states had adopted PHS standards into law.[8]

In 1970, a Senate committee ordered the PHS to do a careful study of the situation. It was not at all clear that the federal government should legislate in an area that had always been subject to local control. In a politically astute move, the PHS examined drinking water protection in states of the most powerful senators on the committee—969 public systems in the states of Vermont, Colorado, Washington, West Virginia, and California.[9] The results were startling. With PHS standards exceeded in over one-third of all samples, the report concluded that forty-one percent of the citizens were drinking "substandard water" and that, nationwide, up to eight million people were drinking "potentially dangerous water." In Washington state alone, two-thirds of the systems had not tested for chemicals in the past year and only 7 of the 127 systems passed the state's bacteriological standards.[10]

At the time of EPA's creation, the limited federal authority over drinking water, along with the Bureau of Water Hygiene in Department of Health, Education, and Welfare, were transferred to EPA. Many of the personnel in this unit were officers in the Public Health Service, the same service that had overseen drinking water standards since 1914. EPA, however, lacked substantive legislative authority to mandate drinking water standards apart from interstate common carriers.

The title of the first congressional legislation proposed in 1971 to provide EPA adequate authority was the Pure Drinking Water Act. The name was changed in future bills to the Safe Drinking Water Act. Whether the original bill name was modeled on the Pure Food and Drug Act—the law that gave the federal government authority to regulate foods and medicines—is unclear, but the name change was significant. It made clear that safe drinking water need not be pure—that public drinking water supplies required management of risk rather than elimination of risk.

In the three years between the first version of SDWA and its ultimate passage, legislators debated over what form the law should take. Should funding be provided by the federal and state governments or by rate payers through water bill charges? Should EPA's standards be technology- or risk-based? How much information should water providers be required to provide consumers about violations? Should they or EPA be subject to citizen suits for these violations? How far should SDWA's reach extend: to the water treatment plant, or further upstream to the water source itself and perhaps even land management practices in the watershed? Should there be a separate office created in EPA to focus on water supply?

THE ARCHITECTURE OF THE SAFE DRINKING WATER ACT

The Safe Drinking Water Act is the primary law safeguarding the tap water we drink. Just months after taking office in 1974, President Gerald Ford signed SDWA into law. Taken together, SDWA was groundbreaking in three key respects. First, it created *uniform* drinking water standards for a wide range of contaminants that were *enforceable* throughout the country. This may seem like common sense today, but it was a radically original idea, recently introduced in the Clean Air Act of 1970 and Clean Water Act of 1972. Second, it provided badly needed government funds through loans and grants for infrastructure. More times than not, poor water quality was due to lack of resources. Third, it directly engaged the public by making the state of our tap water much more transparent. For the first time, water suppliers were required to send out regular reports on water quality and, perhaps more important, immediately notify customers when serious violations occurred.

The law was subsequently amended in 1986 and 1996. The major provisions of the original law adopted in 1974 are set out below.

Water Systems Covered by SDWA

Through its history, the United States has developed a dauntingly complex array of public water systems. There are now over 150,000 public water systems (PWS) scattered throughout the country, ranging from the Los Angeles utility that serves over four million people to the Winterhaven Mobile Estates that serves fewer than thirty customers. Most of these are publicly owned, with about twenty percent under private control.

In determining who shall be subject to the law, SDWA covers PWS that regularly provide drinking water to at least twenty-five people or fifteen service connections for at least sixty days per year. While this definition ensures protection for most of the country, it excludes private wells, the primary source of drinking water for about fifteen percent of the country (forty-five million people) and a large part of rural America's population. Table 6.1 sets out the great variety of PWS in 2015.[11]

Roughly 80% of PWS are small, serving under 500 people. While dominant in terms of number, these small systems serve only 4% of the national population. As we shall discuss later, with poor access to capital and technical capacity, small PWS face significant challenges complying with SDWA. By contrast, large PWS serving over 100,000 people comprise only 0.2% of the number of systems but serve 44% of the population.

Contaminants

Perhaps the greatest challenge facing EPA under SDWA concerns which contaminants the law should regulate, and which remain outside legal control. SDWA charges EPA to assess the risk posed by contaminants and their likelihood to occur in PWS.

Potential contaminants for regulation are first placed on the Contaminant Candidate list. This includes drinking water contaminants that are known or anticipated to occur in PWS but are not subject to SDWA regulations. If national occurrence data are needed as part of EPA's decision-making on whether to regulate a new contaminant (or not), EPA can require monitoring through the Unregulated Contaminant Monitoring Rule (UCMR).[12] After extensive review, the agency focuses on those posing the greatest risks and may decide to commence the regulatory process of establishing maximum contaminant level goals (MCLGs)—the highest concentration of the contaminant in water that causes no known or anticipated adverse effects and allows an adequate margin of safety. For many contaminants, such as microbes and carcinogens, this number is zero.

It may not be practical to eliminate these contaminants, though, so the agency carries out a risk assessment and considers the costs to achieve the mandated reduction. SDWA is one of the few environmental laws with an explicit cost-benefit analysis requirement and an ancillary impacts analysis requirement (requiring EPA to consider both co-benefits and countervailing risks, such as increasing the concentrations of other contaminants). Guided by

Table 6.1. Variety of US public water systems in 2015

Public Water System Type	*<=500*	*501–3,300*	*3,301–10,000*	*10,000–100,000*	*>100,000*	*Total*
Community Water System (e.g., Boston)	27,755	13,517	4,692	3,885	427	**50,546**
Population	4,665,458	19,399,740	28,908,735	110,902,376	139,721,996	303,598,305
Non-Transient Non-CWS (e.g., school)	15,415	2,506	149	17	1	**18,088**
Population	2,150,257	2,674,483	829,469	456,067	203,375	6,313,651
Transient Non-CWS (e.g., gas station)	80,447	2,822	84	13	2	**83,368**
Population	7,236,224	2,660,200	453,342	306,814	2,100,003	12,766,583
Total Systems	**123,617**	**18,845**	**5,195**	**3,915**	**430**	**152,002**
Total Population	**14,041,939**	**24,734,423**	**30,191,543**	**111,675,257**	**142,025,374**	**322,678,539**

Data from the President's Council of Advisors on Science and Technology, "Science and Technology to Ensure the Safety of the Nation's Drinking Water," December 2016.

the instruction that the standard "maximizes health risk reduction benefits at a cost that is justified by the benefits," EPA then sets a maximum contaminant level (MCL). This is the legal standard for the National Primary Drinking Water Regulations (NPDWR), and it is as close to the MCLG as feasible. The EPA is supposed to periodically reevaluate the stringency of the standards, revising them in light of new data and considering new contaminant candidates to add.

Put simply, if the presence of a regulated contaminant in a drinking water sample does not exceed the NPDWR, then drinking water from the tap is legally determined to be safe. States can increase the stringency of MCLs, setting even stricter standards. California, New York, and New Jersey, in particular, regularly set their own standards or set standards that are stricter than EPA's.[13]

EPA's setting of standards for fluoride provides a useful example. Based on studies conducted by the National Academy of Sciences, EPA set the MCLG for fluoride at 4 mg per liter. EPA was subsequently sued both by the Natural Resources Defense Council (arguing that the standard was too high because it would cause crippling skeletal fluorosis) and the South Carolina Department of Health and Environmental Control (arguing that the standard was too low because of naturally occurring fluoride in the water). EPA challenged the NRDC claims by defending its assumptions about daily drinking water consumption by sensitive subgroups of the population, and arguing that dental fluorosis is not an adverse health effect under SDWA. In response to South Carolina, EPA argued that its MCLG was set to protect those who drink more than average amounts of water. EPA's regulation was upheld by the D.C. Circuit.[14]

In addition to NPDWR, EPA is also authorized to set National Secondary Drinking Water Regulations. The secondary standards are not binding on water systems but, rather, guidelines for contaminants that may have cosmetic impacts (such as discoloring teeth), or aesthetic impacts (such as dirty taste, odor, and color).

Source Water Protection

While SDWA's concern is ultimately with tap water, part of the law focuses on protecting source waters to ensure that water does not get contaminated in the first place. Thus, the Underground Injection Control Program (UIC) regulates wells that inject fluids underground (generally into porous geologic formations). Groundwater accounts for about one-fifth of PWS source water across the country, so underground injection merits special attention. There is far more underground injection to dispose wastes or recover minerals than people realize, with municipal, agricultural, commercial, and industrial entities injecting millions of gallons per year of wastewater, brine, or water mixed with chemicals into the over 700,000 wells across the country. In recent years, much of this injection has resulted from the rapid increase in hydraulic fracturing (fracking) which was exempted from SDWA coverage in 2005.

EPA grouped injection wells into five classes ranging from waste disposal wells (Class I) to wells injected into underground sources of drinking water (Class V). Specific regulations apply to each well class. The regulations must ensure injection practices that protect public health and prevent contamination of underground sources of drinking water.

Enforcement

The decision over who enforces is addressed in a similar manner to other federal pollution laws—through cooperative federalism. Under a practice known as "primacy," EPA delegates responsibility to states for primary implementation and enforcement authority. States must adopt their own enforceable standards that are at least as strict as EPA's standards. This includes collecting water samples at designated intervals and locations to determine compliance, and then enforcing adequately when violations occur. Every state except Wyoming has been granted primacy and receives grants from EPA to help cover a portion of their program costs. If a system violates EPA/state rules, it is required to notify the public. States report violation and enforcement information to EPA every quarter, which allows EPA to look over primacy states' shoulders to ensure they are following through. This process clearly failed in EPA's lax oversight of the MDEQ in Flint.

Like other pollution laws, SDWA has a citizen suit provision. "Any person" may file a civil action against a party "alleged to be in violation" of SDWA's provisions or against EPA for failure to perform a nondiscretionary duty.[15] The court may award litigation costs if it deems that appropriate. There has been remarkably little use of the citizen suit provision, orders of magnitude less than under the Clean Air Act or Clean Water Act. The possible causes for this difference are discussed later in the chapter.

Funding

The final basic question for SDWA concerns who pays. From ancient Rome through today, safe drinking water begins and ends with infrastructure. Critical to the provision of safe drinking water, infrastructure is expensive to build and maintain, and the nation's infrastructure is massive. Water needs to be moved from the more than 75,000 reservoirs and rivers to treatment plants and then to our faucets. These built structures and over two million miles of buried pipes never inspire a second's thought on the part of the public until they fail. Such willful ignorance creates a real problem, however, because our nation's water infrastructure has become increasingly enfeebled. Following the lead of the Clean Water Act, SDWA provided billions of dollars in grants for the construction and upgrading of treatment plants.

DRINKING WATER PROTECTION FROM 1986 TO 1996

Contaminants

As described above, SDWA's reach extends both to regulated contaminants (through MCLs) and unregulated contaminants (through candidate contaminants that may eventually have MCLs). This seems straightforward, until one realizes that there are more than 85,000 chemicals in use. After the first decade, EPA had regulated only twenty-three contaminants. The slow pace of determining MCLs was largely due to the complicated nature of establishing defensible standards. Assembling the scientific record and fully complying with the requirements of the Administrative Procedure Act resulted in it taking years to develop and promulgate MCLs.[16]

Impatient with EPA's pace in determining MCLs, Congress took a much more prescriptive approach in the 1986 amendments (much as it did in the amendments to the Resource Conservation and Recovery Act two years earlier), and put in place a very ambitious timetable. The amendments provided EPA a list, mandating the agency to establish MCLs for eighty-three contaminants in the first five years, and then an additional twenty-five MCLs every three years thereafter.

EPA greatly increased the rate of establishing MCLs, but this approach was criticized as rigid and inflexible. Contaminants that may have seemed serious risks in 1986 may seem less important in light of new knowledge. In the meantime, new contaminants of concern emerged, such as the pathogen cryptosporidium that killed scores of people in an outbreak in Milwaukee in 1993. This was a high-profile event that increased pressure on EPA to show results. Such a breakneck pace, though, risked poorly developed MCLs. EPA soon fell behind, missing deadlines and being sued as a result. This led to a major shift in the 1996 amendments, which abandoned the timetable approach.

The Lead and Copper Rule described in the introduction to this chapter was issued in 1991. It posed a novel challenge because the contaminant was rarely present in the source water but, rather, was introduced by lead pipes and solder at the end of the distribution system. As a result, the Lead and Copper Rule is the only drinking water regulation that requires sampling in homes under specific procedures. Additional action is required if more than 10% of water samples exceed the "action level" of 15 ppb. If systems are still above the action level after installing corrosion control treatment, they must replace 7% of lead service lines (LSLs) annually, though the utilities could count LSLs as being replaced if a sample from the line tested below the action level. LSL replacement could stop if samples were below the action level for consecutive six-month periods. A formal revision of the rule was proposed in 2019.

Source Water Protection

The 1986 amendments also created the Wellhead Protection Program. This is a voluntary program encouraging states to protect the areas around water supply wells from contaminants that threaten groundwater.

In 1989, EPA issued the Surface Water Treatment Rule, providing a clever approach for source protection by focusing on upstream watersheds. The rule required treatment of surface water sources for large PWS.[17] Filtration could be avoided, however, if a watershed control program minimized microbial contamination of the source waters. New York City estimated it would cost \$3–\$6 billion to build a treatment plant. Taking advantage of this waiver, the city instead negotiated a comprehensive Memorandum of Agreement with communities in the Catskills and Delaware watersheds—the distant sources of the water pumped to the city. The agreement provided for acquisition of environmentally sensitive lands, strong watershed rules, and a comprehensive protection program. The first waiver was granted in 1993 and has been regularly renewed ever since. By investing in "green infrastructure" rather than the "grey infrastructure" of a treatment plant, New York City found a less-costly protection strategy that had major conservation benefits. This case has become the classic example of payments for ecosystem services.

DRINKING WATER PROTECTION FROM 1996 TO 2006

Contaminants

The 1996 amendments brokered a series of compromises over funding, treatment standards, and deadlines. Congress responded to the strong calls for EPA to slow down so the agency could be more thorough and strategic, with a particular concern over the costs imposed on smaller water systems with limited ability to raise funds for treatment. Setting standard after standard risked exceeding the financial capacity of small water systems. Better to ensure that new standards warranted the investments. Thus, the mandatory schedules for MCL development from the 1986 amendments were removed. EPA was given the authority to select which contaminants required MCLs. For the first time, EPA was allowed to consider treatment technologies in place of performance standards. And progress was made developing standards that had been stalled: radon, disinfection by-products, and sulfates, among others.

Better regulation would require a more rigorous understanding of the relative costs and risks. Hence the removal of the deadlines was coupled with the requirement that EPA conduct an analysis of the costs to water suppliers and the benefits to public health of proposed MCLs.

Seeking to address the high compliance costs that small water systems said threatened their viability, the 1996 amendments authorized states to issue variances to any size system that: (1) cannot afford best available technology and, (2) cannot feasibly connect with another water source. Instead, these systems needed to comply with a new standard, known as the Best Available Affordable Technology (BAAT) that may fail to meet an MCL but does not pose an unreasonable risk to health. States were required to review these variances every three years.

Seeking to increase transparency and improve the public's understanding of its drinking water supply, the 1996 amendments required PWS to deliver Consumer Confidence Reports (CCRs) every six months.[18] CCRs provide information on violations of drinking water regulations and contaminant levels. Since the Flint crisis, they must include additional information on corrosion control efforts and lead action level exceedances that require corrective action. This requirement for public self-reporting has been effective. A study of 517 Massachusetts PWS from 1990 to 2003 found that those utilities mailing CCRs directly to their customers reduced total violations by between 30% and 44% and reduced the more severe health violations by 40–57%.[19]

Risk assessment and management lie at the very core of SDWA's mandate. The statute both instructs the agency to act when there is a "meaningful opportunity for health risk reduction" but also to determine whether the benefits of the MCL "justify" the costs. As a result, there is an inescapable degree of imprecise judgment in setting many of the standards. This was especially clear in the promulgation of arsenic standards.

Arsenic is a naturally occurring chemical, particularly in parts of the Southwest. The PHS set a standard for arsenic in 1942 at 50 ppb. The 1996 amendments required EPA to set an MCL by 2001. Near the end of the Clinton administration, EPA proposed reducing the level to 10 ppb. There was significant pushback to this stricter standard from communities who argued that the costs of compliance would be infeasible or even impossible for smaller water systems. They warned that water bills could increase $200 or $300 a month to pay for capital costs and operation and maintenance costs. As one official from Lewiston, Maine, memorably argued during the debate over the 1996 amendments, as a result of compliance with stricter drinking water standards, "We will have the cleanest water in the state and the dumbest kids."[20] In other words, forcing communities to devote significantly greater resources to treating drinking water would divert funds from arguably more important needs (in this case, from education). This is an example of a risk-risk dilemma, where managing one risk heightens other risks, and is particularly difficult to manage in poor communities. [21]

The incoming George W. Bush administration viewed the arsenic rules as midnight regulation, signed just before Clinton left office. Concerned over the projected $200 million compliance costs, one of the administration's first acts was to suspend the more stringent standard and authorize a second review of the potential adverse health effects by the National Academy of Sciences. There was a fear that the rules had been rushed through and a genuine concern over the potential costs for small water systems that served communities that traditionally voted Republican.

The Bush (43) administration immediately came under intense criticism from not only environmentalists but also many Republicans. As the staunchly conservative *Wall Street Journal* thundered, "you may have voted for him, but you didn't vote for this in your water."[22] The administration ultimately gave way, sticking with the 10 ppb standard. President Bush later acknowledged that repealing the standard had been a terrible mis-step so early in his presidency.

Looking beyond the awful media coverage, the key point is that the science could not fully answer the challenge of standard setting for arsenic. In the EPA's analysis for the new regulation, the calculated benefits were extremely uncertain, with estimates ranging from 6 lives saved through the new standards to 112. Cass Sunstein, a law professor and the Obama administration's chief reviewer of agency regulations, looked carefully at the history of the arsenic regulation and concluded, somewhat with his hands in the air, that "EPA could make many reasonable decisions here, and in the range below 50 parts per billion and above 5 parts per billion, there is no obviously correct choice."[23] The dilemmas of inexact science and risk-risk trade-offs are not unique to arsenic. Many drinking water contaminants, including fluoride, disinfection by-products, and perchlorates, pose similarly difficult challenges.

While EPA has issued a number of revised standards and treatment rules since the 1996 amendments, it has not regulated any new contaminants in drinking water.[24] In addition, most of the standards have not been revised since being added in the 1970s and 1980s. It's important to recognize, though, that this has not been for lack of effort by the EPA. Adding or revising an

MCL is onerous and can be controversial. Since many Superfund sites choose MCLs as the basis for the cleanup standards (known as ARARs), the implications of where the standards are set go far beyond the tap.

For example, efforts to regulate perchlorate, a chemical that harms the thyroid, commenced in the George W. Bush administration. The Department of Defense was concerned that strict standards for perchlorate in drinking water could greatly increase the cost of Superfund cleanups of the contaminant at their bases. As a result, the DOD made use of the interagency consultation process to push for establishment of a National Academy of Science panel to study the issue. The review both slowed the process and recommended a scientifically valid and less stringent reference dose. EPA was under a court deadline to finalize it by 2020, more than a decade after the process began. In July, 2020, however, EPA announced that perchlorate did not meet the criteria for regulation as a drinking water contaminant and determined not to issue a perchlorate standard.

A key point of this story, true not only for SDWA but for many of EPA's statutory authorities, is that the agency is often not the only or even the most important decision-maker in establishing MCLs. Depending on the administration and the issue, other agencies with more political clout, or groups within the White House, can strongly influence the regulatory process. (See Chapter 13).

Funding

As part of the deal to abandon strict deadlines for MCLs, more money was provided for small systems, addressing their difficulty in issuing bonds with poor credit ratings. Following the model of the Clean Water Act, the 1996 amendments supplanted its grants program with the Drinking Water State Revolving Fund (DWSRF). Congress provided grants to states and territories, with the recipients adding a twenty-percent match. States can set aside up to thirty-one percent of this amount for specified purposes such as technical assistance to small systems and land acquisition for source water protection. Each state's program uses the remaining capital to make low interest loans for infrastructure projects. The loan is revolving because payments coming in are then lent out as new loans for other projects.

Source Water Protection

SDWA's authority to protect surface waters remained limited, with some strengthening of information requirements. The 1996 amendment mandated states to create source water assessments, identifying the susceptibility of their PWS to contamination. Each assessment must be made available to the public. The hope is that these findings will spur states and communities to put in place source water protection programs. There is no authority to require action, in large part because land use control has long been jealously guarded as a local government power. As a result, SDWA has no real way to address contamination of source waters from nonpoint pollution such as pesticides and fertilizer. This lack of authority has been subject to serious criticism following contamination from algal blooms. Congress, however, has not expanded SDWA's authority over land use practices that contaminate source waters. As a result, USDA and OSHA have arguably done more for source water protection than SDWA

The most important change in source water protection occurred in 2005. Injections from hydraulic fracturing were exempted from SDWA, except where diesel fuel is utilized, in the 2005 Energy Security Act. The amendment is commonly called the "Halliburton Loophole" because of the role played by Vice President Dick Cheney, former head of Halliburton.[25] Few at the time recognized the explosive growth of fracking in the following decade, or the patchwork of state laws that would arise to address aquifer contamination from fracking bans in some states to weak monitoring requirements in others.

DRINKING WATER PROTECTION FROM 2006 TO TODAY

Contaminants

Unlike the early MCLs, the current drinking water contaminants are ubiquitous and at very low levels. This is the case not only for newly recognized threats from compounds such as PFOA and PFAS (released from fire-fighting foams and Teflon production), but also for the much larger category of what has become known as "emergent contaminants." Evidence has mounted that some chemical contaminants may disrupt the development of humans and animals by fooling our endocrine system. The endocrine system controls the production and release of hormones—the chemical signals that regulate critical aspects of our development and behavior. Endocrine disruptors, a class of synthetic compounds, can mimic hormones and potentially interfere with the endocrine system and sexual development. About fifty chemicals have thus far been shown to have the capacity to act as endocrine disruptors. Chemically stable and difficult to remove with conventional drinking water treatment methods, endocrine disruptors' presence in our drinking water and its likely impact on human populations remain highly contentious.

Levels of pharmaceuticals and personal care products in our drinking water have also caused concern. Millions and millions of people ingest pharmaceutical products every day of the year, drugs treating a dizzying range of conditions from cancer, arthritis, bacterial infections, and hair loss to blood pressure, depression, and high cholesterol. These drugs are specifically designed to change our bodies' chemistry, so their presence in the water we drink has caused alarm in some quarters. And these drugs are surely present in our water. In a widely publicized study, the Associated Press documented the presence of fifty-six pharmaceuticals or their by-products in treated drinking water, including in the water of metropolitan areas supplying more than forty million people across the nation.[26]

There are no regulations requiring testing for the presence of endocrine disruptors or pharmaceuticals in drinking water or limiting their concentration. The Associated Press study contacted sixty-two major drinking water providers. Twenty-eight of those, just under half, tested for drugs in water. Those not testing included facilities serving some of our nation's largest cities—New York, Houston, Chicago, and Phoenix.[27]

The risk of emergent contaminants may be real, but it is largely unknown. A review of the literature in a peer-reviewed scientific journal was inconclusive.[28] Scientific progress has created two sorts of problems, both difficult to manage. The first, seen with endocrine disruptors and pharmaceuticals, is that we are introducing compounds into our environment and drinking water sources that quite literally did not exist decades ago. So how can we assess the unknown? The second problem is that our detection capability has dramatically improved. We can now identify traces of pollutants at excruciatingly tiny levels, at parts per trillion and some even at parts per quadrillion. Yet our progress in detection of harmful compounds has not been matched by equal progress in our ability to link the presence of these compounds at very low levels with the actual risks they pose to us.

Since the Flint tragedy in 2015, the risks from lead in drinking water have become only too well known. High levels of lead have also been found in the drinking water in Newark, Washington DC, and other cities. In 2019, EPA issued proposed revisions to the Lead and Copper Rule, revisions that had been under development since 2011. In simple terms, the revised rule requires water systems to create a public inventory of Lead Service Lines (LSLs). Systems must "find and fix" homes with lead levels above 15 ppb. The tap sampling procedures have been revised to make it harder to game the system by running the tap before testing. And the rule strengthens communication, requiring water systems to notify a customer within 24 hours if a sample exceeds 15 ppb. Systems must also now test for lead levels in schools and day care centers. The main controversy has been over the LSL replacement provisions.

Under the revised rule, water systems must replace the system-owned part of the LSL when customers replace their line. For systems with samples between 10 ppb-15 ppb, the system must work with the state to set an annual replacement goal. Systems with samples above 15 ppb must replace a minimum of 3% of the number of LSLs annually. Much of the criticism has focused on the new rate of 3% instead of the earlier rate of 7% annual replacement. In its defense, EPA has argued that it closed the major loophole of systems being able to avoid LSL replacement if a sample from the line tested below the action level for consecutive six-month periods.

Enforcement

SDWA is designed with multiple redundancies. The local water providers, both public and private, provide the first line of protection. They operate the treatment plant and supervise the infrastructure for water delivery. Because of widespread primacy, the local utilities are supervised by state authorities to ensure compliance with the standards and procedures for sampling and testing. The EPA provides the final check. It determines the water-testing schedules and the methods that must be used to ensure compliance. Regional EPA offices look over the shoulders of the state regulators, ensuring adequate compliance monitoring and enforcement. If a contaminant poses an "imminent and substantial endangerment" to human health and the state/local authorities have not acted to protect the health of people, then EPA has emergency authority to step in and take appropriate enforcement action. This authority had been delegated to regional EPA administrators but rarely exercised. The process was revised following the Flint crisis to involve the Office of Enforcement and Compliance Assurance more directly.

There has been significant noncompliance under SDWA, with violations in three to ten percent of systems every year. A series of articles in the *New York Times* in 2009 reported that more than twenty percent of the water treatment systems across the country had violated key provisions of SDWA.[29] EPA Administrator Lisa Jackson candidly acknowledged that "in many parts of the country, the level of significant noncompliance with permitting requirements is unacceptably high and the level of enforcement activity is unacceptably low."[30] A highly publicized 2015 study by the National Resources Defense Council (NRDC) reported 80,834 violations of SDWA, including both health-based violations and monitoring/reporting violations.[31] Violations occurred in all fifty states and all US territories, covering 77 million people, roughly one-quarter of the country's population.

The most comprehensive peer reviewed study to date analyzed data from 17,900 community water systems from 1982-2015.[32] Figure 6.1 shows the study results, demonstrating the continuing frequency of violations (DBP refers to the Disinfection By-Product Rule; CWS to Community Water Systems).

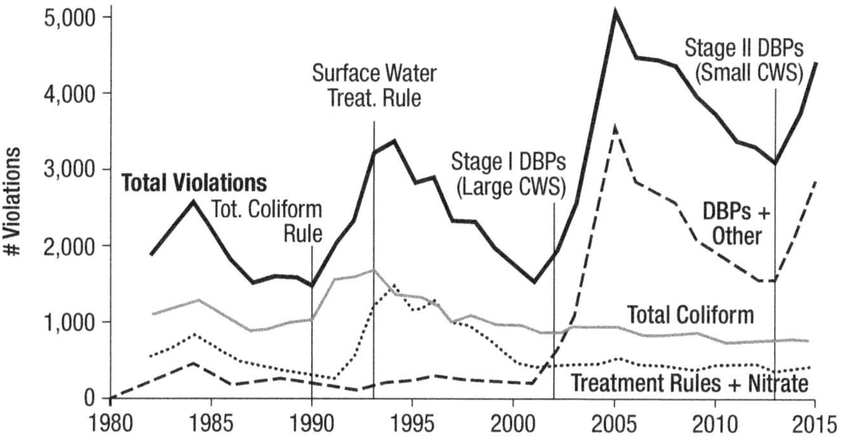

Figure 6.1. Analysis of 17,900 Community Water Systems from 1982–2015. ***Maura Allaire, Haowei Wu, and Upmanu Lall, "National Trends in Drinking Water Quality Violations," Proceedings of the National Academy of Sciences 115, no. 9 (February 27, 2018): 2078–83.***

There is disagreement over whether smaller systems suffer greater noncompliance. The NRDC study reported that very small systems, such as those in rural and more sparsely populated areas, had a higher percentage of health-based violations. The peer-reviewed study described above concluded that violation incidences were much higher in rural than urban areas, but that small systems did not have significantly different rates of violation than larger systems. EPA similarly reported in 2018 the rate of noncompliance did not significantly differ according to the size of the system—7.1% of the smallest systems had violations compared to 6.7% of the largest systems. Only one-fifth of these systems were persistently in violation, meaning that most of the noncompliant systems changed from year to year.

A key question is why there have been such large numbers of violations. On its face, there is significant compliance and enforcement activity. In 2016, for example, there were almost 60,000 site visits to PWS uncovering 39,580 violations, of which 4,470 (11%) were serious violations.[33] This resulted in 30,478 enforcement actions by EPA and state authorities.[34]

Researchers have suggested that the public nature of most PWS may be an important factor for the noncompliance rates. One large empirical study of the Clean Air Act and SDWA found that public entities were in noncompliance significantly more often than private firms yet were less likely to be penalized for violations.[35] This finding is also consistent with the surprising ineffectiveness of citizen suits.

SDWA's citizen suit provisions are virtually identical to those in the Clean Water Act (CWA). Any citizen may commence a civil action against any person (including the United States) alleged to be in violation of any requirement under the statute. There is a sixty-day notice requirement and the court may award costs of litigation to any party as the court determines appropriate.

During the first four decades of SDWA, there was virtually no litigation under SDWA's citizen suit provision. Indeed, there were only twenty-two suits over the first forty-three years. There has been an increase since the Flint crisis, but the number of suits is startlingly low. Consider that there have been thousands of CWA citizen suits over the same period and the two statutes have the same citizen suit provisions. The same imbalance is also true for Notice of Intent (NOI) to sue the EPA. From 1995-2003, there were only 10 NOI under SDWA compared to 270 under the CWA.[36] Some citizen suits have been effective. Litigation by the Bull Run Coalition in the late 1980s and more recent litigation by Riverkeepers have been moderately effective getting EPA to meet statutory deadlines, but these are the exceptions that prove the rule.

Both statutes require self-reporting of violations. Indeed, SDWA violations are easier to find than CWA violations. As described earlier, the 1996 amendments required PWS to deliver Consumer Confidence Reports (CCRs) every six months. CCRs provide information on violations of drinking water regulations and contaminant levels. Since the Flint crisis, they must include additional information on corrosion control efforts and lead action level exceedances that require corrective action. This requirement for public self-reporting has been effective yet it has not driven citizen suits.

Why so few? It doesn't correlate with numbers of government enforcement actions. An average of one citizen suit every two years seems less a case of "The Dog That Didn't Bark" but rather "The Case of the Missing Dog."

In speaking with agency officials, environmental groups, and scholars, a number of explanations for the low number of suits have been suggested. The first is the difficulty of suing your own PWS. Often, violations occur because of infrastructure problems that result from inadequate funds. Cash-strapped systems are much more likely to be in noncompliance than better-funded PWS. Lack of resources is more often the driver of noncompliance than malfeasance. If the lawsuit is successful, it will likely mean higher rates to come into compliance. These increases could be particularly significant and challenging for smaller water utilities that cannot easily issue a bond or raise rates. This is in marked contrast to CWA, where citizen suits routinely target private companies.

Part of the answer may lie in the fact that SDWA simply has not been a focus of environmental groups. There is no doubt that SDWA is a neglected statute in law schools. It is rarely covered in environmental law casebooks, rarely taught in courses, and rarely written about by scholars, except in passing. Prior to Flint, SDWA received almost no attention in the environmental law community. This was equally true for foundations, who rarely funded drinking water projects. NRDC was the only major environmental group with a significant focus on national SDWA concerns prior to Flint.

With few national or local environmental groups funded and focused on drinking water quality, one would expect few citizen suit or lobbying efforts. This stands in marked contrast to the many waterkeeper and other organizations monitoring water quality and litigating under the CWA. This is magnified by the fact that civil penalties are available for citizen suits filed under CWA but not under SDWA. Without the threat of large fines for non-compliance, PWS are less likely to settle, making civil suit litigation more expensive.

Finally, SDWA provides no enforcement mechanism against the sources of contamination. Whether nitrates in agricultural areas or cyanotoxins from algal blooms, SDWA is not designed to get at the real parties to blame for much source water pollution. The drafters of SDWA clearly regarded land use as the domain of local government and (as with the CWA) provided no real power for EPA to address nonpoint source pollution. As a result, it is often more effective to use CWA or nuisance suits to get at drinking water problems than SDWA.

Source Protection

An ounce of prevention may be worth a pound of cure but, out of concern for local land use powers, Congress provided EPA little direct authority to protect source waters. The consequences of this have been made clear in a number of drinking water disasters. In 2014, thousands of gallons of an industrial chemical used for treating coal leaked from the Freedom Industries facility in Charleston, West Virginia, down the bank into the Elk River, located just a mile upriver from the intake point for the region's drinking water treatment plant. Residents quickly noticed the licorice smell and a few hours later were officially warned not to drink or cook, wash, or bathe with the water. A state of emergency was declared in nine counties. Schools, hospitals, restaurants, hotels, and more closed. About 300,000 residents were affected. Later that year, a half- million residents of Toledo, Ohio, were warned not to drink their water because of a toxin called microcystin caused by an algal bloom from agricultural nutrient runoff.

In a creative 2015 lawsuit, the Des Moines Water Works sued thirteen drainage districts in Iowa for operating without appropriate Clean Water Act discharge permits and for the injuries suffered from having to remove high levels of nitrates from source waters.[37] The case was dismissed in 2017, with the court finding that the drainage districts had unqualified immunity from damage claims and injunctive relief, and that the drainage districts had no power to redress the Water Works' injuries.[38] Notably, the lawsuit did not have any SDWA claims.

The net result is that SDWA assigns primary authority to water utilities for ensuring safe drinking water, but they have virtually no authority over sources of water contamination. Neither EPA nor the utilities can regulate nonpoint sources pollution from farms. Thanks to the Halliburton amendment they cannot regulate fracking. And they cannot regulate the storage of dangerous chemicals near water supplies. As a result, water utilities are placed in the position of cleaning up water that has already been contaminated.

It would be much more efficient to avoid the contamination in the first place. This dynamic occurs throughout environmental law, and pits pollution control (cleaning after the fact) against pollution prevention (avoiding harm in the first place). Yet the power of the farm lobby largely prevents this from taking place.

Funding

While a rough measure, every two minutes a major water line bursts in the United States. It may be in Topeka, Kansas, or Tucumcari, New Mexico. In our nation's capital, Washington, DC, the rate is about one pipe break a day.[39] The massive pipes that supply New York City are leaking thirty-six million gallons per day.[40] Engineers fear that their structural integrity has become so compromised that draining the pipes for repair would cause them to buckle and collapse under the weight of the soil on top. Overall, roughly sixteen percent of the nation's piped water is lost from leaks and system inefficiencies—seven billion gallons of treated water every day.

The cause in all these cases is the same: inadequate investment in our pipes and treatment plants. Some of our water and sewer lines date from the Civil War. Most were built by our grandfathers' and great-grandfathers' generations.

Despite the obvious importance, gaining funding to rebuild our water and sewer lines remains elusive. We are starving our water system of funds and have been doing so for years. Part of the reason is the invisibility of the water system, part is the lack of public understanding over how antiquated our infrastructure has become, and part is the refusal to pay for what the system really costs. Perhaps the failure to invest in infrastructure should not be surprising. These arteries and veins of our water system are invisible, buried beneath roads, fields, and buildings. The only time we think about them is when they fail. And the sums required to remedy the decades of underfunding are massive. It costs about $200 per foot of replacement pipe, $1 million every mile.[41] New York City's Third Water Tunnel, currently scheduled for completion in 2020, will span more than 60 miles and meet the growing water demands of more than 9 million area residents, but it comes with a $6 billion price tag.

Since 1997, the State Revolving Fund has distributed more than $26 billion in grants and loans to improve water treatment and delivery systems. Congress appropriates roughly $1 billion per year. That's impressive, until one realizes that EPA has estimated $472 billion in infrastructure needs through 2030.[42] The American Water Works Association has estimated the cost at $1 trillion. You don't need higher-order mathematics to spot the problem. To be sure, these are large sums, but compared to what? How much would it cost were our water distribution and treatment systems to fail?

There are two primary sources of funding for drinking water infrastructure: rate payers and government. Funds raised from water customers cover the lion's share of operation and maintenance as well as capital costs. Larger systems rely on debt financing through bonds for large-scale capital projects. This obviously is infeasible for small systems that are cash strapped.

Rate-based financing, though, only goes so far, for it can be very difficult to raise rates significantly. Most people seem to assume that cheap water should be ours by right and that government, somehow, should find the means to pay for it on its own. To those in the water business, our unwillingness to make the proper level of investment is foolhardy. George Hawkins, former head of the District of Columbia Water and Sewer Authority, makes a telling comparison: "People pay more for their cell phones and cable television than for water. You can go a day without a phone or TV. You can't go a day without water."[43]

When Hawkins approached the District of Columbia's City Council to ask for a modest rate raise, though, he was raked over the coals. Jim Graham, a council member, proclaimed, "This rate hike is outrageous. Subway systems need repairs, and so do roads, but you don't see fares or tolls skyrocketing. Providing inexpensive, reliable water is a fundamental obligation of government. If they can't do that, they need to reform themselves, instead of just charging more."[44] Graham was unhelpfully silent on how the water utility can reform itself to provide the money necessary for maintenance and upgrades on a decaying system.

The second source of funding, which has proven critical for infrastructure, is federal grants and loans. The Drinking Water State Revolving Fund

(DWSRF) was added in the 1996 amendments. From 1998 to 2016, the federal government invested about $19 billion in the DWSRF, which has resulted in more than $32.5 billion going to water system projects across the nation. In 2018 Congress passed the America's Water Infrastructure Act (AWIA). This reauthorized the DWSRF, increasing its budgets with $1.174 billion authorized in 2019, $1.3 billion in 2020, and $1.95 billion in 2021. The loan amortization period was also extended from twenty to thirty years (and from thirty to forty years for disadvantaged communities).

Congress has also passed legislation creating new funding programs. The Water Infrastructure Finance and Innovation Act of 2014 (WIFIA) provides low-interest, long-term federal loans to communities for large water infrastructure projects. The Water Infrastructure Improvements for the Nation Act of 2018 (WIIN) was directed at small and disadvantaged communities, with a focus on lead-related issues. This act provided $20 million for lead testing in school and childcare programs, $10 million for reduction in lead exposure, and $20 million for infrastructure, managerial, and financial training in small and disadvantaged communities. This is particularly significant since many small water systems struggle with operations and maintenance.

Perhaps the greatest immediate funding challenge is posed by lead service lines. There are over six million lead service lines in the country, connecting homes to the large water mains running underneath the streets. As explained in the Flint story, lead service lines are not necessarily a problem so long as corrosion inhibitors are kept at correct levels in the water. If the water becomes corrosive, though, or the protective layer is dislodged, then lead can dissolve into tap water. Replacing these lines is further complicated by the fact that the utility only owns the lines up to the property line. Households own the lines from the sidewalk to the home. Washington, DC launched a large partial lead service line removal project, replacing only the service lines from the water mains to the edge of the property line, but learned that this was worse than doing nothing because it dislodged the protective layer inside the pipe and introduced even more lead into water than before.

Numbers are inexact, but about 15-22 million citizens get their water through lead service lines. Utilities are not required to remove the entire lead service line, and it will be expensive to do so. After months of negotiation, Congress appropriated over $120 million for lead service line replacement in Flint. The American Water Works Association estimates that it will cost up to $30 billion to replace the over five million lead service lines across the nation.[45] This is no small undertaking, given that PWS don't even have an inventory of where those lines are located in communities. Is this too much to spend for a problem that can be avoided by properly treating the water with corrosion inhibitors? And who should pay for it—the federal government, states, cities, or private parties?

A fundamental challenge facing many cities is the shortcoming of the rate-based funding system. Many small systems do not have the rate-paying base to support upgrades in infrastructure or treatment technologies. In larger cities with a shrinking population base, a vicious cycle of rising costs for decaying infrastructure drives up rates for those who can least afford it. Consolidation of water systems has been posed as one remedy, but rates of consolidation have remained low for both business and local political reasons.

There are no easy answers to these challenges. Taken together, the DWSRF, WIFIA, AWIA, and WIIN represent important funding measures, particularly in an era of legislative gridlock. But the levels remain far below the hundreds of billions of dollars that EPA and the water industry deem necessary to maintain infrastructure, much less modernize it.

Indeed, there has been a remarkable lack of innovation in the water sector compared to other utilities, such as electricity generation. While modern treatment technologies, such as granular-activated carbon, membranes, and ultraviolet light or ozone for disinfection, are commercially available, they are the exception rather than the rule. Most PWS rely on mid-twentieth-century technologies and older. On their face, the water and electricity sectors share key similarities—natural monopoly, regulatory oversight, and risk aversion. Yet there are also key differences. There are more investor-owned utilities in the electricity sector and greater competition through regional grids.[46]

As a comprehensive study of the two sectors concluded:

> Most public water suppliers are governed either by local government officials (e.g., members of city councils) or by elected boards (e.g., the board members of irrigation districts). In voting for such officials, members of the local public generally seek three goals: reliability, safety, and low water prices. Elections for water officials are seldom contested except where these goals are threatened. . . . A number of these factors—high fragmentation, public ownership, political pressure for low water rates, and reliability concerns—as well as other issues, inhibit innovation.[47]

The core strategy of the CAA and CWA on technology forcing and best available technologies may also explain the difference, since there is no regulatory driver for sectoral innovation.

Source Protection

In 2010 EPA added a new class of wells in its Underground Injection Program. Responding to concerns over climate change, the agency promulgated regulations for Class VI wells. These are intended for the purpose of long-term storage of carbon dioxide, also known as carbon capture and storage. As with the other aspects of the UIC program, in practice the states administer the wells.

LOOKING FORWARD

EPA's management of drinking water can be viewed as a glass half empty or half full. On the positive side, provision of safe, reliable drinking water is routinely provided throughout the United States. We do not give a second thought when taking a sip from a nearby faucet in Portland, Oregon, or Portland, Maine, in Springfield, Illinois, or Springfield, Missouri. Thanks to SDWA, our tap water is clearly safer than before the law's passage. This is something to be celebrated, indeed it is a historic achievement, and one that billions of people throughout the world still do not enjoy.

At the same time, this success has led to a situation where safe water is largely taken for granted. It only takes a Flint disaster to make clear that this is a misplaced assumption. There are very real challenges posed by algal blooms, emerging contaminants, lead service lines, and source water protection, made all the more challenging because of inadequate funding and spotty enforcement.

Continued protection of our drinking water will require vigilance and perhaps a transformation. We are used to enjoying safe water and paying monthly bills as "consumer drinkers." Fundamental protection of our drinking water will not occur, however, unless we take on the role of "citizen drinkers." The central message of the Flint tragedy is that we cannot assume drinking water will be provided without meaningful oversight, particularly for those communities with the least political power. Going into the next fifty years, we must use our political process to demand effective protection through better enforcement of SDWA, adequate funding for our water infrastructure, and renewed scrutiny of activities threatening our source waters.

EPA has much to be proud of in protecting our precious drinking water, yet much remains to be done.

NOTES

1. Abby Goodnough, Monica Davey, and Mitch Smith, "When the Water Turned Brown," *New York Times*, January 23, 2016.
2. Merrit Kennedy, "Lead-Laced Water in Flint: A Step-By-Step Look at the Makings of a Crisis," *NPR.org*, April 20, 2016.

3. Marc A. Edwards et al., "Engineers Shall Hold Paramount the Safety, Health and Welfare of the Public—But Not if it Threatens Our Research Funding?" *flintwaterstudy.org*, October 10, 2016.

4. Robert D. Morris, *The Blue Death: Disease, Disaster, and the Water We Drink* (New York: Harper Collins, 2007), 162.

5. Patrick Gurian and Joel A. Tarr, "The First Federal Drinking Water Quality Standards and Their Evolution: A History From 1914 To 1974," In *Improving Regulation: Cases in Environment, Health, and Safety*, eds. Paul S. Fischbeck and R. Scott Farrow (Washington, DC: Resources for the Future, 2001).

6. Francis H. Chapelle, *Wellsprings: A Natural History of Bottled Spring Waters* (Camden, NJ: Rutgers University Press, 2005), 15.

7. Joseph Race, *Chlorination of Water* (New York: John Wiley & Sons, 1918), 63.

8. Gurian and Tarr, "The First Federal Drinking Water Quality Standards," 43, 53.

9. Ibid.

10. Ibid.

11. President's Council of Advisors on Science and Technology, *Report to the President: Science and Technology to Ensure the Safety of the Nation's Drinking Water* (Washington, DC: PCAST, December 2016), 25. "Community Water Systems provide drinking water to the same people year-round. . . . Non-Community Water Systems serve customers on less than a year-round basis. [Non-Transient Non-Community Water Systems] serve at least 25 of the same people for more than six months in a year but not year-round (e.g., schools or factories that have their own water source) . . . [Transient Non-Community Water Systems] provide water to places like gas stations and campgrounds where people do not remain for long periods of time."

12. This requirement was added in the 1996 amendments. The Unregulated Contaminant Monitoring Rule requires that EPA issue a new list every five years of up to thirty unregulated contaminants that PWS must monitor.

13. The difference in stringency can be significant. This can also complicate setting ARARs for Superfund cleanups since the choice needs to be made whether to rely on EPA or state standards.

14. NRDC v. EPA/South Carolina Dept. of Health and Environmental Control v. EPA, 812 F.2d 721 (D.C. Cir. 1987).

15. 42 U.S.C. §300j-8.

16. Vic Kimm, former head of the EPA Drinking Water program, interview by author, January 31, 2020.

17. US Environmental Protection Agency, "Surface Water Treatment Rules," *epa.gov*, accessed March 16, 2020, https://www.epa.gov/dwreginfo/surface-water-treatment-rules.

18. The 2018 America's Water Infrastructure Act (AWIA) changed the reporting requirement to every six months for systems serving more than ten thousand people.

19. Lori Snyder Bennear and Sheila M. Olmstead, "The Impacts of the 'Right to Know': Information Disclosure and the Violation of Drinking Water Standards,"

Journal of Environmental Economics and Land Management, 56, no. 2 (2008): https://doi.org/10.1016/j.jeem.2008.03.002.

20. Sue E. Umshler, "When Arsenic is Safer in Your Cup of Tea Than in Your Local Water Treatment Plant," *Natural Resources Journal* 39, no. 3 (Summer 1999).

21. This dilemma is also present in chlorination of water, which sets the risk of pathogens vulnerable to chlorine against carcinogenic compounds (trihalomethanes) which are created by chlorinating water with organic material. See generally, John D. Graham and Jonathan B. Wiener, *Risk vs. Risk: Tradeoffs in Protecting Health and the Environment* (Cambridge: Harvard University Press, 1997).

22. Cass R. Sunstein, "The Arithmetic of Arsenic," *Georgetown Law Journal* 90 (2001).

23. Sunstein, "The Arithmetic of Arsenic," 2258.

24. EPA has issued revisions since 2000 to the arsenic rule, the total coliform rule, and the lead and copper rule, as well as process-based standards such as the filter back wash rule and disinfection byproduct rule.

25. "The Halliburton Loophole," *New York Times,* Opinion, November 2, 2009, https://www.nytimes.com/2009/11/03/opinion/03tue3.html.

26. Jeff Donn, Martha Mendoza, and Justin Pritchard, "Pharmaceuticals Lurking in U.S. Drinking Water," *MSNBC.com*, March 10, 2008.

27. Seven endocrine disruptors were included in the national monitoring under the Third Unregulated Contaminant Monitoring Rule (UCMR3) and were detected in very low numbers.

28. Sara Rodriguez-Mozaz and Howard S. Weinberg, "Meeting Report: Pharmaceuticals in Water—An Interdisciplinary Approach to a Public Health Challenge," *Environmental Health Perspectives* 118, no. 7 (July 1, 2010): 1016.

29. Charles Duhigg, "Millions in US Drink Dirty Water, Records Show," *New York Times*, December 7, 2009.

30. Ibid.

31. Kristi Pullen Fedinick et al., *Threats on Tap: Widespread Violations Highlight Need for Investment in Water Infrastructure and Protections* (Washington, DC: NRDC, 2017), https://www.nrdc.org/sites/default/files/threats-on-tap-water-infrastructure-protections-report.pdf.

32. Maura Allaire, Haowei Wu, and Upmanu Lall, "National Trends in Drinking Water Quality Violations," *Proceedings of the National Academy of Science* 115, no. 9 (February 27, 2018): 2078–83.

33. US Environmental Protection Agency, "Analyze Trends: Drinking Water Dashboard," *epa.gov*, accessed March 16, 2020, https://echo.epa.gov/trends/comparative-maps-dashboards/drinking-water-dashboard?yearview=CY&view=activity&criteria=basic&state=National.

34. US Environmental Protection Agency, "Providing Safe Drinking Water in America: National Public Water Systems Compliance Report," *epa.gov*, last updated April 9, 2020, https://www.epa.gov/compliance/providing-safe-drinking-water-america-national-public-water-systems-compliance-report.

35. David Konisky and Manuel P. Teodoro, "When Governments Regulate Governments," *American Journal of Political Science* 60, no. 3 (July 2016): https://doi.org/10.1111/ajps.12221.

36. James R. May, "Now More Than Ever: Trends in Environmental Citizen Suits at 30," *Widener Law Review* 10, no. 1 (2003): 31.

37. MacKenzie Elmer, "Des Moines Water Works Won't Appeal Lawsuit," *Des Moines Register*, April 11, 2017.

38. Des Moines Water Works v. Sac County, 2017 WL 1042072 (N.D. Iowa 2017).

39. Charles Duhigg, "Saving U.S. Water and Sewer Systems Would Be Costly," *New York Times*, March 14, 2010.

40. Ken Belson, "Plumber's Job on a Giant's Scale: Fixing New York's Drinking Straw," *New York Times*, November 22, 2008, http://www.nytimes.com/2008/11/23/nyregion/23tunnel.html.

41. "New York Third Water Tunnel," *PBS.org*, 2001, http://www.pbs.org/wgbh/buildingbig/wonder/structure/ny_third_water.html.

42. US Environmental Protection Agency, *Drinking Water Infrastructure Needs Survey and Assessment: Sixth Report to Congress,* EPA-816-K-17-002 (Washington, DC: EPA, March 2018), https://www.epa.gov/dwsrf/epas-6th-drinking-water-infrastructure-needs-survey-and-assessment.

43. Duhigg, "Saving U.S. Water and Sewer Systems."

44. Ibid.

45. "Replacing All Lead Water Pipes Could Cost $30 Billion," *Water Tech Online*, March 11, 2016, https://www.watertechonline.com/home/article/15549954/replacing-all-lead-water-pipes-could-cost-30-billion.

46. Newsha K. Ajami, Barton H. Thompson, Jr., and David G. Victor, *The Path to Water Innovation* (Washington, DC: The Hamilton Project, 2014), https://www.hamiltonproject.org/papers/the_path_to_water_innovation.

47. Ibid.

Chapter Seven

Addressing Land Disposal of Wastes

Marcia Williams

The Clean Air Act and Clean Water Act were successful in curbing emissions of wastes into air and water, but the two laws contributed to pollution of the third media: land. In the 1970s the quantity of solid waste nationally was estimated to be between two and four billion tons per year and was growing at a rate of eight percent per year.[1] Land-based units were necessary to manage wastewater and concentrated waste streams that had previously been discharged directly into surface water bodies. Likewise, sludge and particulates containing hazardous constituents, previously emitted into the air or water, were now collected in pollution control devices or treatment units and placed into land disposal units. Thus, land in America became the last unregulated sink for disposal of environmental pollution.

Congress did not fully appreciate the mass transfer of pollution that would occur due to the Clean Air Act and Clean Water Act, but EPA played a critical role in informing Congress of this unpleasant reality. Using authority established in the 1965 Solid Waste Disposal Act (SWDA), as amended in 1970 by the Resource Recovery Act (RRA), EPA collected data on the disposal of wastes and reported to Congress on the swelling pollutant transfer that was occurring between environmental media.[2] EPA's role in the early 1970s was limited to one of information gathering and sharing. The fifty states were in the lead for ensuring the proper management of solid wastes, whether those wastes were managed on-site at their point of generation or off-site at a commercial or municipal treatment, disposal, or recycling facility. The states were also responsible for enforcing against entities that engaged in improper waste disposal practices.

In the 1970s, EPA tracked the progress made by states in implementing their programs, most of which had originated with federal grants and technical assistance authorized under the 1965 SWDA. EPA highlighted the challenges states were facing, including resource shortages and the need for additional technical support and training.[3] Most states were focused on the subset of wastes called municipal wastes, those generated by households and businesses that either were sent to public sewers at a public treatment plant or sent directly to public land disposal sites. Pre-1970, few states had implemented even basic protections for managing these wastes. States were instead focused on establishing rudimentary municipal waste permit programs and stopping dumping of wastes at non-permitted locations. States generally paid much less attention to the methods used by industry to manage industrial wastes on their own property. While limited public-sector resources were one reason for deference to industry, many states were also concerned that, if they cracked down on industrial waste management, more permissive states nearby might become a more appealing home for industry. Thus, the need for national regulation of industrial wastes, particularly those that were potentially hazardous, became a major issue in Congress in the early 1970s.

As required by Section 212 of the 1970 RRA, EPA collected information on the subset of solid wastes that were potentially hazardous, issuing an informative report to Congress in 1973 entitled *Disposal of Hazardous Wastes*.[4] EPA found that hazardous waste generation was growing, hazardous waste disposal to land was increasing, current expenditures by generators managing hazardous waste was low relative to what was needed to be environmentally protective, technology generally existed to manage these wastes more protectively but economic incentives to do so were lacking, and adequate regulation of these wastes at the federal, state, and local level was largely nonexistent. EPA also developed a set of "damage cases" associated with mismanagement of potentially hazardous industrial wastes.[5] The types of damage cases were highly variable, including situations where poor waste management had resulted in groundwater contamination, explosions or fires, and direct contact poisoning. Armed with this information, Congress recognized the need for a special focus on hazardous waste, a subset of solid wastes that could cause significant adverse impacts due to their "quantity, concentration, or physical, chemical, or infectious characteristics. . . ."[6] Thus, technical information on potentially hazardous wastes, collected and reported by EPA, set the stage for passage of the 1976 Resource Conservation and Recovery Act.

In the final days before passage of RCRA, the need for it was described as follows in Congress:

> It is true that since 1965 there has been a Solid Waste Disposal Act. The Federal Government's role, however, in that Solid Waste Disposal Act has been extremely limited. EPA could issue guidelines and issue publications, but they could not issue any regulations. Consequently, the state of solid waste is worse today than it was when that Act became law in 1965.[7]

In signing RCRA into law, Republican President Gerald Ford cited the hazardous waste disposal aspects of the law as "one of the highest priority environmental problems confronting the Nation."[8]

This chapter explores EPA's role in implementing two new statutes enacted by Congress to address the disposal and re-use of waste: the 1976 Resource Conservation and Recovery Act (RCRA) and the 1984 Hazardous and Solid Waste Amendments to RCRA (HSWA).[9] The chapter examines the reasons for increasing congressional mistrust of the executive branch, including EPA, and the resulting impact on the direction of the RCRA program. Despite these challenging circumstances, EPA, through its technical and policy work under several presidential administrations, transformed increasingly prescriptive demands from Congress into a successful program. The concluding section of the chapter explores some remaining challenges and reforms that are worthy of consideration in the years ahead.

ARCHITECTURE OF THE RESOURCE CONSERVATION AND RECOVERY ACT OF 1976

RCRA was introduced in the US Senate by Representative Jennings Randolph (D-WV) on July 21, 1975, with bipartisan support, and passed the Senate on June 30, 1976, by a vote of 88-3. The House of Representatives passed the bill on September 27, 1976 with a 367-8 majority. President Ford signed the bill into law on October 21, 1976. The two big concerns driving its passage were the growing subset of waste considered hazardous as well as the widespread open dumping of all solid waste on land without consideration of environmental consequences.

With the passage of RCRA, Congress communicated a lack of faith in complete state-level control over the pace and scope of waste management regulation. Table 7.1 summarizes the basic architecture of RCRA, which included two major subtitles—one for hazardous waste and the other for all remaining solid waste. What Congress envisioned for hazardous wastes was a "cradle to grave" management system from its point of generation until final disposal. This necessitated creating definitions for the legal subset of solid wastes that were to be classified as "hazardous." It also put the federal government in the position of prescribing a protective hazardous waste management program that the states, not EPA, would implement.[10] States desperately wanted access to EPA's resources and guidance but quickly began to chafe at having to implement their programs in accordance with highly prescriptive federal requirements.

EPA found itself in a challenging position. Authorizing state partners to implement the permitting and enforcement aspects of the program was critical if meaningful nationwide improvements were to be achieved. However, insofar as states chose not to implement the program the way EPA envisioned, Congress left EPA with only a very blunt instrument to address the problem—EPA could withdraw the state's authority to implement the hazardous-waste provisions of RCRA in lieu of EPA, leaving regulated entities in those states with the complex obligation of complying simultaneously with overlapping and uncoordinated federal and state regulations. As EPA learned the hard way, the blunt tool was politically untenable, leaving EPA with only persuasion and grant money as inducements to get implementation underway.

A separate and less prescriptive framework was established for management of the larger universe of non-hazardous solid wastes. That framework relied upon a federal definition of what constituted minimum protective land disposal while still allowing states to tailor their programs in a far more flexible way than was provided for hazardous wastes. Congress banned the land disposal of any waste that failed to meet the minimum protective standards. Statutory provisions also reflected the congressional goal of increasing the re-use, rather than disposal, of both solid and hazardous waste.

EPA'S INITIAL IMPLEMENTATION OF THE 1976 RCRA STATUTE

Shortly after RCRA's enactment in late 1976, EPA issued various advanced notices of proposed rulemaking (ANPRMs), scheduling public meetings and special meetings with states in order to obtain diverse input on how the agency should proceed. For hazardous wastes, there was no good framework to copy or build upon, as only a few states had begun to develop programs. Some states had developed solid waste regulatory programs, but these programs were quite variable in scope and approach and largely in their infancy. Despite the lack of perfect models, the statute imposed tight deadlines on EPA for completing both solid waste and hazardous waste rulemakings.[11]

EPA engaged in similar public outreach related to the new non-hazardous solid waste RCRA requirements. The key issues were state solid waste planning and EPA's grants to support it, the closure of open dumps, and the development of criteria to define minimum protections. Again, EPA raised numerous broad questions about what "adverse effects" the solid waste criteria should address and how the criteria should address protection of groundwater, surface water, and air quality. EPA also asked commenters about how to develop an accurate open dump inventory, ways to ensure open dumps got

Table 7.1. Key Architecture of the 1976 RCRA Statute

General Topic	*Key Provisions*
Hazardous Waste	• Identification of the subset of solid waste to be regulated as hazardous waste • Standards for generators of hazardous waste • Standards for transporters of hazardous waste • Standards for owners and operators of hazardous waste treatment, storage, and disposal facilities (TSDFs) • Permit requirements for TSDFs • Federal authorization of approved State hazardous waste programs to operate in lieu of Federal program • Federal enforcement with fines of up to $25,000/day and criminal provisions
Non-Hazardous Solid Waste	• Criteria to define sanitary landfills and prohibit open dumps • Identification of open dumps • Upgrading of all open dumps within five years of open dump inventory • Federal funding for approved state solid waste planning
Resource Conservation	• Specifications for secondary materials • Market development for recovered materials • Federal procurement guidelines to purchase products with recycled content
Studies	• Waste stream composition and re-use opportunities • Mining waste • Sludge (both municipal and industrial)
Other Key Provisions	• Integration with other environmental laws to avoid duplication • Citizen suits for failure to comply with RCRA solid or hazardous waste provisions • Federal facilities subject to all federal, state, and local waste requirements unless a presidential exemption was obtained • EPA ability to take action when waste results in an imminent and substantial endangerment • Public participation in development of all EPA waste programs and regulations

closed in a timely manner, impediments to the timely closure of open dumps, and inputs on the scope and timing for the state solid waste plans envisioned by RCRA.

Table 7.2 includes issues typical, but not inclusive, of those EPA addressed in its early public outreach on hazardous waste. There was wide attendance at EPA's 1977 public meetings and extensive submission of comments to EPA. In addition to broad participation from industrial and municipal waste genera-

Table 7.2. Examples of Early RCRA Hazardous Waste Regulatory Issues

General Topic	*Issue*
Hazardous Waste: Definitions	• What tests best define wastes that present flammability, corrosivity, and reactivity concerns in landfills? What other broad characteristics are necessary and what test methods exist? • How should EPA coordinate RCRA's requirement to list specific waste streams as hazardous with RCRA's requirement to develop broadly applicable hazardous waste characteristics? • Many wastes are heterogeneous or can separate into phases. How should a representative sample be obtained? • Do secondary materials that are being reclaimed or re-used classify as waste regulated by RCRA?
Hazardous Waste: Generators	• There are over 700,000 generators of hazardous waste. What monthly volume cut-off should be used to define those generators initially covered by RCRA's regulations? • Do generators need to keep records to support decisions that wastes are not RCRA hazardous? • How should EPA track the movement of hazardous wastes from the generating location to an off-site TSDF?
Hazardous Waste: Transporters	• How should EPA's RCRA requirements coordinate with Department of Transportation (DOT) requirements? • Should different types of transporters have different requirements?
Hazardous Waste: TSDFs	• Which standards can apply to all TSDFs vs ones that require tailoring to specific types of TSDFs? • What types of location, design, and operating requirements are needed? • How should EPA coordinate RCRA requirements at TSDFs with requirements in place (or planned) under the CAA or CWA? • Should requirements differ for existing facilities and new facilities?
TSDF Permits	• Who is required to obtain a permit and when should exemptions be given? • What information needs to be included in a permit application? • Should different types of permits be issued for different types of TSDFs? • How should EPA address public opposition to siting of TSDFs? • Can RCRA permit systems be integrated with other permits? • What conditions should be attached to allow existing facilities to continue operating prior to receiving a permit?

General Topic	*Issue*
Authorization for States to Implement the Federal Hazardous Waste Program	• Where did state programs have to be consistent with the federal requirements and where could they differ? • Logistically how can states take over RCRA implementation while EPA is still in the process of developing its RCRA regulations?

tors—some of whom managed their own wastes in on-site facilities—there was widespread interest from the developing commercial solid and hazardous waste industry, industry trade associations, local governments running land disposal facilities, states, and environmental groups. Given the variety of topics and extensive EPA public comments, EPA was not able to meet the (arguably unrealistic) statutory 18-month rulemaking deadlines. EPA did not issue proposed regulations on solid waste until early 1978; the proposal on hazardous wastes, where the issues were more contentious, followed in December 1978. Further delay occurred because, due to the extent of stakeholder interest, the agency found it prudent to hold another round of public meetings in 1979.[12] Final guidance for (non-hazardous) state planning on solid waste management was issued in mid-1979; the final criteria for protective land management of non-hazardous waste occurred in the fall of 1979.[13]

Significant pieces of the hazardous waste regulations were finalized in phases in 1980 although portions of the program addressing standards for permitted hazardous waste facilities were not completed until 1982. In finalizing the 1980 hazardous waste regulations, EPA deferred hazardous waste classification of certain high volume wastes from coal-fired electric power plants, oil and gas production facilities, cement kilns, and mining. Congress then intervened in October 1980 with legislation that exempted such "special wastes" from hazardous waste regulation until EPA prepared in-depth reports to Congress, which I discuss later in the chapter.

The Basic RCRA Regulatory Framework for Non-Hazardous Solid Waste

RCRA authorized EPA to implement a grant program for state solid waste management planning. Plans were intended to contain each state's fundamental strategy for implementing RCRA's mandate to update the protectiveness of solid waste management facilities and eliminate open dumps. In order to aid states, the law required EPA to develop criteria that could differentiate disposal facilities that were environmentally acceptable and those that were not.[14] The unacceptable facilities were classified as open dumps and states were required to close these facilities within five years. EPA was required to publish an annual inventory of existing open dumps for the purpose of informing both Congress and the public.

States had primary responsibility to close open dumps, but Congress authorized citizens to file suits to enforce against any open dump that was not operating under a state compliance schedule or was operating inconsistently with an approved state compliance schedule. Thus, Congress made citizens the back-up enforcers to the states. After providing notice to a state, EPA was also allowed to issue "imminent and substantial endangerment" orders on a case by case basis to close open dumps that were out of compliance.

EPA defined the solid waste criteria to include eight distinct health and environmental topics—floodplains, endangered and threatened species, surface waters, groundwater, waste application to land used for production of food-chain crops, disease vectors, air, and general safety (including the existence of explosive and toxic gases, bird hazards, public access, and fires). For each of the topics, the agency identified protective performance guidelines. The agency structured the topics with flexibility, recognizing that state and local implementing agencies would apply the criteria to widely varying types and locations of facilities as well as a variety of different types of solid wastes. (See Figure 7.1).

Early Implementation Challenges for the RCRA Non-Hazardous Solid Waste Program

In July 1981, the Government Accounting Office (GAO) reviewed the status of the non-hazardous solid waste management program.[15] EPA had awarded states over $47 million from October 1977 to March 1981 to develop state plans and a state open dump inventory, but GAO found that the progress was slow. As of June 1981, no state plans had received EPA approval and the May 1981 Open Dump Inventory was woefully incomplete.[16] The GAO noted that EPA's ability to continue funding these plans was limited; without federal funding, state progress would be significantly impacted. EPA did not disagree with the GAO's findings but noted that, without statutory authority to develop the open dump inventory itself and without adequate funding, progress would be severely impacted.

Due to lack of congressional funding, EPA eliminated financial grant assistance for state and local solid waste planning beginning in 1982. As of that time, the state efforts to get open dumps identified and upgraded or closed had made limited progress and several thousand known open dumps, largely

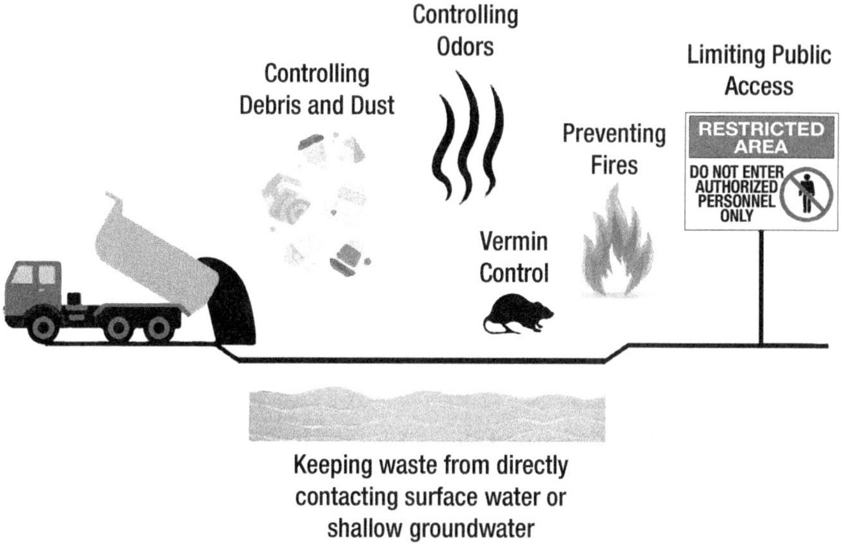

Figure 7.1. Concerns about Open Dumps in the 1970s and Earlier. ***Author-generated***

accepting municipal waste, remained operational. In many states, the state open-dump inventories focused only on identifying municipal solid waste disposal sites; the very large number of industrial, agricultural, mining, and other non-hazardous solid waste disposal sites were not identified or evaluated. Likewise, because of the resource-intensive demands of RCRA's hazardous waste program, EPA made no real progress completing the studies that Congress required on different large volume "special waste" streams, all of which were statutorily required to be completed in the early 1980s but each of which was just starting or still on the "to do" list as of 1983.

The Basic RCRA Framework for Hazardous Waste

EPA had to build a federal hazardous waste regulatory system from scratch without the benefit of well-functioning state models.[17] For wastes classified as hazardous, RCRA envisioned a "cradle to grave" management system that applied at each of the following points in a waste's life cycle: (1) at the point a hazardous waste is first generated, (2) at the generator's site, (3) to transporters carrying the hazardous waste off-site, (4) to entities storing the waste prior to recycling or reusing it, and (5) to entities storing, treating, or disposing of the waste. EPA also had to develop a process that allowed states to apply to

EPA for delegation to implement the RCRA regulatory requirements in lieu of the federal government.

RCRA implementation was so complicated that literally hundreds of manuals, guidance documents, and regulatory interpretive letters were issued by EPA to further define and clarify the program.[18] This section highlights a few of the many challenging choices that EPA made during the early development of the framework. In making these choices, EPA was faced with balancing a simpler regulatory framework against a more accurate regulatory framework.

Approach to Hazardous Waste Identification: Definition of Solid Waste

RCRA provided only general definitions of what constituted a solid waste and a hazardous waste. EPA's task was to further expand these definitions in ways that generators of waste could clearly understand whether their waste materials were covered under the comprehensive hazardous waste regulations. Since Congress had established that hazardous waste was a subset of solid waste, EPA's first challenge was to determine what constituted a solid waste. This turned out to be a very challenging question.

Congress defined solid waste to include discarded or abandoned materials, whether that material was physically solid, liquid, or a contained gas. Today, RCRA practitioners readily accept the fact that a liquid or a contained gas is a "solid waste." However, in 1980, this was a difficult concept to accept. The statutory definition was focused on capturing discarded materials without regard to their physical form. The statute did not tie the concept of a discarded material to whether that material was physically solid or liquid. Congress did, however, specifically exempt a handful of discarded materials that were regulated under other statutes. As an example, Congress excluded solid or dissolved material in domestic sewage since this material was already regulated under the Clean Water Act. A similar rationale was used to exempt effluent discharged under a Clean Water Act point source permit. The reasons for other EPA exemptions were varied and included both materials that were not deemed to result in environmental harm as well as discarded materials that, due to their nature, would be challenging to regulate under EPA's hazardous waste framework.

The concept of discard seems straightforward at first, but EPA found it difficult to apply in the case of secondary materials that generators were recycling or reusing.[19] In some cases, those materials resembled raw materials. By recycling or reusing them, generators were engaging in resource conservation and reducing the amount of waste discarded in the US. Upon more careful analysis, certain types of recycling or reuse more closely resembled disposal of some (or all of) the hazardous components found in the material.

For example, many entities wanted to use certain nitrogen-containing wastes as fertilizers, even though they contained high concentrations of heavy metals that did not beneficially contribute to the product.

EPA's challenge was to distinguish between recycling/reuse that resembled normal product manufacture and recycling/reuse that incorporated significant aspects of discard of hazardous constituents. EPA wanted to find a way to identify the latter group of materials as solid waste to ensure that the material would be protectively managed until the material was recycled. In situations where the recycling activities themselves involved discard, EPA would regulate them as hazardous waste treatment. While those types of decisions could be made fairly routinely if done on a case by case basis, there were thousands of potential wastes that could be recycled or reused in an unlimited number of ways. As EPA noted in the preamble to its 1985 final regulation on what types of wastes were considered hazardous waste even if they were going for recycling:

> We believe, however, that the grant of authority in RCRA over recycling activities is not unlimited. Specifically, we do not believe our authority extends to certain types of recycling activities that are shown to be very similar to normal production operations or to normal use of commercial products. We also do not accept the argument that a potentially harmful recycling practice is invariably subject to regulation under Subtitle C since potential environmental harm is not always a determinative indicator of how closely a recycling activity resembles waste management.[20]

EPA designed an approach that evaluated the waste-like nature of the recycling based on evaluating the type of secondary material being recycled as well as the way in which it was being recycled. (See Figure 7.2). The benefit of EPA's approach was it followed the principle of capturing activities that resembled discard by defining solid waste in a way that allowed generators of secondary materials to self-evaluate the status of their secondary materials. For secondary material recycling that fell outside of RCRA jurisdiction, EPA took the position that the recycling must be legitimate, not sham. EPA placed the burden of showing that recycling was legitimate on the waste generator. EPA included preamble language, guidance documents, and interpretive memoranda that discussed some indicators of legitimate recycling. More recently, EPA has incorporated the most important legitimacy factors into the definition of solid waste regulations.[21] The question of when secondary materials get regulated under RCRA has spawned a significant amount of litigation and continues to do so.[22]

EPA used a tailored approach - covered certain material/ recycling activity combinations as RCRA regulated but excluded others based on discard characteristics - 40 CFR 261.2	<u>Type of Material</u>	<u>Recycling Material</u>
	• Byproduct	• Use on ground
	• Sludge	• Energy recovery
	• Spent material	• Reclaim
	• Off-specification commercial product	• Accumulate for future potential use
	• Scrap metal	• Use directly without reclaim
	• Inherently waste-like	

Figure 7.2. EPA's Approach When Recycling Falls under RCRA. ***Author-generated***

Definition of Hazardous Waste

Given the broad definition of solid waste, EPA needed to determine which specific solid wastes should be classified as hazardous waste to provide a practical definition that generators could use to determine whether their wastes fit within those EPA would subject to hazardous waste regulatory requirements. This was a difficult problem. The statute required that EPA identify a set of characteristics of hazardous waste as well as a list of specific hazardous wastes that, by narrative definition, would be subject to hazardous waste requirements.

In the late 1970s, there were over fifty thousand chemicals in commerce in the US.[23] Those chemicals might be discarded in their pure form or could be found in either low or high concentrations mixed with other chemicals or with naturally occurring materials such as water or soil. If EPA possessed information on the toxicity of each chemical and the properties that determine how the chemical would behave when discarded, EPA could have developed a hazardous waste definition based solely upon concentrations of each chemical in the waste that would result in environmental harm, assuming the chemical was discarded in a solid waste landfill or lagoon or burned in a solid waste incinerator. However, such information was available for only a very limited number of chemical substances. See Chapter 9 on TSCA, which explains why so many chemicals in commerce lack basic toxicity information. Thus, EPA had to develop a different way of identifying the subset of solid waste it would define as hazardous waste.

EPA began by collecting significant information on the types and characteristics of wastes generated by individual industrial sectors, including information on how the wastes were being managed. EPA looked at whether there were incidents of harm or damage from current management practices. EPA recognized that non-industrial locations could generate hazardous waste, but the agency's initial focus was on the large volume of industrial waste that was understood to require management more rigorous than that provided by existing solid waste management facilities that were largely designed to accept municipal refuse.

EPA also proceeded to identify a set of general characteristics that would cause a waste to meet the statutory definition of a hazardous waste. To ensure that generators could determine whether their wastes met these characteristics, EPA sought characteristics that would allow for straightforward test methods or narrative definitions that could be applied based on normal generator knowledge of its waste. EPA ultimately chose four characteristics: ignitibility, corrosivity, reactivity, and toxicity.[24] The toxicity characteristic was initially limited to fourteen chemical constituents for which EPA had adequate toxicity data and information to suggest that the constituents, at or above specified concentrations, could result in groundwater contamination if they were co-disposed with municipal solid waste in a municipal landfill overlying a groundwater aquifer. The characteristic toxicity test was designed to simulate this specific mismanagement scenario. The choice of this mismanagement scenario reflected its widespread use as of 1980.

In order to provide certainty for waste generators, EPA also listed some specific hazardous wastes because they met one of the four general characteristics. However, EPA's main focus was on listing wastes that were not adequately captured by the characteristics, especially wastes that were acutely toxic and wastes that had the potential to result in chronic toxicity if mismanaged.

EPA began the listing process by identifying a set of underlying hazardous constituents, largely taken from lists of hazardous compounds or pollutants addressed in other statutes.[25] EPA then developed categories of listed hazardous waste, based on evaluating the constituents in the waste and their concentrations, with consideration of a set of other factors as considered appropriate.[26] The three broad categories were wastes from non-specific sources, wastes from specific sources, and discarded commercial chemical products. In each case, the regulations define, by narrative definition, which specific wastes are covered by the listing.

A background document for each listed waste was published that provided EPA's rationale and supporting data. These background documents included a description of the industry (or industries) generating the waste, a description of the activity (or activities) that generated the waste, a summary of the waste composition and concentration, a description of plausible waste management

Not Specific to Type of Business/Industry	Specific to an Industry	Unused Commercial Chemical Products
1. Waste: spent halogenated solvents such as TCE and still bottoms from their recovery	1. Waste: waste water treatment sludge	1. Waste: Benzene when present as a sole source active ingredient in an unused product or off specification product or a spill residue or container residue
2. Example generator-small plating shop or large semi-conductor manufacturer	2. Plants in inorganic pigments industry when making chrome yellow or orange pigments	2. Any concentration
30+ like this	**100+ like this**	**1,000+ like this**

Figure 7.3. Three Types of Listed Hazardous Wastes: Examples. ***Author-generated***

methods, and a summary of the adverse effects of the hazardous constituents in the waste along with environmental effects information and chemical fate and transport data (where available). Initially, EPA listed over one hundred industry-specific waste streams and twenty-five waste streams that were not industry-specific. In addition, EPA listed hundreds of chemical substances that, if discarded in pure or technical grade form, were classified as listed hazardous waste. None of these waste listings was specific to a particular entity or location. If an entity generated waste that fit within the narrative description of the listed hazardous waste, the generator was obligated to manage it as a RCRA hazardous waste.

EPA did provide a process whereby individual generators could petition to exclude ("delist") a specific listed waste from a particular location if the generator could demonstrate that the specific waste did not meet the criteria used by EPA to initially list it and that the waste did not pose a threat to health or the environment. Delisting recognized that, within the group of wastes that met the narrative listing description, there could be individual wastes that, due to their composition, did not present meaningful risks. EPA established delisting as a regulatory process, and it required significant data collection on the part of the applicant.

In developing its initial definition of hazardous waste, EPA needed to address the question of when a waste was required to be evaluated for hazardous waste status and whether a waste that was hazardous could ever be re-classified as non-hazardous. EPA specified that generators were required to evaluate each solid waste at its point of generation and to determine at that point whether it met a hazardous waste characteristic or was covered by a hazardous waste listing. A new point of generation occurred when a hazardous waste was mixed with other solid wastes or when a hazardous waste was treated in some fashion.[27] EPA approached the question of how to evaluate these mixtures or treatment residuals differently for characteristic and for listed hazardous waste.

For characteristic hazardous wastes, EPA required the waste generator to re-evaluate the characteristics for each new mixture or treatment residual. If the mixing or treatment removed the characteristic, the waste was no longer a characteristic hazardous waste. However, listed hazardous waste decisions were based on more complex analyses. Once the initial hazardous waste was mixed with other wastes or treated, the waste description no longer met the narrative listing description. In order to ensure that generators did not exit the hazardous waste system simply by performing mixing or treatment that did not address the underlying hazards of the waste, EPA created a separate set of rules for listed hazardous waste. These rules were called the mixture and "derived from" rules. Under these rules, listed hazardous wastes continued to carry the original listings when they were mixed or treated unless generators went through the delisting process described above. Few did. As EPA noted in the preamble establishing these rules:

> We know of no other effective regulatory mechanism for dealing with waste mixtures containing listed hazardous wastes. Because the potential combinations of listed wastes and other wastes are infinite, we have been unable to devise any workable, broadly applicable formula which would distinguish between those waste mixtures which are and are not hazardous.[28]

Importantly, after almost a decade of litigation on aspects of the mixture and derived from rules, a panel of the United States Court of Appeals for the District of Columbia Circuit ruled that EPA had failed to give the public sufficient notice and opportunity for comment when promulgating the "mixture and derived from" rules.[29] EPA re-promulgated the rules to avoid disruption to the RCRA program. However, the status of "mixture and derived from" wastes generated prior to the re-promulgation of these regulations was dependent upon the status of the mixture and derived from rules in individual states.[30] Many EPA enforcement cases that were in progress at the time of this decision could not be completed since wastes that violated RCRA requirements were frequently mixtures of a listed waste and one or more other solid wastes.

Recognizing the breadth of the definition and the costly consequence of mistakenly defining a waste as hazardous, EPA also made use of exclusions to correct for errors of overinclusion. Some of these exclusions were grounded in statutory definitions or legislative history, such as the initial exclusion of high-volume special wastes (e.g., mining waste) or the household hazardous waste exemption.[31] Other exclusions were identified by EPA. An example is waste containing chromium that is nearly exclusively trivalent in form and that is generated from an industrial process using trivalent chromium. These trivalent chromium wastes would fail the toxicity characteristic which was based on total chromium. EPA determined that wastes containing trivalent chromium from certain industrial processes would not be expected to result in the types of harm presented by wastes containing hexavalent chromium or chromium that was likely to convert to hexavalent chromium when discarded. Thus, these EPA-identified exclusions were frequently included to correct a situation where a hazardous waste characteristic captured a subset of waste that did not meet EPA's promulgated criteria for classification as a hazardous waste.[32]

EPA addressed the question of the role of compliance cost in the development of RCRA regulations. This had been the source of a significant number of public comments. In its May 1980 preamble, EPA provided its rationale for concluding that RCRA prohibited EPA from considering compliance costs as a basis for "lessening the standards it considers necessary to ensure protection of human health or the environment" (p. 33089). EPA did conclude, however, that it was able to consider cost-effectiveness in choosing among alternatives that met the statutory requirements.

Scope of Hazardous Waste Generator Coverage

In the mid-1970s limited information was available about the volumes and sources of hazardous waste. In developing the initial regulatory framework, EPA wanted to focus on effectively controlling larger sources of hazardous waste. EPA was able to collect information indicating that there were an estimated 760,000 entities generating a combined total of over 60 million annual tons of hazardous waste. Over 5 percent of the entities produced more than 97.7 percent of the total known quantity of hazardous waste, and they were largely from the manufacturing sector. Also, 695,000 of the generators produced less than 1,000 kg/month which, in total, constituted only one percent of the annual hazardous waste volume. A high percentage of these entities were from outside the manufacturing sector. EPA concluded that, "the enormous number of small generators, if brought entirely within the Subtitle C regulatory system, would far outstrip the limited agency resources necessary to achieve effective implementation."[33]

EPA received extensive comments on this topic. Many commenters wanted EPA to find a way to incorporate waste quantity into the definition of a hazardous waste or develop a way to use degree of hazard of the waste in the definition. EPA considered in detail whether it could develop different tiers of hazardous waste with different monthly generation cut-off levels. After considering this approach in some detail, EPA was unable to develop it, given the almost infinite variety of waste types with different volume ranges and constituents.

Thus, for practicality and environmental-protection reasons, EPA limited the initial cradle to grave regulations to those generators with 1,000 kg/month or more of hazardous waste. EPA determined that by focusing both EPA and state resources on large-quantity generators during initial implementation of the regulations, the resulting implementation and enforcement efforts would achieve better environmental protection. At that time, EPA stated that it intended to phase in rulemaking for generators above 100 kg/month of hazardous waste within two to five years. EPA also provided some additional safeguards for entities generating very small quantities of the subset of acutely toxic hazardous wastes. Entities generating 100 to 1,000 kg/month of hazardous waste were required to limit the quantity of on-site accumulation and ensure that their wastes go to facilities that are approved by the State to handle municipal or industrial wastes. In other words, EPA prohibited these wastes from being handled at solid waste facilities that classified as open dumps or from being unsafely accumulated at their generation location.[34] Thus, the smaller generators were not completely excluded from EPA regulation.

Hazardous Waste Management Framework

To achieve cradle to grave management of hazardous wastes, EPA developed regulatory requirements for waste generators, transporters, and facilities that treated, stored, or disposed of the hazardous waste (TSDFs). Congress provided a very general framework for the scope of these controls in Sections 3002 through 3005 of RCRA. Congress also required these entities to notify EPA under RCRA Section 3010 within ninety days of when EPA classified a waste as hazardous. Without such a notification, these entities were prohibited from continuing to transport or manage the waste.

EPA then developed regulations to fill in the details provided by the statutory requirements. The process was extremely time-consuming, due in part to the need to develop generic approaches for a wide range of different wastes, different types of waste generators, and different types of waste management methods. With the initial set of regulations, EPA chose not to cover certain types of waste management units that were perceived to result in lower environmental risks such as tank-based wastewater treatment units and tank-based elementary neutralization units. EPA also chose not to prescribe detailed requirements for most hazardous waste recycling processes, although storage or

Table 7.3. Key Hazardous Waste Management Requirements for Regulated Entities

Regulated Entity	*Coverage of Requirements*
Hazardous Waste Generators RCRA §3002 40 CFR 262 Goal: properly identify waste as hazardous and prevent its mismanagement while allowing generators reasonable flexibility to accumulate or treat wastes in a set of prescribed ways without obtaining a permit.[1]	• Characterize each waste at point of generation to determine if Subtitle C was applicable; get a hazardous waste ID • Self-implementing on-site requirements for less than ninety-day storage in tanks or containers–training, labelling, inspections, recordkeeping, spill response • Self-implementing for waste satellite accumulation locations—limits on amounts and locations • Requirements before shipping waste off-site and use of licensed waste transporters and a hazardous waste manifest; track safe arrival of waste at receiving facility. • Prepare a biennial report on waste generation
Hazardous Waste Transporters RCRA §3003 40 CFR 263 Goal: ensure that hazardous waste gets to the facility designated by the generator	• Obtain hazardous waste ID numbers • Only accept hazardous waste with proper hazardous waste manifests and fill in appropriate manifest information • Only transport to the generator-designated facility • Meet all DOT requirements • Controls on transfer facility activities • Proper management of any spills or releases
Hazardous Waste Treatment, Storage and Disposal Facilities RCRA §3004[2] RCRA §3005 40 CFR 264 40 CFR 265 40 CFR 270	• Get an EPA ID. Apply for a Part A permit and when requested, a Part B permit • Develop a waste acceptance plan—only accept waste matching the manifest that is covered by the waste acceptance plan; perform waste analysis as required by the plan. • General facility standards—security, inspections, training, location standards, contingency plans and emergency procedures, preparedness and prevention • Return copy of manifest to generator and address any manifest discrepancies • Groundwater monitoring for land-based TSDFs

Regulated Entity	*Coverage of Requirements*
Goal: ensure sufficient TSDF management controls to prevent the creation of any future Superfund sites	• Facility closure and post-closure requirements • Financial assurance requirements • Individual design and operational standards based on type of facility—containers, tanks, surface impoundments, waste piles, land treatment, landfills, incinerators, thermal treatment, other treatment, underground injection • Operate in compliance with self-implementing Part 265 design and operational standards for hazardous waste prior to receiving the Part B permit; address releases to groundwater • Operate in compliance with Part 264 design and operating requirements for hazardous waste and conditions in the permit; address any releases to groundwater • Changes to facility operation limited prior to Part B permit issuance; changes in facility operation require Part B permit modification after permit issuance. Permits extremely detailed.

1 In the preamble to its February 26, 1980 generator regulation, EPA explained its rationale for allowing generators ninety days of accumulation time, stating it was a balance between the congressional desire not to interfere with the generator's production processes and the need to provide adequate environmental and health protection. EPA's research had indicated that for most industries, wastes are removed from the site of generation within ninety days, 45 Fed. Reg. 12722 (February 26, 1980).

2 RCRA §3004 provided a comprehensive framework applicable to owners and operators of TSDFs. RCRA §3005 established the requirement for these facilities to obtain permits. However, Congress recognized that it would take time to permit the over five thousand hazardous waste treatment, storage, and disposal facilities (TSDFs) that were operating as of the effective date of the regulations. Thus, Congress specified that if a facility was in existence as of the date RCRA was enacted and properly applied for a Part A permit, the facility owner/operator would be treated as having been issued such a permit. These facilities were known as "interim status" facilities. Because EPA did not believe it would have the time to oversee the implementation of these requirements at each interim status facility, EPA looked for requirements that would not require substantial facility capital expenditure given that EPA expected it could modify the requirements significantly at the time a RCRA permit was issued. Thus, EPA considered the TSDF interim status standards to be a set of minimum requirements that could be self-implemented by the TSDF owner/operator until such time as those qualifying interim status facilities obtained a RCRA permit.

pre-treatment of wastes destined for recycling were regulated. Table 7.3 very briefly describes the original RCRA cradle to grave regulatory framework.

The Partnership Between EPA and the States

Congress envisioned state authorities as the primary implementers of RCRA. Any state that wanted to administer and enforce the RCRA hazardous waste program in lieu of the federal EPA could apply to EPA and receive authorization A state needed to have a program that was equivalent in scope to the federal program, not be inconsistent with the federal program, and have sufficient capability to enforce the federal RCRA program, including the issuance of RCRA permits.[35]

EPA issued regulations covering state authorization as part of its 1980 consolidated permitting regulations. These regulations clarified that states could have programs that were more stringent than the federal RCRA regulations as long as they were not inconsistent with the federal program. EPA also clarified that EPA had authority itself to enforce any aspect of the delegated state RCRA program. EPA kept its own authority to issue RCRA Section 7003 imminent and substantial endangerment orders and RCRA Section 3007 orders requiring regulated entities to provide additional information. EPA also retained ability to comment on state-issued RCRA permits and to enforce any permit conditions that EPA believed were appropriate to incorporate into the permit but that the state chose not to incorporate. Once EPA approved a state's authorization, if EPA determined that an authorized state was not fully implementing and enforcing its authorized program and did not take timely corrective action, EPA committed to withdrawing the authorization and replacing it with a federal RCRA program.[36]

Once the state authorization regulations were promulgated, EPA spent considerable time implementing this process.[37] Review of state authorization packages was time consuming and the authorization process often involved iterative state submissions and EPA reviews. In some cases, states needed to modify their regulations; in other cases, they needed to obtain supplemental authority from their state legislature. States used a range of approaches. Some states adopted EPA's regulations by reference, with or without undertaking any separate public notice and comment. Other states implemented regulations that were structured differently than EPA's or used their own combinations of regulations and statutory provisions. Even states that adopted EPA's regulations by reference often included a subset of requirements that were more stringent than EPA's regulations.

The more a state's regulations differed in structure and scope from EPA's regulations, the more time consuming it was to complete the authorization process. California illustrates this point. When RCRA passed, California was one of the few states that already had a basic hazardous waste program. As EPA implemented the federal RCRA regulations, California continued to use its existing framework to incorporate aspects of the federal program. The end result in California was a framework that was so complex that it was difficult to determine how it compared with the federal program on a requirement by requirement basis. Throughout the 1980s, both the federal and California hazardous waste regulations applied to regulated parties.

California was one of the last states to receive RCRA authorization for the base RCRA program. That didn't occur until 1992, over a decade after EPA completed the initial RCRA regulatory structure and over five years after the large majority of states had received RCRA authorization. California's authorization occurred only after the state completed a major revamp of its administrative regulations, changing them so that it was possible to determine how and where the state program was similar and where it was more stringent or broader in coverage.

Once a state received final RCRA authorization, an even more complex process controlled what happened to new RCRA regulations promulgated by EPA. These newly promulgated RCRA regulations were effective in non-RCRA authorized states but they were not effective in authorized RCRA states until the state modified its state regulations, submitted a request to EPA to amend its authorized program, and received EPA authorization for the new regulations. The updates were supposed to occur within a year for new regulations that required only a state regulatory change, or within two years where a state required a statutory modification, but those timeframes were not realistic. History shows that it often took years (even a decade) for states to obtain state authorization for RCRA requirements promulgated after the initial federal set of regulations. During this window of time, new EPA RCRA regulations were not effective in RCRA-authorized states.

In summary, the EPA-state partnership was somewhat strained. The authorization process itself was time-consuming. Progress was also slow because some states lacked resources to make progress, some states lacked the political will to aggressively implement the program, some states disagreed philosophically with the approach, and some objected to the limited flexibility that EPA had built into the program.

The Hazardous Waste Enforcement Framework

The 1976 RCRA statute provided strong enforcement provisions. Violations that remained uncorrected thirty days after notice to the regulated entity could result in an administrative order or a civil action. Not only were penalties initially established at $25,000/day for each violation and each day of continued noncompliance, EPA Administrator was authorized to suspend or revoke a violator's RCRA operating permit.[38] Congress also incorporated criminal penalties for a range of poor behavior including transporting or disposing of hazardous waste at a facility without a permit and making any false statements in key RCRA submissions. Criminal convictions could include up to two years of jail time and fines of up to $50,000 per day per violation.

Congress also provided other tools designed to achieve the hazardous waste compliance goals of the statute. EPA and authorized states were granted access to facilities where hazardous waste was generated, stored, treated, or disposed of and regulatory officials could collect samples and information. Additionally, Congress included a citizen suit provision that allowed any person to use the courts to enforce against an entity in RCRA non-compliance. This included suits against EPA if it failed to perform a non-discretionary requirement. Congress also provided EPA with the ability to sue any entity who was or had handled, stored, treated, transported, or disposed of hazardous waste or solid waste if there was evidence that the waste presented an imminent and substantial endangerment. Given that this provision was crafted to apply to both solid and hazardous waste, it was not dependent upon the completion of EPA's hazardous waste regulatory framework.[39]

Early Hazardous Waste Implementation Challenges

The complexity of the early RCRA regulations presented a large number of implementation issues for EPA, the states, and regulated entities. New questions and public comments continued to arrive as regulators and regulated parties tried to implement the regulations. The issuance of the regulations was only a starting point for getting information to the regulated entities and the state and regional implementers on precisely how the regulations should be applied. EPA headquarters worked to develop appropriate guidance manuals and training materials and responded to oral and written requests on how to apply regulations to specific circumstances.[40] And, both EPA and states spent significant amounts of time prior to 1984 in getting states authorized to implement the RCRA hazardous waste program.

The result was that during the early 1980s, the pace of field implementation was slow. EPA regional offices were working with states to identify regulated hazardous waste generators and TSDFs that failed to notify under RCRA, and working with states to identify the universe of TSDFs that would be required to obtain permits. EPA also spent time monitoring state activities to ensure implementation was consistent with federal requirements. Three years after the issuance of the 1980 RCRA regulations, virtually none of the 5,000 interim-status TSDF facilities had obtained RCRA permits. Few interim status facilities had implemented basic groundwater monitoring or obtained necessary financial assurance. Significant RCRA enforcement actions were also quite limited prior to 1984.

In hindsight, two steps could have been taken that would have made program implementation smoother. First, EPA needed a high-quality data system to facilitate implementation. The absence of a quality-controlled information system that captured key information on each hazardous waste generator and each hazardous waste TSDF nationwide slowed the implementation process. Had such a system existed and contained accurate information on facility wastes and operations, government inspections, and enforcement information, EPA and states would have been able to better evaluate the effectiveness of the existing program and the need for program modifications.

A second step forward would have been widespread access to EPA's regulatory interpretive decisions. Such a system would have allowed all RCRA-regulated entities and the states to quickly learn about how EPA was interpreting RCRA. EPA headquarters did establish permit assistance teams to help address challenging permitting issues such as how to decide where to place groundwater monitoring wells at land-based TSDFs. Likewise, a hotline established by EPA answered questions from regulated entities and states about the application of the regulations. Also, EPA headquarters responded to a couple of hundred incoming letters annually on a range of regulatory questions. Today this information is largely automated and relatively easy for any regulated entity to obtain. However, throughout the 1980s and into the 1990s, the only entities benefitting from this information were the entities that had initiated the inquiry. There was no easy way for other regulated entities and the states to know about or obtain this information. This further slowed regulatory compliance.

THE 1984 HAZARDOUS AND SOLID WASTE AMENDMENTS (HSWA)

As discussed above, the implementation of RCRA's 1976 provisions took much longer than initially envisioned. Members of Congress and their staff were disturbed that in 1984, eight years after the passage of RCRA, uncontrolled or poorly controlled land disposal of both non-hazardous solid waste and hazardous waste remained common. Open municipal solid waste dumps were being placed on schedules to upgrade but these open dumps were still operating. Approximately 1,500 hazardous waste land disposal facilities and 200 hazardous waste incinerators needed to be permitted under EPA's promulgated hazardous waste permit regulations. As of late 1983, less than ten land disposal TSDFs had obtained a full RCRA hazardous waste permit with comprehensive protections for groundwater; the numbers of incinerators and hazardous waste storage facilities with RCRA permits was likewise very small. Congress was concerned that if progress were not made faster, more abandoned hazardous waste sites would be spawned, which would balloon the cost of the Superfund program that Congress created in 1980 (see Chapter 8).

The slow initial pace of RCRA program implementation was further impacted by the November 1980 national elections. When Democrat Jimmy Carter lost his re-election bid to Republican Ronald Reagan, the new administration brought a philosophy of "regulatory relief" to Washington. Reagan's landslide victory coincided with a 12-seat GOP gain in the Senate, where the GOP seized the majority, and a 34-seat GOP gain in the House, where the large Democratic majority declined significantly.

All changes in White House control tend to result in some loss of EPA momentum as political appointees transition, but the situation in 1980 was more dramatic than usual and was perceived as particularly problematic by congressional committees overseeing EPA's implementation of RCRA. The Reagan administration's deregulatory agenda was illustrated by the issuance of Executive Order 12291 (1981) and strong centralized oversight of EPA and other agencies by the White House Office of Management and Budget.[41] President Reagan selected Anne M. Gorsuch to head EPA and Rita Lavelle as the political appointee to oversee the implementation of RCRA and the new Superfund law. Under their tenure, EPA experienced budget cuts, significant morale issues for career staff, and a reduction in enforcement cases.[42] Implementation of RCRA slowed, since RCRA entailed more regulation, not less. Given the critical juncture of RCRA program implementation, the timing could not have been worse.

The severe 1980-1982 recession hurt Reagan's popularity, and the perceptions of management and corruption at the Gorsuch-led EPA created political opportunities for the Democrats. In the 1982 elections, Democrats won back 27 House seats and added an additional Senate seat. Legislators in both parties believed that more legislation was needed to accelerate implementation of RCRA.

Democratic Senator George Mitchell of Maine, one of the principal Senate sponsors of HSWA, stated (excerpt): "It has become evident that a strong congressional expression of disapproval of EPA's slow and timid implementation of the existing law is necessary, as well as a clear congressional directive mandating certain bold, preventive actions by EPA which will not be taken otherwise, despite the existing, broad authorities contained in RCRA."[43]

Democratic Congressman James Florio of New Jersey, one of the key House sponsors of HSWA, summarized the situation as follows:

> In 1983, five and one-half years after the mandatory deadline for promulgation of RCRA standards and permits, the 98th Congress began a reauthorization process for RCRA. There was still no enforceable system for regulating the disposal of hazardous waste and little prospect for one soon. The problems recognized in 1976 had become common knowledge and, by 1983, evidence of the dangers was even more compelling. Not surprisingly, Congress made clear that it would not allow the delays to continue. Any confidence that EPA could be trusted to act expeditiously had long since evaporated.[44]

The stage was set for congressional passage of HSWA, one of the most prescriptive environmental laws in US history. HSWA was also precedent-setting in the ways in which it limited EPA implementation discretion and utilized provisions that implemented automatically if EPA failed to meet statutory deadlines.[45]

Architecture of HSWA

Congress gave clear direction that the nation must move away from its continued preference for land disposal of hazardous waste, an approach that was continuing to prove difficult to adequately control. Congress also required EPA to expand both the wastes that were classified as hazardous and the range of entities that were covered by the cradle-to-grave hazardous waste management system. Given the improved analytical techniques that fed an evolving knowledge of groundwater contamination present at hazardous waste TSDFs, Congress determined that owners and operators of those facilities must identify and remediate any such releases to levels protective of health and the environment. And, Congress filled what it saw as numerous remaining gaps in the existing RCRA regulatory safety net.

What was unique about HSWA was the specificity with which it directed EPA how to achieve these goals. Congress specified over seventy different regulatory fixes, almost all of which were required to be completed by the end of fiscal year 1988. Rather than create flexibility for EPA in the face of a four-year period to act, Congress also included inflexible deadlines for a subset of key provisions. Thus, if EPA did not complete the required regulatory program, legislative provisions would implement automatically (so-called "hammers"). Congress also bypassed the slow process of state policy-making by making RCRA regulations effective in all fifty states as soon as the congressional deadlines or EPA effective dates took effect. EPA became the enforcer of those regulations until such time as the states modified their authorized state programs. This simple change resulted in the implementation of new, more stringent hazardous waste regulations years before they otherwise would have been implemented.

Table 7.4. Key Provisions in HSWA

Broad Topic	*Key Provisions*
Hazardous Waste	• Land disposal TSDFs without prescribed financial assurance, adequate groundwater monitoring systems, and complete permit applications required to cease operation by November 1985.[1] Closure permits for all land disposal TSDFs that had operated after 1982 were required to address site-wide releases. • Land disposal of hazardous waste prohibited by congressionally specified dates (between 1986 and 1990) depending upon specific hazardous waste code, unless wastes first treated with best demonstrated available technology; storage of untreated hazardous waste prohibited for more than 12 months.[2] • Minimum technology requirements, including more stringent double liner systems and groundwater monitoring, at all interim status and permitted land disposal TSDFs. • Site-wide investigation and cleanup of all releases above protective levels at all interim status and permitted TSDFs, including releases from site-wide non-hazardous waste units, whether they were operating or closed; EPA could use TSDF permits or new EPA order authority to accomplish this.[3] • Adding 100 to 1,000 kg/month generators to the hazardous waste regulatory system. • Requiring EPA to expand the universe of listed and characteristic hazardous wastes.[4] • Requiring much stronger regulation of industrial boilers and furnaces using hazardous waste for fuel or material recovery. • Prohibiting certain behaviors such as liquids in landfills. • Imposing air emission standards on waste treatment units and wastes stored in containers, surface impoundments, and tanks.
Non-Hazardous Solid Waste	• Strengthening requirements (liners, groundwater monitoring, corrective action for releases) at solid waste management facilities that accept any amount of household hazardous waste or small quantity generator hazardous waste.
Studies	• Study to evaluate the protectiveness of the exemption covering mixtures of domestic sewage and other wastes that reach a POTW through the sewer system. • Studies on underground storage tanks (UST). • Study on hazardous waste from educational institutions. • Study on adequacy on non-hazardous waste criteria to protect groundwater.
Other Key Provisions	• Elevating waste minimization to national policy status and implementing provisions to achieve the policy" as a bullet under the broad category "Other Key Provisions. • Regulating underground storage tanks containing both petroleum and chemical products to address evolving knowledge of significant groundwater contamination from these sources; critical due to the exemption of petroleum from CERCLA coverage.[5]

Broad Topic	Key Provisions
	• Expanding citizen suit authorities under RCRA Section 7002 in situations of imminent and substantial endangerment.[6] • Expanding citizen suit authorities to seek fines to the US Treasury for regulatory and permit compliance violations. • Mandatory inspections of TSDFs operated by federal or state governments.[7]

1 Due to the inability of many interim status TSDFs to obtain financial insurance or due to their failure to install adequate groundwater monitoring systems, over two-thirds of interim status land disposal facilities ceased operation on this date.

2 This provision was the lynch pin in Congress' view that the US had to shift away from land disposal of hazardous waste. It became imperative for EPA to complete the development of technology-based standards for each type of waste by the statutory deadlines or an automatic prohibition to land disposal for that waste automatically went into effect. For wastes EPA defined as hazardous after the date of HSWA, EPA was given a fixed time period with a hard date to complete a technology-based treatment standard. Development of these technology standards was extremely time consuming and generated significant public comment. However, EPA met these deadlines.

During the rulemaking process, EPA attempted to combine these technology-based treatment approaches with risk-based limits to the treatment standards. EPA believed that there was little benefit to requiring treatment beyond what was necessary to protect health and the environment. However, Congress rejected EPA's efforts to limit the scope of the technology standards, communicating that at this time Congress had little confidence in the accuracy of risk-based determinations.

3 This program has many parallels to the CERCLA investigation and remedial process. RCRA corrective action, covering site-wide and off-site releases above protective levels, has been implemented both through issuance of TSDF permits and through EPA order authorities. It has relied upon extensive EPA guidance documents, developed in the late 1980s, on how to perform remedial investigations and how to select protective cleanup remedies. These guidance documents and corrective action implementation approaches have been designed to be consistent with CERCLA remedial approaches. While portions of the corrective action program have been incorporated into regulations, the details of the program remain largely implemented through guidance.

There have been several important cases addressing the scope of RCRA corrective action. One was American Iron & Steel v. EPA, 886 F.2d 390 (D.C. Cir. 1989). That case addressed whether the large volume wastes covered as "special wastes" were covered by RCRA corrective action if they were present on-site at a TSDF. The Court decided that these wastes, while exempt from classification as hazardous waste, were not exempt from coverage under RCRA corrective action. In United Technologies Corp. v. EPA, 821 F.2d 714 (D.C. Cir. 1987), the Court determined that for purposes of corrective action, a "facility" included not just the waste facility itself but all contiguous property owned by the same person who owned the facility. This decision had widespread ramifications for many federal facilities with regulated TSDFs.

4 EPA listed additional hazardous wastes but also made dramatic expansions in the definition of a characteristically toxic hazardous waste in 1990. EPA was able to expand the toxicity characteristic beyond the hazardous constituents included in 1980 due to the progress made in fate and transport modeling of the subsurface along with EPA's completion of risk-based analysis for many organic compounds found in groundwater.

5 In advance of EPA's 1987 regulatory deadline, Congress imposed a prohibition on installation of new steel USTs without adequate corrosion protection. Congress did provide significant specificity on the design and operational content of the UST regulations but left EPA with flexibility on the precise framework for implementing a nationwide program to address the over two million USTs. As with hazardous waste, Congress allowed states to apply to EPA for authorization to implement the UST regulatory program as long as their programs were equally stringent as the federal program. The development of the UST program was a major EPA accomplishment. Given the large number of USTs, EPA relied heavily on standards that could be self-implementing along with strong requirements for financial assurance by UST owners and operators.

6 The citizen suit provisions of RCRA have been used by both citizens and governments to address both non-compliance and imminent and substantial endangerment claims. These suits have frequently been filed in connection with toxic tort suits. A recent line of RCRA §7002 lawsuits has argued that particulate air releases from manufacturing operations that land on the ground can be addressed as solid waste under RCRA. Such an interpretation, when taken broadly, would require entities with particulate emission air permits to also obtain RCRA permits. Seemingly, this type of interpretation would go against the RCRA §1006 to avoid statutory duplication. To date, EPA has not weighed in on this important RCRA interpretive issue. Neither has Congress. For example, see Little Hocking Water Association v. DuPont, Case No. 2:09-cv-01081 (S.D. Ohio 2015). Also see Center for Community Action and Environmental Justice v. Union Pacific Corp., No. 2:11-cv-08608, 2012 WL 2086603 (C.D. Cal. 2012), which reached a different conclusion on coverage of air particulates.

7 While federal facilities were clearly subject to RCRA requirements, implementation of RCRA at federal facilities continued to be challenging, particularly in situations where states were authorized to implement RCRA. In October 1992, Congress further amended RCRA (Pub. L. No. 102-386, known as the 1992 Federal Facility Compliance Act or FFCA) to clarify that both EPA and authorized states have the ability to sue the federal government for RCRA fines and penalties. This resolved one of the last remaining issues being raised by federal facilities on the impact of sovereign immunity and the collection of non-compliance penalties under RCRA. The FFCA also clarified that EPA could issue RCRA §3008(a) enforcement orders against federal facilities in the same manner as such actions were brought against other regulated entities. The FFCA also required EPA to issue regulations clarifying when military munitions became waste subject to RCRA.

Table 7.4 captures many, but not all, of the numerous new requirements present in HSWA. Footnotes to the table entries discuss some of the issues that EPA addressed during implementation of individual HSWA requirements. Because of the specificity of these statutory provisions and the tight deadlines, the agency's main focus was on ensuring that deadlines were met and that automatic statutory hammers did not occur. This observation is not intended to take away from the significant EPA work required to put HSWA requirements into place.

With strong bipartisan oversight efforts in both the House and Senate, most of the core HSWA regulatory framework was completed by EPA by the early 1990s. Since that time, the overall RCRA regulatory framework has remained largely in place. EPA has mainly focused on specific areas of the RCRA regulations that could be strengthened or refined. Frequently these actions arose out of requests by regulated entities or environmental groups. For example, while EPA has kept the main structure for the definition of solid waste and the definition of hazardous waste in place, it continues to refine the regulations, where it can, to further encourage recycling or improve protection.

EPA has also focused on streamlining the management framework, without compromising environmental protectiveness, as it applies to specific types of hazardous wastes or hazardous waste generators. As an example, in the early 1990s, EPA introduced the concept of Universal Wastes to avoid adverse impacts on recycling. Universal wastes, such as batteries and fluorescent lamps, refer to captured wastes that are generated in a wide variety of settings other than just the industrial settings typically associated with hazardous waste. EPA developed a more streamlined approach for these wastes, allowing more flexible accumulation and transportation provisions, all designed to get the wastes safely to a recycling or treatment facility.[46] A similar initiative was EPA's recent promulgation of regulations for pharmaceutical waste. That rule recognized that waste pharmaceuticals were ending up in sewer systems and waterways in part because the existing hazardous waste structure did not result in optimized collection of waste pharmaceuticals from the wide range of pharmacies, retailers, healthcare facilities, and households where they were generated. The final rule, effective in 2019, recognizes the importance of a robust reverse distribution system.

OVERALL PROGRESS IN EPA IMPLEMENTATION

Since the passage of RCRA in 1976, the country has developed a strong professional cadre of waste professionals, both inside and external to government. This core of professionals has been instrumental to EPA and states in their successful implementation of RCRA and HSWA. They have driven the development of a competent commercial waste industry (non-existent before the early 1980s) and allowed hazardous waste generators to incorporate RCRA requirements and resource recovery into business operations. Key areas of expertise include environmental management systems, auditing, hydrogeology, waste treatment technology, waste remediation and risk assessment, and process waste minimization and product sustainability. Numerous US colleges and universities have a wide variety of degree programs and certificate programs relevant to resource recovery, product sustainability, and waste management—topics that were virtually non-existent prior to 1980.

RCRA has evolved into an important groundwater-protection statute. Its prospective requirements for solid and hazardous waste management facilities and underground storage tanks holding petroleum and chemicals have prevented current sources from adversely impacting groundwater. These programs have also addressed or are in the process of addressing historical releases at thousands of locations where groundwater contamination already occurred. EPA has issued various reports discussing program accomplishments.[47] The purpose of this section is to provide a broad overview of how far this program has come over the last thirty-five years.

RCRA Subtitle D Implementation and Accomplishments

With regard to non-hazardous solid waste, significant progress has been made. The existence of open dumps remained a significant problem in virtually every state until the late 1980s, even though their existence was prohibited by Congress as of 1976. Today, such facilities are no longer in operation. A 1995 GAO study found that as of December 1994, forty-six states had either developed solid waste management plans or were in the process of doing so. Some states limited the plans to municipal wastes, but other states dealt more broadly with the universe of municipal and non-hazardous industrial wastes.[48]

During the 1980s, EPA undertook significant data collection on the kinds of solid waste generated in the US and the types of units managing that waste.[49] This information became widely available in the mid-to-late 1980s and drove additional state non-hazardous waste control activities. EPA has also issued very detailed guidance for states and regulated entities on protective management approaches for non-hazardous industrial waste facilities.[50]

EPA also completed the required "special waste" studies identified by Congress in the 1980 amendments to RCRA, completing most of those studies between the late 1980s and the end of the 1990s.[51] These efforts resulted in reports to Congress and made it clear that the volume of solid waste generated in the US dwarfed the amount of hazardous waste generated.[52] For the most part, EPA has not undertaken federal regulations on these large volume wastes, leaving regulation to the states. However, EPA has provided significant information to states to help upgrade state management programs for some of these large volume wastes. In the late 1980s, EPA used the information from its mining waste studies to regulate additional wastes from the smelting and refining industry as RCRA hazardous waste.

EPA decided in the early 1990s to defer to state regulators' handling of the large volume of coal combustion wastes at coal-fired electric-utility plants. The agency revisited this decision in 2000 after completing additional study on the management of coal combustion wastes at non-utility locations. EPA's change in direction resulted in part from information provided by environmental interest groups who argued that state regulatory programs were uneven in protecting groundwater from these CCR wastes, particularly when the wastes were managed in large ash ponds or used as structural fill without proper safeguards. Then, in December 2008, a massive coal ash spill at TVA's Kingston Fossil Plant in Tennessee released about a billion gallons of coal fly ash slurry into neighborhoods and rivers. The environmental tragedy cost TVA more than a billion dollars to remediate and became a galvanizing event in ensuring more stringent federal standards for managing coal combustion residuals (CCR). EPA proposed new federal regulations in 2010 and finalized them in 2015.

The final regulations established minimum national CCR standards under RCRA Subtitle D, which means that the decisions on permitting and enforcement would be solely within the purview of the states. However, on December 16, 2016, Congress stepped in and provided EPA with additional federal authority as part of the Water Infrastructure Improvements (WIIN) Act. This law modified RCRA by requiring that the federal CCR regulations be implemented through a permit program and states were now required to demonstrate that their permit program would be at least as protective as the federal CCR program.[53] EPA refined and strengthened the federal requirements when environmentalists persuaded the DC Circuit Court of Appeals that the rule was not sufficiently protective of public health and the environment.

The development of minimum federal standards for such large volume non-hazardous wastes remains an important area of interest. There is still considerable state to state variability in regulatory structures, implementation, and enforcement. As a result, there continues to be an interest in stronger EPA leadership and control among environmental and citizen groups.[54]

Separately, pursuant to HSWA, EPA upgraded environmental-protection requirements for all non-hazardous solid waste facilities that accepted hazardous waste from households or small quantity hazardous waste generators, wastes that were previously exempt from RCRA's comprehensive hazardous waste requirements. The new EPA requirements are multi-faceted and cover thousands of facilities. They include groundwater monitoring with mandatory corrective action to address groundwater releases, financial assurance requirements, location standards, closure and post-closure care requirements, and facility design and operational enhancements.[55] Facilities subject to these new stringent requirements that did not satisfy them were classified as open dumps and their continued operation was prohibited. These non-hazardous solid waste landfill regulations were first promulgated in 1991. States were required to obtain approval of their municipal solid waste landfill programs if they wanted to exercise any flexibility in the implementation of the 1991 federal regulations. Virtually all states upgraded their state municipal solid waste landfill requirements and received EPA approval to implement these regulations in lieu of the federal solid waste landfill regulations.[56] Effective dates of the regulations varied depending upon size of landfill and specific regulatory provisions. By 1996, these criteria were also applied to land-based non-municipal solid waste facilities receiving any amount of hazardous waste excluded by EPA from its hazardous waste regulatory framework.[57]

In the late 1980s, EPA began a non-regulatory program to encourage municipal solid waste resource conservation and recovery, publishing an *Agenda for Action* in 1989.[58] This document laid out EPA's waste management hierarchy, focusing on source reduction—meaning reduce the generation of waste in the first place—as the preferred approach followed by recycling. The initial goals of the program included a twenty-five percent source-reduction/recycling goal by 1992. Expansive improvements have occurred in recycling materials from the municipal solid waste stream. National rates have increased from very low levels to over thirty-five percent and some states have achieved much higher rates. After years of continued growth, per capita generation of municipal solid waste has remained stable over the last two decades.[59] The agency has continued to provide leadership in this area and continues to publish detailed information on materials recovery opportunities and accomplishments.

Subtitle C Hazardous Waste Implementation and Accomplishments

In the decade after the passage of HSWA, EPA was able to put in place the large majority of the HSWA regulatory program. Hazardous wastes are no longer managed in land-based units unless the wastes have first been treated to dramatically reduce the hazardous nature of the waste. And, when managed in land-based units, the units have liners, leachate collection systems, and sophisticated air and water monitoring systems to detect and correct problems in a timely manner. Hazardous waste TSDFs have been permitted or are undergoing proper closure under prescriptive enforcement orders. A review of state hazardous waste generation reports found significant reductions in the amount of hazardous waste generated over the last three decades.[60] The number of active land disposal facilities has also been reduced dramatically. With around fifteen hundred such facilities in existence in 1984, over one thousand of these facilities ceased operation as of 1986. Today there are less than fifty active permitted hazardous waste disposal facilities.

Importantly, about seventy percent of both operating and closed TSDFs have evaluated the existence of on-site and off-site releases and have completed construction of necessary corrective actions to address releases of hazardous constituents to soil or groundwater facility-wide. Equally important, ninety-five percent of TSDFs have ensured that human exposures from historical releases are controlled and eighty-nine percent of TSDFs have controlled the migration of contaminated groundwater.[61] And, since the mid-1980s, EPA and states have implemented effective hazardous waste enforcement programs with strong criminal and civil enforcement components.

Underground Product Storage Tank Program

In conjunction with the states, the RCRA underground storage tank program has addressed almost two million underground product tanks. About 1.8 million of these tanks have been properly closed. Over seventy percent of approximately 550 thousand active USTs are in significant operational compliance with technical requirements. Cleanups have been initiated at over eighty-eight percent of UST locations where releases have been identified and cleanups are ongoing at all but about four percent of remaining UST release locations.[62]

REMAINING CHALLENGES AND OPPORTUNITIES

Much has been accomplished in the last five decades. To keep the RCRA program maximally effective without added costs that are not commensurate with the protection achieved, creativity is required. This final section provides a sampling of ideas concerning challenges that remain and opportunities for reform.

Most large industrial facilities have learned to effectively incorporate RCRA requirements into normal business operations. However, EPA's RCRA hazardous waste program remains extremely challenging to implement for small businesses and municipal organizations. It is also challenging for larger businesses whose core work differs from the plant-based industrial manufacturing sector which drove EPA's design of the initial hazardous waste regulatory framework. Improved regulatory models are needed for these other types of hazardous waste generators such as retail and service entities, including service entities that do not generate hazardous waste at fixed locations.

Accessible and high-quality data systems on regulated hazardous waste entities remain elusive. What is needed are national and state data systems that include information on hazardous waste generators by generator size and type, waste type, and management method as well as inspection and compliance status of individual hazardous waste generators and TSDFs. Similar data on non-hazardous solid waste generators and management facilities, including all types of recycling facilities, is also lacking. Some of this information is collected by states or EPA in annual or biannual reports. However, the quality of the data is unknown because it is not verified, and the data are not generally available for public use in performing a wide range of analyses. Such information would allow the federal government and the states to learn over time and facilitate reform suggestions from stakeholders, think tanks, and academics. Such data systems would also enable proper prioritization of future risk-reduction and cost-effectiveness improvement opportunities.

States have issued operating- or post-closure permits to the large number of RCRA TSDFs, but these permits were for five or ten years at most, and timely review and renewal of permits has lagged. Additional EPA oversight and expedited procedures are important for sustained environmental protection. The lack of deadlines for issuance of timely permit renewals should be addressed. In some cases, facilities continue to operate on permits that have been expired for ten years or more.

As RCRA has matured, the variability between state RCRA program stringency has continued to widen. Equally important, there are numerous inconsistencies between how different states interpret similar regulatory language. This is not necessarily a problem, but it could be. EPA review of these issues, in concert with the states, could lead to implementation improvements for entities doing business nationally.

Finally, many interesting, unresolved waste management issues justify innovative thinking and pilot efforts. Examples include:

- New approaches to ensure facilities in post-closure care are adequately funded, including consideration of a single public or private agency with management authority for these sites.

- Approaches for addressing hazardous waste generated as a result of public disasters such as major wildfires, earthquakes, tornados, and hurricanes.
- Opportunities to better coordinate RCRA and TSCA in order to evaluate the hazardous waste status of new wastes and classify them as part of the TSCA new chemical review process.

With long-term research and planning, there is every reason to believe that EPA will further improve the cost effectiveness of the hazardous waste program, expand protective mechanisms nationwide for many additional classes of non-hazardous waste, identify more streamlined approaches to remediate contaminated sites, and achieve additional success with resource recovery. Some of these remaining improvements will undoubtedly rely on regulations, but EPA has expanded its toolbox in recent years to complement its RCRA regulatory program with information and data sharing, improved guidance for regulated entities, training, and effective and innovative voluntary programs.

NOTES

1. US Congress, House, Committee on Interstate and Foreign Commerce, *Resource Conservation and Recovery Act: Report (to Accompany H.R. 14496)*, 94th Cong., 1975-1976, H. Rep. 94–1491, 6239.

2. Solid Waste Disposal Act of 1965, Pub. L. No. 89–272, 79 Stat. 997 (1965). The 1970 Resource Recovery Act amended the SWDA and required additional federal study and grants on a variety of resource recovery topics and hazardous waste, but did not fundamentally change the federal government role framed in the 1965 law. Until the formation of EPA in 1970, this program was administered by the Department of Health, Education, and Welfare and the Department of Interior.

3. See US Environmental Protection Agency, *State Activities in Solid Waste Management, 1974*, by Ralph J. Black, EPA-530-SW-158 (Washington, DC: EPA, June 1975). An earlier version of this report included inputs from states and interstate groups on recommended future approaches for solid waste management. These recommendations were based on an understanding that landfills would remain a primary disposal alternative and that to address them, Congress needed to place a higher legislative priority on the solid waste problem, on parity with congressional focus on air and water. See US Environmental Protection Agency, *State Activities in Solid Waste Management: Reports to the Federal-State Solid Waste Management Conference, October 9-11, 1973, Kansas City, Missouri* (Washington, DC: EPA, 1974), https://nepis.EPA.gov/Exe/ZyPDF.cgi/9101SOU0.PDF?Dockey=9101SOU0.PDF.

EPA's October 1975 report concluded that, "The vast majority of all solid waste is disposed of on the land. Virtually no concrete data exists to really quantify much less qualify current management practices. Data does indicate, however, that well over 90 percent of municipal and industrial solid wastes are disposed of in an environmentally unacceptable way on the land. These poor disposal practices result in air pollution from open burning, health impacts from disease vectors and water/land pollution from leachates formed in improperly sited, designed and operated sites," H. Lanier Hickman, Jr., *Activities of the Office of Solid Waste Management Programs, Fiscal Year 1975* (Washington, DC: EPA, October 1975), https://nepis.EPA.gov/Exe/ZyPDF.cgi/9101M979.PDF?Dockey=9101M979.PDF.

4. US Environmental Protection Agency, *Report to Congress: Disposal of Hazardous Wastes*, EPA530-SW-115 (Washington, DC: EPA, June 30, 1973), https://nepis.EPA.gov/Exe/ZyPDF.cgi/10003IEJ.PDF?Dockey=10003IEJ.PDF.

5. For example, EPA issued a report on September 5, 1975 entitled *Report on Hazardous Waste Damage Inventory*, summarizing data accumulated to date on damage incidents. In September 1976, EPA's Emery Lazar, who had actively worked to collect and summarize EPA's damage cases, presented a paper on "The Potential for National Health and Environmental Damage from Industrial Residue Disposal" at the National Conference on Disposal of Residues on Land, sponsored by EPA. EPA continued to update and expand this damage incident inventory over the next five years.

6. RCRA §§1003 and 1004.

7. 122 Cong. Rec. H32598 (September 27, 1976) (statement of Rep. Skubitz).

8. US Environmental Protection Agency, "Press Release: New Law to Control Hazardous Wastes, End Open Dumping, Promote Conservation of Resources," *EPA.gov*, December 13, 1976, https://archive.epa.gov/epa/aboutepa/new-law-control-hazardous-wastes-end-open-dumping-promote-conservation-resources.html.

9. There have been other legislative amendments to RCRA between 1978 and today but none as significant as the 1984 amendments. I have mentioned additional legislative amendments in chapter footnotes where appropriate.

10. In the early 1980s with an absence of measurable hazardous waste permitting and enforcement progress, congressional staffers overseeing RCRA began asking why EPA couldn't take a stronger implementation role. However, under the Reagan administration, such an approach was not seen as politically tenable.

11. The statute required EPA to complete regulations on guidelines for the preparation of state solid waste management plans by April 1977. It required EPA to complete criteria for protective solid waste land disposal by October 1977. And, it required EPA to complete its identification of hazardous waste within eighteen months of the statute's enactment. Similar deadlines were placed on developing most of the other regulatory requirements for hazardous waste generators, transporters, and TSDFs.

12. For example, EPA received over twelve hundred sets of comments on its proposed December 1978 hazardous waste regulations, constituting a stack of text over seven feet high. US Environmental Protection Agency, "Statement on Hazardous Waste Management," *Administrator's Third Quarterly Report on the Status of Development of Regulations Under the Resource Conservation and Recovery Act of 1976*, by Douglas M. Costle (Washington, DC: EPA, 1979), 6.

Before finalizing these proposed regulations, EPA held over eighty-five public meetings across the US with state/local/regional governments, industry, environmental groups, and other interested entities. As a second example, in order to finalize the

1978 proposed solid waste criteria that defined protective solid waste management, EPA held five public hearings and eleven public meetings. EPA received a substantial number of written comments including expansive comments from state and local implementation partners.

13. 44 Fed. Reg. 45066 (July 31, 1979) and 44 Fed. Reg. 53438 (September 13, 1979).

14. EPA's solid waste criteria served as the minimum standards necessary to ensure that these solid waste facilities would provide "no reasonable probability of adverse effects on health or the environment" (RCRA §4004).

15. United States General Accounting Office, *Solid Waste Disposal Practices: Open Dumps Not Identified, States Face Funding Problems: Report to the Honorable Albert Gore, Jr., House of Representatives*, RCED-81-131 (Washington, DC: GAO, 1981).

16. As of June 1981, the GAO determined that twenty-nine states had submitted plans to EPA for approval and eighteen other states had submitted draft or partial draft plans. The GAO also noted that the 1981 Open Dump Inventory only listed 1,209 open dumps nationally. The GAO noted that, based on its research, Louisiana alone estimated over 1,700 open dumps although it had only reported the existence of 41.

17. California instituted a hazardous waste regulatory program in the mid-1970s, but the program suffered from numerous implementation issues and challenges regarding which wastes were actually classified as hazardous. Many of the existing sites permitted to accept hazardous waste in the 1970s in California ended up as Superfund sites subject to additional cleanup requirements. No other states had a complete hazardous waste framework as of the late 1970s.

18. A good starting point is the *RCRA Orientation Manual* (2014) on EPA's website, available at https://www.epa.gov/hwgenerators/resource-conservation-and-recovery-act-rcra-orientation-manual. The agency has developed a RCRA Online electronic database that includes thousands of letters, memoranda, publications, and questions and answers issued by EPA's Office of Resource Conservation and Recovery since 1980.

19. EPA did not formally define what it meant by secondary materials in its regulations. Rather, in the preamble to the 1985 definition of solid waste final regulation, EPA stated that it used the term secondary materials broadly to mean a material that potentially could be a solid and hazardous waste when recycled.

20. 50 Fed. Reg. 614–16 (January 4, 1985).

21. EPA has always noted that there is no single factor that can define legitimate recycling. Rather, EPA has listed important criteria of legitimacy including the extent to which the secondary material is effective for its claimed use, whether or not the secondary material is used in excess of the amount considered necessary, and whether the secondary material is as effective as what it is replacing. One of the key EPA interpretive memoranda on this topic was issued on April 26, 1989, by Sylvia K. Lowrance, Director of the Office of Solid Waste, https://rcrapublic.epa.gov/files/11426.pdf.

22. Important early cases included American Mining Congress v. EPA, 824 F.2d 1172 (D.C. Cir. 1987); American Petroleum v. EPA, 906 F.2d 729 (D. C. Cir. 1990);

American Mining Congress v. EPA, 907 F.2d 1179 (D.C. Cir. 1990); Owen Electric Steel Co. of South Carolina v. Browner, 7 F.3d 146 (4th Cir. 1994). There have been numerous other cases addressing the meaning of discard. Because the specific facts of the situation can impact the analysis, new cases with different fact patterns have continued to be filed.

23. This estimate is based on the number of chemicals placed on the initial 1979 Toxic Substances Control Act (TSCA) chemical substances inventory as having been in commerce in the US currently or in the recent past. The number of chemical substances on the inventory has grown significantly since that time.

24. Other possible characteristics such as carcinogenicity or infectious properties were considered but rejected due to inadequate ability to develop a clear test or definition that generators could self-apply for waste characterization.

25. The list of underlying constituents is found in 40 C.F.R. 261, Appendix VIII, and contains substances shown in scientific studies "to have toxic, carcinogenic, mutagenic, or teratogenic effects on humans or other life forms" 45 Fed. Reg. 33084, 33121 (May 19, 1980). There are over four hundred substances listed.

26. The factors are included in 40 C.F.R. 261.11. These factors include the presence and concentration of the listed hazardous constituents as well as a large number of other factors including persistence, volume of waste involved, whether the waste was likely to be mismanaged, and the severity of the health or environmental impacts of mismanagement.

27. EPA defined treatment in 40 C.F.R. 260.10 as "any method, technique, or process, including neutralization, designed to change the physical, chemical, or biological character of composition of any hazardous waste so as to neutralize such waste, or as to recovery energy or material resources from the waste, or so as to render such waste non-hazardous, or less hazardous; safer to transport, store or dispose of; or amenable for recovery, amenable for storage, or reduced in volume."

28. 45 Fed. Reg. 33084, 33096 (May 19, 1980).

29. Shell Oil Co. v. EPA, 950 F.2d 741 (D.C. Cir. 1991). In promulgating the 1980 RCRA regulations, EPA added the mixture and derived from rules to address significant comments it had received to its early regulatory proposals.

30. Some states took notice and comment on their mixture and derived from rules and in those states, the state regulations remained in place. This was not the case in a large number of states.

31. EPA excluded mining waste and several other large volume waste streams based on the 1980 congressional amendments to RCRA which specifically required additional study before such wastes could be regulated under RCRA Subtitle C. EPA's decision in the initial 1980 RCRA regulations to exclude household hazardous waste from regulation under RCRA's cradle to grave Subtitle C regulatory framework was based on language in the Senate Report on RCRA which stated that the hazardous waste program was not to be used to control disposal of substances used in households or to exert control over general municipal waste based on the presence of such substances. The precise form of the exemption was crafted by EPA after public comment. See 45 Fed. Reg. 33066, 33099 (May 19, 1980).

32. See 40 C.F.R. 261.10. EPA identified impacts to health or the environment as appropriate criteria for any waste classified as a characteristically hazardous waste.

33. EPA discussed this issue in the preamble to its May 19, 1980 hazardous waste regulations, 45 Fed. Reg. 33066, 33102–103. The issue was also discussed in the late 1978 proposed hazardous waste regulatory preamble where EPA asked for public comment.

34. Again, EPA discussed its thinking on this decision in the May 19, 1980 final hazardous waste regulatory preamble referenced above. EPA acknowledged the choice it was making: "The principal element of this issue is how to balance the need to protect human health and the environment from the adverse impact of potential mismanagement of small quantities of hazardous waste with the need to hold the administrative and economic burden of management of these wastes under RCRA within reasonable and practical limits," 43 Fed. Reg. 58970 (December 18, 1978).

35. Consistency with the federal program primarily focused on ensuring that states did not implement provisions that adversely impacted the interstate movement of hazardous waste.

36. This provision has not proved to be an effective deterrent. Many states have not updated their RCRA programs in a timely manner. The detailed withdrawal process and the politics that get infused into it have precluded EPA from using this tool. EPA has established annual reviews of state program implementation and addressed implementation deficiencies with state agreements that discuss needed actions in exchange for the receipt of federal hazardous waste grant dollars.

37. As of 1982, few states had hazardous waste programs comparable to those covered in EPA's 1980-1982 regulations. EPA's authorization process also involved working with states to get necessary enabling legislation and providing grant funds so that states could attract personnel resources to support an effective hazardous waste program.

38. The amount of civil penalties associated with RCRA violations adjusts to reflect inflation. As of 2019, the maximum RCRA civil penalty amounts increased to $74,552 per day, per violation, for penalties that occurred after November 2015.

39. EPA relied upon this provision prior to the passage of CERCLA. According to EPA, as of October 1981 the agency had filed approximately sixty judicial enforcement actions including ones utilizing RCRA §7003, 47 Fed. Reg. 109072, 10978 (March 12, 1982).

40. These outreach tools were designed to ensure consistency and substantial equivalence across states and EPA regions, the primary implementers.

41. Executive Order 12291, 46 Fed. Reg. 13193, 3 C.F.R. (February 17, 1981), 127, https://www.archives.gov/federal-register/codification/executive-order/12291.html.

42. For example, see Brady Dennis and Chris Mooney, "Neil Gorsuch's Mother Once Ran the EPA. It Didn't Go Well," *Washington Post*, February 1, 2017, https://www.washingtonpost.com/news/energy-environment/wp/2017/02/01/neil-gorsuchs-mother-once-ran-the-epa-it-was-a-disaster/.

43. 130 Cong. Rec. S9151 (July 25, 1984) (statement of Sen. Mitchell). Similar views were expressed in the House by its HSWA sponsors. During 1983 and early

1984, various congressional hearings were held, and studies were performed by a variety of interested parties. One such study that received significant attention was a March 1983 study by the Office of Technology Assessment, entitled *Technologies and Management Strategies for Hazardous Waste Control*, available at https://govinfo.library.unt.edu/ota/Ota_4/DATA/1983/8323.PDF. Among other topics, this report focused on ways in which technology could help reduce the hazardous waste land disposal problem.

44. See James J. Florio, "Congress as Reluctant Regulatory: Hazardous Waste Policy in the 1980s," *Yale Journal on Regulation* 3, no. 2 (1986): 367.

45. There are numerous excellent references on the context and importance of HSWA. Two examples are Richard C. Fortuna and David J. Lennett, *Hazardous Waste Regulation—The New Era: An Analysis and Guide to RCRA and the 1984 Amendments* (New York: McGraw-Hill, 1987); and William L. Rosbe and Robert L. Gulley, "The Hazardous and Solid Waste Amendments of 1984: A Dramatic Overhaul in the Way America Manages its Hazardous Wastes," *Environmental Law Reporter* 14, no. 12 (1984): 10458–67.

46. EPA finalized its Universal Waste regulation in 1995, 60 Fed. Reg. 25492 (May 11, 1995). It has since modified the rule to add certain additional categories of universal waste. EPA also allows states to decide upon other wastes that can be managed under their authorized universal waste regulations.

47. For example, see US Environmental Protection Agency, *RCRA's Critical Mission & the Path Forward*, EPA-530-R-14-002 (Washington, DC: EPA, June 2014).

48. US Government Accountability Office, *Solid Waste: State and Federal Efforts to Manage Nonhazardous Waste*, RCED-95-3 (Washington, DC: GAO, February 1995).

49. See US Environmental Protection Agency, *Report to Congress: Solid Waste Disposal in the United States*, EPA530-SW-88-011 (Washington, DC: EPA, October 1988). The study was completed pursuant to a requirement in the 1984 RCRA Amendments. The report estimated more than eleven billion tons of solid waste was produced annually in the US. More than ninety-five percent was industrial nonhazardous waste, oil and gas waste, mining waste, and municipal solid waste.

50. See US Environmental Protection Agency, *Guide for Industrial Waste Management*, EPA-530-R-03-001 (Washington, DC: EPA), first issued in 1999 and updated since that time. A current version is available at https://www.epa.gov/sites/production/files/2016-03/documents/industrial-waste-guide.pdf.

51. The 1980 RCRA Amendments placed deadlines on the Reports to Congress for each of the "special wastes" with reports due between late 1982 and late 1983, depending upon the waste category. Given the extensive scope of these reports and the ongoing efforts to complete the hazardous waste regulatory framework, these studies were not completed until many years beyond the congressional deadlines.

52. With the exception of coal combustion residuals, where EPA developed minimum national management standards and mining waste, where EPA identified certain wastes as regulated hazardous waste, EPA generally recommended that states continue to regulate the special wastes under state solid waste programs.

53. WIIN also requires EPA, if appropriations are available, to implement a permit program in states that do not apply for and receive EPA approval for their state CCR program.

54. For example, in 2016, the Natural Resources Defense Council and a set of other interested parties, filed an action to have EPA undertake federal standards for the management of oil and gas wastes. This action was not successful. However, interest in applying federal non-hazardous or hazardous frameworks covering oil and gas exploration, development, and production wastes continues.

55. See US Environmental Protection Agency, *Criteria for Solid Waste Disposal Facilities: A Guide for Owners/Operators*, EPA-530-SW-91-089 (Washington, DC: EPA, 1993) for a summary of the detailed requirements for solid waste disposal facilities accepting household or small quantity hazardous waste, https://www.epa.gov/sites/production/files/2016-03/documents/landbig.pdf.

56. EPA issued the State Implementation Rule covering approval of state solid waste programs in 1998.

57. The federal solid waste program focused on land-based disposal and not on recycling for material or energy reuse or treatment that was not land-based. Those areas remained under state leadership and different states have regulated more or less broadly in these areas.

58. US Environmental Protection Agency, *The Solid Waste Dilemma: An Agenda for Action*, EPA-530-SW-89-019 (Washington, DC: EPA, February 1989), https://nepis.epa.gov/Exe/ZyPDF.cgi/1000199O.PDF?Dockey=1000199O.PDF.

59. US Environmental Protection Agency, Office of Land and Emergency Management, *Advancing Sustainable Materials Management: 2015 Fact Sheet*, EPA-530-F-18-004 (Washington, DC: EPA OLEM, 2018), https://www.epa.gov/sites/production/files/2018-07/documents/2015_smm_msw_factsheet_07242018_fnl_508_002.pdf.

60. In 1985, there were approximately 270 million metric tons of hazardous waste generated in the US. Within a decade, the amount has been reduced to approximately 30 million metric tons. See US Environmental Protection Agency, "Quantity of RCRA Hazardous Waste Generated and Managed," *Report on the Environment*: *Hazardous Waste* (Washington, DC: EPA), https://cfpub.epa.gov/roe/indicator.cfm?i=54.

61. US Environmental Protection Agency, "Measuring Progress at Resource Conservation and Recovery Act (RCRA) Corrective Action Facilities" *EPA.gov*, last modified May 22, 2019, https://www.epa.gov/hw/measuring-progress-resource-conservation-and-recovery-act-rcra-corrective-action-facilities#2018.

62. US Environmental Protection Agency, *UST Program Facts: Data About the Underground Storage Tank (UST) Program* (Washington, DC: EPA OLEM, December 2019), https://www.epa.gov/sites/production/files/2017-11/documents/ust-program-facts.pdf; US Environmental Protection Agency, Office of Land and Emergency Management, *Underground Storage Tank Program: 25 Years of Protecting our Land and Water* (Washington, DC: EPA OLEM, 2009), https://www.epa.gov/sites/production/files/2014-03/documents/25annrpt-screen.pdf.

Chapter Eight

Cleanup of Uncontrolled Waste Sites

Gene Lucero and Marcia Williams

INTRODUCTION

During the 1970s, a number of high-profile sites brought attention to one of the risks associated with decades of uncontrolled waste disposal—abandoned waste sites. One of the most significant was Love Canal. The Love Canal site became symbolic of a problem whose solution did not easily fit within the existing environmental framework, including the 1976 Resource Conservation and Recovery Act (RCRA) and the 1972 Clean Water Act (CWA).

Love Canal was a neighborhood located within the city of Niagara Falls in the northwestern region of New York State. The neighborhood covered thirty-six square blocks in the southeastern corner of the city, with the canal running through the area. In the 1920s the canal became a dump site for the city's municipal refuse. Twenty years later, Hooker Chemical Company (now Occidental Petroleum Corporation) purchased the site from the city of Niagara Falls, obtained permission from the local government to dump industrial wastes there, and expanded the site into a seventy-acre disposal site. Over a fifteen-year period, approximately 19,800 tons of chemical wastes from the manufacturing of dyes, perfumes, and solvents used for rubber and other purposes were disposed there. The chemicals were encased in drums and buried at a depth of 20–25 feet.

After Hooker Chemical closed the waste dump with a clay cap and vegetation, it made plans to turn the area into a park. However, ultimately Hooker deeded the property to the school board for one dollar, given that the school board was considering obtaining the property through condemnation. Portions of the property were developed for schools and other portions for houses for low- and middle-income families near and on the former disposal areas. Over time, the chemicals in the dump seeped out of the containment structures, and heavy rainstorms led to widespread contamination in the area. Contamination seeped into the basements of some residences, and illnesses and ailments were quickly attributed to exposure to these wastes.

One of the parents in the area, Lois Marie Gibbs, became an activist in 1977 when she discovered that her son's elementary school was built adjacent to the canal. She became a well-known national environmental advocate for stronger environmental laws and regulations. The Love Canal story and Lois Gibbs' role in it was publicized in newspapers and on national television and at congressional hearings. President Carter declared the Love Canal site a national disaster in 1978, leading to more resources devoted to its cleanup.

Love Canal was not the only high visibility, uncontrolled waste site that garnered publicity during the 1970s. In this chapter, we explore how Love Canal, and many sites like it, led to a huge new responsibility for EPA: the cleanup of uncontrolled waste sites throughout the United States. Our focus in the chapter is how EPA responded to the new authorities and responsibilities that Congress gave the agency under CERCLA.

We begin the chapter by exploring how, in the later part of the 1970s, Congress and EPA began to assess the gravity of the abandoned and uncontrolled site problem, the administration's role in the passage of new statutory authority, and the architecture of the law that was passed to address the problem: the Comprehensive Environmental Response, Compensation, and Liability Act (CERCLA) of 1980. We then explore the turbulent period from 1981 to 1986 when the Reagan administration's CERCLA goals were out of step with congressional expectations. Against this backdrop, career EPA employees moved forward to develop the CERCLA regulatory framework and the technical and enforcement tools needed to move forward with actual site cleanup. Despite the friction between the Reagan administration and Congress, important steps forward were made. However, this friction, the slow pace of early site cleanup progress, and the recognition that certain statutory ambiguities needed resolution led Congress to pass major amendments to CERCLA in 1986. The chapter also discusses how EPA chose to implement some of the key provisions in those amendments. We conclude with observations about EPA accomplishments over the last 40 years and future challenges.

Dimensions of the Problem

As explained in the previous chapter, the 1976 Resource Conservation and Recovery Act authorizes EPA to regulate the active generation, storage, transportation, treatment, and disposal of hazardous waste. But in the 1970s a serious gap in EPA's regulatory fabric was discovered—the agency did not have clear authority to deal with hazardous substances spilled on land or to respond to historically discarded wastes that had resulted in contamination but were no longer under the control of the entities that had originally discarded the waste. As recently as 1977, there was no real understanding of how big a problem these kinds of sites presented.

EPA's understanding of what the problem entailed and what type of program was needed to address it came slowly. In 1977, EPA promulgated regulations under the Clean Water Act to address oil and hazardous substance spills in water, but those regulations were enjoined nation-wide by the federal courts. The leadership at EPA during Carter's presidency concluded that a legislative fix was needed, and their efforts eventually led to the enactment of the Section 311 Spill Program under the Clean Water Act in late 1977. As will be shown later in this chapter, much of the legal architecture of the CERCLA program is drawn from the design of Section 311.

While there were a handful of notorious sites that garnered public and media attention, such as Love Canal, EPA did not know how many such sites there were. In 1977, EPA headquarters asked EPA Regions and their state counterparts about other similar problems that they knew about. The resulting list formed the foundation of what would eventually become the National Priorities List (NPL) mandated by the CERCLA statute.

The sites that EPA identified had been created by a wide range of activities, many of them lawful at the time. Chemical and waste disposal onto and into the land was a common activity that led to contamination; there were many other former disposal sites that EPA identified with similar impacts as Love Canal, such as the Stringfellow Acid Pits in Riverside, California.

However, the environmental impacts of all known sites were diverse. Routine disposal from other industrial operations into streams and waterways also created hazards such as PCB contamination in the Hudson River in New York and in Waukegan Harbor, an industrial suburb of Chicago on Lake Michigan. Such chemicals affect the aquatic environments adversely, and in some cases the marine conditions concentrate the contaminants, resulting in unsafe levels in fish being caught and consumed regularly by people living near the waterways. Elsewhere there was acidic drainage from former mining sites and leftover mine tailings that harmed the biota of receiving waters in many parts of the country.

Some cases of widespread contamination were the results of improper or illegal storage or disposal of hazardous waste, such as the Valley of the Drums in Kentucky or the abandoned recycling site in Seymour, Indiana. However, other known cases represented contamination problems that EPA or the states did not have much experience addressing, such as the basin-wide contamination in drinking water aquifers that resulted from solvents and other chemicals being released from a myriad of industrial and commercial businesses in industrial areas such as the San Fernando and San Gabriel Valleys in arid Southern California. There were also problems of radionuclide contamination from research labs and the nuclear armament industry that made, used, or stored radioactive materials.

As the agency gained a sense of how widespread and serious the problem was, it created a task force of its best and brightest to look at how best to address it, whether it could use current laws to address the problem and, if not, what type of legislation might be needed. At many sites, EPA and the Department of Justice (DOJ) initiated litigation to compel the parties responsible to take response actions or to provide funding for such actions, relying on authority in Section 311 of the CWA, or the imminent and substantial endangerment authority in section 7003 of RCRA. Novel approaches, such as relying on the Rivers and Harbors Act of 1899, were also tried.

There were some successes, but there were many issues that arose with such litigation. Did the agency's legal authority allow it to reach back to responsible parties whose actions occurred before the statute was enacted? If there were multiple parties responsible for contamination, did the government have to bring a case against all of them and be prepared to establish their respective shares of liability? Or could the government sue only a few of such parties? Was liability strict or did the government have to establish negligence or creation of a nuisance to go forward? What if there were problems at the site that needed an immediate response (e.g., open drums or pits, recent spills)? If EPA used its own resources and monies to take action, could the agency recoup its remediation costs from responsible parties? Without new legislation, it would have taken many years, possibly decades, to obtain clear answers to these questions.

LEGISLATIVE HISTORY OF CERCLA

By mid-1978, as Love Canal was becoming a congressional focus, Congress asked EPA for the locations of existing hazardous waste sites including ones that were thought to pose a potential threat. In November 1978, EPA provided a key estimate: 838 of an estimated 32,254 sites could cause a significant imminent hazard. The Government Accounting Office (GAO) was asked to testify to Congress in June 1979 on its view of EPA's estimate of the extent of the environmental risks from uncontrolled sites. Based on interviews with state and EPA personnel, GAO concluded that (1) many closed or abandoned disposal sites, as well as active sites, threaten health and the environment, (2) little had been done to identify the sites, address the damage, or prevent further contamination, (3) Congress had not authorized funding for site identification and remediation and that inadequate funds for this type of work were available from either facility owners or State and local governments, and (4) EPA estimate was developed without a reliable methodology and was highly uncertain and inadequate. GAO concluded its congressional testimony by stating:

> No adequate assessment has been made of the number and location of existing and closed sites currently threatening the public health and the environment. The problem of environmental cleanup because of past disposal practices has not been resolved and emergencies [such as the Love Canal in New York] will continue to occur in the future even when the Act [RCRA] is fully implemented.[1]

Shortly thereafter, the Subcommittee on Oversight and Investigations of the House Committee on Interstate and Foreign Commerce undertook a preliminary national survey to determine the location of hazardous waste sites and whether they currently posed a hazard. This survey focused on waste generation and management at fifty-three of the largest domestic chemical companies. The information was intended to provide inputs as Congress began to debate the problems posed by inactive and "orphaned" waste disposal sites.[2] While significant information was collected demonstrating the extensive number of historical waste disposal locations for industrial waste, the extent of the problem remained highly uncertain.

The agency's experiences informed its decision, during the end of the Carter administration, to seek new legislation to provide EPA with authority to take response action on its own, to clarify its enforcement authority and to provide it with funding to develop its own response capacity. While the Democratic Party had a substantial majority in both the House and Senate, the Carter administration had an uneven record of working with Congress. Moreover, EPA was already implementing several major new environmental laws, and it was a tough time for this small regulatory agency to push for another large, expensive program to address a new set of environmental problems. In addition, the economy was troubled: inflation was high, interest rates were high, and the rate of unemployment was growing toward the end of President Carter's term in office. In effect, there was little appetite for a new program that would have to be funded with general revenues, likely requiring increased taxes.

The agency's solution was to propose funding that would be generated from a tax on petroleum and chemical feedstocks, not from increased taxes on the general public. The rationale was that these were the materials that eventually became the chemicals and waste products that were causing environmental contamination. As described later in this chapter, the proposed tax was coupled with EPA authority to take response actions and recover the costs it expended from responsible parties—a notion first embedded in Section 311 of the Clean Water Act—so as to continue to renew its initial funding. But not everyone was enamored of the EPA proposal.

There were several events that almost derailed the legislation. The first occurred during the interagency process that the federal government uses to vet proposed legislation. The final vote was 22–2 against the legislative proposal. EPA's vote was one of the two votes for moving forward; the other was from the Office of Management and Budget (OMB)—the only other vote EPA had to have. The Deputy Director of OMB particularly liked the funding mechanism, which was now being called by the name "Superfund." A press conference for President Carter to announce the introduction of the legislation was scheduled, and the process seemed to be moving forward. However, as opposed to the Deputy Director, the Director of OMB started to pay more attention to the proposal, and found that he particularly disliked the proposed funding mechanism. OMB's position on the legislation abruptly changed and the president's press conference was cancelled.

In what turned out to be fortunate timing, EPA's budget meeting with the president and OMB was scheduled within a few days. As reported by Tom Jorling, EPA's Assistant Administrator for Water and Hazardous Substances, before the meeting started OMB Deputy Director took the opportunity to bring up the president's press conference that had been recently cancelled. Always detail-minded, the president had noticed the change and asked what had happened. Jorling reported that upon hearing about the disagreement over the funding mechanism, the president's reaction was to say emphatically, "This is crazy." In short order, the near-moribund legislative proposal was resuscitated and sent to Congress. In June 1979, President Carter asked Congress for legislation that would establish a $4 billion fund to enable the federal government to respond to Love Canal and similar hazards at other inactive and abandoned sites.

Progress in Congress was not smooth. Intense lobbying against the legislation came from both the chemical and petroleum industries, who would pay the Superfund taxes. Numerous organizations raised probing questions about the enforcement and cost recovery concepts. Different versions of the legislation began to circulate in the House and Senate.

EPA knew that passing such legislation was unlikely unless significant public pressure for the legislation was generated. With help from its allies in Congress, EPA became involved in more congressional hearings on the scope of abandoned hazardous waste sites in America and news coverage increased. The NGOs, including citizen groups affected by sites like Love Canal and activists like Lois Gibbs, amped up the pressure.

By this time, however, the country was embroiled in the Iran hostage crisis (due to the hostile occupation of the US embassy in Tehran by Islamic extremists). President Carter was in a tough re-election fight with Republican Ronald Reagan, who, based on his critical comments about what the environmentalists and EPA were doing, was considered no friend of the environment. Reagan won the bruising election, the Republicans won a majority of seats in the Senate, and, once again, Superfund seemed down for the count and unlikely to get up again.

Less than a month later, President Carter went on TV to announce that he was calling Congress back to deal with two issues: the debt ceiling needed to be raised, and he wanted the Superfund legislation to be passed. Doug Costle, President Carter's EPA Administrator, told a small group of us from the Denver Regional Office (who were all watching the president's speech) that he made a special trip to the White House to convince the president to add Superfund to his "lame duck" agenda for the short interval from November to December between the end of one Congress and the start of the next one.

At the instruction of congressional leaders—including John Culver of Iowa and Edmund Muskie of Maine in the Senate, and James Florio of New Jersey in the House—a group of congressional and EPA staffers worked together over the following weekend on a version of the legislation that could be passed. The result was an intriguing but imperfect bill, with misspellings, poor definitions, ambiguities, and some very significant gaps.

One of the mysteries of the process was whether some special overture to the Reagan Transition Team was needed. Nonetheless, the incoming president did not object to the legislation and Congress acted favorably on both bills. On December 10, 1980, President Carter signed the Superfund legislation into law. President Carter has since said that passing the Superfund statute was one of the major accomplishments of his presidency.

Responsibility for implementing the Superfund statute passed to the new Reagan administration and, like the passage of the legislation that spawned CERCLA, the process did not go smoothly.

Legal Architecture of CERCLA (1980)

The statute established a $1.6 billion fund, 88% of which was funded by industrial fees and 12% funded by general federal revenue.[3] Unlike RCRA, this statute was framed as a federal-led program, not a state-delegated program, and it was intended to focus on the worst uncontrolled waste sites in the country.

The primary congressional goal of the 1980 statute was to have the president clean up inactive or abandoned sites that could result in health or environmental risks as well as respond to accidents, spills, or emergency releases of chemicals. EPA was given primary authority to manage the program, either undertaking cleanups and response actions itself or requiring responsible parties to respond. The secondary CERCLA goal was that the cleanup should be paid for by those responsible, whether or not those entities were negligent.[4] Joint responsibility for this objective was assigned by the president to EPA and the Department of Justice.

The statute is structured to allow EPA to undertake short-term response actions to respond to emergencies (i.e., immediate and planned removal actions usually under $50,000 and 6-months duration) as well as longer-term, more permanent cleanups (i.e., remedial actions). The trigger for EPA action is a release or potential release of pollution into the environment in the form of a hazardous substance or a contaminant that may present an imminent and substantial endangerment. EPA can undertake these actions themselves and recover their response costs from responsible parties, enter into consent agreements with responsible parties to perform the work, or order responsible parties to perform the necessary response actions.[5] The statute identifies four classes of potentially responsible parties (PRPs): (1) current owners and operators of a facility, (2) former owners and operators of a facility during the time that a hazardous substance was disposed there, (3) persons who owned or possessed hazardous substances and arranged for their disposal or treatment at a facility, and (4) entities that accepted hazardous substances for transport to disposal or treatment facilities that they selected.[6]

To address broader CERCLA goals, the 1980 statute required EPA to amend the National Contingency Plan, previously promulgated in 1973 under the Clean Water Act. It also required EPA to create a National Priority List (NPL) of sites that would be evaluated and addressed under CERCLA. EPA was required to identify at least four hundred such sites and update the list at least annually, providing an opportunity for public notice and comment on the NPL sites. Unless a site was on the NPL, EPA could not use Superfund dollars to implement a remedial action at that site.

CERCLA also required organizations to report releases of hazardous substances above EPA-determined reporting levels. Additionally, the statute required EPA to collect information from current and former operators of facilities that stored, treated, or disposed of RCRA hazardous waste to provide EPA with information on those activities and locations. Transporters who selected these facilities were also subject to this reporting.

The Gorsuch Era

The agency's efforts to implement the new law were complicated by a dysfunctional team that led EPA in the early years of the Reagan administration.

Reagan's first EPA administrator was Anne M. Gorsuch (the mother of current Supreme Court Justice Neil Gorsuch). She was bright, an accomplished attorney, a former elected official in Colorado, and politically conservative and anti-regulation in her perspective. She sought to reduce the size of the agency, curb regulations of business, and allow states more flexibility to decide issues. As EPA noted in its summary of the *History of Superfund*: "Superfund got off to a rocky start. CERCLA was signed by President Jimmy Carter shortly before he left office. The incoming Reagan administration viewed Superfund as a five-year program which would not be reauthorized, and which warranted few resources."[7]

Gorsuch's management style led to numerous problems that were disclosed in the press and exploited by the Democratic majority in the House of Representatives. Her efforts to reduce EPA budget and to eliminate or reduce the significance of certain programs were not popular with the Democratic majority and not popular within EPA. Probably most disruptive was that she established a small group of former and current EPA employees to develop a reorganization plan for the agency, which resulted in new organizational units with new leadership. For example, the enforcement personnel (attorneys and technical staff) who had historically been in EPA Enforcement Office (or Enforcement Division in EPA Regions) were now separated into legal and technical units under different reporting lines. These attorneys, who had often led EPA's enforcement efforts in the past, found that they were no longer in charge. To add to the disruption, many senior managers were re-assigned to new unrelated positions, sometimes in different parts of the country. These steps guaranteed that not much would get done at EPA for a while and that Gorsuch would not be a popular leader for EPA staff, who quickly nicknamed her "The Ice Queen."

Management of the Superfund program at this time was particularly challenging. Rita Lavelle was appointed by the president to be the assistant administrator for solid waste and emergency response, a position created by the new statute. Lavelle had experience in Governor Reagan's administration and in California business and politics. At EPA, she was responsible for implementing the new CERCLA law, including allocation of the $1.6 billion in Superfund cleanup monies. Lavelle did not have much experience running large and complex organizations and was not Gorsuch's choice for this position. Some found Lavelle's decisions to be rash and ill-considered, and tried to rein her in, but Lavelle regularly used her connections to key presidential advisors who she knew from her time in California government to support her actions. Decision-making at the highest level in the Superfund program often became a slow, nasty turf fight within the agency.

Gorsuch's objective of having a five-year-limited Superfund program that would then pass to state responsibility also induced some unhelpful and unpopular management practices. The size and magnitude of the cleanup problem needed to be managed, so regions and states were encouraged to limit types of sites that would be complicated and expensive to address, such as contaminated regional groundwater sites and contaminated water body sediment sites (e.g., bays and rivers). Any site where the contamination problem could be managed under other statutes (e.g., CWA, RCRA, or the Atomic Energy Act) should be kept out of the Superfund process. The costs of remediation also needed to be managed, so partial, less-expensive remedies that contained the problem or limited exposures were preferred over long-term, more expensive remedies that attempted more complete or aggressive solutions. And finally, virtually every decision that required expenditure of Superfund monies had to be approved by EPA Headquarters, a practice distinctly at odds with the delegation practices of previous administrations. Outside observers were not wrong to conclude that the administration was purposefully slowing down the identification of NPL sites and the rapid implementation of remedial actions at those sites to avoid expansion of the CERCLA program after the original funding mechanism had expired.[8]

What broke the Gorsuch administration, however, involved "enforcement-sensitive" documents generated by Superfund enforcement cases. These were largely cases started under the Carter administration which had been amended to add Superfund claims once CERCLA was enacted. Allegations of improprieties involving some of the cases were regularly being leaked from agency staff to Congress and the media. Consequently, Congress initiated its own investigations and, as part of the process, subpoenaed a large number of documents from EPA and DOJ. DOJ senior management took the position that, as a result of the president's executive privilege, Congress could not constitutionally subpoena the documents; they would only get what the president chose to make available. Since senior managers at both EPA and DOJ were concerned that sensitive enforcement evidence and strategy would leak out of Congress, they persuaded the president to direct that documents containing such information not be provided. As a result, for the next several months hundreds of person-hours were dedicated to reviewing enforcement case documents and determining which contained "enforcement-sensitive" information. Gorsuch was sent to the Hill to deliver the message and, in the process, became the main defender of the president's executive privilege claim.

At the same time, awards of Superfund monies were increasing, and large grants were often being timed to help the political campaigns of friends of the administration. George Deukmejian was running for California Governor and, as he was a personal friend, Lavelle did not want the announcement of a Superfund grant of more than $6 million in federal funds for the Stringfellow Acid Pits Superfund Site to confer a political win on the current Governor

Jerry Brown and the Democratic Party. Quietly, she convinced others that she should delay the award.

One of the PRPs at the Stringfellow Site was Aerojet General, a former employer of Lavelle. Because that relationship created a potential conflict of interest, she had been asked on the record in her Senate confirmation hearing if she would recuse herself from any matters involving Aerojet. She agreed. However, besides involving herself in the award of Superfund monies in the Stringfellow case, it turns out that Lavelle also regularly called the Aerojet general counsel to report on developments in the Stringfellow matter and other enforcement cases against Aerojet. These contacts came to the attention of congressional investigators when the Aerojet general counsel happened to mention the calls during his interview as part of the overall investigation of EPA. In fact, he had notes of all of Lavelle's calls to him. Among other things, it appeared that the claim of Executive Privilege was being used to protect criminal behavior. Once the circumstances became known, the Administrator had no choice but to fire Lavelle.

Lavelle was furious. Apparently, she was not aware of what others knew and believed her firing was a move orchestrated by her enemies in the agency. In anger, she took the position that only the president could fire her and refused to leave. But Lavelle was no longer welcome at the White House, and the announcement of her firing by the president was announced the next business day. Still angry, Lavelle contacted several congressional members and offered to testify about the shameful goings-on at EPA. At two separate hearings, she was asked pointed questions about her Aerojet contacts, to which her answers were not truthful. Shortly thereafter, the president released all the subpoenaed documents, Lavelle was indicted and convicted of perjury, Administrator Gorsuch resigned, and many other EPA political appointees were asked to leave.[9]

The issues surrounding Gorsuch and Lavelle exacerbated congressional mistrust of EPA, and made it even more difficult for EPA to implement the highly ambitious and complicated law. Even after President Reagan chose William Ruckelshaus, a well-respected former Administrator of EPA, to return to the leadership of EPA, there was ongoing tension between EPA and Congress on CERCLA implementation. Each decision by EPA was heavily scrutinized and, when the time to reauthorize Superfund came around, this mistrust motivated many of the changes Congress wrote into the Superfund Amendments and Reauthorization Act of 1986.

Implementation Progress

Even though early implementation of CERCLA was burdened with management challenges and fraught with technical and legal implementation issues,[10]

EPA did make some progress implementing the new law from 1981 to 1986. Very shortly after the passage of CERCLA, EPA was faced with finalizing a ranking system that would be used to prioritize sites for response, developing the initial list of NPL sites, and issuing a regulation to explain the process EPA would use to undertake response actions and make decisions regarding remedies. The statute placed tight timeframes on each of these requirements. In addition to these deadlines, EPA was faced with making immediate cleanup progress at sites that were already known to the agency as high priority sites.

An important accomplishment was the July 1982 regulatory framework established within the National Contingency Plan ("NCP"). EPA finalized amendments to the NCP to incorporate the procedures that EPA planned to utilize to implement response actions under CERCLA. The revised NCP "is designed to make federal action reasonably predictable by both the regulated community and the general public which the statutes are intended to protect."[11] The amended NCP describes the different organizations that respond to hazardous substance releases and how these entities coordinate. It also describes the ways in which releases are discovered and evaluated, the criteria and methods for performing hazard ranking of sites, the criteria for determining whether a removal or remedial action will occur, the procedures to be followed in performing removal and remedial actions and selecting the remedy, and the nature of records that EPA will establish to support its actions.

EPA developed a multi-step framework for achieving protection of human health and the environment. The basic CERCLA investigation process, as illustrated in Figure 8.1, begins with a preliminary assessment supplemented with a site investigation where necessary. If that review indicates potential risks, the next step involves a more detailed remedial investigation and a feasibility study to determine options for addressing risks. Ultimately, all the information is evaluated and a proposed and final record of decision (ROD) is completed. Remedial design and then implementation of the remedial action follows the completion of a ROD. Once a remedial action is complete—usually defined as when all remedy construction is complete—a site can be deleted from the NPL.

While the NCP explains the processes necessary to reach a decision on an appropriate response action, it does not dictate the specific response action that must be performed at a site. EPA makes those decisions based on data collected during the site investigation and remedy evaluation process.[12] EPA noted that it would use the same factors to determine a Superfund-financed remedy as a responsible party remedy. The statute provides EPA with total discretion to select a remedy and implement it or impose the requirement to implement it on responsible parties. Generally, to avoid letting challenges to its decisions bog down the program in litigation, EPA took the position that

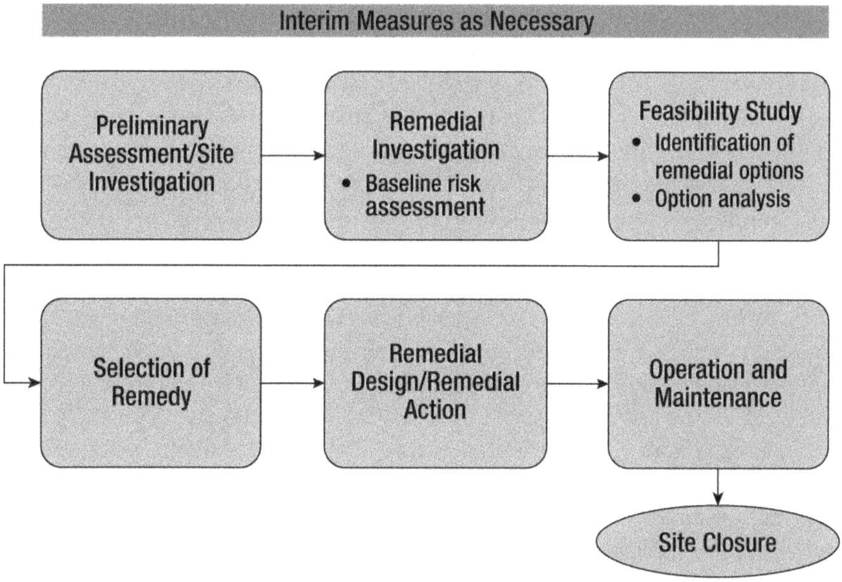

Figure 8.1. Defined Remedial Framework to Ensure Protection of Human Health and the Environment. ***Author-generated***

neither PRPs nor the public could appeal EPA's selected remedy until after remedy implementation is completed.

EPA incorporated its Hazard Ranking System (HRS) into the proposed NCP, and requested public comments. Extensive comments were received and then addressed in the 1982 final NCP, including the Hazard Ranking System as Appendix A of the NCP.[13]

The original National Priorities List—identifying 406 sites—was promulgated by EPA on September 8, 1983. The NPL includes federal facilities (e.g., military bases and nuclear facilities) as well as a wide range of nonfederal sites. Nonfederal sites not only included traditional manufacturing or disposal sites but also included areas of broadly dispersed contamination such as regional groundwater contamination. EPA emphasized that even if a site was listed on the NPL based on the HRS ranking, an NPL listing did not mean that the site would end up with remedial action. Rather, the detailed investigation that followed listing could conclude that the release was either more or less problematic than what was known at the time of listing. EPA continues to update the list of NPL sites.

EPA issued regulations covering CERCLA release reporting obligations between 1981 and 1985. As a result of EPA's April 15, 1981 notice on the

CERCLA Section 103(c) reporting requirement for historical hazardous waste management locations, EPA received notifications of hundreds of additional potentially contaminated sites. These sites were added to its database of contaminated sites to begin the process of preliminary assessment. EPA also completed regulations finalizing the list of hazardous substances along with reportable quantities for each hazardous substance between 1983 and 1985. This ensured the ongoing reporting of new or newly discovered hazardous substance releases.

In addition to developing CERCLA implementation regulations in the early 1980s, EPA continued to work on individual uncontrolled sites. Even before the passage of CERCLA, EPA had obtained information on a large number of potential hazardous substance release sites. By the time CERCLA passed, EPA had already started to prioritize those sites using an early version of the hazard ranking approach that it modified and incorporated into the final 1982 NCP.[14] Based on that ranking process, EPA had identified 115 sites with releases or threatened releases that the agency was evaluating for initial funding decisions.

In the early 1980s, while EPA was still developing the CERCLA regulatory framework and the first NPL, the agency relied heavily on the Fund to implement CERCLA with EPA in the lead on most sites. One primary reason for this was that EPA was in the early process of developing detailed guidance documents to support the CERCLA decision process. Most of these critical documents were not developed until the 1985 to 1988 timeframe. This included guidance on appropriate ways to evaluate exposure and risk and the development of more sophisticated analytical methods and quality control standards for the large number of hazardous substances. Until EPA gained its own experience with appropriate technologies and approaches for different types of site remediation, it was reluctant to let private parties take the lead. Other reasons included the need to establish positions in early litigation on some legal questions that Congress had been silent on in the original statute, such as whether the CERCLA liability structure was joint and several (i.e., the federal government did not have to sue all PRPs and establish their individual shares of liability), and to confirm that PRPs did not have a right to have pre-enforcement judicial review of EPA's decisions on appropriate response actions.

In 1983, it became clear that the size of the Fund—even though $1.6 billion seems like a huge sum—would be insufficient if EPA did not begin to better leverage PRP resources.[15] (The industry tax was not renewed as of 1985 and by 1995 all taxing authority for Fund replenishment had expired.) If PRP's paid for cleanups, EPA would not have to expend its limited Superfund monies.

Consequently, EPA issued guidance on the use of CERCLA Section 106(a) orders in late 1983 and a CERCLA Settlement Policy in late 1984.

At this time, EPA was proceeding with a mix of Fund-financed cleanups and enforcement-led cleanups by PRPs. The shift to a stronger enforcement bias tracked with the release of additional EPA technical guidance providing extra information on remedial assessment and decision-making. Additional guidance on evolving EPA site investigation and remediation was included in EPA's proposed February 1985 modifications to the NCP regulations.[16] By 1989, with the benefit of EPA's implementation experience, the agency had clearly shifted to an "enforcement first" policy, primarily using the Fund as leverage to achieve enforcement settlements.

Mid-Course Corrections Effected in the 1986 Amendments

To get CERCLA passed in the lame-duck session of 1980, Congress had to move fast to come up with passable legislation, which led to certain ambiguities that did not get addressed in the final statute. In addition, Congress had to punt on some issues it could not get agreement on in the time available. By 1984, as the time to consider whether to reauthorize CERCLA began to approach, both the new leadership at EPA (both Ruckelshaus and his eventual successor, Lee Thomas) and Congress had parts of the Superfund program they wanted to fix.

One set of problems centered on the lessons EPA and DOJ had learned from the Hazardous Waste Task Force experience. To optimize the powerful enforcement tools Congress had provided, EPA and DOJ needed to make sure that the enforcement process did not get bogged down in endless and expensive litigation. Early on, the statute was interpreted by the courts as imposing strict and retroactive liability. Courts also determined that the bar for what constituted an actual or potential imminent and substantial endangerment was reasonably low. Because there were differing opinions, the federal government took a bit longer to establish by court decision that the statute imposed joint and several liability, meaning that EPA could select a subset of the potentially responsible parties to perform the necessary response actions or fund the recovery. Establishing these positions simplified EPA's burden of proof, but brought new questions to the forefront.

Meanwhile, courts had more trouble reaching consensus on other issues. For example, did the PRPs who performed the work or reimbursed EPA's costs have a right to seek contribution from the non-complying or non-participating PRPs? If so, when did this right accrue? Another question that troubled several courts was whether the federal government's position was right that PRPs could not challenge the choice of response action or the issuance of an administrative order until the government initiated its own action to enforce its decision in court. Some courts were concerned that these positions raised due process questions. As a result, EPA worried that adverse decisions on these types of liability and process issues could seriously handicap its efforts to maximize the use of its enforcement tools. The eventual solution was for Congress to add some new enforcement and settlement provisions, including ones specifying what the effects of PRP settlements were (e.g., contribution protection) and the right of performing PRPs to seek contribution, and setting out when judicial challenges to EPA decisions were barred (pre-enforcement bar).[17]

Congress had its own CERCLA reauthorization concerns. It was not satisfied with the pace or quality of EPA's implementation of CERCLA. Specifically, the primary concern of many congressional representatives who participated in the early reauthorization process was that EPA still did not have a handle on the total number of sites that would ultimately require response under CERCLA, making it impossible to estimate the likely cost of the overall program. For example, as of 1985 EPA was estimating that eventually about 2,000 sites would end up on the NPL. The Office of Technology Assessment, tasked by Congress to examine this issue, placed the estimate at 10,000 sites (not including federal facility sites).[18] Neither number was well supported nor was there an accurate way to estimate total required remedial funds, total EPA manpower, or the time it would take to complete the program.[19]

The problem, in part, was that there were more potential sites than anyone had imagined in 1980, and with each passing year of CERCLA implementation, the average cost to investigate and remediate sites continued to increase dramatically. For example, as EPA gained more experience with remediation, the average cost estimated for groundwater remediation increased from \$50,000 to \$100,000 to \$1,000,000 per site in four short years. The congressional solution was to establish required numbers and deadlines for preliminary assessments and site investigations, remedial investigations/feasibility studies, and physical on-site work through November 1990. Such mandatory actions, if missed by EPA, could be enforced by states or NGOs.

Perhaps the longest and most difficult discussion in the 1986 CERCLA reauthorization process involved the ultimate cleanup goals for the Superfund program. EPA's early remedies were highly dependent upon short-term risk reduction rather than permanent solutions. For example, many early response actions involved transfer of wastes from an uncontrolled site to a commercial land disposal site (i.e., a Treatment, Storage, and Disposal Facility (TSDF)). While this transfer was an improved short-term result, the long-term safety of land disposal remedies was considered an open question. Although this early approach had been driven by Administrator Gorsuch's preference to have a limited federal Superfund program, the approach continued to be recommended after her departure. Should short-term cleanup remain the priority?

Or should a more thorough cleanup be prioritized? Theoretically, the number of sites that might be addressed by Superfund was much larger than originally estimated and the time to determine what was needed and to implement a response action had become much longer than originally predicted, especially if the goal of remediation was not just risk reduction but rather the achievement of a "complete cleanup."

Exacerbating the problem, the original 1980 statute did not prescribe any cleanup standards for Superfund remediation nor set out any process to develop cleanup standards. EPA attempted to address this issue of "how clean is clean" by propounding a policy in the 1985 NCP that required applicable or relevant and appropriate requirements (ARARs) be applied to Superfund cleanups. Applicable requirements were those that applied to the contamination or the choice of remedy as a matter of law or regulation. Relevant and appropriate requirements may not legally apply, but would be appropriate for the specific circumstances. In the reauthorization decisions, Congress validated this approach by incorporating it into the 1986 Amendments to Superfund. But because of the mistrust Congress held for EPA, based on its early implementation of Superfund, Congress also added in a number of restrictions on how cleanup was to be approached. The 1986 amendments created a preference that the federal government seek to attain standards that eliminate the risk (e.g., achieving cleanup of aquifer groundwater to background or drinking water standards), unless the attainment of those standards is impracticable. There is also a statutory presumption that permanent remedies and innovative treatment technologies should be used in remediating hazardous waste sites.

Unfortunately, these decisions sidestepped what was then, and still is, the largest problem facing EPA and other government entities attempting to implement Superfund: What should the proper goals be for a governmental cleanup program? Stated another way, how big and aggressive should governmental cleanup efforts be? By the mid-1980s the agency was getting a sense of what it knows now: that achieving cleanup to background or no-risk levels is not only hugely expensive at many sites, but will take decades to achieve. Estimates for regional groundwater and sediment remediation, for example, now regularly exceed $100 million at Superfund sites and have even approached a billion dollars at some sediment sites. Some regional groundwater remedies may need to run for fifty to one hundred years in their effort to achieve drinking water maximum contaminant levels (MCLs) in the aquifer groundwater. As criticisms of the program over the last decade or more have pointed out, neither EPA nor the states have the financial or human resources to implement all such remedies that might be appropriate. As a result, the government has had to look to PRPs to both finance and manage these sites, leading to a contentious and resource-intensive process of negotiations and interactions that results in slow cleanups. Relying on long-term management by private parties for whom this is not part of their core business expertise remains risky. Unfortunately, the changes Congress made to the cleanup objectives effectively removed EPA's flexibility to go in a different direction.

When Congress ultimately passed the Superfund Amendments and Reauthorization Act (SARA) of 1986, the final compromise legislation clarified some important issues as discussed above. Additionally, the 1986 amendments:

- Stressed the importance of citizen participation at sites.
- Made federal facilities subject to CERCLA in the same way as any non-governmental site and required the federal government to clean up any hazardous waste sites they owned or operated. Federal facility remedial activities were not allowed to use the Fund. Importantly, federal facility cleanups were required to involve state and local agencies and the public in cleanup decisions and EPA was given authority to review federal agency remedy decisions.[20] Several years later Congress waived sovereign immunity in the Federal Facilities Compliance Act so states could enforce their requirements against federal facilities as well.
- Required the Agency for Toxic Substances and Disease Registry (ATSDR) and EPA to prepare a list of the most common hazardous substances at NPL sites and prepare toxicological profiles on those substances at a rate of twenty-five per year. ATSDR was also required to perform health assessments at NPL listed facilities within a year of listing.
- Clarified under what conditions a subsequent purchaser or corporate successor would become liable for acquisition of contaminated property, whether a Superfund site or not. As a result, many parties engaged in private business transactions involving contaminated property felt compelled to address any necessary remediation in the transaction or at least the allocation of liabilities for such contamination.
- Supplemented the size of the Fund.

Post-1986 Implementation and Impacts

Although CERCLA is designed as a federally led program, its provisions provided a strong and sufficient impetus for states to develop comparable programs. States, for example, are required to use the Hazard Ranking System to evaluate the threats posed by releases in the state and assign priorities to those releases for response activities. EPA then reviews and consolidates these state priority lists. The NCP has stated that to the extent practicable, each state will have at least one site ranked among the highest priority release sites. CERCLA also provides for state participation in remedial actions that will require long-term and more costly actions for cleanup. States are required to provide information on costs including future site maintenance costs.[21]

Of particular importance, beginning in the early 1980s, CERCLA became a model for the development of state remedial statutes. The 1986 amendments accelerated modernization of state laws. A 1991 review of state Superfund programs found that twenty-nine states had funds and enforcement authorities and were conducting programs for removals and remedial actions at non-NPL sites. Twelve additional states had legal frameworks in place although, at the time of the study, there was limited ongoing remedial work under those authorities. The remaining eleven states had no, or very limited, enforcement authorities or funds for non-NPL work. Twenty-four states also reported use of state priority site lists.[22]

In 1996, Congress passed legislation amending CERCLA to protect lenders and fiduciaries from liability so long as they did not participate in the management of a facility contaminated with hazardous substances. In 1999, Congress also provided relief from CERCLA liability to recyclers of certain materials such as glass and metal as long as the recycler met a set of defined conditions. In 2002, Congress provided liability relief from certain very small contributors of hazardous substances at NPL sites if those wastes were disposed of prior to April 1, 2001. This 2002 statute also provided a liability exemption for property owners whose land is adjacent to a Superfund site and for prospective purchasers of property known to be contaminated if those purchasers conducted "all appropriate inquiry" and met a set of other prescribed obligations (e.g., providing access and cooperating with entities undertaking any required remediation). EPA has provided guidance on these obligations.

EPA has continued to update the NCP as needed to incorporate both statutory changes and improvements based on implementation experience. In 1990, EPA updated the HRS to incorporate SARA requirements including a new soil exposure pathway. The 1990 HRS also made numerous changes to the original exposure pathways (e.g., groundwater, surface water, and air) based on more developed exposure and risk assessment information and models. In 2017, EPA again updated the HRS to incorporate a vapor intrusion exposure pathway.

EPA has also continued to undertake enhancements to its CERCLA program. Three initiatives are mentioned as examples. First, EPA made a concerted effort to integrate its processes and outcomes between the RCRA corrective action program and the CERCLA program. This has ensured that cleanup outcomes between these two programs are consistent, precluding regulated parties from statute shopping. Second, EPA put considerable effort into developing risk-based environmental screening levels for a wide range of hazardous substances and media in the mid-1990s, expanding and updating this information over time. More recently, these updates have included risk-based environmental screening levels for sediment. This has facilitated better consistency of remedial outcomes and set the stage for a wide range of voluntary cleanup programs. These environmental screening levels removed significant uncertainty that had impeded cleanup outside of mandatory programs requiring extensive federal or state oversight. Third, EPA developed presumptive remedies for a series of common contamination scenarios. These presumptive remedy guidance documents helped speed up remedial decisions for many types of sites. Recently, EPA issued guidance on evaluating and remediating contaminated sediment sites, one of the most highly complex types of remedial sites.

Despite more than forty years of experience implementing CERCLA, EPA continues to confront new and unresolved issues.[23]

WHAT EPA HAS ACCOMPLISHED

In 1980 when CERCLA was first enacted, the basic knowledge and tools to undertake sophisticated subsurface assessments of contaminated property risks and select permanent remedies to control those risks were completely lacking. Even prioritizing sites was challenging without the data/tools to quantitatively or qualitatively evaluate the range of exposure pathways. Knowledge was limited to undertaking relatively simple risk reduction tasks such as removal of leaking drums or installing access controls. Thus, it is unsurprising that EPA's initial efforts to clean up complex sites were slow and plodding. What is surprising is how much has been accomplished in the last four decades. Significant accomplishments include:

- EPA has collected data that indicate that 487 Superfund sites are in reuse, generating over $43 billion in sales and employing over 150,000 people with annual employment income of over $11 billion. EPA points out that the revenue being generated at these sites is far in excess of the dollars spent to clean the sites up. [24]
- EPA data indicate that alternative energy facilities are located at 50 Superfund sites providing an installed capacity of over 316 megawatts.
- EPA data show that (as of the end of FY2017) 1,475 NPL sites have completed remediation or achieved control of all human exposures to protective levels.

- The work performed by EPA to develop tools for site investigation and remediation has led to both mandatory and voluntary cleanups at thousands of non-NPL sites. As of 2001, an estimated 29,000 sites had been remediated by states.[25] Moreover, the site assessments prepared to screen contaminated sites for NPL listing are utilized directly by states and federal entities for non-NPL cleanup. A 2012 effort to estimate the benefits of the CERCLA site assessment program, prepared by the Association of State and Territorial Solid Waste Management Officials (ASTSWMO) with EPA assistance, found that over 9,000 state cleanups were complete with another 11,000 underway. These were in addition to the 1,700 NPL sites.[26] CERCLA's focus on contaminated properties has now been integrated into virtually all significant business transactions. Primarily, this impacts transfer of contaminated property but can also impact leases, loans, and other business transactions. Many states have contaminated property transfer disclosure and/or due care requirements, but the cost of contaminated property acquisition creates momentum to identify and ensure funding for cleanup even without mandatory legislation. This has resulted in development of standards for "all appropriate inquiry" and tools for implementing private party site assessments.
- From a dearth of trained and capable individuals with expertise in contaminated property, there is now a large professional community of knowledgeable professionals. There are also many individuals who have gained experience in the management and strategic aspects of property remediation.
- The ability to measure the benefits of remediating contaminated properties has improved. In the early days, measurements focused on how many assessments had been completed and how much money had been committed to cleanup. There are always opportunities to expand and improve success metrics, but today's metrics are able to consider the economic benefits of achieved remediation, the number of sites where human exposures have been controlled, and other more direct program benefits.

FUTURE CHALLENGES

CERCLA and related federal and state programs have been dynamic over the last several decades. Various pilot approaches have been tried to speed up the program, improve citizen input into the program, and emphasize the need for innovative partnerships. In many ways, the properties being cleaned up today are more complex (e.g., harbor and river sediment sites, expansive regional groundwater sites, mining sites) than those that were the focus in the 1980s. Many entities have expressed thoughts about ways to improve

CERCLA. Others have spent time focusing on changing the relationship between CERCLA and the wide raft of federal and state programs that supplement CERCLA. But there are still challenges to be tackled and opportunities to be pursued. The following paragraphs provide the authors' thoughts on some remaining challenges.

In recent years, EPA has reduced its efforts to identify and hold responsible more complete sets of PRPs at multi-party sites. Additionally, in recent years EPA has also been reluctant to issue CERCLA Section 106 orders to non-cooperative PRPs at these multi-party sites as long as one or more PRPs steps up to perform the remediation. This is leading to unnecessary and costly contribution litigation and fails to provide proper incentives for PRPs to continue to enter into consent agreements.

The time may be appropriate for EPA to re-visit questions of whether all sites require the same level of cleanup. As an example, should all Superfund contaminated groundwater sites be cleaned up to MCLs or would it be equally beneficial to allow cleanup of the aquifer to less stringent levels coupled with wellhead treatment that assures water withdrawn from the aquifer for drinking water supply meets drinking water standards before delivery. This latter approach is commonly used by municipal water suppliers for non-NPL contaminated groundwater sites. Both could protect the public equally, but the current Superfund approach—driven by the preference for permanent remedies—is far more expensive and takes longer. More generally, are there benefits to achieving 80% of public health objectives more quickly at more sites than achieving 100% cleanup at far fewer sites? The answers to these questions should not be pre-determined, but the analysis of relative costs/benefits could be very useful. This is a particularly important question given that today's remaining federal Superfund sites, and state Superfund-like cleanups, tend to be more complex, time-intensive, and expensive than early Superfund sites. And, with the continuing identification of new contaminants like PFAS with extremely low drinking water advisory levels, it is imperative to move quickly to determine whether a new type of approach would be appropriate for this class of emerging contaminants that could dwarf the dollars and resources spent on Superfund to date.

A remaining challenge is that many Superfund sites are located in distressed communities that have high proportions of low-income and minority populations.[27] Approximately fifty-six million people in the US live within three miles of a Superfund site; about fifteen million people live within one mile of a site. The data in Table 8.1 illustrate that a disproportionate share of people living near sites are minority, impoverished, linguistically isolated, and have less than a high school education. Both Congress and EPA have recognized the environmental justice issue as it relates to Superfund sites,

Figure 8.1. Demographic Profile of Population Living Near Superfund Sites

Indicator	*Population within 1-mile of all sites*	*Population within 3-miles of all sites*	*U.S. Population*
Minority (all races and ethnicities except "non-Hispanic white")	49.3%	49.7%	38.4%
Below poverty level	16.7%	16.7%	14.7%
Linguistically isolated	8.4%	8.1%	5.2%
Less than a high school education	16.3%	15.8%	13.5%
Under 5 years of age	6.7%	6.6%	6.3%
Over 64 years of age	12.3%	12.7%	14.1%
Total population	15,140,827	52,658,478	320,098,094

Source: "Population Surrounding 1,836 Superfund Remedial Sites," *epa.gov*, updated October 2017, https://www.epa.gov/sites/production/files/2015-09/documents/webpopulationrsuperfundsites9.28.15.pdf.

but no consensus has been reached as to appropriate responses and how these responses would affect the other goals of the Superfund program. Should EPA's risk assessments, remedy selection at sites, or enforcement priorities be adjusted in light of environmental-justice concerns? Should EPA give preference to environmental-justice considerations when allocating Superfund trust monies to cleanups? Should the National Ranking System of waste sites incorporate environmental justice information in some systematic way?

EPA and states have required many types of waste facilities to have financial assurance mechanisms in place during site operations to address potential future cleanup requirements at those facilities. However, financial assurance has not been required for entities that generate waste and send it to a range of off-site locations. Moreover, financial assurance for certain categories of production facilities, while considered under CERCLA Section 108(b), has never been implemented. Pursuit of these approaches could provide insurance for the future.

Many NPL sites will be in a final operation and maintenance mode for decades. This is particularly true for large regional groundwater sites. Management of these sites is not the core strength of PRPs whose businesses are unrelated to long-term remedial management. Moreover, EPA oversight of these sites may not be the best use of EPA resources. There could be benefits to establishing a public corporation that could manage these long-term sites. These benefits could include more cost-effective O&M, more consistencies in determining when site remediation can be considered complete, and reduction in the impact of PRP bankruptcies.

A public database on remedial sites that contains accurate information on key remedial activities, costs, resources, and other relevant information would greatly help improve future program implementation and allow for far better understanding of program costs and benefits. EPA's existing public databases have limited information and continue to have significant data quality issues.

Emerging pollutants make it unlikely that any completed cleanup is ever really "finished." Now is the time to develop strategies for addressing potential emerging contaminant issues at ongoing and completed CERCLA and related remedial program sites. Federal leadership in the emerging contaminant area is needed to avoid duplicative work at the state level and the development of programs differing widely in scope and standards.

It is clear that PRPs at CERCLA sites are liable for remediation whether or not those entities were negligent at the time contamination occurred. However, the existence of contaminated property and the identification of PRPs at those properties has resulted in expansive amounts of toxic tort litigation, focused on obtaining punitive negligence decisions around historically contaminated properties. Efforts to make sure that CERCLA cleanup actions, and voluntary cleanup actions, aren't utilized improperly in tort matters would be beneficial.

Most analysis of CERCLA has focused on non-federal NPL site; however, there are large numbers of federal facility sites, many of which are extremely complex. Federal facility sites are not listed on the NPL. The pace of completion, public involvement, and quality of cleanups for federal facility sites should be evaluated with statutory revisions implemented if needed.[28]

CONCLUSION

From 1980 forward, the CERCLA program resonated with the public as addressing high risk environmental problems and thus has commanded a large share of EPA resources. The same view has not always been shared by experienced EPA professionals.[29] An interesting question is whether the disconnect between public and EPA risk perceptions is in part due to public outrage over contaminated sites (e.g., Love Canal and Stringfellow), along with the extremely high degree of discord that developed between Congress and EPA's political leadership in the early 1980s, the formative years for CERCLA. Certainly, whatever decision-making flexibility existed in the 1980 CERCLA statute was severely curtailed with the 1986 amendments, which were driven by a deep congressional mistrust of EPA's leadership after the 1980 Reagan administration appointed Anne M. Gorsuch as EPA

Administrator and Rita Lavelle as the Assistant Administrator for solid waste and emergency response. The congressional reaction was to greatly diminish EPA discretion. The ramifications of the narrowed discretion have continued to impact EPA's ability to make major changes that address the numerous criticisms of CERCLA and the opportunities to improve it based on four decades of experience with its implementation.

The CERCLA experience has fostered public and industry awareness of the adverse impacts and multi-faceted costs of improper waste management. Moreover, because the public expectations for CERCLA have been unrealistically high from the start, EPA's implementation approaches have borne the brunt of significant criticism over the breadth, pace, cost, and cost-effectiveness of the programs and their accomplishments.

In retrospect, EPA did an impressive job implementing the CERCLA statute, but it has certainly evolved into a complex program with limited flexibility to tailor cleanups to local circumstances and to shorten time-consuming processes. Costs to reach remedy decisions for complex sites are now tens to hundreds of millions of dollars per site and required studies and processes can delay site cleanup progress for years. The incorporation of all other state, local, and federal environmental protections into each CERCLA cleanup—i.e., the evaluation of ARARs, considered a reasonable concept in the early years of CERCLA implementation—has greatly added to process complexity and may no longer be needed with the more sophisticated risk-based media/contaminant screening levels. Whether the political will can be generated to attempt such major adjustments in the country's program to address uncontrolled waste sites remains to be seen.

NOTES

1. Henry Eschwege, *Environmental Protection Agency and State Hazardous Waste Management Programs* (Washington, DC: GAO, June 4, 1979), https://www.gao.gov/assets/100/99095.pdf. The relevant discussion begins on page 8.

2. Waste Disposal Site Survey, commonly referred to as the Eckhardt Survey (named for Congressman Bob Eckhardt) and issued in October 1979. This survey found that of the 3,383 sites identified in the survey, 32% were reported as closed for disposal of waste. In fact, 26% of the surveyed sites had closed after 1976, the year RCRA was enacted and these closed sites were estimated to have accepted over 100 million tons of waste, much of it managed in land-based units. It was immediately noted by Congress that these closed sites would not be regulated or monitored under the prospective RCRA hazardous waste regulatory program. See Staff of H. Subcomm. on Oversight and Investigations, Comm. on Interstate and Foreign Commerce, 96th Cong., Waste Disposal Site Survey Report (Comm. Print 1979), https://archive.org/stream/wastedissit00unit/wastedissit00unit_djvu.txt.

3. Christian Miles, University of North Georgia, wrote a 2014 paper on the timeline of CERCLA passage, providing his analysis of the factors that impacted both the timing and legislative changes necessary to get CERCLA enacted, https://digitalcommons.northgeorgia.edu/cgi/viewcontent.cgi?article=1400&context=ngresearchconf.

4. The initial Superfund tax was based on amount of chemicals produced, not on the amount of chemicals released to the environment.

5. EPA can recover its costs for response actions involving hazardous substances, a term defined in the statute and incorporated with specificity into 40 C.F.R. 302 of the regulations. Congress was clear that petroleum, including crude oil or any fraction thereof, is not a hazardous substance. EPA also has authority to undertake response actions involving pollutants and contaminants, but unless a release involves a hazardous substance, EPA cannot recover its costs from potentially responsible parties.

6. EPA career staff preferred to use the term "potentially responsible party" or "PRP" in place of "responsible party" to acknowledge that many parties' liability was due to their relationship to the contamination (e.g., current owners of the facility), not because they actively or negligently caused or contributed to the contamination problems. The 1986 amendments incorporated the terminology into the statute.

7. US Environmental Protection Agency, Office of Solid Waste and Emergency Response, *History of Superfund,* 9200.5-008B (Washington, DC: EPA OSWER, November 1990), https://nepis.epa.gov/Exe/ZyPDF.cgi/91003GNT.PDF?Dockey=91003GNT.PDF.

8. For example, see Superfund observations in James J. Florio, "Congress as Reluctant Regulator: Hazardous Waste Policy in the 1980's," *Yale Journal on Regulation* 3, no. 2 (1986): 363+.

9. Lois Romano, "Rita Lavelle, Dumped," *Washington Post,* March 5, 1983, https://www.washingtonpost.com/archive/lifestyle/1983/03/05/rita-lavelle-dumped/45256854-7ca3-4df4-8031-5a56793be499/?utm_term=.4696eee8e178; David Burnham, "Reagan Dismisses High EPA Official," *New York Times,* March 8, 1983, https://www.nytimes.com/1983/02/08/us/reagan-dismisses-high-epa-official.html; Joe Sargis, *UPI,* September 4, 1985, https://www.upi.com/Archives/1985/09/04/Rita-Lavelle-a-former-EPA-official-convicted-of-perjury/9641494654400/.

10. An April 20, 1982 statement by GAO's Henry Eschwege before the Senate Subcommittee on HUD-Independent Agencies of the Senate Committee on Appropriations noted that "Implementation of the program during its first 15 months has been hampered by a lack of final policies and guidance. To date there have been few Superfund-financed remedial action accomplishments," https://www.gao.gov/assets/110/100133.pdf; see also Henry Eschwege, *EPA's Progress in Implementing the Superfund Program* GAO/CED-82-91 (Washington, DC: GAO, June 2, 1982), https://www.gao.gov/assets/140/137792.pdf.

11. 47 Fed. Reg. 10972 (March 12, 1982).

12. In the preamble to the proposed 1982 NCP, EPA stated that based on its experience with RCRA Section 7003, "the agency has decided that a flexible standard for determining the appropriate extent of remedy is the best standard at this time. As the agency gains greater knowledge regarding cleaning up releases of hazardous substances, more specific standard may be appropriate."

13. EPA updated the HRS when it updated the NCP in 1990, further expanding the exposure pathways that were evaluated.

14. EPA had identified around nine thousand sites by this time, placing these sites in a database known as the CERCLA Information System (CERCLIS). By 1986, the number of CERCLIS sites, each of which needed to receive a preliminary assessment, had grown to more than twenty-five thousand.

15. US Government Accountability Office, *Superfund: Funding and Reported Costs of Enforcement and Administration Activities*, GAO-08-841R (Washington, DC: GAO, July 2008).

16. 50 Fed. Reg. 5862 (February 12, 1985). One of the major modifications in this proposed NCP was the decision that CERCLA actions should be consistent with pertinent federal or state environmental or public health standards. EPA attached a copy of this draft policy to the NCP proposal. Another example was the reliance on operable units to speed up investigation and remediation. The concept of operable units was designed to allow work to go forward on portions of a NPL site while the remainder of the site continued with investigation and remedy selection. A third example was the restructuring of removal response actions. In general, many of the changes proposed in this NCP were based on EPA's implementation experience and were designed to improve and speed up site remediation.

17. The statute did not provide any set factors for allocation, other than providing that equitable factors could be used in the allocation decisions Congress was leaving these decisions to the courts.

18. US Congress, Office of Technology Assessment, *Superfund Strategy*, OTA-ITE-252 (Washington, DC: OTA, April 1985), https://www.princeton.edu/~ota/disk2/1985/8526/8526.PDF.

19. US General Accounting Office, *EPA's Preliminary Estimates of Future Hazardous Waste Cleanup Costs Are Uncertain,* GAO/RCED-84-152 (Washington, DC: GAO, May 1984), https://www.gao.gov/assets/150/141530.pdf.

20. In 1988, EPA and the DOD/DOE developed model language for all federal facility Superfund cleanup agreements and that language included a mechanism for resolving any disputes.

21. EPA did not issue guidance on this until March 1982 and GAO, in a 1982 statement, found that state officials considered the delay in guidance to have impacted the ability to proceed with certain Fund-financed remedial actions.

22. Environmental Law Institute, with funding from EPA, developed a series of these reports between 1989 and 2001. These reports demonstrate an increasingly strengthened set of state remedial programs, many with provisions beyond those in CERCLA. The total number of sites nationwide tracked in these programs peaked in 1993 at around one hundred thousand sites and has been reduced since then.

23. An example of a challenging new issue is per and polyfluoroalkyl substances (PFAS), a class of compounds that are not currently classified as federal hazardous substances.

24. US Environmental Protection Agency, "Superfund Remedial Annual Accomplishments," *epa.gov,* https://www.epa.gov/superfund/superfund-remedial-annual-accomplishments.

25. Environmental Law Institute, *An Analysis of State Superfund Programs: 50-State Study, 2001 Update* (Washington, DC: ELI, November 2002), 7, https://www.eli.org/sites/default/files/eli-pubs/d12-10a.pdf.

26. Association of State and Territorial Solid Waste Management Officials, *Superfund Site Assessment Program: Benefits Beyond NPL Listing, Phase II* (Washington, DC: ASTSWMO, March 2012), http://www.astswmo.org/files/policies/CERCLA_and_Brownfields/2012.03.19-Site_Eval-Phase_II_Report-FINAL.pdf.

27. US Environmental Protection Agency, "Population Surrounding 1,836 Superfund Remedial Sites," *epa.gov*, last updated October 2017.

28. For example, see US Government Accountability Office, *Hazardous Waste Cleanup: Numbers of Contaminated Federal Sites, Estimated Costs, and EPA's Oversight Role,* GAO-15-830T (Washington, DC: GAO, 2015), https://www.gao.gov/assets/680/672464.pdf.

29. In 1987, EPA Administrator Lee Thomas asked a set of experienced EPA professionals to participate on a task force that would rank which of the agency's many environmental programs addressed the highest environmental risks. The results of that study indicated that the RCRA and CERCLA programs were considered areas of medium or low risk compared to other EPA program areas. In contrast to the ranking by the task force of EPA career personnel, public opinion has perceived these two programs as high priority from a risk perspective. See US Environmental Protection Agency, *Unfinished Business: A Comparative Assessment of Environmental Problems, Overview Report*, 000R87901 (Washington, DC: EPA, February 1987), https://nepis.epa.gov/Exe/ZyPDF.cgi/2001635G.PDF?Dockey=2001635G.PDF.

Chapter Nine

Regulation of Chemicals, Pesticides, and Genetically Engineered Organisms

John D. Graham and Penelope A. Fenner-Crisp[1]

OVERVIEW

The last two hundred years have witnessed enormous growth and diversification of chemical technologies beginning in Western Europe and the US and now a global phenomenon. Our lives have been fundamentally transformed in every way imaginable: chemical science has provided innovations that comprise nearly all of the goods and basic infrastructure of industrial societies, the built environment, and consumer products. Innovation in chemical technology has reaped such enormous benefits for society that it is impossible to imagine that we could support the billions who now inhabit planet Earth with natural materials alone.

There have also been negative side effects of the explosion in use of synthetic chemicals, several which gave impetus to EPA regulation. The well-intentioned use of the insecticide DDT harmed non-target species such as the bald eagle by thinning a bird's eggshells, which in turn killed embryos. An organochlorine called vinyl chloride was used as an intermediate in the manufacture of plastics; workers exposed to vinyl chloride developed angiocarcinoma, a rare form of liver cancer, as well as brain and lung cancers, lymphoma, and leukemia. The widespread use of lead in paint products and as a cheap anti-knocking agent in gasoline caused inadvertent harm to exposed children in the form of impairment to neurological health; the ultimate result was a lowering of educational attainment and lifetime earnings among exposed children.

Central questions for Congress included how the federal government should anticipate and address such negative side effects of chemical technologies and what roles EPA should play. This chapter tells the fifty-year story of EPA regulation of chemicals and pesticides.

It is truly a tale of two cities in that the three primary statutes, the Federal Insecticide Fungicide and Rodenticide Act (FIFRA) coupled with the Federal Food Drug and Cosmetic Act (FFDCA) and the Toxic Substances Control Act (TSCA), were enacted in completely different eras and have provided EPA with vastly different authorities. In other respects, the laws are similar, as they all seek to prevent or mitigate "unreasonable" adverse effects on human health and the environment. In contrast to the other laws that EPA administers, they are generally less well understood, even by other offices at EPA; they often receive more criticism than support, not only within the agency but among stakeholders generally. Despite this criticism, this chapter explores how EPA has used these statutes to profoundly affect the practices of regulated industries, including consumers.

We start with the FIFRA/FFDCA story, since it began long before EPA was created, and then consider the TSCA story, insofar as it was a new EPA assignment added by Congress in 1976, and has undergone major revision in the last five years. We then consider EPA's role in biotechnology regulation, which draws from some of the FIFRA/FFDCA and TSCA experiences. The chapter concludes with a review of EPA's influential role in global efforts to manage chemical risks. The globalization of commerce has prompted efforts to control the risks of exported and imported products, with important ramifications for trade relationships.

THE FIFRA/FFDCA STORY

The purpose of the Federal Insecticide Act of 1910 was not to protect the environment but to protect farmers and users from fraudulent or adulterated products. The US Department of Agriculture (USDA) was put in charge of implementation. In 1938, Congress enacted the Federal Food Drug and Cosmetics Act (FFDCA), which directed the Food and Drug Administration (FDA) to regulate levels of unavoidable poisons in food as well as pharmaceuticals and cosmetics.[2] The 1954 Miller Amendment to FFDCA Section 408 directed FDA to regulate food additives, including pesticide residues, by establishing tolerances (maximum allowable residues), which are enforceable standards disallowing excessive residues of specific pesticides in specific foods.[3] This requirement applied only to raw agricultural commodities. A 1958 amendment to FFDCA introduced the so-called Delaney Clause into a different part of FFDCA (§409). The Delaney Clause effectively compels a zero tolerance for a pesticide (or other food additive) known to cause cancer in animals or people. Section 409 of the 1958 amendments also included a requirement for a tolerance in processed food, but only if the pesticide residue in that processed food was expected to exceed the tolerance level in the related raw agricultural commodity.[4] The ramifications of the Delaney Clause for pesticides, and the paradox it created, were not fully understood at the time, since it was not yet known that numerous pesticide products would test positive for cancer in laboratory animal studies or how many uses of common pesticides would be caught up in the dissonance in tolerance-setting between Section 408 and 409.

Legislative action on the environmental aspects of pesticides did not occur until 1947 when the original version of FIFRA was enacted.[5] Pesticide manufacturers were required to register pesticidal products with USDA, which was authorized to consider ecological as well as human health risks. As defined in FIFRA, "pesticides" are substances that are marketed as having the ability to kill or repel "pests"; they include insecticides, fungicides (which kill molds and fungi), herbicides (weed killers), and rodenticides (rat and mouse killers). Pesticides now include genetically engineered plants with pesticidal or pest-resistant properties. While other substances may have pesticidal properties, only those substances marketed for these uses are regulated as pesticides.

In 1962, Rachel Carson's famous book *Silent Spring* drew public attention to the debate about pesticide risks, including the ecological impacts of DDT.[6] In 1967, the non-profit Environmental Defense Fund (EDF) was established in New York City and several EDF attorneys began to raise ecological concerns about the use of DDT on Long Island, New York. Their advocacy led to a county-wide ban on DDT use in 1967 and the Governor of New York followed with a state-wide ban in 1970. EDF also petitioned the USDA and FDA to ban DDT, but the federal agencies refused, which led to complex litigation. Meanwhile, President Richard Nixon decided in 1970 to establish EPA, which led to the transfer of pesticide regulatory duties from USDA and FDA to EPA. USDA and FDA retained some FFDCA enforcement responsibilities.

As described in Chapter 1, one of the new agency's first official decisions was a cancellation of the registration for DDT. Another petition landed on the EPA administrator's desk on December 3, 1970—twenty-four hours after the agency was officially established. The petition from EDF called for the ban of Aldrin and Dieldrin, two insecticides in the same chemical class as DDT that were used against soil insects that damage corn and other crops and used for other purposes, such as a termiticide. Aldrin and Dieldrin were widely used in the 1950s but, by 1970, their use had declined to less than ten percent of the corn acreage in the US, in part because insects were developing resistance to them. EDF argued that these substances, like DDT, posed unreasonable risks to the environment.

EPA Administrator William Ruckelshaus decided in March 1971 to propose cancellation of their registrations, even though there were some divisions of opinion within the agency. The scientists who were transferred into EPA from USDA were not convinced that the science justified cancellation; their view was affirmed by a committee of scientists assembled by the National Academies of Sciences. The attorneys in EPA's Office of General Counsel, who believed the industry shouldered the scientific burden of proving safety, were more convinced by the EDF arguments.[7] Before a final decision was made, Congress passed a series of important amendments to FIFRA.

Architecture of 1972 FIFRA Amendments

Farm interests, pesticide manufacturers, and environmental advocates were all dissatisfied with the structure of FIFRA and they knew that EPA was having some difficulty implementing it. They did not agree on how it should be amended. What emerged from Congress in 1972 was a compromise that reflected the divergent interests.

As a starting point, Congress in 1972 clarified that all pesticides, those already in use as well as new ones, must be registered with EPA. A registration is a license issued by the agency that permits the sale and distribution of a specific product, in prescribed amounts, for specific uses. The application for a registration must include information on the product's chemical composition, packaging, and labeling. If EPA grants an application, the product must be classified as appropriate for use by anyone or only for "restricted use," meaning the applicator must be trained and certified. "Re-registration" is defined as an EPA-led process where the case for registration is re-evaluated based on up-to-date information; it could lead to more or fewer uses, different methods of application, or an agency decision to continue, cancel, or suspend the registration.

A suspension is reserved for cases of "imminent hazard" and, while temporary, is enforceable immediately. Suspensions occur rarely. Cancellation, which may be involuntary or voluntary, is not temporary. Involuntary cancellations, initiated by EPA, may include a more deliberate process that offers the registrant, if requested, the opportunity for a public hearing, USDA consultation, and an opinion from the FIFRA Scientific Advisory Panel. Cancellation of a use or some uses or, in rare cases, all uses and the registration of the chemical is required if the agency makes a determination of "unreasonable adverse effects," where "unreasonable" is a risk-benefit balancing test that considers the economic and other benefits of the pesticide as well as the product's risks to human health and the environment and other adverse effects. The risk-benefit test permits consideration of so many factors that it does not, by itself, provide much practical guidance to the agency. If the agency is concerned about a substance but not certain as to the appropriateness of cancellation or suspension, the agency is authorized to undertake a "special review" of the substance while its use continues. Approximately one hundred chemicals have been subjected to a special review since the 1970s, but only a handful in the past thirty years. Voluntary cancellation, initiated by the registrant, is managed by a simpler administrative process—notice-and-comment—using the Federal Register as the principal communication device.

As we shall see, two provisions in 1972 FIFRA proved to be unworkable: (1) all existing pesticides in commerce—at the time, there were at least thirty thousand products making use of several hundred active ingredients—must undergo re-registration and classification between October 1974 and October 1976; (2) if the agency cancels or suspends a registration, EPA must make indemnity payments to registrants for their economic losses and arrange for the proper disposal of unused product.

Implementation Challenge

The 1972 FIFRA amendments placed enormous responsibilities on the young agency, but the Nixon administration and Congress did not respond with an adequate level of appropriations for the agency's pesticides program. Moreover, the office was finalizing the high-profile decisions on Aldrin and Dieldrin at the same time that it started work on a plan to implement the new re-registration responsibility in the 1972 amendments.

In August 1973, EPA finalized the cancellation of the Aldrin and Dieldrin registrations, while explaining that the evidence did not rise to the level of "imminent hazard," which would have led to suspension. The agency then reversed itself in 1974 and issued a suspension, based on new evidence of carcinogenicity in animal studies conducted by the National Cancer Institute; a legal challenge from industry was rejected by a federal court in 1975.

The agency's plan for implementing the re-registration requirements was not finalized until 1975-1976, but was overly optimistic. The agency assumed that the data in their files on each pesticide accurately reflected the results of properly conducted safety studies, that the data had been thoroughly reviewed by the agency when initially received, and that any adverse effects reported had been noted and addressed with appropriate regulatory action. The plan recognized that there might be some data gaps and proposed to issue "conditional re-registrations" and review them later when the missing data were collected and submitted to the agency.

As the agency began to apply the plan to several re-registration cases, it learned of serious data problems. In fact, FDA informed EPA in the spring of 1976 of disconcerting results from an audit of the work performed by a major private contract laboratory. FDA found serious inadequacies and outright fraud in some experiments. Many of the studies of concern were central to the registrations that the agency was about to review for re-registration.[8] The agency also calculated that, given the program's resources and the poor condition of the obsolete registrations, it would take the agency more than ten years to complete the re-registration task. A decision was made to go back to Congress for additional amendments to FIFRA.

Congress responded in 1978 with amendments that addressed some of EPA's concerns. The deadline for completion of the re-registration process was removed and replaced with "as soon as practicable" language. Congress focused agency review on the several hundred active ingredients rather than the many thousands of registered products. The agency was given new authority to compel registrants to conduct testing according to the agency's guidance, as by then a series of standardized testing guidelines, underpinned by the newly developed Principles of Good Laboratory Practices, were being crafted to inform data generators how to conduct studies that would be acceptable to the agency. The authority was backed up with the power to suspend the registration if requested data were not supplied. And registrants were permitted to engage in cost sharing in response to data requests from the agency.

By the end of the 1970s, EPA had banned virtually all uses of the organochlorines used as insecticides: DDT, Aldrin, Dieldrin, Chlordane, Heptachlor, and Mirex (EPA did not cancel the Aldrin/Dieldrin termiticide use until 1987). It took some time for the ecological benefits in the bird population to be realized, but twenty years later they were shown by scientific studies to be "significant."[9] The last organochlorine for which all uses were cancelled was endosulfan in 2010.

Looking forward briefly, the program gave priority to the organochlorines but most or all uses of other well-known pesticide products were also cancelled due to unreasonable risk: DBCP (1979), EDB (1983), all food uses of Alar (1989), carbofuran (2009), and aldicarb and methyl parathion (2010). We consider EDB and Alar below, because of their broader importance in the agency's history.

High-visibility bans are important to reaffirm the agency's credibility as a regulator, but much of the program's success does not occur through bans. It occurs as industry reconsiders which products and uses to continue and defend. It also occurs through a gradual process of "safer" pesticides, where new products and uses are often—but not always—safer than the ones replaced.

Turmoil in the Early Reagan Years

The transition from the Carter administration to the Reagan administration led to temporary turmoil throughout the agency, including in the pesticides office. Congressional investigations of the agency's activities ensued. President Reagan's first EPA administrator, Anne Gorsuch, and her Senate-confirmed head of the pesticides and toxics program, John Todhunter, refused to move forward on several activities that the agency had initiated under President Carter. One of the most controversial issues concerned the soil fumigant ethylene dibromide (EDB), also known as 1,2-dibromethane (an organobromine compound).[10]

EDB is injected into soil prior to planting and acts to kill nematodes, small parasitic worms that attack the roots of plants. It is also used as a fumigant to control insects and molds in grain milling machinery and flour mills and on stored grain products.

In 1975, the National Cancer Institute demonstrated that EDB exposures in laboratory animals induce excess tumor rates. That disturbing finding followed 1973 studies showing that EDB exposure is associated with genetic mutations and reproductive damage in laboratory animals.

EDF was concerned about the slow response of the Carter EPA and petitioned the agency to cancel or suspend the EDB registration. Near the end of the Carter administration (December 1980), the agency issued a cancellation proposal for some uses but Administrator Gorsuch and Assistant Administrator Todhunter simply sat on the proposal. Congressional inquiries established that Todhunter was downplaying the views of the agency's scientists and espousing his own assessment of the safety of EDB.[11] The issue became more complicated in 1981 when the state of California engaged in a massive EDB fumigation program to control the Mediterranean fruit fly. The Japanese government was insisting that imported produce from California be fumigated before it arrived.

As public furor over the Gorsuch-led EPA grew prior to the 1982 midterm congressional elections, EPA announced in October that another of the organochlorine insecticides, toxaphene, would also be banned. It was a substitute for DDT used to protect cotton crops in the south. William A. Butler of the Audubon Society accused EPA of taking action for political advantage "just prior to the election."[12] Congress came close to banning the chemical itself in frustration over the ineffectiveness of the Gorsuch EPA.

When President Reagan replaced Gorsuch with Ruckelshaus in 1983, the EDB issue entered a new phase because of massive publicity concerning the detection of EDB as a groundwater contaminant in several states (California, Hawaii, Florida, and Georgia). Ruckelshaus responded quickly in October

1983 with an emergency suspension of EDB's registration as it relates to soil fumigation; the other uses of EDB were subject to a cancellation proceeding.

In late 1983, the State of Florida detected EDB in food products, which caused the state to halt the sale of certain cake mixes, pancake mixes, and a variety of consumer products that contained more than one part billion (ppb) of EDB (1 ppb was the chemical detection limit). The industry sued the state of Florida on the grounds that the 1 ppb threshold was far too stringent and urged EPA to reduce public panic by establishing a national policy. A spokesman for the Natural Resources Defense Council (NRDC), a non-profit advocacy group in New York City, asserted that there is no safe level of EDB. In February 1984, EPA announced interim voluntary guidelines for the states to use in order to ensure that food was safe to eat.

EPA's aggressive action on EDB and two other substances (2,4,5-T/Silvex and dinoseb) caused EPA to receive indemnity claims of $40 million from companies incurring losses. Under the 1972 law, there was no dedicated funding for such payments. The federal government paid out $20 million to the manufacturers of 2,4,5-T and EDB from the Treasury Department's Judgement Fund.

The 1988 FIFRA Amendments

Congressional mistrust of EPA, the indemnity issue, and lack of adequate agency resources to complete re-registrations all contributed to another round of amendments to FIFRA. The congressional General Accounting Office (GAO) also conducted an independent investigation in 1986 and determined that legislative action was necessary to fix the program.[13] The 1988 amendments are sometimes described pejoratively as "FIFRA lite," but they gave an important boost to the agency's pesticides program.[14]

Congress specified an ambitious and detailed nine-year schedule for completion of the pre-1984 pesticide re-registrations. The challenge for the agency was made more feasible by three key provisions: the burden of doing much of the preliminary administrative work on each re-registration was shifted from EPA to the registrant, while EPA retained the authority to decide whether a re-registration was warranted and, if so, what the terms of use would be; new fees on the industry were authorized that were projected to raise at least $425 million for the program over the nine-year life of the re-registration activity; and the agency burdens to make indemnification payments and dispose of unused product were removed.[15]

The 1988 FIFRA amendments brought new life to the program. The imposition of the fees and the strengthened data requirements and enforcement tools forced industry to examine its chemical inventory. Many products were voluntarily dropped because the market value to a company was not worth the fees and/or the data burdens. The industry knew that EPA now had the funding to hire additional scientific and regulatory personnel, upgrade its IT capability, and deploy regulatory tools and clear congressional direction to suspend active ingredients when data were not submitted on time. Additionally, some companies were concerned about the cost and implications of what the new toxicology studies might show, forcing many companies to drop active ingredients or specific uses before EPA took regulatory action. Still, EPA progress on re-registration did not occur quickly and was not completed within the proscribed time frame. There was a lot of catch up work, both inside the agency and by industry, to get the re-registration packages where they needed to be.

The Alar Episode

NRDC was concerned that EPA was moving too slowly to regulate older pesticides and, when performing risk assessments, was not taking adequate account of the vulnerability of infants and children. NRDC prepared an extensive report on this subject that featured a plant-growth regulator called Alar that was sprayed on apple trees to enable farmers to harvest all the apples at the same time.[16] The health concern was the breakdown product of Alar, Unsymmetrical dimethylhydrazine (UDMH), which tends to concentrate in certain apple products such as apple juice and apple sauce. Several years earlier, EPA had considered a cancellation of Alar but instead required the industry to conduct a high-quality animal study; in the interim, the amount sprayed on trees was reduced by fifty percent.[17]

In February 1989, CBS's prime-time "60 Minutes" television program picked up the issue and ran an extensive segment highlighting NRDC's concern about the safety of children. EPA's assistant administrator for pesticides and toxic substances, Dr. Jack Moore, was offered an opportunity to respond. Moore acknowledged recent animal studies showing excess tumors due to Alar exposure but indicated that, given the low levels of exposure on food, the risks were not provocative enough to be designated an imminent hazard. NRDC countered that the situation was unacceptable because children could be exposed to Alar for years until EPA finally cancelled the registration for the product.

Public reaction to the "60 Minutes" program, and offshoot media stories, was far greater than NRDC, EPA, industry, or the producers of "60 Minutes" could have imagined.[18] Parents were upset because they thought it was good that their children were drinking apple juice. Hollywood actress Meryl Streep entered the fray with an affirmation of the concerns that NRDC was expressing.

School boards in Los Angeles, New York, Chicago, Atlanta, and other cities banned apples and apple products from their cafeterias. Supermarkets came under pressure to remove apples from their shelves. For apple farmers, the public panic was damaging to their businesses. The producer of Alar, Uniroyal, simply pulled the product's food uses off the market rather than try to defend them in the midst of public panic. Whether doomed by future congressional or EPA action or consumer fears, Uniroyal knew the product had little commercial future although Alar continues to be registered for non-food uses on containerized ornamental plants in commercial greenhouses, shade houses, and nurseries.

There is a wide range of views on what the proper lessons from the Alar episode are. NRDC won a key point: infants and children were put on Congress's agenda for the next amendments to FIFRA.

The 1996 Food Quality Protection Act

In 1992, GAO gave testimony to Congress that, once again, painted a rather bleak picture of the nation's pesticide regulatory programs. It pointed to a pesticide re-registration effort that, at that time, had succeeded in the reevaluation of only two of the older pesticides on the market. Other shortcomings were difficulties in removing unsafe pesticides from the marketplace, lack of an early warning system for pesticide damage, and increasing pesticide contamination of groundwater. Improvements were also suggested in food residue monitoring, import notices to other countries, farm worker safety protections, and pesticide data management.[19]

NRDC lawyers were arguing that FIFRA and FFDCA had different and inconsistent legal standards for the safety of a pesticide. Under FIFRA, the standard was "protection against any unreasonable adverse effects on the environment"; under FFDCA, it was a "reasonable certainty of no harm" except in the case of carcinogens, for which the zero-tolerance Delaney Clause was invoked in some cases. In practice, this complexity meant that the economic benefits of pesticides and other tradeoffs were often considered by the EPA in decision-making about pesticide registrations. NRDC argued for a health-only standard of safety.

Building on the concerns of NRDC and GAO, a scientific review of EPA pesticide risk assessment practices was undertaken by the National Academies. In a report titled *Pesticides in the Diets of Infants and Children*, NAS concluded that EPA's process for assessing risk and establishing tolerances was insufficiently protective of children. Among other failings, it did not account for their unique dietary and other exposure patterns or that many pesticides create harm in the body via common mechanisms of action.[20]

In 1996, Congress responded with the Food Quality Protection Act (FQPA), which amended FFDCA as well as FIFRA and, for the first time, established strong coordination between the two statutes.[21] FQPA gave the agency one uniform standard to use in setting tolerances: "reasonable certainty of no harm." During risk assessment, FQPA required EPA to consider information on the aggregate of all non-occupational exposures to consumers, including food and drinking water, and exposures from lawn, household, and other uses when setting tolerances. The law also required EPA to consider available information on cumulative effects of pesticide residues and other substances that have a common mechanism of toxicity.

On top of these new considerations, Congress directed EPA to use an additional ten-fold (10X) safety factor (known as the FQPA 10X Safety Factor) during the decision-making process to take into account the potential for pre- and post-natal toxicity, in addition to the two standard default 10X factors—one for interspecies extrapolation and the other for intraspecies variability—commonly used in EPA risk assessment.

Risk assessment of chemicals, including pesticides, traditionally relies heavily on animal studies to predict effects in humans. To make those predictions in a health-protective way, risk assessors apply safety or uncertainty factors when converting the quantitative results of animal studies to the possible outcomes in humans. Absent chemical-specific information, the common use of the 10X factor to account for potential differences between animals and humans (interspecies) and the 10X factor to account for variability of response in the human population (intraspecies) have been shown to be reasonable assumptions in most cases.

Other safety/uncertainty factors may be used to convert an effect level into a no-effect level or to account for what happens after long-term exposure based upon what happens after a short-term exposure. These factors are seldom used in pesticide risk assessment because the manner in which the required studies are conducted resolves these issues.

A fifth safety/uncertainty factor—for database deficiencies—may also be needed. This factor would be used if key information is missing. In essence, the FQPA 10X Safety Factor serves this purpose because it is to be applied on the assumption that there is key information missing on whether or not the pesticide being assessed has the potential to produce pre- or post-natal toxicity.

In effect, Congress enlarged the composite standard default safety factor from 100X to at least 1000X, which meant that tolerances would be stricter and more protective, if approved at all. The agency was allowed to eliminate or reduce this additional 10X FQPA factor but only if it could make a finding that reliable data indicated a different factor would be safe for infants and children.

Under FQPA, all 9,721 tolerances that were on the books at the time the law was passed were to be reassessed for safety for children and other consumers within ten years. Then, EPA was to establish a "registration review" program to assure that all pesticides would be re-reviewed at least every fifteen years. Other provisions were designed to encourage use of safer pesticides and biological controls.

In 2008, EPA made the encouraging announcement that it had completed a review of all older pesticides initially registered before November 1, 1984 (as required by the 1988 FIFRA), and assured that the registrations met the new standards under the 1996 FQPA. In all, EPA organized 1,150 pesticide active ingredients into 613 "cases" or related groups. Of these, 384 were re-registered and 229 (37%) were cancelled prior to the completion of re-registration (including pesticides that were not supported for re-registration). Likewise, by September 2007 EPA completed reassessments of all the 9,721 tolerances on the market in 1996. Of these, 2,401 (27.4%) were revoked and many more were reduced. Additionally, because of concerns about aggregate and cumulative risks, a number of pesticide uses in household and veterinary products also were cancelled. The class of organophosphate insecticides incurred a substantial number of voluntary cancellations due to the new tolerance-setting procedures under the FQPA. EPA's success in re-registration was a significant accomplishment.

In 2007 the EPA began the new process of registration review, which requires that each registered pesticide be reviewed at least every fifteen years to determine whether it continues to meet the FIFRA standard. All pesticides registered prior to October 1, 2007 must be reviewed by October 1, 2022. This amounts to 725 "cases" comprised of 1,140 pesticide active ingredients used in thousands of formulations.[22]

Challenges

EPA's pesticide program has come a long way from the day in which it was considered to be slow and inefficient; it is now recognized as one of the agency's most productive programs. It nonetheless still faces a number of challenges; especially as judicial and international pressures collide with the deregulatory posture of the Trump administration.

An Obama-era 2015 order from EPA to cancel remaining uses of the insecticide chlorpyrifos, on the basis of epidemiological data on child health risks, was revoked in 2017 by President Trump's first EPA administrator Scott Pruitt. The Ninth Circuit Court of Appeals instructed EPA in 2019 to reconsider the revocation.[23] After reconsideration, Trump's second EPA administrator, Andrew Wheeler, reaffirmed in 2020 that the agency would consider the issue by the end of the scheduled registration review period (2022).[24] Corteva, a spinoff of the Dow-DuPont merger and a major producer of chlorpyrifos, announced in February 2020 that it would discontinue production of the insecticide by the end of 2020. In the previous decade, the company's share of the global chlorpyrifos market declined from seventy-five percent to twenty-five percent.[25] While EPA refused to ban the product, both the state of California and the European Union banned it.

Meanwhile, pesticide regulators globally have been roiled by competing assessments of the cancer-causing potential of another widely used product, the herbicide glyphosate (trade name Roundup).[26] Use of glyphosate increased as a consequence of new genetically engineered crops that are tolerant to glyphosate. Increasing use has increased levels of human exposure and the perception of potential risks.

In March 2015 the World Health Organization's International Agency for Research on Cancer (IARC) determined that glyphosate is a probable human carcinogen, but neither EPA nor regulatory authorities in Canada, Australia, New Zealand, Japan, and Europe concur with IARC's stance.[27] In addition, a different standing expert panel at the World Health Organization (the FAO/WHO Joint Meeting on Pesticide Residues) does not consider glyphosate to possess human carcinogenic risk via the human diet, a challenging situation for WHO.[28]

On the ecological assessment front, EPA has continued to experience conflicts over how pesticide registrations should comply with provisions of the Endangered Species Act and recent judicial decisions. The agency is working to identify new approaches in line with recommendations from the National Academies.[29] Also, while many highly toxic organophosphate and carbamate insecticides are used less frequently as a result of FQPA, an alternative class of insecticides, the neonicotinoids, is alleged to be a cause of colony collapse disorder in European honey bees, a major pollinator for agriculture in the US. Other non-target insects that are well-loved, like the monarch butterfly, also have been alleged to be harmed by currently registered pesticides, not just the neonicotinoids. EPA Administrator Wheeler has nonetheless proposed to continue neonicotinoid use in the US market, though with greater precautions. In 2018, the European Commission banned several neonicotinoids.[30]

Over time, there is also increasing pressure from invasive species or changes in geographic ranges of insects that are of concern to agriculture and public health. For example, the spotted lanternfly is moving rapidly across the northeastern and mid-Atlantic US, and there currently are only a few effective pesticides on the market to treat them (e.g., natural and synthetic pyrethroids, carbaryl, malathion, neem oil, and insecticidal soaps).[31] Likewise, as a result of global warming, we are witnessing the expansion of favorable conditions for the *Aedes aegypti* mosquito, a vector for a number of arboviruses like dengue, Zika, chikungunya, and yellow fever.[32] Recent mosquito control efforts in Florida involving pesticide applications were met with public skepticism and concern that the pesticide risks might have been too high.[33] There seems to be only limited industry interest in developing alternative public health pesticides, although EPA is reviewing some new product-approval requests on the mosquito issue.

THE TSCA STORY

The origins of the Toxic Substances Control Act of 1976 can be traced to the formal 1970 legislative program of President Richard Nixon.[34] The idea for the bill came not from EPA (which was not created by Nixon until late 1970) but from an obscure White House office called the Council on Environmental Quality (CEQ) that was created by the National Environmental Policy Act (NEPA) of 1969. CEQ's primary function is to help federal agencies with the environmental impact statements required of future projects throughout the economy. The founding chair of CEQ, Russell Train, also used his White House position to flag emerging environmental issues where President Nixon could have an impact. (Train later became the second administrator of EPA under GOP Presidents Nixon and Gerald Ford). Prior to his role at CEQ, Train was instrumental in the development of two national environmental organizations: the World Wildlife Fund and the Conservation Foundation.

Train and his staff were concerned that each industrial toxin of public concern—mercury, vinyl chloride, lead, and PCBs—was viewed as an isolated problem. There was no cumulative learning about how to deal with "toxics" proactively and from an integrated systems perspective. CEQ felt that legislation was necessary to ensure that industry planned for the proper environmental management of chemical exposures before the chemicals were placed into commerce.

When CEQ's draft legislation was placed in the Nixon administration's interagency review process, most offices in the Nixon administration filed no objections, but officials from the Department of Commerce objected strenuously. They argued that the draft bill should not see the light of day because it was inconsistent with basic principles of capitalism.

The Office of Management and Budget (OMB), which routinely manages interagency conflicts, refereed the differences of opinion between CEQ and Commerce. Ultimately, OMB compelled the two parties to go into a room and not adjourn until a resolution was reached. The final version of Nixon's draft TSCA bill included detailed legal contributions from Commerce designed to protect industry from over-regulation as well as CEQ's overarching legislative vision.

Once the draft legislation was submitted to the relevant House and Senate committees, it did not attract much interest. CEQ realized that a stronger statement of rationale for the bill was needed. In April 1971 CEQ released a white paper on TSCA reform that pointed to several broad trends in the US economy that were of concern. The use of industrial chemicals was growing rapidly—both invention of new chemicals and new uses of older chemicals—but the environmental impacts were poorly understood. There were increasing indications that some chemical exposures were linked to cancer. CEQ argued that existing environmental laws address pollution only after it is occurring rather than preventively when new chemicals are put into commerce.[35]

Coincidentally, the timing of the CEQ initiative was aligned with a separate biomedical initiative from the Nixon White House that later became known as Nixon's "War on Cancer." It expanded efforts in prevention and treatment aimed at reversing the alarming increase in the reported incidence of cancer. When TSCA was passed five years later (1976), EPA Administrator Train described it as "one of the most important pieces of 'preventive medicine' ever passed by Congress."[36]

The CEQ initiative caught the eye of John Tunney, a freshman Democratic senator from California who chaired the relevant subcommittee of the Senate Commerce Committee. CEQ was pleased to learn of his interest and briefed his staff on the intricacies of the legislative proposal. Later, Train testified at public hearings before Tunney's subcommittee.

Stakeholder reaction to the CEQ initiative was largely indifferent. The established environmental groups (e.g., Audubon Society) were skeptical because the bill could be seen as a disruption of the federal clean air and clean water laws that were enacted in the 1960s. The business community had more pressing issues at the time. The big chemical companies (Dow Chemical Company and DuPont) saw nothing in the bill that they could not manage, but the small chemical companies were frightened. They feared that new chemicals might be subject to the same costly toxicity testing procedures that were applied to pesticides under FIFRA. The only group actively advocating for the bill was the large labor union AFL-CIO, which was concerned about worker exposures to toxins on the job.

With little movement in the House of Representatives, Senator Tunney saw an issue that he could champion. He recruited as a co-sponsor a senior Republican senator from Kansas, James B. Pearson. Once a strong conservative, Pearson became more moderate later in his career and collaborated with Democrats on civil rights measures and bipartisan resolutions against the US bombing of Laos and Cambodia during the Vietnam War.

Tunney pushed the bill for several years without much progress. What helped his cause was the growing public concern about the environment that unfolded in the early 1970s. The case for the legislation was boosted by mass media coverage of PCB contamination of the Hudson River, the threat of stratospheric ozone depletion by chlorofluorocarbons, and the accidental contamination in Michigan of agricultural products by a flame retardant made of polybrominated biphenyls (PBBs). Tunney and his allies argued that there were more than one hundred industrial chemicals on the market that needed study or regulation such as vinyl chloride, asbestos, mercury, and bis(chloromethyl) ether (BCME). The scope of the legislation was broadened to provide new EPA authority to regulate existing chemicals as well as new chemicals.

After unsuccessful tries in consecutive sessions of Congress, the bill ultimately passed the Senate and House with widespread, bipartisan support. GOP President Gerald Ford signed the new law in October 1976.[37]

Architecture of the Original TSCA

As defined in TSCA, "chemical substances" are "any organic or inorganic substance of a particular molecular identity, including any combination of these substances occurring in whole or in part as a result of a chemical reaction or occurring in nature, and any element or uncombined radical."[38] Thus, the term "chemical substances" includes an incredibly wide spectrum of molecules as well as genetically engineered organisms with certain chemical properties.[39] On the other hand, the fine print of TSCA granted carve outs for numerous substances that were already regulated under other laws administered by EPA and other federal agencies. In effect, TSCA "chemicals" were defined largely as what they were not, as substances that had not been regulated (or could be regulated in the future) under prior statutes (which dealt with food additives, pesticides, cosmetics, pharmaceuticals, medical devices, radionuclides, alcohol, tobacco, and firearms). In the end, a late-1970s version of the TSCA Inventory, which EPA initiated before the law was passed, contained sixty-two thousand chemicals with hugely varying production volumes, so there was plenty of work for EPA and other agencies to do.

For new chemicals, pre-manufacturing notices (PMNs) must be submitted to the agency. If the agency does not raise questions or request additional information within ninety days, the manufacturer is permitted to enter the chemical into commerce. (Normally, industry does not move forward until EPA "drops" its review). The PMN must include basic information about the chemical: the identity of the submitter, the chemical identity, some physical-chemical properties, projected production volume, planned uses, potential exposures and environmental fate. No toxicity tests are required, but must be submitted if voluntarily conducted.

For both existing and new chemicals, the agency is authorized to require additional safety testing if the uses of the chemical may pose an "unreasonable risk" to public health or the environment. If the agency believes risks are or may be unreasonable, it has a wide range of regulatory options: a ban on manufacturing and sale, limits on manufacturing volume, permission only for specific uses, limits on exposures, and warning labels or recordkeeping requirements to facilitate future safety assessments. CEQ staff saw the unreasonable-risk test as appropriate since it seemed to have worked well under FIFRA, and thus this test was placed in the original bill proposed by the Nixon administration.

The unreasonable-risk test is a risk-benefit balancing standard, but it was coupled with an important wrinkle added by lawyers at the Commerce Department. In the process of ensuring adequate protection from unreasonable risk, the agency was required to choose the "least burdensome" regulatory option, a phrase suggested by attorneys at the Department of Commerce. No such phrase is used in FIFRA where unreasonable-risk is used.

EPA is instructed not to regulate under TSCA if other EPA-administered laws are adequate to address the risk. In this respect, TSCA is often seen as a "gap-filling" statute. EPA is also authorized to defer regulation to other federal agencies (e.g., the Occupational Safety and Health Administration [OSHA] or the Consumer Product Safety Commission [CPSC]) under certain conditions.

The innovative feature of TSCA was the preventive policy objective. Prior to 1976 no laws existed anywhere in the world that went upstream to prevent adverse chemical effects via regulation of the manufacture, processing, and importation of chemicals. The preference for end-of-pipe solutions had dominated chemicals policy over the years and left many public health and environmental risks unaddressed. TSCA implementation was assigned to EPA's Office of Prevention, Pesticides, and Toxic Substances, now known as the Office of Chemical Safety and Pollution Prevention.

Implementation Snafus

EPA has had somewhat less difficulty implementing the few provisions of TSCA that target specific chemicals. TSCA contained a requirement that EPA restrict the use of PCBs, and EPA did so. Later TSCA was amended to specifically regulate limited aspects of asbestos use (1986, Title II), and Radon (1988, Title III). EPA did so. In 1992, Congress amended TSCA to regulate lead in housing, and the agency followed suit. PCBs, asbestos, and lead are referred to collectively by the EPA as "national program" chemicals; the radon program is located in EPA's Office of Air and Radiation. The 2016 TSCA amendments added specific provisions related to mercury export and disposal, and EPA has already followed through. The chemical-specific amendments, while more prescriptive, have usually—though not always—resulted in effective action by the EPA.

On the huge discretionary agenda concerning new and existing chemicals, EPA has struggled. As was the case under FIFRA, Congress's willingness to give EPA open-ended assignments was not matched with the appropriations necessary to implement Congress's original vision.[40] While the goal of preventing unreasonable risks is the same for new and existing chemicals, the implementation challenges—and the technical and political challenges for the agency—are quite different.

The PMN process functioned but without much directed toxicity testing of new chemicals. Lacking toxicity data and any analysis by a company that a new chemical was safe, the agency was provided only a set of basic physical and chemical properties to determine whether to let the chemical come on to the market (the approval was self-implementing after ninety days). Annually EPA received between 1,500-3,000 PMNs. EPA staff developed a Quantitative Structure Activity Relationship (QSAR) modeling system and other predictive tools to attempt to identify chemicals most likely to be toxic to human health or the environment. This required a considerable amount of scientific judgment, but EPA's modeling tools are now buttressed by a substantial amount of data and validity checks.

In 1994, GAO found that of the 23,971 new chemicals that had been reviewed by that point, action to reduce risks was taken on only about ten percent or 2,431 chemicals.[41] According to EPA, by 1999 it had reviewed over thirty thousand TSCA submissions for new chemical substances. Because the process is pre-manufacturing, EPA expended the same amount of effort for a chemical that would go into market as for one that never would. Around ninety percent of PMNs addressed chemicals that were never brought to market. Early on, the agency addressed this inefficiency with a measure called a Significant New Use Rule (SNUR). In the new chemicals program, it has been an effective mechanism for gradual introduction and control of new chemicals that trigger exposure or health concerns. In this instance, a SNUR would require manufacturers (including importers) or processors to notify EPA at least ninety days before beginning any activity that EPA has designated as a "significant new use." These new use designations are typically those activities prohibited by the original Section 5 order: for instance, a proposal to increase the number and nature of uses to which the chemical would be put, and/or an increase in volume of production over that projected in the original PMN. With each increase, EPA can then ask for more toxicity and other data to fill out the chemical's profile as the potentially exposed population grows. The required notification initiates EPA's evaluation of the conditions of use associated with the chemical substance within the applicable review period. SNUN review would be the same as described above. Over time, industry expressed concern that new chemicals, which sometimes are more benign, seem to be subject to more scrutiny at EPA than widely used older ones.

EPA's efforts to gather new information about existing chemicals under TSCA, GAO found, were unproductive. Under TSCA, in order for EPA to require industry to develop and submit data, the agency is required to write "test rules" that make a finding of "unreasonable risk." The requirement to complete a full rulemaking to accomplish information gathering ("testing") was quite cumbersome and few test rules were ever fully promulgated.[42]

EDF demonstrated that there was a very high level of ignorance within industry about the toxicity of even high production volume (HPV) chemicals (i.e., at least one million pounds produced per year).[43] EPA did a complete assessment and found that no publicly available basic toxicity information existed for forty-three percent of all high-volume chemicals and only seven percent of these chemicals had full sets of basic toxicity data publicly available.[44] In response, the chemical producers, EDF, and EPA joined in an effort to fill these data gaps. Industry devoted several years to voluntarily developing "screening level" test data for the approximately 2,800 HPV chemicals in commerce in the US. An updated EDF study in 2007 found that job was far from finished.[45] Little activity occurred after that assessment was made available.

Setback on Asbestos

During the Clinton administration, EPA used TSCA authority to outline an ambitious regulatory strategy to reduce the public health risks from exposure to asbestos throughout the US economy. Asbestos seemed like a promising precedent for action because it was featured in the legislative debate around TSCA and because epidemiological studies had already established a causal relationship between chronic worker exposures to asbestos and debilitating diseases such as mesothelioma and lung cancer.

On October 17, 1979, EPA issued an advance notice of proposed rulemaking (ANPRM) that announced the agency's broad investigation of the need to regulate commercial and industrial uses of asbestos under section 6 of

TSCA.[46] The agency also proposed a regulation to address public concerns about asbestos in school buildings.[47] The work was not completed when President Carter lost his re-election bid to the Republican challenger, California Governor Ronald Reagan.

Like what happened in the agency's pesticide program, efforts to implement TSCA under new EPA Administrator Anne Gorsuch slowed considerably. The agency was able to finalize a rule on asbestos in schools,[48] and reporting rules were issued that helped the agency gather data to perform a national risk assessment of asbestos.[49] Progress toward a proposed rule stalled as the agency's leadership authorized open-ended negotiations with industry over a possible voluntary regulation. Key Democrats on EPA's oversight committees criticized the Reagan administration for dragging its feet on asbestos regulation.

After the 1982 midterm elections, when Ruckelshaus returned to EPA leadership, work on the proposed rule proceeded in earnest. A key issue that required resolution was whether EPA should refer the asbestos issue to other federal agencies such as OSHA, the Mine Safety and Health Administration (MSHA), and CPSC, as authorized under TSCA, or whether EPA should proceed with the proposed rule, which was also permitted under TSCA. After deliberation, the agency made an interim policy determination that the proposed rule should proceed in house: there was too much exposure to asbestos occurring outside of OSHA and MSHA regulatory authority; a single federal rule under TSCA would be a more efficient solution than piecemeal rules established under other authorities; and OSHA and MSHA, due to their statutory constraints, did not have authority to issue the most effective solutions (e.g., complete or partial bans on asbestos use in various sectors of the economy). The agency's interim policy position was communicated by Administrator Ruckelshaus to Congressman John Dingell, chair of the agency's oversight committee in the House of Representatives, in a letter dated April 23, 1984.

In May 1984 EPA submitted to OMB the proposed rulemaking package for interagency review as required under President Reagan's 1981 Executive Order on regulatory relief. The ambitious draft proposal called for a ban on asbestos use in several industry sectors. EPA was requesting OMB clearance to seek public comment on the proposed rule.

Over the next six months OMB's Office of Information and Regulatory Affairs (OIRA) staff engaged in an increasingly acrimonious debate with EPA staff over the merits of the proposed rule. The heart of OIRA's concerns were the quality of the cost-benefit analysis prepared by EPA to support the rule, the huge variation in the cost-effectiveness of a ban for different uses of asbestos, and the legal analysis underpinning EPA's decision not to refer the entire issue to other federal agencies. By late October OIRA and EPA had reached a total impasse. Since the agency was not permitted by presidential order to move forward without OIRA clearance, the agency withdrew the package and made a public announcement that the asbestos issue would be referred to OSHA and CPSC.

The public announcement precipitated cries of outrage from key members of Congress and the public. It seemed inconceivable to pro-regulation advocates that EPA's five years of work on the issue would simply be thrown away. Sensing the adverse reaction, EPA withdrew the referral announcement and decided to reconsider the agency's course. Nonetheless, Congressman Dingell initiated in 1985 an in-depth investigation of OIRA's "interference" through his Subcommittee on Oversight and Investigations.[50]

A year later (January 1986), EPA secured OIRA's clearance of a proposed rule that called for a ban on asbestos use in five product categories (roofing felts, flooring felts, floor tile, cement pipe, and fittings), as well as a possible ten-year phase out of other major uses of asbestos. Some current uses of asbestos (e.g., asbestos in brake linings) were not covered because the agency was not aware of appropriate substitutes. Stronger labels were proposed on all products not subject to the proposed ban. In order to ensure that the rulemaking process was rigorous, EPA made the unusual decision to undertake a formal rulemaking that entailed cross examination of experts as well as normal public hearings.

EPA's cost-benefit analysis showed that the economic value of asbestos use was much smaller in some industrial applications than in others. For several months EPA considered, but ultimately rejected as impractical, OIRA's suggestion to place a cap on asbestos use in the economy with opportunity for companies to buy and sell asbestos-use permits. In the final rule, EPA also decided against a market-based phase-out of asbestos use, as had been used by EPA when the phase-out of lead was accelerated in the early 1980s. The agency's policy preference for use-by-use prohibitions made it difficult for the agency's attorneys to defend the action as the "least burdensome" alternative under TSCA.

Two years later (1991), the agency was stunned and demoralized when a unanimous three-judge panel of the Fifth Circuit Court of Appeals in New Orleans overturned the final rule as it applies to existing uses of asbestos.[51] The highly critical opinion nonetheless permitted the agency to prohibit new uses of asbestos in the future.[52] The judges were clearly not convinced by the agency's cost-benefit analysis or unreasonable-risk determination. Nor were bans throughout the industry seen as the "least burdensome" alternative. EPA did not take further action to regulate uses of asbestos under TSCA until Congress gave EPA specific authority to do so.[53]

The asbestos nightmare for EPA had two far-reaching implications. First, the agency concluded that the "unreasonable risk" and "least burdensome" tests in TSCA made it very difficult for the agency to take aggressive regulatory actions on any existing chemicals under TSCA. Whether this conclusion was valid, or an over-reaction, is a matter of some dispute (e.g., the "least burdensome" test may have been more constraining than the "unreasonable-risk" test). Second, Congressman Dingell's concerns about OIRA's interference stimulated widespread deliberation about the merits of continuing the OIRA review process. Other agencies, such as OSHA, also voiced strong concerns about OIRA review.[54]

Ultimately, OIRA review was retained, as it is seen as a presidential prerogative that can be used in different ways by different presidents.[55] In conjunction with reauthorization of the Paperwork Reduction Act, reforms were adopted in 1990 to make the OIRA review process more accountable, transparent, and focused. The OIRA administrator post was made subject to Senate confirmation; written documents exchanged between OIRA and the agencies are placed in the public record at the conclusion of interagency review; OIRA's meetings with stakeholders are disclosed publicly; and OIRA review of rules was focused on "significant rules." EPA adjusted to the reality that cost-benefit review by OIRA would continue, especially when Democratic President Bill Clinton reaffirmed a cost-benefit role for OIRA in 1993.

Innovation in Chemical Risk Management

Ever creative, EPA staff identified alternative pathways to risk management via means not foreseen in TSCA, such as right-to-know and pollution-prevention policies. In 1986, Congress gave the EPA additional authority when it enacted the Emergency Planning and Community Right to Know Act (EPCRA).[56] The agency's Toxics Release Inventory (TRI) under EPCRA required manufacturing facilities with ten or more employees to report releases and transfers of several hundred toxic chemicals that were specifically listed by Congress. TRI became a model for similar "pollutant release and transfer registries" (or PRTRs) worldwide. Congress also gave EPA authority to add new facilities and chemicals to the list, and to delist chemicals and facilities.

The TRI was a major success in terms of providing information to the public and in reducing pollution in the US.[57] For the "core" set of chemicals from industries that have reported consistently over time, total releases on- and off-site decreased by 45.5 percent between 1988 and 1999, a reduction of 1.46 billion pounds. During the same time, the category of total production waste did not change much. Under TRI, EPA made efforts to expand the universe of chemical reporting by lowering reporting thresholds for a number of persistent bio-accumulative and toxic (PBT) chemicals, adding 236 chemicals and chemical categories for reporting to the TRI, and expanding right-to-know by adding the following new industry groups to TRI: metal mining, coal mining, electric utilities, commercial hazardous waste treatment, chemicals and allied products-wholesale, petroleum bulk terminals and plants-wholesale, and solvent recovery services.[58]

The 1990 Pollution Prevention Act (PPA) defined pollution prevention as "the use of materials, processes, or practices that reduce the use of hazardous materials, energy, water, or other resources and practices that protect natural resources through conservation or more efficient use."[59] The PPA established a pollution prevention effort in EPA's chemicals office and required that "source reduction" efforts (e.g., prevent pollution rather than install pollution control equipment to reduce emissions) occur in each office in the agency. It required EPA to establish a pollution prevention strategy to promote source reduction and recycling and the collection of such information on the TRI. It provided resources for state and local pollution prevention programs and the promotion of use of pollution prevention by industry.

EPA also made significant progress in the development of pollution prevention tools such as environmental accounting, financing, resource exchanges, and state-based efforts. Another outgrowth of this effort was "Design for the Environment" (now called "Safer Choice"), a voluntary program that works with various sectors of chemical users (like dry cleaners and printers) to compare existing and alternative products, processes, and practices in order to find the best ways to enhance product performance and reduce risks to human health and the environment.[60] Within EPA, efforts were made to incorporate pollution prevention into permitting programs and compliance efforts. EPA developed guidance on environmentally preferable purchasing to encourage "green" purchasing practices by the entire US government.

After enactment of the Pollution Prevention Act (1990), EPA—building on prevention initiatives in California and other states—developed the concept of "green chemistry" and put in place processes to spread it through the chemical industry. Interest groups were created within the American Chemical Society, new university curricula were launched, and a Green Chemistry Challenge Award is given annually and highlights the importance of developing innovative new processes that are safe and environmentally friendly across the chemical life cycle. Under this program, the EPA carries out partnerships with a number of industries that are significant users of chemicals, including printing, adhesives, automotive refinishing, printed wiring board manufacturers, computer display, textile and garment care, and cleaning product formulators. These projects employ life cycle methods and technology assessments to analyze environmental impacts, performance, and costs of alternatives for producing products.

The Case for TSCA Reform

In a series of reports in 1994, 2005, and 2009, the General Accounting Office informed Congress that legislative reform of TSCA was needed.[61] Several areas of reform were emphasized.

TSCA broadly directs the EPA to assure that the public will be protected from "'unreasonable risks' to health and the environment," but this standard is so vague that it provides little practical guidance. It came to be interpreted as entailing in-depth formal analyses including risk assessment (the severity and magnitude of health and environmental effects) and economic analysis (the economic benefits of the use of the substance as well as the availability, risks, and costs of switching to alternatives). In the case of PCBs, radon, and lead, Congress saw fit to conclude that unreasonable risks did indeed exist and gave EPA very specific direction for how to address those risks. Without a specific direction from Congress, the presumption for an existing chemical was that it is safe unless EPA made a regulatory finding to the contrary. In contrast, new chemicals were reviewed by EPA prior to manufacture within the ninety-day window. GAO suggested that the new vs. old distinction was too stark in TSCA.

All rulemaking under TSCA turned out to be difficult, partly because of competing stakeholder pressures and partly because of lack of clear congressional direction and deadlines. Rulemaking to manage risks under TSCA Section 6—even for chemicals with well-characterized toxicities like asbestos—was hamstrung by requirements for extensive analyses of the costs and benefits of regulatory alternatives. From 1976 to 1994, GAO found that EPA had regulated few chemicals under TSCA, listing only five (PCBs, chlorofluorocarbons, dioxin, asbestos, and hexavalent chromium), and noted that the act itself required the regulation of one of the five, PCBs. In only two cases, PCBs and asbestos, did the EPA take a comprehensive approach to regulation and in one of these cases, asbestos, the rule was overturned in court. The TSCA requirement to prefer the "least burdensome" alternative was framed as a barrier; after the Fifth Circuit's 1991 decision, EPA took no major Section 6 actions under TSCA.

GAO also found that referral of chemical risks to other agencies like OSHA, for control of adverse exposures to workers, did not work well either. By 1994, EPA had formally referred only four chemicals to other agencies: 4,4'-methylenedianiline (OSHA 1985), 1,3-butadiene (OSHA 1985), glycol ethers (OSHA 1986), and dioxin in bleached wood pulp and papers used for food packaging (FDA 1990).

Public access to information on chemicals was hampered by the strict confidential business information (CBI) provisions of TSCA. GAO pointed to the breadth of CBI protections and the significant costs to EPA in assessing claims made by manufacturers under the law. In 1998, sixty-five percent of the information filings directed to the agency through TSCA were claimed as confidential. At that time, submissions under the Inventory Update Rule showed that even about twenty percent of facility identities—seemingly innocuous information—were claimed as confidential. Approximately forty percent of TSCA substantial-risk notices had chemical identity claimed as confidential. EPA could nonetheless access the information, but the states and other interested parties did not have access to TSCA information that was claimed as confidential. EPA was empowered to deny spurious claims of CBI, but there were little to no resources dedicated to this task. GAO concluded that the CBI provisions of TSCA needed to be fixed.

By 2005 both the European Union (EU) and Canada modernized their chemical-regulatory systems, though in very different ways.[62] The EU required virtually all industrial chemicals to be registered in the REACH program with a new chemicals agency (ECHA) in Helsinki, Finland, and industry was required to prepare safety assessments in support of each chemical use. Canada's management plan focused regulatory efforts on a limited set of priority chemicals.

The EU program was particularly important even though Congress decided not to replicate it in the US. The EU had a significant impact on the thinking of leaders at global chemical companies such as Dow, DuPont, and BASF. The fact that the EU required massive data submissions caused big chemical companies to realize that TSCA was not only outdated, but that EPA would fall far behind their EU counterparts in terms of knowledge and understanding of chemicals. Once the global industry learned to live with the EU system, the future demand for more information and data from EPA was seen as less onerous. US companies also recognized that the EU was actively persuading some developing countries to replicate their system. The US-based chemical industry—including the consumer-product associations—became convinced that it was in their interest to have a reformed TSCA, even if it was not exactly like the EU system.

Further stimulating the reform movement was a series of high-profile attacks on chemicals through social media and the mass media. Flame retardants such as PFOS and PFOA were featured in the attacks since they were in existing products with insufficient safety information. Additionally, there were a series of orchestrated attacks aimed at hurting sales of those products.

Those attacks highlighted the inability of EPA to effectively regulate under TSCA and the inability of industry to point to EPA's regulatory system as a guardian of safety. The flame retardants became to TSCA reform what Alar was to FIFRA/FFDCA reform. If TSCA reform was done properly, the industry believed it would undercut the efforts of anti-chemical activists to blacklist low-risk chemicals in the marketplace.

With industry as well as environmental groups seeking TSCA reform, legislation was inevitable. Congress considered the EU and Canadian reforms in the policy debate over how to amend TSCA.[63]

The Frank R. Lautenberg Chemical Safety Act for the 21st Century

A strong bipartisan effort was marshalled in Congress and led to passage of the Lautenberg Chemical Safety Act (LCSA) by a GOP-led Congress. It was signed into law by President Obama on June 22, 2016. The law was named after Democratic Senator Frank R. Lautenberg of New Jersey, a long-time advocate of TSCA reform who passed away three years before the law was enacted.

What industry gained from reform was limited preemption of state and local regulations and the ability to refer publicly to EPA's new chemical decisions as an indication of safety if EPA agreed with the industry's scientific position. Environmentalists gained changes to the statutory standards, deadlines for action under the program, and revised procedures related to CBI. Here are the key provisions and some of EPA's progress on each of them.

New Risk-Determination Standard

The old "unreasonable-risk" standard was broken into two steps: the first step, risk determination, is based upon whether a chemical use poses unreasonable risk to human health and the environment while excluding consideration of costs and other non-risk factors; those factors are considered only in the second risk-management step (described below). EPA is required to consider risks to sensitive populations, including infants, children, and pregnant women.

Priorities and Deadlines for Chemical Assessments

Congress set deadlines for establishing prioritized lists of existing chemicals for assessments. EPA selected the first ten chemicals to undergo risk evaluation and also met deadlines for releasing initial scoping documents (2017) and problem formulation documents (2018). Chemicals deemed to be high priority must undergo full risk evaluations, also according to a proscribed timeline. The risk evaluation process may last no longer than three years, with a possible one-time, six-month extension.

Standard and Deadlines for Risk Management

When unreasonable risks are identified, EPA must take final risk management action within two years, or four years if an extension is needed. Restrictions imposed must be sufficient to ensure protection of susceptible and highly exposed populations. Costs and availability of alternatives must be considered when determining appropriate action to address risks but, most importantly, EPA is no longer required to select the "least burdensome" option.

Testing Authority

As is the case for pesticides, EPA now has the authority to "call in" test information for prioritizing or conducting risk evaluations on a chemical; the agency can use test-order and consent-agreement tools rather than cumbersome rulemakings. The use of non-animal alternative testing methodologies is encouraged, and EPA is not bound to use only the standardized animal testing methodologies that are used to test pesticides and pharmaceuticals in the US.

Fast Track for Persistent, Bioaccumulative, and Toxic (PBT) Chemicals

Action, including bans and phaseouts, must begin as quickly as possible for PBTs but no later than five years after the final agency determination that the PBT criteria have been met.

New Procedures for New Chemicals

Review of the 500-1000 new chemicals entering commerce each year still must occur under a ninety-day pre-manufacture notice (PMN) process; however, now the PMN cannot be approved unless EPA can make an affirmative finding on the safety of a new chemical for requested uses. Like the old TSCA, the petitioner is not required to submit a basic set of safety data to support EPA in making the safety finding. For the period from June 22, 2016 through October 1, 2020, of the 3,452 cases received, the reviews of 2,947 have been completed. These include PMNS, MCANs, and SNUNs (Significant New Use Notifications). Two hundred and fifty-five were deemed incomplete or invalid. The remaining 250 are still in review.[64]

New CBI Standards

CBI claims may not be extended to information obtained from health and safety studies. Further, most CBI claims now must be substantiated and, when a chemical identity is claimed as CBI, a non-CBI structurally descriptive generic name must be provided; EPA has already implemented this process. EPA is now required to review all CBI claims for chemical identity, as well as a representative sample of at least twenty-five percent of other claims, within ninety days of receipt. Other CBI claims can also be reviewed by the agency based on specific events, such as a Freedom of Information Act (FOIA) request, for prioritization, or for risk management under TSCA section 6. CBI claims now automatically expire after ten years unless they are re-substantiated. When a CBI claim for a chemical identity is approved, the EPA must now give that chemical a unique identifier that allows for linking data across EPA's many data systems (e.g., reports of adverse effects). TSCA CBI now may be shared with non-federal authorities including states, subdivisions of states, tribes, emergency responders, and health care professionals if they can preserve CBI.

Unfortunately, EPA appears to be off to a rocky start on the CBI issue. The first existing chemical draft risk evaluation under the new law, for Pigment Violet 29, was released for public comment in November 2018. It was based solely upon health and safety data considered to be proprietary. The agency relied upon robust summaries prepared for the EU's REACH program to craft its hazard profile of the chemical. Following a significant outcry from stakeholders, EPA acquired and released summary and full study reports provided by the manufacturer. However, in the report of the rodent reproductive toxicity study used by EPA as the basis for its hazard characterization, the raw data for each individual animal were blacked out, leaving no opportunity for independent analysis. Thus, the controversy over disclosure of health and safety studies under TSCA is likely to continue.

Fees

EPA's authority to collect fees from industry to support TSCA was expanded with the intent of providing EPA with a sustainable level of funding to support TSCA implementation. EPA is now collecting increased fees for PMN reviews and will collect fees for EPA-initiated and manufacturer-requested existing chemical risk evaluations. Importantly, the fees collected will go not to the US Treasury (where they had been going) but will go directly to support EPA's implementation of TSCA.

Preemption of State and Local Laws

There is a substantial federal preemption provision but with complex carve-outs. States can continue to act on any chemical, or particular uses or risks from a chemical, that EPA had not yet addressed prior to June 2016; existing state requirements in effect on August 31, 2003 were preserved. The law reserved state environmental authorities related to air, water, and waste disposal and treatment. States and the federal government can co-enforce identical regulations. As a stopgap, the law provides states with mechanisms to take action when EPA fails to take final actions to address a chemical risk and/or under certain specific conditions. EPA has identified the next twenty high priority chemicals and thus preemption is in effect for that subset until EPA completes the multi-year process of risk evaluation.

Mercury

As mentioned earlier, Congress gave EPA new authority to regulate mercury, and such authority has already been used by EPA to buttress mercury reporting.

Areas of Progress and Challenge

Pursuant to the Lautenberg Act, EPA issued a 2018 rule modernizing the agency's inventory of industrial chemicals. Next came the first major update of the inventory in forty years.[65] Of the 86,405 chemicals on the inventory in 2020, only 48% were found to be actively in commerce and therefore subject to regulation under TSCA. Of these, about 20% have identities that are claimed as CBI.[66]

EPA met the deadline for finalizing a Prioritization Process Rule that defines how it will identify high-priority chemicals for risk evaluation as well as low-priority chemicals for which no evaluation is warranted at the present time. It also published a final Risk Evaluation Process Rule that establishes the process EPA will use to determine whether or not chemicals present an unreasonable risk to health and the environment. Both of the framework rules were challenged in the Ninth Circuit Court of Appeals by environmental groups because EPA was asserting its authority to limit the number of uses covered in an assessment.

The Court's rulings, issued in November 2019, were mixed. It dismissed the petitioners' argument that TSCA requires EPA to evaluate the risk from all uses of a chemical substance collectively and make a risk finding on the substance as a whole rather than a use-by-use determination. It did not agree with the petitioners' argument that the risk evaluation rule impermissibly allows the EPA to assert discretion to exclude certain conditions of use from the scope of its risk evaluation. However, it did agree that EPA's exclusion of legacy uses and associated disposals from the definition of "conditions of use" was unlawful.[67] This ruling obligates EPA to include an assessment of legacy uses and disposal (if there are any) when finalizing the risk evaluations for the first ten chemicals currently going through the assessment process and in all risk evaluations going forward.

In the future, the agency faces a tension between the risk-evaluation timelines prescribed by Congress and the law's goal to achieve high quality risk evaluations. The risk assessment of a priority chemical could encompass scores of conditions of use and multiple population groups (e.g., workers, non-occupational users, bystanders, and the general public). It remains to be seen how effective the Lautenberg amendments to TSCA will be.

BIOTECHNOLOGY PRODUCTS REGULATION

Genetically modified organisms (GMOs) are products of biotechnology into which genetic material is intentionally and specifically introduced using a variety of technological processes. More broadly, genetic modification includes genetic engineering but also includes procedures not regulated by the government, like chemical and radiation mutagenesis and selective breeding of plants and other organisms. This is a relatively new area of regulation for EPA, not even envisioned when EPA was established in 1970.

GMOs are increasingly the technology of choice for the manufacture of chemicals and pesticides. With GMOs comes the potential for gene spread into the ecosystem, impacts on non-target organisms, and inadvertent contamination of the food supply or the environment.

The White House Coordinated Framework

Products of biotechnology began to be developed and commercialized in the 1980s. The 1986 Coordinated Framework for the Regulation of Biotechnology was developed under the leadership of the White House Office of Science and Technology (OSTP), which sought to delegate regulatory responsibility to agencies for biotechnology products using existing statutory frameworks. Under the coordinated framework, GMOs used as chemicals or as pesticides were to be regulated by EPA under TSCA and FIFRA, respectively.

In 1992 the framework was modified by OSTP to emphasize that such products should not be regulated on the basis of the process by which they are made but, instead, on the basis of the "characteristics of the organism, the target environment, and the type of application." In January 2017, OSTP published an update to the coordinated framework that basically reaffirmed EPA's roles in regulating biotechnology products.[68]

As a practical matter, EPA has not found it easy to implement the OSTP focus on risk rather than process of production. The agency has required that it be notified prior to small-scale field tests of GMO products without requiring any similar notification of the small-scale field tests for the same product developed by conventional breeding techniques. Since the OSTP is broad-level guidance, it does not necessarily constrain EPA regulatory activity where the agency judges that regulation is appropriate. It should be noted that crop field trials are required in all cases for agricultural use pesticides. They are conducted to determine the magnitude of the pesticide residue in or on raw agricultural commodities (RACs), and to reflect pesticide use patterns that could lead to the highest possible residues. The pesticide must be applied at known application rates and in a manner similar to the use directions intended for the pesticide label. Data are normally required for each crop, or the representative crops of each crop group, for which a tolerance (or tolerance exemption) and registration is requested and for each RAC derived from the crop.

Outside the government, the National Academies of Sciences warned federal agencies in 2017 that society is on the cusp of commercializing a broad array of new types of biotechnology products. New risk analysis tools and other technical approaches may be required. EPA and other agencies may need to make use of the flexibility available under its statutes to minimize regulatory gaps and position novel products under suitable statutory frameworks.[69] NAS therefore recommended that EPA and other agencies prepare for action by increasing their scientific capabilities in this arena as well as carrying out pilot projects to advance the understanding and use of ecological risk assessments and benefit analyses for unfamiliar and complex new biotechnologies.

So far, EPA has not significantly buttressed its scientific capacities in this area. Given how appropriations and hiring are determined, this shortcoming is at least as much a congressional and OMB problem as it is an agency problem.

Plant Incorporated Protectants under FIFRA

In 2001 the EPA issued a final rule for the regulation of pesticides in plants under FIFRA, so-called "plant incorporated protectants" (PIPs).[70] Procedures were established for the evaluation of pesticides that are incorporated into plants using the techniques of biotechnology. The safety evaluations include consideration of both environmental and human health impacts. In 2000, the NAS listed what those hazards might be:

- Ecological risks: impacts on non-target organisms, gene flow to weeds or other crops, and development of pesticide resistant organisms.
- Health risks: allergenicity, toxic compounds in plants, and potential for long-term health impacts.[71]

EPA's assessment processes for PIPs strive to address all of these issues. As is the case with other pesticides, EPA regulates market entry via registration; product sponsors submit evidence to demonstrate that the product will not cause unreasonable adverse effects on health or the environment under its proposed conditions of use. EPA can allow unregistered products to be field tested under Experimental Use Permits (EUPs).

EPA approved thirty-eight PIPs from 1992 through 2018. Of these, five (all for corn) have been cancelled.[72] Most of those remaining (33) are products that incorporated genes that encode Bt (*Bacillus thuringiensis*) proteins, which are insecticidal toxins, and four provide virus resistance. These products have been developed for a limited number of high-volume crops: corn (13); cotton (9); soybean (5); potato (3); and one apiece for papaya and plum. Use of the Bt proteins has been challenged because of the ability of many target pests to develop resistance to them, which is managed through the planting process as well as "stacking" multiple Bt genes into the same plant. One (Event 176) has been withdrawn from the market because it expressed high enough levels of Bt toxin in pollen to raise theoretical concerns for non-target organisms like monarch butterflies. A second (Cry9C or StarLink) was pulled from the market because of unresolvable concerns regarding potential allergenicity. Others have been successful even though there is an issue with resistance developing in target organisms and a need for numerous technical solutions to prevent resistance—a conundrum applicable to conventional chemical pesticides as well.

In summary, while genetically engineered foods are controversial with the public, both domestically and internationally, to date the experience with plant-incorporated pesticides has been limited to just a few technologies and crop families. The explosion of innovation in this field may pose unexpected challenges for EPA's pesticide program in the future.

Biotechnology Products under TSCA

EPA has made significant progress with the regulation of new GMOs that produce (or are used as) chemicals under TSCA. A 1997 rulemaking provides the fundamental basis for these activities.[73] An important aspect of the rule is to identify organisms with the potential for pathogenicity or for adverse ecosystem effects. For new microorganisms, EPA established two separate processes. To commercialize an intergeneric microorganism, industry must submit a Microbial Commercial Activity Notice (MCAN) at least ninety days prior to commercialization. Prior to the Lautenberg Act, between FY 1998 and 2016, only 102 MCANs were filed with EPA and all but two were dropped from review. Thirty-three Experimental Release Applications (TERAs) were filed; all but three were approved by EPA. In order to introduce microorganisms into the environment for field tests, industry must file a TERA at least sixty days prior to a field test. The 2016 TSCA amendments for PMNs thus affected the review of MCANs. Under the amendments, EPA considers a recipient microorganism not to present an unreasonable risk if a determination is made of low human health hazard and low environmental hazard associated with the microorganism itself as well as the introduced genetic material. In 2020 EPA issued a rule defining certain GMOs as unlikely to present an unreasonable risk to human health and the environment.[74]

Overall, from the perspective of the agency's fifty-year history, EPA regulation of GMOs is at its early stages but there is no groundswell of opposition suggesting that EPA is ineffective. The challenge is to balance the need for innovation with the need to protect human health and the environment.

GLOBAL AGREEMENTS ON CHEMICAL REGULATION: INTERSECTIONS WITH TRADE AND COMMERCE

In recent decades, global production and distribution of chemicals in commerce has skyrocketed. Rather than regulate chemicals solely on a country-by-country basis, efforts have been launched to harmonize regulations around the world. A number of global agreements have been crafted to control global and transboundary risks. A challenge for EPA is to participate formally in these activities, since the United States Senate has become, over time, increasingly skeptical of international treaties. Without Senate ratification of treaties, official US participation is impossible. Several examples of important international activities are provided in this section.

Sometimes the international collaboration occurs informally, with participation by industry and governments. For example, for a company to successfully launch a new active ingredient (pesticide) for widespread use on a crop that will be traded globally, simultaneous approvals by multiple governments is preferred. These informal efforts began in 1990, and the work continues today as nations around the world upgrade their regulatory programs. Companies work with EPA and other national regulatory programs to get simultaneous approvals. EPA has been a leader in informal harmonization efforts. To formalize this kind of activity, international agreements are sometimes established.

Stockholm Convention on Persistent Organic Chemicals

In May 2001, the Stockholm Convention on Persistent Organic Pollutants (POPs) was signed by parties.[75] The treaty, which came into force in 2003, initially took measures to protect health and the environment from twelve POPs or groups of POPs, including provisions to add additional POPs to the treaty and prevent the introduction of new POPs into commerce. Over time, seven more POPs were added to the initial list of twelve. The treaty provides for technical and financial assistance to developing countries and countries with economies in transition. The US signed but never ratified the agreement, which now includes 182 parties. EPA does not formally participate but collaborates on information provided through allied governments such as Canada.

Organisation for Economic Co-operation and Development (OECD) Mutual Acceptance of Data System

OECD is an international organization based in Paris, France. One mechanism for international regulatory harmonization is a set of OECD council decisions that comprise the OECD's Mutual Acceptance of Data (MAD) System. It has two components: OECD Guidelines for the Testing of Chemicals and OECD Principles of Good Laboratory Practice (GLP). The guidelines program develops and validates internationally agreed upon test protocols by which data are generated in satisfaction of regulatory requirements.

GLP is a managerial concept covering the organizational process and the conditions under which laboratory studies are planned, performed, monitored, recorded, and reported. Its principles are required to be followed by test facilities carrying out studies to be submitted to national regulatory authorities for the purposes of assessment of chemicals and their uses relating to the protection of humans and the environment. All OECD member countries as well as other adherents to MAD must accept study data generated according to OECD test guidelines. Three criteria are crucial: The study must have been conducted according to OECD test guidelines and OECD principles of GLP; the study must have been conducted in a test facility which has been inspected by a national GLP compliance monitoring program; and the national GLP compliance monitoring program must have undergone a successful evaluation by OECD. The US is a full adherent to the MAD system and EPA has been an influential participant in the activities.

Rotterdam Convention on Prior Informed Consent

The Rotterdam Convention on the Prior Informed Consent Procedure for Certain Hazardous Chemicals and Pesticides in International Trade was signed in 1998 and came into force in 2004.[76] The convention requires that chemicals and pesticides that have been added to the convention because they are banned or severely restricted in at least one country in each of two regions shall not be exported, unless explicitly agreed by the importing country. It also includes pesticide formulations that are too dangerous to be used in developing countries. FAO and UNEP jointly provide the secretariat to the convention as well as the interim procedure. The US signed but never ratified the agreement, which now includes one hundred and sixty parties globally. As of October 2018, a total of fifty-one chemicals were on the list of banned or cancelled chemicals, including thirty-six pesticides and fifteen industrial chemicals.[77] EPA can participate in this convention only informally.

Minimata Convention on Mercury

The US and ninety other countries are party to this convention—adopted in 2013 and housed within UNEP—that seeks to reduce use and emissions of mercury globally. Global sources comprise seventy percent of mercury deposition in the US. The convention requires all parties to eliminate and reduce mercury use and emissions in mining, coal-burning, products, and in chemical manufacturing. It also addresses the supply and trade in mercury, safe disposal practices, and cleanup of contaminated sites. The United States was the first country to officially join the convention and EPA is an active participant.[78]

Globally Harmonized System (GHS) of Classification and Labeling of Chemicals

Finalized in 2002, the GHS was an outgrowth of the UN Conference on Environment and Development Agenda 21. Prior to the development of the GHS, there were a variety of confusing systems for labeling chemicals in transport. Under the auspices of the UN, the work was coordinated by the Inter-organization Programme for the Sound Management of Chemicals (IOMC), Coordinating Group for the Harmonization of Chemical Classification Systems (CG/HCCS), with technical input from the International Labour Organization (ILO), the Organization for Economic Cooperation and Development (OECD), and the United Nations Economic and Social Council's Sub-Committee of Experts on the Transport of Dangerous Goods (UNSCETDG). The GHS has been adopted by many countries including the

US and most of our trading partners. The GHS classifies chemicals by severity and type of hazard and provides standardized labels so that these hazards (physical, health, or environmental) can be clearly communicated to all who may have contact with them in transport and in commerce.[79] EPA has been an influential participant in GHS since its inception.

Trade Agreements

The World Trade Organization and international trade agreements have long sought to reduce non-tariff barriers to trade. Some of these barriers are purely discriminatory practices, but legitimate health and safety standards for chemicals and pesticides also create trade barriers and thus have surfaced on the radar screens of trade negotiators. Under the WTO, so-called "technical barriers to trade" (TBT) must be administered in a way that does not discriminate against producers from other countries. Regulators are to focus on the risks of the product itself, and not the process used to manufacture the product.

The Trump administration negotiated a replacement of the North American Free Trade Agreement called the US-Mexico-Canada Agreement (USMCA). It includes complex provisions in a new Chapter 28, "Good Regulatory Practices." The numerous analytic requirements in Chapter 28, along with the ability of industry to bring cases to the USMCA dispute resolution process, may have an impact on product regulation generally in the US. Since the USMCA was ratified by all three countries as of March 2020, it could have an impact on EPA regulation in the years ahead.

CONCLUSION

There is a certain logic to the similar construction of FIFRA/FFDCA and TSCA, three statutes that regulate chemical products. All allow for EPA review before a product can enter into commerce and periodically thereafter. The greater stringency of FIFRA/FFDCA compared to TSCA is understandable if one considers that pesticides are designed to be biologically active (i.e., kill) and have a narrowly defined use; industrial chemicals are not generally designed to be biologically active—though certainly can be—and have multiple uses. TSCA reform in 2016 mirrored, in some ways, the 1996 FIFRA/FFDCA reform (i.e., the focus on vulnerable subpopulations, periodic review of existing products, and a risk-determination without regard to costs). When considering regulatory alternatives, both laws continue to embrace risk-benefit analysis through the unreasonable-risk test.

The tale of EPA's fifty-year history in pesticide and chemical regulation is filled with both successes and setbacks. The pesticide program, already operational at USDA and FDA, got off to a strong start at EPA in the 1970s, building on the credibility that Ruckelshaus's DDT decision provided the young agency. The re-registration effort was not completed as rapidly as envisioned, but now, with several refinements to FIFRA and FFDCA and a well-trained technical staff, the program is quite productive. Chemicals regulation at EPA evolved quite differently: an ambitious new assignment for EPA, a slow start with limited resources, a cumbersome statute, and a hard-fought loss in the Fifth Circuit on existing uses of asbestos. The drafting of the 1976 statute gave more tools for EPA to succeed with new chemicals than with existing chemicals. Agency creativity, technical and legal, produced progress on new chemicals, the TRI program, pollution prevention, and green chemistry. The future is promising with the new Lautenberg amendments to TSCA but the devil, if there is one, will be in the details of implementation. Both programs may need a significant infusion of new expertise on biotechnology issues. The pressures to address regulatory issues globally will only intensify, and EPA has had the credibility worldwide to make a difference in global deliberations, if only it can be sustained.

NOTES

1. The authors acknowledge helpful comments from John Applegate, Jim Barnes, Nancy Beck, Keith Belton, Terry Davies, Linda Fisher, Art Fraas, and David Konisky. Appreciation is also expressed for the efforts of Lynn Goldman, who prepared a paper for our first workshop, which we used as background material for development of the chapter. Dr. Goldman was not able to join us for the entire book project because of the unexpected demands on her time caused by COVID-19.
2. Federal Food Drug and Cosmetics Act, Subtitle 4: Cosmetics, U.S.C. 21 (1938).
3. Pub. L. No. 518, 68 Stat. 511 (1954).
4. Federal Food Drug and Cosmetics Act, Chapter IV: Food, U.S.C. 21 (1958).
5. Federal Insecticide, Fungicide, and Rodenticide Act Amendments, 7, Pub. L. No. 80–102 (June 25, 1947).
6. Rachel Carson, *Silent Spring* (Boston, MA: Houghton Mifflin, 1962).
7. Phillip L. Spector, "Regulation of Pesticides by the Environmental Protection Agency," *Ecology Law Quarterly* 5 (1976): 233.
8. Scott Ferguson and Ed Gray, "1988 FIFRA Amendments: A Major Step in Pesticide Regulation," *Environmental Law Reporter* 19 (1989): 10074, fn 39.
9. For an accessible review of those studies, including references to the peer-reviewed literature, see Susan Wayland and Penelope Fenner-Crisp, *Reducing Pesticide Risks: A Half Century of Progress* (Washington, DC: EPA Alumni Association, March 1, 2020).

10. The EDB story is based on Mark R. Powell, *The 1983-1984 Suspensions of EDB Under FIFRA and the 1989 Asbestos Ban and Phase-out Rule Under TSCA: Two Case Studies in EPA's Use of Science*, discussion paper 97–06, revised edition (Washington, DC: Resources for the Future, March 1997).

11. Congressional Research Service, *Ethylene Dibromide (EDB)*, IP0280E (Washington, DC: CRS, January 31, 1985), EveryCRSReport.com.

12. Irvin Molotsky, "EPA Plans to Curb Use of Toxaphene, A Pesticide," *New York Times*, October 17, 1982, 25.

13. US General Accounting Office, *Pesticides: EPA's Formidable Task to Assess and Regulate Their Risks*, RCED-86-125 (Washington, DC: GAO, April 18, 1986).

14. Federal Insecticide, Fungicide, and Rodenticide Act Amendments, 7, Pub. L. No. 100-532 (October 25, 1988).

15. Ferguson and Gray, "1988 FIFRA Amendments," 10070.

16. Bradford Sewall and Robin M. Whyatt, *Intolerable Risk: Pesticides in Our Children's Food* (New York: Natural Resources Defense Council, February 27, 1989).

17. Philip Shabecoff, "EPA Won't Ban Use of Chemical on Apples," *New York Times*, January 23, 1986.

18. David Shaw, "Alar Panic Shows Power of Media to Trigger Fear," *Los Angeles Times*, September 12, 1994.

19. US General Accounting Office, *Pesticides: Thirty Years Since Silent Spring-Many Long-standing Concerns Remain*, GAO/T-RCED-92-77 (Washington, DC: GAO, 1992).

20. National Research Council, *Pesticides in the Diets of Infants and Children* (Washington, DC: National Academies Press, 1993).

21. Food Quality Protection Act of 1996, Titles 7 and 21, Pub. L. No. 104-170 (August 1996).

22. US Environmental Protection Agency, "Registration Review Process," *epa.gov,* accessed April 30, 2020, https://www.epa.gov/pesticide-reevaluation/registration-review-process; US Environmental Protection Agency, "Re-registration and Other Review Programs Predating Pesticide Registration Review," accessed April 30, 2020, https://www.epa.gov/pesticide-reevaluation/re-registration-and-other-review-programs-predating-pesticide-registration.

23. League of United Latin American Citizens (LULAC) v. Wheeler, No. 17-1636 (9th Cir. en banc, April 19, 2019).

24. Lisa Friedman, "EPA Won't Ban Chlorpyrifos, Pesticide Tied to Children's Health Problems," *New York Times*, July 18, 2019.

25. Lisa M. Campbell, Timothy D. Backstrom, and James V. Aidala, "Corteva Announces it Will Cease Production of Embattled Insecticide Chlorpyrifos," *National Law Review*, February 14, 2020.

26. David Cox, "The Roundup Row: Is the World's Most Popular Weedkiller Carcinogenic?" *The Guardian*, March 9, 2019.

27. Holly Yan, "The EPA Says Glyphosate, the Main Ingredient in Roundup, Doesn't Cause Cancer. Others Aren't So Sure," *CNN.com,* May 3, 2019, https://www.cnn.com/2019/05/01/health/epa-says-glyphosate-is-safe/index.html.

28. Food and Agriculture Organization of the United Nations and World Health Organization, *Joint FAO/WHO Meeting on Pesticide Residues, Geneva 9-16 May 2016: Summary Report* (May 16, 2016), 2, https://www.who.int/foodsafety/jmprsummary2016.pdf.

29. National Research Council, *Assessing Risks to Endangered and Threatened Species from Pesticides* (Washington, DC: National Academies Press, 2013).

30. Britt E. Erickson, "Neonicotinoid Pesticides Can Stay in the US Market, EPA Says," *Chemical and Engineering News*, February 3, 2020.

31. Anne E. Johnson, Deborah McCullough, and Rufus Isaacs, "Spotted Lanternfly: A Colorful Cause for Concern," *MSU Extension: Invasive Species*, May 7, 2019, https://www.canr.msu.edu/news/spotted-lanternfly-a-colorful-cause-for-concern.

32. US Centers for Disease Control and Prevention, "Zika Virus: Potential Range in the US," *cdc.gov*, accessed April 29, 2020.

33. Cinnamon S. Bloss et al., "Public Response to a Proposed Field Trial of Genetically Engineered Mosquitoes in the United States," *Journal of the American Medical Association* 318, no. 7 (August 15, 2017): 662–64.

34. The next several paragraphs of legislative history are based on a review of congressional hearing transcripts and a telephone interview with former CEQ staff member J. Clarence "Terry" Davies, April 18, 2020.

35. US Council on Environmental Quality, *Toxic Substances*, white paper (Washington, DC: CEQ, April 1971).

36. US Environmental Protection Agency, "Train sees New Toxic Substances Law as 'Preventive Medicine,'" *epa.gov*, October 21, 1976, www.epa.gov/history/topics/tsca/03.htm.

37. Linda-Jo Schierow, *The Toxic Substances Control Act (TSCA): Implementation and New Challenges*, RL 34118 (Washington, DC: CRS, July 28, 2009).

38. Toxic Substances Control Act, 15, Pub. L. No. 94–469 §2601 et seq. (October 1976).

39. David Markell, "An Overview of TSCA, Its History and Key Underlying Assumptions, and Its Place in Environmental Regulation," *Washington University Journal of Law and Policy* 32 (January 2010): 333.

40. Mark A. Greenwood, "TSCA Reform: Building a Program that Can Work," *Environmental Law Review* 39 (January 2009): 10036–37.

41. US General Accounting Office, *Toxic Substances Control Act: Preliminary Observations on Legislative Changes to Make TSCA More Effective,* T-RCED-94-263 (Washington, DC: GAO, July 1994).

42. US General Accounting Office, *Chemical Regulation: Options Exist to Improve EPA's Ability to Assess Health Risks and Manage Its Chemical Review Program*, GAO-05-458 (Washington, DC: GAO, June 2005).

43. Richard A. Denison, *Toxic Ignorance: The Continuing Absence of Basic Health Testing for Top-Selling Chemicals in the United States* (New York: Environmental Defense Fund, 1997).

44. US Environmental Protection Agency, Office of Pollution Prevention and Toxics, *Chemical Hazard Data Availability Study: What Do We Really Know about*

the Safety of High Production Volume Chemicals? (Washington, DC: EPA OPPT, April 1998).

45. Richard A. Denison, *High Hopes, Low Marks: A Final Report Card on the High Volume Chemical Challenge* (New York: Environmental Defense Fund, July 2007).

46. 43 Fed. Reg. 8562 (1979).

47. 45 Fed. Reg. 61966 (1980).

48. 47 Fed. Reg. 23360 (1982).

49. 47 Fed. Reg. 33198 (1982); 47 Fed. Reg. 38780 (1982).

50. United States Congress, House, Subcommittee on Oversight and Investigations, Committee of Energy and Commerce, *EPA's Asbestos Regulations: Report on a Case Study on OMB's Interference in Agency Rulemaking*, 99th Congress, 1st sess., 1985.

51. Warren E. Leary, "Appeals Court Strikes Down Major Parts of Federal Asbestos Ban," *New York Times,* October 22, 1991.

52. US Environmental Protection Agency, Technical Amendment in Response to Court Decision on Asbestos: Manufacture, Importation, Processing and Distribution Prohibitions, 59 Fed. Reg . 33208 (June 28, 1994).

53. US Environmental Protection Agency, "EPA Actions to Protect the Public from Exposure to Asbestos," *epa.gov*, accessed April 8, 2020.

54. Alan Morrison, "OMB Interference with Agency Rulemaking: The Wrong Way to Write a Regulation," *Harvard Law Review* 99 (1986); Harold H. Bruff, "Presidential Management of Rulemaking," *George Washington University Law Review* 57 (1989); Steven T. Kargman, "OMB Intervention in Agency Rulemaking: The Case for Broadened Record Review," *Yale Law Journal* 95, no. 8 (1986).

55. Elena Kagan, "Presidential Administration," *Harvard Law Review* 114, no. 8 (2001).

56. The Emergency Planning & Community Right-To-Know Act (EPCRA), U.S.C. 11011 et seq. (1986).

57. James T. Hamilton, *Regulation Through Revelation: The Origin, Politics, and Impacts of the Toxics Release Inventory Program* (New York: Cambridge University Press, 2005).

58. US Environmental Protection Agency, Addition of Facilities in Certain Industry Sectors; Revised Interpretation of Otherwise Use; Toxic Release Inventory Reporting; Community Right-to-Know; Final Rule, 62 Fed. Reg. 23834 (May 1, 1997); US Environmental Protection Agency, Persistent Bioaccumulative Toxic Chemicals: Lowering of Reporting Thresholds for Certain PBT Chemicals; Addition of Certain PBT Chemicals; Amendments to Proposed Addition of Dioxin and Dioxin-like Compounds Category; Toxic Chemical Release Reporting; Chemical Right-to-Know, 49 C.F.R. Part 372, Final Rule, 64 Fed. Reg. 58666-753 (1999).

59. The Pollution Prevention Act (PPA), 42 U.S.C. §§13101 and 13102 et seq. (1990).

60. US Environmental Protection Agency, *Cleaner Technologies Substitutes Assessment: A Methodology and Resources Guide*, EPA-744-R-95-002 (Washington, DC: EPA, 1996).

61. US General Accounting Office, *Toxic Substances Control Act: Preliminary Observations on Legislative Changes to Make TSCA More Effective*, T-RCED-94-263 (Washington, DC: GAO, July 1994); US General Accounting Office, *Chemical Regulation: Approaches in the United States, Canada, and the European Union*, GAO-06-217R (Washington, DC: GAO, 2005); US General Accounting Office, *Chemical Regulation: Options for Enhancing the Effectiveness of the Toxic Substances Control Act*, GAO-09-428T (Washington, DC: GAO, 2009).

62. Adam D. K. Abelkop and John D. Graham, "Regulation of Chemical Risks: Lessons for Reform of the Toxic Substances Control Act from Canada and the European Union," *Pace Environmental Law Review* 32, no. 1 (2015): 108-224; Adam D. K. Abelkop et al., "Regulating Industrial Chemicals: Lessons for US Lawmakers from the European Union's REACH Program," *Environmental Law Reporter* 42, no. 11 (November 2012): 1042–65.

63. Agnes Botos, John D. Graham, and Zoltan Illes, "Industrial Chemical Regulation in the European Union and the United States: A Comparison of REACH and the Amended TSCA," *Journal of Risk Research* 22, no. 10 (2018): https://doi.org/10.1080/13669877.2018.1454495.

64. US Environmental Protection Agency, Office of Pollution Prevention and Toxics, "Statistics for the New Chemicals Review Program under TSCA," *epa.gov*, accessed October 8, 2020, https://www.epa.gov/reviewing-new-chemicals-under-toxic-substances-control-act-tsca/statistics-new-chemicals-review#stats.

65. US Environmental Protection Agency, Office of Chemical Safety and Pollution Prevention, "EPA Releases First Major Update to Chemicals List in 40 Years," *epa.gov*, 2019.

66. US Environmental Protection Agency, "TSCA Chemical Substance Inventory," *epa.gov*, accessed March 15, 2020.

67. Safer Chemicals, Healthy Families v. EPA, 943 F.3d 397 (9th Cir. 2019).

68. Robbie Barbero et al., "Increasing the Transparency, Coordination, and Predictability of the Biotechnology Regulatory System," *whitehouse.gov*, January 4, 2017.

69. National Academies of Sciences, Engineering, and Medicine, *Preparing for Future Products of Biotechnology* (Washington, DC: National Academies Press, 2017).

70. US Environmental Protection Agency, Regulations Under the Federal Insecticide, Fungicide, and Rodenticide Act for Plant-Incorporated Protectants (Formerly Plant-Pesticides), 66 Fed. Reg. 37771–817 (July 19, 2001).

71. National Research Council, *Genetically Modified Pest-Protected Plants: Science and Regulation* (Washington, DC: National Academies Press, 1990).

72. US Environmental Protection Agency, "Current and Previously Registered Section 3 Plant-Incorporated Protectant (PIP) Registrations," *epa.gov*, October 24, 2018, https://www.epa.gov/ingredients-used-pesticide-products/current-and-previously-registered-section-3-plant-incorporated.

73. US Environmental Protection Agency, Microbial Products of Biotechnology; Final Regulation Under the Toxic Substances Control Act; Final Rule, 62 Fed. Reg. 17909–958 (1997).

74. US Environmental Protection Agency, Microorganisms: General Exemptions from Reporting Requirements; Revisions to Recipient Organisms Eligible for Tier I and Tier II Exemptions, Final Rule, 85 Fed. Reg. 13760 (2020).

75. Stockholm Convention on Persistent Organic Pollutants, May 22, 2001, 2256 U.N.T.S. 119; 40 I.L.M. 532 (2001).

76. Rotterdam Convention on the Prior Informed Consent Procedure for Certain Hazardous Chemicals and Pesticides in International Trade, September 10, 1998, 2244 U.N.T.S. 337.

77. Conference of the Parties to the Rotterdam Convention on the Prior Informed Consent Procedure for Certain Hazardous Chemicals and Pesticides in International Trade, Geneva, Switzerland, April 29–May 10, 2019.

78. US Environmental Protection Agency, "Minamata Convention on Mercury," *epa.gov*, March 11, 2019, https://www.epa.gov/international-cooperation/minamata-convention-mercury.

79. United Nations, *Globally Harmonized System of Classification and Labelling of Chemicals (GHS)*, 2nd ed. (Geneva: UN, 2007), http://www.unece.org/fileadmin/DAM/trans/danger/publi/ghs/ghs_rev02/English/00e_intro.pdf.

Chapter Ten

Environmental Science at EPA: Providing Good Science for Relevant Policy

Terry F. Yosie and Bernard D. Goldstein

After resigning as President Reagan's EPA administrator in March 1983, Anne Gorsuch coauthored a book in which she stated that she had done more for science at EPA than any of her predecessors.[1] Presentation of a slide with this quote to an audience of environmental scientists who had lived through the Gorsuch era could be counted on to elicit a combination of gasps and derisive laughter. Yet it is hard to imagine the memoir of any former EPA administrator saying that she or he had intentionally distorted science to achieve their policy goals or did not base EPA regulations on the best available science. Our point is that the extent to which science and technology provide a credible foundation for EPA's policies cannot be judged on the basis of what is said, but of what is done.

INTRODUCTION

Since its inception in 1970, EPA has depended upon scientific information to establish regulatory standards, policies, and guidance. This has been the fundamental role of environmental science throughout EPA's history, even while different administrations have demonstrated varying degrees of commitment to investing in scientific research and maintaining core skill competencies necessary for evidence-based decisions. During the past fifty years, science at EPA (more so than other science agencies) has experienced competing and contradictory expectations and demands from regulatory officials, political appointees, politicians, and the general public. Of fundamental importance is recognition that, no matter how well science may be conducted and presented, EPA's decisions are ultimately based upon legal and broader political and societal considerations and judgments that are informed by science but not determined by it. How EPA's scientists and policy-makers reconciled, or failed to reconcile, these diverse factors is an important part of the agency's history.

The availability of scientific and technical data has varied greatly in quality and amount depending on the nature of the health or environmental problem(s) under review. Over time, EPA has made ongoing investments in research germane to its mission and has continued to upgrade its processes to ensure a higher quality of scientific data available to policy-makers (most of whom are politically appointed non-scientists and exhibit varying levels of scientific understanding). These upgrades included data quality guidelines and Good Laboratory Practices, competitive extramural research funding (conducted by non-EPA research scientists), and expanded internal and external peer reviews.

For reasons discussed below, the authors conclude that maintaining a distinct scientific organization within EPA has considerable merit. This requires maintaining core nonpolitical, professional staff competencies across a range of scientific issues, committing to publication of research results in independent, high reputation scientific publications, and preserving independent external advisory processes to attain credible scientific excellence in both research planning and results.

Of particular importance in considering EPA's organizational structure is that it is both a generator of scientific information as well as a consumer of data to develop enforceable regulatory policies and standards. This duality of data creation vs. policy relevance is not directly confronted by the major governmental organizations tasked with generating science, such as the National Institutes of Health (NIH) and the National Science Foundation (NSF).

EPA has struggled to manage important challenges, including obtaining sufficient research funds; maintaining core scientific skills; resolving conflicts over research priorities; sustaining funding on specific health or environmental problems over time; understanding the emergence of new technologies or commercial products with insufficient assessments of their potential risks until contamination has occurred; presenting scientific uncertainties and accompanying analyses of risk to policy-makers and more general stakeholders; defining the role of the precautionary principle in policy-making; and addressing changing societal expectations for greater transparency that challenge the legitimacy of evidence-based decisions. These challenges have resulted, in part, from legal, political, cultural, and technological changes in society concerning research methods and the degrees of freedom policy-makers should possess in making judgments about scientific data and its application to decision-making.

This chapter adopts an analytical framework for evaluating the implementation of EPA's scientific mission based upon three sets of issues: 1) assessing specific dynamics within EPA and the scientific community that identifies research needs and generates scientific information, 2) defining specific scientific debates and drivers that had a material and long-term impact on EPA decision-making, and 3) evaluating the scientific input and its relevance and value to EPA's decision-making processes. The chapter specifically addresses structural and cultural tensions inherent in planning environmental science at EPA. It examines the applications of science in nine policy debates and decisions, identifying both successes and limitations (recognizing that the Office of Research and Development, EPA's central research planning and management unit, is not the exclusive source of scientific data for policy-making). The chapter concludes with an assessment of ongoing and future scientific and organizational challenges.

Overall, this evaluation of how EPA generates and applies environmental science concludes that decision-making stemming from evidence-based approaches has greatly contributed to the improvement of the nation's air, land, and water quality. Such progress has often been contentious within the scientific community as debates evolved over data quality and methods and standards of evidence to be used in regulatory policy-making. In the political arena, competing interest groups increasingly invoke scientific and pseudoscientific arguments as they vie for influence over specific EPA policy decisions. In recent years, the American public has become more skeptical of the scientific community as various forms of "denialism" are organized to oppose treatment of public water supplies, and climate change mitigation and adaptation, and other issues. While EPA has not always consistently applied consensus-based scientific processes in its decision-making, environmental science is a critical component for implementing current programs and in safeguarding future public health and the environment.

EMERGENCE OF EPA'S SCIENCE AND TECHNOLOGY LABORATORIES

The consolidation of federal organizations in 1970 resulted in EPA inheriting eighty-four sites—half of which were laboratories. Congress provided $35 million for EPA to build an environmental research center in Cincinnati, while EPA developed its plans for laboratory facilities. The eventual result was three different types of laboratories:

1. Those that report to each of the ten EPA regions and primarily focus on environmental monitoring, including the development of unique analytical processes that are available nationally. Their analytical expertise is often

focused on challenges posed by regional environmental conditions, such as the deserts of the Southwest.

2. Those that report to program offices and specifically focus on programmatic needs. An example is the National Vehicle and Fuel Emissions Laboratory of the EPA's Office of Air and Radiation. This laboratory not only provides automotive emission testing services required for certifying vehicles but is also involved in developing new technologies.
3. Those that report to the Office of Research and Development and perform research related to EPA's needs, which we describe in more detail below. Over time, ORD has had a variable coordinating and oversight function for regional and program office laboratories.

ORGANIZATION OF THE OFFICE OF RESEARCH AND DEVELOPMENT

Until the recent closure of the Las Vegas laboratory, EPA had fourteen separate active research laboratories in twelve locations for more than forty years. These laboratories, and a handful of research stations, originally were organized under functional groupings of health, ecosystem, monitoring, and engineering, with corresponding headquarters components responsible for management of the laboratories and synthesis of information. Geographical concentration of those laboratories performing air pollution research in Raleigh, NC, and water pollution research in Cincinnati, OH, at first kept some degree of focus on environmental media consistent with program office orientation.

In the mid-1990s, under Assistant Administrator Robert Huggett, ORD reorganized in keeping with the risk paradigm and developed new external research and fellowship programs.[2] In addition, each national research laboratory was directed to establish an associate director for ecology position. Subsequently, national program directors were established in assigned areas of emphasis, such as water, to assess research needs based on evaluations within, and external to EPA to present to ORD management for priority-setting guidance and decisions. This organizational structure has become more complex by the addition of new function-focused entities. National research programs have been formed to focus on specific crosscutting areas and direct planning and funding oversight in such areas as Air, Climate and Energy, Human Health Risk Assessment, and Sustainable and Healthy Communities. These are grouped together under the direction of a deputy assistant administrator for science. This individual is also responsible for the Office of Science Policy, which is aimed at insuring that ORD's scientific activities are responsive to the needs of the program offices and regions, as well as external stakeholders, including involvement in ORD's environmental justice, tribal, and international activities.

Another change was the establishment of the position of science advisor, based upon a 1992 recommendation by the National Academy of Science to "ensure that EPA policy decisions are informed by a clear understanding of relevant science."[3] The NAS committee envisioned the role to be similar to that of a general counsel reporting to the EPA administrator. Since being formally instituted, the position's responsibilities, organizational status, and reporting relationships have changed with each administrator who may or may not appoint someone for the position. Generally, the science advisor function has been carried out by the same person occupying the role of assistant administrator for research and development. In the name of streamlining, the current Administrator Andrew Wheeler has moved to abolish the position.

DOES EPA NEED A SCIENCE AND TECHNOLOGY COMPONENT?

Despite EPA's policy-making being so highly dependent upon science and technology, there is no inherent requirement for it to have an in-house research and technology development component. By comparison, for the Occupational Safety and Health Administration (OSHA), research and technical support is provided by the National Institute for Occupational Safety and Health (NIOSH), which is part of the Department of Health and Human Services (HHS). Having different congressional and executive oversight and budgetary review processes, OSHA and NIOSH often pursue different objectives that are in separate administrative orbits.

Placing science and technology in a separate agency has disadvantages. Regulatory agency leadership has far less say about the direction of research in relation to their programmatic and regulatory needs; the leadership of the separate science agency has fewer vantage points to prevent policy directions veering from the foundation of defensible science; and there is less opportunity for both formal and informal communication that is such an important part of intra-agency planning. However, it has the advantage of having its science less susceptible to arm-twisting aimed at influencing or challenging scientific findings to conform to policy goals. The attempts at persuasion can be conducted directly or indirectly by agency policy leaders who have significant influence over the leadership, budget, promotion, research priorities, or new facilities of the research organization.

The proximity to regulatory office policy-makers requires EPA's scientists to carefully adopt and maintain those processes that lead to scientific consensus in a democratic society—in particular, unbiased external scientific review. Recognition of this need for external scientific review has led to congressional actions such as the formation of the Clean Air Scientific Advisory Committee and of the Science Advisory Board in 1977 and 1978, respectively.

One can consider the different placement of science at EPA and at OSHA, both formed in 1970, to be an experiment in structuring regulatory agency science management. Based on the results obtained over the past fifty years, there can be little doubt that EPA has had greater success than OSHA in developing science-based regulations.

Unfortunately, EPA has experienced episodes of inappropriate distortion or avoidance of scientific consensus, such as with global climate change. The Trump administration annually proposes EPA budgets for congressional approval (not adopted to date) that significantly disinvest in environmental research and other programs. Using its own administrative authorities, the administration's political appointees continue to convert EPA's science from well accepted, consensus-based approaches to imposition of confrontational political and legal frameworks. These frameworks have emerged outside of the independent, mainstream scientific community and lack scientific credibility.

EPA's researchers also receive a number of staff- and budget-intensive assignments that are unplanned. These include responses to congressional concerns about asbestos in schools; Persian Gulf oil fires during operation Desert Storm; Exxon Valdez ecological assessments and cleanup responsibilities; Hurricane Katrina and Harvey emergency response actions; Deep Water Horizon testing of dispersants and air and water quality monitoring; lead contamination in the Flint, Michigan, water supply; PFAS water measurements; and numerous other examples. Rarely are special appropriations provided for these activities.

The US government has numerous science and technology agencies with no direct regulatory authority and with separate budgets. These include NIH and NSF, which themselves have components that focus on developing science related to the environment, such as the National Institute for Environmental Health Sciences (NIEHS). NIEHS also has the lead role in the National Toxicology Program, whose membership includes FDA, EPA, and NIOSH, among others. NIEHS and NSF also are more able to fund studies in areas that EPA's leadership or its congressional oversight committees might otherwise wish to avoid—recent examples being global climate change and the health and social implications of unconventional shale gas development. But neither NIH nor NSF has ORD's obligation to provide scientific and technical information and advice on the broad range of EPA's science-based regulatory activities. This need to respond to the breadth of activities covered by EPA's mandates itself justifies the existence of an in-house scientific organization (principally through ORD).

TENSIONS INHERENT IN INCLUDING A SCIENCE AND TECHNOLOGY ORGANIZATION WITHIN A REGULATORY AGENCY

The tensions described below are among those inherent in the structure of a regulatory agency that contains a science and technology component. They are all manageable in ways that will differ depending upon the agency's mission and by the relative influence of external interests. All require thoughtful oversight.

Basic vs. Applied Research: Shorter vs. Longer Term Needs

EPA's scientific and technical needs and activities are aimed primarily toward the applied end of the continuum between basic and applied science. Many of EPA's research scientists would prefer to answer more basic longer-term questions, while most regulatory program offices are too besieged by short-term statutory and court deadlines to generally consider longer term needs. The focus of ORD's scientific and technical staffs should be on recognizable mission-oriented activities. However, there are reasons that ORD's portfolio also should include selective, future-oriented risks, including the importance of identifying potential health and environmental risks related to innovative technologies and problems of emerging importance. Examples are, respectively, ORD's activities to understand the potential risks of nanotechnology (per congressional directive, EPA's nanotechnology research was restricted to ecological impacts), and early efforts beginning in the Carter administration to address the consequences of what then was called global warming. Anticipation of future regulatory needs often includes developing laboratories or otherwise attracting staff with expertise in newer techniques who will be essential to future regulatory activities, such as the recruitment of molecular biologists necessary for understanding the potential risks of genetic engineering. These molecular biologists have also contributed toward the development of new toxicological screening techniques.

Budgetary considerations have at times led EPA to prematurely terminate hard to replace research capabilities. Examples include the early 1980s decision to eliminate a laboratory group studying non-ionizing radiation based upon the simplistic assumption that a single NAS review downplaying the potential adverse effects of electric transmission towers would end this issue, and the failure to spend the final ten percent of a multi-million dollar study which precluded analysis of a study of the effects of shale oils in laboratory animals.

Longer-term research and technology success also depends upon attracting bright young scientists and engineers which justifies EPA's support of fellowship programs—particularly those that lead to the research fellows spending time at EPA. While the ability to recruit and retain young talent is a major challenge for scientific organizations—public, private, and non-profit—around the world, it is especially acute at EPA as the Trump administration's proposed budget reductions and opposition to independent environmental science have particularly impacted EPA's ability to maintain or replenish core scientific skills. Leadership is also needed at the top. Perhaps coincidentally, the two administrations perceived to be the most antagonistic towards independent science, that of Ronald Reagan (until he replaced Anne Gorsuch with William Ruckelshaus) and Donald J. Trump, have been the only two administrations that have not designated a nominee for AA/ORD. As of this writing, more than three years into his term, there is no indication of whom President Trump might nominate as assistant administrator for research and development.

Setting the Research Agenda

Setting the research agenda in a regulatory agency is a process that is driven by policy and legal objectives, as well as scientific feasibility and content. To the policy-maker wrestling with decision deadlines, research activities are expected to align with regulatory priorities. ORD's leaders know that their Office of Management and Budget examiners and congressional oversight and budget committees appropriately will be asking EPA's regulatory program offices about the responsiveness of ORD to EPA's regulatory priorities. Yet scientific feasibility should also be an important part of priority setting. In specific instances, EPA might be better served by devoting ORD resources to a lower-ranked priority, if such research would be much more likely to narrow uncertainties bedeviling the decision process, while new science was unlikely to help resolve a higher-ranked priority. Timeliness is also crucial. Decisions about what research to pursue depend upon how quickly answers are likely to be obtained in relation to a decision deadline mandated by Congress or by the judiciary. Accordingly, setting EPA's research agenda fosters continued communication between the program offices and ORD, with particular attention to nuances of the very different languages and planning needs of regulators and scientists. Over time, this development often has reduced the discretion of research program managers over budgeting and research prioritization and provided more influence to regulatory program offices.

Additional considerations also inhibit EPA's ability to determine the success of its efforts. Perhaps the most direct way to find out if a pollutant has an adverse effect in humans is to change exposure levels in a defined population, while following the health or environmental endpoints of concern. Changing exposure levels occur as a result of regulation. But, not surprisingly, the regulator wants ORD to focus on getting information for its next challenge, rather than studying whether the previous regulation made a difference. That is why congressional provisions that force reevaluation of standards, such as the Clean Air Act's NAAQS provisions, are highly effective in spurring policy-relevant research.

The relation of the extent of scientific certainty to setting the research agenda comes with the recognition that the time-consuming nature of performing and reviewing science can be used by politically appointed policymakers to avoid acting, allegedly awaiting more definitive evidence. Examples include yet another study to determine whether global climate change is real, whether lead affects the nervous system of children, or whether benzene causes human leukemia.

ORD also has the responsibility to consider research needs that transcend the agency's various program offices. An example from 1984 concerns the ranking of better screening tools for the early detection of reproductive and developmental toxins. Each program office thought this important, but not of sufficient importance to be funded above their lowest ranking media-specific priority. Success in obtaining funding for this research from the EPA leadership was a recognition of ORD's crosscutting role in an agency that has long battled against its silos.

Further, while the research agenda favored by the academic scientific culture is one that tends to reward publishable outcomes showing effects, for EPA's regulatory offices, a legitimate research agenda topic may be based on responding to public concern even though scientists believe an adverse effect is highly unlikely. Maintaining public confidence in EPA as an institution is a pragmatic objective that transcends individual research planning debates.

The Role of EPA's Extramural Research

The breadth of science and technology needed to support EPA's mission has made ORD's funding of an extramural program particularly attractive to extending EPA's credibility and scientific responsiveness. The funding processes used, and the extent of budgetary support offered, has varied widely through the years. Earlier in EPA's history, the choice of extramural projects and the scientists to conduct them was characterized by an informality and insularity which led to establishment of more structured processes and organizational components. In 1995 EPA formed the Science to Achieve Results (STAR) program which has supported funding on topics of specific interest to EPA through competitive awards as individual grants or as centers based upon requests for applications. The STAR program was initially funded at $100 million but had dwindled to approximately $55 million by 2018.

The STAR program was endorsed by a 2003 National Research Council review. A thorough reevaluation by NRC in 2017 found that EPA had developed high-quality procedures for priority-setting which help integrate STAR within EPA's research programs. Overall, it was judged a productive program with an impressive number of publications and high level of use of the research output by EPA and related organizations. The NRC Committee also noted research that potentially led to reductions in compliance costs to industry and state and local governments. Criticisms included problems associated with EPA's management of the database of research outputs and uses, and the need for improved communication about program outputs. The NRC reviewers also found the EPA fellowship program to be valuable. They expressed concern about its merger into the overall NSF fellowship program, a concern that is justified.[4]

Three issues are central to considering the value of EPA's extramural program. Foremost is EPA's need to attract high quality external researchers rather than those who are unsuccessful in competing for research funding from agencies such as NIEHS or NSF. Rigorous peer review is central to establishing EPA's extramural funding as having sufficient cachet to be recognized by the academic peer structure for which obtaining grants is often an essential component of academic success. Secondly, the need for high standards has budgetary implications in terms of the relatively fixed overhead to run the extramural program. If the external funding levels are relatively low, then the percentage of the budget that must go to administering the program becomes sufficiently high as to raise questions about its efficacy. Thirdly, ORD needs to manage the goal of obtaining research relevant to EPA's mission without stifling the creativity and innovation of the leading scientists that EPA hopes to attract while also serving the public interest.

Consensus vs. Confrontation

EPA uses science both to develop regulatory standards and to defend its decisions against eventual lawsuits from industry and environmental non-governmental organizations—often both. The processes of incorporating science into these two applications are very different. The standard approach for science is consensus; for legal processes, it is confrontation. Expert committees charged with analyzing and synthesizing scientific information as a basis for decision processes are routinely formed by numerous national and international organizations. They are structured to obtain a consensus scientific position by processes which include selection of expert members appropriately balanced by disciplines and previous opinions; avoidance of conflicts of interest; careful statement of the committee's task; selection of unbiased committee staff; and standardized approaches toward selecting literature to be considered and for the review and reporting of committee findings.

In contrast, US legal processes involving scientific issues primarily involve confrontation in which the lawyers of both sides choose scientists who are at opposite ends of the spectrum of scientific opinions. Ethical well-trained lawyers are expected to advance only those arguments that are best for their client(s), and to work hard to dismantle the arguments of the opposing lawyer. Inherent in this legal approach is both the selection of those scientists who are most likely to credibly support their client and the discrediting of the scientists chosen by the opposing side. Fairness is aimed for through processes focused on achieving impartiality, including rules about admissible evidence and the selection and actions of the judge and jury. In the case of EPA, the decision-maker who receives the advisory committee report is usually the EPA administrator who has been chosen through a political process.

Legal confrontation related to complex scientific issues, such as often occurs in toxic tort cases, utilizes a strategy known as corpuscularization.[5] In contrast to weight of evidence approaches, in which relevant studies are given consideration, corpuscularization consists of considering any lack of perfection in any study advanced by the other side as grounds for completely discarding the study rather than attempting to place the findings, with proper attention to their limitations, in a coherent whole. As described in more detail below, the inherent inability of epidemiological studies involving environmental exposures to conform to the gold standard of a double-blind randomized control trial, as required by FDA for a new pharmaceutical agent, results in each individual environmental study having some potential for confounding data and thus susceptible of being totally discarded in a legal process. Further, discarding science inconvenient to policy goals can be seen in the Trump EPA's attempt to misuse transparency as a way to throw out any study for which the raw data are not available to be exhaustively reanalyzed by industry consultants, as has occurred with formaldehyde. This concern is exacerbated by the fact that misuse of transparency requirements can also jeopardize the personal privacy of study participants and, consequently, violate ethics practices for scientific research.

Through the years, controversies engendered from EPA's science-based decisions have led to attacks on, and deliberative reconsideration of, the processes by which science is analyzed and synthesized by EPA. These include whether science not subjected to peer review is acceptable, how the information is to be organized and presented to the public, how members of external scientific advisory committees are chosen, and whether scientific advisory processes should work under the same rules as regulatory decision-making (such as the requirement for response to each written comment).[6] These deliberations have occurred over a relatively prolonged period and through iterative procedures, allowing input by the scientific community and by stakeholders. All have in common identification of potential problems and consideration of alternatives for problem correction. In contrast, under the Trump administration, the disruption in these processes is unprecedented, with major changes occurring by fiat rather than by due deliberation involving stakeholders, including EPA's Science Advisory Board (SAB).

Misuse of the SAB is particularly evident in Administrator Wheeler's ongoing approach to institute the transparency rule. In seeming violation of its congressional charter to be involved in major EPA science-based comments, the SAB was not consulted before sending out the proposed rule for public comment. Mr. Wheeler subsequently asked the SAB to meet by phone to address the limited question of how to maintain the confidentiality of personal identification information and business information once the raw data are turned over to EPA. In essence, this question limits SAB's role to that of a lab technician who enables the function of a specialized piece of laboratory equipment but has no say in whether it is the right piece of equipment to answer the question, or how the measurements should be interpreted. Compounding the issue is that the SAB, much to its surprise, was not asked at its August 27, 2019 meeting for a consensus report on how best to maintain confidentiality. Rather, each member was asked to write their individual comments at the end of the meeting so that EPA could choose among them. As EPA leadership has had the opportunity to alter the membership selection process, for which it has been chided by a Government Accountability Office (GAO) report,[7] it will have the opportunity to choose among the comments of SAB members who are likely to be friendly to its political goals.

In general, the recent changes can be interpreted as moving from consensus to confrontation, thereby enhancing the likelihood that the EPA administrator will be given a scientific opinion that is biased to support preconceived policy views, rather than providing the collective judgment of EPA's scientific professionals and of the independent scientific community. For example, former

Administrator Pruitt's policy (embraced by his successor Andrew Wheeler) disqualified external scientists from service on the SAB or other science advisory committees if they received EPA research funding, using the rationale that such a circumstances constituted a conflict of interest. Such a policy ignored the fact that EPA's then existing conflict of interest procedures were robust and vigorously applied and represented good scientific practice. The exclusion of EPA-funded external scientists significantly altered the available pool of credible, independent scientists from SAB service. Less qualified scientists, many with direct financial relationships to industries subject to EPA regulation, took their place, but were declared by EPA to be conflict-free.

Analyzing the Weight of Evidence as a Means of Providing Input into the Regulatory Decision Process

The concept of weight of evidence refers to the relative amount and kind of information that supports or undermines a scientific hypothesis or policy proposal. Because it depends upon data derived from different studies that utilize a variety of methodologies, weight of evidence is necessarily judgmental in nature and is expressed in both qualitative and quantitative terms. Evaluating uncertainty is inherent in any weight of evidence determination.

Weight of evidence issues pervade many EPA science-based decisions and are particularly controversial for putative carcinogens. Central to understanding the management of this issue is to recognize the following principles, using carcinogenicity as an example:

1. some, but far from all, chemicals are capable of causing human cancer;
2. epidemiological evidence that a chemical can cause human cancer in essence represents a failure of EPA regulatory approaches which are primarily based on using toxicological evidence derived from in vitro or animal studies to prevent development or release of the chemical—a policy of waiting to regulate until humans develop cancer is not ethically or socially acceptable;
3. evidence related to chemical carcinogenicity comes from multiple sources and disciplines, including in vitro mutagenesis studies, two-year high dose animal exposures, and chemical structure activity relationships and epidemiology;
4. evidence that individual chemicals or chemical mixtures can cause human cancer falls on a continuum that ranges from minuscule to compelling;
5. approaches that classify chemicals into groups based on their likelihood of causing cancer (e.g., possible, probable, or known categories of carcinogens; or groups 1, 2a, b, 3, 4) are helpful for regulatory purposes, but

inherently require establishing lines which demarcate risk categories along the continuum of evidence;

6. for those chemicals that the evidence places close to these demarcation lines, small differences of opinion among knowledgeable scientists in interpreting the literature can move the chemical across the two classifications. Accordingly, these small differences, particularly if they have significant impacts on specific industries, can be highly controversial;
7. as there is no way to completely avoid having chemicals that are at or near these dividing lines, there will always be controversy about the results of weight of evidence deliberations on carcinogenicity for at least certain chemicals; and
8. ORD and similar agencies should focus their research agendas on those chemicals that are at or near the dividing line in the expectation that additional information will move the chemical up or down the continuum so as to more clearly delineate the proper classification.

Mismatch between the Desire of Scientists for Precision and the Needs of Risk Managers

The first step in any quality control process is to determine the data quality objective. The DQO for measuring environmental pollutants should be set by the risk manager based on the intended use of the data. By themselves, scientists responsible for developing analytical tools for measuring pollutants often will attempt to obtain the greatest precision and accuracy that is technically feasible rather than the level of precision required for regulatory purposes. Similarly, providing detailed uncertainty analysis for risk estimates is frequently requested by NAS committees without evidence that such information makes a difference in the decision process. A radar gun in the hands of a state trooper does not need to reproducibly measure the miles per hour of a speeding car to two decimal places in order to decide if a car has exceeded the limit.

TENSIONS INHERENT TO ENVIRONMENTAL SCIENCES

A number of issues are specifically germane to the environmental health sciences and affect EPA's decisions and stakeholders' interpretation of those decisions. They include:

1. Challenges to the ability to perform fully controlled scientific studies on humans in a polluted community

The gold standard for epidemiological research is the drug or medical device study required for FDA approval. In such studies human volunteers suffering from a disease for which a new pharmaceutical agent may provide relief are randomly assigned to the drug or a placebo. The assignment is not known to either the volunteer or the treating physician until the results are analyzed at the end of the study.

EPA cannot ethically support such classic double-blind randomized control studies of the effects of pollutants on susceptible populations. Imagine the public opinion fallout from asking a population to be randomly exposed to a pollutant. Instead, environmental health research usually depends upon taking advantage of "natural" experiments in which differences in pollutant levels reflect local conditions that differ geographically or temporally. Unidentified confounders are far more likely to interfere with the accuracy of the findings for such studies than in a randomized double-blind trial. Other differences are that, in a classic gold standard pharmaceutical study, the number of study participants is chosen to conform to the needed power of the study to detect a predetermined effect, and the extent of exposure to the new pharmaceutical is determined by the investigator. In contrast, the population size of an environmental health study is often determined by proximity to a source, such as release of a chemical from a smokestack or from an overturned railroad tanker car, and the extent of individual exposure is often far less certain. Accordingly, replication of the findings in environmental studies is necessary—preferably by different investigators in different locations, using different methodologies such that the only commonality is exposure to the agent of concern. Controlled human exposures to toxic agents can occur in the laboratory setting, but are usually limited to healthy subjects rather than the sensitive populations of concern to the regulator (although EPA does perform limited, controlled exposure studies for some risk groups such as asthmatics and elderly healthy individuals). While more controlled assessment of ecosystems is possible in greenhouses, field research is often confounded by uncontrolled vagaries such as the weather.

2. The need to estimate effects that challenge the possibility of scientific validation.

The public demand for protection against relatively low levels of risk has led to EPA regulations that require the estimation of risks at the range of 1 in 100,000 or 1 in 1 million lifetime-risk-levels that are usually far too low to be the subject of epidemiological studies. The issue is further complicated by the fact that, with the rare exception of asbestos causation of mesothelioma, the environmental agent being regulated is not the sole cause of the endpoint of concern. For example, benzene is not the sole cause of leukemia. However, the risk of benzene-induced leukemia can be estimated using scientific methods that are central to the field of risk analysis, including understanding the mechanisms of carcinogenesis and the toxicology of benzene. As a result, there is no exact replication of an epidemiological study, even though biostatistical associations across epidemiological investigations can be meaningful and further strengthened when integrated with results from controlled human and animal studies. In summary, and where possible, environmental science research must integrate several sets of inquiry across animal toxicology, human clinical, and epidemiological fields of study.

3. Ethical issues related to community-based research

Alleged ethical transgressions have led to EPA or congressionally imposed limitations in the ability to perform community-based studies, particularly related to environmental justice issues. Two examples are: the Baltimore Lead Paint Study,[8] a Johns Hopkins University evaluation of the relative effectiveness on reducing children's blood lead levels of various lead-reducing techniques in inner city housing with existing lead paint; and the Children's Environmental Exposure Research (CHEER) study, which assessed exposure and effects of ongoing household use of pesticides on children. The Baltimore study witnessed a successful class action lawsuit against Johns Hopkins and the university researchers involved in the research. The CHEER study, which was condemned by Senator Barbara Boxer as "appalling, unethical and immoral," resulted in congressional action limiting EPA's research activities.

Both of these cases raise significant challenges for research scientists, including how to design and communicate the results of specific studies, especially when research issues overlap with societal concerns over inequality, access to health care, and the well-being of minority populations. In an age of growing transparency and use of social media, scientists are also more vulnerable to charges of unethical behavior from politicians and activist groups more broadly. The outcome of these and similar studies is that environmental health scientists now shy away from research aimed at determining the extent of individual exposures or effects due to community or household environmental conditions that are otherwise legal. This challenge should also motivate EPA and academic scientists to innovate methodologies to obtain necessary data to support future public health decision-making.

DEBATES AND DECISIONS SHAPING THE EPA'S USE OF SCIENTIFIC INFORMATION

Throughout its history, EPA has conducted research and prepared scientific assessments of varying degrees of sophistication and robustness. Such research and assessments reflected the institutional capacities and skill sets within EPA at different times and the existing state of knowledge of the scientific community at large. These factors have proven to be highly consequential in shaping and supporting individual policy decisions. An examination of critical scientific debates and decisions across the EPA's history yields insights into several important issues, including: the role of scientific quality and peer review in regulatory decision making; how new information is evaluated for its relevance to regulatory policy-making; emergence of newer scientific methods and tools; and the evolution of new policies and procedures governing the administration and evaluation of scientific data. Over time, these and other factors have become very important in guiding public perceptions of the credibility and legitimacy of EPA's decisions.

There are abundant examples of specific science policy debates and decisions; this chapter will focus upon nine select, yet especially impactful, cases over the course of several decades. These are not case studies but, rather, representative syntheses that illustrate longer-term impacts on the decision-making processes of EPA as an institution. They include, in approximate chronological order:

1. The Community Health and Environmental Surveillance System (CHESS) Studies

CHESS emerged as a coherent multi-city epidemiological research program in 1970 and was designed to monitor the health status of populations in relation to varying environmental conditions. Consistent with the sense of national urgency to reduce air pollution levels at that time, CHESS studies were designed, implemented, and reported with great haste. Within five years, eighty-three separate data sets were compiled. Shortcuts included absence of a pilot phase to identify complications in planning inter-related sets of pollution studies; postponement of quality assurance of CHESS data; underestimation of the size and complexity of the CHESS program; failure to provide sufficient staff resources and funding; and insufficient internal and external peer review.[9]

Individual CHESS reports were assembled into a CHESS Monograph that addressed sulfur oxides, nitrogen oxides, and other pollutants. As this information also supported a process to update individual National Ambient Air Quality Standards (NAAQS), it generated substantial external comments and controversy across the scientific community, affected interest groups and other stakeholders. The result was a series of high-profile reevaluations within EPA and a major investigation led by the House Committee on Science and Technology and its chair, Congressman George Brown (the *Brown Report*).[10]

Several major, longer-term consequences emerged from the CHESS studies controversy. EPA has never again implemented an epidemiological program comparable in scope and magnitude to CHESS. Suspicions continued to linger for many years among industry groups (as reflected in testimony before the Clean Air Scientific Advisory Committee during its review of air quality criteria documents for NOx, SOx, and Particulate Matter) that individual CHESS data sets were being used to support future ambient air quality standards development. Following the *Brown Report*, the US Congress enacted the 1978 Environmental Research and Development Demonstration Authorization Act (ERDDAA) that established new requirements for research planning and management, and statutorily created the Science Advisory Board with expanded independent peer review authority over research and its application to the standard-setting process.

2. 1979 NAAQS Ozone Revision

EPA is required by the 1970 Clean Air Act and subsequent amendments to review NAAQSs every five years to account for changing scientific information. The vehicle for conducting this scientific reassessment is preparation of an air quality criteria document, followed by public comment and review by the Science Advisory Board. Significant public controversy emerged in the revision of the ozone NAAQS due to several converging factors: A committee of the Science Advisory Board publicly reviewed two drafts of the ozone criteria document, but there was no consensus "closure" statement from the committee that documented its final advice to EPA; reports emerged that economic advisors to President Jimmy Carter persuaded the EPA Administrator Douglas Costle to relax the final primary, or health-based, ozone standard from the original 0.08 parts per million (ppm) for one hour to a proposed level of a one-hour 0.10 parts ppm to a final promulgated standard of a one-hour 0.12 ppm on January 26, 1979.

The messiness of the process, the scientific controversy over the appropriate level for the ozone NAAQS, and EPA's decision not to submit the actual standard for the Science Advisory Board's review (despite language in ERDDAA authorizing the SAB to provide such input) prompted the American Petroleum Institute, the City of Houston, and other petitioners to sue EPA. In its October 1981 term, the US Supreme Court upheld EPA's ozone decision and, while acknowledging that EPA made procedural errors in not submitting the final standard for SAB review, did not conclude that such errors materially impacted the outcome of the final standard.[11]

In parallel to this litigation, and in recognition of the fact that updates of other NAAQS were in progress, EPA and the SAB jointly and publicly discussed and subsequently adopted revisions that reshaped the standard-setting process for the next four decades. These revisions included: more specific delineation of the roles and responsibilities for preparation and review of air quality criteria and other documents in NAAQS development; formalization of the role of the Clean Air Scientific Advisory Committee (CASAC), established by the 1977 Clean Air Act Amendments, to implement the SAB's statutory role for independently reviewing the scientific basis of NAAQS; and adoption of a formal "closure" memo process that summarizes CASAC's scientific findings and recommendations prior to an EPA's administrator's decision to promulgate a final standard(s). CASAC was also authorized to comment on any proposed NAAQS criteria or standard and, following the 1979 ozone decision, it has offered its scientific advice on proposed ranges for a NAAQS as developed by the air pollution regulatory staff.[12]

3. The Form of the NAAQS Standards

The numerical level of a NAAQS standard receives much attention, not only because of its importance for compliance, but because it is a readily understandable measuring stick of whether the standard has been relaxed or made more stringent. Another important component of the standard is its form which includes averaging time, how and where it is measured, and the frequency with which a measured level must be above the standard before the locality is judged to be in exceedance. EPA's scientific assessments and its scientists have prioritized this issue and made frequent changes in the form of NAAQS standards. The science leading to changes in the forms of the standards for ozone is described below.

The form of the ozone standard has been changed in different ways. It was originally a photochemical oxidants standard based on measuring the oxidizing potential of the air. This was mostly due to ozone, but also included other potentially harmful oxidizing agents, e.g., peroxyacylnitrates (PAN). The advent of a versatile and robust monitor that was specific to ozone led to the change in the standard from photochemical oxidants to ozone. Also noteworthy is that the subsequent significant decline in studying the effects of non-ozone airborne oxidants illustrates how changing the regulatory standards alters research priorities.

In 1997 the ozone standard averaging time was changed from one hour to eight hours. This reflected better understanding of ozone toxicity, a broader ozone monitoring network facilitated by the new ozone measurement technique, and changing cultural patterns leading to urban sprawl and increased automobile use. Moreover, it was increasingly recognized that children were at particular risk to ozone. As children were likely to be outdoors playing much of the warm summer days that atmospherically led to high ozone levels, and their play led to higher respiratory rates thereby increasing ozone uptake, the one-hour standard was no longer appropriate.[13] This understanding of changing population exposure profiles provided an important trigger for additional health studies to address specific health effects.

There has also been a change in the definition of how many measurements above the standard are permissible before regulatory action begins. For ozone, the goal is to avoid having unusual atmospheric conditions trigger regulatory action. Changes in the number of allowable exceedances result in more or less stringency without changing the apparent specific numerical level of the standard.

4. Formalization of the Science Advisory Board's role in research planning and peer review of the scientific basis of EPA policy decisions

Both CHESS and the Ozone NAAQS exposed major fault lines in EPA's processes for research planning and assessment in support of policy-making and led to major institutional changes governing the conduct of external peer review. While EPA had established the Science Advisory Board in January 1974 as a staff office within the Office of Research and Development, the passage of ERDDAA 1978 transferred the SAB to the Office of the Administrator and provided for the board to report directly to the administrator and relevant congressional oversight committees.

In addition to the SAB's role in reviewing air quality criteria, subsequent controversies over the interpretation of scientific assessments for multi-media cancer risk assessments for perchloroethylene, trichloroethylene, methylene chloride, acrylonitrile, PCBs, dioxins, and other compounds—and, specifically, major disagreements between EPA's Cancer Assessment Group and the Science Advisory Board—intensified momentum to institute more formal peer review procedures across the agency and expand the number of such reviews.

These efforts culminated in a memorandum circulated by the administrator to all senior EPA officials on February 8, 1982, entitled, "Improving the Scientific Adequacy of Agency Regulations and Standards." The memorandum established an agency-wide process for identifying a minimum of fifteen to twenty-five high priority rulemakings whose scientific basis would be reviewed by the SAB. It further required that EPA program staff prepare a "scientific issues staff paper" that assessed all major scientific issues and studies associated with a proposed regulatory action, including significant areas of scientific uncertainty.

This memorandum continued to be updated by subsequent EPA administrators and served as a principal mechanism for planning SAB reviews for the subsequent decades until the arrival of Administrator Scott E. Pruitt in 2017 and his successor Andrew Wheeler in 2018.

Based upon the ERDDAA 1978 and Clean Air Act Amendments of 1977 as they pertain to the SAB and CASAC, respectively, the memorandum cemented the SAB's role as EPA's primary source of independent peer review and led to more frequent and structured dialogue between the board and EPA administrators and other senior officials. While not formally addressed in this memorandum, the SAB's review of ORD research plans and priorities also expanded in subsequent years. Altogether, the number of SAB scientific reviews increased from approximately a dozen annually in the early 1980s to approximately seventy per year by the end of that decade. By contrast, the number of SAB formal reviews plummeted to three in fiscal year 2019.

Anne Gorsuch's term as administrator (1981-1983) witnessed the preparation of "hit lists" of SAB appointees and other scientists who were removed from serving on advisory panels or receiving research funding. The return of William D. Ruckelshaus as administrator from 1983-1985 reestablished the practice of selecting independent scientists and engineers to the SAB and other panels (some of them were re-recruited from the hit lists) and adoption of more rigorous conflict of interest requirements. Such commitments continued in future decades until Administrators Pruitt and Wheeler abandoned these widely accepted scientific practices and instituted new appointment procedures that resulted in less scientifically qualified SAB members and the selection of individuals with conflicts of interest.

EPA has maintained a host of other scientific advisory bodies in addition to the Science Advisory Board. For example, the Scientific Advisory Panel has historically advised pesticide program managers on specific registration decisions; and ORD Assistant Administrator Robert Huggett established a Board of Scientific Counselors (BOSC) in the 1990s to review specific research plans, laboratory organization, and staffing needs. BOSC was dismantled by Administrator Pruitt in 2017, but then was reinstated by Administrator Wheeler with new membership. These other advisory panels were not generally statutorily based, nor did they report to the EPA administrator.

5. Preparing Risk Assessment Guidelines to Bridge Scientific Data with Policy Frameworks

As EPA's research program and regulatory agenda expanded in the 1970s and 1980s, policy-makers began to encounter two additional sets of science-related challenges: how to make decisions on a growing number of individual pollutants that exhibited some similar risk characteristics (e.g., halogenated solvents, heavy metals), and how to prepare scientific assessments for an expanding universe of health and ecological endpoints of concern.

An important innovation that responded to these challenges was the development of risk assessment guidelines. EPA published its initial set of

Interim Procedures & Guidelines for Health Risk and Economic Assessments of Suspected Carcinogens in 1976. They were subsequently circulated for comments by the Science Advisory Board and numerous federal agencies and later helped catalyze the formation of an Interagency Regulatory Liaison Group (IRLG) in 1977 that sought to harmonize various risk assessment protocols and regulatory policies among four health agencies (including the Consumer Products Safety Commission, EPA, FDA, and the Occupational Safety and Health Administration). Publication in 1983 of the National Research Council's (NRC) report on *Risk Assessment in the Federal Government: Managing the Process* further formalized the risk assessment process by developing an analytical framework consisting of hazard assessment, exposure assessment, dose response assessment, and risk characterization.

EPA adopted NRC's risk framework in 1983 and developed a series of guidelines for additional endpoints in subsequent years. These included guidelines for cancer, exposure, developmental risk, mutagenicity, neurotoxicity, reproductive toxicity, complex mixtures, and ecological risks mutagenicity, EPA has periodically updated some, but not all, of these guidelines and submitted them for SAB and public review.

The value of risk assessment guidelines is that they provide a science-based bridge that links research data to decision frameworks of direct relevance to policy-makers. Risk guidelines provide common definitions of key concepts and terminologies, define protocols to select applicable data, provide advice for interpreting key studies, explain methods used to extrapolate scientific data to endpoints of concern through both quantitative and qualitative approaches, and provide a formal structure to organize data that is relevant to risk assessment and subsequent policy-making.

6. Revisions to the Particulate Matter (PM) NAAQS, 1980-1997

EPA's original decisions to set NAAQS occurred during a time of great national urgency. High and unhealthy levels of photochemical oxidants, particulate matter and other criteria pollutants and individual toxic substances blanketed urban and regional atmospheres. In the case of particulate matter (PM), EPA quickly compiled and assessed available scientific studies and promulgated the PM NAAQS in 1971. The specific PM indicator that was measurable in the field, and became the basis for enforcement actions, was Total Suspended Particulates (TSP). TSP represented a mass concentration of PM in community air and cast a broad net of implementation actions to reduce PM levels across the US.

Accumulating scientific research in the fields of atmospheric chemistry, animal toxicology, human clinical studies, and epidemiology, and enactment of the 1977 Clean Air Act Amendments, led EPA to reassess the TSP standard. Between 1980-1987, EPA published and revised several drafts of air quality criteria documents and also released a staff paper that translated available scientific data into policy options. Both sets of documents were reviewed by the public and CASAC, which prepared a closure memo for the EPA administrator that summarized its advice.

Newer scientific information led EPA to publish a revised approach to PM standard-setting in 1987. That year, EPA promulgated a PM10 NAAQS, a recognition that smaller-sized PM can enter the thorax and penetrate the lower respiratory tract and cause or worsen diseases such as asthma, bronchitis, cancer, and emphysema. Specifically, PM10 refers to particles with an aerodynamic diameter of less than or equal to ten microns in size. In 1997, following public and CASAC review, EPA further revised the PM10 standard to PM2.5 microns or less. The 1997 decision emerged from compelling scientific results obtained through the Six Cities studies that used prototype PM2.5 samplers and from other publications that concluded excess mortality at the existing NAAQS levels set in 1987. EPA further revised the PM NAAQS to focus on particle sizes of 2.5 microns or less. This new standard was also made possible by the development and validation, in which EPA scientists participated, of monitoring equipment sufficiently robust to be used by state and local authorities.

A broader trend from the 1980s to the present day has been a greater emphasis upon longer-term exposures (regulated through an annual PM standard) at increasingly lower levels. Recent research also found endpoints of concern beyond the respiratory system, particularly cardiovascular risks.

PM standard setting has responded to changing scientific information that documents that the physical and chemical composition of the atmosphere can greatly change over time. Particulate matter decision-making clearly demonstrates that selecting the appropriate pollutant indicator (e.g., TSP, PM10, PM2.5) is an essential factor in public health protection. A major co-benefit of steadily reduced PM concentrations is the reduction of many individual atmospheric toxic substances. EPA's sustained commitment to assessing and adjusting the adequacy of PM standards represents one of the major public health successes in the history of the agency.

7. Global Risk Assessment and Risk Management: The Case of Stratospheric Ozone Depletion

Throughout its history, most of EPA's policy initiatives focused on pollution within the US. Simultaneously, the skills and capabilities acquired enabled EPA's participation in bilateral, regional, and global pollution abatement evaluations and actions. Major trans-US initiatives included efforts with Canada to reduce acid deposition and pollution of the Great Lakes;

chemicals' assessment and management with the European Union and the Organization for Economic Cooperation and Development; collaboration with Russia and China on research, pollution monitoring, and air, water, and waste management; and participation in important international convocations, such as the Basel Convention, the Montreal Protocol, and the Intergovernmental Panel on Climate Change.

In the 1970s, researchers Sherwood Rowland and Mario Molina published important studies documenting the deterioration of the stratospheric ozone layer that provided a significant barrier to the exposure of humans, animals, and vegetation to a potentially harmful spectrum of ultraviolet radiation.[14] The primary mechanism for such deterioration was determined to originate from the widespread commercial use of chlorofluorocarbons (CFCs), a class of chemical compounds that proved highly effective as propellants for consumer products, air conditioning systems, refrigerants, and other cooling applications. CFCs, once released, had a long-term residence time in the atmosphere and could reach the stratosphere (extending up to thirty-two miles above the earth's surface). The work of Rowland and Molina (subsequently awarded a Nobel Prize) initially was vigorously disputed by the global chemical industry, but subsequent publications authored by them and by other scientists reinforced the credibility of their work regarding measurable deterioration of upper atmospheric ozone levels.

EPA maintained a skeleton capability to address stratospheric ozone depletion as it was neither an important funder of research on this topic nor did its regulatory staff define it as a priority problem (except for specific initiatives taken by the Office of Toxic Substances to ban CFCs in spray cans). A few staff within the agency's Office of Policy Analysis began to compile and assess the growing body of scientific literature funded by other agencies (the National Aeronautics and Space Administration and the National Institutes of Health, for example) to estimate public health and environmental impacts due to the loss of stratospheric ozone. They calculated both the magnitude and the costs of effects ranging from increases in melanoma to declining agricultural productivity in the US and globally. Their assessment of stratospheric ozone depletion risks and economic costs met with considerable skepticism by scientists from ORD and EPA program offices, but it received important backing from a special committee of the Science Advisory Board in its closure letter to Administrator Lee Thomas.

Non-ORD science and a risk assessment prepared by policy office staff was atypical of the process normally applied within EPA to assess health risks. As public concerns over the health implications of stratospheric ozone depletion increased in the US and internationally, the policy office's risk assessment performed a highly significant interagency function by facilitating the US government's scientific consensus that subsequently guided the international negotiations leading to the 1987 Montreal Protocol. Looking back, this has proven to be the most successful international environmental agreement in history as ozone depletion has receded. Further, the Montreal Protocol continues to perform double duty in responding to climate change as CFCs and successor products are highly potent greenhouse gases.

EPA continues to have an important role in implementing Montreal Protocol requirements. As it encounters other important health and environmental problems that exist beyond the domain of expertise of ORD and traditional regulatory policy, it will need to strengthen its ability to develop new strategies for acquiring necessary information beyond the boundaries of traditional research planning and regulatory approaches.

8. Methyl tert-Butyl Ether (MTBE) in Gasoline

The addition of MTBE to gasoline represents a failure of EPA to take into account the issue of an enormous increase in population exposure from an existing chemical in a timely fashion, while failing to develop a sufficiently robust scientific foundation to assess health and environmental risks. Particularly problematic was the single-minded focus by political appointees in EPA's Air Office beginning in 1989 on promoting this marked increase in MTBE for the addition of an oxygenated chemical to gasoline. The MTBE issue unfortunately also demonstrated the stovepipe nature of EPA's regulatory approaches—in essence a policy designed to clean the air resulted in contaminating surface and ground water supplies.

The 1990 Clean Air Act Amendments mandated the use of oxygenates to reduce the level of carbon monoxide emitted during the combustion of motor fuels. The Amendments also set numerical limits for oxygenated fuels to displace ozone precursors and air toxics such as benzene, toluene, and xylene (BTX). The two major candidates were MTBE and ethanol, the former supported by the petrochemical industry and the latter by agricultural interests. EPA as well as environmental groups generally supported MTBE, in part because it would be more rapidly available in the very large amounts needed. Known facts not sufficiently considered were that MTBE in trace amounts contaminates drinking water and is highly resistant to the usual biodegradative processes for hydrocarbons. Further, almost any addition of oxygen to a hydrocarbon makes it more water soluble and, therefore, able to more rapidly move from a spill site to drinking water sources.

At the same time that the EPA Air Office was advocating the use of MTBE, the EPA Water Office had a major program to address groundwater contamination from leaking underground gasoline storage tanks. This so-called LUST program was optimistically targeted to be completed in the late

1990s, while the addition of MTBE to gasoline occurred in the early 1990s. Inevitably, leakage of gasoline which contained ten to fifteen percent MTBE led to significant contamination of water sources.

Two important health-related factors added to the controversy. As a chemical long in use, relatively little new toxicity testing was required. A consent decree under the Toxic Substance Control Act led to an industry-sponsored two-year animal study that was not reported until after MTBE use began, and which showed increases in certain cancers. Similar findings were reported by a study in Italy. In addition, individuals complained of a variety of non-specific symptoms, such as headache and queasiness, related to exposure to MTBE in gasoline.[15] The petrochemical industry, having already made significant investment in MTBE, subsequently funded numerous studies to debunk these findings. An EPA review of the health issues was followed by reviews by the Health Effects Institute, the National Academy of Sciences, the White House Office of Science and Technology Policy, and various states. Eventually MTBE was phased out of use, but not before significant damage to the nation's water supplies and an industry write-off of over $1 billion of investment costs.

Over one hundred million Americans were exposed to MTBE. One of the lessons of the MTBE episode, that the extent of human exposure needs to be taken into account in determining the extent of toxicity testing required *before* allowing the use of a chemical, has been incorporated into the 2016 amendments to the Toxic Substance Control Act (officially known as the Frank Lautenberg Chemical Safety for the 21st Century Act).

9. Scientific Assessment of Shale Gas Risks

The story of the assessment, or lack of assessment, of shale gas drilling risks is ongoing. Advances in oil and gas exploration and production technology, often characterized as unconventional gas drilling (UGD), led to a boom in drilling for previously inaccessible shale layers from which substantial amounts of gas and oil could now be extracted. Part of the developing technology was the addition of chemical agents, many of them proprietary, to the water used for hydraulic fracture to facilitate release of shale gas. Much of this occurred in populated areas, such as southwestern Pennsylvania, where unfamiliarity with the technology, coupled with communication blunders by industry and its government supporters, led to substantial public opposition and to statewide or local restrictions on UGD.[16]

The issue of hydraulic fracturing also illustrates the evolution of processes for reviewing and commenting on scientific information as shaped by the World Wide Web, social media, and changing external advocacy of science policy debates. Anti-fracking groups were galvanized by social media, which rapidly spread videos of a flowing water faucet set afire by a homeowner striking a match, as well as other alarming information. The shale gas industry, which has a very weak peer structure as compared to the chemical or petrochemical industries, hurt its credibility through aggressive responses. This included resistance to the disclosure of chemical constituents used in shale gas extraction and insistence that no health research was needed as they had been doing hydro-fracturing for sixty-five years with complete safety, which contradicted their own assertion to the public that the technology was new.

The net result illustrated what is known as the social amplification of risk. This concept contains two major factors that lead to an increased perception of risk: lack of familiarity with the risk and lack of trust in those providing information.[17] New York State's banning of UGD activities also illustrates the increasing role of a precautionary approach in environmental health decision-making. Governor Cuomo's stated reason for the ban was that the head of the New York State Department of Health had summarized a thorough review of the health literature on UGD with a classic precautionary statement that the existing evidence did not establish that the UGD process was safe. Similarly, the Supreme Court of Pennsylvania, in a decision inimical to the interests of the UGD industry, stated that the commonwealth had failed in its responsibility to obtain the needed research.[18]

The UGD issue also raised questions about EPA's role in public health protection. President Barack Obama formed a Shale Gas Advisory Committee whose tasks included advising on public health issues. It was led by the Department of Energy, with specified inclusion of the Department of Interior and EPA. Health and Human Services was not included, with EPA insisting it could cover the health issues. Yet not one of the seven external members of President Obama's committee had any background in public health or related fields. The resulting report almost completely neglected the needed public health research. EPA's subsequent activities in this area were limited by Congress and relatively devoid of public health content. (The lack of expert external advice on UGD was not restricted to the federal government. In two similarly tasked committees organized by the governors of Maryland and Pennsylvania, with a total of forty-five members, there was also no one with a public health background.)[19] ORD's role was heavily constrained by Congress which solely authorized a study of the potential effects of UGD on drinking water resources. Thomas Burke, then acting assistant administrator of ORD, in conjunction with the critical reviews of EPA's Science Advisory Board, moved the final report toward a public health assessment, although the potential for public health impact was not directly assessed.[20] Further, despite the obvious public concern, research on UGD or hydraulic fracturing was not listed as a priority by EPA's extramural program. Fortunately, NIEHS has supported research into the potential human health impact of UGD. The UGD issue identifies a major challenge for EPA to gain significant credibility and reputation as a primary source of public health expertise and research. (See further discussion below about the EPA's role in public health.)

ONGOING AND FUTURE CHALLENGES

From Command and Control to Risk Assessment-Risk Management and Onward Toward Sustainability

EPA's fifty-year history has evolved in three separate but continuing phases. The agency's establishment in 1970 occurred at a time of heightened public and, hence, political concern over deteriorating air quality, contaminated water bodies, polluted lands, and endangered fish, wildlife, and other species. There was substantial bipartisan support for the enactment of new and broad powers for EPA to control pollution sources, primarily from stationary and mobile sources. EPA's principal strategy for implementing this public and statutory mandate was to develop and enforce regulatory controls that were legally binding on specific sectors of the economy. This "command and control" approach is the foundation of the key statutes providing EPA with its legal authority to regulate pollution and formed EPA's primary conception of its mission and implementation of environmental management that continues to the present day.

Environmental science issues played a peripheral, if supporting, role in this initial phase of EPA's history because of the urgency imposed by statutory and court deadlines and the need to reassure the public that its concerns were being addressed by executive action. By the late 1970s, as many baseline regulatory controls were being instituted across air, land, and water media, support increased to integrate environmental science more directly into regulatory decision-making. Momentum built for this outcome for two major reasons: the growing availability of scientific information allowed decision-makers to develop more targeted solutions to environmental problems, and a growing public awareness of the costs of environmental regulation that provided EPA and many stakeholders with a desire to ensure that regulatory policy was based on higher quality data that documented risks of concern.

While command and control as a regulatory philosophy served as the bedrock of EPA's decisions, the publication of the NRC's 1983 report on *Risk Assessment in the Federal Government: Managing the Process* provided an important new rationale and set of tools for organizing risk analyses in support of policy decisions.[21] The report separated the process of evaluating risks from actions that EPA could take to manage them. EPA adopted this "risk assessment/risk management" framework in 1983. While it did not substitute for command and control regulation, it provided a framework to evaluate risks and identify policy options before implementing regulatory controls for many of EPA's most important decisions. EPA's leadership in advancing risk assessment methods and tools for individual environmental problems has continued.

Initially with stratospheric ozone and more recently with a focused evaluation of global megatrends, both the scientific and policy debates are shifting to the need to respond to problems that are simultaneously systemic and global. These include climate change, water scarcity, overconsumption of natural resources, and proliferation of waste streams (such as plastics in the oceans), to name a few. The concept of "sustainability" has emerged in recent decades as a means to articulate the connectivity of these present-day trends with the longer-term consequences to humans and ecosystems over multiple generations. Sustainability, unlike command and control and risk assessment-risk management, more explicitly addresses environmental, economic, and societal issues and impacts as part of an integrated process of evaluation and response.

Sustainability comprises the third phase of EPA's evolving mission, and the agency has begun to implement specific sustainability policies on a case-by-case basis, as well as introduce the concept in recent versions of its strategic plan. In the process of evaluating the applicability of sustainability to current programs, there is a growing recognition by professional staff that many current tools—e.g., risk assessment, cost-benefit analysis, life-cycle analysis, social cost of carbon evaluations, ecosystem productivity assessments, public-private partnership agreements—are very adaptable across the spectrum of command and control, risk assessment-risk management, and sustainability policy frameworks. EPA has received important analytical and institutional support to advance sustainability into its core mission from the National Academy of Sciences,[22] the private sector, environmental organizations, and universities. During 2017–2019, both Administrators Pruitt and Wheeler have rolled back the development of the sustainability framework and specific tools to apply it within individual agency programs (such as the social cost of carbon in assessments of climate change).

The evolution of EPA's decision-making frameworks has been accompanied by growing societal pressures to set the environmental policy agenda. This trend has taken a variety of forms over the years, including expanded public participation in formal rulemaking processes, the maturation of stakeholder processes and expansion of their voices through increased participation in social media and across the Internet. These trends have impacted the planning and implementation of scientific research by driving change through the use of sensor technology to measure pollution, demands for increased access to data, and expectations that both communities and individuals will have an expanded voice in determining research priorities. As a result, EPA faces both a clear challenge and an opportunity to expand its collaboration with bottom-up stakeholder perspectives, including those of minority communities, as a means to build credibility, relevance, and trust in assessing and implementing public health and environmental needs.

The Organization of ORD in Relation to EPA's Mission: The Public Health Context

Two branches of the US Public Health Service were moved into the newly formed EPA in 1970: The Division of Air Pollution and the Division of Water Pollution. Similarly, for the majority of states, environment health authorities, which historically had been part of public health agencies since the nineteenth-century sanitary revolution, also have been moved into newly formed agencies focused on the environment. However, public health has continued to be a significant portion of EPA's mission throughout its history.

The core concepts of public health include distinguishing among primary, secondary, and tertiary preventive modalities. Primary prevention, the highest preference, involves approaches that prevent a risk of adverse consequences from occurring, e.g., banning tobacco use. Secondary prevention focuses on early detection and treatment, such as preventing strokes through screening programs for high blood pressure. Tertiary prevention deals with care for those affected, a rare role for EPA.

While primary prevention is the desirable outcome, it is hardest to measure. Arguably, EPA's major contribution to environmental health has been the development and standardization of scientific techniques that provide regulators with the means to prevent the development and release of harmful chemicals. There is almost an infinite number of potential chemical structures from which industry can choose. For each new chemical that is developed for marketing there are perhaps ten or more that are seriously considered. During this development phase, the potential for exposure and for adverse effects in humans or the general environment is explored in relation to avoiding harm and the ensuing legal liability, as well as the need for EPA and international approval. Exploration includes toxicological and ecological tests that evaluate such undesired endpoints as mutagenicity and environmental persistence and that are recognized by EPA as providing information relevant to marketing approval. We do not know how many humans have not been harmed or ecosystems not affected because the chemicals were never developed or marketed due to the tests developed by ORD in conjunction with the potential presence of EPA's regulatory review requirements.

In contrast, risk assessment and risk management mostly fit under the heading of secondary prevention. We identify what is already a problem, e.g., the potential for adverse effects due to the level of a pollutant in air or water and devise regulatory means to bring the levels down. Developing the science necessary to quantitatively estimate risk has been exceptionally valuable to EPA's activities, including priority setting, and is reflected in many of the laws EPA enforces. EPA's recognition of this value led to reorganizing ORD under the risk paradigm. Such reorganization arguably has lessened ORD's focus on primary prevention, something that may have slowed EPA's investment in developing molecular toxicology tools to predict adverse effects of a new or existing chemical.

Particularly disappointing is that neither the European Union's REACH (Registration, Evaluation, Authorization and Restriction of Chemicals) program nor the 2016 TSCA amendments have placed much emphasis on the need to develop new evaluation tools. A major impetus for both the EU and US approaches has been the recognition of the relative lack of thorough toxicological testing of existing chemicals in commerce. Despite imposing, perhaps, a billion dollars of testing costs, almost no attention in the EU or US has been given to the commensurate use of government funds to improve the test procedures, which are not infallible. For example, if one assumed that current tests for reproductive and developmental toxicity were 99% effective, an unreasonably high estimate, then for every 10,000 reproductive and developmental toxins tested, one hundred such toxins would not be excluded from the market.

EPA's investments, along with those of NIEHS and the NTP (National Toxicology Program), have led to advances in molecular toxicology.[23] Briefly, techniques have been developed that explore the response of subcellular genetic pathways to toxins. For example, certain pathways may reflect the usual response to agents that cause inflammation, while other pathways respond to agents that affect the endocrine system. Two major challenges are the need to more precisely pin down the implications of the observed molecular changes to human or ecosystem health, and the need to better explain to EPA regulators and stakeholders whether there is, or should be, a distinction between "normal" adaptive responses and adverse effects. The exquisite details provided by molecular toxicology magnify an old issue that has faced EPA regulators. For example, the EPA administrator may be told by industry that a relatively low level of an air pollutant that causes a two percent narrowing of airways should not be considered in standard setting because merely going from indoors to outdoors on a cold day can lead to ten percent narrowing of the airways. In contrast, environmental groups may tell the administrator that to an asthmatic child who might have thirty percent airway narrowing during an asthma attack, an additional two percent caused by an air pollutant could significantly alter the child's health status. EPA also has recognized that integration of epidemiological findings into traditional risk assessment is an important public health challenge.[24]

Another reason for concern about EPA's public health credentials has to do with staffing decisions. Many of the initial ORD staff were USPHS (US Public Health Service) commissioned officers. Unfortunately, due in part to lessened career prospects at EPA, many returned to the Department of Health and Human Services, which led to a decline in commissioned PHS officers from approximately 650 to 240 by 1986 and to less than 50 presently.[25] ORD has worked to counteract this decline in familiarity with public health concepts by developing an Environmental Public Health Division within its National Health and Environmental Exposure Laboratory, although this organizational structure is in transition, and by developing a fellowship agreement with the Association of Schools and Programs in Public Health.

Meeting Challenges to EPA's Science: The Precautionary Principle

The precautionary principle has been advanced by the European Union as a key driving force in establishing environmental controls. It has been adopted by many US environmental groups and by various local agencies (such as the Berkeley City Council). It was described at the 1992 United Nations Conference on Environment and Development as follows: "Where there are threats of serious or irreversible damage, scientific uncertainty shall not be used to postpone cost effective measures to prevent environmental degradation."[26] A central facet of the precautionary principle is to put the onus for demonstrating safety on industry rather than on government. While forcefully advocated by the EU, including being used as the basis for protecting EU agriculture by banning agricultural products from the US and developing countries, there is little evidence that it is used more frequently in the EU than in the US (see Chapter 13). For example, the 1990 Clean Air Act Amendments related to air toxics would fit well under the precautionary principle in that, instead of EPA having the burden to prove harm, regulated sources have the responsibility to demonstrate safety. Further, instead of basing controls on the level of risk, the amendments instituted maximum available control technology requirements almost irrespective of the level of risk.

The role of science in the precautionary principle has been much debated. The debate is often complicated by its many different definitions which often revolve around attempting to calibrate how much scientific uncertainty is needed for action. The various definitions are often grouped under "strong" and "weak," with the strong often requiring little more than observing an association between a potential cause and a reported effect to serve as a basis for action. As the precautionary principle becomes increasingly incorporated in international treaties, trade negotiations, and in national and local governance, its potential impact on environmental health sciences becomes even more important.

The precautionary principle raises another issue pertinent to EPA research that is often overlooked. Decisions invoking the precautionary principle are inherently provisional, as is recognized in some of its definitions. If the science were reasonably certain, there would be a lesser need to utilize the precautionary principle. Also inherent is that decisions made under the precautionary principle impose significant economic or social costs. If the costs were trivial, the environmental threat alone would be sufficient for action. Thus, the more precaution exhibited in environmental policy, the greater the likelihood that erroneous decisions with significant unnecessary costs will be made. Accordingly, being precautionary should lead to more research to determine if the action is correct. However, it does not appear that further research has ever led the EU to change a decision based on the precautionary principle.

The failure to perform post-hoc research on the efficacy of regulatory decisions is not limited to the EU. After making contentious regulatory decisions, EPA policy-makers naturally would prefer ORD to focus on research related to a forthcoming decision rather than evaluate the effectiveness of past decisions. Yet, after a regulatory determination is made may be the best time to perform the research. One has the opportunity to enlist a population in advance of a foreseeable change in exposure and observe what happens. The Health Effects Institute, a boundary organization supported by both EPA and American automobile makers, has funded a series of studies to assess the impact of EPA's regulatory decisions on health. This approach should be expanded to other types of EPA policies, including ecological impacts.

The private sector frequently opposes the application of the precautionary principle in regulatory decision-making on the grounds that it inserts value judgments in lieu of science. Ironically, there are many applications of the precautionary principle in industry's own governance and operations. The American Chemistry Council's Responsible Care founding principles, dating from the mid-1980s, explicitly endorse the adoption of precautionary approaches in environmental, health, and safety management. Other examples across the private sector include the adoption of redundancy factors in construction standards and utilization of safety factors in toxicity testing.

Meeting Challenges to EPA's Science: Unforeseen Issues

One of the more difficult challenges facing environmental scientists is timely forecasting of a new or emerging environmental problem about which EPA will be expected to respond. Examples include nanotechnology and rapidly resolving the question of whether it was safe to use an unprecedented volume of dispersants during the Deepwater Horizon oil spill. Unquestionably, unforeseen challenges will continue to occur. Many of them will be related to global climate change, such as the need to assess disease vectors, the availability of potable water supplies, and other issues.

EPA's responsiveness will be hampered by recently approved or planned actions by Administrators Pruitt and Wheeler. As just one example, assume that ORD has correctly identified an emerging issue and competitively funded scientists to begin analysis of the problem. Under the new rules, these scientists, who arguably are the most knowledgeable about the new issue, would be prohibited from giving scientific advice to EPA.

Conducting Consensus-based Science in an Era of Political Polarization

This chapter has evaluated the multiple tensions inherent in managing research in a regulatory agency and the adaptations of EPA management to improve both the quality and policy relevance of research conducted by the agency and, more broadly, the scientific community. Numerous successes can be documented (some of which are identified in this chapter) even while new challenges have emerged.

The most significant of the recent challenges confronting EPA and other scientific agencies of government lies in the substitution of ideologically based legal and advocacy approaches to science in contrast to the established consensus-based approach. Scientists have never spoken with one voice. Historically, this has been a major strength in ensuring that multiple perspectives and criteria are applied to evaluating the validity and limitations of scientific information either as individual studies or in aggregated form such as EPA risk assessments. This evidence-based diversity had built and sustained public confidence over many decades in the underlying integrity of information used as a foundation for enforceable and, at times, expensive-to-implement policies and standards. Though never free of dispute or controversy, the consensus-based approach to science has enjoyed the broad support of the scientific community across academia, business, and environmental organizations, and civil society in general.

The consensus-based methods of scientific investigation and evaluation are presently under direct attack by the chemical and fossil fuel industries, think tanks funded by these interests, and their colleagues who occupy senior level positions within the current administration's EPA, other government agencies, and the White House. Their alternative, developed over many years of challenging consensus scientific judgments over the risks of tobacco smoke (directly inhaled or via secondhand smoke), stratospheric ozone depletion, and, most prominently, climate change, has been to substitute ideological norms and standards evolved through legal and advocacy processes (previously discussed in this chapter) in lieu of peer reviewed, evidence-based practices adhered to by the scientific community.

The differentiation between ideological approaches to policy-making and consensus-based approaches based upon science can be illustrated in the following examples:

1. Whereas the broad and diverse scientific community weighs multiple kinds of evidence to develop consensus judgments around risk and uncertainty, groups espousing an ideological framework for policy-making arrive at an agenda that cherry-picks subsets of scientific data that support their position to delay or avoid controls of harmful pollutants. Examples of the latter include recent debates over chlorpyrifos, climate change, and exposures to mercury emissions.
2. Ideological proponents are able to generally communicate with a common voice around a core set of desired outcomes—objecting to the legitimacy of the federal government (or other levels of government) in regulating contaminants, supporting evaluations of regulatory costs (but not benefits), and espousing proof of harm over probability of harm. By contrast, properly managed scientific community debates that are conducted through workshops, conferences, and peer review processes do not have a regulatory outcome in mind a priori and invite credible scientists with diverse points of view to exchange their perspectives on evidence and risk.
3. Qualified experts who are published in reputable peer-reviewed publications form the backbone of consensus-based scientific evaluations, whereas the ideological school manufactures opinions in op-eds, blogs, commissioned papers, and, less frequently, peer-reviewed publications. Given the nature of scientific deliberations and subsequent government rulemaking processes, ideological advocates have numerous opportunities to advance their point of view and ample funding to do so.

Since 2017, the goals of deregulatory ideologists have expanded to directly attack the means by which independent scientists have participated with EPA. Their initiatives have included:

- EPA, in 2018, has finalized a decision to exclude recipients of EPA research grants as participants in scientific panels that advise the agency on the scientific basis of regulatory policies and standards. The rationale for such exclusion is that funded scientists would have a conflict of interest even though EPA has maintained rigorous ethical standards (comparable to those of other government scientific agencies and nongovernmental bodies) to identify and prevent such conflicts from ever arising or taking remedial action once identified. Further, the exclusion of university scientists fails to take into account that academia has its own processes to inhibit biased opinions that are not based on the best science. Peers on an EPA consensus committee are likely to be those who review the academic scientist's manuscripts or grant applications or are asked for letters of recommendation by appointment and promotion or award committees.

- From 2017-2019, EPA terminated the service of independent scientists serving on its Science Advisory Board and other science advisory bodies. Two results of these actions are a substantial diminution of expertise necessary to evaluate risks from pollutants across air, land, and water media. Second, EPA's administrator appointed replacements lacking the credibility and stature of their predecessors, with many of them affiliated with industry groups, consultant organizations dependent upon industry funding, or ideological organizations whose views they represented on many of the issues they have been appointed to advise the administrator.
- The Trump administration has proposed dramatic reductions in overall EPA funding and research budgets and staffing levels for the past several years. Congress has not followed through on these proposals in the appropriations process.[27] However, due to retirements and attribution, EPA no longer maintains the core competencies of expertise necessary to evaluate and control public health and environmental risks across many issues.

The scientific community, including EPA, also faces a significant and growing challenge in reconciling its current methods for conducting and communicating research with the changes in social and political behaviors enabled by the technological platforms of social media. This challenge manifests itself in several ways: the communication of nonauthoritative or pseudoscientific voices to influence the outcome of scientific evaluations; insertion of less scientifically based hypotheses to challenge consensus-based scientific conclusions; and efforts to intimidate qualified scientists from serving on EPA scientific advisory committees by mobilizing social media criticism of their independent views. Government-employed scientists at EPA and other agencies are limited in their ability to respond to these developments because of the nonpolitical nature of their work and ethical constraints.

Not only EPA, but the entire scientific community faces similar challenges to its credibility and authority in applying evidence-based approaches to public health decisions. This erosion in scientists' stature, in addition to those issues presented above, also include a series of high profile controversies—such as corporate deceit in the failure to disclose risks from Vioxx, the opposition to vaccines, disparagement of genetically modified goods, and skepticism of data documenting global climate change—that have contributed to reduced public confidence in the ability of scientists to contribute solutions to major societal problems. This "denialism," in the words of one major analyst, replaces "the rigorous and open-minded skepticism of science with the inflexible certainty of ideological commitment" and corresponds with the decline in public trust of established organizations in general.[28] No more vivid example of this challenge exists than the political and ideological opposition to evidence-based approaches for responding to the SARS-CoV-2 (COVID-19) pandemic.

Three approaches have emerged that can strengthen scientists' ability to continue their important work even while contending with social media maelstroms. They include:

1. Staying focused on the fundamentals of their professional methods, standards, and responsibilities. It is important to maintain a resolute commitment to the appropriate design and implementation of scientific studies (including application of the most recent methodologies and ethical standards); adhere to robust internal and external peer review; practice transparency in research methods and communication of results (to the extent appropriate to the goal of validating environmental health studies; collaborate with colleagues across multiple institutions over time; and avoid financial or other conflicts of interest.
2. Linking the reported results of specific studies to a broader narrative that advances understanding of specific environmental problems across scientific disciplines and among nontechnical audiences, including policymakers, elected officials and their staffs, journalists, and civic society organizations and citizens. Such a narrative would establish an important context for how science is relevant to the objectives of these audiences and how they, in turn, can become more informed consumers of scientific information. As an example, the Health Effects Institute has historically provided explanatory text to explain the broader implications of its major studies.
3. Integrating EPA's science results and programs with broader information networks that promote scientific understanding and accuracy. There are numerous civil society organizations—professional societies, individual schools and educational institutions, business and environmental organizations—that are interested in scientific information and perform a valuable role in advancing the scientific literacy of their members and society

at large. They also serve as important conduits of information to scientists' direct stakeholders such as policymakers, Congress, and state and local governments. EPA should develop a formal strategy of collaborating with these types of organizations.

Both the scientific community and the public are committed to improving environmental quality for their own and successive generations. Currently, scientists have the means to better inform the citizenry and, in so doing, help marginalize those voices that advocate policies not based on evidence-based scientific methods.

In reflecting upon the fifty years of environmental science at EPA, and the tensions, successes, and challenges embedded in the agency's history, several factors emerge as critical to its future success. These include: leadership commitment to quality and ethics in research management and day-to-day decision-making; expanding participation with "boundary organizations" that incorporate individual sectors of society (academia, business, non-governmental organizations, communities); increasing collaboration with stakeholders at all levels of society; incorporating the perspectives and needs of minority populations in research design and policy; and rethinking the narrative of EPA's role in society (including a reevaluation of how best to utilize social media and other communications platforms), while optimizing the knowledge and empowerment of citizens to use credible scientific information to strengthen environmental protection at all levels of society.

This chapter will end, as it began, with an anecdote originating from the Gorsuch era. When President Reagan was reelected in 1984, the Heritage Foundation, a conservative think tank whose opinions were much valued in the first Reagan administration, updated its influential "Mandate for Leadership."[29] In the section on EPA, the Heritage authors chided the president for replacing Gorsuch with the more liberal Ruckelshaus. Their sole criticism of Gorsuch was for reducing support for EPA's science, which they pointed out was necessary for intelligent change. Whether the broad-based nonpartisan support for science at EPA will revive, or be seen as a relic of the past, will be a critical factor for success in rebuilding public confidence in EPA and in reviving the agency's own sense of purpose and professionalism to implement its important mission.

NOTES

1. Anne Gorsuch and John Greenya, *Are You Tough Enough* (New York: McGraw-Hill, 1986). Gorsuch was EPA's fourth administrator and served from 1981-1983.

2. Dorothy E. Patton and Robert J. Huggett, "The Risk Assessment Paradigm as a Blueprint for Environmental Research," *Human and Ecological Risk Assessment: An International Journal* 9, no. 5 (2003):1337-48, DOI: 10.1080/10807030390240364.

3. National Research Council, *Strengthening Science at the U.S. Environmental Protection Agency: Research-Management and Peer-Review Practices* (Washington, DC: The National Academies Press, 2000), https://doi.org/10.17226/9882.

4. National Research Council, *The Measure of STAR: Review of the U.S. Environmental Protection Agency's Science To Achieve Results (STAR) Research Grants Program* (Washington, DC: The National Academies Press, 2003), https://doi.org/10.17226/10701; National Academies of Sciences, Engineering, and Medicine, *A Review of the Environmental Protection Agency's Science to Achieve Results Research Program* (Washington, DC: The National Academies Press, 2017), https://doi.org/10.17226/24757.

5. Thomas O. McGarity, "On the Prospect of 'Daubertizing' Judicial Review of Risk Assessment," *Law & Contemporary Problems* 66, no. 4 (2003): 155–266.

6. National Research Council, *Strengthening Science*; US Environmental Protection Agency, *Safeguarding the Future: Credible Science, Credible Decisions*, EPA-600-9-91-050 (Washington, DC: EPA, March, 1992); US Environmental Protection Agency, *Reducing Risk: Setting Priorities and Strategies for Environmental Protection*, SAB-EC-90-021 (Washington, DC: EPA, Sept, 1990).

7. US Government Accountability Office, *EPA Advisory Committees: Improvements Needed for the Member Appointment Process* (Washington, DC: GAO, July, 2019), 19-280, https://www.gao.gov/assets/710/700171.pdf.

8. David R. Buchanan and Franklin G. Miller, "Justice and Fairness in the Kennedy Krieger Institute Lead Paint Study," *American Journal of Public Health* 96, no. 5 (2006): 781–7.

9. US Environmental Protection Agency, "CHESS Briefing," Internal Document, November 20, 1979.

10. U.S. Congress, House, Committee on Science and Technology, Subcommittee on Special Studies, Investigations, and Oversight, Subcommittee on the Environment and the Atmosphere, *The Environmental Protection Agency's Research Program with Primary Emphasis on the Community Health and Environmental Surveillance System (CHESS), An Investigative Report*, 94th Cong., 2nd sess. (Washington, DC, November 1976).

11. American Petroleum Institute v. Douglas M. Costle, 665 F.2d 1176 (D.C. Circ. 1981).

12. "Review and Revision of National Ambient Air Quality Criteria and Standards: Draft Guidance Document," Memorandum from Matthew B. Van Hook, EPA Office of General Counsel, to Terry F. Yosie, Science Advisory Board, February 4, 1981.

13. Peter J. A. Rombout, Paul J. Lioy, and Bernard D. Goldstein, "Rationale for an Eight-Hour Ozone Standard," *Journal of Air Pollution Control Association* 36, no. 8 (1986): 913–17.

14. Mario J. Molina and F. S. Rowland, "A Stratospheric Sink for Chlorofluoromethanes: Chlorine Atom-Catalyzed Destruction of Ozone," *Nature* 249 (1974): 810-12, https://doi.org/10.1038/249810a0.

15. Serap Erdal and Bernard D. Goldstein, "Methyl tert-Butyl Ether as a Gasoline Oxygenate: Lessons for Environmental Public Policy, Annual Review of Energy and the Environment 25 (November 2000): 765-802; Bernard D. Goldstein, "MTBE: A Poster Child for Exposure Assessment as Central to Effective TSCA Reform," *Journal of Exposure Science and Environmental Epidemiology* 20, no. 3 (2010): 229–30, PMID: 20407449.

16. Bernard D. Goldstein, "Flowback," *The Environmental Forum* 33, no. 1 (2016): 25–9. There were also major divisions within the oil and gas industry, with larger, more integrated companies displaying a willingness for greater transparency compared to smaller, more independent operators.

17. Roger E. Kasperson et al., "The Social Amplification of Risk: A Conceptual Framework," *Risk Analysis* 8, no. 2 (June, 1988): 177–87.

18. Goldstein, "Flowback."

19. Bernard D. Goldstein, Jill Kriesky, and Barbara Pavliakova, "Missing from the Table: Role of the Environmental Public Health Community in Governmental Advisory Commissions Related to Marcellus Shale Drilling," *Environmental Health Perspectives* 120, no. 4 (April 2012): 483–6, doi: 10.1289/ehp.1104594.

20. US Environmental Protection Agency, *Hydraulic Fracturing for Oil and Gas: Impacts from the Hydraulic Fracturing Water Cycle on Drinking Water Resources in the United States*, EPA-600-R-16-236F (Washington, DC: EPA, 2016).

21. National Research Council, *Risk Assessment in the Federal Government: Managing the Process* (Washington, DC: The National Academies Press, 1983), https://doi.org/10.17226/366.

22. National Research Council, *Sustainability and the U.S. EPA* (Washington, DC: The National Academies Press, 2011), https://doi.org/10.17226/13152; National Research Council, Committee on Scientific Tools and Approaches for Sustainability, *Sustainability Concepts in Decision-Making: Tools and Approaches for the US Environmental Protection Agency* (Washington, DC: The National Academies Press, 2014), https://doi.org/10.17226/18949.

23. National Research Council, *Toxicity Testing in the 21st Century: A Vision and a Strategy* (Washington, DC: The National Academies Press, 2007), https://doi.org/10.17226/11970; Robert J. Kavlock et al., "Accelerating the Pace of Chemical Risk Assessment," *Chemical Research in Toxicology* 31, no. 5 (March 2018): 287–90, https://doi.org/10.1021/acs.chemrestox.7b00339.

24. Maureen R. Gwinn et al., "Chemical Risk Assessment: Traditional vs Public Health Perspectives," *American Journal of Public Health* 107, no. 7 (July 2017):1032–9, doi: 10.2105/AJPH.2017.303771.

25. Bernard D. Goldstein, "EPA as a Public Health Agency," *Regulatory Toxicology and Pharmacology* 8, no. 3 (1988): 328–34.

26. United Nations, "Rio Declaration on Environment and Development," *Report of the United Nations Conference on Environment and Development, Rio de Janeiro, June 3–14* (New York: UN, 1992).

27. Congressional Research Service, *US Environmental Protection Agency FY2019 Appropriations,* IF11067 (Washington, DC: CRS, March 28, 2019).

28. Michael Specter, *Denialism: How Irrational Thinking Hinders Scientific Progress, Harms the Planet, and Threatens Our Lives* (London: Penguin Books, 2009), 3.

29. Stuart M. Butler, Michael Sanera, and W. B. Weinrod, *Mandate for Leadership II: Continuing the Conservative Revolution* (Washington, DC: The Heritage Foundation, 1984).

Chapter Eleven

How Economics Has Contributed to EPA

Richard D. Morgenstern

INTRODUCTION[1]

Key to assessing the contribution of economics to the US Environmental Protection Agency is an understanding of both the evolving practices of the discipline and how these practices have helped shape actual policies. Unsurprisingly, both the practices and the influence of economics have changed dramatically over the past half century.

In the early years, agency economists focused on the potential for new regulations to disrupt industry and the overall economy. Neither benefits, (damage) analyses, nor market-based mechanisms were part of EPA's early toolbox. In fact, apart from limited academic writings, relatively little was known in the early years about the net social costs of environmental rules or about alternatives to direct or traditional regulation.

Over time, in concert with growth in the academic discipline of environmental and resource economics, the agency conducted broader and more data-driven assessments of the social costs of environmental protection, including some estimates of the distribution of environmental harms and of the remedies crafted to reduce them. To address the potential trade-offs among regulatory outcomes, EPA adopted a neoclassical net benefits framework, often referred to as Kaldor-Hicks criterion, wherein a regulation or other policy is deemed to be a societal improvement if those made better off could hypothetically compensate those harmed by the rule, even if actual compensation does not occur. Thus, uncompensated costs can be justified by improvements in health and the environment. The agency generally eschewed normative or advocacy analyses in favor of the more mainstream positive economics, focusing on cause-and-effect behavioral relationships.

Over the years, EPA's growing capacity to conduct quality economic studies put it solidly in the top tier of federal regulatory agencies. Despite the limited statutory support for economic criteria, history reveals numerous instances where economic analyses have helped inform and shape major regulatory and policy decisions. The focus on marginal (as opposed to average) costs and benefits is now firmly established at EPA, as is the embrace of market mechanisms. Behavioral responses to regulation are routinely considered, along with the value of information, the value of a statistical life, the analysis of risk and uncertainty, and the use of big data. Discounting of future costs and benefits is also now routine. While not strictly an economic tool, the agency's broadscale priority-setting efforts based on comparative risk assessment can be traced to the efforts of EPA economists.

At the same time, given the historical resistance of the environmental community and Congress to the use of economics in environmental decision-making, it would be imprudent to overstate the role economics has played at EPA over the past fifty years. Despite the record number of well-trained economists currently employed at the agency and, until recently, the growing use of independent peer review, the agency's economics studies of health and environmental benefits are often criticized by industry for double-counting or otherwise overstating damages. Some analyses are also challenged by environmentalists, typically for overestimating costs and underestimating the gains from regulation. At the time of this writing (spring 2020), certain economic approaches are under attack by the Trump administration which is seeking to downplay both the conduct and use of benefits analysis in some key areas. Nonetheless, over the five decades covered in this chapter, there has been a strengthened, but still tentative, embrace of mainstream economics at EPA.

Initially, it is useful to define some basic terms. An economic cost is commonly defined as the sum of the money, time, and other resources needed to make something or perform a service. Economists use the term to measure the burdens associated with one course of action versus another. Although they are not additive, other aspects of costs that can enter into regulatory decisions include cost-effectiveness (dollars per ton removed or life saved), job loss, industrial plant closures, and affordability. Benefits consider the physical changes in health and welfare (wellbeing), as well as the monetary expression of these physical changes, including the value of a statistical life (VSL) or life year (VSLY). Economic incentive or market-based policies rely on market forces as opposed to direct regulation—sometimes referred to as "command and control"—to alter producer and consumer behavior. Examples of incentive-based mechanisms include banking and trading, and taxes/subsidies.

Although not the sole province of economists, the distributional effects of environmental harms, as well as the policies to reduce those harms, are often evaluated via economic techniques. *Behavioral economics* examines the effects of psychological, cognitive, emotional, cultural, and social factors on the economic decisions of individuals and institutions.

During the agency's first decade (1970-80), cost and cost-effectiveness analyses, assessments of affordability, potential job losses, industrial plant closings, and regulation-induced price increases all factored into agency decision-making. Early consideration of market-based mechanisms can be traced to the late 1970s, as can the initial research on the measurement of health and environmental damages. White House and interagency reviews were also initiated in the agency's first decade.

At the beginning of EPA's second decade, the agency's economics capacity expanded along multiple dimensions. The 1981 Reagan Executive Order (EO) 12291 mandated benefit-cost studies as part of the newly required Regulatory Impact Analyses (RIAs) for major new rules.[2] Although the order was heavily motivated by business concerns about regulatory overreach, EPA's response was broad-based and rigorous, aimed at developing a science-based approach for informing policy and regulatory decisions. The agency's policy office, along with several program offices, hired economists and harnessed an expanding academic discipline to estimate the health and environmental benefits as well as the costs of new regulations.

The history of economics at EPA is marked by a number of high-profile developments, including support for some controversial rules, a major expansion in the use of market mechanisms, early attempts at an evidence-based approach to priority-setting across programs, and research studies to better understand the realized, as opposed to the expected, costs and benefits of key initiatives. Support for economics by political appointees at EPA and the White House has ebbed and flowed over the years. Most recently, the Trump EPA has revisited some long-settled practices, particularly in the calculations of benefits, in their push to reduce regulatory burdens.

This chapter begins with brief reviews of the legal constraints on the use of economics across the different statutes and the role of the White House and interagency reviews in shaping EPA policies. From there the focus moves to a discussion of the key economic issues relevant to agency decisions, initially examining in some detail the first decade, before turning to the post-1980 period. The next section reports on select developments in the conduct and use of economics in the Trump administration, followed by a summary of major trends in economics at EPA over the fifty-year period. The final section identifies challenges for the future.

BACKGROUND

Statutory Role for Economic Analysis of Environmental Regulation

Following his second stint as EPA administrator, William Ruckelshaus reflected on certain of the agency's statutory goals: "The nation was committed to a sort of pie in the sky at some future date . . . each time a new generation of clean technologies came into use, the response from EPA had to be: 'That's great—now do some more' whether that 'more' made any sense as an environmental priority or not."[3]

While Ruckelshaus's "pie in the sky" characterization is clearly applicable to goal-setting in the 1970 Clean Air Act (CAA) and the 1972 Clean Water Act (CWA), it does not apply to all mandated activities. Most statutes contain provisions that allow economics to be used for some aspects of standard-setting and permitting, which translate the goals into legally enforceable limits for individual facilities.[4] At the same time, EPA is accorded considerable flexibility via the Chevron doctrine, which holds that courts will defer to an agency's reasonable interpretation of a statute the agency is charged with administering.[5]

Table 11.1 summarizes the patchwork quilt of opportunities to use economics in EPA decision-making for the major environmental statutes. As shown, most laws allow some consideration of costs, particularly as they affect feasibility, affordability, or cost-effectiveness. The National Ambient Air Quality Standards (NAAQS) are a clear exception, reinforced by a 2001 Supreme Court ruling where the court explicitly upheld the notion that costs may *not* be used as a factor in establishing the primary health and secondary welfare NAAQS, which aim to protect public health with "an adequate margin of safety."[6]

Of the major environmental statutes EPA administers, only the amended Safe Drinking Water Act (SDWA) explicitly embraces benefit-cost analysis. The original Toxic Substances Control Act (TSCA) and the Federal Insecticide, Fungicide, and Rodenticide Act (FIFRA) are generally interpreted to allow benefit-cost analysis. The use of economics in these three statutes reflects varied media-specific and evolving congressional views. With growing concerns about the impact of new rules on small drinking water systems, Congress amended the SDWA in 1996 to allow benefit-cost analysis as part of the regulatory process. The agency was also instructed to estimate the potential for widespread harm in the absence of regulation as opposed to the sole reliance on calculations of harm to individuals, and to demonstrate that its actions would reduce those risks. Maximum contaminant levels (MCLs) are to be set "as close as feasible" to the maximum contaminant level goal (MCLG), where feasibility is defined as the use of the best technology and

Table 11.1. Economic Analysis Allowable under the Environmental Statutes

	Benefit-related factors			*Cost-related factors*			
	Pollution reduction	*Health*	*Welfare*	*Technical feasibility*	*Affordability*	*Cost-effectiveness*	*Benefit / cost*
Clean Air Act (CAA)							
NAAQS / primary		X					
NAAQS / secondary			X				?
Hazardous air pollution		a	a	b	b	b	b
Automobile engines	c	c	c	c	c	c	c
Fuel standards*	c	c	c			c	c
New source standards	X			X	X	X	X
Clean Water Act (CWA)							
Effluent guidelines, industrial sources	X	?	?	X	X	X	?
Safe Drinking Water Act (SDWA)							
Maximum contaminant levels		X	X	X	X	X	X
Toxic Substances Control Act (TSCA)		X	X	X	X	X	X
Lautenberg Chemical Safety Act	X	X	X				
Resource Conservation and Recovery Act (RCRA)		?	?	X	?	?	?
Federal Insecticide, Fungicide and Rodenticide Act (FIFRA)		X	X		X	X	X
Food Quality Protection Act (FQPA)		X					

?: Uncertain if allowable under this statute.
a: Only marginally relevant in the initial MACT (maximum available control technology) phase; principally relevant for residual risk phase.
b: Affordability, etc. are relevant only within a narrow framework for MACT determinations; these factors plus B/C considered in going beyond MACT.
c: Statute contains many specific directives limiting considerations of costs, health, and welfare.
*: Energy Independence and Security Act of 2007 established an aggressive Renewable Fuels mandate (as an amendment to the CAA). Mandates were initially set in EISA 2005; EISA 2007 set the more aggressive quantity requirements.
Source: This table builds off of Robert W. Hahn, "United States Environmental Policy: Past, Present, and Future," *Natural Resources Journal* 34, no. 2 (1994): 331; the only modifications made to Hahn's table incorporate the 1996 Amendments to the Safe Drinking Water Act. Hahn's table, in turn, was derived from Arthur Fraas, "The Role of Economic Analysis in Shaping Environmental Policy," *Law and Contemporary Problems* 54, no. 4 (1991); and Francis Blake, "The Politics of the Environment: Does Washington Know Best?" *American Enterprise* (March/April 1991).

treatment approaches, taking cost into consideration. The EPA administrator is required to explain any decision to deviate from the benefit-cost balance, but is allowed to do so.

Congress passed the Food Quality Protection Act of 1996 (FQPA) amending the FIFRA regulatory provisions for pesticide residues on foods and animal feed to remove the consideration of cost and replace the "unreasonable risk" provisions with a "safety" requirement that tolerances assure "a reasonable certainty of no harm." Consideration of cost as part of the unreasonable risk determination is still allowed under other provisions of FIFRA. In a similar spirit, a key provision of the Frank R. Lautenberg Chemical Safety for the 21st Century Act (2016), removed cost considerations from the determination of "unreasonable risk" across all sections of TSCA.

Beyond these major EPA-administered statutes, the Energy Independence and Security Act (EISA) of 2007 established an aggressive mandate for renewable fuels as an amendment to the Clean Air Act. EISA permits EPA to use both cost and benefit factors in establishing the feasibility of alternative annual levels of renewable fuels to be blended into gasoline.

Since 1981 various efforts have been made in Congress to mandate a benefit-cost test for new environmental and other social regulation.[7] To date, none has been enacted into law. At the same time, Congress has established an expedited process to override a regulation and taken other steps to limit the power of regulatory agencies, although these are not explicitly tied to a benefit-cost test.[8,9,10]

Historical Role of Interagency Review of EPA Regulation

The role of the White House, OMB, and other federal agencies in reviewing EPA rules has been controversial since the agency's earliest days. In 1971 the Nixon administration established the Quality of Life Review which focused on environmental regulations. The aim of the Nixon program, according to a report issued over two decades later by the Clinton OMB, was "to minimize burdens on business . . . [since] . . . the significant growth in the amount and kinds of regulation created a counter political development that ultimately produced a companion program to evaluate the regulatory system." [11]

The Council on Wage and Price Stability (CWPS) was established by President Ford in 1974 to address concerns about stagflation and slow economic growth. Ford also issued Executive Order 11821, requiring government agencies to prepare inflation impact statements before promulgating costly new rules. According to the Clinton-era OMB Report,

> The economists at CWPS quickly concluded that a regulation would not be truly inflationary unless its costs to society exceeded the benefits it produced. Thus

the economists turned the inflation impact statement into a benefit-cost analysis . . . one of the legacies of this approach was that it slowly built an economic case against poorly conceived regulations, raising interest particularly among academics and students who began to use the publicly available analyses in their textbooks and courses.[12]

When President Carter came to office in 1977, EPA and other regulatory agencies opposed Executive Office review of agency rules while the president's economic advisers favored them as a means of limiting inflationary pressures and assuring that regulatory burdens on the economy were adequately considered. Reflecting these competing views, EO 12044, issued in March of 1978, established general principles for agencies to follow when issuing rules deemed to have "major economic consequences for the general economy, for individual industries, geographical regions, or levels of government." The Carter administration also set up the Regulatory Analysis Review Group (RARG) staffed by the CWPS and the Council of Economic Advisors (CEA), with the goal of reviewing the economic analyses of up to ten regulations per year and placing comments in the public record.[13]

Within EPA there was considerable pushback to the RARG reviews, however, as documented in an internal memo issued by the Office of Air and Radiation in 1978:

The RARG methodology . . . focuses on aggregate health impacts and not on the health of sensitive individuals . . . [It] avoids complex judgments regarding medical evidence by arbitrarily assigning no value to less conclusive indications of health risk associated with low levels of exposure. The RARG approach selects only the most conclusive studies for use in the cost model and assigns no value to uncertain risks at lower levels.[14]

The earlier cited Clinton-era OMB report interprets the RARG and other Carter administration actions as "help[ing] to institutionalize both regulatory review by the Executive Office of the President and the utility of benefit-cost analysis for regulatory decision makers."[15]

During the 1980 presidential campaign, Ronald Reagan made regulatory relief (not reform) one of his four pillars for economic growth, along with reducing government spending, tax cuts, and steady monetary growth. EO 12291, issued by Reagan twenty-eight days after his inauguration, emphasized more formal and comprehensive centralized regulatory oversight and modified existing executive branch reviews in at least three significant ways: 1) by requiring that agencies prepare benefit-cost analyses for major regulations and stipulating that new rules should maximize net benefits (social benefits minus social costs) to the extent allowed by the underlying legislation; 2) by replacing CWPS with OMB's Office of Information and Regulatory

Affairs (OIRA) as the agency responsible for centralized review; and 3) by requiring agencies to send their proposed and final regulations along with the benefit-cost analyses in draft form to OMB for review prior to issuance. The Task Force on Regulatory Relief, chaired by then-Vice President George H. W. Bush, was to oversee the process and serve as an appeal mechanism if the agencies disagreed with OMB's recommendations.[16,17] Unsurprisingly, these new requirements were not well received at EPA.[18]

As Bill Ruckelshaus has reflected:

> The OMB . . . was not impressed with the congressional mandate to get on with environmental protection regardless of cost, as some of the statutes demanded. This situation acted as a serious impediment to the effectiveness of the EPA administrator, who was immediately responsible to Congress to carry out its wishes. The OMB staff was removed from that responsibility and somewhat insulated as a result of cover in the White House . . . No matter which political party is in office, this tension will persist. I couldn't resolve it [in my first stint as EPA administrator]. . . . When I went back to the agency in 1983, I got right back in the middle of it! The *same people were there*! The *same* people in the agency, the *same* people in OMB, fighting each other over what should happen to these standards![20]

Following the election of President Clinton in 1992, there was an active debate in the new administration on the fate of EO 12291. Would it continue? Would it be modified to limit the role of benefit-cost analysis? A decision came in September 1993 with the issuance of EO 12866, which continued the basic EO 12291 framework, retained the requirement for analysis of benefits and costs—quantified to the maximum extent possible—and embraced the principle that the benefits of regulations should *justify* (not maximize) the costs. It also gave somewhat greater emphasis to equity in regulatory decision-making and reduced the number of non-major rules required to be submitted in advance to OMB. To increase the openness and accountability of the process, a ninety-day period was established for OMB review of proposed rules, along with a requirement that all review-relevant documents exchanged between OIRA and the agency be made available to the public. The basic structure established by President Reagan and affirmed by President Clinton remains in place today, as every president in the past four decades has embraced benefit-cost analysis as a tool for decision-making. Interestingly, at least one prominent commentator, Georgetown University Law professor and former Obama-appointed head of the agency's policy office, Lisa Heinzerling, argues that the Obama administration strengthened the dominance of benefit-cost analysis "by insisting on interpretations of environmental statutes that embraced cost benefit tests at every opportunity."[19]

As discussed later, as discussed later in the chapter, it is President Trump who weakened the role of benefit-cost analysis in EPA.

THE EARLY EPA YEARS

The 1970s-era legislation and the founding of EPA itself are widely seen as a response to public outcry about polluted air and water. Apart from some early academic writings, relatively little was known about the costs and benefits of environmental protection in 1970.[21] Nonetheless, in his initial organization of the agency, Bill Ruckelshaus established the Office of Planning and Management (OPM) and its Economic Analysis Division (EAD) to provide broadscale economic expertise and oversight for the agency. Most of the early economics staff in OPM held MBA degrees—many of them from top-tier schools. Initially, there were only a few PhD-level economists in the agency, including those who had come from the Department of Agriculture when EPA was established. In addition, a small economic analysis group, including several PhD economists who had joined EPA from the Public Health Service (mostly located in Raleigh, North Carolina), was established in the Office of Air Quality Planning and Standards (OAQPS) within the agency's Office of Air and Radiation.

Early on, these business and economic analysts focused on the costs, cost-effectiveness, and affordability of new regulations, as well as on the potential for adverse impacts such as price increases, job losses, and plant closings. Hoff Stauffer, a young Stanford MBA recruited from the management consulting firm McKinsey &Co., served as the first EAD director. He recruited a small staff of high-powered analysts and also established a network of outside experts, including consulting firms and academics, as EPA contractors to bolster the in-house economics capabilities.

As part of the agency's internal regulatory review process, OPM staff regularly assessed the costs and economic impacts of proposed regulations, based on information provided by the program offices or, sometimes, OPM internal analyses. These economic analyses were generally included in decision packages that went to the administrator, whether or not they were mandated by legislation. Thus began a dual role of the policy office—one that would become increasingly controversial over time. That is, policy staff would sometimes support regulatory action by providing technical assistance to program offices and, sometimes, offer independent policy views in options selection meetings with the administrator. Over the years, the program offices recognized the value of owning the analyses themselves and started building or strengthening their internal economic staffs, often recruiting economists from OPM or OMB to serve as leaders or senior analysts.[22]

The OPM group also served as an in-house think tank for evaluating alternative approaches for achieving agency goals. Roy Gamse, a Harvard MBA, succeeded Stauffer as EAD director and later went on to become deputy assistant administrator for planning and evaluation in the Costle era. He recalls briefing Deputy Administrator Robert Fri early in his tenure on the idea of using a national emissions tax to reduce sulfur dioxide emissions—as proposed in the form of a "Pure Air Tax" by the Nixon administration in 1972.[23] Following the 1973 OPEC oil embargo, the OPM group also developed expertise in energy policy and participated actively in interagency debates about possible US response options.

Former EPA Administrator Russell Train has noted that:

> [A] major factor we had going for us [1973-77] was good economic analysis. I think we had about the best in the government. . . . As a result, when I would go into a meeting at the White House on auto emissions or other subjects, we always had better economic data than the other side. We even did better than the Department of Commerce. I always thought this fact was extremely influential in our successes.[24]

Alvin Alm, who headed OPM in the early 1970s and returned as deputy administrator in the 1980s, concurred with Train's assessment of the quality of the economics staff and specifically cited the agency's work on the cost-effectiveness and economics impacts of the Effluent Guideline regulations for industrial water pollution.[25]

Concurrent but separate from the economics-oriented activities in OPM and the program offices, the Office of Research and Development (ORD) started developing its own economics expertise. In 1972 Stanley Greenfield, the first ORD assistant administrator, recruited a former RAND colleague and MIT PhD in economics, Alan Carlin, to establish an environmental research division with a heavy economics focus. At its peak, the ORD group employed fifteen to twenty analysts, including several PhD economists, to work on a range of issues including the valuation of crop damage and other categories of environmental benefits, economic incentive measures, and broad economic trends.[26]

A particular focus of the ORD group was the use of stated preference methods to value environmental amenities such as clean water for fishing and recreation. Later research used similar methods to value damages to human health. Another ORD research area involved the use of economic-incentive approaches to control pollution. ORD issued grants to universities and other expert groups to conduct long-term research on a range of environmental economic issues. This economics research function moved to the policy office in the early 1980s, although ORD continued some economics research in its joint EPA/NSF Research program. A 1998 review found that since 1970, the agency had funded over four hundred and fifty economics-oriented studies aimed at improving methods for measuring environmental costs and benefits as well as the design of economic incentive mechanisms.[27]

When Doug Costle—who had previously served as an assistant director at the Congressional Budget Office and as head of the Connecticut Department of Environmental Quality—became EPA administrator in 1977, he recruited a strong group of assistant administrators, including Bill Drayton, to head the OPM. Drayton, who had worked with Costle in Connecticut and was also previously an associate at McKinsey & Co., continued the tradition established by his predecessors of focusing on the marginal costs and effectiveness (not the benefits) of regulatory options and projecting the microeconomic impacts on regulated companies, industries, employees (jobs), and consumers. Costle and Drayton also continued the practice of involving economic staff from OPM and relevant program offices in briefings of the program assistant administrators and the administrator/deputy administrator.[28] Periodically, OPM reported on the cumulative costs and economic impacts of EPA regulations to the administrator and, as required, in testimony before Congress.

During the Costle/Drayton era, the OPM and the program offices expanded the type of economic expertise in the agency by hiring a number of PhD economists.[29] However, since most regulatory decisions hinged on technical and financial characteristics of specific industries, MBAs with strength in industrial and financial analysis continued to conduct or manage most of the economic analyses.

In a 2001 interview, in response to a question about how he defended the agency against claims that EPA was strangling the economy, Administrator Costle asserted:

> [M]uch of that was overstated . . . my approach was to assemble the best economic staff I could and take industry critics head-on. I asked Bill Drayton to do a study of the five most expensive rules that EPA had ever adopted. I wanted a comparison of agency forecasts of the likely expense of compliance with industry's forecasts and with the actual costs. . . . In four of the five cases, both the government and industry had significantly overestimated the actual costs. In one case, both industry and government underestimated the costs by a magnitude. In the four cases where we overestimated, our costs were closer to reality than industry's. And where we both underestimated, again our figures were closer to actual costs.[30]

Arguably, the most important regulatory innovation of the Costle/Drayton era was their emphasis on economic-incentive mechanisms to achieve regulatory objectives. Notwithstanding the (failed) Nixon-era proposal for a national

Pure Air Tax, Costle and Drayton spearheaded a major effort to introduce emissions bubbles and offsets to give individual facilities more flexibility to choose where and how to achieve required reductions in lieu of meeting uniform standards. A Regulatory Reform group was established within OPM to support this effort.[31]

In fact, the history of agency policies on emissions bubbles and offsets extends back to a failed Nixon administration attempt (1973) to allow large industrial plants that "modified" their operations to avoid NSPS requirements. Subsequently, in the Train era, EPA allowed emissions growth in nonattainment areas to be offset by emissions at other area facilities under certain limiting conditions. EPA's 1979 Bubble Policy went further, allowing existing sources to treat all stacks or vents at a given industrial facility as though enclosed in a single bubble and to reduce emissions where they chose, as long as overall emissions were reduced as required. Subsequent revisions toward the end of the Costle/Drayton era permitted existing source trades across plants or industries for the same pollutant.[32] A key element of all these early flexibility policies, however, was the requirement for EPA to preapprove proposed trades or related actions, a potentially expensive and time-consuming process. It wasn't until the lead phasedown program introduced in the mid-1980s that EPA allowed trading without preapproval of individual transactions.

Strong support for economic-incentive approaches came from academic economists over the objection of many agency lawyers and environmental advocacy groups who saw them as allowing companies to pay to pollute and thereby not clean up. This was a more potent argument in the pre-lead phasedown days when the benefits analysis wasn't advanced enough to allow determination of the value of the earlier or, possibly, larger emissions reductions that might be achieved via use of banking and trading.[33] Clearly, it wasn't the shortage of PhD economists that limited the use of incentive approaches. Rather, it was general skepticism and political inertia. To their credit, the leaders of these reform efforts persevered in advancing the case for incentive-based approaches.

Another economics-oriented initiative during this period was the embrace of financial analysis to support civil penalties for noncompliance with Clean Air and Clean Water Act rules. In the late 1970s, OPM developed an initiative which later evolved into the BEN model to calculate the economic benefits a firm obtained from noncompliance.[34] The BEN model focuses on two types of savings for noncomplying firms: those accrued by delaying capital expenditures for environmental compliance, and those resulting from not operating pollution control equipment during the period of noncompliance.[35] Over time, this initial effort led to the development of several other models including ABLE, which relates to cash flow and other metrics regarding a firm's ability to pay, and MABLE, which considers the financial strength of noncomplying municipalities. These models are currently managed by the agency's enforcement office.[36]

Despite the modest but growing contributions of economists throughout the 1970s, it is important to note the stated concerns among some nongovernment economists about the performance of EPA programs. For example, in an essay published in the early 1980s, Robert Crandall, a respected Senior Fellow in the Brookings Economics Studies Program, claimed that the agency's air pollution program was both ineffective and inefficient.[37]

THE POST-1980 EXPANSION OF EPA'S CONDUCT AND USE OF ECONOMIC ANALYSIS

Economics at EPA got a major boost with President Ronald Reagan's 1981 issuance of EO 12291, which expanded efforts to apply economic methods to regulatory decision-making. Specifically, Reagan sought to go beyond the principal focus on costs and require explicit consideration of benefits stated in monetary terms, when feasible. In effect, he was arguing that for a regulation to be acceptable, low costs alone are not sufficient. Rather, one must also demonstrate measurable gains to human health and the environment.

Despite many twists and turns, advances, and setbacks over the following four decades, economics has clearly established a much larger seat at the environmental policy table than previously. Increasingly, high quality, peer-reviewed RIAs and other economic studies are performed throughout the agency and the results used to shape agency decisions.

By the end of 2019, the agency employed almost sixty PhD economists, roughly double the 1996 levels (the last year of a full staff census), and an estimated six to eight times more than in the early 1970s.[38] Hundreds of additional EPA staff have master's level economics training or MBAs. EPA also routinely draws on economists in academia, think tanks, and consulting firms to develop new analytic techniques and analyze both the benefits and costs of environmental rules. Environmental and natural resource economists have served on specialized subcommittees of the Science Advisory Board.[39] Even with the general growth in agency staffing over the years, the large-scale expansion in the number of economists involved in EPA analyses clearly stands out.

In the early days, the vast majority of agency economists directly involved in regulatory activity worked in the policy office. Today that office remains a central player on economic issues and currently houses the National Center for Environmental Economics (NCEE). At the same time, every major program office now has its own economists on staff, many of whom work collaboratively with their policy office peers.

Clearly, measuring the influence of economic analysis in the regulatory process is far more challenging than simply counting heads. One indicator of the expanded influence of the discipline can be found in the 2008 publication Retaking Rationality: How Cost-Benefit Analysis Can Better Protect the Environment and Our Health, by NYU Law Professors Richard Revesz and Michael Livermore. While observing that many benefit-cost analyses have been used to roll back or stop environmental and public health protections, including stricter fuel efficiency standards and the ban on asbestos, the authors argue that these assessments can just as easily justify or rationalize proposed new environmental rules. For example, they cite the Court of Appeals for the Ninth Circuit finding that the Bush-era EPA had failed to account for the greenhouse gas reductions that result from tighter fuel-efficiency standards, noting that "if they had included the benefits of those reductions . . . [it] . . . would have led to more efficient vehicles on the market."[40] This embrace of benefit-cost analysis stands in contrast to those opposing the application of economic analysis to environmental policy-making, largely on moral or ethical grounds.[41]

Since 1981, EPA has developed more than one hundred and fifty RIAs on major regulations.[42] Less comprehensive economic studies have been performed for hundreds more non-major rules. Most of the RIAs are complex technical studies, hundreds of pages in length, costing several million dollars each. While some RIAs have been prepared internally, largely by program office economists, most of them are written by contractors and consultants under the supervision of agency staff. These studies generally integrate multidisciplinary scientific literature by toxicologists, epidemiologists, biologists, chemists, engineers, and economists.[43] Guidelines issued by EPA's policy office seek to achieve consistency in methods and approaches used across the agency, although a number of studies have found substantial variability in the overall quality of these economic analyses and in the adherence to agency and OMB guidelines.[44]

Questions have also been raised about potential political bias in the use of economic analysis. In an attempt to quantify such biases, a 2014 paper I published with my Resources for the Future colleague Art Fraas examined specific arguments advanced by OMB on the strengths and weaknesses of RIAs over the period 1997-2012. Overall, we found that while most arguments fell within the mainstream of economic thinking, Republican administrations focused more on uncounted costs of regulation at both the firm and societal level, while uncounted benefits have often been given greater emphasis in Democratic administrations.[45] Beyond OMB views, high level political figures have spoken out on environmental economic issues, although such statements are not necessarily determinative of the views of an entire administration.[46]

To help understand some specifics of the expansion of economics at EPA over the years, the next several sections review three major economics success stories: the phasedown of lead in gasoline; the development of the acid rain program (ARP); and the establishment of the social cost of carbon (SCC). These cases stand out because they all involve large-scale health and/or environmental gains, they occurred under both Democratic and Republican presidents, and each represents a different contribution by agency economists. Not coincidently, all three of the major initiatives involve air or climate issues—the areas where economic analysis has been used most extensively at the agency. Subsequent sections chronicle selected contributions of economics on water, waste, and pesticide issues—areas where economics plays a growing but historically smaller role.

Lead Phasedown

EPA regulation of lead in gasoline began in the early 1970s, motivated by the destructive potential of lead on the catalytic converters required by the agency to meet emission standards for hydrocarbons, nitrogen oxides, and carbon monoxide.[47] Regulation of the lead content of motor fuels reduced exposure to lead itself, although gasoline was not seen as a significant source of the few violations of the lead NAAQS, the only relevant EPA standard at the time.

By the early 1980s, regulatory requirements were in place for large petroleum refiners for both the production of unleaded gasoline and an overall limit on the lead content of leaded fuels. Small refiners faced more lenient standards. In early 1982, following a recommendation from the vice president's Task Force on Regulatory Relief, and a controversial meeting between EPA Administrator Anne Gorsuch and a small New Mexico refinery seeking compliance relief, EPA proposed to delay pending new rules that would have tightened the standards for both large and small refiners. In response to strong opposition within the agency as well as from environmental groups and public health officials, in late 1982 a final rule lowered the allowable lead content of leaded gasoline for most refiners and phased out special provisions for small refiners by mid-1983.

Less than a year after the 1982 rulemaking, and following the return of Bill Ruckelshaus as EPA administrator, Alvin Alm, then serving as deputy administrator, asked the agency's policy office to study the benefits and costs of further reducing lead in gasoline. A small team headed by Joel Schwartz and Albert (Nick) Nichols, under the direction of Milton Russell and me, produced a major study, eventually released in the form of an RIA, which quantified benefits in monetary terms in three major categories: children's health effects related to lead, reduced maintenance costs for automobiles, and the ozone co-benefits associated with the reductions of various tailpipe emissions.[48] While limited information prevented quantification or monetization of other adverse effects of lead in gasoline, policy office research on a previously unstudied health effect, namely, reduced blood pressure levels for adults, was conducted and published as part of the overall lead phasedown effort. Costs were estimated based on a linear programming model originally developed for the Department of Energy.

The final RIA estimated that in the first year of implementation (1986) the new rule would prevent 172,000 children from exceeding the 25ug/dl blood lead action level established by the Centers for Disease Control.[49] The monetized benefits of the proposed rule were estimated to exceed costs by roughly a factor of three-to-one. If the new studies linking elevated lead levels to high blood pressure and consequent cardiovascular disease in adults were included, the benefit-cost ratio was more than ten-to-one.

The final regulation, in the form of a tradable performance standard jointly developed by the Policy Office and the Office of Mobile Sources, included innovative provisions for the banking and trading of lead rights while dramatically slashing the use of lead in leaded gasoline in less than a year. The estimated costs were twenty percent less than alternative approaches that did not use market mechanisms.[50] The banking provisions, which allowed lead credits to be saved for later use, provided incentives for early reductions to help meet the new regulatory requirements. Unlike the textbook cap-and-trade program later developed for the SO_2 program, there was no formal allocation of permits. Instead, the regulation implicitly awarded property rights on the basis of current gasoline production levels. The rigor of the RIA was widely seen as an important factor in gaining quick OMB and White House support in an administration heavily oriented to regulatory relief. Subsequent analysis revealed that the trading and banking provisions had, in fact, speeded compliance and also provided significant incentives for diffusion of cost-saving technologies.[51] The proactive nature of the RIA and the support of senior agency management have also been cited as key factors in the success of the lead phasedown effort.[52]

Several studies have examined the impact of the lead phaseout on an ex post basis. Reyes (2007) finds robust evidence that lowered exposure to lead in the late 1970s and early 1980s explains fifty-six percent of the drop in crime rates in the 1990s.[53] A 2018 paper by Aizer et al. documents the positive effects on the test scores of minority children associated with lead phasedown.[54] A 2019 paper by Hollingsworth and Rudik examines the automotive racing exemption in the rule and finds that each leaded race significantly increases the prevalence of elevated blood lead levels in children and the elderly mortality rate.[55]

A 2017 review by Schmalensee and Stavins identified several overall lessons from the lead phasedown program:[56]

- It served as a proof of concept, showing that a tradable emission rights system could be environmentally effective and economically cost effective.
- It demonstrated that transaction costs could be small enough to permit substantial trade. As Schmalensee and Stavins note, "requiring prior government approval of individual trades had raised transactions cost and hampered trade in EPA's Emissions Trading Program in the 1970s (a set of emission-reduction-credit systems), while the lack of such requirements was an important factor in the success of lead trading."[57]
- It revealed the importance of banking, which contributed a significant share of the gains from trade.

Acid Rain Program (ARP)

Starting in the late 1970s, there was growing concern that forests and aquatic ecosystems were being damaged by acid deposition—due largely to the long-distance transport of SO_2 and NOx emissions from coal-fired power plants. Pressure for action came from NGOs, northeastern states, and the Canadian government, concerned about the transboundary flows of acid rain precursors and other pollutants. Unlike lead phasedown, where the debate and analysis were largely conducted inside EPA, the acid rain issue was actively considered by Congress, EPA, and the NGO community for over a decade. More than seventy bills were introduced in the 1980s to rollback SO_2 emissions by six to twelve million tons per year, many of which included specific requirements for scrubbers at the dirtiest plants and for the extension of the 1977 Clean Air Act NSPS emissions standards to existing sources.[58] Economic studies were conducted by academics, industry, and EPA on the cost of meeting the new requirements, which differed dramatically among individual electric generating units, depending on the type of coal burned, facility age, and other factors. Arguably, it was the interplant cost differences that limited the appeal of one-size-fits-all methods and opened the door to a more flexible market-based approach.

Even before President George H. W. Bush's 1989 inauguration, staff at EPA and other agencies, along with the vice-president's office—under the leadership of Bush's close associate, later to become counsel to the president, C. Boyden Gray—set to work on a set of proposed amendments to the Clean Air Act. Recall that Bush had campaigned to be the "environmental president" and to look to the marketplace for innovative solutions. Project 88, chaired by Senators Timothy Wirth (D-CO) and John Heinz (R-PA) and directed by Harvard Professor Robert Stavins, stimulated widespread discussion in the environmental policy community about market-based approaches. Alone among major environmental groups, the Environmental Defense Fund supported an emissions trading approach. In spring 1989 the administration advanced a proposal that embodied emissions trading. Ultimately, Congress adopted Title IV of the 1990 Clean Air Act Amendments, structurally quite similar to the administration's proposal, which mandated a fifty-percent reduction in SO_2 emissions from 1980 levels via cap-and-trade to provide regulated sources with the flexibility to select the most cost-effective approach to reduce emissions. Importantly, the legislation included specific provisions for implementation of the program, including the scope of covered sources, the emissions cap, allowance allocation, and targets and timetables.

Arguably, most of the technical decisions about the stringency and design of regulations were dictated by Congress in the quite detailed statutory provisions of Title IV. Implementation, of course, fell to the agency, in this case the OAR's Clean Air Markets Division (CAMD). In several rulemakings and guidance documents issued throughout the 1990s, the agency faced choices about how much to rely on private markets and how much to require administrative preapprovals. Most experts now agree that the agency made quite sound choices in these cases, generally deferring to the market.[59]

Overall, the success of the ARP represents a major turning point in EPA regulatory activity, especially in the air program. Building on the earlier offset and bubble programs, as well as lead phasedown, the ARP laid the groundwork for later OAR market-based initiatives, including the highly effective NOx Budget Trading Program.[60]

The success of the ARP in reducing emissions and achieving environmental goals at relatively low cost—well below predicted levels—has been widely chronicled.[61,62] Interestingly, the substantial public health gains associated with the ARP were not fully understood when the program was established, although early agency analysis suggested they could be significant.[63] A recent analysis found that the "Acid Rain Program caused lasting improvements in ambient air quality," reducing mortality risk by five percent over ten years.[64]

Schmalensee and Stavins (2017) identify several lessons from the ARP that generally reinforce findings from the lead phasedown program:[65]

- It is valuable to put final rules in place well before the beginning of the first compliance period, as was done two years prior to the 1995 initial phase with the SO_2 allowance trading program (to provide some degree of certainty to regulated entities, facilitate their planning, and limit price volatility in early years).
- As with the lead trading program, the absence of requirements for prior approval of trades reduced uncertainty for utilities and administrative costs for government, and it contributed to low transaction costs and substantial trading.
- As in the lead trading program, banking was extremely important, accounting for more than half of the program's cost savings.
- A robust allowance market can be fostered through a cap that is significantly below business-as-usual (BAU) emissions, combined with unrestricted trading and banking.
- Allocation of free allowances can be used to build political support, an important reminder for later programs focused on climate change.
- Intra-sector emissions leakage can be minimized, as it was in this program, by including all nontrivial sources within the sector.
- High levels of compliance can be ensured through accurate emissions monitoring and significant penalties for noncompliance.

Social Cost of Carbon

Following the 2007 Ninth Circuit Appeals Court finding that a weakened fuel efficiency rule was "arbitrary and capricious" because of the failure to consider the value of CO_2 reductions, economists from EPA, the National Highway Traffic Safety Administration (NHTSA), and other federal agencies began efforts to develop monetary values for these reductions based on the framework established under EOs 12291 and 12866.[66] An interagency working group was established in 2009 in the Obama administration, especially when it became clear that the House-passed Waxman Markey legislation for a national, economy-wide cap-and-trade scheme would not be approved in the Senate and that targeted policies were the only practical means of achieving near-term emission reductions. With a wide array of potential policies to be considered, including energy efficiency standards in buildings, motor vehicles, and appliances, it was important to identify the most cost-effective options.

The SCC represents the monetized damages of a one-ton increase in CO_2 emissions, including changes in agricultural productivity, human health, property damages, power systems, ecosystems, and other effects. The interagency working group sought to estimate the SCC in a rigorous manner, taking account of the long-lived nature of CO_2 and other greenhouse gases and the global breadth of the damages. The group was composed of economists and scientists from multiple federal agencies. Staff from EPA's policy office took the lead in the modeling analysis. The report of the Interagency Working Group on the social cost of carbon, issued in 2010, developed a range of SCC values using three integrated assessment models, multiple socioeconomic and emissions scenarios and discount rates, and a probability distribution for equilibrium climate sensitivity. For emissions occurring in 2010, the central SCC value was $21 per ton of CO_2 emissions, with sensitivity analyses ranging from $5 to $65 (2007 dollars per ton of emissions). By 2020, the central value rose to $26 per ton of CO_2. Subsequent revisions raised the central value to $42 per ton of CO_2 for 2020. Importantly, these estimates represented the global benefits of CO_2 reductions, not simply those for the US. Using similar methods, EPA subsequently developed social cost estimates for emissions of methane and nitrous oxide.[67] A number of other countries have followed the US lead and developed comparable estimates and EPA has used the SCC to support various rulemakings.[68] As discussed later in this chapter, an early action by the Trump administration involved a major downward revision of the SCC.

The Agency-Wide Impacts of RIAs

Beyond the three major applications of economics to agency rulemaking discussed so far, several scholarly studies have examined how economic analyses have helped shape rulemakings across the agency. Fraas (1991) examined economic analyses conducted in the 1980s and found that while better RIAs can make a major contribution to the decision-making process, a number of them have not provided the analysis required by EO 12291. "The most common problems," he noted, "are that they fail to consider suitable alternatives to the selected regulatory action, and they fail to quantify benefits."[69]

In a provocatively titled paper, "Reinventing the Regulatory State," Pildes and Sunstein (1995) evaluate the significance of EO 12866 and its predecessor (EO 12291) by focusing on regulatory institutions, along with regulatory means and ends. As regards the presence of an institution to oversee and coordinate regulatory policy, they see OIRA as "highly salutary . . . [at least potentially] by encouraging early consultation and taking advantage of information from affected persons at early stages of agency action . . . to help reduce agency-OIRA conflicts."[70] Interestingly, they argue for splitting the RIA process into two stages, the first focusing on a quantitative cost-benefit assessment with as much disaggregation as feasible in order to indicate how costs and benefits are distributed over various groups and interests. In the second stage, they propose that "agencies should take into account differences between expert and lay value frameworks, concerns for equity, the expressive dimensions of the choice, and other relevant values not subject to the cost-benefit approach."[71] Unfortunately, the authors do not explicitly explain how either stage has or could alter regulations.

A mid-1980s agency report examined the fifteen major rules requiring RIAs plus a few analyses prepared for nonmajor rules issued over the previous several years. Apart from lead phasedown, the report identified various rule improvements, including both cost reductions and benefits enhancements in excess of $3 billion per year, and specific regulatory options adopted to achieve the desired degree of environmental benefits at lower cost than the initial proposals, primarily in the hazardous waste and toxics substances programs. At the same time, the report notes, "for many of these analyses, the necessary scientific and/or economic data were either inadequate or unavailable. In [some cases, however] EPA simply did not thoroughly carry out all of the specific types of analyses called for in the RIA guidelines."[72]

Morgenstern (1997) organized a dozen regulatory case studies of RIAs developed over the 1985–94 decade. Most studies were prepared by current or former EPA staff who were involved in the original analyses. In reviewing these studies, Morgenstern and co-author Mark Landy found that the group of RIAs had made significant contributions to the final rules although, as they note, "in most cases the authors do not argue that the changes [some of which were small] . . . occurred solely because of the economic analyses. Nor do they argue that the same or similar changes might not have occurred for other reasons."[73]

In all twelve RIAs examined by Morgenstern and Landy, specific cost savings were identified, including a reduced number of products covered by the rule, and the substitution of monitoring of indicator pollutants for broadscale monitoring. Beyond lead in gasoline, four of the case study authors attribute specific benefit-enhancing measures to the economic analysis: lead in drinking water, reformulated gasoline, Navajo Generating Station, and the organic chemicals effluent guidelines.

Typical rule changes included decreased emission or discharge rates, expanded coverage of source categories, and a shortened time period for emitters to come into compliance. One RIA helped identify a potential cross-media transfer of VOCs from water to air, which stimulated subsequent efforts to address these emissions under the Clean Air Act. In some cases, changes were made which also enhanced the administrative feasibility of the rules and increased the likelihood of compliance. For the asbestos rule, the RIA identified various products that could be removed from the marketplace at low to moderate cost.[74] In several cases where the economic analysis did not explicitly strengthen the rule, it helped support the regulation in the face of OMB and public scrutiny.

In the case of CFCs, the analysis demonstrated the extent of the expected stratospheric ozone depletion and revealed that low-cost alternatives existed for many uses. The analysis also made the case for the use of tradable permits among US producers and laid the groundwork for the excess profits taxes on CFC producers later adopted by Congress. The most immediate impact of the analysis was to support Administrator Lee M. Thomas' efforts in support of the government's 1987 adoption of the Montreal Protocol to the Vienna Convention.

Interestingly, John Bachman, former associate director for Science/Policy and New Programs, Office of Air Quality Planning and Standards, Office of Air and Radiation, reports a case where an RIA may have discouraged an EPA administrator from relaxing the PM standard.[75]

Beyond its use in addressing air pollution and global environmental problems, economic analysis has been adopted by other major agency programs. An important application in the waste programs is the so-called subtitle D rule, which covers municipal solid waste landfills. Promulgated in 1991, the subtitle D rule involved seven years of study by EPA. A number of issues emerged over the study period, including baseline questions which, in turn, created uncertainty about the rule's incremental costs above those previously imposed by state and local governments, the protectiveness of the statutory minimum option (that relied on corrective action to clean up groundwater contaminated by leaking landfills), the economic impact on small communities, the value of clean groundwater, and the impact of leaking sites on local property values. In the end, the regulation mandated only a single liner (as opposed to the double liners required at hazardous waste facilities subject to Subtitle C regulation), although even less stringent options were legally possible.[76]

McGartland (2013) chronicles a number of important instances of EPA's use of economics, including the case of the pesticide Alar, the trade name for daminozide, a chemical used to keep fruit firm and full-colored beyond its natural shelf life.[77] Arguably, the economic analysis revealed important flaws in the agency's process for registering pesticides. As previously noted, before the 1996 amendments FIFRA required the agency to balance the risks and the economic benefits of such chemicals. Prior to the 1980s expansion of economics at the agency, the pesticide office would compare the estimated risks with the benefits of a particular pesticide—defined as the changes in farm income associated with use of the pesticide. As McGartland notes:

> There were two major problems with this approach. First, the regulator should be focused on incremental reductions in risk. If EPA canceled the registration

of a particular pesticide, farmers would turn to substitute pesticides, so the risk associated with substitution needed to be incorporated as well. Second, changes in farmers' incomes were not a proper measure of the benefit of using—or the cost of canceling—the pesticide.[78]

In the mid-1980s, when McGartland and other policy office economists started working with the pesticide office to develop a benefit-cost analysis, they estimated that the incremental cost per cancer case avoided from a total Alar ban was relatively low. Within the program office there were concerns about the losses in farm income associated with banning Alar because some apple growers were heavily reliant on the chemical. Concerns were also raised about the uncertainty of the risk estimates. Principally based on their economic analysis, McGartland and other policy office staffers argued for full cancellation of Alar. In the end, the pesticide was permitted to remain on the market, pending further review and data development. It wasn't until the negative publicity from a story on CBS's *60 Minutes* and Congressional testimony by Meryl Streep that the main producer voluntarily removed the pesticide from the market. Arguably, the public reaction to the risk posed by Alar was excessive. As McGartland notes, however, "economists were in a position to say that the panic could have been avoided if EPA had regulated Alar even with the limited data available. With this case, it became clearer to EPA managers that economic analyses did not always support weakened regulation."[79]

The strengths and weaknesses of economic analysis as applied to Clean Water Act (CWA) issues are illustrated in the case of the regulations on the design and operation of cooling water intake structures for power plants and industrial facilities, as mandated under Section 316(b) of the CWA. Typically, these structures pull large numbers of fish and shellfish (or their eggs) into the machinery, killing or injuring them by heat, physical stress, or the chemicals used to clean the cooling system.

EPA actions to issue Section 316(b) rules date back to 2004 and 2006, although both of the early regulations were successfully challenged in court. In 2014 EPA re-promulgated key regulatory provisions to replace the suspended 316(b) requirements.

The 2014 rule required more than one thousand large power plants and manufacturing facilities to choose among multiple options to reduce mortality of aquatic organisms. A key issue was whether or not to mandate minimum controls across all facilities, as in predecessor regulations, or to rely strictly on the site-specific determinations.

Most of the controversy surrounding the economics of the rule involved the estimation of benefits, tied to reductions in the kills or injures of aquatic organisms. By reducing these kills, the rule would increase the number of fish, shellfish, and other organisms in the affected water bodies, and produce recreational, commercial fishing, and other user benefits.[80] Estimates were also developed for nonuse or passive use values that are independent of any current or anticipated use of the resource, reflecting human values associated with existence and bequest motives, i.e., the willingness to pay (WTP) for the knowledge that an ecosystem is functioning without the effects of human activity, or to convey the functioning ecosystem to future generations. The agency used several different valuation methods to develop these estimates, including market data and benefit-transfer approaches from studies involving stated preference and other WTP methods. Several regional analyses were also performed, and benefit categories that were not quantifiable or monetized were identified. In addition, damages associated with the increased CO_2 emissions were estimated based on the SCC.

EPA analyzed a range of costs associated with the cooling water intake rule and characterized a number of key uncertainties. Total benefits were estimated to be about $33 million annually at a three-percent discount rate although, as the agency noted, "some potentially significant benefit categories have not been fully monetized, and thus the national monetized benefits are likely to understate substantially the rule's expected benefits to society."[81] Total annual costs to society were estimated to be roughly an order of magnitude more than the monetized benefits, $275–297 million, depending on the discount rate used.

The incompleteness of the benefits estimates and the (implicit) assignment of zero value to some important but difficult to quantify impacts were key issues for debate within the agency. Some EPA staff argued that efforts to conduct the needed stated preference surveys were hampered by budget limitations and the difficulty of obtaining OMB approvals under the requirements of the Paperwork Reduction Act. Ultimately, the rule was reissued in 2014 without a mandate for minimum controls across all facilities. After extensive litigation, it was ultimately upheld by the Second Circuit Court of Appeals.

A further example where economic analysis played a significant role in the agency's water-related agenda is the arsenic in drinking water rule, initially issued at the end of the Clinton administration, subsequently withdrawn by the George W. Bush administration, and later reinstated by the Bush administration without significant changes. Recall that the 1996 revision to the Safe Drinking Water Act authorized the agency to adjust the MCLs upwards, above the technically feasible level, if the benefits do not justify the costs.

Anyone who has read an Agatha Christie novel knows that arsenic is extremely toxic at high doses. The key question for the regulators, however, was how strong a carcinogen it is at low doses. Scientists debated whether the cancer risk from low levels of exposure were proportional to the risks at higher levels or whether serious risks only arise after concentrations reach a certain threshold. A National Research Council (NRC) report identified several international studies that found significant cancer risks at low levels and a number of domestic papers that found no measurable risks.[82] In an extensive review of the evidence, Sunstein (2001) argues that "[with these results] . . . it would not have been entirely astonishing for the NRC to find that the evidence was too inconclusive to support a new rule."[83] In the end, the NRC recommended that EPA lower its current standard of fifty parts per billion (ppb). Critics attacked the NRC study on various grounds, including the fact that the key Taiwanese paper underlying the recommendations was based on quite different cooking and nutritional practices than were used in the US. The absence of a single report of a US arsenic-induced cancer case supported that critique.

Given the underlying uncertainty about the cancer risks, the RIA projected 0-112 "lives saved" from the proposed reduction of the standard to 10 ppb. The costs were estimated to range from $0 to $560 million, with the highest costs per household (by far) falling on smaller, rural water systems often serving lower-income populations. Overall, the agency estimated that the costs of the 10 ppb standard ranged from $2 million to $60 million higher than the monetized benefits. Estimated benefits were closest to costs at a 20 ppb standard. A detailed study by Robert Hahn and Jason Burnett at AEI-Brookings estimated costs were more than $100 million above the monetized benefits.[84]

Interestingly, Hahn and Burnett raised questions about the usefulness of their own cost-benefit analysis. In contrast, Sunstein argued that the wrong lesson to draw from this RIA is that:

> [A] specification of benefits and costs tells us little that we did not already know . . . [Rather] an effort to trace both costs and benefits can inform inquiry, making decisions less of a stab in the dark. This is indeed a substantial gain. Once the range is specified, a judgment of value, and not of fact, will be [required]. But the judgment of value will be easier to identify once we understand what we do not know. A real virtue of cost benefit analysis is that it helps to explain exactly why the choice of regulation in the case of arsenic is genuinely difficult . . . it is a large improvement over the "intuitive toxicology" seen in the public reaction to the decision.[85]

Comparative Risk Studies

During their relatively brief second stint at the agency, Administrator Bill Ruckelshaus and his deputy, Alvin Alm, commissioned a task force of career staff to compare the risks associated with major environmental problems beyond existing control levels. While not an economic analysis *per se,* the 1987 report of the seventy-five person agency-wide task force, *Unfinished Business,* embodied a risk- and evidence-based approach to priority setting. The principal finding was that the "rankings by risk do not correspond well with EPA's current program priorities."[86] Climate change and air pollution were ranked as relatively high risks while hazardous and solid waste issues were ranked lower. Administrator Lee Thomas, who previously helmed EPA's waste program, quickly embraced the agency-wide perspective of *Unfinished Business*, describing it as "a credible first step toward a promising method of analyzing, developing and implementing environmental policy."[87]

Early in his EPA tenure, Administrator William K. Reilly asked the SAB to review *Unfinished Business.* The resulting SAB report recommended that EPA target opportunities for the greatest risk reduction and that a stove-pipe approach to environmental protection was no longer suited for use in addressing real world environmental problems. The SAB also noted some of the difficulties in using comparative risk assessment in priority setting.[88] Subsequently, the agency applied the comparative risk approach in its internal budget process and to priority-setting challenges in several locales around the US, including Santa Clara, California, and Denver, Colorado. It was also used in Agency for International Development-funded demonstration projects in eastern Europe and various developing countries.

Studies on the Costs and Benefits of the Clean Air Act

In an amendment introduced by Senator Daniel P. Moynihan (D-NY), Congress added Section 812 to the 1990 Clean Air Act Amendments, requiring EPA to conduct periodic, scientifically reviewed studies on the effects of the Act on the "public health, economy, and the environment of the United States." Previously, the agency did not face a specific mandate to conduct ex post analyses of the public health and environmental benefits of its rules. The first two 812 analyses, covering the periods 1970–1990 and 1990–2010, found that monetized benefits of the Clean Air Act far exceeded costs, driven by large PM mortality and lead benefits.[89] Throughout their lengthy preparation, the studies were scrutinized by an expert SAB subcommittee of economists, air quality modelers, epidemiologists, and other health experts, chaired by economist Richard Schmalensee of MIT.[90] In March 2011, EPA issued the third prospective study, which examined the results of the CAA from 1990 to 2020. The central benefits estimate in this study also exceeded costs by a wide margin.

The 812 studies faced criticism from outside economists concerned about the baseline assumption that all air quality improvements since 1970 are properly attributable to the CAA, and for the agency's failure to disaggregate the analysis sufficiently to determine if even higher net benefits could have been achieved by alternative policies.[91] Administrator Carol Browner and other agency leaders were quite supportive of these analyses and cited them in multiple budget and programmatic requests to Congress.

A number of studies looking back at the performance of individual rules issued under authority of multiple environmental statutes have been published since the late 1990s. While the emphasis on individual rules limits the ability to make broad statements about entire statutes, it does strengthen the basis for ascertaining the effect of specific regulations in a causal manner. Harrington et al. (2001) and Harrington (2006) compared the ex ante estimates of regulatory costs to those realized ex post for a set of rules for which data were available.[92] While these studies found cases of both overestimation and underestimation of costs across several different samples of rules, on average total costs were overestimated. Interestingly, the same studies found that the average cost per ton of emissions or discharges reduced are reasonably accurate, defined by the authors as +/- 25 percent. The authors suggest that one reason for the different findings regarding total and average costs is that regulated firms reduced emissions or discharges less than expected, which helps explain the overestimates of expected total costs. Other factors are also likely at work, including unanticipated technological innovation and inaccurate baseline information on current emission levels.

Other retrospective studies have used quasi-experimental methods to develop a counterfactual (control group) against which to examine the costs (or benefits) of EPA regulations.[93] Typically, these studies—mostly focused on the Clean Air Act—compare the performance of regulated firms to similar entities not subject to the same regulation. Due to the complexity of establishing a suitable control group, these analyses are often difficult (and expensive) to carry out. It is not feasible to summarize this literature here, but recent research reveals cases where regulation has been more effective than expected. Other research identifies rules which have failed to attain the anticipated goals. On the cost side, examples of both underestimates and overestimates are also found in this literature. Unintended consequences of regulation have been quantified as well, including job losses, increases in the market power of regulated firms, and inequity in the distribution of costs or benefits across demographic groups. Areas designated nonattainment under the Clean Air Act have suffered employment losses and reduction in industrial output as a result of the spatially oriented approach to regulation.

EPA itself has undertaken several retrospective analyses of regulatory costs, with the stated aim of improving ex ante cost estimation.[94] These analyses explore various hypotheses about differences between *ex ante* and *ex post* cost estimates. They also involve a number of empirical studies that seek to understand why and how the discrepancies arise. While the work is still in its infancy, it represents a promising path forward for developing more accurate ex ante analyses of future rules.

Economic Incentives across the Agency

As discussed throughout this chapter, interest in market-based mechanisms can be traced as far back as the early 1970s, including the Nixon era proposal for a Pure Air Tax and, most importantly, to the issuance of EPA's Bubble Policy in the Costle era along with initiatives regarding pollution offsets, banking, netting, and trading. The lead phasedown program (1985) was the first market mechanism to allow such transactions without prior EPA approval. Project '88, chaired by Senators Heinz and Wirth and organized by Harvard professor Robert Stavins, had a major impact on the thinking about market mechanisms within the agency, as well as in the broader environmental policy community. Administrator William K. Reilly established an agency-wide task force to consider additional opportunities for using economic incentives. The task force developed options for various incentive-based initiatives, including pollution fees and taxes, trading and marketable permits, deposit-refund systems, liability mechanisms, information-based programs, subsidies, and other approaches that could be applied in the areas of municipal solid waste, climate change, water resource management, and multi-media activities.[95] Some of these were later adopted by EPA or by state and local authorities.

The Evolving Role of the Policy Office

From EPA's earliest days, the agency's policy office conducted economics-oriented studies of agency rules. Often these studies supported individual program office initiatives. Other times they were crosscutting in nature, e.g., the early studies on *The Cost of a Clean Environment,* which estimated the aggregate costs of environmental protection across all programs.[96] As the agency's conduct and use of economic methods evolved over time to include benefits analysis, general equilibrium modeling, and other specialized approaches, the policy office often took the lead in developing guidance materials and assisting individual program offices in the use of these techniques. From the earliest days, the policy office also reviewed and critiqued analyses and regulatory proposals made by program offices and, from time to time, developed independent policy proposals.

Early on, Bill Ruckelshaus encouraged wide-ranging discussion within the agency about options for addressing environmental problems. Often critiques advanced by the policy office—then headed by a presidentially appointed Senate-confirmed assistant administrator—sparked important debates between the economic efficiency-oriented policy office, and program offices charged with implementing individual statutes. Sometimes those debates resulted in changes to the design or scope of individual rules or policies, such as the lead phasedown regulation discussed earlier. Sometimes the policy office arguments were rejected or just resulted in fine-tuning the rules or simply sharpening the supporting arguments. In interviews conducted for this chapter, a number of current and former program office analysts expressed their appreciation for the policy office reviews and the advance warning they provided for comments from OMB or the public, although this was not a universally held view. Interestingly, in his oral history project interview, Administrator Bill Reilly lamented that the policy office played a relatively small role in the early agency deliberations on the 1990 Clean Air Act Amendments.[97]

Beginning in the late 1970s with the Council on Wage and Price Stability and, later, the OMB reviews of agency regulations, the policy office also got involved with the program offices in interacting with OMB and, sometimes, other White House offices. By the mid-1980s, there was growing resistance inside EPA to the policy office's engagement with the interagency process. In response, EPA Administrator Lee M. Thomas issued a memorandum clarifying that the relevant program offices, which by this time had developed more experience with economics, were solely responsible for individual rules as they worked their way through the full regulatory process, including the interagency reviews. Arguably, the Thomas memorandum, which remains in effect today, was a sound management decision, aligning accountability and control in the hands of the program offices. At the same time, it was widely seen as limiting the influence of the policy office.

As regards the internal debates that were generated by the policy office reviews of individual regulations, not all EPA administrators saw great value in the process, especially when word would leak to the press about the different options under consideration. In those cases, the internal debates were seen as weakening the administrator's flexibility in decision-making, and/or providing ammunition to OMB or others opposing specific regulatory provisions.

It is difficult to pinpoint exactly when the policy office's role in independently reviewing individual rules was scaled back. Based on my own recollections and interviews with current and former staff, the change is most clearly linked to an agency reorganization plan advanced by Administrator Carol Browner which sought, among other goals, to better integrate economic analyses directly into program office activities. As part of this mid-1990s reorganization, Administrator Browner also established EPA's National Center for Environmental Economics (NCEE) and attached it directly to the office of the administrator. Further, she shifted the coveted presidential appointee Senate-confirmed position, long held by an assistant administrator for policy, to the Office of International Affairs. Since that time, the policy office's activities have been more heavily weighted toward regulatory support, with less emphasis on independent regulatory review.[98]

Trends in the Net Benefits of EPA Rules

There is no simple way to assess overall trends in the contribution economics has made to EPA's effectiveness or efficiency in managing the environment. Although it is clouded by changes in the scientific understanding of the impacts of environmental contaminants, especially the effects of fine particles on human mortality, one rough metric of trends in the net benefits of EPA rules (the difference between total benefits and total costs) can be found in OMB's annual *Reports to Congress on the Benefits and Costs of Federal Regulations and Agency Compliance with the Unfunded Mandates Reform Act.*[99] The 2017 report estimates \$343.5 billion (2001 dollars) in total benefits vs \$45.3 billion (2001 dollars) in costs for the major EPA rules issued for the period 2006-2016, roughly a seventy-percent increase in the real net benefits compared to the major rules issues in the prior decade (1995-2005).[100] Thirty-nine different major rules were issued in each of the two decadal periods. By far, air regulations—driven by PM mortality—comprised the bulk of the benefits for both periods (ninety-six to ninety-seven percent). Various commentators and the OMB reports themselves are replete with caveats about the uncertainty of the estimates.[101]

THE TRUMP ERA

In his campaign for the presidency, Donald Trump spoke repeatedly about excessive regulation by EPA and other federal agencies, similar to the language used by candidate Ronald Reagan almost four decades earlier. Compared to Reagan, however, Trump has moved more aggressively to scale back EPA regulations. Whereas Reagan supported mainstream economics, the Trump administration tried to change some of the basic math of benefit cost analysis. Recall Bill Ruckelshaus' often cited comment about risk assessment being like a captured spy: "if you torture it long enough, it will tell you anything you want to know."[102]

Initial Actions

Initially, the Trump administration delayed or proposed to revoke a range of existing rules, primarily air pollution and climate change regulations issued in the last year of the Obama Administration. The principal rationale for these revocations was the claim of high costs. EO 13771, "Reducing Regulation and Controlling Regulatory Costs," issued a mere ten days into the Trump Administration, called for the removal of two regulations for every new one promulgated, without regard to the benefits of the rules. Professor Lisa Heinzerling, a long-time critic of benefit-cost analysis, has labeled the Trump approach as "cost nothing" analysis.[103]

Social Cost of Carbon

The earliest effort by the Trump administration to reduce the agency's benefits estimates is the recalculation of the SCC (described below). Other significant revisions have also been undertaken, most notably those involving ancillary or co-benefits of air pollution and the monetization of ecological benefits.

The revisions to the SCC are among the most extreme of the Trump administration's attempts to alter economic analysis. In the RIA supporting repeal of the Clean Power Plan, the Trump EPA argued that the Obama administration used too low a discount rate (which gives greater weight to future benefits). The Trump EPA also argued that the Obama administration inappropriately included non-US benefits in the calculation. The Trump EPA added a new scenario using a higher (seven percent) discount rate. Further, they limited the calculations to include only those benefits accruing directly to the US.[104] Together, these changes lowered the 2020 values for the SCC to \$6 or \$1 per ton, depending on the discount rate (three percent and seven percent, respectively)—a huge reduction from the previous central value of \$42 per ton of CO_2 for 2020 (all in 2007 dollars).

Although the addition of an estimate based on a seven-percent discount rate is, arguably, consistent with past regulatory guidance under OMB *Circular A-4*, the mainstream economics view is that such a high discount rate is inappropriate for estimating the inter-generational damages associated with long-lived gases like CO_2. Similarly, counting only direct domestic US benefits from carbon mitigation ignores the inherently global commons nature of climate change and the prospect that regulatory actions taken by the US may influence policies of other nations. In fact, every nation finds itself in a situation where the benefits of its actions will spill over to other countries.

The failure to subject these new SCC calculations to peer review further undermines their legitimacy.

Co-Benefits of Regulation

Long-standing EPA and OMB guidance documents reflect the broad consensus within the economics community regarding the treatment of ancillary co-benefits in regulatory analyses.[105] For example, existing OMB guidance states that "analytic priority should be given to those ancillary benefits and countervailing risks that are important enough to potentially change the rank ordering of the main alternatives in the analysis. . . . Like other benefits and costs, an effort should be made to quantify and monetize ancillary benefits and countervailing risks."[106]

While it is clearly appropriate to seek rigorous assessment of potentially more cost-effective means of achieving regulatory benefits, arbitrarily limiting consideration of these benefits, as the Trump EPA has done in several recent regulatory actions, is indefensible. For example, in a December 2018 Notice of Proposed Rulemaking for the mercury air toxics rule (MATS), EPA sought to reverse a prior agency finding that regulation of hazardous pollutants (HAPs) is "appropriate and necessary."[107] Although the magnitude of the PM co-benefits resulting from the control of mercury are not in dispute, EPA proposed to ignore these benefits to support its conclusion that the benefits of the MATS are less than the costs. Numerous experts, with diverse views on regulation, have spoken out against the agency decision to exclude these co-benefits, arguing that all significant costs and benefits should be counted.[108] There are concerns about the appropriate baselines or possible rebound effects.[109] In the case of the MATS, EPA has not presented a better, more cost-effective way to achieve these benefits.

Other Rules

Three other climate-related regulatory actions by the Trump administration involving co-benefits and/or the SCC are also noteworthy for their inconsistent use of economics: the proposed revisions to the Corporate Average Fuel Economy (CAFE) Standards, the withdrawal of the Clean Power Plan, and the draft of the proposed replacement rule, the Affordable Clean Energy (ACE) rule. Each one of these actions represents a challenge to long-established principles of economic analysis. In the CAFE revision, despite an administration that has questioned the use of ancillary benefits, we see strong reliance on estimates of negative safety benefits (so-called dis-benefits) to justify relaxation of fuel efficiency standards. Further, the RIA gives considerable weight to a recent (and not widely reviewed) estimate of the rebound effect and the negative ancillary benefits associated with the added congestion and the additional vehicle miles traveled. In contrast, the case for withdrawing the Clean Power Plan seems to rest heavily—some might say exclusively—on the cost analysis. Ancillary benefits are given short shrift, despite the substantial increase in PM mortality associated with the withdrawal of the rule.

To the Trump EPA's credit, the RIA for the proposed ACE does include a benefits analysis based on standard agency approaches for treatment of ancillary benefits, although it relies on the revised values of the SCC. On a plain reading, the RIA would support the most stringent of the three options considered. The fact that the agency proposed and, ultimately, promulgated a less stringent option which leaves a lot of foregone net benefits on the table calls into question their adherence to the welfare-maximizing provisions of the existing Executive Orders on regulatory analysis.

Beyond these changes to air pollution and climate-related rules, the Trump EPA has also made other changes that departed from established approaches in other areas. For example, the decision to rescind the 2015 Waters of the United States (WOTUS) rule issued by the Obama administration—which increased the amount of wetlands subject to federal regulation under the Clean Water Act and replace it with a new, less stringent regulation in 2017—hinges on the exclusion of annual wetlands-related benefits which the EPA and Army Corps of Engineers jointly estimated two years earlier ranged from $300 million to $500 million. As a distinguished group of economists note in *Science Magazine*, "we find no defensible or consistent basis provided by the agencies for the decision to exclude what amounts to the largest category of benefits from the 2017 RIA."[110]

Further, it is important to call out the Trump administration's efforts to scale back the influence of mainstream economists in the review of EPA studies. In June 2018, the agency abolished the Environmental Economics Advisory Committee (EEAC), a group that had operated for more than twenty-five years within EPA's SAB where it had served as an important source of peer review for the agency's economic analyses.[111] Fortunately, in the spring of 2020 the agency established an *ad hoc* committee of respected economists and other experts to review the agency's updated *Guidelines for Preparing Economic Analyses*.

TRENDS OVER FIFTY YEARS

In looking back over the fifty-year history of economics at EPA, a number of points emerge:

1. Notwithstanding the statutory limitations, and the early resistance to economic analysis, EPA has successfully embraced a neoclassical, net benefits analytic framework and integrated economics into numerous regulatory and policy decisions. Clearly, EPA ranks in the top tier of federal regulatory agencies for the quality of its economic analyses.
2. The nature of economic analyses conducted at EPA has broadened considerably over the years, moving from a strict focus on costs, cost-effectiveness, economic impacts, and affordability to include what are, arguably, a more fundamental set of issues, e.g., estimation of the benefits of new regulations and a comparison of benefits and costs. While all EPA offices have attempted to quantify and monetize the benefits and costs of new rules, the greatest advances have come in the analysis of health damages, the primary endpoints in air and drinking water regulation. Substantial progress has also been made in monetizing the potential damages from climate change. Efforts to monetize the benefits in other areas have been undertaken as well, although they are generally less advanced.
3. While the initial decision by President Reagan to introduce benefit-cost analysis into decision-making was a push for deregulation, the agency's strong response, building on the growing academic field of environmental and resource economics, has supported new regulatory initiatives in many areas. As Revesz and Livermore note: "the politically driven biases that tilt cost-benefit analysis against regulation arise from a historical accident, not an inherent flaw."[112] The quite substantial increase in the number of economists employed at the agency and the presence of economists on various subcommittees of the Science Advisory Board have added capacity and legitimacy to the agency's economics work.
4. Over the years, market mechanisms have been used to address a growing number of environmental challenges. While many of these initiatives have involved air pollution, successful programs have been developed in other media as well, especially at the state and local levels. Examples include the privatization of some wastewater systems and the pricing of municipal solid waste. Unsurprisingly, there is still resistance to these approaches in some quarters.[113]
5. Further, EPA has embraced economics-oriented approaches along multiple dimensions not directly related to benefit-cost analysis. Examples include cross-agency priority setting, the use of big data to study the performance of existing rules, and the analysis of risk and uncertainty.
6. While the bulk of the economics-trained staff initially resided in the agency's centralized policy office, over the years most program offices established in-house economics capabilities of their own. The current focus of the centralized policy office is heavily oriented to providing technical support to the program offices. Independent assessment of regulatory op-

tions from economists not tied to program offices are now less common than in earlier years.

7. The Trump administration has emphasized cost reductions and de-emphasized the health and welfare benefits of regulation. Examples of efforts to revamp the basic elements of environmental and resource economics include the recalculation of the SCC, and the downplaying of ecological and co-benefits. These actions face strong opposition from the mainstream economics community.
8. OMB reviews of EPA rules and RIAs have been controversial throughout the agency's history. While the process is still greatly frustrating to EPA staff, there is now more transparency and openness than previously.

CONCLUSION

This historical review has highlighted various developments affecting EPA's conduct and use of economics over the agency's first half century. The advantage of hindsight is just that—the capacity to review past practices. At the same time, earlier developments may not be especially useful predictors of the future. The field of environmental and resource economics is quite vibrant. Undeniably, there are many factors that drive the focal points and types of analyses emphasized in the policy process. The 2020 presidential election will certainly influence both the conduct and use of economics in environmental decision-making in the coming years.

Several economics-oriented challenges merit special emphasis. First and foremost, in my view, is the importance of restoring the integrity of economics to EPA analyses and decision-making processes. Such a move would strengthen both the agency's legal defenses as well as its standing in the court of public opinion. Re-establishing mainstream economics would also support the development of new climate change policies issued under authority of the Clean Air Act or, possibly, new legislation.

If Congress were to enact new climate relevant authorities, EPA might be able to consider broader and more efficient instruments to reduce emissions, including economy-wide carbon pricing mechanisms. Clean energy standards on industry or other sectors might be considered as well. New legislation directly authorizing efforts to address climate change would not diminish the importance of conducting rigorous analysis of any proposed new policy approaches, but such legislation would unshackle the agency from relying so heavily on the ancillary or co-benefits as justification for climate policies.

Two other future challenges for economics at EPA merit final comment. First, there is growing interest in expanding the analysis and evaluations of the distributional impacts of major environmental programs and problems, including the potential for disproportionate burdens on low-income households, communities of color, or specific areas of the country. Who wins from environmental policies? Who loses? Arguably, economics has something to contribute to addressing these questions. EPA has already carried out some work in this area, but much more remains to be done.

Finally, it is important to emphasize the importance of institutional learning. Currently, there are growing, but still quite limited, efforts to look back at existing regulations to evaluate the impacts of environmental regulation from an ex post perspective. Despite the expansion of environmental economics over the past five decades, most of the current efforts involve ex ante analysis. A key challenge to any future EPA will be to carry out (or support) systematic assessments that compare ex ante estimates of policy impacts with ex post retrospective determinations of major environmental rules. The late Senator Daniel Patrick Moynihan deserves credit for championing such efforts. Rigorous evaluation of past rules will provide a much-needed means for validating (or not) the ex ante analyses. It will also yield evidence of both the successes and shortcomings of environmental regulation, including any unintended consequences. High quality retrospective analyses can help shape future regulation and policy and also reveal appropriate analytic frameworks that can be applied to forward-looking ex ante assessments. Fortunately, the data and methods are now more available than ever to carry out these studies. To EPA's credit, they have begun work in this area. Much more is needed.

NOTES

1. The author acknowledges helpful comments and insights from Frederick Allen, Alan Bassala, John Bachman, Carol Browner, Alan Carlin, Alex Cristofaro, Devra Davis, Roy Gamse, John Graham, Arthur Fraas, Linda Fisher, Robert Fuhrman, Alan Krupnick, Michael Livermore, Al McGartland, William Reilly, Michael Shapiro, and participants in various Indiana University review meetings (2019).

2. A major regulation is defined as one with annual costs or benefits in excess of $100 million.

3. William D. Ruckelshaus, "Stopping the Pendulum," *Environmental Toxicology and Chemistry* 15, no. 3 (1996): 230, https://doi.org/10.1002/etc.5620150301; see also Cary Coglianese, "The Limits of Consensus: The Environmental Protection System in Transition: Toward a More Desirable Future," *Environment: Science and Policy for Sustainable Development* 41, no. 3 (1999): 28-33, DOI: 10.1080/00139159909604620.

4. Cost and benefit information may also be used in enforcement actions under most statutes, since these are largely the province of states, which are generally granted discretion in this area.

5. Chevron USA v. NRDC, 467 U.S. 837 (1984).

6. Whitman v. American Trucking Associations, Inc., 531 U.S. at 465 (2001). Specifically, the court found that it was "fairly clear that this text does not permit the EPA to consider costs in setting the standards." More recent decisions have added important qualifications. For example, in Michigan v. EPA, 576 U.S. 743 (2015), a challenge to a CAA regulation on hazardous air pollutants, the Supreme Court ruled that the agency must consider costs when deciding to regulate rather than later in the process of issuing the rule.

7. John D. Graham and Paul R. Noe, "A Paradigm Shift in the Cost-Benefit State," *The Regulatory Review*, April 26, 2016. For example, S. 1080, the "Regulatory Reform Act of 1981," passed the Senate in 1982 by a vote of 94-0, but it was not acted upon in the House. In 1995, as part of the "Contract with America," the House passed H.R. 1022, the "Risk Assessment and Cost-Benefit Act of 1995," but the companion bill, S. 343, the "Comprehensive Regulatory Reform Act of 1995," died in the Senate after a long floor debate and three unsuccessful cloture votes in the summer of 1995. Since then similar legislation has been introduced, although none has been enacted into law.

8. For example, the Congressional Review Act (CRA), which provides an expedited process for Congress to override a regulation, was adopted as Subtitle E of the Contract with America Advancement Act of 1996 (Pub. L. 104–121) and signed into law by President Clinton on March 29, 1996. The CRA empowers Congress to review, by means of an expedited legislative process, new federal regulations issued by government agencies and, by passage of a joint resolution, to overrule a regulation. Once a rule is thus repealed, the CRA limits its reissuance in substantially the same form. Congress has a window lasting sixty legislative days to disapprove any given rule by simple majority vote; otherwise, the rule will go into effect at the end of the period. The Data Quality Act (DQA) or Information Quality Act (IQA), was enacted in 2001 as a two-sentence rider in a spending bill. While the DQA has been criticized as providing a vehicle for special interest groups to challenge regulations on the grounds of not meeting information quality requirements, a 2004 Report by the Congressional Research Service found it had a limited effect on regulation.

9. Consolidated Appropriations Act, Pub. L. 106–554 §515.

10. See US Congressional Research Service, *The Information Quality Act: OMB's Guidance and Initial Implementation,* RL32532 (Washington, DC: CRS, August 19, 2004), https://fas.org/sgp/crs/RL32532.pdf. CRS stated that "In April 2004, OMB provided Congress with a report on the implementation of the DQA during FY2003. The report said the agencies received only about thirty-five substantive correction requests during the year, and said it was "premature to make broad statements about both the impact of the correction request process and the overall responsiveness of the agencies." Many other correction requests listed in the report were on minor issues or involved matters that had been dealt with before the IQA was enacted. OMB indicated there was no evidence that the IQA had affected the pace of rulemaking. However, OMB Watch (a public interest group) said OMB's report was "seriously flawed" in that it understated the number of correction requests and did not disclose that nearly three-quarters of the requests were from industry. A major test of the IQA's effectiveness is whether agencies' denials of correction requests are subject to judicial review.

In June 2004, a US District Court ruled that the act does not permit judicial review regarding agencies' compliance with its provisions, and the Department of Justice issued a brief stating that the IQA does not permit judicial review. The Competitive Enterprise Institute filed a lawsuit to prevent dissemination of EPA's *Climate Action Report 2002* published May 2002, claiming the research did not meet requirements of the Federal Data Quality Act (FDQA). The case was dismissed in November 2003.

11. US Office of Management and Budget, "Chapter I: The Role of Economic Analysis in Regulatory Reform," Report to Congress on the Costs and Benefits of Federal Regulation, 62 Fed. Reg. 39354 (July 22, 1997), https://obamawhitehouse.archives.gov/omb/inforeg_chap1.

12. Ibid. In fact, the conclusion that regulation isn't inflationary unless costs exceed benefits is controversial since improved health or ecosystems are not generally counted in official price statistics. Thus, even net beneficial rules would drive up prices. Arguably, the operative word in the OMB statement is "truly" since in the grander scheme of economic welfare all benefits would be counted. Of course, if the OMB statement refers simply to the priority given to different rules, it is reasonable for them to focus on rules that do not have net benefits.

13. Interestingly, EPA Administrator Costle later commented that RARG's effect on rulemaking "if any, was probably to sharpen us up in doing our homework. We were never contravened." See US Environmental Protection Agency, "Douglas M. Costle: Oral History Interview," EPA 202-K-01-002, *epa.gov*, August 1996, https://archive.epa.gov/epa/aboutepa/douglas-m-costle-oral-history-interview.html.

14. Walter Barber, *Memorandum to Assistant Administrator for Air and Radiation David Hawkins on the President's Council on Wage and Price Stability Regulatory Analysis Review Group (COWPS/RARG) Critique of the Proposed NAAQS for Ozone* (Research Triangle Park, NC, November 8, 1978), cited in John Bachman, "Will the Circle Be Unbroken: A History of the U.S. National Ambient Air Quality Standards," *Journal of the Air & Waste Management Association* 57, no. 6 (2007): 679.

15. OMB, *Costs and Benefits of Federal Regulation.* The report also cites a Court of Appeals decision (Sierra Club v. Costle, 657 F. 2d 298 (1981)) which found that a part of the president's administrative oversight responsibilities was to review regulations issued by his subordinates.

16. In 1990, President Bush revived the Reagan Task Force on Regulatory Relief—now called the Competitiveness Council—and placed Vice President Quayle in charge.

17. At the same time, EO 12291 clearly stated that the order did not create an enforceable legal right. In effect, it cannot be used as a basis for litigation.

18. For example, in his post service interview, Administrator William Reilly said: "By and large . . . we were able to work through many, if not most, of our regulations with the OMB process reasonably well. That was not true of a relatively small number which got a large amount of public attention, I think, as much for the way the issue was framed and dealt with by OMB as for their substantive view. It is profoundly frustrating to an EPA Administrator to go through all of the careful control processes of arriving at a regulatory decision or proposal and to respect all of the rules against *ex parte* contact—make sure any contact with the regulated community is recorded,

noted, memorialized, public, on the record—and then to have it go to the White House and see many of the same parties engaged in influencing other people who have influence over such decisions without any public record, without any acknowledgment that this is going on. The secrecy that characterized that process, I think, is a source of great mistrust and, potentially, of corruption. Corruption in the sense that it violates process, not that it involves anyone taking any money." See US Environmental Protection Agency, "William K. Reilly: Oral History Interview," EPA 202-K-95-002, *epa.gov*, September, 1995, https://archive.epa.gov/epa/aboutepa/william-k-reilly-oral-history-interview.html.

19. Lisa Heinzerling, "Cost-Nothing Analysis: Environmental Economics in the Age of Trump," *Colorado Natural Resources, Energy & Environmental Law Review* 30, no. 2 (2019): 291.

20. US Environmental Protection Agency, "William D. Ruckelshaus: Oral History Interview," EPA 202-K-92-0003, *epa.gov*, January 1993, https://archive.epa.gov/epa/aboutepa/william-d-ruckelshaus-oral-history-interview.html. In a similar vein, former Deputy Administrator Alvin Alm, commenting on his second EPA stint (he also served as assistant administrator for OPM during the early 1970s) stated that: "junior [OMB] people have a lot of power, particularly to delay decision-making . . . During the time I was there . . . you never really knew where things were . . . it seemed like the issues would wind up in OMB . . . unless there was . . . real pressure like a court deadline." See US Environmental Protection Agency, "Alvin L. Alm: Oral History Interview," EPA 202-K-94-005, *epa.gov*, 1993, https://archive.epa.gov/epa/aboutepa/alvin-l-alm-oral-history-interview.html.

21. For a materials and energy balance approach, see Robert U. Ayres and Allen V. Kneese, "Production, Consumption and Externalities," *American Economic Review* 59, no. 3 (1969): 282-97; for the theory and empirical basis for environmental protection, see Anthony C. Fisher, John V. Krutilla, and Charles J. Cicchetti, "The Economics of Environmental Preservation: A Theoretical and Empirical Analysis," *American Economic Review* 62, no. 4 (1972): 605–19.

22. For example, Gail Coad then Dave Gibbons (effluent guidelines), Ed Brandt (Pesticides), and Judy Nelson (Toxics) all worked at OMB.

23. Roy Gamse, personal communication with author, January, 24, 2019; See William D. Ruckelshaus, *Statement before the Subcommittee on Air and Water Pollution, Senate Committee on Public Works* (Washington, DC: EPA, February 16, 1982), 8.

24. See US Environmental Protection Agency, "Russell E. Train: Oral History Interview," EPA 202-K-93-001, *epa.gov*, May 5, 1992, https://archive.epa.gov/epa/aboutepa/russell-e-train-oral-history-interview.html.

25. Train credited Alm with building the economics staff, although in his interview Alm recognized that some of the great analysts were already on board when he arrived. See EPA, "Alvin L. Alm: Oral History Interview."

26. Alan Carlin, personal communication with author, January 16, 2019.

27. Robert C. Anderson, and Paul Kobrin, *Introduction to Environmental Economics Research at the EPA* (Washington, DC: Environmental Law Institute, 1998): 5.

28. Gamse, personal communication.

29. For example, Don Fink, Bob Hamrin, and Anne Smith.

30. EPA, "Douglas M. Costle: Oral History Interview."

31. Gamse, personal communication.

32. The Agency's Final Emissions Trading Policy, issued in 1986, integrated the bubble with offsets, netting, and banking and articulated a common currency for trades, an emissions reduction credit. As the former head of EPA's Regulatory Reform group notes in a recent review article, water trading posed additional challenges, but EPA did issue a draft Water Quality Trading Policy Framework in 1996 and Water Quality Trading Guidance in 2003. See Michael H. Levin, "Lessons from the Birth of Emissions Trading," *BioCycle,* May 2016.

33. In the case of environmental fees, there were practical design issues, such as the difficulty of structuring fees appropriate for mercury or other toxics subject to hotspots versus pollutants, which mix more readily.

34. The noncompliance initiative was based, in part, on an approach used in Connecticut when Administrator Doug Costle was head of the state DEQ.

35. "The model does not attempt to quantify the economic benefits that a firm may have obtained by improving its competitive position due to obtaining these savings . . . [because] . . . this calculation is fraught with difficulties." Robert H. Fuhrman, "The Role of EPA's BEN Model in Establishing Civil Penalties," *Environmental Law Reporter* 21 (1991): 10248.

36. A lengthier discussion of these issues would reveal that some experts do not believe that BEN and other models used in enforcement activities reflect sound economic and financial principles. They point to the limited vetting of the models outside the agency.

37. Specifically, Crandall wrote: "There are no comprehensive studies . . . that demonstrate . . . effectiveness in reducing air pollution. In fact, because of delays, poor enforcement, and imperfectly understood dispersion and transport characteristics, it is possible that the entire program has generated little reduction in air pollution despite expenditures of more than $25 billion per year in this pursuit . . . The data on air quality are so poor that one cannot confidently assert that air quality has improved because of the 1970 Clean Air Act Amendments. It is probable that carbon monoxide and sulfur dioxide concentrations have been reduced, but the reductions in SO_2 may result as much from economic factors as from environmental policy . . . some data for the 1960s demonstrate a more rapid improvement in air quality (other than photochemical smog) than occurred in the 1970s. Although the effectiveness of the policy in reducing air pollution is in doubt, its efficiency is not. There can be little doubt that the reliance upon individual point-source standards, the political deals crafted to secure support for the policy, the distinction between new and old sources, and the haphazard enforcement program have combined to give us an extremely inefficient overall policy . . . EPA data show enormous ranges in the incremental cost of control across sources of the same pollutant." See Robert W. Crandall, "The Political Economy of Clean Air: Practical Constraints on White House Review," In *Environmental Policy Under Reagan's Executive Order: The Role of Benefit-Cost Analysis,* ed. V. Kerry Smith (Chapel Hill: University of North Carolina Press, 1984), 209.

38. The estimate of the current number of PhD economists is from a personal communication with Al McGartland. The 1996 number is from Richard D. Morgenstern,

ed., *Economic Analyses at EPA: Assessing Regulatory Impact* (Washington, DC: Resources for the Future, 1997), 15.

39. The SAB Environmental Economics Advisory Committee was abolished in 2018 although as of spring 2020 it appears it is being reestablished.

40. Richard L. Revesz and Michael A. Livermore, "A Truly Green Economics," *Forbes*, December 2, 2008, https://www.forbes.com/2008/12/02/environment-supreme-court-oped-cx_rr_ml_1202reveszlivermore.html#6a1918ec71f5

41. See, for example, the writings of other prominent scholars who, just a few years earlier, had advanced a more negative storyline about economics: Lisa Heinzerling and Frank Ackerman, *Priceless: On Knowing the Price of Everything and the Value of Nothing* (New York: New Press, 2005). The authors question, among other issues, the quantification, monetization, and discounting of benefits.

42. The one hundred and fifty major regulations probably represent about two percent of the total number of rules promulgated by the agency over the period, albeit a much larger share of the costs. The two-percent figure is taken from an internal memo from OPPE Deputy Assistant Administrator Jack Campbell to EPA Administrator Lee M. Thomas dated August 1997. It only covers the period 1981–1986.

43. Agency economists were instrumental in developing some of the early analyses later expanded by epidemiologists and others. See, for example, Ostro (1984) and Schwartz and Marcus (1986). Bart Ostro, "A Search for a Threshold in the Relationship of Air Pollution to Mortality: A Reanalysis of Data on London Winters," *Environmental Health Perspectives* 58 (1984); J. Schwartz and A. H. Marcus, "Statistical Reanalyses of Data Relating Mortality to Air Pollution During London Winters 1958-72," *Appendix to Second Addendum to Air Quality Criteria for Particulate Matter and Sulfur Oxides, 1982: Assessment of Newly Available Health Effects Information,* EPA-600-8-86-020F (Research Triangle Park, NC: EPA, December 1986).

44. Robert W. Hahn et al., "Assessing Regulatory Impact Analyses: The Failure of Agencies to Comply With Executive Order 12,866," *Harvard Journal of Law and Public Policy* 23, no. 3 (Summer 2000): 859–89; Robert W. Hahn and Patrick M. Dudley, "How Well Does the U.S. Government Do Benefit-Cost Analysis?" *Review of Environmental Economics and Policy* 1, no. 2 (Summer 2007): 192–211.

45. Arthur Fraas and Richard D. Morgenstern, "Identifying the Analytical Implications of Alternative Regulatory Philosophies," *Journal of Benefit-Cost Analysis* 5, no. 1 (January 2014): 137–71.

46. Examples of high-level government officials who have spoken on environmental economics are C. Boyden Gray, (Reagan/Bush, and Bush/Cheney years) and Al Gore (Clinton/Gore years). Gray, who served as counsel to the Presidential Task Force on Regulatory Relief (chaired by Vice President Bush) and later counsel to the president (1989–93), was quite active on EPA regulatory issues, often in support of less stringent regulation and/or greater use of market mechanisms. Gore's criticism of the use of economics in setting environmental policy was articulated in his best-selling book *Earth in the Balance* (especially Chapter 10) published shortly before he was elected vice president. Al Gore, *Earth in the Balance: Ecology and the Human Spirit*, 1st ed. (Boston: Houghton Mifflin, 1992).

47. For descriptions of the history of the regulation of lead in gasoline, see Albert L. Nichols "Lead in Gasoline," In *Economic Analyses at EPA: Assessing Regulatory Impact,* ed. Richard D. Morgenstern (Washington, DC: Resources for the Future, 1997), 49–86;, Richard G. Newell and Kristian Rodgers, "Leaded Gasoline in the United States: The Breakthrough of Permit Trading," In *Choosing Environmental Policies: Comparing Instruments and Outcomes in the United States and Europe*, eds. Winston Harrington, Richard D. Morgenstern, and Thomas Sterner (Washington, DC: Resources for the Future, 2004); Robert W. Hahn and Gordon L. Hester, "Where Did All the Markets Go? An Analysis of EPA's Emissions Trading Program," *Yale Journal on Regulation* 6, no. 1 (1989): 109–53; Richard Schmalensee and Robert N. Stavins, "Lessons Learned from Three Decades of Experience with Cap and Trade," *Review of Environmental Economics and Policy* 11, no. 1 (Winter 2017): 59–79, https://doi.org/10.1093/reep/rew017.

48. Nichols, Russell, and I are all economists, as were most of the policy office staff who worked on the lead phasedown project. Schwartz has a PhD in physics but worked primarily as a health scientist. Other study authors were Jane Leggett, Ronnie Levin, Bart Ostro, and Hugh Pitcher. See Morgenstern, ed., *Economic Analyses at EPA*.

49. The current CDC blood lead action level is 10 ug/dl.

50. See Nichols, "Lead in Gasoline."

51. Suzi Kerr and Richard G. Newell, "Policy-Induced Technology Adoption: Evidence from the U.S. Lead Phasedown," *Journal of Industrial Economics* 51, no. 3 (2003): 317–43; Hahn and Hester, "Where Did All the Markets Go?"

52. See Nichols, "Lead in Gasoline."

53. Jessica Wolpaw Reyes, "Environmental Policy as Social Policy? The Impact of Childhood Lead Exposure on Crime," *The B.E. Journal of Economic Analysis & Policy* 7, no. 1 (2007).

54. Anna Aizer et al., "Do Low Levels of Blood Lead Reduce Children's Future Test Scores?" *American Journal of Applied Economics* 10, no. 1 (2018): 307–41.

55. Hollingsworth, Alex and Ivan Rudik. 2019. "The social cost of leaded gasoline: Evidence from regulatory exemptions," http://conference.nber.org/conf_papers/f132540.pdf.

56. Schmalensee and Stavins, "Lessons Learned from Three Decades"; Robert W. Hahn and Gordon L. Hester, "Marketable Permits: Lessons for Theory and Practice," *Ecology Law Quarterly* 16 (1989): 368–76.

57. Hahn and Hester, "Where Did All the Markets Go?"

58. For historical review, see Dallas Burtraw and Karen Palmer, "SO_2 Cap-and-Trade Program in the United States: A Living Legend of Market Effectiveness." In *Choosing Environmental Policies: Comparing Instruments and Outcomes in the United States and Europe*, eds. Winston Harrington, Richard D. Morgenstern, and Thomas Sterner (Washington, DC: Resources for the Future, 2004).

59. See A. Denny Ellerman et al., *Markets for Clean Air: The U.S. Acid Rain Program* (Cambridge: Cambridge University Press, 2005).

60. Examples of other CAMD trading programs following the SO_2 trading program include the acid rain industrial source opt-in-program, and the acid rain NOx

averaging program. Outside of CAMD, additional trading and banking programs were developed for diesel engines. The CAA was also responsible for a NOx trading program (RECLAIM) in Southern California. Further, a market for renewable fuel (RIN) credits was made part of the implementation of the Renewable Fuel Standard (RFS) in OAR's Office of Mobile Sources.

61. See Schmalensee and Stavins, "Lessons Learned from Three Decades"; Burtraw and Palmer, "SO_2 Cap-and-Trade Program in the United States"; H. Ron Chan, et al., "The Impact of Trading on the Costs and Benefits of the Acid Rain Program," *Journal of Environmental Economics and Management* 88 (March 2018): 180–209.

62. Interestingly, starting in 2003, the prospect of new air quality regulations as well as a series of federal court decisions delivered a period of high and volatile allowance prices. Later, as new, more stringent regulations affected power plant SO_2 emissions and provided less compliance flexibility than under the Acid Rain Program, the cap-and-trade program ceased to bind on power plants. By 2012, allowances cleared at auction prices below $1 per ton, well below the $1,000 per ton allowance prices of the mid-2000s.

63. John Bachman of OAR noted the importance of early PM research by policy office staffers Bart Ostro, Joel Schwartz, and others on the health effects of fine particles. John Bachman, personal communication with author, January 2019.

64. Alan I. Barreca, Matthew Neidell, and Nicholas J. Sanders, "Long-Run Pollution Exposure and Adult Mortality: Evidence from the Acid Rain Program," *National Bureau of Economic Research*, working paper no. 23524 (June 2017), doi:10.3386/w23524.

65. Schmalensee and Stavins, "Lessons Learned from Three Decades."

66. The 9th circuit decision followed a Supreme Court decision, Massachusetts v. Environmental Protection Agency, 549 U.S. 497, in which twelve states and several cities sued the agency to force the federal government to regulate CO_2 and other GHGs.

67. US Interagency Working Group on Social Cost of Greenhouse Gases, *Addendum to the Technical Support Document for the Social Cost of Carbon: Application of the Methodology to Estimate the Social Cost of Methane and the Social Cost of Nitrous Oxide* (Washington, DC: EPA, August 2016), https://www.epa.gov/sites/production/files/2016-12/documents/addendum_to_sc-ghg_tsd_august_2016.pdf.

68. Specifically, the SCC was used to support several car and truck mileage standards and the (now retracted) Clean Power Plan. It has also played a role in setting standards for pollutants that indirectly affect CO_2 emissions, such as the control of mercury and other air toxics emitted by power plants. The social cost calculations of methane and nitrous oxide have been used in rulemakings affecting the oil and natural gas sector. In all cases, use of the SCC helped make a case for more stringent regulation.

69. Arthur Fraas, "The Role of Economic Analysis in Shaping Environmental Policy," *Law and Contemporary Problems* 54, no. 4 (Fall 1991), 125, https://scholarship.law.duke.edu/lcp/vol54/iss4/5.

70. Richard H. Pildes and Cass R. Sunstein, "Reinventing the Regulatory State," *University of Chicago Law Review* 62, no. 1 (1995): 127, https://chicagounbound.uchicago.edu/uclrev/vol62/iss1/1.

71. Ibid.

72. When the lead in gasoline rule is included, the net benefits rise to more than $10 billion per year. US Environmental Protection Agency, Office of Policy Planning and Evaluation, *EPA's Use of Benefit-Cost Analysis:1981-1986,* EPA-230-05-87-028 (Washington, DC: EPA OPPE, 2018), 2, https://www.epa.gov/sites/production/files/2018-02/documents/ee-0222-1.pdf.

73. Richard D. Morgenstern and Mark K. Landy, "Economic Analyses: Benefits, Costs, Implications," In *Economic Analyses at EPA: Assessing Regulatory Impact,* ed. Richard D. Morgenstern (Washington, DC: Resources for the Future, 1997), 457.

74. In 1991 the 5th Circuit Appeals Court struck down major parts of EPA's ban on asbestos products, ruling that the agency had not adequately considered alternative regulation short of the prohibition. The federal government did not appeal the ruling. See Christine Augustyniak, "Asbestos," In *Economic Analyses at EPA: Assessing Regulatory Impact,* ed. Richard D. Morgenstern (Washington, DC: Resources for the Future, 1997), 171–203.

75. Bachman reports as follows about a 1982 meeting he had with Administrator Anne Gorsuch: "A number of months after the CASAC closed on the SP and made their final recommendations on the standards (January 1982), I received a phone call from a high level EPA political appointee with some instructions for an immediate special briefing limited to this official, Administrator Anne Gorsuch, and me. In this after-hours session, I reviewed the scientific and policy bases for the decision. In response to a question at the end, I noted the results of the then draft PM Regulatory Impacts Analysis (RIA) were not included because they had not been reviewed and contained cost information that could not be considered in the decision. I then summarized the key finding, which though preliminary and uncertain, suggested that the estimated benefits of the PM_{10} standards exceeded the costs even at the lowest end of the ranges of the two standards combined. The administrator was furious. She could not believe that the air office would develop material that would undercut her choice for the PM standards. Almost certainly because of that exchange, we received no official guidance for the proposal before she left the agency, and PM was caught in limbo. This is the only case in which I know that an RIA had a direct influence on an administrator's non-decision regarding the NAAQS." See John Bachman, "Will the Circle Be Unbroken: A History of the U.S. National Ambient Air Quality Standards," *Journal of the Air & Waste Management Association* 57, no. 6 (2007): 682.

76. According to one EPA manager, "staff at OMB . . . did not [believe] . . . the RIA played a strong role in the decision-making process since the most cost-efficient option, according to the RIA, was not chosen. [However, EPA] staff indicate that because of concerns about costs, the analysis played a role in identifying how to keep the final rule costs down . . . by identifying the more inexpensive and more efficient sub-options . . . (the final rule was significantly cheaper than the proposed rule)." Sara Rasmussen, "Municipal Landfill Management," In *Economic Analyses at EPA: Assessing Regulatory Impact,* ed. Richard D. Morgenstern (Washington, DC: Resources for the Future, 1997), 261. Arguably, the decision to require the single liner was used to support subsequent agency decisions to allow recycled batteries,

cleaning supplies, and other household wastes to be deposited in permitted subtitle D municipal landfills.

77. McGartland, a highly respected PhD economist who has served as the director of the National Center for Environmental Economics since its creation in the late 1990s, has in-depth knowledge of Alar, as he worked on the issue while in a staff position in the policy office in the 1980s. See Al McGartland, "Thirty Years of Economics at the Environmental Protection Agency," *Agricultural and Resource Economics Review* 42, no. 3 (2013): 436–52.

78. Ibid., 446.

79. Ibid., 447.

80. Direct benefits include both "market" commodities (e.g., commercial fisheries) and "nonmarket" goods (e.g., recreational angling). Indirect use benefits pertain to impacts on the aquatic ecosystem food web.

81. US Environmental Protection Agency, *Economic Analysis for the Final Section 316(b) Existing Facilities Rule*, EPA-821-R-14-001 (Washington, DC: EPA, 2014), 1–10, https://www.epa.gov/sites/production/files/2015-05/documents/cooling-water_phase-4_economics_2014.pdf.

82. National Research Council, *Arsenic in Drinking Water* (Washington, DC: The National Academies Press, 1999), https://doi.org/10.17226/6444.

83. Cass R. Sunstein, "The Arithmetic of Arsenic," *Georgetown Law Journal* 90 (2001): 2270, https://pdfs.semanticscholar.org/5ca2/433d817159185403e841d1201be800f29616.pdf.

84. Robert W. Hahn and Jason K. Burnett, "A Costly Benefit: Economic Analysis Does Not Support EPA's New Arsenic Rule," *Regulation* 24, no. 3 (Fall 2001), https://ssrn.com/abstract=291806 or http://dx.doi.org/10.2139/ssrn.291806.

85. Cass R. Sunstein, "The Arithmetic of Arsenic," 2302.

86. US Environmental Protection Agency, *Unfinished Business: A Comparative Assessment of Environmental Problems,* 000R87901 (Washington, DC: EPA, 1987), xv.

87. Lee M. Thomas, "Preface," In *Unfinished Business: A Comparative Assessment of Environmental Problems,* 000R87901 (Washington, DC: EPA, 1987), ii. In an interview with the author (April 27, 2019), Thomas noted that the relative priorities established in *Unfinished Business* are as relevant today as they were in 1987. See also Philip Shabecoff, "Report Says Agency Focuses on Lesser Problems," *New York Times,* February 19, 1987, B6.

88. US Environmental Protection Agency, *Reducing Risk: Setting Priorities and Strategies for Environmental Protection*, SAB-EC-90-021 (Washington, DC: EPA Science Advisory Board, 1990).

89. US Environmental Protection Agency, *The Benefits and Costs of the Clean Air Act, 1970 to 1990,* EPA-410-R-97-002 (Washington, DC: EPA, 1997); US Environmental Protection Agency, *The Benefits and Costs of the Clean Air Act, 1990 to 2010,* EPA-410-R-99-001 (Washington, DC: EPA, 1999).

90. The review took place under the auspices of the legislatively mandated Advisory Committee for Clean Air Compliance Analysis. Interestingly, the baseline and disaggregation were actively debated by the committee before release of the retro-

spective report. However, the consensus in the group was that the data and modeling needed to address these concerns did not exist at the time.

91. For a detailed review of the first two studies, see Alan Krupnick and Richard D. Morgenstern, "The Future of Benefit-Cost Analyses of the Clean Air Act," *Annual Review of Public Health* 23 (2002): 427–48, https://doi.org/10.1146/annurev.publhealth.23.100901.140516.

92. For example, see Winston Harrington, Richard D. Morgenstern, and Peter Nelson, "On the Accuracy of Regulatory Cost Estimates," *Journal of Policy Analysis and Management* 19, no. 2 (Spring 2000): 297–322; Winston Harrington, *Grading Estimates of the Benefits and Costs of Federal Regulation, discussion paper 06–39* (Washington, DC: Resources for the Future, 2006).

93. Richard D. Morgenstern, "Retrospective Analysis of U.S. Federal Environmental Regulation," *Journal of Benefit-Cost Analysis* 9, no. 2 (2018): 285–304, https://doi.org/10.1017/bca.2017.17; Janet Currie and Reed Walker, "What Do Economists Have to Say about the Clean Air Act 50 Years after the Establishment of the Environmental Protection Agency?" *Journal of Economic Perspectives* 33, no. 4 (2019): 3–26; Joseph E. Aldy et al., "Looking Back at Fifty Years of the Clean Air Act," working paper 20-01 (Washington, DC: Resources for the Future, 2020).

94. Elizabeth Kopits et al., "Retrospective Cost Analyses of EPA Regulations: A Case Study Approach," *Journal of Benefit-Cost Analysis* 5, no. 2 (2014): 173–193.

95. US Environmental Protection Agency, *Economic Incentives: Options for Environmental Protection*, EE-0315-P21-2001 (Washington, DC: EPA, March 1991), https://www.epa.gov/environmental-economics/economic-incentives-options-environmental-protection-1991.

96. US Environmental Protection Agency, Office of Policy Planning and Evaluation, *Environmental Investments: The Cost of a Clean Environment*, EPA-230-11-90-083 (Washington, DC: EPA OPPE, November 1990), https://www.epa.gov/sites/production/files/2017-09/documents/ee-0294b_all.pdf. For a useful review of this report see Ralph A. Luken and Arthur G. Fraas, "The US Regulatory Analysis Framework: A Review," *Oxford Review of Economic Policy* 9, no. 4 (1993): 96–111.

97. Specifically, Reilly said: "My first nominee was Terry Davies as assistant administrator for policy. He was, I think, the lone Democrat in the crowd and he was the last one agreed to by the White House. White House personnel simply held hostage Terry Davies until they made sure the rest of the complement was to their liking. I think that was a big mistake and they came to regret it. It meant that the Office of Policy Planning and Evaluation had no champion and was not effectively represented in the formulation of the Clean Air Act. It might have been a somewhat different Act had they been included. The staff there was somewhat critical of parts of it. But, as counsel to the president, Boyden Gray used to complain about not having OPPE involved in it, he was quick and generous in acknowledging that it was his and the White House's fault. They hadn't given me Terry Davies until the Clean Air Act had been forwarded to Congress." See EPA, "William K. Reilly: Oral History Interview."

98. As the NCEE website notes, the office serves as consultants to the agency, promotes consistent economics, enhances EPA's economic tools, links science and

policy, and connects with outside experts on priority analytic needs. See "Who We Are," *ncee.org*, http://ncee.org/who-we-are/.

99. US Office of Management and Budget, *2017 Draft Report to Congress on the Benefits and Costs of Federal Regulations and Agency Compliance with the Unfunded Mandates Reform Act* (Washington, DC: OMB, 2017), https://www.whitehouse.gov/wp-content/uploads/2017/12/draft_2017_cost_benefit_report.pdf.

100. These estimates are based on the midpoints of the ranges reported by the OMB.

101. Former OIRA administrator Susan Dudley has argued that the OMB's reported estimates are highly dependent on a few assumptions about PM benefits and that the ranges presented are unlikely to reflect the true uncertainty surrounding them. Susan E. Dudley, "OMB's Reported Benefits of Regulation: Too Good to Be True?" *Regulation* (Summer 2013): 26–30. Also see the criticism that EPA has double counted co-benefits: C. Boyden Gray, "EPA's Use of Co-Benefits," *Engage* 16, no. 2 (2015): 31–33.

102. Ruckelshaus, "Risk in a Free Society," speech at Princeton University February 18, 1984, reprinted in *Environmental Law Reporter*, https://elr.info/sites/default/files/articles/14.10190.htm.

103. Heinzerling, "Cost-Nothing Analysis: Environmental Economics in the Age of Trump," *Colorado Natural Resources, Energy & Environmental Law Review* 30, no. 2 (2019).

104. Gray has labeled GHG reduction outside the US as "foreign co-benefits." See Gray, "EPA's Use of Co-Benefits."

105. US Environmental Protection Agency, *Guidelines for Preparing Economic Analyses* (Washington, DC: EPA, May 2014), https://www.epa.gov/sites/production/files/2017-08/documents/ee-0568-50.pdf; US Office of Management and Budget, *Circular A-4* (Washington, DC: OMB, September 17, 2003), https://obamawhitehouse.archives.gov/omb/circulars_a004_a-4/.

106. OMB, *Circular A-4*, 26.

107. See Advance Notice of Proposed Rulemaking, *Environmental Protection Agency (EPA) Proposed Rule: Increasing Consistency and Transparency in Considering Costs and Benefits in the Rulemaking Process*, Docket ID No. EPA–HQ–OA–2018–0107. Most recently (December 2018), the EPA issued a Notice of Proposed Rulemaking for the mercury air toxics rule which limits consideration of the ancillary benefits.

108. For example, Richard Schmalensee of MIT has stated: "The actual costs and benefits of a proposed new regulation, whether strengthening or weakening environmental protection, are as a matter of basic logic independent of the nominal target of that regulation. It would be illogical and inconsistent with basic economics to ignore what are often called co-benefits—as it would be to ignore some of the costs involved. Indeed, transparency requires that all costs and benefits, co- or not, be made explicit and valued where possible." Richard Schmalensee, Comment on the *Environmental Protection Agency (EPA) Proposed Rule: Increasing Consistency and Transparency in Considering Costs and Benefits in Rulemaking Process,* August 23, 2018, https://www.regulations.gov/document?D=EPA-HQ-OA-2018-0107-1756.

Similarly, Joseph Cordes, Professor of Economics at George Washington University and co-director of the university's Regulatory Studies center, stated that "there is no disagreement in the extensive literature on benefit-cost analysis about the appropriateness of counting indirect effects or co-benefits. To the extent that indirect benefits or costs are true joint products of a regulation or program, and not merely different manifestations of the primary benefit or cost, such effects should legitimately be included as a social cost or benefit." Joseph Cordes, Comment on the *Environmental Protection Agency (EPA) Proposed Rule: Increasing Consistency and Transparency in Considering Costs and Benefits in Rulemaking Process*, August 20, 2018, https://www.regulations.gov/document?D=EPA-HQ-OA-2018-0107-1232.

109. Susan E. Dudley et al., "Consumer's Guide to Regulatory Impact Analysis." The EPA has not argued that the technology used to comply with MATS is not a cost-effective way of also controlling PM emissions. Before issuing a final rule that relied on any such justification, the EPA would of course have to re-propose it.

110. See Kevin J. Boyle, Matthew J. Kotchen, and V. Kerry Smith, "Deciphering Dueling Analyses of Clean Water Regulations: Hundreds of Millions of Dollars in Benefits Were Discarded," *Science* 358, no. 6359 (October 2017). According to the authors, the designation of wetlands-related benefits as unquantified is inconsistent with best practices for conducting benefit-cost analysis. Specifically, "the stated reasons for their exclusion are as follows: Older studies introduce uncertainty because public attitudes toward nature protection may have changed; the studies may not have used the most recent methodological approaches; and the limited number of studies make it difficult to validate the estimates. The 2017 RIA also argues that more recent studies are not available. It is important to note, however, that the 2017 RIA does not apply a consistent criterion for when studies are considered 'too old' to produce reliable benefit estimates. If either the date when data were collected or when a study was published is the standard for inclusion or exclusion (i.e., prior to 2000 in this case), then the standard should be applied uniformly. Yet the benefit measures retained in the 2017 RIA for point sources of pollution are based on data collected in 1983 and published in 1993 . . . Thus, if the stated exclusion rule were applied consistently, this would imply no quantification of benefits for any categories of water-quality effects. But this is incompatible with decades of scientific research on the estimates of economic benefits for water-quality improvements and on the connectivity of streams and wetlands to downstream waterways. . . . Importantly, assuming all or most benefits are unquantifiable, and thus implicitly assigning $0 for excluded benefits, undermines the use of conducting a benefit-cost analysis. The age of studies alone is not a defensible criterion for excluding categories of economic benefits. RIAs related to environmental quality should take advantage of all the credible information available using state-of-the-art benefit-transfer methods to calibrate existing value estimates to meet the needs of each new rule. . . . [Further] . . . our review of the literature uncovered at least 10 studies published since 2000 that could be considered for expanding the body of knowledge on wetland values [see supplementary materials (SM)]. The 2017 RIA correctly notes that methods to measure economic values for changes in environmental quality have advanced over the last three-plus decades. . . . However, the decision pertaining to wetlands-related benefits is inconsistent with best practices

within the current economics literature. Before studies are excluded from consideration, best practice requires documentation that either they did not use methods that would meet contemporary standards or that estimates could not be adjusted to reflect uncertainty based on newer research. The 2017 RIA did not provide such documentation, and well-established methods for conducting benefit-cost analysis suggest that whenever possible, best estimates should be presented along with a description of the uncertainties," 48–49.

111. In response to the dissolution of the EEAC, an outside group of economists set up an independent organization, the External Environmental Economics Advisory Committee (E-EEAC), dedicated to providing up-to-date, nonpartisan advice on the state of economic science as it relates to EPA programs. While this group has no official standing in the regulatory process, it is attempting to use the bully pulpit to subject the agency's economic analyses to rigorous peer review. A first effort by the E-EEAC was the development of an influential critique of the RIA for the MATS rule. See Joseph E. Aldy, Matthew J. Kotchen, Mary Evans, Meredith Fowlie, Arik Levinson, and Karen Palmer, *Report on the Proposed Changes to the Federal Mercury and Air Toxics Standards* (Washington, DC: External Environmental Economics Advisory Committee, December 2019), https://cb4388c0-f641-4b7b-a3ad-281c0e6f8e88.filesusr.com/ugd/669644_35b6835a3c26451680bae954f11d2282.pdf.

112. Revesz and Livermore, "A Truly Green Economics."

113. Recent Supreme Court decisions on CAMR and CAIR could limit market mechanisms in the absence of specific legislation. Concerns about environmental justice have also been raised, e.g., in California.

Chapter Twelve

Politics and EPA

David M. Konisky and Megan Mullin[1]

EPA was created at a momentous time in US politics. The Vietnam War was escalating, large-scale movements to secure civil rights for African Americans and equal rights for women were ongoing, and political and social unrest was erupting in the streets in large cities from Los Angeles to Chicago to Baltimore. Although we tend to look back at this period of time as one of tumult and crisis, in many important areas of public policy, it was also a period of great optimism and promise. This is certainly the case for environmental protection. As Jim Barnes describes in Chapter 1, there was both a rising tide of concern about environmental problems and, just as importantly, a strong collective conviction that the federal government could effectively intervene to solve them. A responsive Congress and executive branch took heed by enacting far-reaching and wide-ranging laws that reshaped environmental policy in the United States for the next half century.

The newly created EPA would be tasked with implementing these new laws and was buoyed in its efforts by several important features of US politics at the time. First, there was general agreement across party lines, at both the elite and mass public levels, regarding the importance of environmental problems. Second, by historical standards, and despite the previously mentioned political unrest, public trust and confidence in government institutions was high. Third, an emerging set of advocacy organizations had the legal and scientific capacity to help defend the mission of the nascent EPA. And, fourth, there was general agreement about the nature of the problems to be confronted and who should bear responsibility—mainly, large business and heavy industry. This widely shared definition of the problem of environmental degradation helped provide clarity as to the appropriate policy interventions.

In sum, the creation of EPA in December 1970 came during a political moment when the new agency enjoyed broad, bipartisan support, built on a widely held belief that EPA's mission "to protect human health and the environment" was both important and urgent. These conditions have changed profoundly over the succeeding five decades, such that the politics surrounding EPA now interfere with the agency's ability to effectively carry out its mission. To be clear, as previous chapters in this book have documented, EPA in many ways has delivered on the promise to improve environmental quality and social welfare for most Americans. But, despite these successes, the agency has become mired in political conflict that now affects nearly every aspect of its work. Some of the conflict reflects broader developments in the American political system, while other aspects are specific to EPA, its mission, and the policy tools it employs. Taken as a whole, the agency has become a political football, with every major decision seemingly shrouded in controversy.

In this chapter, we document changes in environmental politics since EPA's establishment and trace the ways that politics have influenced the agency's ability to administer and enforce environmental laws. Although a wide range of activity external and internal to EPA can fall under the moniker of "politics," our discussion will emphasize the most sweeping and consequential change in the American political system during this period—the growth of partisan polarization among elected officials and in the broader mass public. We begin by demonstrating that polarization has been particularly pronounced on the issue of the environment. We show how polarization saturates EPA's political context, setting the stage for conflict over the agency's activities within Congress and the courts, between states, among stakeholders and the mass public, and within presidential administrations themselves. The stark partisan divide on environmental regulation has produced swings in policy but also has contributed to enduring changes in EPA budget and authority. Being asked to do more with fewer resources leaves more room for discretion in policy implementation, contributing to environmental outcomes that can vary widely across communities. Finally, we discuss the changing nature of the environmental problems that EPA confronts. Because the most pressing contemporary challenges are less visible than those that motivated EPA's formation, they do not arouse widespread public demands for action that could help mitigate polarization's effects.

PARTISAN POLARIZATION ON THE ENVIRONMENT

The Bipartisanship of the "Environmental Decade"

Many scholars of environmental politics and policy refer to the 1970s as the "environmental decade," bracketed by the enactment of the National

Environmental Policy Act in 1970 and the passage of the Superfund law in 1980.[2] Until that time, responsibility for environmental protection had rested largely at the state and local levels, attracting differing levels of interest and seriousness across jurisdictions.[3] For its part, the federal government generally limited its activities to conducting research, providing guidance, and encouraging (but not compelling) performance standards.

During the environmental decade, the US environmental protection system was remade. Congress enacted more than a dozen major statutes, in areas ranging from air and water pollution to chemicals and pesticides to waste management and contaminated site remediation. Table 12.1 lists the major statutes assigned to the fledgling EPA during this time, each of which receives more detailed attention elsewhere in this book.[4] Collectively, these federal programs are striking for their scale, ambition, and largely prescriptive approach to addressing environmental problems.

Table 12.1. Major Statutes Enacted from 1970–1980

National Environmental Policy Act (1970)
Clean Air Act (1970) (amended in 1977)
Federal Water Pollution Control Act Amendments (Clean Water Act, 1972) (amended in 1977)
Federal Environmental Pesticide Control Act (1972)
Safe Drinking Water Act (1974)
Resource Conservation and Recovery Act (1976)
Toxic Substances Control Act (1976)
Comprehensive Environmental Response, Compensation, and Liability Act (1980)

The newly enacted laws are also remarkable for the bipartisan support they received. In the modern era, most consequential laws are passed on partisan votes, often relying on arcane rules of budget reconciliation that enable Congress to bypass the supermajority voting constraints of the US Senate.[5] By comparison, the laws of the environmental decade garnered substantial levels of support from both sides of the political aisle. As illustrations, the legislation that eventually became the 1970 Clean Air Act passed the House by a vote of 374-1 and the Senate by a vote of 73-4 (the final legislation passed each chamber by voice vote),[6] the 1972 Clean Water Act passed the House by a vote of 366-11 and a Senate vote of 74-0,[7] and the 1976 Resource Conservation and Recovery Act passed the House by a vote of 367-8 and the Senate by a vote of 88-3.[8] The ambition of many of these laws is attributable to competition between President Richard Nixon and Democratic Senator Edwin Muskie, who engaged in a "tit-for-tat" legislative negotiation, each attempting to one-up the other in order to appeal to an electorate with a growing environmental consciousness. Even when President Nixon faltered, vetoing the Clean Water Act in 1972 out of concern for its "staggering" cost ($24.6 billion to cover the federal share of upgrading wastewater treatment plants),[9] 113 Congressional Republicans voted with their Democratic colleagues to override the veto.[10]

The bipartisanship of the environmental decade, however, was short-lived. US politics has become more polarized in the decades that have followed, both among political elites and in the general public. This polarization shapes EPA's relations with its external stakeholders, with important implications for its agenda, the policy tools it uses to advance its goals, and the reactions to its activities.

The Rise of Partisan Polarization

Political scientists studying the ideological composition of Congress have shown that the middle of the twentieth century was a period of unusually low levels of party conflict. Republicans and Democrats overlapped in their roll call voting more than at any other time before or since.[11] The environmental decade occurred during the end of this period of depolarization. Since that time, political elites have become more divided—the parties are both internally more homogeneous and farther apart from one another. Issues that previously had split politicians along regional lines started to become absorbed into partisan conflict.

Many factors have contributed to the rise of partisan polarization. A starting point is the 1960s civil rights reforms, which produced a realignment of the South in which conservative, white districts came to be represented by Republicans rather than by Democrats. Meanwhile, expanded opportunities for participation by Black and Hispanic politicians and voters resulted in some districts electing more liberal Democrats than they had before. The decisions these politicians made once in office, combined with broader changes in the political, social, and economic environments, reinforced patterns of polarization and spread its effects across regions and issues.[12] Rising inequality, the growing residential segregation of Americans by party, changes in electoral rules, and the fragmentation of media all have played a role.[13]

Polarization is sharpest among elected office holders and other political elites but over time has spread to ordinary Americans who identify with one of the parties. Issues that have low salience, or importance, are more susceptible to becoming polarized.[14] Thus, as the environment has become less of a priority to the American public, partisans have more readily taken up positions to match those of political elites. There is little evidence to indicate growing divides in policy attitudes among the broader mass public, which raises important questions about representation as politicians and their partisan supporters become more polarized.[15] Increasingly, politicians have incentive to respond to the more extreme preferences of those who vote in primaries rather than to the median voters in their districts.[16]

It is important to note that the overall divergence in party positions across issues has not been symmetric—Republicans have moved farther to the right over recent decades than Democrats have moved to the left.[17] This asymmetric polarization is particularly evident on the environment. With the base constituencies of the Republican party growing more hostile toward government power, regulation, and threats to the fossil fuel economy, it has become politically risky for Republican politicians to take overtly pro-environment stances. While the Democratic party has moved left in seeking over time to more aggressively address environmental risks, Republicans have made a bigger leap by challenging the core of EPA scope and authority. This fundamental partisan conflict dominates every aspect of the agency's political environment.

Polarization in Congress

With respect to the environment specifically, consider first polarization in Congress. The League of Conservation Voters (LCV) has been tracking congressional voting behavior on the environment in a systematic way since 1970. Each year, the LCV identifies a series of votes on what the organization considers to be important environmental decisions, and then tracks whether members of Congress vote to support the organization's position. For example, in 2017, among the votes that the LCV included in its scores was the confirmation vote of former EPA Administrator Scott Pruitt and several votes to allow oil and gas drilling in the Arctic National Wildlife Refuge.[18] The LCV then aggregates these votes into a single score for each representative and senator. Figure 12.1 shows the average score for members of each political party, separately for the House and Senate, from 1970 to 2018. The rise in polarization is striking. The difference in average scores between Republicans and Democrats during the environmental decade was approximately twenty percentage points. Beginning in the late 1980s and early 1990s, this margin began to widen, and over the last decade, the split has grown to as large as eighty points. Although interest group scores may exaggerate differences due to the strategic selection of the votes analyzed, studies of a broader set of votes have found similar levels of polarization.[19]

The stark polarization that now characterizes US national politics is also prevalent at the state level, in some cases even more strongly in state legislatures than in Congress.[20] Increasingly, American politics is becoming

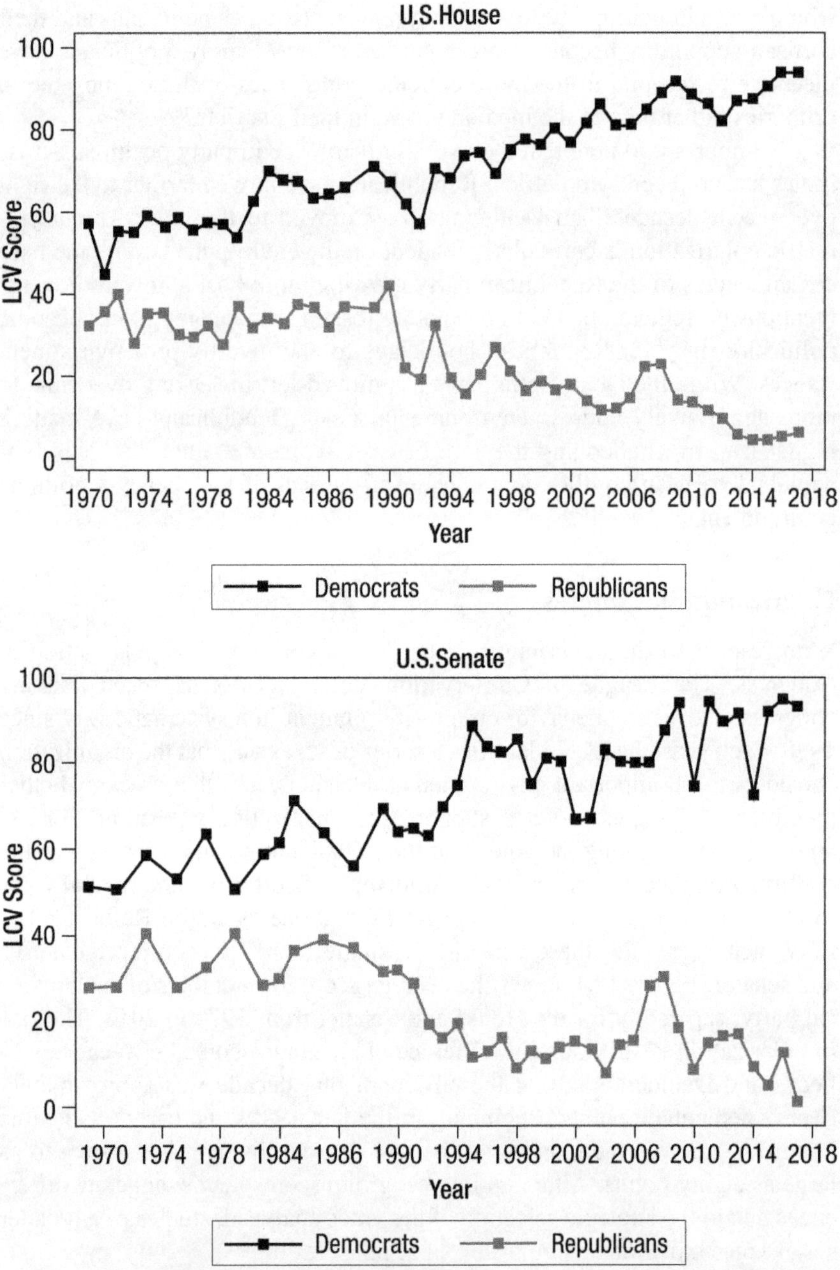

Figure 12.1. League of Conservation Voters Scores, 1970–2018. *Data compiled from League of Conservation Voters Scorecard reports.*

nationalized, with shared partisanship as a force that binds people together more than local issues or regional loyalties.[21] One implication of this nationalization is that the political climate around EPA at the state level begins to resemble its contentious nature at the national level, further complicating the agency's efforts to effectively carry out its mission. We discuss the relationship between the EPA and the states in greater depth later in the chapter.

Polarization in the Mass Public

Large differences in environmental attitudes also exist among self-identified partisans in the general American public. A common measure of Americans' preferences toward the environment is their views about the allocation of government resources. Figure 12.2 displays the trend in one such measure. The General Social Survey (GSS), a national survey conducted by the National Opinion Research Center, has since 1972 included a question that asks a nationally representative sample of Americans whether the federal government is spending too much, too little, or about the right amount of money on the environment. These data show a pattern of polarization that resembles the voting pattern of members of Congress. What had been modest differences between the opinions of Republicans and Democrats during the 1970s and 1980s rose sharply in the 1990s, and polarization continues to grow through today.

The bottom panel of Figure 12.2 demonstrates that among the mass public, environment stands out as an issue of unusually high polarization. During the 1970s and 1980s, the difference between Democrats and Republicans in beliefs about spending on the environment ranged from about five to fifteen percentage points, which is similar to that for education, health, drugs, cities, and foreign aid. However, over the past thirty years, the partisan difference has increased to about twenty-five to thirty points, while remaining about the same for these other issues. Polarization on government spending on the environment is now among the most divisive issues included on the survey, comparable only to military spending and issues of race and welfare.

Noticeable in this figure is the short period of time around 1990 when partisans converged in their support for environmental spending. In 1988, Republican candidate and incumbent Vice President George H.W. Bush spotlighted environmental issues during his presidential campaign, declaring on the shores of Lake Erie, "I am an environmentalist. Always have been . . . and I always will be."[22] Less than six months after taking office, President Bush proposed ambitious revisions to the Clean Air Act to address acid rain and urban smog. With his leadership, the set of amendments eventually passed Congress with overwhelming majorities and broad Republican sup-

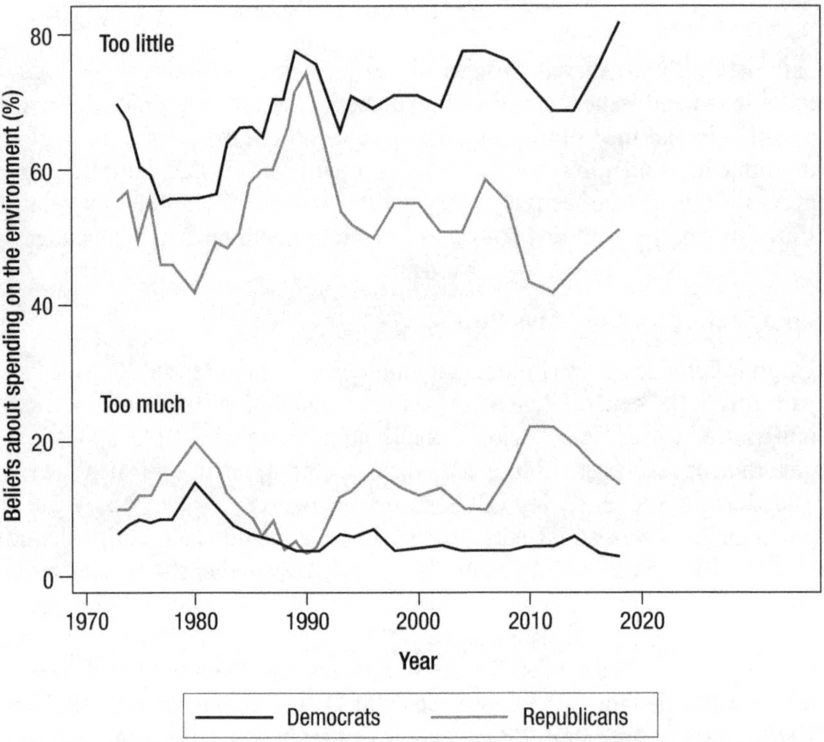

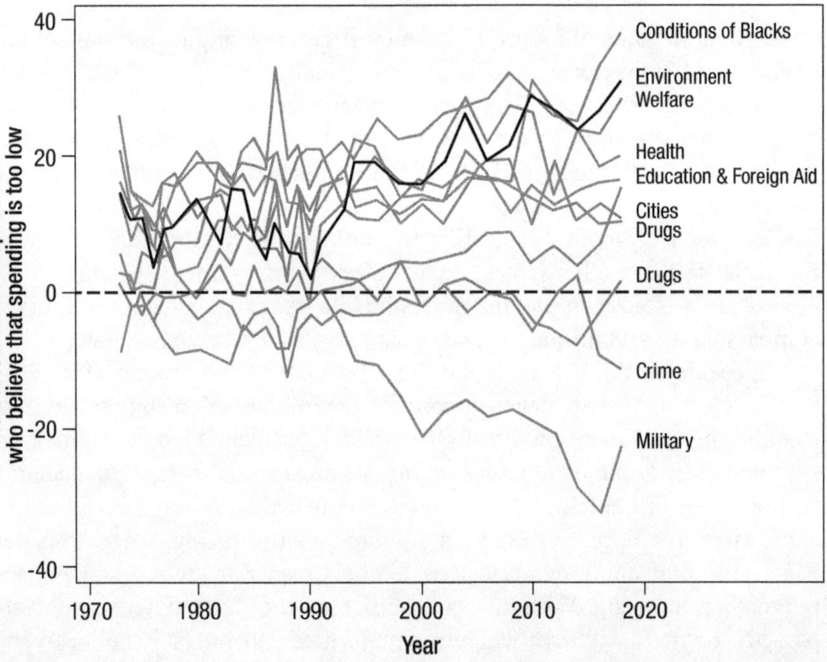

Figure 12.2. Government Spending Priorities, 1970–2018. ***Data from the General Social Survey.***

port. Separate from President Bush's effort in signaling that environment could be a bipartisan issue, other events around this time—especially the historic 1989 Exxon Valdez oil spill in Alaska's Prince William Sound and the heavily marketed global celebrations of the twentieth anniversary of Earth Day—raised the salience of the environment without igniting partisan division. By 1992 President Bush had changed his political strategy to more often emphasize the economic costs of environmental protection, and the gap in opinion among partisans in the mass public not only reemerged, but quickly escalated.[23]

Wider divides in opinion about the environment do not signal rising levels of public concern. In fact, just the opposite seems to be true. Whereas public opinion polls during the 1970s revealed widespread concern about environmental quality, the environment now barely registers in most surveys that ask Americans to indicate the most important problems facing the country. For example, in a poll conducted by the Gallup Organization in 1975, fifty-three percent of Americans identified "reducing pollution of air and water" as one of top three problems requiring action in the United States. This represented a thirty-six percent increase from 1965 and trailed only "reducing crime" among the issues identified.[24] By comparison, across the first three months of 2019, only three to four percent of Americans mentioned environment or pollution in response to a similar inquiry from Gallup.[25] The receding salience of public opinion toward the environment may reflect a version of what economist Anthony Downs referred to as the "issue-attention cycle"—the tendency for surges of public attention to an issue to recede after collective realization of the costs and challenges of fully addressing it.[26]

Polarization in External Political Climate

Three key elements of the external political climate around EPA have transformed over the last fifty years in ways that further politicize environmental policy-making. First, the appointment process for federal judges has become a political battleground, with important implications for the scope of EPA authority. Second, the density of interest groups and other information providers seeking to influence EPA policy has increased, creating a more active and antagonistic set of stakeholders that engages with the agency. And, third, changes in the structure of the news media have fragmented audiences and set up competing narratives about environmental policy issues. We discuss each in turn.

Although politics have always influenced judicial selection and decision-making, polarization has expanded its importance. Ideological consistency is now the primary consideration for presidential nominations to federal courts, and ever since the 1987 blocked Supreme Court nomination of Robert Bork, nominees now consistently receive close ideological scrutiny. Polarization and divided government contribute to confirmation delay,[27] and overall rates of confirmation have fallen: whereas approximately ninety percent of appellate court nominees were confirmed in the 1970s, only about half were confirmed under President George W. Bush.[28] Interest groups have become more active in nomination politics, and nominees are now more ideologically extreme.[29]

These developments have an impact on judicial decision-making. Judges very often reach decisions about legal questions that are in line with their predispositions and policy preferences.[30] This is especially true in the absence of other constraints, such as fidelity to precedent for the lower courts. In an analysis of environmental decisions by the DC Circuit Court from 1970 to 1994, legal scholar Richard Revesz found that the partisanship of a judge's appointing president was a strong predictor of the judge's votes, especially if the judge had a co-partisan on the panel and the case was unlikely to be reviewed by the Supreme Court.[31] The selection of more ideological judges through more ideological processes produces courts that are more divided along ideological lines. For the Supreme Court in recent years, this has meant a large proportion of cases decided by a one-vote margin. In the lower courts, expectations about the ideological direction of a court ruling may influence the behavior of environmental agency personnel who seek to avoid litigation over their decisions.[32]

Regarding the changing interest group community, EPA was established during a period in which the number of interest groups was beginning to skyrocket. In 1970, an estimated 4,000 groups were based in Washington, DC—double the number that had existed in 1950—and the number continued to grow, reaching about 17,000 in 2010.[33] The composition of groups has changed as well, with particular growth in the number of citizen groups (as distinct from labor unions or business-oriented groups, such as trade associations), especially in the area of the environment. During the agency's early years, environmental movement pressure originated mostly from a few major organizations—the Natural Resources Defense Council (NRDC), Environmental Defense Fund (EDF, now Environmental Defense), and the Sierra Club—that had deep expertise and sharp focus on agency activities. These groups participate through the entire policy process—from legislative negotiation and enactment through the regulatory process, the courts, and state implementation. They play an important role inside the Democratic party and often represent the environmental movement to the broader public. Now there are myriad groups with a wide range of priorities, goals, strategies, and capacities pushing EPA toward a stricter regulatory approach.

Environmental advocacy organizations have greatly expanded their capacity. Data collected by political scientists Frank Baumgartner and Beth Leech indicate that there were 119 environmental groups with a combined staff of 316 people at the beginning of the 1960s; by the mid-1990s, these numbers had increased to more than 300 groups and 3,000 staffers.[34] As of 2005, this number had grown further to more than 560 such groups.[35] Other estimates place the total even higher. In his study of environmental organizations, political scientist Christopher Bosso estimated that the full-time staffs of twenty-five major groups in 2000 combined to more than 7,600 people.[36]

Alongside this growth in environmental groups has been a proliferation of organizations that are often outwardly hostile to EPA's core mission. In response to government expansion during the 1960s and early 1970s, the business community became more politically active and organized to advocate for business-oriented tax cuts, deregulation, reductions in social welfare spending, and contraction of labor union rights.[37] New organizations, such as the Business Roundtable in 1972, and strengthened existing entities, such as the US Chamber of Commerce and the National Association of Manufacturers, helped to forward these goals. Corporations also started investing in lobbyists; in 1971, 175 companies had registered lobbyists in Washington, DC, whereas by 1978, almost 2,000 corporate trade associations had lobbyists. Similarly, the number of political action committees associated with businesses increased from fewer than 250 in 1974 to over 1,100 in 1978.[38] Thus, just as EPA was finding its feet as a new federal agency, the business community was ramping up its efforts to challenge the regulations the agency was unveiling. These increases have continued in the decades since. For example, as of 2010, the number of federal political action committees (PACs) exceeds 4,500, nearly 40% of which are affiliated with business firms. In a typical election year, PACs associated with businesses and trade associations account for about two-thirds of all PAC contributions to federal candidates.[39]

At the same time that businesses were becoming more politically active, the conservative political movement that had emerged in the 1950s and 1960s became institutionalized in the form of think tanks such as American Enterprise Institute, The Heritage Foundation, the CATO Institute, and legal organizations including the Pacific Legal Foundation and the Mountain States Legal Foundation.[40] These business groups and conservative movement organizations generally were not established as a direct response to EPA or environmental policy, but their agendas of promoting limited government and free enterprise often conflict with EPA's efforts to administer the laws Congress assigned to the agency. Moreover, their efforts have been buttressed by the political movement that challenges federal environmental policy in the domain of private property rights and Western public lands management. Although this movement—monikered the Sagebrush Rebellion and the Wise-Use Movement, in different iterations—directs its objections primarily toward other federal agencies (e.g., Bureau of Land Management, US Fish and Wildlife Service), it mobilizes activism and funding toward challenging environmental regulation in broad terms, contributing to contestation in the EPA's political landscape. As political scientist Judy Layzer has shown, business community has worked in concert with the conservative movement to construct and disseminate an anti-regulation storyline that challenges EPA decision-making.[41] Their efforts have included a well-documented disinformation campaign aimed at debunking the science about climate change,[42] which further contributed to the spread of competing narratives about EPA and its activities.

These competing narratives have been enabled by changes in the news media—the third important element of EPA's external context. Over recent decades, fragmentation in media audiences has reduced the public's incidental exposure to political news and allowed people to select news sources that cater to their political predispositions. As audiences for broadcast television news and print newspapers have declined, Americans have more opportunity to select the media they consume—opting in to partisan news programming, or opting out of news consumption altogether.[43] The online news media environment fragments audiences not only by partisan orientation but also by interest in particular news topics.[44] While online, specialized media outlets proliferate, traditional outlets for delivering content of general interest are disappearing: over the course of just the last 15 years, an estimated 1,400 American cities and towns lost a newspaper,[45] which in itself may contribute to polarization.[46]

Major changes in media sources covering the environment have occurred as part of these broader developments. According to data provided by the Society of Environmental Journalists, a professional association for journalists reporting on the environment, overall membership has risen since the early 1990s. However, as shown in Figure 12.3, the number of newspaper journalist members has declined significantly, from 358 in 1995 to 170 in 2019.[47]

The content of environmental coverage has also changed. Studies of reporting on climate change, for example, have found that reporting tends to amplify extreme viewpoints, instead of emphasizing convergent agreement.[48] One illustration is that reporters have tended to give an equal voice to individuals doubting the merits of climate science, even when they express viewpoints outside the mainstream.[49]

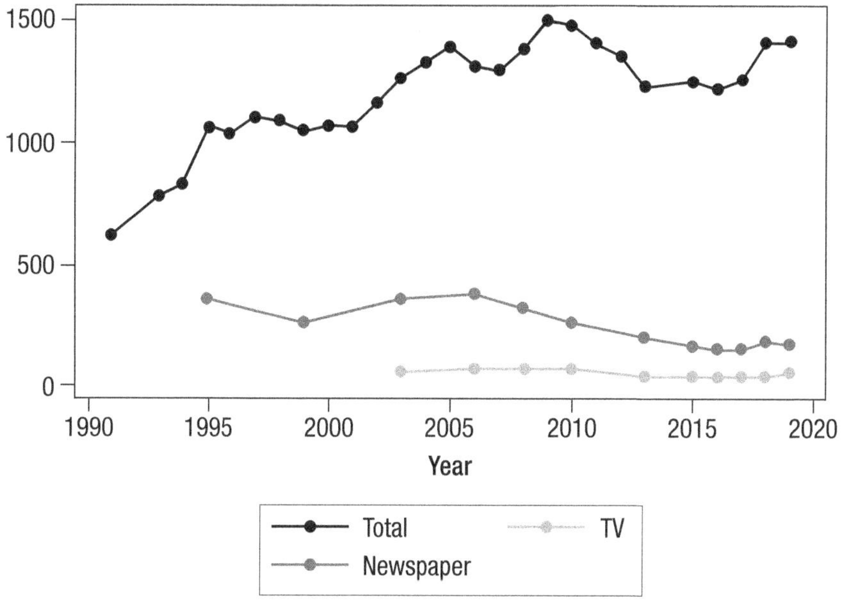

Figure 12.3. Membership in Society of Environmental Journalists, 1995–2019. ***Data provided by the Society of Environmental Journalists.***

CONSEQUENCES OF PARTISAN POLARIZATION FOR THE EPA

Legislative Gridlock

The consequences of the changing political climate for EPA are significant and multi-faceted. First is legislative gridlock, a product of the deep partisan polarization in Congress. As the ideological distance between the parties has grown, Congress has failed to act on a greater proportion of the issues on the national policy agenda. Gridlock across all salient policy issues is about fifty percent more common than it was when EPA was created.[50] On the environment, Congress has produced very little during the forty years following the environmental decade. Most of the major laws have not been revised by Congress in more than two decades; for example, the last major round of amendments to the Clean Water Act occurred in 1987, the Clean Air Act in 1990, the Resource Conservation and Recovery Act in 1996, and the Safe Drinking Water Act in 1996. The only major exception is the recent update to the Toxic Substances Control Act, which was amended in 2016.

There are several implications of Congressional gridlock for EPA. First, broadly recognized problems or gaps in environmental laws remain unfixed.

For example, the drafters of the Clean Air Act did not anticipate that some large sources of air pollution (e.g., coal-fired power plants) that existed prior to the law would still be in operation decades later. As we discuss below, these sources of air pollution continue to adversely affect air quality in many parts of the country, and they are large sources of the greenhouse gases contributing to climate change. Second, problems that Congress elected to ignore (e.g., nonpoint water pollution from agricultural sources), or did not address at all because they were not yet well understood (e.g., climate change), are left uncovered by explicit statutory authority. As a result, EPA relies on ad hoc or voluntary approaches to address these problems, or it stretches the authorities that Congress has granted under existing statutes—setting up political battles in rule making processes and the courts. And finally, congressional gridlock means that EPA often is subject to the efforts of other political actors in setting its policy agenda, as John Graham and Jonathan Wiener discuss more in the next chapter.

Importance of Party Control in Congress

In addition to creating a barrier to lawmaking, the growing partisan divide in environmental policy preferences magnifies the effects of partisan control of Congress. In his study of party issue ownership, political scientist Patrick Egan found dramatic changes in party advantage on the environment over the period 1970-2011.[51] In the 1970s, Americans were slightly more likely to believe that Democrats would do a better job than Republicans at handling the environment, but the Democratic advantage on this issue was smaller than for health care, education, and jobs. Whereas party-issue advantage on other issues has varied in level and even direction over time, on the environment it has only grown, such that Americans more clearly perceive this issue as the domain of one party than for any other issue on the national policy agenda.

The Democrats' issue ownership of the environment has important consequences for the policies that both parties pursue. When Democrats are in power, they are more likely to prioritize the environment, and they may do so in a way that diverges from broad public opinion and instead responds to activists and other more extreme voices in their political coalition. Egan shows that the environmental policy preferences of Democrats who say that the environment is personally "extremely important" to them are far more liberal than the preferences of the average American.[52] And Republican politicians may not feel there is anything to gain from taking on environmental problems—that is, why should Republicans bother prioritizing solutions to environmental problems if voters are unlikely to give them any electoral credit for doing so?

Contrast this to the early days of EPA when its obligations under statutes such as the Clean Air Act and Clean Water Act resulted, in part, from efforts by Republican and Democratic politicians to compete for environmental votes. In the current political environment, it is uncommon for Republican political leaders to discuss, let alone promote, policies intended to mitigate environmental problems. The last Republican presidential candidate who strongly campaigned on an environmental message was George H.W. Bush, and he softened that message when he ran for reelection. During periods of recent GOP control of Congress, the agenda has focused on restricting EPA rather than on expanding its authorities.

Partisanship in Congress also has changed the exercise of oversight activities. In 1981 incoming President Ronald Reagan brought an abrupt end to the environmental decade when he appointed conservative Colorado legislator Anne Gorsuch as EPA administrator. Committed to reducing the EPA's scope and delegating more authority to the states, Administrator Gorsuch oversaw sharp cuts in the agency's budget and reduction in enforcement actions and penalties. Congress held combative oversight hearings in which members from both parties accused the administrator of undermining federal laws—including in the Senate, which was under Republican majority control.[53] Gorsuch ultimately resigned in 1983 in a cloud of scandal related to management of the Superfund program. With congressional investigations underway over the agency's activities, President Reagan replaced Gorsuch by bringing back the first EPA Administrator, William Ruckelshaus.

President Donald Trump's appointment of Administrator Scott Pruitt in 2017 presented a similarly strong challenge to EPA's mission, but in this case, Congress did not provide a similar check. Pronouncing himself a "leading advocate against the EPA's activist agenda," Pruitt in his position as Oklahoma attorney general had sued the agency more than a dozen times over its rulemaking efforts. While leading EPA, Administrator Pruitt pushed to reduce the agency's budget and workforce, weaken enforcement efforts, and roll back a range of regulations. Congress—this time with Republican majorities in both houses—did not approve the entirety of the proposed budget cuts but otherwise did not challenge these efforts to steer the agency in a much more conservative direction.[54] Even as Pruitt came under fire for ethics scandals, response to the charges was strongly partisan, and congressional oversight committees were slow to act. After his eventual resignation, Pruitt was replaced by agency deputy Andrew Wheeler, who shared Pruitt's deregulation priorities.

Use of Executive Authority

Another direct consequence of the legislative gridlock and partisanship in Congress has been a presidential turn toward administrative tools to pursue their environmental policy agendas. Recent presidents have come to office with legislative goals only to be stymied by partisan discord in the House or Senate, forcing them to adjust to an administrative strategy as the only viable alternative. Two examples illustrate this point, one in the area of air pollution during the George W. Bush administration and the other in climate policy during the Barack Obama administration.

Upon entering office in 2001, President Bush's top environmental goal was to improve air quality through cost-effective mechanisms. Initially, the Bush administration pursued this goal through new legislation, referred to as the Clear Skies Initiative, which aimed to reduce emissions from electric utilities through a cap-and-trade program loosely modeled after the successful SO2 program that was created under the 1990 Clean Air Act Amendments—through the leadership of his father, among others.[55] The Clear Skies legislation did not advance in Congress, however, first stymied by Vermont Senator Jim Jeffords, who had recently switched his party affiliation from Republican to Independent, and later, after the Republicans retook the Senate in 2002, by more conservative senators who did not prioritize clean air legislation.[56]

The Clear Skies legislation included provisions to weaken the Clean Air Act's New Source Review (NSR) program, which requires facilities that existed before the 1970 law to upgrade pollution control technology when modifying or upgrading their operations. These facilities were given "grandfather" protections under the 1970 CAA,[57] creating an important gap in air pollution control because these sources release a disproportionate amount of emissions of SO2, NOx, CO2, and other pollutants.[58] Toward the end of President Clinton's second term, EPA pursued aggressive enforcement of what it then viewed to be violations of the NSR program, claiming that facilities were deliberately mischaracterizing major renovations as routine maintenance as a way to avoid upgrading their pollution control systems as required by the NSR program.[59]

The Bush administration sought to alleviate this enforcement pressure, specifically on coal-fired power plants, and more generally to weaken the NSR requirements through legislative fixes as part of the Clear Skies legislation. However, when it became clear that Congress would not enact any such legislation, President Bush instead opted to pursue an administrative strategy through a series of rulemakings, including a 2003 EPA rule to exempt power plants and other facilities making "routine" repairs (defined to mean up to twenty percent of a facility's replacement cost per year) from NSR requirements. These NSR reforms were met by stiff opposition in Congress and a lawsuit filed by national environmental organizations and fourteen states. The DC Circuit Court of Appeals issued an injunction and eventually invalidated the rule entirely, asserting that it was based on faulty interpretation of the CAA.

President Obama followed a similar course in his attempts to fulfill a campaign pledge to address climate change by reducing CO2 emissions from the electric power sector. At first, Democrats in the US House took the lead to devise a cap-and-trade policy as part of broader legislation on energy and climate change. The prospects for legislation on the surface seemed promising, given that Democrats held strong majorities in both chambers of Congress. Although the US House was able to muster sufficient votes to narrowly pass a bill (219-212), colloquially referred to as the Waxman-Markey bill (named after California Democrat Henry Waxman and Massachusetts Democrat Ed Markey), negotiations broke down in the US Senate and the legislation was abandoned in 2010. According to an analysis by political scientist Theda Skocpol, the climate bill's failure was attributable to the Republican party's hardening stance on environmental issues; without a groundswell of public support, the bill's supporters were unable to overcome an organized opposition assembled by the Tea Party and fossil fuel interests.[60]

After winning reelection in 2012, the Obama administration returned its attention to climate policy, although this time—following in the footsteps of President Bush—decided to pursue policy administratively through EPA rulemaking. At a speech at Georgetown University in July 2013, President Obama announced that he was directing EPA Administrator Gina McCarthy to use the agency's authority under the CAA to regulate CO2 emissions from existing coal-fired power plants. This was the beginning of what became the Clean Power Plan, discussed in more detail in Jody Freeman's chapter in this volume. Upon release of the rule, Scott Pruitt (as Oklahoma attorney general) led a group of fossil fuel interests, business organizations, and states in a legal challenge. President Obama's Clean Power Plan met a similar fate as President Bush's NSR reforms. In September 2016, the US Court of Appeals heard arguments, but the court failed to issue a judgment in the case, and has instead issued a series of continuations in light of the efforts of EPA under the Trump administration to rescind and replace the plan altogether. Earlier in the same year, the US Supreme Court issued a nationwide stay on enforcement of the Clean Power Plan, the first time the Supreme Court had ever stayed a regulation prior to a decision from the Court of Appeals.

Presidential reliance on EPA rulemaking to pursue controversial policy goals, as illustrated in these two examples, has important implications. First, it requires the agency to justify policy proposals that may not be fully supported by scientific evidence and may have questionable legal authority.

Second, unlike legislation, pushing through new rules (or rescinding existing rules) does not require building a broad political coalition of support. Third, because rulemaking is less transparent than the legislative process, it favors organized, professionalized advocacy groups that have access and expertise to shape not only content of rules, but which rules come under consideration. The voices of less powerful stakeholders often go unheard and unrepresented in decision-making, perpetuating historical inequities and failures of procedural justice. Finally, rulemaking elevates the importance of internal White House politics, especially by enhancing the role of agencies and offices (e.g., Office of Management and Budget (OMB)) that may have missions and goals that conflict with those of EPA.

Judicial Review

With the rise in legislative gridlock and reliance on executive authority, courts have taken on a critical role in defining EPA authority and obligations. As other chapters in this volume describe, litigation has been central to EPA activities since the agency's founding. EPA pursues enforcement actions through the courts, and citizen suit provisions included in many of the major environmental laws empower third parties to engage directly in the laws' enforcement. The complexity of environmental law and ongoing advances in scientific knowledge create ample opportunity for judicial review of EPA rulemaking, and questions about the consistency of agency decisions with the underlying statutory authority have become all the more heated as polarization has increased.

Courts provide an alternative venue for interest group conflict over environmental policy. Environmental interest groups have long battled with polluting industries and conservative public interest law firms in environmental litigation.[61] Yet although environmental groups generally have been sympathetic to EPA's mission, they often have acted as the agency's strident adversaries. From EPA's earliest years, they indicated a willingness to press the agency, as when the Environmental Defense Fund sued to compel fulfillment of EPA's commitment to identify and regulate hazardous air pollutants under the Clean Air Act. Bringing and joining in lawsuits was an important part of how the "Group of Ten" major environmental groups responded to the Reagan administration's redirection at EPA.[62] Indeed, the key feature that distinguishes environmental groups from other interest groups active in Washington, DC, is their level of participation in litigation.[63] Industry and conservative think tanks and interest groups also have turned to the courts to pursue their own goals, including with use of the SLAPP—the strategic lawsuit against public participation—in an effort to check environmental groups' use of citizen suits.

In the early years after enactment of the foundational statutes assigned to EPA, federal courts tended to exercise aggressive judicial review in an effort to ensure consistency with congressional intent.[64] As time passed, the courts backed off this approach in favor of granting more deference to agency decisions. The Supreme Court established the *Chevron* doctrine in a 1984 decision upholding EPA's Clean Air Act "bubble policy," which allowed firms flexibility in where to reduce their emissions from multiple points within a single facility. The *Chevron* doctrine has become one of the most important features of administrative law, allowing EPA (and other federal agencies) to move forward with rulemakings as long as they are reasonable interpretations of statute in circumstances where Congress itself is not explicit. The scope and character of agency deference is highly contested, however, as what is considered reasonable is subjective. And, as selection processes for federal judges have become more explicitly political, environmental and industry groups have responded by forum shopping to find the most favorable venue for their legal claims. Overall, judicial review of EPA activities now serves to reinforce, not dampen, polarization's divisive pull.

AGENCY INSTITUTIONALIZATION

EPA over fifty years has evolved from a small agency, threaded together from existing federal agencies, to a large bureaucracy with offices throughout the country and staffed by seasoned personnel who have deep experience in rulemaking, enforcement, and scientific assessment. As EPA has institutionalized, it has also encountered extended periods of resource constraints, changing priorities from frequent changes in agency leadership, and intense conflicts with the White House.

EPA Budget Constraints

EPA's responsibilities have expanded in significant ways over the course of the agency's five-decade history, owing to the broad scope of its mandate to implement legislation, new presidential initiatives, economic growth that produces more regulated activity, and the increasing technical complexity of the problems it is required to address. Yet, EPA's budget has not increased commensurately. In most respects, EPA is being asked to do more with less, both in terms of resources and staff.

As shown in Figure 12.4, EPA budget ramped up for most of its first two and a half decades, with temporary disruptions in the mid-1970s and then again during the early years of the Reagan administration. It has remained relatively flat in nominal terms since the early 1990s, ranging from about $7

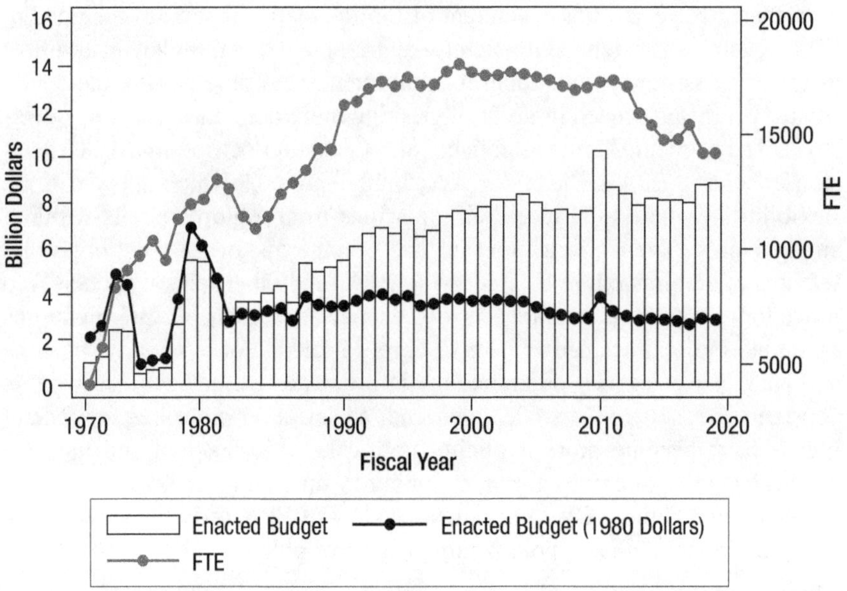

Figure 12.4. EPA Budget and Full Time Equivalent (FTE) Employees, FY1970-FY2019. ***Data compiled from EPA website, 2020.***

billion to $9 billion. In real terms, EPA's budget has been in decline, interrupted only by the one-time influx of appropriations following the Great Recession. The agency's current, inflation-adjusted budget stands at about the same level as in 1980. Staffing levels continued to rise in the 1990s even as real funding levels fell, but over the last decade the number of employees has fallen seventeen percent. Currently, much of EPA's staff is not located in its Washington office, but instead in one of the agency's regional or technical offices in other parts of the country.

The topline budget information disguises the fact that much of the money Congress provides to EPA is not discretionary. About half of the agency's current budget includes appropriations that are dedicated to specific purposes, including pass-through funding for state and tribal assistance and the state-operated clean water and drinking water revolving loan fund programs to finance water infrastructure upgrades, as well as money specifically allocated to remediate contaminated sites under the Superfund program. In fiscal year 2018, of the agency's $8 billion budget, 57% went to just these three purposes.[65] With only the balance of this budget can EPA fund the rest of its operations, including its administration and enforcement of pollution control programs and all of its science and technical activities.

It is difficult to say what an ideal budget might be for EPA; however, with a declining real budget over the past thirty-five years, the agency has had to make difficult choices about where to invest its resources. Moreover, independent estimates have shown that EPA's budget falls well short of what is needed for addressing issues like contaminated properties under the Superfund program[66] and deteriorating water and wastewater infrastructure.[67] Budget constraints also limit the resources available for enforcement, placing more burden on state environmental agencies to make sure that regulated sources are meeting their obligations. Another consequence of the agency's limited budget is that EPA has been less able to expand its agenda to address new and pressing issues, which may be one reason that issues such as nonpoint source pollution and environmental justice—that do not have specific statutory authorities—have been back-burner issues for most of the agency's history.

Despite the fact that EPA's budget amounts to a minuscule portion of the annual federal budget (about 0.2 percent currently), it has been a target for presidents and Congress since the agency's outset. In most cases, EPA budgets have been reduced during periods of Republican presidents and/or Republican majorities in Congress. Contentious fights over EPA budgets have been regular occurrences over the last twenty-five years during periods when Republicans have controlled at least one chamber of Congress. Under the leadership of Newt Gingrich, John Boehner, and Paul Ryan, Republicans in the US House in particular have attempted to reduce, or at least curtail the growth in, EPA's budget. In addition to proposing less money through the regular appropriation process, Republicans have used budgetary riders that target specific areas of EPA spending.[68]

The recurring fights over EPA's budget speak to only one dimension of partisan efforts to shape EPA policy. In turning toward what political scientists call the administrative presidency,[69] executives use their authorities to appoint officials and reconfigure decision-making procedures in order to expand their influence over agency decisions. Both Democrats and Republicans use these tools and authorities and have been doing so since the outset of EPA. In periods of divided government, when the party presiding in the White House does not control both houses of Congress, the EPA and other agencies are answerable to two principals competing for control over the agency's activities. But because the parties have such divergent aims with respect to EPA,[70] the consequences for this agency can be particularly striking.

EPA Administrator Discretion

Presidents have taken different approaches to selecting individuals for EPA's top position. More so than any other position in the federal government, including the chair of the White House Office of Environmental Quality, the EPA administrator has become the government's public point person on environmental policy. The position of EPA administrator requires managing a large bureaucracy and its multi-billion-dollar budget, making decisions about technically complex issues, managing relationships with key players at the White House and other federal agencies, and effectively engaging with diverse stakeholders external to the agency. Appointment of an EPA administrator can be an opportunity to try to align the agency with a president's policy preferences. Research from political scientists has found that career staffers at EPA are among the most liberal of staffers at any federal agency.[71] Thus, for presidents such as George H.W. Bush, Bill Clinton, and Barack Obama who came to office having campaigned to improve environmental protection, the task is somewhat easier since their preferences were more clearly aligned with those of career officials at the agency. For newly elected presidents with agendas to limit the size of government and cut environmental regulation, such as Ronald Reagan, George W. Bush, and Donald Trump, the challenge of moving the agency closer to their preferences is more difficult.

Presidents have chosen EPA administrators with varying professional backgrounds: known principally at the time of their appointment for service in federal government positions (William Ruckelshaus, Doug Costle, Lee Thomas), for running state environmental agencies (Carol Browner, Lisa Jackson, Gina McCarthy), for holding state elected office (Anne Gorsuch, Christie Todd Whitman, Michael Leavitt, Scott Pruitt), for working at environmental advocacy organizations (Russell Train, William Reilly), and for representing industry as a lobbyist (Andrew Wheeler). Only one former EPA administrator, Stephen Johnson, was a career civil servant with the agency itself. Each administrator came to the position with a different set of objectives and policy priorities, as well as differing sets of existing relationships with important stakeholder communities and varying degrees of influence within the White House.

EPA administrators not only manage a president's environmental policy agenda, but also are able to establish their own priorities for the agency. The evolution of EPA environmental justice policy illustrates this opportunity. Environmental justice emerged on EPA's agenda at the tail end of the George H.W. Bush administration. In response to growing evidence that communities of color and low-income communities experience disproportionate burdens from the presence of hazardous waste landfills and incinerators, the location of contaminated sites, and industrial sources of pollution,[72] there was a groundswell of public attention and activism about this issue. Following a meeting with members of the Congressional Black Caucus, political activists, and academics, Administrator William K. Reilly created the Environmental Equity Workgroup in July 1990. This group produced a two-volume report, *Environmental Equity: Reducing Risk in All Communities*, that made a series of recommendations including the establishment of a new Office of Environmental Equity (later renamed the Office of Environmental Justice).[73] Although Administrator Reilly was under no statutory or legal obligation to take on environmental justice, he chose to do so using his discretion. Over the next two decades, his successors also used their discretion to proceed on this issue, but in divergent ways.[74]

EPA's engagement with environmental justice continued during the early years of the Clinton administration, in large measure sparked by President Clinton's signing of Executive Order 12898 (EO 12898), which required each federal agency to "make achieving environmental justice part of its mission by identifying and addressing, as appropriate, disproportionately high and adverse human health or environmental effects of its programs, policies, and activities on minority and low-income populations."[75] Among other provisions, EO 12898 called for the creation of an interagency working group to be led by the EPA administrator; required each federal agency to develop an environmental justice strategy; called for new data collection and analysis on risks to human health broken out by race, national origin, and income; and called for greater transparency and inclusiveness in government decision-making. EPA Administrator Carol Browner expressed interest in pursuing environmental justice, declaring it as one of her top four priorities,[76] and the agency respond to the EO12898 by developing an environmental justice strategy in 1995[77] and publishing an implementation plan the following year.[78]

Environmental justice receded on EPA's agenda in the final years of the Clinton administration and did not reappear during the George W. Bush administration. Implementation of EO 12898 stalled, and numerous reports, including from the GAO and EPA's own inspector general, found that the agency was failing to take environmental justice issues into account in its decision-making.[79] In a 2004 report, the EPA inspector general concluded: "Although the Agency has been actively involved in implementing Executive Order 12898 for 10 years, it has not developed a clear vision or a comprehensive strategic plan, and has not established values, goals, expectation, and performance measurements." The inspector general was specifically critical of EPA's position, articulated in a 2001 memorandum from Administrator Christie Todd Whitman, that the agency was working to achieve environmental justice for everyone. According to the inspector general, this position deemphasized minority and low-income populations, and in so doing moved EPA away from the basic tenets of EO 12898.[80] Studies from various academic scholars have reached similar conclusions, noting the failure of EPA to effectively integrate equity considerations into its permitting, rulemaking, and enforcement activities and to adequately handle petitions made to the agency under the Title VI of the Civil Rights Act.[81]

Environmental justice returned to EPA's agenda during the Obama administration, under the leadership of EPA Administrators Lisa Jackson and Gina McCarthy, each of whom stated that environmental justice was a priority. During these years, EPA developed actions under Plan EJ 2014 to create new policy guidance, assessment and information tools, and public outreach procedures to better integrate environmental justice into its programs, policies, and activities.[82] The agency also slowly began to incorporate equity considerations into decisions in the final years of the Obama administration, building them into rulemaking on toxic emissions from oil refineries and CO2 regulations as part of the Clean Power Plan, as well considering it more regularly as part of regulatory impact analyses.[83]

The ebb and flow of attention to environmental justice across the past twenty-five years illustrates how EPA administrators can use their discretion to shape agency efforts. The leadership and prioritization of issues is especially important on problems that are not mandated for attention by statute or prioritized by influential stakeholders, such as leading interest groups.

On environmental justice specifically, EPA is not under any formal legal obligation to address the disproportionate pollution burdens experienced by many communities of color and low-income. And, the courts have virtually foreclosed the opportunity for citizen groups to sue EPA and other environmental agencies for decisions that create disparate impacts, for example in permitting, unless they can demonstrate intentional discrimination.[84] Moreover, mainstream environmental advocacy organizations, such as EDF, NRDC, and the Sierra Club have not regularly prioritized these communities or the issue of social justice, which is one reason for the historical friction between these organizations and grassroots environmental justice groups. The fact that environmental justice has remained a low priority, even during Democratic presidential administrations, may also suggest the Democrats have not shifted far to the ideological left in their approach to environmental policy-making.

White House Oversight

As an additional check on EPA and other federal agencies, presidents have created offices and procedures within the White House itself that centralize rulemaking and promote closer alignment between agency activity and presidential goals. Many of these institutions were specifically established in response to concerns that the types of social regulation coming out of agencies like EPA conflicted with other priorities such as economic growth.

These efforts began at the outset of EPA. Although President Richard Nixon is rightly credited for creating the agency and signing laws such as the National Environmental Policy Act and the Clean Air Act, the Nixon administration also created obstacles to the early work of EPA. A notable example of these efforts was "Quality of Life Reviews," which were intended to reduce costs of regulation through a process managed by the newly created OMB. Under these reviews, other federal agencies were invited to scrutinize EPA regulations, and OMB required EPA to perform extensive analysis of the costs of proposed regulations.[85] This process led to both delays in the rulemaking process, and, in some cases, substantive changes. The conflicts over Quality of Life reviews escalated to the point that EPA Administrator Ruckelshaus threatened to resign unless Nixon fully empowered the EPA to issue rules without undue OMB interference.[86]

President Nixon also created a commission of industry leaders, called the National Industry Pollution Control Council, that was housed in the Department of Commerce to advise the president on health, safety, and environmental policy. Congressional backlash was severe, and this commission only lasted for a few years before being defunded by Congress.[87] Collectively, these efforts were consequential. John Quarles, EPA's initial general counsel and assistant administrator for enforcement, wrote in his memoir that the "EPA [was] forced to establish a balance in its decisions. It [had] to be sufficiently sensitive to the economic, social, and other impacts of environmental regulations to preserve a degree of harmony with the rest of the government."[88]

There is no better example of a president attempting to shape environmental policy through administrative means than Ronald Reagan, who famously pronounced in his 1981 inaugural address that "[g]overnment is the not solution to our problem; government is the problem."[89] With this goal in mind, according to public administration scholar Bob Durant, the "Reagan administration applied an administrative strategy with a fervor and comprehensiveness unparalleled by its predecessors."[90] One of the president's top priorities was the delegation of programs to state governments. Statutes including the Clean Water Act, the Safe Drinking Water Act, and the Resource Conservation and Recovery Act allow willing states to administer these pollution control laws, provided that states demonstrate they have sufficient legal and administrative capacity to effectively manage the programs. As part of a broader "New Federalism" strategy to empower states, EPA and other federal agencies (e.g., Occupational Health and Safety Administration, the Office of Surface

Mining and Reclamation) hastened formal delegation to state agencies.[91] For example, from 1984 to 1986, more than forty states were delegated authority to enforce the hazardous waste provisions of the Resource Conservation and Recovery Act.[92]

The most important and durable manifestation of the Reagan administration's approach was the further empowerment of the OMB to oversee rulemaking through the signing of Executive Order 12291 (EO 12291). Discussed at greater length in Richard Morgenstern's chapter on environmental economics, EO 12291 required all executive agencies (but not independent regulatory agencies such as the Consumer Product Safety Commission or the Nuclear Regulatory Commission) to perform a Regulatory Impact Analysis (RIA) of all proposed and final major regulations (defined as actions with at least $100 million in costs). These cost-benefit analyses were to be submitted to the Office of Information and Regulatory Affairs (OIRA) within the OMB, which also established the standards for how RIAs were to be done, with the idea that only rules with social benefits that exceed their costs should move forward. At the time that President Reagan issued EO 12291, there were concerns that OMB would potentially usurp the EPA and other agencies' discretion under statutes to promulgate regulations. In defense of the legality of the executive order, EPA's Office of Legal Counsel issued an opinion noting that OMB would only supervise, not displace rulemaking.[93]

The degree to which OMB held to this standard became a hotly debated issue in subsequent years, as the Reagan administration put its regulatory review practices into effect. The concerns were at least fivefold. First, the review process had a "chilling effect," resulting in a reduction of the number of rules submitted by EPA for review, as well as a high number relative to other federal agencies in both the number of rules withdrawn and returned by the OMB for reconsideration.[94] Second, the regulatory review process created by EO 12291 impeded transparency, by allowing OIRA to delay publication of a notice of a proposed regulation until after the agency had responded to OIRA's criticisms, thereby disguising the changes required by OIRA.[95] Third, critics claimed that the OIRA review process provided a forum for industry to offer its views on pending regulatory actions.[96] Fourth, the regulatory review process resulted in serious delays including National Ambient Air Quality Standards for NO2 (five months), standards for asbestos (six months), and standards for high-level radioactive waste disposal (one year).[97] According to one estimate, during the first term of the Reagan administration, of 169 EPA regulations with statutory or court-ordered deadlines submitted for review, the OMB extended its review time beyond the time periods outlined in EO 12291 on eighty-six occasions.[98] And, last, and related to the delays, was that OMB changed the content of regulations and almost always to weaken them.

The Reagan administration's efforts to influence the regulatory process did not go unnoticed. For its part, Congress—particularly the Democratic-controlled House of Representatives—conducted oversight hearings to investigate OIRA procedures. The courts also intervened. In a lawsuit brought by the Environmental Defense Fund against EPA Administrator Lee Thomas for failure to issue timely regulations under the 1984 amendments to the Resource Conservation and Recovery Act, the US District Court for the District of Columbia held that the OMB does not have authority to use its regulatory review under EO 12291 to delay the issuance of regulations beyond the date of statutory deadlines.[99]

To those who seek to reduce EPA's scope of authority, regulatory review and cost-benefit analysis are powerful tools for presidential administrations to align agency goals with White House political priorities. Those who prefer a more powerful EPA tend to see OMB as a tool of political interference from the White House, as it historically has been active when the priorities of the White House diverge with those of EPA. To be sure, there are plenty of occasions since the Reagan administration where OMB and other White House offices have been accused of interfering with EPA rulemaking.

President George H. W. Bush, for example, created the Council of Competitiveness with the objective of assuring that "regulations fulfill the statute with a minimal amount of economic impact."[100] The council, led by Vice President Dan Quayle, included high-ranking officials in the administration, including the Director of the OMB Richard Darman, Chief of Staff John Sununu, economic advisor Michael Boskin, Secretary of Commerce Robert Mosbacher, and Secretary of Treasury Nicholas Brad. During the final two years of the administration, the Council of Competitiveness began to actively work to directly challenge EPA regulations. Largely acting in secret, the council solicited complaints from industry about what it believed to be excessive regulation, analyzed costs and benefits of proposed rules, and worked to delay or refashion any new regulations that it thought were overly burdensome.[101] The Council was particularly active in seeking changes to CAA regulations, but also made revisions to a wetlands delineation manual to limit the reach of federal protections for about half of US wetlands, and changed a regulation on mixed-waste incineration that would have required incinerator operators to do more recycling, among other regulations.[102]

The OMB continued to assert influence on EPA rulemaking during the George W. Bush administration. OIRA Administrator John Graham made several changes to OIRA's review process, including the use of prompt letters to suggest regulatory actions to agencies, a technique that Graham indicates was intended as a "polite nudge" to an agency to give a matter needed attention.[103] In addition, OIRA updated its standards for cost-benefit analysis, insisted on strict adherence to OIRA's ninety-day limit for reviews, increased the size and technical skills of staff, and established new policies to improve transparency.[104] On transparency, Graham issued a memorandum to staff that changed procedures to require that documents and communications with external parties related to OIRA reviews were to be made available online, and moved to provide written comments, also made available to the public, on occasions when OIRA returned rules to agencies for reconsideration.[105] These transparency reforms, however, only applied *after* rules had been entered into the record—that is, only when they were officially sent from an agency to OIRA for review. For critics, this was a problematic approach, especially when coupled with the fact that OIRA frequently insisted that agencies involve OIRA early on in rulemaking, because this informal intervention by OIRA was not covered by the transparency reforms.[106]

An analysis conducted by the GAO concluded that EPA regulations were often changed as part of regulatory review by OIRA. Specifically, the GAO found that OIRA returned twenty-one of the approximately four hundred agency rules it reviewed, which amounted to more than the previous seven years combined. Further, GAO determined that, of the eighty-five draft rules it analyzed carefully, OIRA's review had a significant effect in twenty-five cases. And, in seventeen of twenty-five of these draft rules, OIRA "recommended the revision, elimination, or delay of certain provisions, the addition or revisions of regulatory alternative that provided more flexible and/or less costly compliance options, or the revision of agencies' cost and/or benefits for the rules."[107] Fourteen of these cases were EPA rules, including the elimination of manganese from a list of hazardous wastes, the relaxation of compliance requirements in a proposed rule on pollution discharge elimination systems for large cooling water intake structures at existing power plants, and the revision of estimates of costs and benefits in a proposed rule on emissions from some marine vessels and highway motorcycles.[108] In part because of these actions, the GAO concluded that OIRA had changed the view of its role in the rulemaking process from "counselor" to "gatekeeper."[109]

Complaints about the role of OMB in EPA rulemaking are not limited to actions taken during Republican presidential administrations. During the Obama administration, for instance, EPA officials also were frustrated by what they viewed as interference and delay. Lisa Heinzerling, who served as associate administrator for policy from 2009 to 2010, after leaving this position commented on frequent delays created by the OMB, then run by Cass Sunstein. Specifically, she pointed to delays of three years for issuing EPA's list of "chemicals of concern" under TSCA and of not accepting delivery of a notice of new data pertaining to an EPA proposal to regulate coal ash impoundments.[110]

The key point to emphasize here is that, regardless of the merits of any single intervention by OIRA, EPA clearly must be responsive to its regulatory oversight. The posture that the OIRA takes varies from administration to administration, coinciding with presidential priorities and views on the role of regulation. What is clear, however, is that over the course of EPA's fifty-year history, OIRA has played a more assertive role in agency decision-making.

The Politics of Federalism

The design of EPA and the laws it is designated to enforce create inevitable tension between the agency and state and local governments. One reason is that states and localities are themselves subject to EPA's regulatory actions. Local governments in particular are overwhelmingly responsible for services such as wastewater treatment and drinking water provision that are core areas of EPA oversight. As Jim Barnes describes in the opening chapter of this book, the EPA's first administrator, William Ruckelshaus, made cities such as Atlanta, Cleveland, and Detroit the early targets of EPA action, pointing to the millions of gallons of untreated sewage that the cities were discharging into local waterways. To this day, local governments agencies are often laggards in environmental compliance, often due to constraints in resources and expertise.[111]

A second reason for tension is that federal environmental laws have preempted state authority in many areas and created new mandates, often without funding. In designing the framework for these laws, Congress intended for states to take on the day-to-day implementation of the programs, with EPA providing technical and financial support, oversight, policy development, and leadership. From the beginning, managing relationships with states proved to be a challenge.[112] The new laws created obligations for state and local governments without providing adequate funding to meet those obligations. Over time, relationships became more conflictual as states expanded their capacity for implementing environmental programs but perceived continued growth in unfunded mandates and inflexible demands from EPA.

States' role in implementing federal environmental laws has expanded dramatically over the life of EPA. Delegation occurs most formally when states assume primary authority, or "primacy," over the implementation of particular programs. More and more states have obtained primacy authorization over time, with the result that ninety-six percent of programs that could be delegated to states now have been delegated, according to the most recent compilation of data from the Environmental Council of the States.[113] Another important expansion of state responsibility came in the 1987 reauthorization of the Clean Water Act, which ended direct EPA grants to local wastewater infrastructure projects, replacing them with a state-run revolving loan program. Nine years later, Congress created a similar state program for drinking water infrastructure. These revolving loan funds—in combination, accounting for more than twenty-five percent of the EPA's budget in most years—place the fiduciary responsibility for maintaining support to local infrastructure projects into the hands of states, which may not have the capacity to support it.[114]

For EPA, a key challenge of the delegation model is ensuring some level of consistency in environmental outcomes. States vary in a number of important dimensions that shape their approach to implementation. Similar to the federal level, partisan control of government and the relative power of business and environmental interests can influence the stringency of a state's environmental enforcement.[115] Wealthier states have larger tax bases to support environmental programs.[116] Political institutions such as legislative professionalism can influence the attention that environmental issues receive relative to other state priorities,[117] and the design of environmental agencies helps orient agency personnel toward particular political actors and policy goals.[118] Overall, states vary widely in their environmental effort, and those that have ambitious policies are not necessarily the same as those with high levels of environmental spending or enforcement activity.[119] It is difficult even to assess states' environmental performance, let alone provide effective oversight that can improve performance.

EPA has struggled to provide adequate oversight of state programs. Primacy is granted not just to high-performing state programs, but to virtually all states. Once delegated, it is rare for EPA to take back that authority; the agency simply does not have the resources to assume enforcement responsibilities. In 1993 congressional testimony, then EPA Administrator Carol Browner stated, "[t]here are some States that have seriously considered returning primacy to the Federal government. I will be very honest with you, we don't have the resources to manage even one major State if primacy were to be returned."[120] Even when EPA has initiated primacy withdrawal proceedings, as it did against eight states around this time for management of their drinking water programs, the agency typically has not followed through, instead continuing to work with states to improve performance. Because revoking a state's authority to implement environmental law is usually untenable, EPA directs considerable effort toward improving the performance of state programs. This effort is particularly necessary because of the rising costs of environmental implementation that have landed on states, in many cases putting a considerable stress on state budgets. The decline in EPA's budget has reduced federal funding support for state environmental programs as well as oversight and assistance from EPA personnel.[121] Even when federal and state policy priorities are aligned, scarcity of resources on both sides produces a relationship between EPA and state environmental agencies that is often strained.

Polarization adds to these tensions by sharpening divides both between states and EPA and among states themselves. Political leadership in many states has become more consistently partisan. From the 1970s through 1996, over twenty states were represented in the US Senate by a member from each political party; now only ten states have split delegations. The number of states with divided party control of state government also has fallen by half. Polarization is not the only explanation for this growing state-level consistency in political representation, but it is closely related and aggravates the effects. Rising partisanship at the state level has likely contributed to more conflictual relationships between EPA and the states that vary over time depending on the party that sits in the White House. Divergence between parties also increasingly pits the states against one another on questions of environmental policy.

One measure of these conflicts is the rise of multistate lawsuits against the federal government, chronicled by political scientist Paul Nolette. As shown in Figure 12.5, the environment is an area in which this trend is pronounced. Two-thirds of all multistate lawsuits brought against a federal agency since 1980 have been directed at EPA. State attorneys general are coordinating with one another, nearly always along partisan lines, either to force or to block the agency's enforcement efforts.[122] Joining in these multistate lawsuits helps

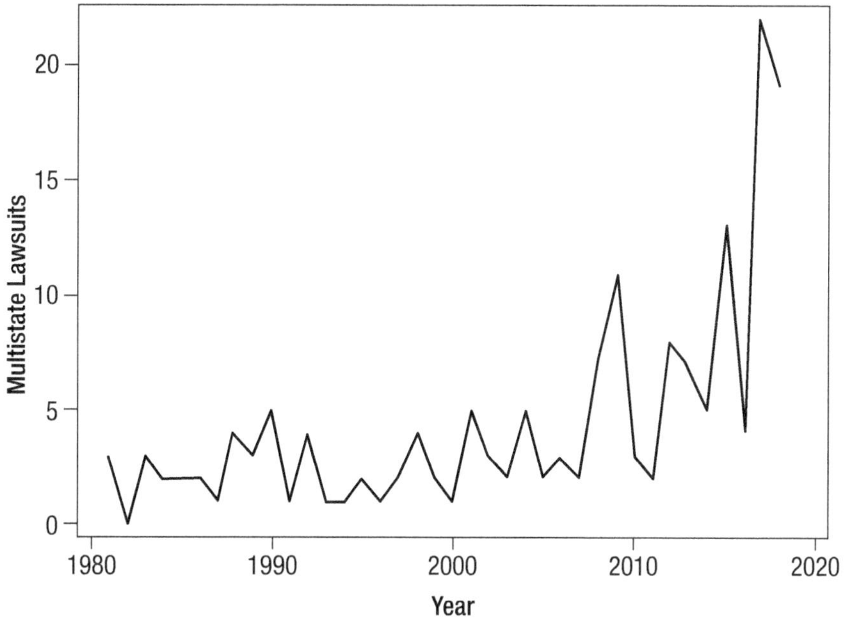

Figure 12.5. Multistate Environmental Lawsuits, 1981–2018. ***Data from State Litigation and AG Activity Database.***

elected attorneys general advance their political goals, even sometimes counter to the preferences of sitting governors. Submission of multistate *amicus curiae* briefs also has been increasing and becoming much more partisan in nature.

Two recent examples demonstrate the significance of these efforts. As Jody Freeman describes in her chapter, the Supreme Court's decision in *Massachusetts v. EPA*, 549 U.S. 497 (2007) serves as the legal foundation for greenhouse gases to be regulated under the Clean Air Act. That decision came about because of a lawsuit filed by Democratic attorneys general in twelve states, along with numerous cities and environmental organizations, and critical to the decision was the Court's determination that states are entitled to "special solicitude" in the determination of standing to bring suit. Additional groups of states filed briefs on both sides of the case. States also have played an important role in the long-running legal battle over the definition of the "waters of the United States" that are subject to protections under the Clean Water Act. In the Supreme Court case *Rapanos v. United States* 547 U.S. 715 (2006), more than thirty states filed a brief arguing for continued federal oversight of wetlands adjacent to tributaries. Ten years later, many of these same states—in several cases, with Democratic attorneys general replaced by Republicans—joined with the agriculture and business communities against the Obama administration's Clean Water Rule (described in more detail in the chapter by Jon Cannon), designed to bring many of those waters under similar protection. State-led lawsuits against the rule stalled its implementation until EPA under President Trump suspended it and proposed its own replacement—a replacement that is now under challenge in another multistate suit.

CONCLUSION

EPA was born out of great optimism about the potential for the federal government to lead the charge in tackling the nation's environmental problems. In retrospect, that optimism seems well-placed; the first five decades of EPA are in many ways a story of success. Air and water quality have improved, blood lead levels are a fraction of what they once had been, and many formerly toxic sites have been remediated and returned to beneficial reuse. During the same period, by many measures, the nation's political conditions have worsened: public trust in government has plummeted, and partisan conflict now overwhelms and stifles nearly every effort to solve public problems. Whereas environmental protection had once been a goal with broad bipartisan support, polarization on the environment is now as severe as on any other public issue.

Looking forward, EPA will continue to operate within the contested, volatile politics brought on by partisan polarization. Polarization complicates relationships with states and other partners, stalls progress in confronting new environmental challenges, and makes it difficult to maintain continuity in policies and programs. All the while, the agency has lost the broad public endorsement it once had for the work of environmental protection.

These politics make all the more difficult two challenges that EPA now confronts. First is the challenge of addressing new, less transparent problems. An estimated twenty million people participated in the first Earth Day in 1970, many demanding that government address the highly visible environmental problems of urban smog, polluted rivers, and poorly managed solid and hazardous waste. Many of these problems could be attributed to specific sources and/or were geographically concentrated, and much of the legislation enacted by Congress during the environmental decade targeted these sources. Examples are abundant: the CAA's performance standards for industrial sources, the CWA's wastewater permit limits for sewage treatment plants, and RCRA's regulation on the disposal of hazardous waste.

Controlling pollution from smokestacks, tailpipes, discharge pipes, and at landfills is not necessarily simple or inexpensive, but the task is more straightforward than addressing pollution from sources such as agriculture and urban stormwater. Moreover, the politics in many respects was easy. Rightly or wrongly, in the years leading up to and during the environmental decade, industry was widely perceived to be the villain. For this reason, at the beginning, directly targeting power plants, oil refineries, chemical manufacturers, and other industrial sources seemed to pose a safe political course for EPA.

In part a victim of its own success, EPA now often finds itself in a very different situation. Many of the problems on its agenda are no longer "easy," with clearly identifiable sources or practical technological fixes. Among the environmental challenges that the agency now must confront include nonpoint source pollution, secondary particulate matter, and climate change. These problems are less transparent and often have diffuse sources. In many cases, the "villains" now are the American public—fertilizing our lawns, eating our dinners, flying to see our families. The technical solutions are more elusive, and the politics are much more difficult since they often involve changing individual behavior. The leading question over the last decade has been about EPA's role in tackling the problem of climate change. Unlike the problems at the agency's formation, public support for a strong federal role in addressing climate change is both divided and weakly held.[123]

The second major challenge is to become more inclusive and address inequities in outcomes. Visible environmental problems have not been eradicated in the United States; they are just seen less often by the media and influential decision-makers because they are concentrated in areas populated by communities of color and people with low incomes. Particulate pollution still reaches dangerous levels, especially around coal plants and in agricultural areas, but communities nationwide also experience health effects from coal ash ponds, mining activity, confined animal feeding operations, failing septic systems, and a variety of other visible hazardous nuisances that often do not receive priority attention within EPA. Some of these problems fit the old model of identifiable sources and practical technological solutions, but policy action has been slow to follow. Addressing these and other challenges disproportionately affecting some communities may require more targeted policies and programs.

Challenges thus still remain for EPA as it hits its five-decade mark. Without question, EPA has become one of the leading public health agencies in the world. Through the policies and programs the agency implements, it has delivered to the American people enormous benefits to public health and environmental quality. The future success of EPA, however, will require the agency to effectively navigate the difficult political conditions in which it now operates. This is no easy task, especially in the current political environment where the White House and EPA leadership regularly question the agency's purpose, the regulatory tools Congress has given it to carry out its mission, and the basic scientific underpinnings of the environmental problems the agency is charged to manage. Over its fifty-year history, EPA has endured similar challenges, and it is likely to do so again.

NOTES

1. The authors are grateful for insightful comments and suggestions from Jim Barnes, Dan Fiorino, John Graham, Phil Sharp, and Jonathan Wiener.

2. Michael E. Kraft and Norman J. Vig, "Environmental Policy in the Reagan Presidency," *Political Science Quarterly* 99, no. 3 (1984): 415-39; Robert Cameron Mitchell, Angela G. Mertig, and Riley E. Dunlap, "Twenty Years of Environmental Mobilization: Trends among National Environmental Organizations," *Society and Natural Resources* 4, no. 3 (1991): 219–4.

3. J. Clarence Davies, III, *The Politics of Pollution* (New York: Pegasus, 1970).

4. Congress also enacted several additional laws during this period in the areas of natural and biological resources whose jurisdiction fell to other federal agencies, including the Coastal Zone Management Act (1972), the Marine Mammal Protection Act (1972), the Endangered Species Act (1973), the Federal Land Policy and Management Act (1976), the Fisheries Conservation and Management Act (1976), the National Forest Management Act (1976), and the Alaska Lands Act (1980).

5. Barbara Sinclair, *Unorthodox Lawmaking: New Legislative Processes in the U.S. Congress*, 3rd ed. (Washington, DC: CQ Press, 2007).

6. "Clean Air Bill Cleared with Auto Emission Deadline," *CQ Almanac*, 1970.

7. Judith A. Layzer, *Open for Business: Conservatives' Opposition to Environmental Regulation* (Cambridge, MA: MIT Press, 2012), 39.

8. Roll call votes from Congress.gov.

9. E. W. Kenworthy, "Senate, House Override Veto of Clean-Water Bill," *New York Times*, October 18, 1972.

10. Annie Snider, "Vetoes by Eisenhower, Nixon Presaged Today's Partisan Divide," *Greenwire*, October 18, 2012.

11. Keith T. Poole and Howard Rosenthal, *Congress: A Political-Economic History of Roll Call Voting* (New York: Oxford University Press, 1997).

12. Marc J. Hetherington, "Putting Polarization in Perspective," *British Journal of Political Science* 39, no. 2 (2009): 413-48; Frances Lee, *Beyond Ideology: Politics, Principles, and Partisanship in the U.S. Senate* (Chicago: University of Chicago Press, 2009).

13. Nolan McCarty, Keith T. Poole, and Howard Rosenthal, *Polarized America: The Dance of Ideology and Unequal Riches* (Cambridge, MA: The MIT Press, 2006); Marcus Prior, *Post-Broadcast Democracy: How Media Choice Increases Inequality in Political Involvement and Polarizes Elections* (New York: Cambridge University Press, 2007).

14. Thomas M. Carsey and Geoffrey C. Layman, "Changing Sides or Changing Minds? Party Identification and Policy Preferences in the American Electorate," *American Journal of Political Science* 50, no. 2 (2006): 464–77; Matthew C. Levendusky, "Clearer Cues, More Consistent Voters: A Benefit of Elite Polarization," *Political Behavior* 32, no. 1 (2010): 111–31.

15. Yphtach Lelkes, "Mass Polarization: Manifestations and Measurements," *Public Opinion Quarterly* 80 (2016): 392-410.

16. Seth Hill and Chris Tausanovitch, "Southern Realignment, Party Sorting, and the Polarization of American Primary Electorates, 1958–2012," *Public Choice* 176, no. 1 (2018): 107–32.

17. Michael Barber and Nolan McCarty, "Causes and Consequences of Polarization," In *Political Negotiation: A Handbook*, eds. Jane Mansbridge and Cathie Jo Martin (Washington, DC: Brookings Institution Press, 2015).

18. League of Conservation Voters, *2017 National Environmental Scorecard: First Session of the 115th Congress* (Washington, DC: LCV, February 27, 2018), http://scorecard.lcv.org/sites/scorecard.lcv.org/files/LCV_Scorecard-2017-Full.pdf.

19. Parrish Bergquist and Christopher Warshaw, "Elections and Parties in Environmental Politics," In *Handbook of U.S. Environmental Policy*, forthcoming, ed. David M. Konisky (Cheltenham, UK: Edward Elgar Publishing, 2020).

20. Boris Shor and Nolan McCarty, "The Ideological Mapping of American Legislatures," *American Political Science Review* 105, no. 3 (2011): 530–51.

21. Daniel J. Hopkins, *The Increasingly United States: How and Why American Political Behavior Nationalized* (Chicago: University of Chicago Press, 2018).

22. Robert Shepard, "Vice President George Bush, Taking a New Campaign Issue," *UPI,* September 1, 1988.

23. "Bush vs. Clinton: What Is an Environmental President?" *Los Angeles Times,* September 27, 1992.

24. Cited in Charles. O. Jones, "Speculative Augmentation in Federal Air Pollution Policy-Making," *Journal of Politics* 36, no. 2 (1974): 438–64.

25. Gallup, "Most Important Problem," https://news.gallup.com/poll/1675/Most-Important-Problem.aspx, accessed September 3, 2019.

26. Anthony Downs, "Up and Down With Ecology—The 'Issue-Attention Cycle,'" *Public Interest* 28 (Summer 1972): 38.

27. Charles Shipan and Megan L. Shannon, "Delaying Justice(s): A Duration Analysis of Supreme Court Confirmations," *American Journal of Political Science* 47, no. 4 (2003): 654–68; Nolan McCarty and Rose Razaghian, "Advice and Consent: Senate Responses to Executive Branch Nominations 1885–1996," *American Journal of Political Science* 43, no. 4 (October 1999): 1122–43.

28. Sarah A. Binder, "Consequences for the Courts: Polarized Politics and the Judicial Branch," In *Red and Blue Nation? Consequences and Correction of America's Polarized Parties, Volume Two*, eds. Pietro S. Nivola and David W. Brady (Washington, DC: Brookings Institution Press, 2008).

29. Charles M. Cameron, Jonathan P. Kastellec, and Jee-Kwang Park, "Voting for Justices: Change and Continuity in Confirmation Voting 1937–2010," *The Journal of Politics* 75, no. 2 (2013): 283–99.

30. Jeffrey A. Segal and Harold J. Spaeth, *The Supreme Court and the Attitudinal Model Revisited* (Cambridge University Press, 2002).

31. Richard L. Revesz, "Environmental Regulation, Ideology and the D.C. Circuit," *Virginia Law Review* 83, no. 8 (1997).

32. Brandice Canes-Wrone, "Bureaucratic Decisions and the Composition of the Lower Courts," *American Journal of Political Science* 47, no. 2 (2003): 205–14.

33. Anthony J. Nownes, *Interest Groups in American Politics: Pressure and Power* (New York: Routledge, 2012).

34. Frank R. Baumgartner and Beth L. Leech, *Basic Interests: The Importance of Groups in Politics and Political Science* (Princeton, NJ: Princeton University Press, 1998), 108.

35. Grant Jordan et al., "Tracking Interest Group Populations in the US and UK," In *The Scale of Interest Organization in Democratic Politics: Data and Research Methods*, eds. Darren Halpin and Grant Jordan (London: Palgrave MacMillan, 2012), 150.

36. Christopher J. Bosso, *Environment, Inc: From Grassroots to Beltway* (Lawrence, KS: University of Kansas Press, 2005), 92.

37. Joseph G. Peschek, *Policy-Planning Organizations: Elite Agendas and America's Rightward Turn* (Philadelphia: Temple University Press, 1987), 190–91.

38. Layzer, *Open for Business*, 50.

39. Nownes, *Interest Groups in American Politics,* 164.

40. Layzer, 48–58.

41. Ibid.

42. Robert J. Brulle, "Institutionalizing Delay: Foundation Funding and the Creation of US Climate Change Counter-Movement Organizations," *Climatic Change* 122, no. 4 (2014): 681–94; Justin Farrell, "Network Structure and Influence of the Climate Change Counter-Movement," *Nature Climate Change* 6, no. 4 (2016): 370; Naomi Oreskes and Erik M. Conway, *Merchants of Doubt: How a Handful of Scientists Obscured the Truth on Issues from Tobacco Smoke to Global Warming* (New York: Bloomsbury Publishing, 2011).

43. Prior, *Post-Broadcast Democracy*; Kevin Arceneaux and Martin Johnson, *Changing Minds or Changing Channels? Partisan News in an Age of Choice* (Chicago: University of Chicago Press, 2013).

44. David Tewksbury, "The Seeds of Audience Fragmentation: Specialization in the Use of Online News Sites," *Journal of Broadcasting & Electronic Media* 49, no. 3 (2005): 332–48.

45. Charles Bethea, "Shrinking Newspapers and the Costs of Environmental Reporting in Coal Country," *The New Yorker*, March 26, 2019.

46. Joshua P. Darr, Matthew P. Hitt, and Johanna L. Dunaway, "Newspaper Closures Polarize Voting Behavior," *Journal of Communication* 68, no. 6 (2018): 1007–28.

47. Data provided to authors from Society of Environmental Journalists on April 1, 2019.

48. Maxwell T. Boykoff, "We Speak for the Trees: Media Reporting on the Environment," *Annual Review of Environment and Resources* 34 (2009): 431–57.

49. Maxwell T. Boykoff and Jules M. Boykoff, "Balance as Bias: Global Warming and the US Prestige Press," *Global Environmental Change* 14, no. 2 (2004): 125–36.

50. Sarah A. Binder, "Polarized We Govern?" (Washington, DC: Center for Effective Public Management, Brookings Institution, 2014), https://www.brookings.edu/wp-content/uploads/2016/06/BrookingsCEPM_Polarized_figReplacedTextRevTableRev.pdf.

51. Patrick J. Egan, *Partisan Priorities: How Issue Ownership Drives and Distorts American Politics* (Cambridge: Cambridge University Press, 2013), 71.

52. Egan, *Partisan Priorities*.

53. Dale Russakoff, "EPA Chief is Assailed at Hearing," *Washington Post,* February 16, 1983.

54. David M. Konisky and Neal D. Woods, "Environmental Federalism and the Trump Presidency: A Preliminary Assessment," *Publius: The Journal of Federalism* 48, no. 3 (2018).

55. During his election campaign, then candidate Bush pledged to include carbon dioxide as part of a four-pollutant bill, but once becoming President, he reversed course and excluded carbon dioxide from the Clear Skies initiative.

56. John D. Graham, *Bush on the Home Front: Domestic Policy Triumphs and Setbacks* (Bloomington, IN: Indiana University Press, 2010).

57. Richard L. Revesz and Jack Lienke, *Struggling for Air: Power Plants and the "War on Coal"* (New York: Oxford University Press, 2016).

58. US Government Accountability Office, *Air Emissions and Electricity Generation at U.S. Power Plants*, GAO-12-545R (Washington, DC: GAO, April 18, 2012).

59. Graham, *Bush on the Home Front*.

60. Theda Skocpol, "Naming the Problem: What It Will Take to Counter Extremism and Engage Americans in the Fight against Global Warming," paper presented at the *Symposium on The Politics of America's Fight Against Global Warming, February 14, 2013, Harvard University*.

61. Gregory L. Hassler and Karen O'Connor, "Woodsy Witchdoctors versus Judicial Guerrillas: The Role and Impact of Competing Interest Groups in Environmental Litigation," *Boston College Environmental Affairs Law Review* 13 (1986): 487–520.

62. Andrew B. Whitford, "The Structures of Interest Coalitions: Evidence from Environmental Litigation," *Business and Politics* 5, no. 1 (2003): 45–64.

63. Matthew Grossmann, "Environmental Advocacy in Washington: A Comparison with Other Interest Groups," *Environmental Politics* 15, no. 4 (2006): 628–38.

64. Robert Glicksman and Christopher H. Schroeder, "EPA and the Courts: Twenty Years of Law and Politics," *Law and Contemporary Problems* 54, no. 4 (1991): 249–309.

65. US Environmental Protection Agency, *FY 2019 EPA Budget in Brief*, EPA-190-R-18-002 (Washington, DC: EPA, February 2018), https://www.epa.gov/sites/production/files/2018-02/documents/fy-2019-epa-bib.pdf, accessed September 3, 2018.

66. Katherine N. Probst and David M. Konisky, *Superfund's Future: What Will it Cost?* (Washington, DC: Resources for the Future Press, 2001).

67. American Society of Civil Engineers, *2017 Infrastructure Report Card* (Reston, VA: ASCE, 2017).

68. Christopher McGrory Klyza and David J. Sousa, *American Environmental Policy: Beyond Gridlock* (Cambridge, MA: MIT Press, 2013).

69. Richard P. Nathan, *The Administrative Presidency* (Hoboken, NJ: John Wiley & Sons, 1983); Robert F. Durant, *The Administrative Presidency Revisited: Public Lands, the BLM, and the Reagan Administration* (Albany, NY: State University of New York Press, 1992); William G. Resh, *Rethinking the Administrative Presidency: Trust, Intellectual Capital and Appointee-Careerist Relations in the George W. Bush Administration* (Baltimore, MD: Johns Hopkins University Press, 2015).

70. Konisky and Woods, "Environmental Federalism and the Trump Presidency"; David M. Konisky and Neal D. Woods, "Environmental Policy, Federalism, and the Obama Presidency," *Publius: The Journal of Federalism* 46, no. 3 (2016).

71. Joshua D. Clinton et al., "Separated Powers in the United States: The Ideology of Agencies, Presidents, and Congress," *American Journal of Political Science* 56, no. 2 (2012).

72. Evan J. Ringquist, "Assessing Evidence of Environmental Inequities: A Meta-Analysis," *Journal of Policy Analysis and Management* 24, no. 2 (2005).

73. US Environmental Protection Agency, *Environmental Equity: Reducing Risks for All Communities, Volumes 1 & 2*, EPA-230-R-92-008 (Washington, DC: EPA, 1992).

74. For a complete discussion, see David M. Konisky, *Failed Promises: Evaluating the Federal Government's Response to Environmental Justice* (Cambridge, MA: MIT Press, 2015).

75. "Executive Order 12898: Federal Actions to Address Environmental Justice in Minority and Low-Income Populations," 59 Fed. Reg. 7629 (February 16, 1994).

76. Konisky, *Failed Promises*, 41.

77. US Environmental Protection Agency, *The EPA's Environmental Justice Strategy* (Washington, DC: EPA, April 3, 1995).

78. US Environmental Protection Agency, *1996 Environmental Justice Implementation Plan,* EPA-300-R-96-004 (Washington, DC: EPA, 1996).

79. National Academy of Public Administration, *Environmental Justice in EPA Permitting: Reducing Pollution in High-Risk Communities is Integral to the Agency's Missions* (Washington, DC: NAPA, December, 2001); US Environmental Protection Agency, Office of Inspector General, *EPA Needs to Consistently Implement the Intent of the Executive Order on Environmental Justice*, 2004-P-00007 (Washington, DC: EPA, March 1, 2004); US Government Accountability Office, *EPA Should Devote More Attention to Environmental Justice When Developing Clean Air Rules,* GAO-05-289 (Washington, DC: GAO, July 2005).

80. US EPA, *EPA Needs to Consistently Implement*, 10.

81. H. Spencer Banzhaf, "Regulatory Impact Analyses of Environmental Justice Effects," *Journal of Land Use & Environmental Law* 27, no. 1 (2011); Shalini P. Vajjhala, Sarah Szambelan, and Amanda Van Epp, *Integrating EJ into Federal Policies and Programs: Examining the Role of Regulatory Impact Analyses and Environmental Impact Statements*, RFF Discussion Paper 08–45 (Washington, DC: Resources for the Future Press, 2008); Konisky, *Failed Promises*, 41; Colin Provost and Brian J. Gerber, "Political Control and Policy-Making Uncertainty in Executive Orders: The Implementation of Environmental Justice Policy," *Journal of Public Policy* 39, no. 2 (June 2019).

82. US Environmental Protection Agency, *Plan EJ 2014* (Washington, DC: EPA, September 2011), 4.

83. David M. Konisky, "Environmental Justice Delayed: Failed Promises, But Some Hope for the Future," *Environment: Science and Policy for Sustainable Development* 58, no. 2 (2016): 4–15.

84. US Commission on Civil Rights, *Not in My Backyard: Executive Order 12,898 and Title VI as Tools for Achieving Environmental Justice* (Washington, DC: US-CCR, October, 2003), https://www.usccr.gov/pubs/envjust/ej0104.pdf.

85. Mark K. Landy, Marc J. Roberts, and Stephen R. Thomas, *The Environmental Protection Agency: Asking the Wrong Questions*, revised edition (New York: Oxford University Press, 1994), 37.

86. Layzer, 39.

87. Layzer, 39–40.

88. Quoted in Layzer, 39.

89. Ronald Reagan, *First Inaugural Address*, January 20, 1981, https://www.reaganfoundation.org/media/128614/inaguration.pdf, accessed September 3, 2019.

90. Durant, *The Administrative Presidency Revisited*, 49.

91. Robert A. Shanley, *Presidential Influence and Environmental Policy* (Westport, CT: Greenwood Press, 1992), 113. See also Patricia McGee Crotty, "The New Federalism Game: Primacy Implementation of Environmental Policy," *Publius: The*

Journal of Federalism 17, no. 2 (1987): 53–67; Neal D. Woods, "Primacy Implementation of Environmental Policy in the US States," *Publius: The Journal of Federalism* 36, no. 2 (2005): 259–76.

92. US Environmental Protection Agency, "Authorization Status of All Resource Conservation and Recovery Act (RCRA) and Hazardous and Solid Waste Amendments (HWSA) Rules," *epa.gov*, last updated March 31, 2019, https://www.epa.gov/rcra/authorization-status-all-resource-conservation-and-recovery-act-rcra-and-hazardous-and-solid.

93. Proposed Executive Order, "Federal Regulation," 5 Op. O.L.C. 59 (1981).

94. Shanley, *Presidential Influence*, 69.

95. Shanley, 63.

96. Lisa Heinzerling, "Inside EPA: A Former Insider's Reflections on the Relationship Between the Obama EPA and the Obama White House," *Pace Environmental Law Review* 31, no. 1 (2014).

97. Shanley, 71.

98. Robert V. Percival et al., *Environmental Regulation: Law, Science and Policy* (Boston: Little, Brown and Company, 1992), 709.

99. Percival et al., 710.

100. Dana Priest, "Competitiveness Council under Scrutiny," *Washington Post*, November 26, 1991.

101. Norman J. Vig, "Presidential Leadership and the Environment: From Reagan and Bush to Clinton," In *Environmental Policy in the 1990s*, eds. Norman J. Vig and Michael E. Kraft, 2nd ed. (Washington, DC: CQ Press, 1994).

102. Layzer, *Open for Business,* 159–61.

103. John D. Graham, "The Evolving Regulatory Role of the U.S. Office of Management and Budget," *Review of Environmental Economics and Policy* 1, no. 2 (2007).

104. US General Accounting Office, *Rulemaking: OMB's Role in Reviews of Agencies' Draft Rules and the Transparency of Those Reviews*, GAO-03-929 (Washington, DC: GAO, 2003).

105. Graham, *Bush on the Home Front*, 257-8; Heinzerling, "Inside EPA," 335.

106. Heinzerling, "Inside EPA."

107. GAO, *OMB's Role,* 9.

108. Ibid.

109. GAO, *OMB's Role*, 5.

110. Lisa Heinzerling, "Who Will Run the EPA," *Yale Journal on Regulation* 30 (2012): 39-43.

111. David M. Konisky and Manuel P. Teodoro, "When Governments Regulate Governments," *American Journal of Political Science* 60, no. 3 (2016): 559–74.

112. Denise Scheberle, "Environmental Federalism and the Role of State and Local Governments," In *The Oxford Handbook of U.S. Environmental Policy*, eds. Michael E. Kraft and Sheldon Kamieniecki (Oxford: Oxford University Press, 2012).

113. Environmental Council of the States, *Cooperative Federalism 2.0: Achieving and Maintaining a Clean Environment and Protecting Public Health* (Washington, DC: ECOS, 2017).

114. Dorothy M. Daley, Megan Mullin, and Meghan E. Rubado, "State Agency Discretion in a Delegated Federal Program: Evidence from Drinking Water Investment," *Publius: The Journal of Federalism* 44, no. 4 (2013): 564–86; John Morris, "Dirty Water, Clean Water: Infrastructure Funding and State Discretion in Southern States," In *Speaking Green with a Southern Accent: Environmental Management and Innovation in the South*, eds. Gerald Andrews Emison and John C. Morris (Lanham, MD: Lexington Books, 2010), 45–64.

115. Evan J. Ringquist, "Policy Influence and Policy Responsiveness in State Pollution Control," *Policy Studies Journal* 22, no. 1 (1994).

116. Dorothy M. Daley and James C. Garand, "Horizontal Diffusion, Vertical Diffusion, and Internal Pressure in State Environmental Policymaking 1989-1998," *American Politics Research* 37 (2005).

117. Ringquist, "Policy Influence."

118. Matthew Potoski, "Designing Bureaucratic Responsiveness: Administrative Procedures and Agency Choice in State Environmental Policy," *State Policy and Politics Quarterly* 2, no. 1 (2002): 1–23.

119. David M. Konisky and Neal D. Woods, "Measuring State Environmental Policy," *Review of Policy Research* 29, no. 4 (2012): 544+.

120. Quoted in Rena I. Steinzor and William F. Piermattei, "Reinventing Environmental Regulation via the Government Performance and Results Act: Where's the Money?" *Environmental Law Reporter* 28 (1998): 10563.

121. ECOS, "Cooperative Federalism 2.0."

122. Paul Nolette, *Federalism on Trial: State Attorneys General and National Policymaking in Contemporary America* (Lawrence, KS: University of Kansas Press, 2015). Updated data in the figure come from http://attorneysgeneral.org, created and maintained by Nolette. Year indicates resolution date, except lawsuits initiated from 2014 to the time of writing are indicated by initiation date.

123. Patrick J. Egan and Megan Mullin, "Climate Change: U.S. Public Opinion," *Annual Review of Political Science* 20 (2017): 209–27.

Chapter Thirteen

Agenda Setting at EPA

John D. Graham and Jonathan B. Wiener

INTRODUCTION

How does EPA come to do what it does? Can EPA choose its own path? To what extent do other actors, stakeholders, and institutions influence EPA's priorities? Why has EPA historically emphasized some issues at some times, yet other issues at other times?

These questions refer to the phenomenon of "agenda setting," which is distinct from other steps in the policy making process such as options formulation, policy adoption, implementation, enforcement, and evaluation.[1] Some scholars argue that agenda setting is the most important step of all for environmental protection, because a serious environmental problem may go unaddressed indefinitely if policy makers do not put it on their agenda.[2]

Setting the agenda is partly a technical process involving evidence about problems, impacts, technologies, and policy options. But stakeholders may also employ public information campaigns, social media, lobbying, and litigation in the courts. Agenda setting can become a contest to frame public debate, advocate for attention, attribute causes, assign blame, and build a coalition for action.[3]

EPA can exercise leadership, but it cannot do everything. At any given moment, many issues compete for EPA's attention; some are added or elevated on the agenda, while others are demoted. Many factors may influence this process. If a problem becomes highly salient to policy makers and does not trigger political conflict, it may be particularly likely to find its way on to the agenda.[4] Inevitably, given scarce time and effort, there is some triage. Sometimes new issues may "intrude" and push aside previously important items; periodically, the agency undertakes "reprioritization" in light of its limited political capital, budget, and staff.[5] Even when EPA is attempting to be proactive in advancing environmental protection, it faces the challenge of giving more attention to some issues than to others, and the influence of other actors on its agenda.

The term "agenda" is somewhat confusing because agenda items (which are simply issues) vary considerably in scope, time horizon, type, and complexity. This chapter focuses on agenda items that could lead to policy-making by EPA through legislative proposals, international agreements, regulations, voluntary standards, and other measures. Thus, we consider EPA's longer-range agenda, as defined by proposals for new legislation, as well as EPA's operational agenda in developing regulations to implement current environmental laws. We do not address agenda setting as it relates to the agency's enforcement, communications, and human resources functions.

There is no official EPA website that lists the agency's current agenda of policy issues; indeed, it is not always in an agency's interest to be completely transparent about its agenda. In some cases, EPA administrators are quite explicit about issues that are a priority to them (e.g., children's health during the Carter administration, climate change and environmental justice during the Obama administration, and deregulation during the Trump administration). But, as we shall see, the issues that consume EPA's time and effort on a day-to-day basis are not necessarily the personal priorities of the agency's political leadership because there are many competing pressures on EPA leadership.

Part 1 of this chapter looks inside the federal government at the processes that influence EPA's agenda. The primary question we address "internally" is: How much does EPA set its own agenda for policy measures, given that it is constantly pressured by other federal institutions, notably the Congress, the courts, and the White House?

Part 2 of this chapter examines external conditions that shape the federal government's environmental agenda. Here, "external" refers to societal forces operating outside of the federal government, such as public opinion, media coverage, scientific knowledge, technological change, interest-group activity, state governments, and international relations.

In Part 3, we describe a complex historical example of EPA agenda-setting, in which EPA—amidst a variety of both internal and external dynamics—emerged as a central player. This example highlights EPA's policy entrepreneurship in national and global efforts to phase out the chemical pollutants linked to depletion of the stratospheric ozone layer. EPA's agenda setting and policy making efforts led to the US national ban on CFCs in aerosol spray cans in 1978 and the international agreement known as the Montreal Protocol on Substances that Deplete the Ozone Layer in 1987.

To inform this chapter, we gathered information from several sources: laws, rules, and court decisions; EPA documents; academic literature; interviews with practitioners from all periods in the agency's fifty-year history (listed in the Appendix); and our own experiences in the federal government during the Bush (41), Clinton (42), and Bush (43) administrations.

PART 1: INTERNAL DYNAMICS WITHIN THE FEDERAL GOVERNMENT

External conditions help shape EPA's agenda, but governmental actors must make the agenda-setting decisions. Here we explore the extent to which EPA sets its own agenda and how much the Congress, the White House, and the federal judiciary influence EPA's agenda.[6]

A subtheme of Part 1 is that specific personalities, sometimes called policy entrepreneurs, can play important roles in agenda setting.[7] Sometimes those actors are employed by EPA (as leaders or staff), while in other cases they work at the numerous other governmental and non-governmental organizations that interact with the agency. In short, people matter in the agenda-setting process.

The Congress

The practitioners we interviewed believe that it is the Congress, not the agency leadership, that generally determines EPA agenda. Their beliefs are consistent with an influential body of political science theory that gives primacy in the US to the power of the legislature to instruct agencies, compared to the powers of the executive branch and the judiciary.[8] There are several mechanisms or levers that Congress uses to control EPA: authorization, appropriation, and informal political influence. Each is discussed below.

The scope of a federal agency's agenda is defined by the grant of legal authority in the laws that the agency is directed to administer. EPA cannot act on issues that are outside the scope of its legal authority (unless an extra-legal action item goes unchecked by Congress and the courts). Within EPA's grant of authority, Congress defines which actions are mandatory and which are discretionary. While Congress has told EPA to tackle numerous issues, there are well-known and important pollution problems that Congress has never given EPA strong regulatory authority to address (e.g., indoor air pollution, and non-point sources of water pollution such as runoff from farms).

The growing power of Congress from the 1960s to the 1980s was accentuated by a deepening public mistrust of the executive branch—notably after the Vietnam War pursued by the Johnson and Nixon administrations, and the Watergate scandal leading to Nixon's resignation in 1973. Interestingly, EPA was created in 1970 by a first-term Republican president (Richard Nixon) seeking to claim or neutralize an issue championed by a potential Democratic challenger (Senator Edmund Muskie of Maine).[9] But there was skepticism as to whether the Nixon administration was really serious about environmental protection.[10] Since there is a long history of congressional mistrust of the executive branch, especially on environmental issues, a large share of EPA's agenda is specified in environmental laws and is mandatory in nature.

EPA's resources (budget and staff) are typically insufficient to administer all of the laws EPA is authorized to administer. Appropriations and authorization committees are distinct power centers in the Congress, and those committees are not always aligned in their viewpoints. EPA's annual appropriation from Congress delineates how much money will be allocated to specific programs and activities. EPA does not have general authority to move appropriated funds from one purpose to another. If EPA has no budgetary authority for a new agenda item, it is difficult for the agency to work on that item. In some situations, a provision—sometimes called a "rider"—in EPA's appropriation will disallow use of funds for a specific purpose, or direct precisely how the funds must be allocated (e.g., a grant to an outside organization).

The policy sentiments of members of Congress place a further informal constraint on what issues the agency might address. If EPA ignores the informal political boundaries defined by the will of powerful members of Congress, the agency can be punished in many ways: delays or denials of Senate confirmation of agency nominees; formal investigations of the agency; embarrassment of EPA leadership at oversight hearings; and riders or cuts in the next year's appropriation.

There are frequently different viewpoints within the Congress, including many members who have no personal opinion on what issues EPA should address, so the agency leadership is likely to give particular weight to the views of a few key members: the House and Senate leadership (majority and minority) and the chairs and ranking minority members of its authorizing and appropriations committees. During the agency's fifty-year period, there was a multi-decade period of power acquisition by congressional committees and their chairs and professional staff.[11] Recently there has been a trend among House and Senate leadership to consolidate power, but committee chairs remain influential.[12] Understanding the elusive will of Congress is not always easy but it does play an influential role in shaping EPA's agenda.

The roles of professional staff in Congress are worthy of elaboration because they can have a powerful influence over which issues EPA does and does not address. The same specialized staff often work on committees for many years, even when the membership of the committee changes due to elections. The committee staff are often lawyers, whereas the agency staff are often scientific, policy, economic, and technical experts, as well as lawyers; such differences in training may lead to some difficulties in mutual understanding. Committee staff are not beholden to EPA for information but can obtain information from the Library of Congress, the Congressional Research Service, the Government Accountability Office (GAO), and the Congressional Budget Office (CBO), as well as from stakeholders, lobbyists, advocates, and academics about what is (or is not) happening at the agency. Thus, if the agency's leaders want to add or subtract items from its agenda, it is crucial that they make an effort to persuade key committee staff to adopt the agency's point of view.

Of all the levers possessed by Congress, the statutory directive, sometimes coupled with a deadline for action, is the most straightforward technique used by Congress to set EPA's agenda. The federal environmental laws, beginning in the 1970s, contain numerous such prescriptions.

The first major environmental law EPA was tasked with administering, the Clean Air Act (CAA) of 1970, contained several agenda-setting directives, most notably requirements that EPA list key pollutants and set national ambient air quality standards (NAAQS) for them, and also reduce tailpipe emissions of named pollutants from new cars by ninety percent within six years. The Clean Air Act Amendments of 1977 contained a host of additional mandatory assignments. The Clean Water Act (CWA) of 1972 directed EPA to adopt technology-based standards to reduce effluents from industrial point sources, and to set water quality standards for uses designated by the states. The Safe Drinking Water Act (SDWA) of 1974 instructed EPA to set maximum levels for contaminants in public drinking water systems. The Resource Conservation and Recovery Act (RCRA) of 1976 specified how EPA must regulate solid and hazardous waste facilities, and the Comprehensive Environmental Response, Compensation, and Liability Act (CERCLA) of 1980 instructed EPA to ensure that numerous abandoned waste disposal sites were cleaned up.

After the election of conservative Ronald Reagan in 1980 and the tumultuous tenure of EPA Administrator Anne M. Gorsuch (1981-1983), Congress sought to constrain executive discretion further. The next three environmental laws passed by Congress—the Hazardous and Solid Waste Amendments (HSWA) of 1984, the Superfund Amendments and Reauthorization Act (SARA) of 1986, and the Clean Air Act Amendments (CAAA) of 1990—contained some of the most prescriptive provisions in the history of US environmental law.

Since the 1990s, Congress has become more polarized on partisan lines, and legislative gridlock is now commonplace. Still, some new environmental laws have been enacted by Congress after 1990: the Safe Drinking Water Act Amendments of 1996 gave EPA both more responsibility to list contaminants and publish exposure data and more authority to set maximum contaminant levels based on analysis of risks, costs, and benefits; the Food Quality Protection Act of 1996 directed EPA to provide a special margin of safety to protect children from pesticide residues on foods; the 2005 and 2007 energy laws and the 2008 farm bill directed EPA to mandate blending of renewable fuels, such as ethanol, with gasoline; and the 2016 Lautenberg Chemical Safety Act directed EPA to accelerate risk assessment and management of industrial chemicals. Despite the pervasive partisan polarization in Congress after 1990, each of these laws was passed with large bipartisan majorities in both the House and Senate.

In most of these laws, Congress created nondiscretionary duties for EPA to enact regulations by specified deadlines, often to achieve highly ambitious environmental goals. A major driver of this legislative approach was that, without a clear direction from Congress, EPA might become bogged down in difficult technical and economic debates and have a tendency to delay tough decisions due to competing political pressures. Moreover, Congress was aware that, inside the executive branch, the Office of Management and Budget (OMB) was asking EPA for further analyses unless the measure was nondiscretionary and faced a strict deadline. Thus, Congress used nondiscretionary mandates and deadlines to force regulations to be issued that it feared might otherwise never be issued or would be unduly delayed.

The influences of appropriations language and the will of Congress are illustrated by the Clinton administration's struggle to address climate change in the late 1990s. Vice President Al Gore led the Clinton administration's international effort in support of the 1997 Kyoto climate protocol, which set targets for industrialized (but not developing) nations to reduce greenhouse gas emissions. President Clinton did not submit the protocol for Senate ratification when it became apparent that there was widespread bipartisan opposition in Congress. Then a member of Congress, Joe Knollenberg (R-MI), fearing that the Clinton-Gore administration might proceed to implement the Kyoto Protocol without Senate ratification, used his perch on the House Appropriations Committee to block the Clinton administration. Knollenberg championed a rider on appropriations bills for two fiscal years (1999-2000) that prohibited federal agencies from using funds "to propose or issue rules, regulations, decrees, or orders for the purpose of implementing, or in preparation for implementation of, the Kyoto Protocol." This language did not necessarily preclude EPA from using its CAA authority to regulate greenhouse gas emissions, but it may have caused some staff in the Clinton EPA to be more cautious about making climate policy without statutory authorization.[13]

An alternative view is that the Clinton EPA had no intention of mandating GHG reductions, as the administration preferred voluntary plans to reduce emissions.

There was a legislative effort from 1995 to 1997 to give EPA more authority to set its own agenda through the use of analytic tools such as comparative risk assessment and cost-benefit analysis. Congress chose not to enact comparative-risk legislation, in part because some members feared that such legislation might weaken the progress the agency was making under the environmental laws passed in the 1970s and 1980s.

As important as Congress is as an agenda setter, there are situations where Congress—intentionally or inadvertently—allows the executive branch or the judiciary to determine EPA's agenda. The most obvious cases are where Congress writes flexible or ambiguous laws, which has the practical effect of giving EPA some agenda setting power. We consider some of those situations below when we discuss agency agenda setting.

Overall, Congress has powerful levers to shape EPA's agenda. Our interviewees agreed that Congress has been the primary actor driving EPA's agenda, and one interviewee estimated that roughly 80–85% of the activity at EPA is driven by Congress. Through statutory commands, appropriations, oversight, and other mechanisms, Congress often determines which issues EPA addresses or how ambitiously.

The Courts

In US administrative law, judicial review is often seen as a downstream check on agency issuance of unlawful regulations or enforcement actions. The trend in the 1970s was for courts to expect more thoroughness from all federal agencies in the gathering and interpretation of evidence in support of final regulations. This came to be called the "hard look" doctrine of judicial review. But courts also began to play an influential role upstream in setting the agenda of regulatory agencies. Some of this trend applied to all federal agencies; other aspects are rooted in the specific ways that modern environmental laws were crafted.

The Administrative Procedure Act (APA) of 1946 was designed to enhance the opportunity for the public to participate in the federal rulemaking process.[14] The APA requires each federal agency to "give an interested person the right to petition for the issuance, amendment, or repeal of a rule" (5 USC section 553(e)). Further, the APA empowers federal courts to review decisions not to act (as well as to act), including the power to "compel agency action unlawfully withheld or unreasonably delayed" as well as to vacate "arbitrary" or "capricious" agency actions (5 USC section 706).

Historically, the federal courts have been reluctant to intrude upon the agency's agenda-setting discretion. Forcing an issue onto EPA's agenda requires judicial intervention into how the agency is managed and how budgets and personnel are allocated by agency leadership. Thus, if someone petitions an agency to initiate rulemaking, the courts typically permit the agency to decline if it gives defensible reasons. Deference to the agency may be appropriate because the statute affords discretion and the agency has greater expertise than the court on the topic of the petition. If the topic area is one where market conditions and technology are changing rapidly, the agency may be the institution best equipped to review and update policies over time.

Despite the typical judicial deference to agency priority setting, there are cases where federal courts have held that EPA, in its response to a petition, behaved unlawfully. In effect, the "hard look" doctrine that courts applied to final regulations began to be applied to EPA's responses to rulemaking petitions. Judge Bazelon observed in 1971 that the "power [of courts to set aside agency actions] has come into more frequent use, and with it, the requirement that administrators articulate the factors on which they base their decisions. . . .[C]ourts are increasingly asked to review administrative action that touches on fundamental personal interests in life, health, and liberty."[15]

A prominent example of a court decision impelling EPA to add to its agenda was the 1972 case that launched the "PSD" program (Prevention of Significant Deterioration of air quality). EPA had begun setting national ambient air quality standards (NAAQS) under the Clean Air Act (CAA) section 109, and requiring states with air dirtier than the NAAQS to adopt state implementation plans (SIPs) to attain the NAAQS under section 110. But EPA had not yet been requiring states with air cleaner than the NAAQS to keep their air clean. CAA section 109 said the NAAQS were to be set at the level requisite to protect public health and welfare, and the 1970 CAA had no specific provisions for non-degradation of cleaner air. CAA section 116 authorized states to set standards that are more stringent than the NAAQS if states chose to do so, implying that the states could choose not to do so. Still, in *Sierra Club v. Ruckelshaus*, a federal district court held that the policy goals expressed in CAA section 101, to "protect and enhance the quality of the Nation's air," obliged EPA to require states to prevent the significant degradation of air quality that is cleaner than the NAAQS.[16] Five years later, this PSD policy was codified by Congress in the 1977 CAA Amendments.[17]

Sometimes the courts reject EPA's denial of a rulemaking petition. One of the most important court cases in EPA history was a US Supreme Court decision in 2007, *Massachusetts v. EPA*, on EPA's authority to regulate greenhouse gases under the CAA.[18] This case arose from a petition by a coalition of states, citizens, conservation groups, and environmental advocacy groups. The petitioners requested in October 1999 that the Clinton EPA limit greenhouse gas emissions. EPA did not respond to the petition during the Clinton administration (although EPA's then general counsel, Jonathan Cannon, issued a memorandum finding that EPA did have the authority to regulate greenhouse gases under the CAA). After taking office in 2001, the Bush (43) EPA sought public comment on the issues raised by the petition, while obtaining an assessment of scientific knowledge and uncertainties about climate change from the National Research Council of the National Academy of Sciences.

In September 2003 the Bush (43) EPA denied the rulemaking petition on the grounds that (1) the Clean Air Act does not authorize EPA to issue regulations to address greenhouse gas emissions contributing to global climate change, and (2) even if EPA had such authority, EPA has policy discretion and it would be unwise to exercise it because the CAA is not well designed to address greenhouse gases, and such domestic policies could conflict with international climate treaty negotiations.

In a 5-4 decision, the US Supreme Court rejected EPA's decision, ruling that the CAA does authorize EPA to regulate greenhouse gases and that EPA must confront the question whether greenhouse gases would reasonably be anticipated to "endanger public health and welfare" under the CAA. The Court's decision did not itself mandate that EPA regulate greenhouse gases (only that it confront the endangerment question), and thus it left unclear when a court may compel an agency to elevate the priority given to one issue among the many over which the agency does have statutory authority. After efforts to enact new climate legislation in Congress failed in 2009–2010, this 2007 Supreme Court decision enabled EPA under the Obama administration to proceed with several CAA rulemakings related to climate change, notably the Clean Power Plan and GHG standards for motor vehicles.

Starting with the Clean Air Act of 1970, a suite of federal environmental laws included stronger "citizen suit" provisions that are applicable when EPA fails to implement nondiscretionary requirements.[19] These provisions allow environmental advocacy groups to become agenda enforcers, helping Congress oversee EPA implementation of priorities established in legislation.[20] Early on, observers viewed citizen suits as generally effective in prodding EPA to fulfill congressional mandates to protect the environment.[21] Later, some observers worried that the accumulation of numerous statutory provisions with nondiscretionary duties, subject to enforcement by citizen suits, may unduly shift EPA's agenda-setting discretion to litigants and courts, without sufficient sensitivity to the multitude of issues that EPA must weigh in setting priorities. In general, though, the practitioners we interviewed see nondiscretionary duties as an effective way to avoid the inaction that might have occurred had EPA been granted a wide range of discretion about whether to issue protective regulations.

The tensions over EPA discretion versus citizen suits are exhibited in EPA's efforts to avoid being compelled by litigation to regulate local air quality directly from the federal level, preferring to let the states have this role. In the 1970s, after EPA found some state implementation plans (SIPs) for air pollution to be inadequate, EPA issued several federal implementation plans (FIPs), but these FIPs were challenged in court by the states and were held to have exceeded EPA's authority to compel action by the states. Then in the 1980s, environmental groups persuaded the courts to compel EPA to disapprove California's SIP for its South Coast Air Basin on the grounds that it was not stringent enough. EPA reluctantly issued a FIP in 1990, but then sought to avoid enforcing it due to the enactment of the CAA Amendments of 1990. In 1992 the Ninth Circuit ordered EPA to go ahead with its FIP nonetheless, but in 1995 Congress passed a special rider allowing EPA to rescind its FIP, after which California adopted a new SIP which EPA approved by 1999.[22] This history illustrates that, unless Congress intervenes, the courts can force EPA to address issues that the agency might prefer the states to address.

Agenda-setting lawsuits are often resolved by the parties before a judicial opinion is issued. The resolutions may occur in the form of a settlement (which is not approved by the court but may lead to a stay of the lawsuit) or a judicial consent decree (a contract between the petitioner and the agency that is approved by the court, often with criteria for performance reviews over time). The content of settlements and consent decrees may go beyond a mandatory timetable for EPA to execute a nondiscretionary duty. There are cases where EPA has agreed—sometimes with enthusiasm—to revamp its rulemaking or implementation approach under the settlement. The 1972 Clean Water Act directed EPA to list and regulate "toxic pollutants" to ensure an ample margin of safety. When EPA failed to implement this provision on schedule, multiple citizen suits were filed against the agency. In the "Toxics Consent Decree," EPA agreed to regulate toxics on an industry-by-industry basis through technology-based controls, instead of health-based standards on each pollutant. This approach was later codified by Congress in the Clean Water Act Amendments of 1977.[23]

Such "sue-and-settle" agreements became controversial. In March 1986, the Department of Justice (DOJ) issued a memorandum from Attorney General Edward Meese restricting the DOJ, when representing EPA in such lawsuits, from entering into settlements or consent decrees that interfere with EPA's discretionary authority to develop its rules. The policy in the 1986 memo was later formalized in the Code of Federal Regulations in 1991.[24] More recently, a GAO study examined the thirty-two major rules issued by EPA from May 31, 2008, to June 1, 2013, under seven key statutes, and found that only nine of them were issued following deadline lawsuits, concluding that "[t]he effect of settlements in deadline suits on EPA's rulemaking priorities is limited."[25] In October 2017, President Trump's first EPA Administrator, Scott Pruitt, issued a letter seeking to end what he called the practice of "sue-and-settle" in which EPA agrees with litigants to rulemakings, outside of normal legislative and administrative procedures. Experts continue to debate whether such settlements are distorting EPA's agenda and inviting costly new rulemakings or are sensible resolutions that save costs and conserve EPA resources compared to prolonged litigation.[26]

The nondiscretionary clauses in environmental laws are particularly important during presidential administrations that have a zealous anti-regulation philosophy. The Trump administration sought to minimize the flow of new regulations from agencies, and eliminate two existing regulations for each new one that is adopted. In the case of EPA, however, the Trump administration has been directed by federal courts to proceed with nondiscretionary regulatory duties that the Trump administration tried to ignore. The fact that some environmental laws compel periodic re-evaluation of existing standards has also compelled the Trump administration to initiate rulemaking proceedings on issues that might otherwise not be reconsidered at all.[27] Thus, even in an administration that seems hostile to EPA's regulatory missions, environmental groups can access the judiciary to force rulemakings that flow from nondiscretionary duties in environmental laws.

The President

The White House (in any administration) does not necessarily share the perspective that federal agencies are simply implementers of a congressional agenda. White House oversight of a department's policy agenda arises from the president's political accountability (both credit and blame) for the impacts of agency policies. The president also aims to pursue his or her own policy agenda, and hence there have been persistent efforts by presidents of both parties to steer EPA action.[28] Some go further to advocate the "unitary executive" theory under which all cabinet agencies—including EPA—report to the president, and the Constitution grants the president control of the executive branch.[29]

The picture might be different if EPA had been created by Congress as a so-called "independent agency," like the Federal Reserve Board or the Nuclear Regulatory Commission. The leaders of these multi-member commissions are appointed by the president for fixed terms of office, and have some restrictions on the power of the president to remove them from office (though this varies by agency and its effect may be contested).[30] The White House typically has less control over the policy initiatives of these independent agencies than it has over Cabinet departments.

The Nixon administration made a conscious decision *not* to establish EPA as an agency independent of White House oversight (in part to avoid giving Congress greater sway), even though William Ruckelshaus, EPA's first administrator, worked hard to build the agency's reputation for independence from political influences. The word "independent" can be confusing because many observers believe that EPA is (or should be) independent of political influence, but here the word independence refers to the ability of the White House to control or influence EPA's agenda. Congress has never passed legislation formally classifying EPA as a cabinet-level department, despite several efforts to do so, but most presidential administrations include the EPA administrator at meetings of the cabinet. Most importantly, the EPA administrator serves at the pleasure of the president, which means that EPA's decision-making is, as a practical matter, ultimately under presidential control.

Presidential influence on—and accountability for—agenda setting at EPA is most apparent when a presidential candidate campaigns on an EPA-related initiative, wins the election, and then proceeds as president to fulfill the campaign commitment. This was the pattern under President George H. W. Bush (41), a Republican, who pledged in the 1988 campaign to enact a new Clean Air Act, notably to reduce acid rain. He won the election, and ultimately succeeded in working with the Democrat-majority Congress to pass the CAA Amendments of 1990. Likewise, candidate Barack Obama, a Democrat, pledged in 2008 to make climate change a legislative priority. The subsequent legislative proposal (the Waxman-Markey bill) passed the House but not the Senate, and the Obama administration then used executive authority to ensure that climate change was high on EPA's agenda. More recently, candidate Donald Trump pledged to repeal much of Obama's climate agenda; once in office, Trump issued executive orders for that purpose, and Trump's EPA undertook to repeal or replace the Obama EPA climate policies with less stringent and less costly requirements.[31] Thus, agenda setting by EPA and the White House may be coordinated—primarily by the White House staff and the president's political appointees at EPA—to match the president's policy agenda and to build the president's popularity with base constituents or with the public at large.[32]

Given the president's political accountability for EPA initiatives, the Executive Office of the President (EOP) has taken concerted steps during EPA's history to shape, promote, and constrain EPA's agenda. EOP efforts to control Cabinet departments and agencies are a key part of the "administrative presidency."[33] At least since the creation of EPA and the wave of modern environmental legislation in the 1970s, every president of both political parties has attempted to manage EPA.

One approach is to deploy the White House Council on Environmental Quality (CEQ) as an oversight mechanism to ensure that EPA's priorities are in sync with the president's priorities. CEQ is a small unit in the EOP comprised primarily of political appointees with deep loyalty to the president. The CEQ chair and EPA administrator may, depending on the initiative, compete with each other—or be aligned with each other—during White House deliberations. With regard to EPA's agenda, the influence of the CEQ chair varies enormously from one administration to the next—relative to EPA, CEQ was far more influential under Bush (43) than it was under Obama.

A second approach is to subject EPA initiatives to review by the policy offices in the White House. In the Bush (43) administration, and also to a large extent in the Clinton administration, both the Domestic Policy Council (DPC) and National Economic Council (NEC) reviewed and commented on significant EPA initiatives during the interagency review process. Although the White House offices are small, they are typically staffed with political operatives who are highly loyal to the president, have good connections with the president's constituencies, and know how the president's allies in Congress might react to an EPA initiative.

Third, the White House may employ the powers of OMB to ensure that EPA's agenda is aligned with presidential priorities. Each year EPA and OMB negotiate EPA's budget request from Congress, and OMB uses this process to send clear signals to EPA as to which initiatives are approved and which are not. With respect to regulatory policies, OMB's Office of Information and Regulatory Affairs (OIRA) has authority under longstanding executive orders, issued by presidents of both parties, to review major rules and their impacts.[34] When OMB was unable to obtain Senate confirmation of an OIRA administrator under Bush (41), the White House created the Council on Competitiveness, led by Vice President Dan Quayle, to provide political leadership for regulatory oversight. Unlike CEQ, OIRA has a substantial career staff with significant policy-analysis expertise and knowledge of the agency's programs. But OIRA review typically occurs after an agency has developed a proposed rule, so OIRA has less influence on agency agenda-setting unless OIRA gets involved earlier in EPA policy-making process or sets clear expectations as to what kinds of initiatives will be approved.[35]

Despite the growing influence of the administrative presidency, there are limits to presidential control of EPA's agenda. Presidential executive orders cannot override statutory laws enacted by Congress. One study of agenda setting at EPA found that two factors overshadowed all others in shaping the rulemaking agenda at EPA during the Clinton and Bush (43) administrations: statutory prescriptions from Congress and judicial orders and consent decrees.[36] The president's political appointees at EPA cannot change those two factors, nor can the administrative presidency. The president can propose new legislation, but that takes time and bills may not be enacted, especially in a polarized Congress. The president and political appointees can try to change agency policies, but those changes may be challenged in court—as, for example, were both the Obama EPA's climate policy (the Clean Power Plan (2015)), and the Trump EPA's replacement (the Affordable Clean Energy rule (2019)). The Supreme Court has repeatedly held that the Administrative Procedure Act (5 USC 706) requires agencies to avoid "arbitrary" actions and to give reasoned explanations for their policy choices.[37] The Trump administration's efforts to deregulate, at EPA and other agencies, have been slowed and constrained by numerous court rulings upholding challengers' allegations that these rule changes violate the APA requirements of reasoned rulemaking and other statutory strictures.[38]

The Agency

If Congress, the judiciary, and the president are such powerful actors in the agenda setting process, does that mean that EPA has zero power to define its own agenda? No. To appreciate EPA's limited yet important role, it is helpful to briefly recall the history of the field of public administration.

This field took shape in the late 19th century and early 20th century, as the size of the federal government was expanding. Scholars observed that expert civil servants in the federal government have a central role to play in the new administrative state.[39] While recognizing that it is Congress, a body of elected officials, which is the ultimate agenda setter—because Congress writes the laws that put issues on the agenda of each federal agency and define the scope of the agency's authority and the tools it can use—these scholars saw legislative action as political, and an agency's administration of legislation as more professionalized and evidence-based and thus more free from politics.

Expert civil servants also play a role in agenda setting. Once Congress creates a new agency (or, as occurred in the case of EPA, confers authority on the president to reorganize agencies into a new one—see Chapter 1), and defines its mission(s) through authorizing statutes, some but not all of the agenda-setting function is accomplished. Elected legislators, and the president, lack the time and expertise (and foresight of future developments) to specify all of the issues that a federal agency will need to address. In order to carry out the laws passed by the Congress, experts in federal agencies need to implement their statutory responsibilities, mediate presidential instructions, and also respond to public concerns and to new developments in science, technology, and society. Thus, public administrators define part of the agenda within their budget and statutory authority, recognizing that some of the agency's agenda is legally mandatory and some reflects the priorities of the White House. There still remains some room for agency agenda setting, while recognizing that the agency's political leadership is subject to both external and internal influences.

Because EPA was not created by legislation, but by presidential reorganization, and because EPA acts under an array of statutes, EPA has both multiple constraints and also some room to maneuver. One way that EPA defines its own agenda is by drafting new legislation which is later enacted by Congress and thus drives EPA's subsequent agenda. During the Carter administration, EPA staff worked on legislation to clean up abandoned hazardous waste sites. EPA drafts ultimately became part of the CERCLA Superfund Law in 1980. During the George H. W. Bush (41) administration, EPA staff also played a key role in drafting some provisions of the Clean Air Act Amendments of 1990. Another example occurred in the Reagan administration, when EPA responded to the growing evidence of the danger of high levels of radon in homes by developing the "Radon Action Plan," a program that was eventually included in legislation passed by Congress. The Plan provided technical guidance to states, workplaces, schools, and homeowners on how to monitor radon levels and what to do if the levels of radon are unsafe.

Working within the scope of existing environmental laws, EPA can also set its own agenda in cases where Congress has provided EPA with some discretion as to whether a problem should be subject to regulation or how it should be regulated. Under the Reagan administration, EPA accelerated the phase-out of lead in gasoline in response to a public-health benefits analysis rather than a statutory deadline. Under the Bush (43) administration, EPA used discretionary Clean Air Act authority to extend low-sulfur fuels regulation to the off-road diesel engines used in construction, mining, and agriculture. In the Obama administration, EPA developed a federal regulation of coal ash residuals under RCRA even though the agency had no nondiscretionary obligation to do so. Likewise, the Obama EPA sharply increased the stringency of GHG standards for cars and light trucks from model years 2017 to 2025 under discretionary authority provided by Congress in 2008. The deregulation-minded Trump EPA also raised eyebrows when it announced plans for discretionary new regulations to slash pollution from heavy-duty trucks.

Other cases of EPA agenda setting have arisen where EPA works with industry, environmental groups, and/or the states to address a problem with a voluntary solution that is not compelled or authorized by statute. Throughout the 1990s, EPA established several voluntary programs: to label and reduce energy use, such as "Green Lights," "Climate Wise" and "Energy Star"; to undertake safety testing on "High Production Volume" chemicals; to encourage businesses to go "Beyond Compliance," show "Environmental

Leadership," and join "Project XL" (excellence and leadership); and to make "33/50" percent extra reductions in toxic pollution.[40] In other cases, voluntary measures by industry are undertaken as a substitute for EPA regulation. It may not appear to the public that EPA is setting an agenda, since the industry is acting on its own, but the industry may be acting because it knows the issue is on EPA's agenda or will be placed there if the industry does not act. EPA's routine activities to protect the public health from pesticides and toxic substances often work in this way.

An even more systematic attempt at agenda-setting was the 1987–1992 "risk-ranking" project undertaken at the initiative of EPA Administrators Lee Thomas and William K. Reilly. These risk rankings were contained in a prominent 1987 report, "Unfinished Business" and a sequel, "Reducing Risk."[41] Table 13.1 shows the final ranking of ecological risks produced by EPA in 1987. One of the insights of this agency-wide risk-ranking exercise was that climate change (global warming) warranted greater EPA attention than it had received, in light of its major risks, whereas hazardous waste management (driven by the RCRA and CERCLA laws) was receiving a disproportionately large share of agency resources. The late Senator Daniel Patrick

Table 13.1. Summary Ranking of Ecological Risks

Rank	*Environmental Problem*
1	• Stratospheric ozone depletion
	• CO2 and global warming
2	• Physical alteration of aquatic habitats
	• Mining, gas, oil extraction and processing wastes
3	• Criteria air pollutants
	• Point-source discharges
	• Non-point source discharges and in-place toxics in sediment
	• Pesticides
4	• Toxic air pollutants
5	• Contaminated sludge
	• Inactive hazardous waste sites
	• Municipal waste sites
	• Industrial non-hazardous waste sites
	• Accidental release of toxins
	• Oil spills
	• Other ground water contamination
6	• Radiation other than radon
	• Active hazardous waste sites
	• Underground storage tanks

Source: US Environmental Protection Agency, Office of Policy Analysis, *Unfinished Business: A Comparative Assessment of Environmental Problems,* 000R87901 (Washington, DC: EPA, 1987), 48.

Moynihan was impressed with these efforts and sought unsuccessfully to pass legislation requiring EPA to periodically rank risks and report the results to Congress. However, EPA's risk-ranking exercises could not easily change the agency's actual agenda, given the statutory prescriptions, congressional preferences, and judicial review described above.

PART 2: EXTERNAL CONDITIONS

EPA and the federal government do not operate in a societal vacuum. Their day-to-day activities are shaped by a variety of external conditions. We highlight below several societal forces that play important roles in influencing the federal government's environmental agenda.

Public Opinion

In a representative democracy, public opinion on environmental issues can significantly influence EPA's agenda. Since EPA's inception, a strong majority of the US public has exhibited favorable attitudes toward environmental protection. Except during economic recessions, a majority has favored giving greater priority to environmental protection than to economic growth. But

Table 13.2. Do you think the US government is doing too much, too little or about the right amount in terms of protecting the environment?

	Too much %	*Too little%*	*Right amount %*	*No opinion %*
2019 Mar 1-10	8	61	31	1
2018 Mar 1-8	9	62	28	1
2017 Mar 1-5	11	59	26	3
2016 Mar 2-6	12	57	29	2
2015 Mar 5-8	16	48	34	1
2014 Mar 6-9	17	48	34	1
2013 Mar 7-10	16	47	35	2
2012 Mar 8-11	17	51	30	2
2011 Mar 3-6	16	49	33	2
2010 Mar 4-7	15	46	35	4
2006 Mar 13-16 ^	4	62	33	1
2005 Mar 7-10 ^	5	58	34	3
2004 Mar 8-11 ^	5	55	37	3
2003 Mar 3-5 ^	7	51	37	5
2000 Apr 3-9	10	58	30	2
1992 Jan 5-Mar 31	4	68	26	2

^ Asked of a half sample
Source: Data acquired by David Konisky from *Gallup Poll Monthly, February 1989-2002.*

surveys rarely find environmental concerns among the highest ranked issues on the minds of US voters.

The environmental issue was relatively more important to the public in the first half of EPA's history than in the second half because the public responded to salient environmental problems and tragedies (some of which were then ameliorated by EPA policies), and the environmental advocacy movement, working through the mass media, was able to arouse public concerns about the environment. For example, the advocacy group Environmental Action entered the political sphere in the 1970s with its "Dirty Dozen" campaigns.[42] In each election cycle, they would target twelve members of Congress with poor voting records on environmental issues and seek to defeat them. A big success occurred in 1970 when their efforts contributed to the defeat of seven of the twelve targeted incumbents. Their subsequent campaigns contributed to the defeat of four incumbents in 1972 and eight incumbents in 1974. There were many factors that led to these election results but, in the 1970s, a member's environmental voting record did become recognized as a sensitive matter during election campaigns.

Over time, however, it became more difficult to arouse public anger about the environment, in part because EPA and the states were successful in solving some of the most acute and visible environmental problems. Moreover, industry and conservative groups learned from the successes of environmental groups and began to be more aggressive in opposing the expansion of federal regulation of the private sector. As explained in Chapter 12, the environment was not as high on the list of public concerns in the second twenty-five years of EPA's history as it was in the first twenty-five years.

Nevertheless, unusual events—surprises or crises—may become "civic moments" that focus attention, open policy windows, and help advocates overcome normal obstacles to collective action.[43] Among the features that galvanize public attention to such events are dramatic stories: compelling narratives that, once told via mass media and amplified through social media, help mobilize collective action.[44]

In the history of EPA and environmental policy, salient crises have been noteworthy in spurring policy change.[45] Oft-cited examples include the Santa Barbara oil spill and the Cuyahoga River catching fire in 1969; the discovery of hazardous waste at Love Canal in 1978; the Bhopal, India, chemical facility accident in 1984; and the Exxon Valdez oil spill in 1989. Of course, not all crises spur policy, and not all policies arise from crises.[46] One must take care to avoid the fallacy of post hoc ergo propter hoc—erroneously attributing subsequent outcomes to a prior event, even though other factors might have been more influential in the outcome. And when crises do spur policy, the types of policy responses can vary greatly, depending on the specific characteristics of the event, the contest to frame the public narrative, the political context in which these occur, and the institutional mechanisms in place for learning and responding.[47]

Frequently cited examples of crisis events that were amplified in the news media and followed by new lawmaking—effectively raising water pollution on the legislative and agency agendas—were the 1969 oil spill in Santa Barbara, California, the declaration that Lake Erie was dead, and the Cuyahoga River catching fire. These events and news coverage were followed by the creation of EPA in 1970 and the enactment of the 1972 Federal Water Pollution Control Act (the Clean Water Act (CWA)). But the story is not so simple. The CWA was not enacted until more than two years after these events; in the meantime, Congress enacted other laws including the National Environmental Policy Act (NEPA) in 1969 and the Clean Air Act (CAA) in 1970 (as well as a Water Quality Improvement Act that was more modest than the subsequent CWA). The Cuyahoga River had actually caught fire numerous times over several decades; although the 1969 fire was not the largest, it signaled the continuing problem of river pollution in Cleveland, where the new mayor Carl Stokes sought local and national support to combat water pollution in low-income communities.[48] National news coverage of the Cuyahoga River on fire in *Time* magazine in 1969 even used a photograph from a larger fire that had occurred seventeen years earlier, in 1952, evidently without noting the photo's earlier date, thereby amplifying the 1969 fire's influence on national public attention.[49] The series of river fires had come to be viewed as more worrisome over time, as public opinion shifted from favoring industry to seeking greater environmental quality.[50] Meanwhile, the "Earthrise" photograph taken from the Apollo 8 space capsule orbiting the Moon in 1968 had portrayed the Earth as a fragile blue orb, helping to frame the growing environmental movement.[51]

Partisan politics also played a role. The Republican Nixon administration created EPA, and took executive action in late 1970 to address water pollution, which may also have further motivated Democratic leaders in Congress to prepare a new bill (the CWA). Party leaders competed with each other to address water pollution more comprehensively while Congress sought to prevent the president from taking credit and expanding executive power.[52] Thus, a simple linkage between the 1969 Cuyahoga River fire to the 1972 CWA may be a kind of "fable" that contains "useful truths" while omitting many complications.[53]

Later crises further illustrate how stimulation of public concern sets the stage for policy responses. The 1984 chemical disaster in Bhopal, India, took on special interest in the US because the same chemical was a contaminant of concern in the Konawa Valley, West Virginia. Congress responded with the

Emergency Planning and Community Right-to-Know Act in 1986 (including its Toxics Release Inventory), and then with a new provision of the Clean Air Act Amendments of 1990 requiring chemical facilities to assess their accident risks (section 112(r) creating the Risk Management Program (RMP)). After the chemicals accident in West, Texas, in April 2013, the Obama administration issued a rule to strengthen the RMP in January 2017, and the Trump administration subsequently issued a revised rule rescinding much of that regulation in November 2019.

The 1989 Exxon Valdez Oil Spill in Prince Edward Sound, Alaska, was followed by enactment of the 1990 Oil Pollution Act. The 2010 BP Deepwater Horizon Oil Spill was followed by reorganization of the relevant bureaus in the Interior Department, but not major legislative change.[54] Still, the BP Deepwater Horizon oil spill did oblige staff at EPA, other agencies, and the White House to drop other priorities and focus on that immediate crisis. Indeed, the 2010 spill caused the Obama administration to shelve expansive plans for licensing new offshore oil drilling, plans which some had seen as part of a possible deal to enable a new national climate bill to pass the Congress (it did not).

The terrorist attacks of September 11, 2001 also influenced EPA's agenda. A month later, the agency took on new responsibilities to help clean up an anthrax attack on the Hart Senate Office Building in Washington, D.C. Many of the agency's priorities were put on hold for months as the agency's leaders helped develop plans to measure air quality in New York City and advised the city and state on appropriate cleanup efforts from the collapse of the World Trade Center buildings.[55]

Solid waste was not high on EPA's agenda in the early 1970s. Then, after RCRA was enacted in 1976 (in part, as RCRA itself recites, to respond to the rising tide of solid wastes resulting from measures to reduce air and water pollution), frightening revelations of hazardous waste under residential neighborhoods and children's playgrounds—in towns like Love Canal, New York, and Times Beach, Missouri—appeared to spur enactment of CERCLA in 1980. These focusing events pressed EPA and Congress to elevate wastes on the policy agenda, and at the same time they opened a policy window for advocates—inside EPA and Congress, as well as in non-governmental organizations—to advance stronger waste management and cleanup on EPA's agenda. After the enactment of RCRA and CERCLA, a scandal at EPA over misfeasance in the hazardous waste program was exposed to the public in the early 1980s, leading to the resignation of Administrator Anne Gorsuch and criminal prosecution of other EPA officials. Congress then supplemented RCRA and CERCLA with the HSWA in 1984 and SARA in 1986, adding numerous highly prescriptive instructions to EPA. More recently, the tragic

2008 coal ash spill at a TVA plant in eastern Tennessee, and another on the Dan River in North Carolina in 2014, gave a new sense of urgency to EPA's languishing effort to regulate coal ash under RCRA, and led to new regulations, cleanup measures, and penalties.

Overall, as explained in Chapter 7, solid and hazardous waste grew to become a very high priority for EPA spending, staffing, rulemakings, enforcement actions, and public relations. Still, some studies have suggested that the public health benefits from waste cleanup activities may have been modest (compared to other issues such as air pollution, ozone depletion, and climate change), and the cleanups have not been sufficiently targeted to help the low-income and minority communities burdened by wastes.[56] At the same time, since Congress created some dedicated funding for Superfund cleanups, the priority given to abandoned sites did not necessarily draw EPA resources away from air pollution and other agency programs.

Media Coverage

The agenda of an agency like EPA is influenced by stories in the mass media that activate stakeholders and shape public opinion. In recent years, the explosion of communications on social media has added a new dimension to the media influences on EPA's agenda.

The role of news media coverage in shaping EPA's agenda and new lawmaking can be multifaceted. The effect of media influence can constrain EPA's own agenda choices, hold EPA accountable to public scrutiny for its policy implementation, and sometimes open windows of opportunity for EPA to elevate issues. For EPA, good communication may be essential to its agenda setting, policy formulation, and implementation. In the eyes of the White House, a principal objective of EPA activity may be to manage environmental issues so that the president is helped (or at least not harmed) politically. Presidents become frustrated when controversies at EPA distract the administration from focusing on more important presidential goals. In this vein, President Reagan brought William Ruckelshaus back to lead EPA in 1983 to rescue the administration and the agency from a slew of adverse media coverage associated with the resignation of Administrator Anne Gorsuch.

A classic illustration of news media influence in the 1980s, discussed in more detail in Chapter 9, concerns EPA's alleged failure to adequately regulate a chemical called Alar that was sprayed on trees by apple farmers to regulate growth and allow ripening to occur at the same time. CBS's "60 Minutes" television program frightened many parents in America when it aired a prime-time story of how the health of children may be threatened when they consume apple products containing Alar residue. The Natural

Resources Defense Council (NRDC) and environmental journalists used the Alar story as a potent symbol of the need to modernize federal regulation of chemicals used in agriculture based on risk assessments that address exposures to children. Congress ultimately responded with amendments to EPA process for registering agricultural chemicals, including a special mandated safety factor for children: The Food Quality Protection Act of 1996. But Alar was not the only driver of that law, as the agricultural chemical industry was also seeking, and obtained, relief from the antiquated zero-risk Delaney clause of the 1950s.

Media coverage alone does not necessarily make an issue a priority at EPA. At least since the late 1980s, environmental journalists have written numerous stories that highlight the risks of global warming, the important role of greenhouse gases emitted by human activities (including cars, electric power plants, and farms), and the crucial need for the United States to play a global leadership role. Despite this coverage, EPA's policy response to climate change has been quite limited in the US until the Obama administration. In fact, both the George W. Bush (43) and Donald Trump administrations were willing to incur substantial negative press coverage in their determined efforts to block or relax regulations aimed at curtailing emissions of greenhouse gases. Thus, media coverage is only one of several factors that influence whether EPA decides to tackle an environmental concern.

Scientific Knowledge

From the agency's inception, new scientific knowledge has had a major impact on the environmental movement and the agenda of EPA. In *Silent Spring* (1962) Rachel Carson assembled a growing body of scientific evidence linking synthetic pesticides to ecological harm, termed them "biocides" because their adverse effects are rarely restricted to the target pest, and showcased evidence that some chemicals bioaccumulate in the food chain, worsening their environmental footprint. Although Carson's book was controversial at the time of publication, in 2006 it was named by *Discover* magazine as one of the twenty-five greatest science books of all time. The concerns raised by Carson became focal points for EPA's increasingly rigorous risk assessments of agricultural and industrial chemicals.

The enactment of the 1970 CAA was partly spurred by industry's preference for uniform national rules rather than a patchwork of state by state rules, and by presidential campaign rivals Nixon and Muskie competing to please the rising tide of green voters.[57] That raises the question why around 1970 the voting public was favoring stronger environmental rules. Part of the answer is related to public opinion: the emerging national environmental movement (the first Earth Day was held in 1970), the baby boom and demographic changes, the counter-culture critique of capitalism, the first photographs of Earth from space (notably "Earthrise" in 1968), and more.[58] There was also new scientific knowledge from atmospheric chemistry pinpointing how pollution from cars and factories was contributing to urban smog, and how inhalation of lead in gasoline was a threat to the neurologic health of children.

EPA's intensified control of air pollution since 1990 has been less in response to crisis events and public outrage, and more in response to advances in scientific knowledge about the adverse health effects of inhaling soot and smog. The Clinton EPA, under the leadership of Carol Browner, established the first air-quality standards for fine particulate matter (particles smaller than 2.5 microns—PM2.5), and established national low-sulfur fuel requirements to reduce particle emissions from highway diesel engines. The Bush (43) EPA, under the leadership of administrator Christie Todd Whitman, rejected industry requests to relax the highway diesel standards, and went further and extended the standards to off-road diesel engines. Public health analyses showed that EPA diesel standards would, once fully implemented, save thousands of lives per year from respiratory-system diseases; economic analyses showed that the public health benefits of diesel-pollution controls, measured in economic terms, would far exceed the costs to industry and consumers.

The evolution of scientific knowledge is not predictable, and the same subject, such as safe levels of smog in the air, can be subject to new environmental health data and shifting scientific opinions. During the Carter administration, EPA relaxed the air-quality standard for ozone (smog) because scientists believed that standard was overly stringent, but then, based on new, better-designed studies, EPA tightened the ozone standard in the Clinton administration and again in the Obama administration. For a more in-depth exploration of the influence of science at EPA, see Chapter 10.

Technological Change

New technologies may solve past environmental problems but may create new risks for EPA to manage. When EPA regulates or restricts use of industrial chemicals, it often finds that the substitute chemicals pose their own risks. The phase out of lead in gasoline, which served as an octane booster, was a boon for children's health, but one of the primary substitute octane boosters, the chemical MTBE, was ultimately banned when it was found leaking from underground gasoline storage tanks and creating an offensive odor in polluted communities. Today the main octane enhancer is corn-based ethanol, which is blended with gasoline. EPA in 2020 released a major scientific report identifying environmental risks associated with corn production, ethanol refining, and transport of ethanol to gasoline stations.[59] Thus, EPA must play a continuing role in identifying and managing risks when one technology replaces another in the marketplace.

Nanotechnology and biotechnology were only dimly understood when the agency was created in 1970, but regulation of both processes have become visible parts of EPA's agenda. Because biotechnology can be used in so many economic sectors of the economy, it was for many years addressed by EPA, the FDA (Food and Drug Administration), the USDA (US Department of Agriculture), and other agencies under their statutes for pesticides, foods, and other topics, as part of an umbrella policy adopted in 1986 known as the "Coordinated Framework." In 2016, Congress enacted the National Bioengineered Food Disclosure Law, calling on the USDA to establish labelling rules for foods. Emerging new technologies such as synthetic biology, automated vehicles, and artificial intelligence may soon be important elements of EPA's agenda.

EPA regulation itself can stimulate industry to invest in research and development (R&D) that discovers new technologies, refines existing technologies, and finds more sustainable production processes. When under pressure from EPA and state regulators, the pulp and paper industry in the US found that the dioxin discharges to surface water could be more effectively addressed through industrial process changes than through the traditional end-of-pipe effluent controls. More recently, in the automotive arena, EPA's granting of waivers to California's zero-emission vehicle program stimulated the commercialization of plug-in electric vehicles that rely on advances in lithium-ion battery technology. As a result, EPA does not have to rely entirely on post-combustion treatment systems to control tailpipe pollution from cars. In the near future, electric vehicles and automated vehicles (self-driving cars) may reduce energy use and emissions, depending on how the electricity is generated and how many vehicles are on the roads. EPA's agenda has become more receptive to integrated reforms of industrial practices and products, even though the systems of regulation established by Congress did not always envision or readily accommodate such fundamental innovation.

Another type of technological change can also influence EPA's agenda: innovation in the methods of monitoring to measure pollution, environmental quality, exposures, and health impacts. As monitoring technology improves, the cost of gathering exposure information declines, which can help identify new environmental problems, resolve debates about past alarms, and open new opportunities to regulate more cost-effectively.[60] The ability to install continuous emissions monitoring devices on electric power plants helped make possible EPA's 1990 Acid Rain program and its cap-and-trade policy design. The current era of "big data," including vast new supplies of information and computing power, may broadly influence EPA's agenda and policies. Personal exposure sensors made widely available at low cost, perhaps built into cellphones, clothing, or accessories, may soon enable much more detailed measurement of actual human exposures, contributing to better analyses of health effects from exposures to different substances, and improving understanding of the distribution of environmental health impacts and associated environmental justice concerns.

The process of technological innovation—some of it stimulated by EPA policies and some occurring due to market forces—has a feedback effect on EPA's agenda. While regulation of coal plants has been a priority in much of EPA's fifty-year history, the agenda in EPA's future may include regulation of environmental risks associated with the supply chains supporting solar panels, wind turbines, and utility-scale energy storage systems.

Interest Groups

EPA's agenda is also influenced by interest groups—organizations that advocate for the interests of their members. Interest groups include environmental advocacy groups, consumer advocacy groups, labor unions, and businesses and their industry trade associations. They each use political, informational, legal, and other strategies. In addition, state and local governments, and foreign governments, sometimes function as advocates to EPA on behalf of their citizens' interests.

Some of the factors discussed above—including public opinion, news media coverage, and scientific and technological advances—are catalyzed by interest groups. Interest groups conduct public information campaigns to influence public opinion and politicians. Classic examples include NRDC's efforts and CBS's "60 Minutes" coverage on Alar, as noted above, and the ethanol industry's efforts to promote the virtues of biofuels, thereby overcoming the resistance from the petroleum industry.

During the history of EPA, environmental advocacy groups have capitalized on salient "focusing" events that galvanized public attention and opened "policy windows" or "civic moments."[61] Acting as "policy entrepreneurs," environmental groups have periodically framed the narrative of blame and opportunity, pushed issues onto EPA's agenda, and devised innovative policy solutions.[62]

The US environmental-policy agenda reflects not only the interests of environmental advocacy groups but also the efforts of well-organized industry groups or specific companies to gain competitive advantage. Industries that sell the same product (such as cars) in national markets have supported national uniform pollution standards that avoid a costly state-by-state patchwork.[63] And regional industry segments—and regional government officials—have backed EPA rules that limit the loss of industry and jobs from their regions. EPA's sulfur regulations under the 1977 Clean Air Act imposed scrubber technology standards that protected high-sulfur eastern coal against low-sulfur western coal.[64] The PSD policy to keep cleaner states clean was backed by members of Congress from dirtier rustbelt states, in part to protect the rustbelt against competition from the sunbelt.[65] Manufacturers of new technologies have backed rules to phase out older technologies in order to confer advantages on those who manufacture the newer substitutes (e.g., see the story of industry reaction to chlorofluorocarbon regulation in Part 3 of this chapter). Sometimes the most potent lobbying in favor of new rules arises from unexpected coalitions of environmentalists and industry subgroups seeking the same rules for different reasons.[66] Both industry and environmental groups favored a rewrite of the 1976 Toxic Substances Control Act in 2020, but EPA's implementation of the new law under the Trump administration has been quite controversial.

When governments of states or foreign countries act as interest groups, they can be especially potent because they often have significant resources, legal expertise, motivated leaders, well-organized staff, and numerous points of contact with EPA, Congress, and the White House. The US states play important roles in enacting their own laws, lobbying federal actors, implementing federal and state laws, and challenging or defending federal environmental laws and EPA rules in court. States sometimes adopt early laws that lead EPA to learn from state experience, which may put new approaches on EPA's agenda (e.g., EPA has often adjusted its agenda after California regulates motor vehicles and toxic chemicals). Foreign governments can also influence EPA's agenda, such as by seeking or resisting negotiated agreements on international environmental issues. Mexico and Canada have both worked hard to put cross-boundary pollution on EPA's agenda, as both countries have experienced some ecological harm from US industrial practices.

The activities of interest groups are sometimes very predictable, but in other cases they can be somewhat surprising, as we will see in the following case study of EPA protecting the stratospheric ozone layer. We examine policy making as well as agenda setting, since the importance of EPA as an agenda setter in this case cannot be appreciated without addressing the ultimate policy outcomes.

PART 3: CASE STUDY: EPA AGENDA SETTING TO PREVENT DEPLETION OF THE STRATOSPHERIC OZONE LAYER[67]

Ozone (O3) in the stratosphere plays an important role in shielding the Earth's surface from the ultraviolet (UV) radiation emitted by the sun. Ozone depletion, by allowing increased UV to reach the earth's surface, can increase skin cancers in humans and endanger animals and plants (including agricultural crops).

An important example of scientific knowledge influencing EPA's agenda was the 1974 discovery by scientists Mario Molina and Sherwood Rowland that chlorofluorocarbons (CFCs) could deplete the stratospheric ozone layer. CFCs had been invented almost fifty years earlier, in the late 1920s, by Thomas Midgely, a scientist at General Motors. They were a non-toxic replacement for toxic refrigerants such as ammonia. The inexpensive and apparently non-reactive characteristics of CFCs made them "wonder chemicals," ideal for a wide variety of uses, including air conditioning, home heating and cooling, refrigeration, aerosol spray can propellants, medical inhaler devices, fire extinguishers, and more. But Molina and Rowland's landmark paper theorized that, in the upper atmosphere, CFCs could be broken apart by UV radiation from the sun, releasing chlorine ions that react rapidly to deplete stratospheric ozone—a single chlorine atom could destroy as many as 100,000 molecules of O3. They further estimated that if the global CFC industry continued to grow at ten percent per year, up to half of the ozone layer would be destroyed by 2050. Even a ten percent reduction in the ozone layer could cause as many as 80,000 additional cases of skin cancer per year.[68]

These scientific findings came against the backdrop of increasing public awareness of global environmental interconnectedness, including the 1968 "Earthrise" photograph of the Earth taken from Apollo 8 orbiting the Moon, the first Earth Day in 1970, the creation of EPA in 1970, and the first United Nations Conference on the Environment held in Stockholm in 1972.[69]

The US National Academy of Sciences (NAS) convened panels of experts to review the ozone-depletion theory. They determined that ongoing releases of CFCs were a significantly greater threat to stratospheric ozone than nitrogen emissions from future Super Sonic Transport (SST) aircraft.[70] In 1975 the US government formed a Federal Interagency Task Force on Inadvertent Modification of the Stratosphere (IMOS), led by the National Science Foundation and CEQ. In 1977 the UN Environment Programme (UNEP) held the first meeting of its Coordinating Committee on the Ozone Layer (CCOL).

Consumers began to reduce purchases of CFCs; sales peaked in 1974 and then declined for several years. The industry was caught flat-footed by the adverse consumer reactions, and CFC manufacturers turned to questioning the validity of the science linking CFCs to ozone depletion. Led by the new trade group, Alliance for Responsible CFC Policy, industry argued for more study before hasty and costly restrictions were adopted.

The state of Oregon was the first political jurisdiction to restrict the use of CFCs in aerosols, passing legislation in May 1975 that took effect in March

1977. The State of New York followed in the summer of 1975 with a requirement that aerosol sprays be labeled to inform consumers of the possible harm posed by CFCs. Building on these efforts, the Natural Resources Defense Council in June 1975 petitioned three federal agencies (EPA, the Consumer Product Safety Commission (CPSC), and the FDA) to ban uses of CFCs in aerosol sprays.[71]

Coordinating the agendas of three federal agencies was no easy task, especially since the White House had little authority over CPSC. In July 1975, CPSC declined the NRDC petition on the grounds that there was insufficient scientific evidence. EPA and FDA delayed a decision until the above-mentioned NAS studies were completed. When both studies validated the ozone-depletion theory, EPA and FDA signaled their intent to regulate, decisions made under the administration of Republican President Gerald Ford. EPA delayed a bit to wait for the Toxic Substances Control Act (TSCA), which had been undergoing debate in Congress for several years, to be enacted in October 1976, near the end of Ford's term. TSCA provided new authority for EPA to address the CFC issue.

EPA proposed regulation in May 1977 under TSCA at the onset of the administration of Democratic President Jimmy Carter. In March 1978 EPA and the FDA both issued final rules banning nonessential uses of CFCs in aerosol spray cans while essential uses, such as medical inhalers, were exempted. The banned uses amounted to about eighty percent of aerosol sprays, and manufacturers switched to substitutes such as pump sprays and hydrocarbon propellants.

Globally, the US acted to protect the ozone layer before the rest of the world. Sweden was also prompt to act, announcing intentions to ban aerosol sprays in January 1978, a few months prior to EPA and FDA final rulemaking actions, but the Swedish action did not take effect until 1979.

For the many non-aerosol spray applications of CFCs, Congress supplied EPA discretionary authority to regulate under the 1977 CAA amendments, but EPA did not take prompt action. Industry resisted regulation, as the cost of substitutes for air conditioning, refrigeration, and other uses was higher than the cost of aerosol spray substitutes. Moreover, the production of CFCs in other countries made further unilateral action by the US look less effective at reducing the global problem and raised interest in an international agreement.

Meanwhile, European governments resisted regulation of CFCs, and pressed ahead with the European SST called the Concorde. British and French officials questioned the science of ozone depletion by CFCs, and worried that US policy on stratospheric ozone was seeking to gain competitive advantage by restricting the European chemicals and aviation industries. Canada and Sweden finalized their bans of CFCs in aerosol spray cans in

1979, the Netherlands adopted a labeling requirement, and in 1980 the full European Community adopted a thirty percent cut in CFCs in aerosols from 1976 levels—though it was not really a binding constraint because production had already declined due to consumer concerns.

Thus, in the 1970s, the US was more precautionary regarding CFCs than was Europe.[72] Indeed, EPA adopted a national ban on CFCs in aerosol sprays just four years after the first publication of the theoretical paper on how CFCs could deplete stratospheric ozone, and before direct observations of such depletion occurring.

In the early 1980s, scientists from several countries began measuring significant actual depletion of stratospheric ozone around the globe, decreases so steep that some experts initially thought their measuring devices must be malfunctioning. In 1985 they found the severe "ozone hole" over Antarctica.

In response, UNEP formed a working group on an international legal response, which led to the negotiation of the 1985 Vienna Convention for Protection of the Ozone Layer. A standoff occurred between the US, Canada, Sweden, Norway, and Finland, who together advocated a 100% (or at least 80%) phase-out of nonessential aerosol uses of CFCs, versus the European Community, which backed just a 30% reduction (in effect, a limit above their current production volumes).

CFC regulation fell in priority at EPA under the troubled leadership of Administrator Anne Gorsuch, but the issue moved higher on the agenda when William Ruckelshaus returned for his second stint as EPA administrator in 1983. The environmental advocacy community was frustrated with the Reagan administration's slow pace of action. NRDC sued EPA in 1983 for failing to follow through on the scientific determination of danger, and sought new regulations under the Clean Air Act.

EPA launched its new "Stratospheric Ozone Protection Plan" in January 1986, including a series of expert workshops, a new risk assessment on cancer and other adverse effects, and options for international agreement and domestic rulemaking. By the end of 1986, negotiations began on the Montreal Protocol on Substances that Deplete the Ozone Layer, which was finalized in 1987.

The Montreal Protocol required substantial agency resources and EPA leadership. European countries eventually agreed to the US proposal for a fifty percent cut and long-term phase-out of CFCs. US manufacturers such as DuPont, who had earlier opposed international controls on CFCs, changed their position in 1986 to support a phase-out in the Montreal Protocol, in part because they now foresaw competitive advantage from making substitutes under a CFC phase-out regime.[73] EPA professional staff played a significant role in persuading US companies to change their position.

Inside the Reagan administration, opposition to EPA's plan emerged from the Interior Department, several White House offices, and OMB. This opposition was overcome by EPA showings on the science of ozone depletion, the risks of adverse ecological effects and millions of cancer deaths worldwide, and the availability of affordable substitutes. A bipartisan yet nonbinding resolution was also passed in Congress favoring EPA's stance. Both the Secretary of State (George Schultz) and the Secretary of Treasury (James Baker) sided with EPA. Persuaded by the case made by EPA administrator Lee Thomas, Republican President Ronald Reagan decided to endorse EPA's approach, one of the most impressive accomplishments by an EPA administrator in the fifty-year history of EPA.

Follow-on agreements in the 1990s tightened the CFC phase-out targets further and began to address substitutes such as HCFCs. A special Montreal Protocol Fund to assist developing countries with substitutes helped engage China and India in the phase-out; they might otherwise have stayed out of the agreement in order to use CFCs to provide cooling and refrigeration to their populations. In 1990, the CAA Amendments expanded Title VI to address the stratosphere, including CAA section 612 which authorizes EPA to regulate CFC substitutes to ensure they "reduce overall risks to human health and the environment" (42 U.S.C. § 7671k(a)).

A complication emerged when it became apparent that prominent substitutes for CFCs, such as HCFCs and HFCs, were strong greenhouse gases.[74] Subsequent international agreements aimed to phase down use of these substitutes, including the 2016 Kigali Amendment (to the Montreal Protocol) on HFCs. In the 1990s, under its authority in CAA 612, EPA had approved HFCs as safer alternatives for CFCs and HCFCs, because HFCs do not deplete ozone. But the issue returned to EPA's agenda because of the GHG concern. The Obama EPA issued new rules under CAA 612 to restrict HFCs because of their climate change impacts. Two smaller HFC manufacturers, Mexichem Fluor and Arkema, sued EPA, and the US Court of Appeals for the DC Circuit partially struck down EPA's rules insofar as they regulate already-installed HFCs, while upholding EPA's authority to prohibit future new uses of HFCs;[75] the court summarily vacated the 2016 rule as well in an unpublished opinion on April 5, 2019. Interestingly, larger manufacturers Honeywell and Chemours sided with EPA in this dispute. In 2018, the Trump administration EPA rescinded the 2015 and 2016 rules in full, which NRDC challenged in court.

This case study of EPA protection of the stratospheric ozone layer illustrates EPA leadership in agenda-setting (and policy making generally), amidst multiple external forces and governmental actors. Particularly in 1976-78 (the aerosol spray ban) and in 1985-87 (the negotiation of the Montreal Protocol), EPA was a key agenda-setting and policy-making actor:

marshalling the evidence, organizing the work, formulating US policy and international agreements, issuing domestic regulations, and setting the global agenda for protecting stratospheric ozone. Without the leadership of EPA, this issue would likely have taken many more years for the world to resolve.

CONCLUSION

Our research, interviews and personal experience lead us to some clear findings about agenda setting at EPA. Inside the government, Congress has played the most powerful rule for fifty years, more important than the White House, the courts, or even the political leadership of EPA. And much of the judicial activity has operated to reinforce the role of Congress, by making sure that EPA implements its non-discretionary duties and makes reasoned responses to rulemaking petitions under the APA. We also find evidence of increasing White House influence over EPA's agenda, especially in the second twenty-five years of EPA's life when the flow of new environmental laws from Congress slowed. Nonetheless, we present numerous examples of EPA persuading Congress to add items to its agenda or EPA using discretionary authority to protect public health and the environment with new regulations or voluntary policies.

The mix of external forces has evolved over the agency's fifty-year period. Public opinion was a much more important factor earlier than later in the agency's history. Nonetheless, crisis events during the agency's entire history appear to have caused temporary surges in public concern that influenced EPA's agenda. EPA must respond to unexpected crises, focusing events, and shifts in public opinion. Such "policy shocks" may divert EPA resources from the agency's long-term agenda for environmental protection toward unanticipated "fire-fighting" exercises, but EPA may also seize the window of opportunity opened by such crises to pursue long-awaited reforms.[76]

Advances in scientific knowledge and technological innovation have also had an influential agenda-setting role, with some of the advances unrelated to EPA policy and others stimulated by EPA policy. An ongoing challenge for the agency's dedicated staff is to keep abreast of such advances, even during periods when the administration seems hostile to the agency's mission or the Congress imposes demands that far exceed the agency's resources.

The agency's agenda has been strongly influenced by policy entrepreneurs (both within and outside of the agency). The activism of national environmental groups is particularly notable. Industry, the states, and foreign governments have also influenced EPA's agenda, occasionally in somewhat surprising ways or through creative coalitions.

It is rare that any federal agency has the opportunity to fully rethink and reset its own agenda. In EPA's entire fifty-year history, we found only one systematic, agency-wide effort to use analytic tools to rank the major environmental problems facing the country in relation to the extent of EPA efforts to address those problems. This was the "risk-ranking" project that began in the late 1980s at the end of the Reagan administration and continued in early 1990s in the Bush (41) administration. This risk ranking project recommended giving higher priority to global environmental issues such as ozone depletion, climate change, and biodiversity, and lower priority to hazardous waste cleanups.

The limited influence of these reports underscores our finding that Congress is the most important agenda setter at EPA. It also suggests that Congress as well as EPA need to participate in future risk-ranking exercises in order for them to have a substantial impact on EPA's agenda.

If there is a perplexing puzzle about EPA's agenda, it is why EPA played such a successful role on the ozone depletion issue but was unable to address climate change until the Obama administration, and much of the Obama-era rules are being removed or relaxed by the Trump administration. Chapter 4 looks at this puzzle in detail. Here we conclude with the observation that it is difficult or impossible for EPA to put any issue—even a compelling one—on its agenda if there is determined opposition from the White House or from Congress.

APPENDIX: INTERVIEWEES AND COMMENTERS

We are very grateful to the following people who assisted us in developing this chapter by answering our questions during personal, telephone, or electronic interviews: Phil Angell, James Barnes, David Doniger, Linda Fisher, Joseph Goffman, Tom Jorling, Janet McCabe, and Bob Sussman. We are also grateful to the following individuals for supplying critical comments on previous versions of this chapter: Terry Davies, Daniel Fiorino, Linda Fisher, and David Konisky. No specific statement in the chapter should be attributed to any of these individuals.

NOTES

1. Agenda setting is the first step in the classic six-step "policy process model" of public administration. See Harold D. Lasswell, "The Policy Orientation," In *The Policy Sciences*, eds. Daniel Lerner and Harold D. Lasswell (Palo Alto: Stanford University Press, 1950); Harold D. Lasswell, *Politics: Who Gets What, When and*

How (New York: Meridian Books, 1958); John W. Kingdon, *Agendas, Alternatives and Public Policies*, 1st ed. (Boston: Little Brown, 1984), 2nd ed. (New York: Harper Collins College, 1995), 3rd ed. (London: Longman Classics, 2003).

2. Michael E. Kraft and Scott R. Furlong, *Public Policy: Politics, Analysis, and Alternatives*, 4th ed. (Washington, DC: CQ Press, 2013), 87.

3. Kingdon, *Agendas, Alternatives and Public Policies*; Kraft and Furlong, *Public Policy*, 87-88; Frederick Mayer, "The Story of Risk," In *Policy Shock: Recalibrating Risk and Regulation after Oil Spills, Nuclear Accidents, and Financial Crises*, eds. Edward J. Balleisen et al. (Cambridge: Cambridge University Press, 2017).

4. Jack L. Walker, "Setting the Agenda in the U.S. Senate: A Theory of Problem Selection," *British Journal of Political Science* 7 (1977): 423–45.

5. Frank R. Baumgartner and Bryan D. Jones, *Agendas and Instability in American Politics* (Chicago: University of Chicago Press, 2010).

6. Marissa Martino Golden, "Who Controls the Bureaucracy? The Case of Agenda Setting," Paper presented at the *National Public Management Research Conference, Washington, DC, October 2003.*

7. James Q. Wilson, "The Politics of Regulation," In *The Politics of Regulation*, ed. James Q. Wilson (New York: Basic Books, 1984), 370–71; William N. Eskridge, Jr., "Politics Without Romance: Implications of Public Choice Theory for Statutory Interpretation," *Virginia Law Re*view 74, no. 2 (March 1988): 285; Christopher H. Schroeder, "Rational Choice Versus Republican Moment Explanations for Environmental Laws 1969–71," *Duke Environmental Law & Policy Forum* 9 (1998); Jonathan B. Wiener and Barak D. Richman, "Mechanism Choice," In *Research Handbook on Public Choice and Public Law*, eds. Daniel Farber and Anne Joseph O'Connell (Cheltenham: Edward Elgar Publishing, 2010), 377–78.

8. Barry Weingast and Mark Moran, "Bureaucratic Discretion or Congressional Control?" *Journal of Political Economy* 91 (1983): 765–800; Mathew D. McCubbins, Roger G. Noll, and Barry R. Weingast, "Administrative Procedures as Instruments of Political Control," *Journal of Law, Economics, and Organization* 3 (1987); Mathew D. McCubbins, Roger G. Noll, and Barry R. Weingast, "Structure and Process, Politics and Policy: Administrative Arrangements and the Political Control of Agencies," *Virginia Law Review* 75 (1989).

9. E. Donald Elliott, Bruce A. Ackerman, and John C. Millian, "Toward a Theory of Statutory Evolution: The Federalization of Environmental Law," *Journal of Law, Economics, and Organization* 1, no. 2 (Fall 1985): 313–40.

10. Richard Lazarus, *The Making of Environmental Law* (Chicago: University of Chicago Press, 2004).

11. James Q. Wilson and John DiIulio, *American Government: Institutions and Policies*, 11th ed. (Boston: Houghton Mifflin, 2008), 338–60.

12. E. Scott Adler and John D. Wilkerson, *Congress and the Politics of Problem Solving* (Cambridge: Cambridge University Press, 2012).

13. Amy Royden, "U.S. Climate Change Policy Under President Clinton: A Look Back," *Golden Gate University Law Review* 32, no. 4 (2002).

14. Cornelius Kerwin, *Rulemaking: How Government Agencies Write Law and Make Policy* (Washington, DC: CQ Press, 2003).

15. Environmental Defense Fund v. Ruckelshaus, 439 F.2d 584, 597–98 (D.C. Cir. 1971).

16. 344 F.Supp. 253 (D.D.C. 1972), *aff'd per curiam*, 2 Envtl. L. Rep. 20,656 (D.C. Cir. November 1, 1972), *aff'd by an equally divided court*, 412 U.S. 541 (1973).

17. Richard L. Revesz et al., *Environmental Law and Policy*, 4th ed. (St. Paul, MN: Foundation Press, 2019), 417–20; B. Peter Pashigian, "Environmental Regulation: Whose Self-Interests are Being Protected?" *Economic Inquiry* 23, no. 4 (1985).

18. Massachusetts v. EPA, 549 U.S. 497 (2007).

19. Celia Campbell-Mohn, Barry Breen, and J. William Futrell, *Sustainable Environmental Law* (Washington, DC: Environmental Law Institute, 1993).

20. For "police patrols and fire alarms" as strategies for Congress to empower non-governmental actors to monitor agency action and litigate to enforce statutes, see Mathew D. McCubbins and Thomas Schwartz, "Congressional Oversight Overlooked: Police Patrols and Fire Alarms," *American Journal of Political Science* 28, no. 1 (1984); McCubbins, Noll, and Weingast, "Administrative Procedures as Instruments"; McCubbins, Noll, and Weingast, "Structure and Process, Politics and Policy."

21. Richard B. Stewart and James E. Krier, *Environmental Law and Policy: Readings, Materials and Notes*, 2nd ed. (Indianapolis, IN: Bobbs-Merrill Company, 1978).

22. Revesz et al., *Environmental Law and Policy,* 397–404.

23. Nicholas A. Ashford and Charles C. Caldart, *Environmental Law, Policy, and Economics* (Cambridge: MIT Press, 2008).

24. 28 C.F.R. §§0.160–0.163.

25. US Government Accountability Office, *Environmental Litigation: Impact of Deadline Suits on EPA's Rulemaking Is Limited*, GAO-15-34 (Washington, DC: GAO, December 15, 2014), https://www.gao.gov/products/GAO-15-34.

26. Robert V. Percival, "The Bounds of Consent: Consent Decrees, Settlements and Federal Environmental Policy Making," *University of Chicago Legal Forum* 1, no. 13 (1987); Henry N. Butler and Nathaniel J. Harris, "Sue, Settle, and Shut Out the States: Destroying the Environmental Benefits of Cooperative Federalism," *Harvard Journal of Law and Policy* 37 (2013): 579-628; John D. Graham and Cory R. Liu, "Regulatory and Quasi-Regulatory Activity Without OMB and Cost-Benefit Review," *Harvard Journal of Law and Public Policy* 37, no. 2 (January 2014): 443–44; Stephen M. Johnson, "Sue and Settle: Demonizing the Environmental Citizen Suit," *Seattle University Law Review* 37, no. 891 (2014); Nina A. Mendelson and Jonathan B. Wiener, "Responding to Agency Avoidance of OIRA," *Harvard Journal of Law & Public Policy* 37 (2014); Ben Tyson, "An Empirical Analysis of Sue-and-Settle in Environmental Litigation," *Virginia Law Review* 100, no. 7 (2014); Janette L. Ferguson and Laura K. Granier, "Sue and Settle: Citizen Suit Settlements and Environmental Law," *Natural Resources and Environment* 30, no. 1 (Summer 2015); Courtney McVean and Justin R. Pidot, "Environmental Settlements and Administrative Law," *Harvard Environmental Law Review* 39 (2015); Travis A. Voyles, "Clearing Up Perceived Problems with the Sue-and-Settle Issue in Environmental Litigation," *Journal of Land Use and Environmental Law* 31 (2016).

27. Keith B. Belton & John D. Graham, "Trump's Deregulation Record: Is It Working?" Administrative Law Review (2019), 71, 803-80.

28. Elena Kagan, "Presidential Administration," *Harvard Law Review* 114, no. 8 (2001).

29. Steven G. Calabresi, *The Unitary Executive: Presidential Power from Washington to Bush* (New Haven, CT: Yale University Press, 2008).

30. Kirti Datla and Richard Revesz, "Deconstructing Independent Agencies (and Executive Agencies)," *Cornell Law Review* 98 (2013).

31. Keith B. Belton and John D. Graham, "Trump's Deregulation Record: Is It Working?" *Administrative Law Review* 71, (2019): 803-80.

32. Brandice Canes-Wrone, *Who Leads Whom? Presidents, Policy, and the Public* (Chicago: University of Chicago Press, 2006).

33. Richard P. Nathan, "The Administrative Presidency," *Public Interest* (Summer 1976); Richard P. Nathan, *The Administrative Presidency* (Hoboken, NJ: John Wiley & Sons, 1983); Kagan, "Presidential Administration"; Richard W. Waterman, "The Administrative Presidency, Unilateral Power, and the Unitary Executive Theory," *Presidential Studies Quarterly* 39, no. 1 (March 2009); William G. Resh, *Rethinking the Administrative Presidency* (Baltimore, MD: Johns Hopkins University Press, 2015).

34. Jonathan B. Wiener and Daniel L. Ribeiro, "Environmental Regulation Going Retro: Learning Foresight from Hindsight," *Journal of Land Use & Environmental Law* 32 (2016).

35. John D. Graham, "The Evolving Regulatory Role of the U.S. Office of Management and Budget," *Review of Environmental Economics and Policy* 1, no. 2 (Summer 2007).

36. Marissa Martino Golden, "Who Controls the Bureaucracy? The Case of Agenda Setting," Paper presented at the *National Public Management Research Conference, Washington, DC, October 2003.*

37. Motor Vehicle Manufacturers Ass'n v. State Farm Mutual Insurance Co., 463 U.S. 29 (1983); Department of Commerce v. New York, 588 U.S. __, 139 S. Ct. 2551 (2019).

38. Belton and Graham, *Trump's Deregulation Record.*

39. Woodrow Wilson, "The Study of Administration," *Political Science Quarterly* 2 (June 1887).

40. Janice Mazurek, "Government-Sponsored Voluntary Programs for Firms: An Initial Survey," In *New Tools for Environmental Protection: Education, Information, and Voluntary Measures*, eds. Thomas Dietz and Paul Stern (Washington, DC: National Research Council, 2002); the Obama administration EPA kept a list at https://archive.epa.gov/partners/web/html/index-5.html.

41. US Environmental Protection Agency, *Unfinished Business: A Comparative Assessment of Environmental Problems,* 000R87901 (Washington, DC: EPA, Office of Policy Analysis, 1987); US Environmental Protection Agency, *Reducing Risk: Setting Priorities and Strategies for Environmental Protection*, SAB-EC-90-021 (Washington, DC: EPA, Science Advisory Board, 1990).

42. University of Michigan, "The Dirty Dozen," *Michigan in the World,* accessed February 7, 2020, https://michiganintheworld.history.lsa.umich.edu/environmentalism/exhibits/show/main_exhibit/earthday/environmental-action-moving-fo/the-dirty-dozen.

43. James Gray Pope, "Republican Moments: The Role of Direct Popular Power in the American Constitutional Order," *University of Pennsylvania Law Review* 139, no. 2 (1990); Thomas A. Birkland, "Focusing Events, Mobilization, and Agenda Setting," *Journal of Public Policy* 18, no. 1 (1998); Thomas A. Birkland, *Lessons of Disaster: Policy Change after Catastrophic Events* (Washington, DC: Georgetown University Press, 2006).

44. Mayer, "The Story of Risk."

45. Birkland, "Focusing Events"; Birkland, *Lessons of Disaster*; Robert V. Percival, "Environmental Legislation and the Problem of Collective Action," *Duke Environmental Law and Policy Forum* 9, no. 1 (1998); Robert Repetto, ed., *Punctuated Equilibrium and the Dynamics of US Environmental Policy* (New Haven, CT: Yale University Press, 2006).

46. Matthew E. Kahn, "Environmental Disasters as Risk Regulation Catalysts? The Role of Bhopal, Chernobyl, Exxon Valdez, Love Canal, and Three Mile Island in Shaping U.S. Environmental Law," *Journal of Risk and Uncertainty* 35, no. 1 (2007).

47. Edward J. Balleisen et al., *Policy Shock: Recalibrating Risk and Regulation after Oil Spills, Nuclear Accidents, and Financial Crises* (Cambridge: Cambridge University Press, 2017).

48. Lorraine Boissoneault, "The Cuyahoga River Caught Fire at Least a Dozen Times, but No One Cared Until 1969," *Smithsonian Magazine*, June 19, 2019, https://www.smithsonianmag.com/history/cuyahoga-river-caught-fire-least-dozen-times-no-one-cared-until-1969-180972444/; David Stradling and Richard Stradling, "Perceptions of the Burning River: Deindustrialization and Cleveland's Cuyahoga River," *Environmental History* 13, no. 3 (2008); Ariel Wittenberg, "Did a Burning River *Really* Fuel Landmark Law's Passage?" *E&E News*, June 18, 2019.

49. Jonathan H. Adler, "Fables of the Cuyahoga: Reconstructing a History of Environmental Protection," *Fordham Environmental Law Journal* 14 (2002); Wittenberg, "Burning River."

50. Stradling and Stradling "Perceptions of the Burning River."

51. William Bryant, "The Re-Vision of Planet Earth: Space Flight and Environmentalism in Postmodern America," *American Studies* 36 (1995); Richard N. L. Andrews, *Managing the Environment, Managing Ourselves: A History of American Environmental Policy* (New Haven, CT: Yale University Press, 2006); Robert Poole, *Earthrise: How Man First Saw the Earth* (New Haven, CT: Yale University Press, 2010).

52. Wittenberg, "Burning River."

53. Adler, "Fables of the Cuyahoga."

54. Balleisen et al., *Policy Shock.*

55. National Research Council, *Reopening Public Facilities After a Biological Attack* (Washington DC: National Academies Press, 2005), chapter 4, at https://www.nap.edu/read/11324/chapter/6.

56. James T. Hamilton and W. Kip Viscusi, *Calculating Risks? The Spatial and Political Dimensions of Hazardous Waste Policy* (Cambridge, MA: MIT Press, 1999).
57. Elliott, Ackerman, and Millian, "Toward a Theory of Statutory Evolution."
58. Bryant, "The Re-Vision of Planet Earth"; Poole, *Earthrise.*
59. US Environmental Protection Agency, Clean Air Act Section 211(v)(1) Anti-backsliding Study (May 2020).
60. Daniel C. Esty, "Environmental Protection in the Information Age," *NYU Law Review* 79, no. 1 (April 2004).
61. Pope, "Republican Moments"; Percival, "Environmental Legislation"; Birkland, "Focusing Events"; Birkland, *Lessons of Disaster*; Repetto, *Punctuated Equilibrium*.
62. Wilson, "The Politics of Regulation," 370–71; Eskridge, "Politics Without Romance," 285; R. Douglas Arnold, *The Logic of Congressional Action* (New Haven, CT: Yale University Press, 1990); Schroeder, "Rational Choice"; Wiener and Richman, "Mechanism Choice," 377-78; Mayer, "The Story of Risk."
63. Elliott, Ackerman, and Millian, "Toward a Theory of Statutory Evolution."
64. Bruce A. Ackerman and William T. Hassler, *Clean Coal/Dirty Air* (New Haven, CT: Yale University Press, 1981).
65. Pashigian, "Environmental Regulation."
66. Bruce Yandle, "Bootleggers and Baptists in the Market for Regulation," In *The Political Economy of Government Regulation*, ed. Jason F. Shogren (Boston: Kluwer Academic Publisher, 1989).
67. This case study draws heavily from the following: Peter Morrisette, The Evolution of Policy Responses to Stratospheric Ozone Depletion," *Natural Resources Journal* 29 (1989): 793-820; James K. Hammitt and Kimberly M. Thompson, "Protecting the Ozone Layer," In *The Greening of Industry: A Risk Management Approach*, eds. John D. Graham and Jennifer Kassalow Hartwell (Cambridge, MA: Harvard University Press, 1997); James K. Hammitt, "Stratospheric Ozone Depletion and Global Climate Change," In *The Reality of Precaution: Comparing Risk Regulation in the US and Europe*, eds. Jonathan B. Wiener et al. (London: Routledge, 2011); Stephen O. Andersen, Marcel L. Halberstadt, and Nathan Borgford-Parnell, "Stratospheric Ozone, Global Warming, and the Principle of Unintended Consequences—An Ongoing Science and Policy Success Story," *Journal of the Air & Waste Management Association* 63 (2013).
68. Mario Molina and F. Sherwood Rowland, "Stratospheric Sink for Chlorofluoromethanes: Chlorine Atom-Catalyzed Destruction of Ozone," *Nature* 249, no. 5460 (1974).
69. Bryant, "The Re-Vision of Planet Earth"; Poole, *Earthrise.*
70. National Research Council, *Environmental Impact of Stratospheric Flight* (Washington, DC: National Academy of Sciences, 1975); National Research Council, *Halocarbons: Effects on Stratospheric Ozone* (Washington, DC: National Academy of Sciences, 1976).
71. David Doniger and Michelle Quibell, *Back from the Brink: How NRDC Helped Save the Ozone Layer* (New York: National Resources Defense Council, 2007).
72. Hammitt, "Stratospheric Ozone Depletion."

73. Jonathan B. Wiener, “On the Political Economy of Global Environmental Regulation,” *Georgetown Law Journal* 87 (1999): 772–73; Wiener and Richman, “Mechanism Choice,” 385–86.

74. Jonathan B. Wiener, “Protecting the Global Environment,” In *Risk vs. Risk: Tradeoffs in Protecting Health and the Environment*, eds. John D. Graham and Jonathan B. Wiener (Cambridge, MA: Harvard University Press, 1995); Andersen, Halberstadt, and Borgford-Parnell, “Stratospheric Ozone, Global Warming.”

75. See Mexichem Fluor, Inc. v. EPA, 866 F.3d 451 (D.C. Cir. 2017).

76. Balleisen et al., *Policy Shock*.

Chapter Fourteen

EPA at Fifty: A Look Back and Forward

David M. Konisky[1]

In his first State of the Union speech delivered to Congress on January 22, 1970, President Richard Nixon declared that: "[t]he great question of the seventies is, shall we surrender to our surroundings, or shall we make our peace with nature and begin to make reparations for the damage we have done to our air, to our land, and to our water? Restoring nature to its natural state is a cause beyond party and beyond factions. It has become a common cause of all the people of this country."[2] President Nixon continued with a long enumeration of policy ideas and program initiatives to address environmental problems ranging from cleaning up the country's waterways from municipal pollution, to preserving open spaces from development, to cutting pollution from cars. Collectively, he described these efforts as "the most comprehensive and costly program" on the environment in the nation's history.

Fifty years later, another Republican president, Donald J. Trump, boasted about the undoing of the very types of policies and programs that President Nixon had promoted a half century prior. In his third State of the Union address, delivered to Congress on February 4, 2020, President Trump celebrated "slashing a record number of job-killing regulations" and a "bold regulatory reduction campaign," that he claimed had made the United States the "number one producer of oil and natural gas anywhere in the world, by far."[3] Setting aside the dubious nature of this assertion,[4] the message that President Trump was sending to Americans was clear. In his view, the laws and regulations that grew out of the original commitments of President Nixon were onerous, unwanted, too costly, and impediments to economic growth and prosperity.

Of course, a lot has transpired in the intervening fifty years, and the path of environmental policy in the United States from the time of President Nixon to the current period of President Trump has been anything but smooth or linear. The US Environmental Protection Agency (EPA) has been the central player in this story. Since its establishment in 1970, through an executive reorganization plan described thoroughly by Jim Barnes in Chapter 1, Congress has regularly tasked EPA with implementing a broad portfolio of policies to improve air and water quality, protect drinking water from harmful substances, manage the disposal of solid and hazardous waste on land, remediate sites from past contamination, control the use of chemicals and pesticides, and so much more.

The chapters of this book have told much of this history, highlighting many of the key successes and setbacks that EPA has encountered along the way. Building on these contributions, the main objectives of this final chapter are twofold. First, I will synthesize what I see as the key themes that have emerged from EPA's first five decades. This discussion will begin by summarizing a set of extraordinary successes that can be largely attributed to the agency's efforts. Most notable among these successes is that EPA has delivered improved environmental quality, which has resulted in immense benefits for human and ecological health. To deliver these benefits, EPA has had to build a substantial scientific, legal, and analytical capacity, and manage an enormous workload established by the ambitious expectations of congressional legislation. In addition, throughout its fifty years, EPA has often shown an adept ability to be innovative in policy design and a willingness to take on powerful economic interests to achieve its goals.

The second goal of this chapter is to emphasize areas of unfinished business for EPA to address in the coming years and decades. Some of the issues on this agenda are "old" challenges, in that they were well understood at the time of EPA's creation in 1970. These problems include: local and interstate air pollution, lead in drinking water, and nonpoint source pollution from agricultural sources. Other problems are "new," having appeared on the agenda at some point in the past few decades such as climate change and environmental justice, or much more recently such as water contamination from PFAS chemicals. The challenge in addressing these problems is complicated by the EPA's limited or unclear authority, as well as their complexity and political sensitivity.

Of even more significance for EPA is an additional challenge. At the time of its creation in 1970, the agency enjoyed support from both Republican and Democratic elected officials, and from a concerned and mobilized public that both clamored for bold action and believed in the agency's mission. Times have changed. As EPA moves into its second half century, it finds itself mired in a politically polarized climate. EPA has persevered through turbulent political waters at various times throughout its history, but most of the time the challenges have come from *outside* the agency (i.e., opposing views from the White House, Congress, industry, etc.). The Trump presidency, however, has brought the challenge from *within*. The leadership of the EPA during the Trump Administration, supported by many in the political conservative movement and many in the industries regulated by the agency, has engaged in a sustained and comprehensive project to both reverse environmental policy achievements of the past and to permanently hamper the ability of future administrations to carry out EPA's mission. The future of EPA will depend on the success or failure of this assault. Lessons from history suggest that EPA will emerge temporarily scathed, but capable of resurgence if there is a return to bipartisan support and adherence to science. With an important unfinished agenda, and the growing urgency of problems like climate change, EPA will again have the opportunity to lead the way in providing environmental protection for the country.

ENVIRONMENTAL PROTECTION ACHIEVEMENTS

Speaking at a conference on the future of EPA held at American University on April 23, 2019, former EPA Administrator William Reilly said, "I don't know of any agency that can point to more indisputable successes, progress, and achievements that you can breathe, that you can drink, that you can touch with your hands, than the Environmental Protection Agency."[5] This statement succinctly captures an undeniable fact about EPA's fifty-year history: the agency has played a central role in delivering extraordinary improvements in environmental protection. These efforts have saved millions of lives, improved the quality of life for many more, and enhanced the quality of the natural environment. Of course, EPA has not acted alone. Congress provided the impetus for almost all of EPA's success through the enactment of countless new statutes during the "environmental decade" of the 1970s. And firms operating in numerous sectors of the economy have developed and invested in pollution control—albeit, often only grudgingly—to limit the impact of their activities. Collectively, the results of these efforts have been astonishing.

Consider air quality. When Congress enacted the modern federal Clean Air Act (CAA) in 1970, many cities in the United States were suffering from severe smog problems, due to virtually unmitigated emissions from large power plants, factories, and other large stationary sources and the exhaust from cars, trucks, and other mobile sources. Left to the discretion of state and local governments, few emission limits or technology standards had been established in most places (notable exceptions were standards for mobile sources in California and a smoke abatement ordinance in Allegheny County, Pennsylvania). With the CAA, Congress created a broad portfolio of policies to change course, including National Ambient Air Quality Standards (NAAQS),

New Source Performance Standards (NSPS), technology-forcing emissions limits for mobile sources, and provisions to limit the release of hazardous air pollutants. Later amendments to the law doubled-down, adding provisions to better control emissions from older stationary sources of pollution, limit SO2 and NOx emissions that were contributing to acid rain, and mandate cleaner gasoline in poor air quality areas, among other provisions. These programs, established by Congress and then implemented by EPA through the development of regulations and the coordination of state plans, resulted in massive improvements in air quality.

Figure 14.1 shows some of the gains, plotting the percentage decline in criteria air pollutants since the passage of the CAA. In total, from 1970 until today, emissions of these pollutants have declined by seventy-four percent. As the graph also shows, this has occurred over a period of time when the population and economy of the country have both grown considerably as has energy consumption and vehicle miles travelled. Also noteworthy is that emissions of carbon dioxide (CO_2), which have not been regulated, have grown by twenty percent over this same period.

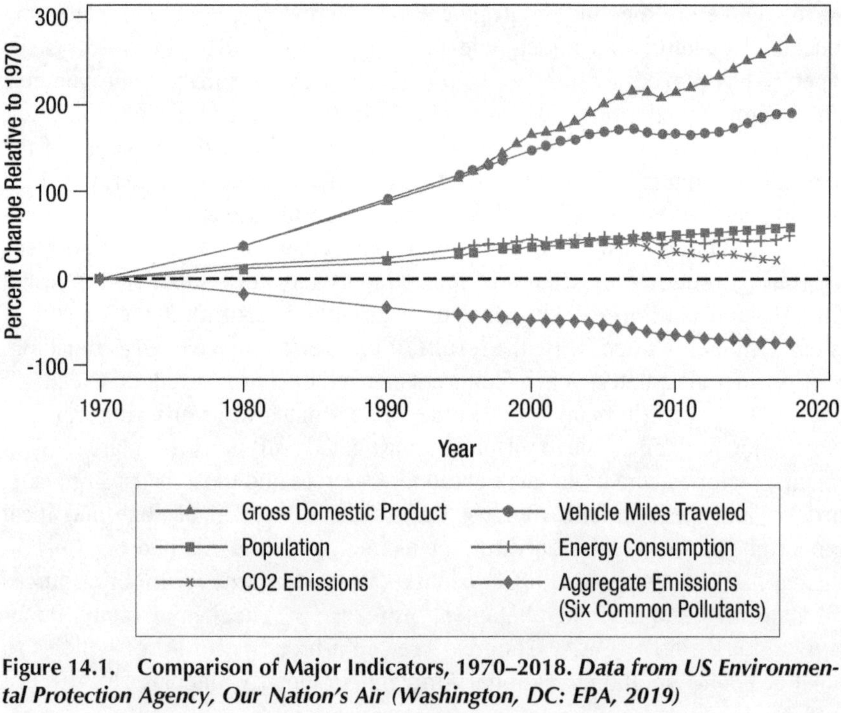

Figure 14.1. Comparison of Major Indicators, 1970–2018. ***Data from US Environmental Protection Agency, Our Nation's Air (Washington, DC: EPA, 2019)***

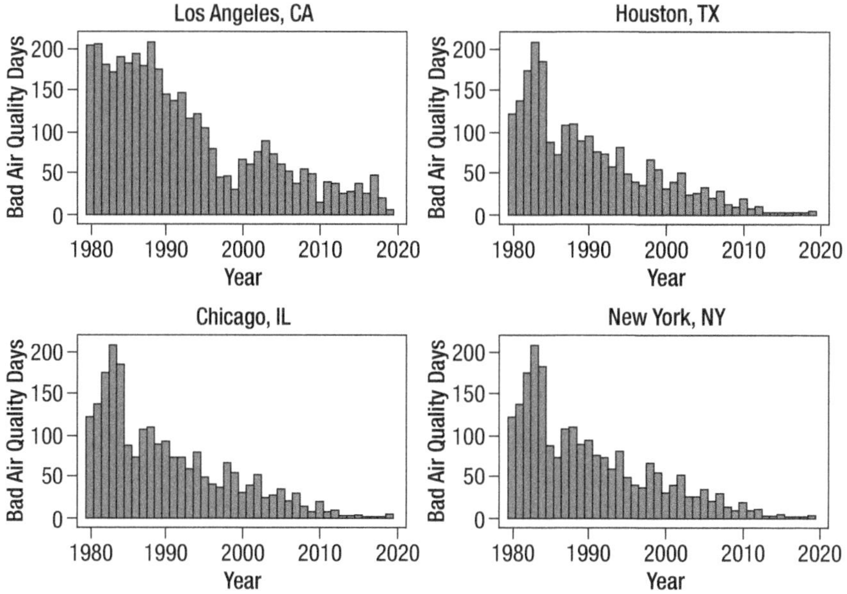

Figure 14.2. Unhealthy air days from AQI, 1980–2019. ***Data from US Environmental Protection Agency, Annual Summary Data of Air Quality by core-based statistical area***

Figure 14.2 further illustrates improvements in air quality, by showing trends in unhealthy air quality days in four major US cities: Los Angeles, Houston, Chicago, and New York. Specifically, using EPA data derived from its air quality monitoring network, the graphs show a clear declining trend in the annual number of days in each city that are classified by the agency as unhealthy, very unhealthy, or hazardous. In Los Angeles, for example, it was common during the 1980s for there to be 150-200 days per year with extremely bad air quality, compared to less than 50 days during the 2010s. Similar trends are shown for the other cities.

Retrospective cost-benefit analyses performed by EPA have estimated that the CAA has resulted in more than $24 trillion in benefits from 1970-2020.[6] These benefits are derived in large measure from millions of premature deaths that have been avoided due to reduced exposure to air pollution, but also improved health and well-being from fewer cases of asthma, bronchitis, heart attacks and cardiovascular disease, and other ailments. And, because measuring benefits is quite challenging, as was discussed by Richard Morgenstern in Chapter 11, these numbers likely under-estimate the full benefits. Not only are these total monetized benefits enormous, but they dwarf the costs of implementation. These same reports place the costs of compliance with air pollution regulations at about $565 billion.[7]

EPA's contributions to environmental protection, of course, extend far beyond air pollution control. In the area of water quality, EPA has helped advance many of the objectives of programs created by the Clean Water Act (CWA) of 1972 and the Safe Drinking Water Act of 1974. For example, point sources of water pollution, from both municipal and industrial dischargers, were not regulated at the federal level before the enactment of the CWA. Under provisions of the law, EPA has overseen a national permitting program, the National Pollution Discharge Elimination System (NPDES), that requires all point sources to obtain a permit to legally discharge pollution into US waterways. Currently, EPA (or, most often, state environmental agencies operating under EPA oversight), has issued approximately seven thousand major NPDES permits and more than one hundred thousand additional minor permits to smaller municipal and industrial point sources. These permits establish source-by-source requirements, built on technology-based, effluent guideline limitations that EPA has established on an industrial sector basis. By one recent accounting, the agency has published 57 such guidelines, which collectively have resulted in the removal of 702 billion pounds of pollutants from US waters.[8]

EPA has also played a major role in helping municipal wastewater treatment facilities upgrade their infrastructure. Prior to the CWA, municipal treatment of wastewater was quite limited. In many cities, big and small, municipal utilities only employed primary treatment (i.e., technologies to remove coarse solids and sediments); across the country, more than forty percent of wastewater plants only used this basic treatment process at the time Congress enacted the CWA. By 2008, ninety-eight percent of wastewater treatment plants had adopted more comprehensive, secondary treatment (i.e., technologies that can remove most organic matter that remains after primary treatment). Enabling this progress was a massive capital investment program managed by EPA and state governments to provide construction grants to municipal wastewater treatment plants. Over the course of two decades, this program provided more than $50 billion in grants to states (it was replaced in 1990 by a loan program, which since has provided an additional $100 billion in financial assistance).[9] Another estimate places the total amount of grants from the CWA to municipal wastewater plants at $650 billion.[10]

Although the CWA has yet to meet its stated goal to eliminate the discharge of pollutants into the nation's waters, the reduction of point source pollution through the NPDES program and investment in new infrastructure has undoubtedly resulted in lower discharges of various pollutants into the nation's rivers, streams, lakes, and oceans. Economists examining various policy components of the CWA have often found that their costs exceed their benefits; however, benefits associated with improving human health, reducing toxic pollution, and protecting coastal areas and surface-groundwater interactions are generally not accounted for in these analyses.[11] Moreover, overall improvements to the quality of US waterways has been slowed by the lack of systematic control of nonpoint source pollution from agriculture and other sources. Nonpoint source water pollution is part of the unfinished business facing the EPA that I discuss later in the chapter.

EPA has also played a major role in reducing health risks associated with drinking water. Over the course of the past fifty years, EPA has used its authority under the SDWA to establish over one hundred national primary drinking standards through either maximum contaminant levels or treatment technology requirements for a variety of microorganisms (e.g., *Cryptosporidium, Giardia, and Legionella*), disinfectants (e.g., chlorine), disinfectant byproducts (e.g., chloroform, Trihalomethanes), organic chemicals (e.g., atrazine), inorganic chemicals (e.g., arsenic, lead, and nitrates), and radionuclides.[12] Public and privately operated water systems that serve at least twenty-five people, which provides service to about three hundred million Americans, must meet these standards and publicly report their achievement (or lack thereof) of these national standards. Although violations are still common—especially for financially constrained, public water utilities operating small systems[13]—this program has undoubtedly resulted in improved drinking water quality for most Americans. According to EPA data displayed in Figure 14.3, over the past twenty years, the percentage of the US population

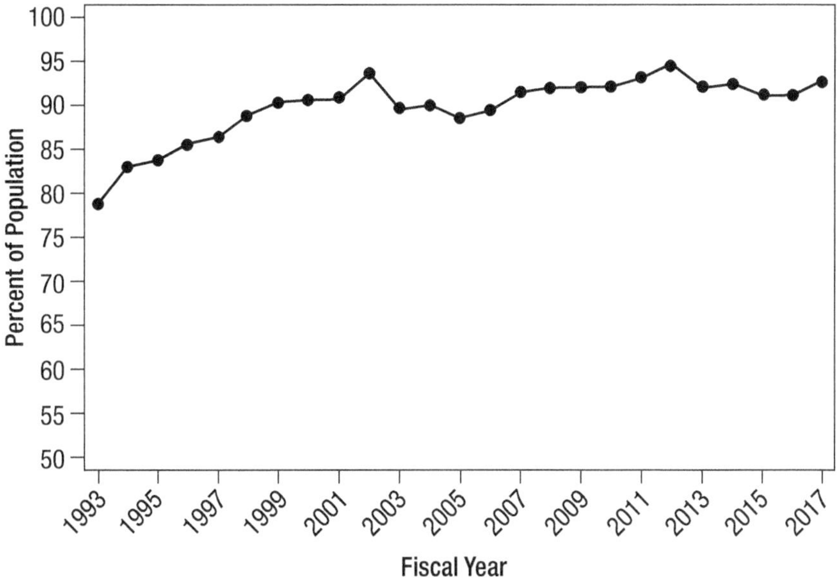

Figure 14.3. Percentage of US Population Served by Community Water Systems with No Reported Violations of EPA Health-Based Standards. ***Data from US Environmental Protection Agency, Report on the Environment* (Washington, DC: EPA, 2018).**

that receives its water from a community water system with no reported violations of SDWA health-based standards has increased—79% in 1993 to 93% in 2017 (data are not available for earlier years).

Similar to the investment of federal resources to enable the upgrading of wastewater treatment plants as part of the CWA, a major achievement under the SDWA has been capital investment to upgrade the nation's drinking water infrastructure. In particular, the 1996 SDWA Amendments created the State Drinking Water Revolving Fund (SDWRF) to provide resources to assist water systems in meeting federal standards. EPA administers this loan program in cooperation with states. According to one recent accounting, the SDWRF has leveraged federal investment of $17.5 billion to provide more than $30 billion to water systems across the United States.[14] Despite this investment, it is important to emphasize that much of the country's current drinking water infrastructure, particularly in older, urban areas, needs major repair or replacement. In 2018, EPA published a report that estimated that, over the next two decades, drinking water utilities will need to invest $473 billion in their systems, which far exceeds the resources available through the SDWRF.[15]

EPA has also played a central role in the transformation of waste disposal. Prior to the enactment of the Resource Conservation and Recovery Act (RCRA) in 1976, the federal government's role in waste management was fairly modest, with most responsibilities falling to state and local agencies. Moreover, waste disposal requirements were quite limited, resulting in what would be considered careless if not negligent practices by today's standards, such as placing waste in unlined landfills or directly in rivers, disposing household trash and more hazardous substances in open dumps, and discharging liquids containing toxic chemicals into unlined evaporation ponds, to name just a few.[16] With the passage of RCRA, as well as the 1984 Hazardous and Solid Waste Amendments, EPA was given the authority to regulate the management of hazardous waste from "cradle-to-grave" (i.e., from the point of generation to the location of disposal) and to provide guidance to states to improve their management and disposal of municipal and non-hazardous waste.

Through EPA implementation of these and other programs, there have been significant declines in the amount of hazardous and solid waste generated, improved disposal standards and practices, and increased municipal and industrial recycling rates.[17] Moreover, there has been a substantial effort through both RCRA's Corrective Action programs and its Underground Storage Tank program to cleanup sites where there has been contamination. By one measure, approximately 18.5 million acres of contaminated lands have been cleaned up in these programs.[18]

EPA's RCRA programs implemented through RCRA are intended to result in the appropriate management and disposal of solid and hazardous waste. One benefit is that landfills and other disposal sites should not result in contamination that threatens human health and/or the environment. Of course, the history of accidental releases and the casual handling and disposal of many harmful chemicals has resulted in tens of thousands of abandoned contaminated sites around the country.[19] Through the Superfund program, enacted by Congress in December 1980, EPA has managed the cleanup of more than one thousand such sites. Congress enacted Superfund in response to the high profile case of Love Canal in Niagara Falls, New York, which resulted in a federally financed relocation of nearby residents who feared that Hooker Chemical's hazardous waste landfill was contaminating their homes, causing higher than normal rates of miscarriages, cancers, and other adverse health effects.[20] The Superfund program was built on the polluters pay principle: those responsible for the historic contamination of sites would be held legally liable and financially responsible for their cleanup. And, in cases for which there was no viable private responsible party to "foot the bill," Congress provided the EPA with resources (first financed through a variety of environmental taxes and now through general revenue) to fund the remediation of these sites.

In addition to Love Canal, many iconic sites have been cleaned up through the Superfund program including General Electric Hudson River (upstate New York), the Valley of the Drums (Brooks, Kentucky), the Murray Smelter (Salt Lake County, Utah), the Industri-Plex (near Boston, Massachusetts), and Times Beach (outside of St. Louis, Missouri). In addition, there are hundreds of much lesser known sites that EPA has either used public resources to remediate or, in most cases, compelled responsible parties to handle themselves. As of February 2020, there are more than 1,335 sites still listed on the National Priorities List (NPL), with another 51 proposed for addition. Of these NPL sites, nearly 800 have completed construction of their remedial activities (i.e., these are sites where the cleanup remedy, such as a landfill or groundwater system, is in place but requires ongoing operation).[21] In addition, over the four decades of the Superfund program, 424 sites have been deleted from the National Priorities List, further demonstrating EPA's progress in managing the Superfund program. The remediation of Superfund sites has proven costly, with sites typically having cleanup costs of millions of dollars, with others reaching tens if not hundreds of millions of dollars.[22] Economic analyses, moreover, have raised questions about whether these costs are justified, either in terms of providing health benefits[23] or in increasing property values for homeowners in close vicinity to sites.[24]

Figure 14.4 shows trends in NPL site listing and cleanup progress over the history of the program. A few patterns are interesting to note. First, includ-

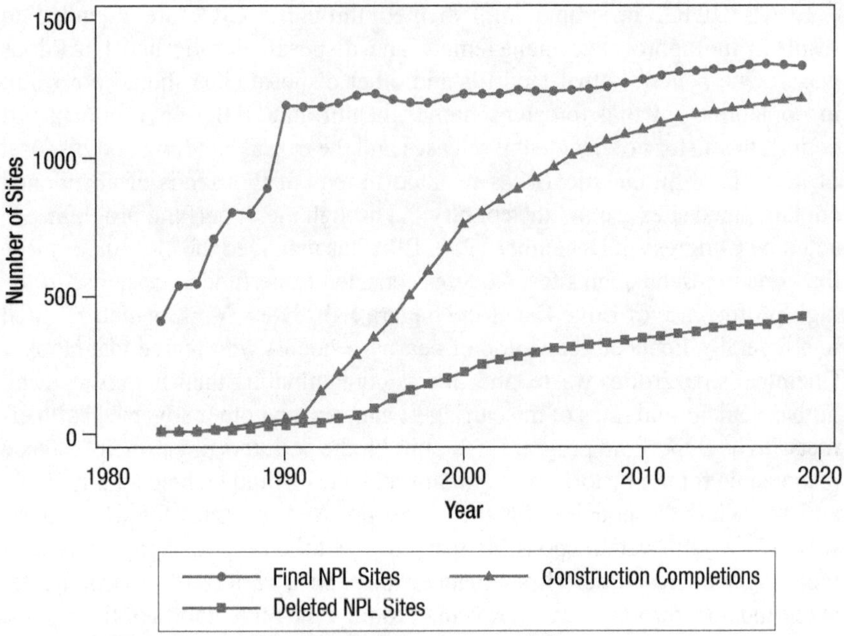

Figure 14.4. Number of NPL Sites by Status at the End of Each Fiscal Year, 1983–2019. ***US EPA, Superfund website, 2020***

ing the initial listing of 406 sites in 1983, most sites were added to the NPL during the first decade of the Superfund program. In more recent years, fewer sites have been added; on average, between 2000 and 2019, the number of new NPL sites each is 16. Second, there has been considerable progress in addressing the contaminated sites that EPA has placed on the NPL, as evidenced by the increasing number of "construction completions" (described above) and the growing number of sites that have been completely deleted from the NPL.

At the time of EPA's founding, public concerns about the effects of pesticides and other chemicals in the environment were reaching their apex. Rachel Carson's book *Silent Spring* was not just a national bestseller; combined with emerging scientific evidence, it helped change the image of chemicals from a mostly positive one focused on innovation and economic promise to an increasingly negative one focused on risks to human and ecological health.[25] The rapidly changing framing of chemicals in the public discourse was reflected in Congress' amendments to the Federal Insecticide, Fungicide and Rodenticide Act (FIFRA) in 1972, which required EPA to evaluate the risks of pesticides to humans, wildlife, and the environment. This created a difficult challenge for EPA given that there were thousands of pesticides already in use and many new ones that were being created for entry into the market.

Over the course of the past five decades, EPA has employed its authorities to ban some pesticides including perhaps most notably DDT and other similar organochlorines, which were well-known to create adverse effects on both humans and wildlife. EPA Administrator William Ruckelshaus's decision to ban the domestic use of DDT in 1972 is widely viewed as an important early moment in EPA's history, demonstrating the willingness of the new agency to forcefully exert its regulatory authority. As a consequence, animal species that were on the brink of extinction at the time, such as the bald eagle, brown pelican, and peregrine falcon have recovered.[26] Among the other accomplishments, EPA evaluated the risks associated with countless pesticides that were already on the market, leading to some being removed by the agency or discontinued by their manufacturers, as well as reviewed thousands of pesticide residue limits on food, with special attention to children as mandated by the 1996 Food Quality Protection Act.[27]

Beyond pesticides, EPA has made further progress to inform understanding about and, when necessary, regulate the use of chemicals under the Toxic Substances Control Act (TSCA). Through TSCA, the agency has evaluated more than fifty thousand new chemicals, at times imposing limits on their use or handling to protect the public. EPA has also used its powers under TSCA to ban some chemicals such as the chlorofluorocarbons (CFCs) that were determined to be depleting the ozone layer and synthetic chemicals like polychlorinated biphenyls (PCBs), the improper disposal of which has contaminated both land and water sources at sites throughout the country. A likely indirect, but difficult to quantify, consequence of bans, FIFRA licensing requirements, and TSCA evaluations is that EPA has sent a strong signal to chemical manufacturers about the benefits of investing in safer chemicals to avoid uncertain or prolonged approval processes.

Building a Capacity to Regulate

This brief overview of EPA's environmental protection achievements over the past fifty years, in the areas of air and water pollution control, drinking water quality, waste disposal, Superfund cleanups, and pesticides and chemicals regulation, illustrates the breadth of the agency's triumphs. By any measure, these achievements, and many more not mentioned, are impressive. Through its actions, EPA has earned a reputation as one of the most capable public health agencies in the world, serving as a model for similar agencies in other countries. To be clear, the agency did not alone generate these improved environmental outcomes. Rather, they came through partnerships with other federal agencies and with state environmental agencies working collaboratively through a model of cooperative federalism in which responsibility was shared across levels of government. EPA also has generally (though not always) had the support of both Republican and Democratic White Houses to pursue implementation of pollution control laws. And, perhaps most importantly, EPA could only bring about these achievements because it was empowered with mandates and clear jurisdiction from Congress through the enactment of ambitious pollution control laws.

All of this said, there was nothing inevitable about EPA's success over the past half century. At the time of the agency's formation, there was some skepticism that an agency lacking Cabinet status and clear independence from the White House would have the political will to take on powerful economic interests.[28] Further complicating matters, EPA's mission intersected with the jurisdictions and interests of other federal agencies, including the Department of Agriculture, the Department of Interior, the Department of Transportation, and the Department of Defense, which created the potential for internal clashes within the executive branch where EPA would have to compete with larger, more politically powerful agencies.

Most importantly, at the time of its establishment, EPA was not envisioned by most people as the type of regulatory agency that it is today. Recall President Nixon created the agency through a reorganization of existing offices that sat in other federal departments. That is, Congress did not originally authorize or empower EPA with a specific set of regulatory authorities, but only did so after the fact through the passage of various federal pollution control laws. And, although the laws clearly granted strong authorities to EPA, at the outset, it was not obvious how the agency would use them. As Jim Barnes writes in Chapter 1, the direction of the agency was set by the initial decisions made by Administrator Bill Ruckelshaus, particularly in the areas of air and water pollution control. In this sense, there is some serendipity to what EPA has become. Had the agency had a different leader in its formative years, a leader less assertive in the use of the agency's newfound regulatory and enforcement powers, EPA may have developed into a different type of agency.

Ruckelshaus' decisions in the early days of the agency went a long way toward setting a tone for the agency in how it would pursue its mission. However, this alone would have been insufficient to generate the scale of environmental protection achievements described above. The chapters of this book have revealed several additional factors that have contributed to EPA's successes. I will highlight four factors in particular: 1) skillful management of its immense portfolio of responsibilities; 2) development of impressive technical capacity (i.e., scientific, legal, economic) to support its decision-making; 3) policy ingenuity; and 4) willingness to take on powerful economic interests. I discuss each in turn.

Administrative Management

This book has provided numerous illustrations of various ways that EPA has effectively managed the enormity of its administrative tasks. For example, consider an early decision the agency made in its implementation of the CWA. EPA faced a dilemma in how to define point sources (e.g., industrial facilities, municipal wastewater plants)—a critical issue given that the CWA required all such sources to obtain a permit to legally discharge pollution into US waterways. As Jonathan Cannon writes in Chapter 5, EPA believed that a literal interpretation of a point source under the law would have required including hundreds of thousands of sources within the NPDES permit regime. After first trying to exempt many of these sources (a decision overturned by the federal courts), EPA instead regulated entire categories of point sources using a general permit authority, rather than a source-by-source approach. With this strategy, the agency (and eventually the states delegated authority to implement the NPDES program) has been able to focus its attention on the largest point sources of pollution.

A second example that further exemplifies how the agency has managed its administrative burden comes from EPA's early implementation of RCRA. As Marcia Williams explains in Chapter 7, at the time that Congress passed the RCRA law, information on the sources and volumes of hazardous waste was extremely limited. An early assessment from the agency determined that there were approximately 760,000 separate generators of hazardous waste which, if all regulated in the same way, would have made it virtually impossible for the agency to effectively implement new hazardous waste regulations. To simplify its task, the agency wrote regulations that focused attention on the activities of "large quantity generators," which was a sensible approach given that the agency had determined that just about five percent of the existing sources accounted for nearly ninety-eight percent of the total quantity of hazardous waste.

To be clear, at times, the weight of the administrative burden has been difficult for EPA to manage. Many of the environmental statutes that the agency implements contain ambitious timelines and requirements that EPA regularly reassess its decisions (e.g., NAAQS must be reviewed every five years). In areas such as chemical assessments under TSCA, the setting of maximum contaminant levels under the SDWA, and the establishment of standards for hazardous air pollutants under the CAA, progress has been much slower, with EPA often acting only after being compelled to do so by court orders. The reasons for slow progress are multi-faceted, having to do with prioritization, scientific uncertainty, and vocal opposition from regulated industry. The agency, furthermore, must manage the regular churn of its responsibilities, while also being able to effectively respond to emergencies (e.g., oil spills, chemical accidents), public health scares (e.g., Alar residues on food, the outbreak of cryptosporidium in Milwaukee), as well as seemingly never-ending legal challenges spurred by lawsuits from both regulated industries and environmental advocacy organizations. As John Graham and Jonathan Wiener write in Chapter 13, EPA's agenda is a product of all these factors, and it has taken skilled leadership of EPA administrators and other senior leadership to "keep the trains (mostly) running on time."

Development of Technical Capacity

A second important reason for EPA's success is that it has developed superb technical expertise throughout the agency to support its core programs. This expertise took time to build, and its development has come in part out of necessity. The US federal courts have shown themselves to be willing to defer to the judgment of EPA, as long as the agency can demonstrate that its decisions are supported by appropriate, high-quality analysis.

A good illustration comes from EPA's implementation of CAA NAAQS, which evolved from a haphazard process in the early 1970s to a formal, comprehensive, and painstaking process in more recent years. In Chapter 2, Bill Pedersen remarks on just how rudimentary was the agency's initial setting of NAAQS. In part compelled by the short timelines set out by the CAA, Pedersen notes that the proposed standards for all six criteria air pollutants came in at less than twenty pages total, and "contained literally no discussion of the scientific conclusions involved or how EPA had reasoned from those conclusions to the standards." The final version, he notes, was "equally summary." As might be expected, EPA was unable to provide the federal courts with a complete and reasoned explanation for the standards as part of a lawsuit brought challenging the scientific basis of the secondary SO2 standard, and ended up withdrawing the rule. In the aftermath of this episode, Pedersen notes that EPA created a more systematic process for establishing NAAQS standards that included detailed reviews by multiple agency offices, external scientific advisors, and the public, and ultimately the creation of a separate dedicated office.

To illustrate the depth of the current process, consider the most recent update to the ozone NAAQS. EPA tightened the primary and secondary standard for ozone from seventy-five parts per billion to seventy parts per billion in 2015. The review of the ambient ozone standard included rigorous, multiyear reviews of science, health risks and exposure, policy options, regulatory impact analysis, and other evaluations that collectively totaled thousands of pages to support the agency's decision to strengthen the standard.[29] Most of this analysis was done by in-house scientists, economists, and other analysts located in EPA's Office of Research and Development and EPA's Office of Air Quality Planning and Standards located in the Research Triangle in North Carolina. In addition, the agency's independent Science Advisory Board weighed in by providing its own guidance to the agency on an appropriate standard. Although the ozone standard was challenged in court by some in industry and many states, the US Court of Appeals for the District of Columbia Circuit upheld EPA's regulation in an August 2019 decision.[30]

The NAAQS case demonstrates how the agency has built up its capacity to support its rulemaking process. As Bernie Goldstein and Terry Yosie comment in their chapter on science and Dick Morgenstern notes in his chapter on economic analysis, the expertise that EPA staff bring to regulatory decision-making is a distinctive and critical feature of the agency.

Policy Ingenuity

EPA has also achieved success through many instances of policy ingenuity and innovation. Examples abound in the area of air pollution control. In the early years of CAA implementation, the agency faced a dilemma. As initial deadlines neared for compliance with the NAAQS, EPA had to identify a way to both meet the standards as well as permit the construction of new pollution sources in areas that were struggling to comply (banning new sources was not a politically tenable option). As Bill Pedersen describes in Chapter 2, EPA developed an "offsets" policy, which it formally codified in a 1976 regulation, that allowed the construction of new sources of pollution as long as the source installed strict controls itself and could obtain new emission reductions from *other* sources to offset its own new emissions. This policy was not specified in the CAA itself, but was an imaginative solution to a vexing policy problem.

EPA's development of its "bubble" policy a few years later shows similar ingenuity. The agency developed the bubble policy in 1979 to help industrial sources of air pollution find more economical approaches to meet their CAA emissions reductions obligations. The policy allows existing sources to treat all of their emissions points (e.g., stacks, vents) as if they were part of a single enclosed system (or bubble), and then reduce their emissions at the individual points they choose. As long as aggregate emissions are reduced as required, EPA would consider a facility to be meeting its obligations. In future years, EPA went further to allow trading across plants for industries for the same pollutant. As was the case with the offsets program, this policy was not spelled out in the CAA, rather it is an example of EPA using its broad authorities to facilitate compliance with the law and the achievement of air pollution control goals.

There is perhaps no better example of policy entrepreneurship in EPA's fifty-year history than its multi-decade effort to address climate change. To be clear, and as I discuss more later in the chapter, EPA has not yet succeeded in creating a durable, robust policy to reduce the greenhouse gas emissions that are causing climate change. While Congress provided the agency with clear authorization to address problems such as air and water pollution, chemicals and pesticides, and solid and hazardous waste, it has not enacted legislation directing the agency to develop programs to address climate change. The closest Congress came to doing so was in 2008, when the US House of Representatives passed the so-called Waxman-Markey bill, but this legislation failed when it was considered in the US Senate.

Despite the lack of a specific congressional mandate, EPA has made itself the federal government's de facto leader on this issue. When climate change first appeared on the public agenda, there was no organizational home for the issue and, as Jody Freeman writes in Chapter 4, when climate change emerged as an issue in the 1970s, it was neither a focus of the Carter White House nor EPA. Yet, over the succeeding years, the enterprising efforts by numerous individuals in the agency began to raise the profile of climate change at the agency and among the broader public. Initially, as Freeman notes, these efforts were led by staff in EPA's Office of Policy, Planning, and Evaluation, which in 1983 began to assemble and circulate internal reports on the issue. Climate change was also elevated by EPA administrators Lee Thomas and William Reilly through their support of risk ranking exercises, as part of which EPA experts characterized the issue as being an important problem to address. In the decade or so that followed, EPA began to unveil a variety of voluntary initiatives aimed at encouraging firms to invest in programs to reduce their greenhouse gas emissions in exchange for recognition from EPA for their efforts (e.g., Green Lights, Energy Start, Climate Leaders). Although these programs were not well integrated with the agency's regulatory programs, they did signal some commitment to at least encourage willing businesses to strive toward reducing their carbon footprint.[31]

Following retrenchment during the George W. Bush administration, EPA during the Obama administration decided to take matters one step further through the design of a broad regulatory program. One of the signature initiatives to address emissions from the electricity sector, was the Clean Power Plan, finalized in 2015, in which EPA used authority it believed it had under existing CAA provisions to limit CO_2 emissions from existing coal-fired power plants. At the time EPA proposed the Clean Power Plan, emissions from electricity generation accounted for about a third of all US CO_2 emissions, with a large proportion coming from the burning of coal.

Of course, by this time, EPA had been regulating criteria and hazardous air pollutants under the CAA for nearly four decades. In those cases, Congress had provided the agency with a clear mandate. In the case of CO_2, while the Supreme Court had pushed the agency to determine if it was in fact a "pollutant" for the purposes of the CAA, the law itself did not prescribe how the agency could do this. In a similar fashion to its crafting of its offsets and bubble policies in the 1970s, the agency interpreted its authorities under the CAA broadly, relying on a lightly used part of the statute as the basis for setting limits on coal plant emissions. Building on the existing cooperative federalism model that has generally worked well in the area of air pollution control, EPA set state-level emission targets but left the details of implementation to state governments themselves. As Freeman details, the Clean Power Plan was challenged by a couple dozen states and many affected industries, and we will never know its legality since the federal courts did not rule on its merits and the question became moot following the Trump administration's rollback. Nonetheless, this example again illustrates how EPA can use its authorities, if it desires, in an innovative way to try to achieve its policy goals.

Willingness to Take on Industry

A final characteristic of EPA decision-making that has contributed to its success has been its willingness, when necessary, to take on powerful sectors of the economy. To be clear, the agency's inclination to take on automakers, the oil and gas industry, electric utilities, and other sectors has waxed and waned over the years, often constrained by the White House and other powerful voices within the executive branch. Moreover, there are numerous occasions when the agency has been able to work collaboratively with regulated industries to achieve environmental improvements. Examples include regulations for the automobile sector on diesel exhaust during both the Clinton and George W. Bush administrations and greenhouse gas standards during the Obama administration for which the agency worked closely with automakers to design a mutually acceptable rule. Taking a fifty-year perspective, however, there also are many instances when, despite strong external opposition, the EPA has pursued aggressive environmental protections.

Perhaps the best example from the early decades of the agency's history is with respect to the creation of pollution control standards for cars and trucks. In the early 1970s, EPA moved forward with aggressive, technology-forcing standards under its recently granted CAA authorities to reduce emissions of hydrocarbons, carbon monoxide, and nitrogen oxides. As John

Graham describes in great detail in Chapter 3, automakers, and domestic companies in particular, strongly resisted EPA standards, using the courts, influential members of Congress, and contrary voices within the White House to object. Despite this pushback, EPA pressed ahead, albeit on a somewhat slower timeline, with standards that resulted in large reductions in pollution from cars and trucks.

Other useful illustrations come from EPA's implementation of the Superfund program. The program has never been particularly popular among businesses in the affected industries, especially given its broad provisions about who can be held responsible for cleanup costs. In the first decade of the program, the EPA made a couple of decisions that exacerbated tensions. First, the agency had to clarify the cleanup standards it would use for National Priorities List sites (the Superfund statute did not specify such standards). As Gene Lucero and Marcia Williams write in Chapter 8, EPA put in place a policy in 1985 that required site cleanup standards be based on applicable or relevant and appropriate requirements—so called ARARS—meaning the agency would set standards based on the provisions of other environmental laws (e.g., MCLs under the SDWA). This approach was later codified by Congress in the 1986 Superfund amendments. Later in the decade, EPA formally adopted an "enforcement first" policy, through which it leveraged the use of public trust fund resources to achieve enforcement settlements with responsible parties. In other words, rather than conduct cleanups first and seek reimbursement, EPA shifted toward forcing responsible parties to take responsibility for costs earlier in the remedial process.

As noted above, EPA's first Administrator Bill Ruckelshaus set a tone early on that the agency would enforce its congressional mandates, embracing a command and control approach as necessary and appropriate to do so. These decisions did not come without some cost. As Megan Mullin and I discuss in Chapter 12, EPA's approach generated a strong backlash from regulated entities as well as political conservatives that objected to the agency's approach. In addition, EPA's willingness to take on powerful economic sectors helped create what has often become an adversarial relationship between EPA and many segments of the regulated community. These byproducts of the agency's approach will only complicate its efforts to address the ongoing and new challenges I discuss next.

UNFINISHED BUSINESS

Looking to the future, there are numerous environmental challenges that EPA will need to address. Several of the challenges are not new, in that they have been on the agency's agenda to different extents for a long time and, in some cases, since the formation of the agency. Other issues are more recent additions to the agenda. The items I emphasize here are not intended to represent a definitive or comprehensive list, and there undoubtedly will be unforeseen issues that arise on the agency's future agenda. Yet, the issues I highlight are instructive in that they represent the diversity and scale of problems that EPA will need to confront in the years and decades to come. All present challenges for the agency, and some will be quite difficult to effectively address, due to a combination of their technical complexity, uncertain or under-utilized legal authority, and political sensitivity.

Air Pollution

Compared to 1970, air quality is unquestionably better in most places in the United States. However, this should not be misunderstood to mean that air quality across the country meets the current health-based standards set by EPA. In fact, in many parts of the country, ambient air quality remains a severe problem. According to the most recent EPA estimates, over one hundred and thirty million Americans—constituting about forty percent of the US population—currently live in counties that are in violation of at least one national ambient air quality standard.[32] Recent analyses that take advantage of new ways to measure air quality, such as satellite imagery, suggest that the actual number of Americans that live in areas failing to meet NAAQS may be substantially higher.[33] Many of the most serious air quality problems occur in large metropolitan areas such as Atlanta, Chicago, Houston, Los Angeles, Pittsburgh, and St. Louis, and, in some places such as southern California, millions of people live in locations that are in violation of multiple standards for criteria air pollutants such as ozone, particulate matter, and NOx. Moreover, while ambient concentrations of criteria air pollutants have declined in recent decades, there has been a recent uptick in concentrations of particulate matter, especially PM2.5 (particulates in the air that have a diameter of 2.5 micrometers or smaller).[34] Specifically, according to EPA's National Emissions Inventory data, between 2016 and 2018, PM2.5 concentrations increased by 5.5 percent. Exposure to PM2.5 is associated with numerous adverse health effects including respiratory and cardiovascular problems that can result in premature mortality. In an analysis of this increase in PM2.5, one study estimated that this increase was associated with an additional 9,700 premature deaths (with a monetized damages value of $89 billion), and attributed the rise in emissions to increases in economic activity and wildfires, as well as declines in CAA enforcement.[35] Despite growing evidence of the health effects of exposure to PM2.5 at concentrations below the current CAA

NAAQS standards, EPA in April 2020 decided not to make the standard more stringent (discussed more later in the chapter).

One specific problem that EPA has struggled with over the course of its fifty-year history is interstate pollution, specifically the long-range transport of pollutants such as SO2 and NOx, which can affect air quality hundreds of miles away from where they are released. An important impetus for Congress in enacting federal air pollution control programs in the 1970 CAA was to address this very problem, given a concern that states themselves had few incentives to curb interstate pollution. Interstate air pollution is an intrinsically challenging problem for EPA to manage, and it was exacerbated by early developments in CAA implementation in which large stationary sources installed taller stacks to help compliance with NAAQS standards (see Bill Pedersen's discussion in Chapter 2). Over the decades, EPA has implemented a variety of programs to address the long-range transport of air pollutants, several coming out of the 1990 CAA Amendments such as the Ozone Transport Commission and the SO2 emissions cap and trade program to address acid rain. Further efforts came during the George W. Bush and Obama administrations through the development of the Clean Air Interstate Rule (CAIR) and the Cross State Air Pollution Rule (CSAPR), respectively, the latter of which is now in full force following years of litigation in the federal courts. EPA, however, has been less effective in responding to complaints from states that say they are unable to meet NAAQS because of pollution coming from outside their borders. States in the northeastern United States in particular have frequently petitioned EPA to intervene, requesting that the agency employ its authorities under the CAA's "good neighbor provision" which enables the agency to impose emissions limits on sources of pollution that are causing noncompliance of NAAQS in downwind states. To this point, EPA has been reticent to use this authority.

Drinking Water

The Flint water crisis, which began in 2014 and became national news a year later, is a stark reminder that there remain vulnerabilities in the US drinking water system. The lead contamination of Flint's public drinking supply was a failure in many respects. Decisions by state government officials, empowered by a controversial fiscal emergency manager law, resulted in the widespread lead poisoning of children and the deaths of a dozen people from an outbreak of Legionnaires disease. The proximate cause of the lead contamination was a decision to use the Flint River as a temporary source for the city's drinking water but not to use corrosion control chemicals to prevent the leaching of lead from service lines. This decision, made primarily to cut the costs of city operations, coupled with failures to properly implement EPA's lead and copper rule, resulted in a full-scale public health crisis. Studies of lead poisoning in Flint children found that elevated blood levels doubled with the switch to the Flint River, and in socioeconomically disadvantaged neighborhoods, levels nearly tripled.[36]

In addition to being a public health crisis, the Flint Water Crisis Task Force, charged by the Governor of Michigan to investigate the causes of the crisis, declared it a case of environmental injustice. The Task Force concluded: "Flint residents, who are majority Black or African American and among the most impoverished of any metropolitan area in the United States, did not enjoy the same degree of protection from environmental and health hazards as that provided to other communities. Moreover, by virtue of their being subject to emergency management, Flint residents were not provided equal access to, and meaningful involvement in, the government decision-making process."[37]

For its part, EPA was slow to react to the crisis. Part of the reason for the tepid EPA response was that officials in Michigan agencies deliberately misled the agency and, in so doing, hindered its ability to react. The breakdown in communication and coordination between EPA and the state of Michigan ruptured the cooperative federalism model that binds together much of the US pollution control system. Without coordination and collaboration, the SDWA and other pollution control laws do not work as intended. Even so, when the EPA's own inspector general evaluated EPA's response to the Flint Water Crisis, they determined that the agency could have used its emergency powers under the SDWA up to six months earlier than it did to intervene in the crisis[38] and that the agency's Region 5 office (located in Chicago) did not have in place appropriate management controls that would have enabled the agency to respond more expeditiously when it learned of Flint and the state of Michigan's failure to implement the Lead and Copper Rule (it is important to note that Miguel Del Toral, an EPA official in Region 5, did ring alarm bells in the early months of the crisis which were not heeded by the agency).[39]

The Flint Water Crisis also illustrates that the US public water system still has weaknesses. The lead problem is particularly challenging. Unlike many pathogens and contaminants that water utilities can effectively manage at their drinking water plants, lead enters drinking water primarily through leaching from lead service lines. To date, the main approach to managing potential lead contamination has been the use of corrosion control chemicals, which works effectively when in place. However, the Flint case, and more recently similar widespread problems in Newark, New Jersey, illustrate limitations with this approach. A more comprehensive strategy would be a large-scale project to replace lead service lines. The expense of such a project is substantial, and EPA does not have anywhere near the resources to fund such an initiative. There is considerable uncertainty in estimates of the number of lead service lines currently in use in the United States, with EPA placing the number somewhere between 6.1 to 10 million. According to one recent analysis, EPA suggests that less than one hundred and fifty thousand of these lines could be replaced using resources from the SDWRF, and that this would take thirty-five years.[40]

The expense of replacing lead service lines highlights a broader challenge for EPA in providing environmental protection. Many of the core US environmental laws recognize the critical need for the investment of federal financial resources. As just mentioned, the 1996 SDWA amendments included a revolving fund to help local governments upgrade their drinking water infrastructure. The CWA, as initially passed, included the provision of billions of dollars in grants to modernize wastewater treatment plants, since extended through a revolving fund to provide low-interest loans. The Superfund program put in place a set of taxes to fill the coffers of a trust fund that EPA could use to clean up contaminated properties. Yet, these programs either fall well short of the demand (in the case of wastewater and drinking water), or no longer provide revenue as designed (the Superfund taxes expired in 1995). A complicating dynamic is that the laws (and usually their accompanying regulations) do not often change, but funding requires ongoing congressional appropriations. These resource challenges, which can only be addressed by Congress, inhibit EPA's ability to achieve its mission.

Other problems also challenge the drinking water system. In Chapter 6, Jim Salzman notes that EPA will have to determine if and how to regulate a list of "emergent contaminants," many of which are ubiquitous and potentially harmful at very low levels. In recent years, a class of synthetic chemicals known as PFAS—Per- and polyfluoroalkyl substances—have (re-)emerged on EPA's agenda. PFAS, colloquially referred to as "forever chemicals" since they are intentionally manufactured to not break down, are found in a wide range of consumer products as well as fire-fighting foams. Research on the health effects of exposure to PFAS is still developing, but studies of two specific chemicals—PFOA and PFOS—point to reproductive and immunological effects, as well as elevated cancer risk.[41] The potential health risks associated with PFAS have been known for decades. As far back as 2000, EPA negotiated a settlement with the chemical manufacturer 3M to phase out the use of PFOS in its Scotchgard products, and DuPont agreed to a similar plan regarding PFOA, which it used in its Teflon products.[42] Several years later during the George W. Bush administration, EPA Administrator Steve Johnson negotiated the 2010/2015 PFOA Stewardship Program, which was a voluntary agreement between EPA and eight major chemical companies to reduce PFOA from facility emissions and product content by ninety-five percent no later than 2010, and to make progress toward eliminating PFOA from emissions and product content by no later than 2015.[43] Despite this history, EPA has yet to regulate PFAS, and only recently did the agency begin to formally consider setting maximum contaminant levels under the SDWA and make an initial recommendation for addressing PFOA and PFOS contamination in groundwater as part of federal cleanup programs (e.g., Superfund, RCRA).[44] Although the agency recommended standard is less stringent than that put in place in several states (e.g., New Hampshire, New Jersey, New York),[45] it is an important initial step since there are more than a thousand sites around the country where there is soil and water contamination from the uncontrolled use and/or improper disposal of PFAS.[46]

Beyond PFAS, EPA will also need to confront other emerging contaminants increasingly found in US drinking water. Jim Salzman notes, for example, that approximately fifty chemical contaminants have been identified as endocrine disruptors. He also notes the presence of high levels of pharmaceutical and personal care products in the drinking water system, exposure to which is poorly understood. As these problems mount, and as scientific advances improve our understanding of their effects on water quality and human health, EPA will need to respond with policy and programs, and have resources from Congress to do so.

Nonpoint Source Water Pollution

The story of the Cuyahoga River in Cleveland catching fire in 1969 is regularly pointed to as a key moment in the history of US environmental policy. As Jon Cannon writes in Chapter 5, the image of a river on fire due to pollution brought newfound attention to the effects of point source discharges from factories and municipalities. Not surprisingly, when Congress enacted the 1972 CWA, it aggressively targeted these sources, and this part of the CWA has resulted in significant reductions of discharges to US waterways. Yet, serious water quality problems persist. Almost five decades after the Cuyahoga incident, another event in Ohio generated national attention. This time, a toxic algae bloom in Lake Erie forced the City of Toledo to shut off drinking water service to five hundred thousand people for several days. This incident, occurring in August 2014, was attributable primarily to nonpoint source pollution from agricultural runoff of fertilizers (e.g., phosphorous), animal feedlots, and leaking septic systems. As the result of the algae bloom, the city's water treatment plant discovered unsafe levels of microcystin, exposure to which can cause gastrointestinal problems and abnormal liver function.[47]

The toxic algae bloom in Lake Erie has become an annual occurrence, and clearly illustrates the problem of nonpoint source pollution, particularly from agricultural sources, that has limited EPA's ability to generate the improvements in water quality contemplated by the CWA. According to the most recently available data from the agency, more than half of the US rivers and streams that have been assessed are "impaired," meaning they are not meeting their designated uses (e.g., drinking water, fishing, swimming, industry, agriculture). Similarly, more than seventy percent of assessed US lakes, reservoirs, and ponds are "impaired" with similar numbers for other types of waterways such as bays and estuaries, coastal shorelines, and wetlands.[48] According to these same evaluations, the major causes of these impairments are nonpoint source pollution from agriculture, as well as urban runoff.[49]

The CWA provides EPA with limited tools for addressing nonpoint source pollution. But, as Jonathan Cannon describes in Chapter 5, the agency has not aggressively employed the tools it does have. For instance, the CWA requires states to develop programs, subject to EPA approval, to control nonpoint source pollution. Analyses of these programs, however, indicate that they have not been particularly effective and that EPA in particular has not performed appropriate oversight.[50] Perhaps the most promising tool available to the EPA is the Total Maximum Daily Load (TMDL) program, which enables the agency to set source-by-source discharge limits for waterways that are not meeting their designated uses. States have the primary responsibility for setting TMDLs, but these are subject to EPA approval and courts have ruled that the agency must set TMDLs if states fail to do so. In some cases, such as the Chesapeake Bay TMDL, EPA has played a major supportive role of state efforts, but it has not done so on a widespread basis. Although using TMDLs to fully address nonpoint source pollution is challenging because compliance with pollutant load allocations for nonpoint sources is voluntary, the agency has not yet employed them to their full potential.[51]

Environmental Justice

Across a great number of indicators, EPA policies and programs have helped to generate significant improvements in environmental quality. Although these improvements have resulted in an enhanced quality of life for most Americans, countless others still experience disproportionate pollution burdens. Environmental justice refers to the uneven distribution of environmental risks (e.g., proximity to unwanted land uses such as industrial sites, solid and hazardous waste landfills, incinerators) and amenities (e.g., parks, safe drinking water), as well as lack of access to and fairness of environmental decision-making processes (e.g., land use siting decisions, issuance of air and water pollution permits). Over the past several decades, research has documented that people of color and low-income in the United States face more of these risks and enjoy fewer of these amenities.[52] Communities in Detroit, Port Arthur (TX), and so-called "Cancer Alley" in Louisiana are just a few where poor people of color live in close proximity to various types of polluting facilities.

Considerable public health and epidemiological research has documented race-, ethnic-, and class-based disparities in pollution exposure and associated adverse health outcomes. For example, numerous studies have shown that communities with more people of color and low-income are more likely to be exposed to high levels of air pollution, as well as experience higher incidence of asthma and other respiratory illnesses.[53] Studies have also shown that these communities often host hazardous waste landfills and other disposal facilities,[54] and are serviced by water utilities that more frequently violate SDWA standards.[55] The reasons underlying these patterns are complex (e.g., housing discrimination, real estate markets, neighborhood demographic transition),[56] most of which fall well beyond the jurisdiction of EPA to address. However, research has also shown that these disparities may be exacerbated by biases in regulatory enforcement efforts, both by EPA and the state environmental agencies to which it has delegated authority to implement programs. Specifically, numerous studies have shown there is less compliance monitoring and fewer penalties issued when facilities violating their permits are located in communities of color and lower socioeconomic status.[57]

As Megan Mullin and I discuss in Chapter 12, EPA's attention to environmental justice has fluctuated over the last few decades, but in general it has not received sustained attention. The issue first appeared on the agency's agenda in the early 1990s, when Administrator William Reilly asked agency staff to investigate environmental equity concerns. Since that time, and across both Democratic and Republican presidential administrations, EPA has failed to develop a comprehensive environmental justice program.

Recent analyses point to several reasons why EPA has not embraced an environmental justice agenda. The first set of reasons are institutional. Since President Clinton signed an executive order on environmental justice in 1994 (Executive Order 12898), EPA has systematically failed to incorporate environmental justice considerations into its core programs and decision-making as the executive order requires (the same is true for other federal agencies). For example, EPA has not consistently considered environmental justice issues in permitting decisions, standard-setting under major laws, regulatory impact analyses, and in enforcement efforts. Moreover, the agency has not effectively administered Title VI provisions of the 1964 Civil Rights Act that are intended to provide opportunities for communities to raise civil rights complaints against state environmental agencies (and other entities) receiving federal financial assistance.[58] In part, EPA's lack of progress on environmental justice reflects limited authority; statutes such as the CAA and CWA do not specifically mandate that EPA consider equity issues. However, the agency does have considerable discretion throughout many of its core functions to pursue such objectives. Over the years, however, the agency has been slow to develop tools and technical guidance for how to incorporate environmental justice into permitting, standard-setting, enforcement, and other kinds of decision-making, and leadership on the issue has generally been lacking. The agency during the Obama administration did make significant strides in these areas. EPA administrators Lisa Jackson and Gina McCarthy each made environmental justice a priority and ushered through Plan EJ 2014 to help the agency develop tools and resources to better address issues of equity and fairness in EPA decision-making, but these administrative actions have been cast aside during the Trump administration.[59]

A second factor that helps explain the lack of attention to environmental justice at EPA pertains to the agency's organizational culture. A recent analysis that involved scores of interviews with EPA officials revealed that regulatory staff in the agency's programmatic offices often view environmental justice as an issue beyond the agency's core mission. For these officials, carrying out the mandates as prescribed by Congress is what matters, and consideration of equity in outcomes or fairness in decision-making requires the diversion of limited resources and jeopardizes what many people view as the agency's neutrality.[60] For these reasons, the small number of EPA staff who do work on environmental justice have historically faced large obstacles in their efforts to focus the agency's attention on these issues. Effectively addressing environmental justice in the future, thus, will require EPA to take on these organizational culture issues, as well as to better utilize its discretionary authorities.

Climate Change

As Jody Freeman writes in Chapter 4, EPA has been engaged on climate change for most of its history. As early as the Carter administration, staff at EPA began to compile scientific assessments of the problem, and the agency has over time put in place various greenhouse gas mitigation programs, ranging from voluntary initiatives in the 1990s and 2000s to proposed regulatory programs in the 2010s. The agency has also been an active participant, and often a leader, in helping other nations take on this issue, as well as in providing technical expertise for US officials in their efforts to craft international agreements. To be clear, EPA has taken these actions mostly at its own initiative. Congress has not explicitly mandated EPA to control greenhouse gas emissions, and the agency has not been given a specific role to assist other government agencies, communities, or individuals in developing climate change adaptation strategies. Thus, from one perspective, the fact that EPA has accomplished what it has is notable.

EPA's efforts to address climate change through regulation during the Obama administration stands out. The agency used its authority under the CAA to set limits on CO_2 emissions from existing coal-fired power plants as part of its Clean Power Plan. In addition, the agency finalized a CAA New Source Performance Standard for new fossil fueled power plants, which would have required any new coal plant to incorporate carbon capture and storage technology. Beyond the electricity sector, the agency worked with the National Highway Traffic Safety Administration (NHTSA) and the state of California to twice set standards to increase fuel economy and reduce greenhouse gas emissions from cars and light trucks, and EPA promulgated two phases of standards to increase fuel economy and lower carbon emissions of medium and heavy duty trucks. The agency also placed restrictions on the use of hydrofluorocarbons which are potent greenhouse gases utilized in air conditioning, refrigeration, and other products. These and other efforts contributed to the US commitment that President Obama pledged for the United States as part of the Paris Agreement on climate change, which was to reduce US greenhouse gas emissions twenty-six to twenty-eight percent below 2005 levels by 2025.

These policies and programs have all been substantially curtailed by EPA in the years of the Trump administration. These rollbacks are discussed more below, but suffice it to say here that, as a consequence, EPA does not currently have in place a serious approach to reducing the greenhouse gas emissions causing climate change. As long as climate change continues to be framed as a problem for the agency to address, and absent a clearer mandate from Congress, the EPA in the future will likely once again return to the types of regulatory approaches pursued during the Obama administration.

These steps alone, however, will not be sufficient to address the full-scale of climate change. To date, EPA has been for the most part focused on the mitigation dimension of the problem, which makes good sense given the historic pollution control orientation of the agency, and the need to reduce greenhouse gas emissions from sources that EPA already regulates for other purposes. However, climate change is a much different type of environmental problem than EPA was designed to address fifty years ago. Climate change affects every sector of the economy, and with strong and growing evidence that the United States has already begun to see its effects (i.e., excessive heat days, extreme weather events, more intense wildfires, etc.), policy attention at EPA (and other federal agencies) will need to emphasize not just mitigation, but also policies and programs to enhance adaptation and community resiliency.

EPA has much to offer in these areas, given its vast expertise and technical capacity in science, economics, and law. But, to do so effectively, Congress will need to equip the agency with additional authorities. The toolkit given to the agency in the 1970s to address air and water pollution, chemicals and pesticides, solid and hazardous waste, and other "traditional" environmental problems is not the same toolkit that the agency will need to help the United States effectively make progress on climate change. A recent report produced by scholars at American University in collaboration with the EPA Alumni Association noted that the regulatory approaches that have produced immense improvements in environmental quality will need to be supplemented with broader use of market-based instruments and new, non-regulatory approaches, such as voluntary initiatives, to fully engage industry, cities and towns, and the public.[61] In addition, EPA will need to strengthen partnerships with other government agencies, particularly state and local governments, who are more closely involved in land use decisions. In this way, EPA will need to reinvigorate environmental federalism to broaden and improve relationships with other levels of government.

Moreover, EPA may need to consider some internal reorganization. The structure of the agency has not changed much since its formation when, quite sensibly, it was organized around major media (e.g., air, water, land) and core regulatory functions (e.g., enforcement, research, and development). Issues such as climate change and environmental justice are not easily divided along these lines and effectively addressing these problems will require initiatives that cut across EPA's current programmatic and office lines. None of this is to suggest that EPA should move away from its traditional responsibilities, as there remains plenty of work in these areas as well. These new efforts should be additive and complementary, not substitutes for what EPA already does.

With so much work that remains unfinished, and at a time when EPA needs reinvestment and reinvention to take on even more complicated problems, the agency finds itself under attack. For the past few years, the Trump administration and EPA leadership itself has pursued an agenda not to strengthen the agency to take on either traditional or new problems, but instead to cripple it from doing so. The current crisis at EPA is an intensification of a political backlash that EPA has now faced for at least several decades. The difference today is that challenge comes from *within* the agency, in a way even more severe than in the 1980s during the Reagan administration. For EPA to successfully fulfill its mission to protect human health and the environment, it will have to overcome this politically driven assault. This is the subject of the rest of the chapter.

THE CURRENT POLITICAL THREAT TO THE EPA, AND THE AGENCY'S FUTURE

Until the election of President Trump, most analysts and historians pointed to the early 1980s as the period in time that presented the most direct political threat to EPA. President Reagan followed up on his campaign commitments to reduce the size of the federal government and to cut regulations by appointing officials to EPA such as Anne Gorsuch (EPA Administrator) and Rita Lavelle (Assistant Administrator for Solid Waste and Emergency Response) who were openly suspicious, if not overtly hostile, to the agency's mission. These officials advocated for deep budgetary and personnel cuts and for easing enforcement of environmental laws. As Megan Mullin and I describe in Chapter 12, a bipartisan effort in Congress resisted this retrenchment, undertaking numerous oversight investigations. Amidst a scandal over handling of the Superfund program, Gorsuch resigned and Lavelle was fired, and President Reagan responded to the scandals, mismanagement, and general political undermining of the agency by bringing back a trusted leader, Bill Ruckelshaus, who had adeptly guided EPA during the agency's formative years. In the course of EPA's fifty-year history, this period of turbulence was only brief and the damage to the agency's capacity to carry out its mission was limited.

In the time since, EPA has regularly faced fierce political opposition to its general mission and to specific decisions from members of Congress, regulated industries, and periodically the White House and other federal agencies. But not since the 1980s have the threats to the agency come so severely from *within* the agency itself, though this time with a potentially more lasting effect. Dissimilar to the 1980s, Congress has not pursued rigorous oversight of EPA. Although there have been more hearings since the Democrats took control of the US House of Representative after the 2018 midterm elections, this oversight has not slowed EPA's deregulatory push. And when President Trump's first EPA Administrator Scott Pruitt was forced to resign due to innumerable scandals, he was not replaced with a trusted environmental leader as President Reagan had done. Instead, President Trump promoted the agency's Deputy Administrator Andrew Wheeler, who, prior to his appointment to the agency, had worked as the chief of staff for a prominent critic of the EPA, Senator James Inhofe, and as a coal industry lobbyist where he had worked to undermine many of the environmental laws that he would now have responsibility to implement.[62]

The past few years at EPA have arguably been the most tumultuous for the agency in its half century history. President Trump campaigned for the presidency in 2016 on an agenda that called for an aggressive and systematic rollback of EPA regulations. His calls for policy retrenchment emphasized EPA rules that he perceived to be holding back the energy industry, and specifically those that he thought were part of a "war on coal."[63] However, once in office, the extent of policy reversals under his administration has extended into nearly every aspect of the agency's jurisdiction, as well as to the fundamental capacity and scientific basis of decision-making that the agency historically has relied on.

Policy Rollbacks

Major news organizations have done extensive reporting on the rollbacks of environmental regulations and policies during the first term of the Trump administration. By one such accounting, as of December 2019 federal agencies had completed or initiated ninety-five separate actions in areas ranging from air and water pollution control to energy exploration and extraction to toxic substances and chemical safety.[64] These deregulatory actions expand beyond the EPA and comprise activities of other federal offices and agencies, such as the Council of Environmental Quality, the Department of Interior, the National Oceanic and Atmospheric Administration, and the Federal Energy Regulatory Commission. In response to lawsuits, the federal courts have often reversed the rollbacks, including a number of EPA actions, such as efforts to delay the compliance deadline for a new ozone NAAQS, to weaken federal standards regulating the disposal of coal ash from power plants, to reverse emission standards for "glider" trucks, and to delay implementation of a rule to strengthen certification requirements and training for handlers of pesticides.[65] In these and other cases, the courts reversed EPA decisions because they lacked either sufficient legal rationale or technical justification. The legal defeats are numerous; by one recent tally, through the first three years of the Trump presidency, about ninety-five percent of the administration's deregulatory actions in the area of the environment had been over-turned by a federal court.[66] Despite this poor record of legal success, the deregulatory efforts have continued unabated.

The list of EPA deregulatory actions during the first term of the Trump presidency is lengthy, touching on virtually every area of EPA decision-making. Examples in the area of air pollution control include canceling a requirement that oil and gas companies report methane emissions, the loosening of a twenty-year-old rule designed to limit toxic emissions from major industrial polluters, revising New Source Review requirements making it easier for some facilities to avoid emissions limits, easing enforcement of rules for excess emission events from facility start-ups, shutdowns, and malfunctions, and weakening air pollution protections in national parks and wilderness areas. In the case of water pollution control, rollbacks include withdrawing proposed rules intended to reduce pollution at sewage treatment plants and to protect groundwater from pollution from some uranium mines, proposing a new rule to exempt some power plants from limits on toxic discharges into waterways, and empowering EPA to issue CWA permits over state objections for projects like oil and natural gas pipelines.[67] With respect to toxic substances and chemical safety, EPA rollbacks include reversing a ban on the pesticide chlorpyrifos despite evidence linking it to health problems in children, narrowing the reach of the 2016 rewrite of the Toxic Substances and Control Act regarding assessments of dry-cleaning solvents, paint strippers, and other toxic chemicals, and undoing a 2017 EPA rule designed to improve safety at sites that use and store hazardous materials that was promulgated after a chemical plant explosion in Texas.[68]

As of this writing, many of these actions are subject to lawsuits, so their legality is yet to be determined. Regardless, taken as a group, these and dozens of other deregulatory actions at EPA comprise a systematic and comprehensive program to not just reduce regulatory burdens on industry, agriculture, and other sectors of the economy, but seemingly to undermine the very public health and environmental protection mission of the agency. Although the policy reversals reflect a change in political preferences of the White House and agency leadership, they are not in response to changes in the underlying problems themselves, and, in all cases, the intent of the policy is to reduce health and environmental protections not enhance them. It is also important to note that these actions have come at the direction of EPA political leadership, often over the objections of career EPA officials, and there have been numerous resignations or early retirements of senior career officials in protest. Moreover, it is also striking that over this same period of time, there are few examples of new actions taken by EPA that, by an objective standard, are clearly designed to improve environmental quality. One example is the agency's "Cleaner Trucks Initiative," which is a regulatory effort underway in collaboration with the California Air Resources Board to update NO_x standards for heavy-duty trucks.[69] But, such examples are few and far between.

To further illustrate the depth of the policy retrenchment, it is useful to summarize EPA's recent decisions to revoke and replace a regulatory plan to reduce carbon dioxide emissions from the electricity sector, to weaken fuel economy and greenhouse gas standards for cars and trucks, and to substantially limit the reach of the clean water protections. These cases have been described in detail in previous chapters of the book, so the summary here will be brief.

One of EPA's signature policies to address climate change during the Obama presidency was a CAA regulation to limit CO_2 emissions from existing coal-fired power plants, known as the Clean Power Plan. The overall goal of the rule was to reduce CO_2 emissions from these plants by thirty-two percent from 2005 levels by 2030. To achieve this national target, EPA established state-by-state limits calibrated to each state's electricity portfolio, and then afforded states wide discretion to formulate plans to meet their limits, allowing emission reductions through three means: 1) efficiency improvements at existing plants, 2) shifting power generation from coal to natural gas plants, and/or 3) generating more electricity from renewable sources such as wind and solar power.

From the outset, the Clean Power Plan was controversial, with objections coming from industry and numerous state governments, many of whom believed EPA was overstepping its legal authority under the CAA. After EPA proposed the rule, future EPA Administrator, and then Oklahoma Attorney General, Scott Pruitt organized a legal campaign to challenge it.[70] By the time the case had reached the US Court of Appeals for the D.C. Circuit, twenty-four states, the coal industry, and several electric utilities had lined up against it, with seventeen states, the District of Columbia, and many environmental organizations lined up in favor. The arguments against the Clean Power Plan were numerous, mostly related to whether EPA had jurisdiction to regulate CO_2 under the CAA, and, if so, if such jurisdiction permitted the agency to require emissions reductions "beyond the fence-line" of a facility. The legal challenges, however, were never resolved by the courts and they became irrelevant when EPA reversed course during the Trump administration.

A couple of months after taking office, President Trump signed an Executive Order instructing EPA to undo the Clean Power Plan. Later in 2017, when EPA announced it was moving to revoke the Clean Power Plan, Administrator Pruitt remarked: "We are committed to righting the wrongs of the Obama administration by cleaning the regulatory slate. Any replacement rule will be done carefully, properly, and with humility, by listening to all those affected by the rule."[71] In June 2019, EPA formally rescinded the Clean Power Plan and replaced it with the Affordable Clean Energy (ACE) rule, which is based on a narrow interpretation of EPA authority under the CAA in which only emissions limits "within the fence-line" of a facility are allowed. Specifically, the ACE rule requires power plants to meet modest emissions targets through improvements in their heat-rate efficiency. EPA's own analysis found that the rule would result in minuscule reductions of CO_2 emissions—0.7 percent below 2005 levels by 2030—falling well short of the 32 percent that the agency had estimated would result from the prior Clean Power Plan. Moreover, while the ACE rule's economic analysis estimated net annual benefits of $730 million, these are just a fraction of the estimated net benefits of the Clean Power Plan, which were between $26-$45 billion. In sum, while the ACE rule may technically comply with legal mandates to regulate CO_2, it is not designed to significantly reduce CO_2 emissions.

EPA during the Trump administration has taken similar actions to unravel Obama-era standards designed to improve the fuel economy and reduce the greenhouse gas emissions from cars and light trucks. In 2012, EPA and NHTSA jointly issued a rule that required automakers to increase the average fuel economy of passenger vehicles to about 54 miles per gallon by 2025. These standards constituted a second round of updates put in place during the Obama presidency, and contributed to that administration's broader efforts to reduce greenhouse gas emissions from cars. The 2012 rule, which affected model years 2017-2025, included a midterm evaluation of the standards for model years 2022-2025 to determine if the standards were achievable. In the waning days of the Obama administration, EPA Administrator Gina McCarthy concluded that automakers could in fact meet the standards, and at a lower cost than previously estimated.[72]

Just two months later, EPA Administrator Pruitt and Department of Transportation Secretary Elaine Chao announced that the agencies would reconsider this determination, later declaring that the standards were actually inappropriate and should be revised.[73] Later that year, EPA proposed a replacement rule, known as the Safer Affordable Fuel-Efficient (SAFE) Vehicles Rule, which substantially reduced the ambition of the 2012 standard. The final version of the rule, put in place in March 2020, requires approximately a 1.5 percent annual increase in the average fuel economy of passenger cars and light trucks, compared to the previous version that had required about a 5 percent increase.[74] By EPA's own estimates, relative to the Obama-era rule, the SAFE Vehicle Rule would result in more pollution of criteria air pollutants from tailpipes as well as more greenhouse gas emissions.[75] In addition, EPA as part of the SAFE Vehicle Rule revoked permission previously granted to California to establish its own, more stringent mobile source pollution standards related to greenhouse gases and fuel economy. California has for decades received a waiver from EPA to establish its own guidelines, and more than a dozen states have adopted these more stringent standards over the years to address their own air quality problems.

The EPA's rewrite of fuel economy standards is notable for at least two reasons. First, the technical analysis provided by EPA to justify the changes received scathing criticism from both academic scholars and

EPA's own analysts. Writing in *Science* magazine, a group of leading environmental economists criticized that analysis released in support of the proposed rule, noting that it "has fundamental flaws and inconsistencies, is at odds with basic economic theory and empirical studies, is misleading, and does not improve estimates of costs and benefits of fuel economy standards beyond those in the 2016 analysis." These economists further claim that if the SAFE rule goes into effect, the result may actually be increased traffic-related deaths and more CO_2 emissions compared to the Obama-era rule. Although the details of the final version of the rule diverged slightly from the proposed version, the critiques have been similar.[76] Similarly, EPA's Science Advisory Board found major errors in the analysis of the proposed rule, noting that "there are significant weaknesses in the scientific analysis of the proposed rule," and that these weaknesses "lead to implausible results regarding the overall size of the vehicle fleet," which is a key assumption on which the rule is based.[77]

One likely explanation for the flawed analysis is that EPA's own internal technical experts, mostly based at the agency's Ann Arbor, Michigan-based National Vehicle and Fuel Emissions Laboratory, were sidelined from the process. Instead, officials with far less experience and expertise at the NHTSA put together the analysis and did so over the objections of EPA's career staff.[78]

A second notable aspect of the rewrite of the fuel economy standards is that several major automakers are opposed. Although the entire industry (minus Tesla), through its trade associations, requested that the Trump administration loosen the 2012 rule to provide more compliance flexibility, the associations later objected to the administration's proposal to "freeze" and instead recommended a gradual tightening of the standards (the final rule seems to have heeded this advice to some extent).[79] Of particular concern to the automakers is that the Trump administration and the state of California could not negotiate a uniform, national rule, which creates the possibility that the industry will face two sets of standards. In a rebuke to the Trump administration, four major automakers—Ford, Volkswagen, Honda, and BMW—negotiated a voluntary agreement in 2019 with California to meet a higher standard than in the Trump final rule, but a less stringent one than the Obama administration had issued (Volvo joined in April 2020).

A third important EPA policy change during the Trump administration is the effort to significantly narrow CWA jurisdiction. Specifically, in January 2020 the EPA finalized a replacement for the Waters of the United States (WOTUS) rule that it had issued a few years prior. The purpose of the WOTUS rule is to clarify which US waterbodies are subject to CWA protection, something that has been the subject of considerable uncertainty and controversy for decades. The issue stems from the ambiguity of the 1972 Clean Water Act and a split 2006 Supreme Court decision in the *Rapanos v. United States* case, which muddled jurisdiction for EPA when issuing pollution permits and for the US Army Corps of Engineers when issuing wetlands permits.

The 2015 rule put in place by EPA during the Obama administration met opposition from agriculture and business interests, as well as political officials who viewed the Obama WOTUS rule to be a vast overreach of federal authority. In leading a lawsuit against the rule, Scott Pruitt (serving at the time as Oklahoma Attorney General) said, "Respect for private property rights have allowed our nation to thrive, but with the recently finalized [WOTUS] rule, farmers, ranchers, developers, industry and individual property owners will now be subject to the unpredictable, unsound, and often byzantine regulatory regime of the EPA."[80] The new rule, known as the Navigable Waters Protection Rule, replaced regulations that had been in place since the Reagan administration and defined the waters of the United States in a much narrower way compared to the Obama-era version. The revised WOTUS rule eliminates federal protections for more than half of all wetlands and nearly a fifth of streams that do not have relatively permanent surface water connections to nearby waterways (states, if they choose, can protect these resources).[81] In announcing the decision, EPA Administrator Wheeler said that the agency and the US Army Corps of Engineers are "providing much needed regulatory certainty and predictability for American farmers, landowners, and businesses to support the economy and accelerate critical infrastructure projects."[82]

Unsurprisingly, EPA's decision to narrow the jurisdiction of the CWA has been met with strong opposition from many environmental organizations, and is certain to face legal challenge. One of the grounds for the legal challenge will be whether there is a sufficient scientific basis to justify EPA's revised interpretation of the CWA. The agency's Science Advisory Board strongly concluded that the rule lacked scientific support. Specifically, the Science Advisory Board found that the agency had completely ignored its own prior analysis of watershed systems and processes, concluding that "the proposed Rule lacks a scientific justification, while potentially introducing new risks to human and environmental health."[83]

The deregulatory actions at EPA during the Trump presidency, as illustrated by the cases of ACE rule, SAFE Vehicles rule, and the Navigable Waters Protection rule, have a couple of common threads. First, the policy retrenchment of the past few years reflects more than just a change in policy direction. It is not at all unusual for agencies to shift focus and revisit past decisions when there is a new presidential administration. But, the recent activities at EPA represent something qualitatively different in their scope and intent, reflecting a deliberate and systematic effort to shift the very mission of the agency from protecting human health and the environment to reducing regulatory burden and curtailing the role of the federal government in providing environmental protection. This motivation is in plain sight, and is illustrated in comments from Administrators Pruitt and Wheeler when announcing the agency's policy reversals. The motivation is also reflected in recent budgets. Take for example EPA's FY2018 budget blueprint, the first budget during the Trump presidency, which called for a thirty percent reduction in EPA spending, as well as a twenty-five percent decrease in the number of employees (subsequent budget proposals called for similar reductions).[84]

A second thread running through EPA's recent deregulatory agenda is a pattern of writing new regulations with dubious technical or scientific justification. In support of its regulations, the agency has repeatedly produced questionable economic and scientific analyses, at times completely sidelining career officials with extensive expertise attained from decades of experience. The agency's Science Advisory Board, which includes many of the Trump administrations' own appointees, has regularly admonished the agency for its errors and for neglecting to base rules on established science. For an agency that has long relied on advancing science to carry out its mission, the diminishment of its use in decision-making is alarming. As I discuss in the next section, the lack of scientific rigor is part of a broader campaign to devalue the importance of science at EPA.

Reducing Scientific Input and Capacity

EPA during the Trump presidency has moved to fundamentally change the use of science in agency decision-making. These efforts are not only to justify policy rollbacks, but also to limit the capacity of *future* administrations. The scope of the changes includes limiting the types of scientific studies that the agency can use and reducing the input from scientists themselves.

Potentially the most consequential effort is a plan that would require EPA to give preference to scientific studies that have publicly available data. Officially, the plan is known as the Strengthening Transparency in Regulatory Science rule, though colloquially it is referred to as the "Secret Science" rule. The agency initially proposed the rule in April 2018, and then released an updated version in March 2020.[85] Critics fear that the rule will be used, for example, to discard or discount landmark studies supporting air pollution control standards, such as Harvard's Six Cities Study, which is especially important in providing scientific justification for regulating PM2.5. Other areas of decision-making that could be affected include rules on lead and water contaminants regulated under the SDWA.[86] Consistent with standard practice in medical and public health research, these types of studies do not release all their individual level data in order to protect the confidentiality of study subjects.[87] In a review of the updated version of the proposal, EPA's Science Advisory Board concluded: "There is minimal justification provided in the Proposed Rule for why existing procedures and norms utilized across the US scientific community, including the federal government, are inadequate, and how the Proposed Rule will improve transparency and the scientific integrity of the regulatory outcomes in an effective and efficient manner." The Science Advisory Board went on to say that: "It is plausible that in some situations, the Proposed Rule will decrease efficiency and reduce scientific integrity, determining if in fact that will be the case requires a thorough and thoughtful examination that is currently absent in the Proposed Rule. Moving forward with altered transparency requirements beyond those already in use, in the absence of such a robust analysis, risks serious and perverse outcomes."[88]

The agency is also taking measures to curtail the input it receives from scientists, including those that serve on external advisory boards. In general, the Trump administration has initiated plans to limit the use of federal advisory committees; in June 2019, the White House issued an order to federal agencies to reduce by one-third the number of federal advisory boards.[89] EPA leadership, for its part, has taken several specific steps in this direction. In October 2017, EPA Administrator Pruitt changed the rules about who may serve on scientific panels that advise the agency. Specifically, the new policy barred scientists who had previously received EPA research grants, but it did not put in place a similar restriction for scientists who had received industry funding (as of this writing, the rules are subject to legal challenge). A Government Accountability Office study that reviewed this policy concluded that this decision shifted the representation on the Science Advisory Board and the Clean Air Scientific Advisory Committee (CASAC) away from academic scientists and toward industry representatives.[90] Also with respect to the Science Advisory Board, Administrator Wheeler proposed to empower the chair of the board, in consultation with the EPA Administrator, to decide which rules deserve scrutiny. This proposal would undo longstanding practice which more broadly includes input from the full forty-four-member panel.[91]

EPA has traditionally relied on these types of independent advisory boards to help it make scientifically based judgments when setting pollution standards. In one striking example of how this has changed in recent years, Administrator Wheeler (at the time, serving in an acting capacity), disbanded two expert panels that reported to the CASAC. Specifically, Wheeler dismissed panels of scientists that reviewed NAAQS for particulate matter and ozone, leaving the review of these standards to the CASAC itself which is not comprised of scientists with the same expertise.[92] This decision has proven consequential. A year after Wheeler did away with the special panel on particulate matter, the CASAC decided to leave the NAAQS annual standard for PM2.5 at its current level. Not only did this decision diverge from EPA staff's recommendation that the standard needed to be tightened to protect human health,[93] but it conflicted with the assessment of the particulate matter panel itself. The scientists on that disbanded panel decided to deliberate on their own accord after having been dismissed, and recommended that the PM2.5 standard be strengthened even more than had been suggested by EPA staff.[94]

EPA during the Trump administration has also made efforts to reduce its internal scientific capacity. As one illustration, the administration defunded thirteen children's health centers located nationwide that EPA has for many years jointly sponsored with the National Institute of Environmental Sciences.[95] More generally, EPA has proposed drastic cuts to the budget of EPA's Office of Research Development, which houses much of the agency's scientists working on air pollution, water pollution, chemicals, and other issues. In its Fiscal Year 2018 budget, EPA proposed reducing its budget for research and development by $200 million, representing a 44 percent decline.[96] Subsequent budgets have proposed similar cuts, though each year Congress has continued funding these programs at much higher levels.

Collectively, these efforts to limit the use of science and the role of scientists threaten the credibility and the capacity of the agency to carry out its mission. What is so striking is that the challenges are coming from *within* the agency itself. As the chapters of this book have made clear, the regulatory decisions of EPA are consequential, and for the entire fifty-year history of the agency, various stakeholders (e.g., industry, environmental groups, the White House, other federal agencies) have frequently raised questions about the scientific and technical justifications for EPA decisions. To buttress its mission, the agency has over the decades invested in its own scientific capacity in response, and this investment has served the agency well. The current efforts are a deliberate effort to diminish if not dismantle this capacity and, in so doing, represent not only an affront to the career staff at EPA, but a disservice to the public that the agency is supposed to protect.

EPA has contributed in immeasurable ways to the vast improvements in environmental quality that the United States has experienced over the past half century. As summarized earlier in the chapter, and in much more depth throughout this book, EPA's implementation of federal environmental laws has generated better air and water quality, safer drinking water, improved handling and use of chemicals, and more careful disposal of waste. EPA has made these contributions through the skillful leadership of numerous Administrators and senior managers and with the dedication of a capable workforce. The agency has brought policy creativity and diligence to its large and complicated workload, and historically done so leveraging the substantial technical expertise it has developed to pursue the agency's mission. Considering the modest size of the agency, both in terms of budget and personnel, EPA's environmental protection achievements are substantial, and the fifty-year history of the agency is mostly a story of success.

Notwithstanding this tremendous progress, there remain many important environmental problems for the United States to confront. This chapter identified a number of these problems, including smog and small particulates in the air, lead and PFAS contamination in drinking water, and agricultural pollution of the nation's waterways. These and other problems can largely be addressed through improved and expanded use of current laws, policies, and programs. Other problems, such as climate change and environmental justice, will require new initiatives and perhaps a broader reimagination of the role of the federal government in providing environmental protection.

As EPA looks towards its next half century, the agency must play a central role in addressing these and other challenges. To do so effectively, however, the politics in and around EPA need to change. As this chapter has described, the current political leadership of the agency threatens its very mission, both in the short-term with its unprecedented policy retrenchment and in the long-term with its calculated and systematic efforts to diminish the use of science and expertise in its decision-making. The agency can likely withstand the current assault on its mission and capacity, but these recent developments will soon need to be reversed if the agency is to avert lasting damage. This can be done with new leadership, additional resources, and a rebuilding of lost human capital and technical capacity. None of this will be easy. The political polarization that generally characterizes American politics now permeates US environmental policy. It would be naïve to suggest that politics can simply be removed from environmental policy. Yet, it is worth harkening back to the time when EPA was established. Not only was there a wide consensus among the American public that environmental protection was important, but there was a belief that the federal government, using science as a guide, was up to the challenge of providing it. And, most importantly, these views were largely shared across the political divide. At a June 2019 congressional hearing,[97] four former EPA administrators—Lee Thomas, William Reilly, Christine Todd Whitman, and Gina McCarthy—all stated that the direction in which EPA leadership has taken the agency during the Trump presidency is unacceptable. These former top EPA officials, three serving under Republican presidents and one serving under a Democratic president, all agreed that an effective and successful EPA will require a return to bipartisan support and a commitment to science. The fifty-year history of the agency suggests that this is sage advice.

NOTES

1. The author thanks Jim Barnes, John Graham, and Megan Mullin for helpful comments and suggestions.

2. Richard Nixon, Annual Message to the Congress on the State of the Union, Online by Gerhard Peters and John T. Woolley, The American Presidency Project, https://www.presidency.ucsb.edu/node/241063.

3. Donald J. Trump, Address Before a Joint Session of the Congress on the State of the Union, Online by Gerhard Peters and John T. Woolley, The American Presidency Project, https://www.presidency.ucsb.edu/node/335440.

4. The US became the leading producer of natural gas in 2011, five years before President Trump took office, and the leading producer in 2018 well before most of the administration's regulatory rollbacks went into effect. See US Energy Information Administration, "The US Leads Global Petroleum and Natural Gas Production with Record Growth in 2018," *eia.gov,* August 20, 2019, https://www.eia.gov/todayinenergy/detail.php?id=40973.

5. Quoted in John E. Reeder, *Moving Forward: Future Directions for EPA and Environmental Protection* (Washington, DC: American University School of Public Affairs, Center for Environmental Policy, December 2019), 3.

6. US Environmental Protection Agency, *The Benefits and Costs of the Clean Air Act, 1970-1990,* Retrospective Study EPA-410-R-97-002 (Washington, DC: EPA, October 15, 1997); US Environmental Protection Agency, *The Benefits and Costs of the Clean Air Act, 1990-2020*, Prospective Study (Washington, DC: EPA, March 1, 2011).

7. EPA, *Benefits and Costs, 1970-1990*; EPA, *Benefits and Costs, 1990-2020.*

8. Jim Hanlon et al., *Water Quality: A Half Century of Progress* (Washington, DC: EPA Alumni Association, April 2020).

9. Hanlon et al., *Water Quality*.

10. David A. Keiser and Joseph S. Shapiro, "Consequences of the Clean Water Act and the Demand for Water Quality," *The Quarterly Journal of Economics* 134, no. 1 (2019): 349-96.

11. David A. Keiser, Catherine L. Kling, and Joseph S. Shapiro. "The Low But Uncertain Measured Benefits of US Water Quality Policy," *Proceedings of the National Academy of Sciences* 116, no. 12 (2019): 5262-69.

12. US Environmental Protection Agency, "National Primary Drinking Water Regulations," *epa.gov,* accessed February 7, 2020, https://www.epa.gov/ground-water-and-drinking-water/national-primary-drinking-water-regulations#Radionuclides.

13. Maura Allaire , Haowei Wu, and Upmanu Lall, "National Trends in Drinking Water Quality Violations," *Proceedings of the National Academy of Sciences* 115, no. 9 (2018): 2078-83; David M. Konisky and Manuel P. Teodoro, "When Governments

Regulate Governments," *American Journal of Political Science* 60, no. 3 (2016): 559-74.

14. Victor Kimm, Joseph Cotruvo, and Arden Calvert, *Drinking Water: A Half Century of Progress* (Washington, DC: EPA Alumni Association, April 2020).

15. More specifically, the EPA estimated that there was a need of $312.6 billion to replace or refurbish aging or deteriorating pipelines, $83 billion to construct, expand, or rehabilitate infrastructure to reduce contamination, $47.6 billion to construct, rehabilitate, or cover water storage reservoirs, and $21.8 billion to construct or rehabilitate intake structures, wells, and spring collectors. See US Environmental Protection Agency, *Drinking Water Infrastructure Needs Survey and Assessment, Sixth Report to Congress* (Washington, DC: EPA, March 2018).

16. Marianne Horinko et al., *Waste Management: A Half Century of Progress* (Washington, DC: EPA Alumni Association, April 2020).

17. Horinko et al., *Waste Management.*

18. Ibid.

19. Katherine N. Probst and David M. Konisky, *Superfund's Future: What Will it Cost?* (Washington, DC: Resources for the Future, 2001).

20. The health effects related to Love Canal are much less clear than is conventionally assumed. See Allan Mazur, *A Hazardous Inquiry: The Rashomon Effect at Love Canal* (Cambridge, MA: Harvard University Press, 1998).

21. US Environmental Protection Agency, "Superfund: National Priorities List (NPL)," *epa.gov,* accessed February 27, 2020, https://www.epa.gov/superfund/superfund-national-priorities-list-npl.

22. Probst and Konisky, *Superfund's Future.*

23. James T. Hamilton and W. Kip Viscusi, "How Costly is 'Clean'? An Analysis of the Benefits and Costs of Superfund Site Remediations," *Journal of Policy Analysis and Management* 18, no. 1 (1999): 2-27.

24. Michael Greenstone and Justin Gallagher, "Does Hazardous Waste Matter? Evidence from the Housing Market and the Superfund Program," *The Quarterly Journal of Economics* 123, no. 3 (2008): 951-1003.

25. Frank R. Baumgartner and Bryan D. Jones, *Agendas and Instability in American Politics* (Chicago: University of Chicago Press, 2010).

26. Susan Wayland and Penelope Fenner-Crisp, *Reducing Pesticide Risks: A Half Century of Progress* (Washington, DC: EPA Alumni Association, March 1, 2016).

27. Wayland and Fenner-Crisp, *Reducing Pesticide Risks.*

28. Bruce A. Ackerman and William T. Hassler, "Beyond the New Deal: Coal and the Clean Air Act," *Yale Law Journal* 89, no. 8 (1980): 1466-1571.

29. US Environmental Protection Agency, "Ozone (O3) Standards: Integrated Science Assessments from Review Completed in 2015," *epa.gov,* accessed March 10, 2020, https://www.epa.gov/naaqs/ozone-o3-standards-integrated-science-assessments-review-completed-2015.

30. Ellen M. Gilmer, "D.C. Circuit Largely Upholds Obama Ozone Standards," *E&E News*, August 23, 2019, https://www.eenews.net/stories/1061043675.

31. Daniel J. Fiorino, *The New Environmental Regulation* (Cambridge, MA: MIT Press, 2006).

32. US Environmental Protection Agency, "Summary Nonattainment Area Population Exposure Report (Green Book)," *epa.gov,* last updated March 31, 2020, https://www3.epa.gov/airquality/greenbook/popexp.html.

33. Daniel M. Sullivan and Alan Krupnick, *Using Satellite Data to Fill the Gaps in the US Air Pollution Monitoring Network*, working paper (Washington, DC: Resources for the Future, 2018).

34. US Environmental Protection Agency, "Our Nation's Air: Status and Trends Through 2018," accessed April 21, 2020, https://gispub.epa.gov/air/trendsreport/2019/#welcome.

35. Karen Clay and Nicholas Z. Muller, *Recent Increases in Air Pollution: Evidence and Implications for Mortality*, No. w26381 (Washington, DC: National Bureau of Economic Research, 2019).

36. Mona Hanna-Attisha, Jenny LaChance, Richard Casey Sadler, and Allison Champney Schnepp, "Elevated Blood Lead Levels in Children Associated with the Flint Drinking Water Crisis: A Spatial Analysis of Risk and Public Health Response," *American Journal of Public Health* 106, no. 2 (2016): 283-90.

37. Flint Water Advisory Task Force, *Final Report* (Lansing, MI: FWATF, March 2016), 54.

38. US Environmental Protection Agency, *Management Alert: Drinking Water Contamination in Flint, Michigan, Demonstrates a Need to Clarify EPA Authority to Issue Emergency Orders to Protect Public Health*, 17-P-0004 (Washington, DC: EPA, October 20, 2016).

39. US Environmental Protection Agency, *Management Weaknesses Delayed Response to Flint Water Crisis*, 18-P-0221 (Washington, DC: EPA, July 19, 2018).

40. US Environmental Protection Agency, *Strategies to Achieve Full Lead Service Line Replacement*, EPA 810-R-19-003 (Washington, DC: EPA, October 2019).

41. US Environmental Protection Agency "Basic Information on PFAS," *epa.gov,* accessed March 16, 2020, https://www.epa.gov/pfas/basic-information-pfas.

42. US Environmental Protection Agency "EPA and 3M Announce Phase Out of PFOS," *epa.gov,* May 16, 2000, https://yosemite.epa.gov/opa/admpress.nsf/0/33aa946e6cb11f35852568e1005246b4?opendocument; Daniel J. DeNoon, "EPA Urges Teflon Chemical Ban: DuPont Agrees to Phase-Out of Worrisome Pollutant PFOA," *WebMD*, January 27, 2006, https://www.webmd.com/a-to-z-guides/news/20060127/epa-urges-teflon-chemical-ban#1; Alina Tugend, "Teflon is Great for Politicians, But is it Safe for Regular People," *New York Times*, October 14, 2006, https://www.nytimes.com/2006/10/14/business/teflon-is-great-for-politicians-but-is-it-safe-for-regular-people.html.

43. US Environmental Protection Agency "Fact Sheet: 2010/2015 PFOA Stewardship Program," *epa.gov,* accessed April 8, 2020, https://www.epa.gov/assessing-and-managing-chemicals-under-tsca/fact-sheet-20102015-pfoa-stewardship-program#what.

44. US Environmental Protection Agency, "EPA Announces Proposed Decision to Regulate PFOA and PFOS in Drinking Water," *epa.gov,* February 20, 2020; US Environmental Protection Agency, "Interim Recommendations for Addressing Groundwater Contaminated with PFOA and PFOS," *epa.gov,* December 19, 2019.

45. Pamela Goodwin, Keith Williams, and Melissa Clarke, "Insight: EPA Moves Toward Setting Drinking Water PFAS Health Standard," *Bloomberg Law Environment & Energy Report*, April 9, 2020, https://news.bloomberglaw.com/environment-and-energy/insight-epa-moves-toward-setting-drinking-water-pfas-health-standard.

46. Jared Hayes and David Andrews, "'Forever Chemicals' in Over 500 NJ Water Systems and Sources – More Than 1,000 Contaminated Sites Nationwide," *Environmental Working Group News*, November 5, 2019, https://www.ewg.org/news-and-analysis/2019/10/forever-chemicals-almost-200-nj-water-systems-and-sources-more-1000.

47. Emma G. Fitzsimmons, "Tap Water Ban for Toledo Residents," *New York Times*, August 3, 2014, https://www.nytimes.com/2014/08/04/us/toledo-faces-second-day-of-water-ban.html.

48. US Environmental Protection Agency, "Water Quality Assessment and TMDL Information," *epa.gov*, accessed March 16, 2020, https://ofmpub.epa.gov/waters10/attains_index.home.

49. EPA, "Water Quality Assessment and TMDL Information."

50. US Government Accountability Office, *Nonpoint Source Pollution: Greater Oversight and Additional Data Needed for Key EPA Water Program*, GAO-12-335 (Washington, DC: GAO, July 2, 2012).

51. US Government Accountability Office, *Clean Water Act: Changes Needed if Key EPA Program Is to Help Fulfill the Nation's Water Quality Goals*, GAO-14-80 (Washington, DC: GAO, January 13, 2014).

52. Evan J. Ringquist, "Assessing Evidence of Environmental Inequities: A Meta-Analysis," *Journal of Policy Analysis and Management* 24, no. 2 (2005): 223-47; Paul Mohai, David Pellow, and J. Timmons Roberts, "Environmental Justice," *Annual Review of Environment and Resources* 34 (2009): 405-30; Spencer Banzhaf, Lala Ma, and Christopher Timmins, "Environmental Justice: The Economics of Race, Place, and Pollution," *Journal of Economic Perspectives* 33, no. 1 (2019): 185-208.

53. See, for example, Michelle L. Bell and Francesca Dominici, "Effect Modification by Community Characteristics on the Short-term Effects of Ozone Exposure and Mortality in 98 US Communities," *American Journal of Epidemiology* 167, no. 8 (2008): 986-97; Benjamin J. Apelberg, Timothy J. Buckley, and Ronald H. White, "Socioeconomic and Racial Disparities in Cancer Risk from Air Toxics in Maryland," *Environmental Health Perspectives* 113, no. 6 (2005): 693-99; Scott L. Zeger et al., "Mortality in the Medicare Population and Chronic Exposure to Fine Particulate Air Pollution in Urban Centers (2000–2005)," *Environmental Health Perspectives* 116, no. 12 (2008): 1614-19; Steven Babin et al., "Medicaid Patient Asthma-related Acute Care Visits and their Associations with Ozone and Particulates in Washington, DC, from 1994–2005," *International Journal of Environmental Health Research* 18, no. 3 (2008): 209-21; Yan Wang et al., "Estimating Causal Effects of Long-term PM2.5 Exposure on Mortality in New Jersey," *Environmental Health Perspectives* 124, no. 8 (2016): 1182-88; Marie Lynn Miranda et al., "Making the Environmental Justice Grade: The Relative Burden of Air Pollution Exposure in the United States," *International Journal of Environmental Research and Public Health* 8, no. 6 (2011): 1755-71; Zhengyan Li, David M. Konisky, and Nikolaos

Zirogiannis, "Racial, Ethnic, and Income Disparities in Air Pollution: A Study of Excess Emissions in Texas," *PLOS ONE* 14, no. 8 (2019).

54. Ringquist, "Assessing Evidence of Environmental Inequities."

55. Yolanda J. McDonald and Nicole E. Jones, "Drinking Water Violations and Environmental Justice in the United States, 2011–2015," *American Journal of Public Health* 108, no. 10 (2018): 1401-7; David Switzer and Manuel P. Teodoro, "Class, Race, Ethnicity, and Justice in Safe Drinking Water Compliance," *Social Science Quarterly* 99, no. 2 (2018): 524-35.

56. Banzhaf, Ma, and Timmins, "Environmental Justice: The Economics of Race, Place, and Pollution."

57. David M. Konisky, "Inequities in Enforcement? Environmental Justice and Government Performance," *Journal of Policy Analysis and Management* 28, no. 1 (2009): 102-21; David M. Konisky and Tyler S. Schario, "Examining Environmental Justice in Facility-Level Regulatory Enforcement," *Social Science Quarterly* 91, no. 3 (2010): 835-55; David M. Konisky and Christopher Reenock, "Regulatory Enforcement, Riskscapes, and Environmental Justice," *Policy Studies Journal* 46, no. 1 (2018): 7-36; Switzer and Teodoro, "Class, Race, Ethnicity, and Justice."

58. David M. Konisky, ed., *Failed Promises: Evaluating the Federal Government's Response to Environmental Justice* (Cambridge, MA: MIT Press, 2015).

59. Konisky, ed., *Failed Promises*.

60. Jill Lindsey Harrison, *From the Inside Out: The Fight for Environmental Justice within Government Agencies* (Cambridge, MA: MIT Press, 2019).

61. Reeder, *Moving Forward: Future Directions for EPA and Environmental Protection*.

62. Coral Davenport, Lisa Friedman, and Maggie Haberman, "E.P.A. Chief Scott Pruitt Resigns Under a Cloud of Ethics Scandals," *New York Times*, July 5, 2018, https://www.nytimes.com/2018/07/05/climate/scott-pruitt-epa-trump.html; Coral Davenport, "How Andrew Wheeler, the New Acting E.P.A. Chief, Differs from Scott Pruitt," *New York Times*, July 5, 2018, https://www.nytimes.com/2018/07/05/climate/wheeler-epa-pruitt.html.

63. David M. Konisky and Neal D. Woods, "Environmental Federalism and the Trump Presidency: A Preliminary Assessment," *Publius: The Journal of Federalism* 48, no. 3 (2018): 345-71.

64. Nadja Popovich, Livia Albeck-Ripka, and Kendra Pierre-Louis, "95 Environmental Rules Being Rolled Back Under Trump," *New York Times*, last modified December 21, 2019, https://www.nytimes.com/interactive/2019/climate/trump-environment-rollbacks.html.

65. Popovich, Albeck-Ripka, and Pierre-Louis, "95 Environmental Rules."

66. NYU Institute for Policy Integrity, "Roundup: Trump-Era Agency Policy in the Courts," *New York University School of Law*, last modified April 20, 2020, https://policyintegrity.org/trump-court-roundup.

67. Popovich, Albeck-Ripka, and Pierre-Louis, "95 Environmental Rules."

68. Ibid.

69. Maxine Joselow, "EPA, Calif. Plan for Trucks: 'Cooler Heads are Prevailing'," *E&E News*, January 30, 2020, https://www.eenews.net/stories/1062210673.

70. Eric Lipton and Coral Davenport, "Scott Pruitt, Trump's EPA Pick, Backed Industry Donors over Regulators," *New York Times*, January 14, 2017, https://www.nytimes.com/2017/01/14/us/scott-pruitt-trump-epa-pick.html.

71. US Environmental Protection Agency, "EPA Takes Another Step to Advance President Trump's America First Strategy, Proposes Repeal of 'Clean Power Plan,'" *epa.gov*, October 10, 2017.

72. US Environmental Protection Agency, *Final Determination on the Appropriateness of the Model Year 2022-2025 Light-Duty Vehicle Greenhouse Gas Emissions Standards under the Midterm Evaluation*, EPA-420-R-17-001 (Washington, DC: EPA, January 2017).

73. US Environmental Protection Agency, *Mid-Term of Greenhouse Gas Emissions Standards for Model Year 2022-2025 Light-Duty Vehicles*, EPA-HQ-OAR-2015-0827 (Washington, DC: EPA, April 2018).

74. US Environmental Protection Agency, "US DOT and EPA Put Safety and American Families First with Final Rule on Fuel Economy Standards," *epa.gov,* March 31, 2020.

75. National Highway Traffic Safety Administration and US Environmental Protection Agency, *Final Regulatory Impact Analysis: The Safer Affordable Fuel-Efficient (SAFE) Vehicles Rule for Model Year 2021-2026 Passenger Cars and Light Trucks* (Washington, DC: NHTSA, EPA, March 2020), https://www.nhtsa.gov/sites/nhtsa.dot.gov/files/documents/final_safe_fria_web_version_200330.pdf.

76. Maxine Joselow, "Trump's Car Rule would Cause more Pollution Deaths," *E&E News*, April 2, 2020, https://www.eenews.net/stories/1062763069.

77. US Environmental Protection Agency, Science Advisory Board, *Science Advisory Board (SAB) Consideration of the Scientific and Technical Basis of the EPA's Proposed Rule titled The Safer Affordable Fuel-Efficient (SAFE) Vehicles Rule 2021-2026 Passenger Cars and Light Trucks*, EPA-SAB-20-003 (Washington, DC: EPA SAB, February 27, 2020).

78. Robinson Meyer, "'We Knew They Had Cooked the Books,'" *The Atlantic*, February 12, 2020, https://www.theatlantic.com/science/archive/2020/02/an-inside-account-of-trumps-fuel-economy-debacle/606346/.

79. Hiroko Tabuchi and Neal E. Boudette, "Automakers Sought Looser Rules. Now They Hope to Stop Trump From Going Too Far," *New York Times*, May 9, 2018, https://www.nytimes.com/2018/05/09/climate/automakers-fuel-economy-trump.html.

80. Curtis Killman, "Oklahoma Attorney General Scott Pruitt Sues EPA—Again," *Tulsa World*, July 9, 2015, https://www.tulsaworld.com/news/local/crime-and-courts/oklahoma-attorney-general-scott-pruitt-sues-epa-again/article_c603ba08-dd62-5b0a-ad3e-e4b8d0e2d977.html.

81. Ariel Wittenberg, "Trump's WOTUS: Clear as Mud, Scientists Say," *E&E News*, February 18, 2019, https://www.eenews.net/stories/1060121251; Ariel Wittenberg, "Democrats Vow to Battle Trump's WOTUS Rule," *E&E News*, January 24, 2020, https://www.eenews.net/eedaily/stories/1062161147.

82. US Environmental Protection Agency, "EPA and Army Deliver on President Trump's Promise to Issue the Navigable Waters Protection Rule – A New Definition of WOTUS," *epa.gov,* January 23, 2020.

83. US Environmental Protection Agency, Science Advisory Board, *Commentary on the Proposed Rule Defining the Scope of Waters Federally Regulated Under the Clean Water Act*, EPA-SAB-20-002 (Washington, DC: EPA SAB, February 27, 2020).

84. US Environmental Protection Agency, *FY2018 EPA Budget in Brief*, EPA-190-K-17-001 (Washington, DC: EPA, May 2017).

85. US Environmental Protection Agency "Strengthening Transparency in Regulatory Science," *epa.gov,* accessed April 29, 2020, https://www.epa.gov/osa/strengthening-transparency-regulatory-science.

86. Kelsey Brugger, "Trump Admin Advances High-Impact 'Secret Science' Rule," *E&E News*, November 12, 2019, https://www.eenews.net/stories/1061531673.

87. Brugger, "Trump Admin Expands Reach."

88. EPA SAB, *Consideration of the Scientific and Technical Basis of EPA's Proposed Rule Titled Strengthening Transparency in Regulatory Science*.

89. Brad Plumer and Coral Davenport, "Science Under Attack: How Trump Is Sidelining Researchers and Their Work," *New York Times*, December 28, 2019, https://www.nytimes.com/2019/12/28/climate/trump-administration-war-on-science.html.

90. US Government Accountability Office, *EPA Advisory Committees: Improvements Needed for the Member Appointment Process*, GAO-19-280 (Washington, DC: GAO, July 8, 2019).

91. Sean Reilly, "Wheeler's Science Advisory Board Revamp Plan Sparks Concerns," *E&E News*, December 10, 2019, https://www.eenews.net/greenwire/2019/12/10/stories/1061775673.

92. Cheryl Hogue, "EPA Scrubs Science Panels on Air Pollution," *Chemical & Engineering News*, October 20, 2018, https://cen.acs.org/environment/pollution/EPA-scrubs-science-panels-air/96/i42.

93. Cheryl Hogue, "US EPA's Science Advisers Split on Tightening Air Pollution Limit," *Chemical & Engineering News*, November 10, 2019, https://cen.acs.org/environment/pollution/US-EPAs-science-advisers-split/97/i44; Sean Reilly, "Trump's Soot Proposal Bucks Advice of EPA Career Staff," *E&E News*, April 14, 2020, https://www.eenews.net/stories/1062872411.

94. Independent Particulate Matter Review Panel, "Advice from the Independent Particulate Matter Review Panel (formerly EPA CASAC Particulate Matter Review Panel) on EPA's Policy Assessment for the Review of the National Ambient Air Quality Standards for Particulate Matter (External Review Draft – September 2019)," letter to EPA Administrator Andrew Wheeler, October 22, 2019, https://ucs-documents.s3.amazonaws.com/science-and-democracy/IPMRP-FINAL-LETTER-ON-DRAFT-PA-191022.pdf.

95. Plumer and Davenport, "Science Under Attack."

96. EPA, *FY2018 EPA Budget in Brief.*

97. United States Congress, House, Committee on Energy & Commerce, "Hearing on 'Critical Mission: Former Administrators Address the Direction of the EPA,'" *energycommerce.house.gov,* June 11, 2019, https://energycommerce.house.gov/committee-activity/hearings/hearing-on-critical-mission-former-administrators-address-the-direction.

Appendix

List of Administrators of US Environmental Protection Agency

Administrator	*Period Served*
William D. Ruckelshaus	December 4, 1970–April 30, 1973
Russell E. Train	September 13, 1973–January 20, 1977
Douglas M. Costle	March 7, 1977–January 20, 1981
Anne M. Gorsuch (Buford)	May 20, 1981–March 9, 1983
William D. Ruckelshaus	May 18, 1983–January 4, 1985
Lee M. Thomas	February 8, 1985–January 20, 1989
William K. Reilly	February 6, 1989–January 20, 1993
Carol N. Browner	January 22, 1993–January 19, 2001
Christine Todd Whitman	January 31, 2001–June 27, 2003
Michael O. Leavitt	November 6, 2003–January 25, 2005
Stephen L. Johnson	May 2, 2005–January 20, 2009
Lisa P. Jackson	January 26, 2009–February 14, 2013
Gina McCarthy	July 19, 2013–January 20, 2017
Scott Pruitt	February 17, 2017–July 6, 2018
Andrew Wheeler	February 28, 2019–present

Note: List only includes EPA Administrators that received Senate confirmation, and excludes those that served in an acting capacity.

Bibliography

"40+ Groups Oppose Attacks on Vital Clean Water Act Safeguard." *Clean Water Action*, April 17, 2018. https://www.cleanwateraction.org/publications/40-groups-oppose-attacks-vital-clean-water-act-safeguard.

"A Costly Order to Auto Makers: Clean Up Car Exhausts by 1975." *US News and World Report*, May 22, 1972.

Abelkop, Adam D. K., Agnes Botos, Lois Wise, and John D. Graham. "Regulating Industrial Chemicals: Lessons for US Lawmakers from the European Union's REACH Program." *Environmental Law Reporter* 42, no. 11 (2012): 1042–65.

Abelkop, Adam D. K., and John D. Graham. "Regulation of Chemical Risks: Lessons for Reform of the Toxic Substances Control Act from Canada and the European Union." *Pace Environmental Law Review* 32, no. 1 (2015).

Ackerman, Bruce A., and William T. Hassler. "Beyond the New Deal: Coal and the Clean Air Act." *Yale Law Journal* 89, no. 8 (1980): 1466–1571.

———. *Clean Coal/Dirty Air: Or How the Clean Air Act Became a Multibillion-Dollar Bail-out for High-Sulfur Coal Producers and What Should Be Done about It*. 23. New Haven: Yale University Press, 1981.

Ackerman, Bruce A., and Richard B. Stewart. "Reforming Environmental Law." *Stanford Law Review* 37 (1985).

Adler, E. Scott, and John D. Wilkerson. *Congress and the Politics of Problem Solving*. Cambridge: Cambridge University Press, 2012.

Adler, Jonathan H. "Fables of the Cuyahoga: Reconstructing a History of Environmental Protection." *Fordham Environmental Law Journal* 14 (2002): 89–145.

Adler, Robert W. "Resilience, Restoration, and Sustainability: Revisiting the Fundamental Principles of the Clean Water Act." *Washington University Journal of Law & Policy* 32, no. 1 (2010).

Aizer, Anna, Janet Currie, Peter Simon, and Patrick Vivier. "Do Low Levels of Blood Lead Reduce Children's Future Test Scores?" *American Journal of Applied Economics* 10, no. 1 (2018): 307–41.

Ajami, Newsha K., Barton H. Thompson Jr., and David G. Victor. "The Path to Water Innovation." Washington, DC: The Hamilton Project, 2014. https://www.hamiltonproject.org/papers/the_path_to_water_innovation.

Aldy, Joseph E., Maximillian Auffhammer, Maureen Cropper, Arthur Fraas, and Richard Morgenstern. "Looking Back at 50 Years of the Clean Air Act." Washington, DC: Resources for the Future, January 2020. https://scholar.harvard.edu/files/jaldy/files/wp_20-01_looking_back_at_fifty_years_of_the_clean_air_act_v2_1.pdf.

Aldy, Joseph E., Matthew J. Kotchen, Mary Evans, Meredith Fowlie, Arik Levinson, and Karen Palmer. "Report on the Proposed Changes to the Federal Mercury and Air Toxics Standards." Washington, DC: External Environmental Economics Advisory Committee, December 2019. https://cb4388c0-f641-4b7b-a3ad-281c0e6f8e88.filesusr.com/ugd/669644_35b6835a3c26451680bae954f11d2282.pdf.

Allaire, Maura, Haowei Wu, and Upmanu Lall. "National Trends in Drinking Water Quality Violations." *Proceedings of the National Academy of Science* 115, no. 9 (February 27, 2018): 2078–83.

American Society of Civil Engineers. "2017 Infrastructure Report Card." Reston, VA: ASCE, 2017.

Andersen, Stephen O., Marcel L. Halberstadt, and Nathan Borgford-Parnell. "Stratospheric Ozone, Global Warming, and the Principle of Unintended Consequences—An Ongoing Science and Policy Success Story." *Journal of the Air & Waste Management Association* 63 (2013): 607–47.

Anderson, James E. *Public Policy-Making*. London: Thomas Nelson & Sons Ltd., 1974.

Anderson, Robert C., and Paul Kobrin. "Introduction to Environmental Economics Research at the EPA." Washington, DC: Environmental Law Institute, 1998.

Andrews, Edmund L. "Bush Angers Europe by Eroding Pact on Warming." *New York Times*, April 1, 2001. https://perma.cc/P97Z-7XT3.

Andrews, Richard N. L. *Managing the Environment, Managing Ourselves: A History of American Environmental Policy*. 2nd ed. New Haven, CT: Yale University Press, 2006.

Apelberg, Benjamin J., Timothy J. Buckley, and Ronald H. White. "Socioeconomic and Racial Disparities in Cancer Risk from Air Toxics in Maryland." *Environmental Health Perspectives* 113, no. 6 (2005): 693–99.

Arceneaux, Kevin, and Martin Johnson. *Changing Minds or Changing Channels? Partisan News in an Age of Choice*. Chicago: University of Chicago Press, 2013.

Arnold, R. Douglas. *The Logic of Congressional Action*. New Haven, CT: Yale University Press, 1990.

Ashford, Nicholas A., and Charles C. Caldart. *Environmental Law, Policy, and Economics*. Cambridge, MA: MIT Press, 2008.

Ashford, Oliver A. *Understanding Climatic Change: A Program for Action*. Washington, DC: National Academy of Sciences, 1975.

Association of State and Territorial Solid Waste Management Officials. "Superfund Site Assessment Program: Benefits Beyond NPL Listing, Phase II." Washington,

DC: ASTSWMO, March 2012. http://www.astswmo.org/files/policies/CERCLA_and_Brownfields/2012.03.19-Site_Eval-Phase_II_Report-FINAL.pdf.

Augustyniak, Christine. "Asbestos." In *Economic Analyses at EPA: Assessing Regulatory Impact*, edited by Richard D. Morgenstern. Washington, DC: Resources for the Future, 1997.

"Auto Emissions Rules Delayed to '76: Relatively Strict Interim Curbs Set." *Wall Street Journal*, April 12, 1973, sec. News Roundup.

Ayres, Robert U., and Allen V. Kneese. "Production, Consumption, and Externalities." *American Economic Review* 59, no. 3 (1969): 282–97.

Babin, Steven, Howard Burkom, Rekha Holtry, Nathaniel Tabernero, John Davies-Cole, Lynette Stokes, Kerda DeHaan, and Deitra Lee. "Medicaid Patient Asthma-Related Acute Care Visits and Their Associations with Ozone and Particulates in Washington, DC, from 1994–2005." *International Journal of Environmental Health Research* 18, no. 3 (2008): 209–21.

Bachman, John. "Will the Circle Be Unbroken: A History of the U.S. National Ambient Air Quality Standards." *Journal of the Air & Waste Management Association* 57, no. 6 (2007): 652–97.

Bachman, John, David Calkins, and Margo T. Oge. *Cleaning the Air We Breathe: A Half Century of Progress*. Washington, DC: EPA Alumni Association, 2017.

Baker, Peter. *Days of Fire: Bush and Cheney in the White House*. New York: Anchor, 2014.

Balleisen, Edward J., Lori S. Bennear, Kimberly D. Krawiec, and Jonathan B. Wiener, eds. *Policy Shock: Recalibrating Risk and Regulation after Oil Spills, Nuclear Accidents, and Financial Crises*. New York: Cambridge University Press, 2017.

Ballentine, Roger. Interview by Jody Freeman, April 16, 2019.

Bannerjee, Neela, Lisa Song, and David Hasemyer. "Exxon: The Road Not Taken." *Inside Climate News*, September 16, 2015. https://perma.cc/2GUK-AXRP.

Banzhaf, H. Spencer. "Regulatory Impact Analyses of Environmental Justice Effects." *Journal of Land Use & Environmental Law* 27, no. 1 (2011): 1–30.

Banzhaf, H. Spencer, Lala Ma, and Christopher Timmins. "Environmental Justice: The Economics of Race, Place, and Pollution." *Journal of Economic Perspectives* 33, no. 1 (2019): 185–208.

Barbash, Fred, and Deanna Paul. "The Real Reason the Trump Administration Is Constantly Losing in Court." *Washington Post*, March 19, 2019. https://perma.cc/LQB5-7KLB.

Barber, Michael, and Nolan McCarty. "Causes and Consequences of Polarization." In *Political Negotiation: A Handbook*, edited by Jane Mansbridge and Cathie Jo Martin. Washington, DC: Brookings Institution Press, 2015.

Barbero, Robbie, James Kim, Ted Boling, and Julia Doherty. "Increasing the Transparency, Coordination, and Predictability of the Biotechnology Regulatory System." whitehouse.gov, January 4, 2017. https://obamawhitehouse.archives.gov/blog/2017/01/04/increasing-transparency-coordination-and-predictability-biotechnology-regulatory.

Barreca, Alan I., Matthew Neidell, and Nicholas J. Sanders. "Long-Run Pollution Exposure and Adult Mortality: Evidence from the Acid Rain Program." *National*

Bureau of Economic Research working paper no. 23524 (June 2017). https://doi.org/doi:10.3386/w23524.

Barringer, Felicity. "A New (and Unlikely) Tell-All." *New York Times*, July 22, 2008. https://perma.cc/HVV3-Z7DG.

Barstow, David, David Rohde, and Stephanie Saul. "Deepwater Horizon's Final Hours." *New York Times*, December 25, 2010. https://perma.cc/WSU5-2UMT.

Batiuk, Richard A., Denise L. Breitburg, Robert J. Diaz, Thomas M. Cronin, David H. Secor, and Glen Thursby. "Derivation of Habitat-Specific Dissolved Oxygen Criteria for Chesapeake Bay and Its Tidal Tributaries." *Journal of Experimental Marine Biology and Ecology* 381, Supplement (December 1, 2009): S204–15.

Baumgartner, Frank R., and Bryan D. Jones. *Agendas and Instability in American Politics*. Chicago: University of Chicago Press, 2010.

Baumgartner, Frank R., and Beth L. Leech. *Basic Interests: The Importance of Groups in Politics and Political Science*. Princeton, NJ: Princeton University Press, 1998.

Beitsch, Rebecca. "DOJ Sues California to Stifle Cap and Trade Program With Quebec." *The Hill*, October 23, 2019. https://perma.cc/L795-WGPM.

Bell, Michelle L., and Francesca Dominici. "Effect Modification by Community Characteristics on the Short-Term Effects of Ozone Exposure and Mortality in 98 US Communities." *American Journal of Epidemiology* 167, no. 8 (2008): 986–97.

Belson, Ken. "Plumber's Job on a Giant's Scale: Fixing New York's Drinking Straw." *New York Times*, November 22, 2008. http://www.nytimes.com/2008/11/23/nyregion/23tunnel.html.

Benford, Robert D., and David A. Snow. "Framing Processes and Social Movements: An Overview and Assessment." *Annual Review of Sociology* 26 (2000): 611–39.

Bergquist, Parrish, Christopher Warshaw, and David M. Konisky, "Elections and Parties in Environmental Politics." In *Handbook of U.S. Environmental Policy*, Forthcoming. Northampton, MA: Edward Elgar Publishing, 2020.

Bethea, Charles. "Shrinking Newspapers and the Costs of Environmental Reporting in Coal Country." *The New Yorker*, March 26, 2019.

Binder, Sarah A. "Consequences for the Courts: Polarized Politics and the Judicial Branch." In *Red and Blue Nation? Consequences and Correction of America's Polarized Parties*, edited by Pietro S. Nivola and David W. Brady, Vol. 2. Washington, DC: Brookings Institution Press, 2008.

———. *Polarized We Govern?* Washington, DC: Center for Effective Public Management, Brookings Institution, 2014. https://www.brookings.edu/wp-content/uploads/2016/06/BrookingsCEPM_Polarized_figReplacedTextRevTableRev.pdf.

Biniaz, Susan. Interview by Jody Freeman, April 14, 2019.

———. "The Paris Agreement at Three Years Old, The Doctor's Report." *Harvard Law School Environmental & Energy Law Program*, December 17, 2018. https://perma.cc/XG35-37RU.

———. "The Paris Agreement—Au Revoir?" *Columbia Law School Climate Law Blog* (blog), May 24, 2019. https://perma.cc/F7X4-AX8Q.

———. *What Happened to Byrd-Hagel? Its Curious Absence from Evaluations of the Paris Agreement.* New York: Columbia University, Sabin Center for Climate Change Law, 2018. https://perma.cc/2AB5-HMEL.

Birkland, Thomas A. "Focusing Events, Mobilization, and Agenda Setting." *Journal of Public Policy* 18, no. 1 (1998): 53–74.

———. *Lessons of Disaster: Policy Change after Catastrophic Events*. Washington, DC: Georgetown University Press, 2006.

Blake, Francis. "The Politics of the Environment: Does Washington Know Best." *American Enterprise*, April 1991.

Bloss, Cinnamon S., Justin Stoler, Kimberly C. Brouwer, Matthew Bietz, and Cynthia Cheung. "Public Response to a Proposed Field Trial of Genetically Engineered Mosquitoes in the United States." *Journal of the American Medical Association* 318, no. 7 (August 15, 2017): 662–64. https://doi.org/doi:10.1001/jama.2017.9285.

Boffetta, Paolo, Carlo La Vecchia, and Suresh Moolgavkar. "Chronic Effects of Air Pollution Are Probably Overestimated." *Risk Analysis* 35, no. 5 (2015): 766–69. https://doi.org/10.1111/risa.12320.

Boissoneault, Lorraine. "The Cuyahoga River Caught Fire at Least a Dozen Times, but No One Cared Until 1969." *Smithsonian Magazine*, June 19, 2019. https://www.smithsonianmag.com/history/cuyahoga-river-caught-fire-least-dozen-times-no-one-cared-until-1969-180972444/.

Bonine, John. "The Evolution of Technology Forcing in the Clean Air Act." *Environmental Reporter*, monograph no. 21 (1975).

Bosso, Christopher J. *Environment, Inc: From Grassroots to Beltway*. Lawrence, KS: University of Kansas Press, 2005.

Botos, Agnes, John D. Graham, and Zoltan Illes. "Industrial Chemical Regulation in the European Union and the United States: A Comparison of REACH and the Amended TSCA." *Journal of Risk Research* 22, no. 10 (2018): 1187–1204.

Boyer, Barry, and Errol Meidinger. "Privatizing Regulatory Enforcement: A Preliminary Assessment of Citizen Suits Under Federal Environmental Laws." *Buffalo Law Review* 34 (1985): 833–964.

Boykoff, Maxwell T. "We Speak for the Trees: Media Reporting on the Environment." *Annual Review of Environment and Resources* 34 (2009): 431–57.

Boykoff, Maxwell T., and Jules M. Boykoff. "Balance as Bias: Global Warming and the US Prestige Press." *Global Environmental Change* 14, no. 2 (2004): 125–36.

Boyle, Kevin J., Matthew J. Kotchen, and V. Kerry Smith. "Deciphering Dueling Analyses of Clean Water Regulations: Hundreds of Millions of Dollars in Benefits Were Discarded." *Science* 358, no. 6359 (October 2017): 49–50.

Bradbury, Stephen G., and Matthew Z. Leopold. Memo to Mary Nichols, September 6, 2019. https://perma.cc/X2WY-RPW7.

Branigin, William. "Obama Reflects on 'Shellacking' in Midterm Elections." *Washington Post*, November 3, 2010. https://perma.cc/ECX9-RBTU.

Brenner, Joanna. "Neil Gorsuch's Late Mother Almost Annihilated the EPA. Is History Repeating Itself?" *Newsweek*, February 1, 2017.

Bresnahan, Timothy, and Dennis Yao. "The Nonpecuniary Costs of Automobile Emissions Standards." *RAND Journal of Economics* 16 (February 1, 1985): 437–55. https://doi.org/10.2307/2555505.

Bries, Lloyd. "Bush Disses Global Warming Report." *CBS News*, June 3, 2002. https://perma.cc/H3UM-LYE3.

British Antarctic Survey. "The Ozone Hole." bas.ac.uk, April 1, 2017.

Browner, Carol M. "Vice President's Clean Water Action Announcement." EPA.gov, March 9, 1991. https://archive.epa.gov/epapages/newsroom_archive/speeches/0679ee1981604445852570la0052e319.html.

———. Interview by Jody Freeman, March 26, 2019.

Bruff, Harold H. "Presidential Management of Rulemaking." *George Washington University Law Review* 57 (1988).

Brugger, Kelsey. "Trump Admin Advances High-Impact 'Secret Science' Rule." *E&E News*, November 12, 2019. https://www.eenews.net/stories/1061531673.

Brulle, Robert J. "Institutionalizing Delay: Foundation Funding and the Creation of US Climate Change Counter-Movement Organizations." *Climatic Change* 122, no. 4 (2014).

Bruner, Jerome. *Acts of Meaning*. Cambridge, MA: Harvard University Press, 1990.

Bryant, William. "The Re-Vision of Planet Earth: Space Flight and Environmentalism in Postmodern America." *American Studies* 36 (1995): 43–63.

Bullen, Dana. "Auto Firms, Denied Delay on Emissions, Weigh Action." *Washington Star*, May 13, 1972.

Burford, Anne M., and John Greenya. *Are You Tough Enough?* New York: McGraw-Hill, 1986.

Burnham, David. "Reagan Dismisses High EPA Official." *New York Times*, February 8, 1983.

Burtraw, Dallas, and Karen Palmer. "SO2 Cap-and-Trade Program in the United States: A Living Legend of Market Effectiveness." In *Choosing Environmental Policies: Comparing Instruments and Outcomes in the United States and Europe*, edited by Winston Harrington, Richard D. Morgenstern, and Thomas Sterner. Washington, DC: Resources for the Future, 2004.

Bush, George H. W. "Address on the Environment." Erie Metropark, MI, August 31, 1988.

Bush, George W. "The State of the Union Address by the President of the United States." Washington, DC, January 31, 2006.

———. Saginaw, MI, September 29, 2000.

"Bush vs. Clinton: What Is an Environmental President?" *Los Angeles Times*, September 27, 1992.

Butler, Henry N., and Nathaniel J. Harris. "Sue, Settle, and Shut Out the States: Destroying the Environmental Benefits of Cooperative Federalism." *Harvard Journal of Law and Policy* 37 (2013): 579–628.

Butler, Stuart M., Michael Sanera, and W. B. Weinrod. *Mandate for Leadership II: Continuing the Conservative Revolution*. Washington, DC: The Heritage Foundation, 1984.

Calabresi, Steven G. *The Unitary Executive: Presidential Power from Washington to Bush*. New Haven, CT: Yale University Press, 2008.

Cameron, Charles M., Jonathan P. Kastellec, and Jee-Kwang Park. "Voting for Justices: Change and Continuity in Confirmation Voting 1937–2010." *The Journal of Politics* 75, no. 2 (2013): 283–99.

Campbell, Lisa M., Timothy D. Backstrom, and James V. Aidala. "Corteva Announces It Will Cease Production of Embattled Insecticide Chlorpyrifos." *National Law Review*, February 14, 2020.

Campbell, Troy H., and Aaron C. Kay. "Solution Aversion: On the Relation between Ideology and Motivated Disbelief." *Journal of Personality and Social Psychology* 107 (2014): 809–24.

Campbell-Mohn, Celia, Barry Breen, and J. William Futrell. *Sustainable Environmental Law*. Washington, DC: Environmental Law Institute, 1993.

Canes-Wrone, Brandice. "Bureaucratic Decisions and the Composition of the Lower Courts." *American Journal of Political Science* 47, no. 2 (2003): 205–14.

———. *Who Leads Whom? Presidents, Policy, and the Public*. Chicago: University of Chicago Press, 2006.

Cannon, Jonathan Z. "A Bargain for Clean Water." *NYU Environmental Law Journal*, Breaking the Logjam: Environmental Reform for the New Congress and Administration Paper, 17, no. 1 (2008).

———. *Environment in the Balance: The Green Movement and the Supreme Court*. Cambridge, MA: Harvard University Press, 2015.

———. Memo to Carol Browner. "Re: 'Electricity Restructuring and the Environment: What Authority Does EPA Have and What Does It Need,'" April 10, 1998.

———. Interview by Jody Freeman, March 5, 2019.

Carley, Sanya, Natalie Messer Betts, and John Graham. "Innovation in the Auto Industry: The Role of the U.S. Environmental Protection Agency." *Duke Environmental Law & Policy Forum* 21, no. 2 (Spring 2011): 367–99.

Carlson, Ann E. "Iterative Federalism and Climate Change." *Northwestern University Law Review* 103, no. 3 (2009): 1097–1161.

Carsey, Thomas M., and Geoffrey C. Layman. "Changing Sides or Changing Minds? Party Identification and Policy Preferences in the American Electorate." *American Journal of Political Science* 50, no. 2 (2006): 464–77.

Carson, Rachel. *Silent Spring*. Boston, MA: Houghton Mifflin, 1962.

Carter, Jimmy. "Energy and the National Goals: A Crisis of Confidence." American Rhetoric, July 15, 1979. https://www.americanrhetoric.com/speeches/jimmycartercrisisofconfidence.htm.

Cass, Ronald A., Colin S. Diver, Jack M. Beermann, and Jody Freeman. *Administrative Law: Cases and Materials*. 7th ed. Philadelphia: Wolters Kluwer, 2015.

Chan, H. Ron, B. Andrew Chupp, Maureen L. Cropper, and Nicholas Z. Muller. "The Impact of Trading on the Costs and Benefits of the Acid Rain Program." *Journal of Environmental Economics and Management* 88 (March 2018): 180–209.

Chapelle, Francis H. *Wellsprings: A Natural History of Bottled Spring Waters*. Camden, NJ: Rutgers University Press, 2005.

Chesapeake Bay Program. "Population Growth." Chesapekebay.net, 2020. https://www.chesapeakebay.net/issues/population_growth.

"Chesapeake Bay Water Quality Continues to Improve." *Water and Waste Digest*, December 19, 2017. https://www.wwdmag.com/pollution-control/chesapeake-bay-water-quality-continues-improve.

Christofferson, Bill. *The Man from Clear Lake: Earth Day Founder Senator Gaylord Nelson*. Madison, WI: University of Wisconsin Press, 2004.

Claussen, Eileen. Interview by Jody Freeman, March 28, 2019.

Clay, Karen, and Nicholas Z. Muller. "Recent Increases in Air Pollution: Evidence and Implications for Mortality." Washington, DC: National Bureau of Economic Research, 2019.

"Clean Air Bill Cleared with Auto Emission Deadline." CQ Almanac, 1970.

Clinton, Joshua D., Anthony Bertelli, Christian R. Grose, David E. Lewis, and David C. Nixon. "Separated Powers in the United States: The Ideology of Agencies, Presidents, and Congress." *American Journal of Political Science* 56, no. 2 (2012): 341–54.

Clinton, William J., and Albert Gore, Jr. "The Climate Change Action Plan." Washington, DC: Executive Office of the President, 1993.

Coglianese, Cary. "The Limits of Consensus: The Environmental Protection System in Transition: Toward a More Desirable Future." *Environment: Science and Policy for Sustainable Development* 41, no. 3 (1999): 28–33. https://doi.org/10.1080/00139159909604620.

Colburn, Jamison E. "Coercing Collaboration: The Chesapeake Bay Experience." *William & Mary Environmental Law and Policy Review* 40, no. 3 (2016).

Connaughton, James. Interview by Jody Freeman, June 13, 2019.

Coppess, Jonathan. "Upon Further Review: The Decision on EPA's RFS Waiver Authority." *Farmdoc Daily* 7, no. 151 (August 18, 2017).

Cordes, Joseph. "Comment on the Environmental Protection Agency (EPA) Proposed Rule: Increasing Consistency and Transparency in Considering Costs and Benefits in Rulemaking Process," August 20, 2018. https://www.regulations.gov/document?D=EPA-HQ-OA-2018-0107-1232.

Corrigan, Richard. "Success of New Agency Depends Upon Ruckelshaus' Direction." *National Journal* 2, no. 47 (November 28, 1970).

Cox, David. "The Roundup Row: Is the World's Most Popular Weedkiller Carcinogenic." *The Guardian*, March 9, 2019.

Crandall, Robert W. "The Political Economy of Clean Air: Practical Constraints on White House Review." In *Environmental Policy Under Reagan's Executive Order: The Role of Benefit-Cost Analysis*, edited by V. Kerry Smith. Chapel Hill: University of North Carolina Press, 1984.

Creech, Elizabeth. "Saving Money, Time and Soil: The Economics of No-Till Farming." *USDA Blog* (blog), November 30, 2017. https://www.usda.gov/media/blog/2017/11/30/saving-money-time-and-soil-economics-no-till-farming.

Cummins Inc. "Cummins First to Receive EPA Certification: ISX Engine Certified to October 2002 On-Highway Standard." Cummins, Inc.: Investor Overview, April 2, 2002. Investor.cummins.com.

Currie, Janet, and Reed Walker. "What Do Economists Have to Say about the Clean Air Act 50 Years after the Establishment of the Environmental Protection Agency?" *Journal of Economic Perspectives* 33, no. 4 (2019): 3–26.

Daley, Dorothy M., and James C. Garand. "Horizontal Diffusion, Vertical Diffusion, and Internal Pressure in State Environmental Policymaking 1989-1998." *American Politics Research* 37 (2005): 615–44.

Daley, Dorothy M., Megan Mullin, and Meghan E. Rubado. "State Agency Discretion in a Delegated Federal Program: Evidence from Drinking Water Investment." *Publius: The Journal of Federalism* 44, no. 4 (2013): 564–86.

Darr, Joshua P., Matthew P. Hitt, and Johanna L. Dunaway. "Newspaper Closures Polarize Voting Behavior." *Journal of Communication* 68, no. 6 (2018): 1007–28.

Datla, Kirti, and Richard L. Revesz. "Deconstructing Independent Agencies (and Executive Agencies)." *Cornell Law Review* 98 (2013).

Davenport, Coral. "How Andrew Wheeler, the New Acting E.P.A. Chief, Differs from Scott Pruitt." *New York Times*, July 5, 2018. https://www.nytimes.com/2018/07/05/climate/wheeler-epa-pruitt.html.

———. "The Man Who Could Put Climate Change on the Agenda." *National Journal*, April 4, 2013. https://perma.cc/9U3L-6UZA.

———. "Nations, Fighting Powerful Refrigerant That Warms Planet, Reach Landmark Deal." *New York Times*, October 15, 2016. https://perma.cc/P8JT-463R.

Davenport, Coral, Lisa Friedman, and Maggie Haberman. "E.P.A. Chief Scott Pruitt Resigns Under a Cloud of Ethics Scandals." *New York Times*, July 5, 2018. https://www.nytimes.com/2018/07/05/climate/scott-pruitt-epa-trump.html.

Davies, III, J. Clarence, ed. *Comparing Environmental Risks: Tools for Setting Governmental Priorities*. Washington, DC: Resources for the Future, 1996.

———. *The Politics of Pollution*. New York: Pegasus, 1970.

———. Interview by John D. Graham and Penelope Fenner-Crisp, April 18, 2020.

Davis, Devra. *When Smoke Ran Like Water: Tales Of Environmental Deception and the Battle against Pollution*. 1st ed. New York: Basic Books, 2002.

Denison, Richard A. *High Hopes, Low Marks: A Final Report Card on the High Volume Chemical Challenge*. New York: Environmental Defense Fund, 2007.

———. *Toxic Ignorance: The Continuing Absence of Basic Health Testing for Top-Selling Chemicals in the United States*. New York: Environmental Defense Fund, 1997.

Dennis, Brady, and Chris Mooney. "Neil Gorsuch's Mother Once Ran the EPA. It Didn't Go Well." *Washington Post*, February 1, 2017, sec. Climate and Environment. https://www.washingtonpost.com/news/energy-environment/wp/2017/02/01/neil-gorsuchs-mother-once-ran-the-epa-it-was-a-disaster/.

DeNoon, Daniel J. "EPA Urges Teflon Chemical Ban: DuPont Agrees to Phase-Out of Worrisome Pollutant PFOA." WebMD, January 27, 2006. https://www.webmd.com/a-to-z-guides/news/20060127/epa-urges-teflon-chemical-ban#1.

Denzau, Arthur T., and Michael C. Munger. "Legislators and Interest Groups: How Unorganized Interests Get Represented." *American Political Science Association* 80 (1986).

DeShazo, J. R., and Jody Freeman. "Timing and Form of Federal Regulation: The Case of Climate Change." *University of Pennsylvania Law Review* 155, no. 6 (June 2007).

Dickinson, Tim. "Climate Bill, R.I.P." *Rolling Stone*, July 21, 2010. https://perma.cc/4ZN9-3C44.

DieselNet. "US EPA Upholds the Consent Decree Schedule." dieselnet.com, June 8, 2001. https://dieselnet.com/news/2001/06epa.php.

Dockery, Douglas W., C. Arden Pope, Xuebing Xu, Jack D. Spengler, James H. Ware, Martha E. Fay, Benjamin G. Ferris, and Frank E. Speizer. “An Association between Air Pollution and Mortality in Six U.S. Cities.” *The New England Journal of Medicine* 329, no. 24 (December 9, 1993): 1753–59. https://doi.org/10.1056/NEJM199312093292401.

Doniger, David. “Remembering John Hoffman, Ozone Defender and Climate Protector.” *NRDC Expert Blog* (blog), October 2012. https://perma.cc/3NHB-ZH88.

———. Interview by Jody Freeman, April 29, 2019.

———. Email to Jody Freeman, November 1, 2019.

Doniger, David, and Michelle Quibell. *Back from the Brink: How NRDC Helped Save the Ozone Layer*. New York: National Resources Defense Council, 2007.

Donn, Jeff, Martha Mendoza, and Justin Pritchard. “Pharmaceuticals Lurking in U.S. Drinking Water.” *MSNBC.Com*, March 10, 2008.

Dower, Roger C., and Richard D. Morgenstern. “Energy Taxation in the United States: A Case Study of the BTU Tax Proposal.” *International Journal of Global Energy Issues* 10, no. 2 (1998).

Downs, Anthony. “Up and Down with Ecology: The Issue-Attention Cycle.” *The Public Interest* 28 (1972): 38–50.

Doyle, Jack. *Taken for a Ride: Detroit’s Big Three and the Politics of Pollution*. New York: Four Walls Eight Windows, 2000.

Drayton, William. “Getting Smarter About Regulation.” *Harvard Business Review* 59, no. 4 (1981): 38–53.

———. Interview by Jody Freeman, May 9, 2019.

Dudley, Susan E. “OMB’s Reported Benefits of Regulation: Too Good to Be True?” *Regulation*, Summer 2013, 26–30.

———. Letter to Stephen L. Johnson. “Regulating Greenhouse Gas Emissions Under the Clean Air Act,” July 10, 2008. https://perma.cc/28TH-JUBW.

Dudley, Susan E., Richard Belzer, Glenn Blomquist, and Timothy Brennan. “Consumer’s Guide to Regulatory Impact Analysis: Ten Tips for Being an Informed Policymaker.” *Journal of Benefit Cost Analysis* 8, no. 2 (Summer 2017): 187–204.

Duhigg, Charles. “Millions in US Drink Dirty Water, Records Show.” *New York Times*, December 7, 2009. https://www.nytimes.com/2009/12/08/business/energy-environment/08water.html.

———. “Saving U.S. Water and Sewer Systems Would Be Costly.” *New York Times*, March 14, 2010.

Durant, Robert F. *The Administrative Presidency Revisited: Public Lands, the BLM, and the Reagan Administration*. Albany, NY: State University of New York Press, 1992.

Easterbrook, Gregg. “Christie Todd Whitman May Have the Most Thankless Job in Washington.” *New York Times*, August 23, 2001. https://perma.cc/X6G2-WXER.

———. “Hostile Environment.” *New York Times Magazine*, August 19, 2001. https://perma.cc/XS9C-E28G.

———. “William Reilly: Rebuilding the EPA From the Ashes Into a Political Force to Reckon With.” *Los Angeles Times*, June 2, 1991. https://www.latimes.com/archives/la-xpm-1991-06-02-op-183-story.html.

"Ecology Leader Charges Sellout." *New York Times*, April 12, 1973.

Editorial Board. "With a Whimper." *New York Times*, July 22, 2010. https://perma.cc/8SU6-W4UE.

Edwards, Marc A., Amy Pruden, Siddhartha Roy, and William J. Rhoads. "Engineers Shall Hold Paramount the Safety, Health and Welfare of the Public — but Not If It Threatens Our Research Funding?" flintwaterstudy.org, October 10, 2016.

Egan, Patrick J. *Partisan Priorities: How Issue Ownership Drives and Distorts American Politics*. Cambridge: Cambridge University Press, 2013.

Egan, Patrick J., and Megan Mullin. "Climate Change: U.S. Public Opinion." *Annual Review of Political Science* 20 (2017): 209–27.

Ellerman, A. Denny, Paul L. Joskow, Richard Schmalensee, Juan-Pablo Montero, and Elizabeth M. Bailey. *Markets for Clean Air: The U.S. Acid Rain Program*. Cambridge: Cambridge University Press, 2000.

Elliott, E. Donald, Bruce A. Ackerman, and John C. Miller. "Toward a Theory of Statutory Evolution: The Federalization of Environmental Law." *Journal of Law, Economics and Organizations* 1, no. 2 (1985).

Elmer, MacKenzie. "Des Moines Water Works Won't Appeal Lawsuit." *Des Moines Register*, April 11, 2017.

"Environment: Verdict on DDT." *Time*, June 26, 1972.

Environmental & Energy Law Program. "Review of New Source Review Changes in Affordable Clean Energy (ACE) Proposal." *Harvard Law School Environmental & Energy Law Program*, October 29, 2018. https://perma.cc/QGS2-YV6J.

Environmental Council of the States. "Cooperative Federalism 2.0: Achieving and Maintaining a Clean Environment and Protecting Public Health." Washington, DC: ECOS, 2017.

Environmental Integrity Project. "New Report: EPA Enforcement at Record Low in 2018." *EnvironmentalIntegrity.Org*, February 26, 2019. https://environmentalintegrity.org/news/new-report-epa-enforcement-at-record-low-in-2018/.

Environmental Law Institute. "An Analysis of State Superfund Programs: 50-State Study, 2001 Update." Washington, DC: ELI, November 2002. https://www.eli.org/sites/default/files/eli-pubs/d12-10a.pdf.

"EPA Alumni Association Members Survey Report." Washington, DC: American University School of Public Affairs, Center for Environmental Policy, April 2019.

"EPA Media Summary." ABC Radio, April 11, 1973.

Erdal, Serap, and Bernard D. Goldstein. "Methyl Tert-Butyl Ether as a Gasoline Oxygenate: Lessons for Environmental Public Policy." *Annual Review of Energy and the Environment* 25 (November 2000): 765–802.

Erickson, Britt E. "Neonicotinoid Pesticides Can Stay in the US Market, EPA Says." *Chemical and Engineering News*, February 3, 2020.

Eskridge, Jr., William N. "Politics Without Romance: Implications of Public Choice Theory for Statutory Interpretation." *Virginia Law Review* 74, no. 2 (March 1988): 275–338.

Esposito, John C., and Ralph Nader. *Vanishing Air: The Ralph Nader Study Group Report on Air Pollution.* New York: Grossman Publishers, 1970.

Esty, Daniel C. "Environmental Protection in the Information Age." *New York University Law Review* 79, no. 1 (April 2004): 115–211.

Ewing, Jack. "Researchers Who Exposed VW Gain Little Reward from Success." *New York Times*, July 24, 2016.

Expert Panel on the Role of Science at EPA. "Safeguarding the Future: Credible Science, Credible Decisions." Washington, DC: EPA, March 1992.

Fabricant, Robert E. Memo to Marianne L. Horinko. "EPA's Authority to Impose Mandatory Controls to Address Global Climate Change under the Clean Air Act," n.d.

Fact Sheet: President Obama's Climate Action Plan. Washington, DC: White House Office of the Press Secretary, 2013. https://perma.cc/3KBD-JCV3.

Farber, Daniel A. "Politics and Procedure in Environmental Law." *Journal of Law, Economics, and Organization* 8, no. 1 (March 1992): 59–81.

Farman, Joseph C., Brian G. Gardiner, and Jonathan D. Shanklin. "Large Losses of Total Ozone in Antarctic Reveal Seasonal ClOx/NOx Interaction." *Nature* 315, no. 6016 (1985): 207–10.

Farrell, Justin. "Network Structure and Influence of the Climate Change Counter-Movement." *Nature Climate Change* 6, no. 4 (2016).

Ferguson, Janette L., and Laura K. Granier. "Sue and Settle: Citizen Suit Settlements and Environmental Law." *Natural Resources and Environment* 30, no. 1 (Summer 2015). https://www.americanbar.org/publications/natural_resources_environment/2015-16/summer/sue_and_settle_citizen_suit_settlements_and_environmental_law.html.

Ferguson, Scott, and Ed Gray. "1988 FIFRA Amendments: A Major Step in Pesticide Regulation." *Environmental Law Reporter* 19 (1989).

Fiorina, Morris P., Paul E. Peterson, D. Stephen Voss, and Bertrand Johnson. *America's New Democracy*. 3rd ed. New York: Penguin Academics, 2006.

Fiorino, Daniel J. *The New Environmental Regulation*. Cambridge, MA: MIT Press, 2006.

Fisher, Anthony C., John V. Krutilla, and Charles J. Cicchetti. "The Economics of Environmental Preservation: A Theoretical and Empirical Analysis." *American Economic Review* 62, no. 4 (1972): 605–19.

Fitzsimmons, Emma G. "Tap Water Ban for Toledo Residents." *New York Times*, August 3, 2014.

Flint Water Advisory Task Force. "Final Report." Lansing, MI: FWATF, March 2016.

Florio, James. "Congress as Reluctant Regulator: Hazardous Waste Policy in the 1980's." *Yale Journal on Regulation* 3, no. 2 (1986). https://digitalcommons.law.yale.edu/yjreg/vol3/iss2/6.

Flournoy, Alyson. "Supply, Demand and Consequences: The Impact of Information Flow on Individual Permitting Decisions under Section 404 of the Clean Water Act." *Indiana Law Journal* 83 (2008).

Flugge, M., J. Lewandrowski, J. Rosenfeld, C. Boland, T. Hendrickson, K. Jaglo, S. Kolansky, K. Moffroid, M. Riley-Gilbert, and D. Pape. "A Life-Cycle Analysis of the Greenhouse Gas Emissions of Corn-Based Ethanol." Washington, DC: ICF, USDA, January 30, 2017.

Food and Agriculture Organization of the United Nations, and World Health Organization. "Joint FAO/WHO Meeting on Pesticide Residues, Geneva 9-16 May 2016: Summary Report," May 16, 2016. https://www.who.int/foodsafety/jmprsummary2016.pdf.

Fortuna, Richard C., and David J. Lennett. *Hazardous Waste Regulation—The New Era: An Analysis and Guide to RCRA and the 1984 Amendments*. New York: McGraw-Hill, 1987.

Foster, Wade. "Parsing Rapanos." *Environmental Law Review Syndicate*, April 7, 2018. http://www.velj.org/elrs/parsing-rapanos.

Fraas, Arthur. "The Role of Economic Analysis in Shaping Environmental Policy." *Law and Contemporary Problems* 54, no. 4 (Fall 1991). https://scholarship.law.duke.edu/lcp/vol54/iss4/5.

Fraas, Arthur, and Richard D. Morgenstern. "Identifying the Analytical Implications of Alternative Regulatory Philosophies." *Journal of Benefit-Cost Analysis* 5, no. 1 (January 2014): 137–71.

Freeman, A. Myrick. "Environmental Policy Since Earth Day I: What Have We Gained?" *Journal of Economic Perspectives* 16, no. 1 (Winter 2002): 125–46.

Freeman, Jody. "The Obama Administration's National Auto Policy: Lessons from the 'Car Deal.'" *Harvard Environmental Law Review* 35 (2011).

Freeman, Jody, and Adrian Vermeule. "Massachusetts v. EPA: From Politics to Expertise." *Supreme Court Review* 2007, no. 1 (2007).

Friedman, Lisa. "EPA Won't Ban Chlorpyrifos, Pesticide Tied to Children's Health Problems." *New York Times*, July 18, 2019.

Fuhrman, Robert H. "The Role of EPA's BEN Model in Establishing Civil Penalties." *Environmental Law Reporter* 21 (1991).

Gaba, Jeffrey M. "Federal Supervision of State Water Quality Standards under the Clean Water Act." *Vanderbilt Law Review* 36 (1983).

Gallup. "American's Concerns about Water Pollution Edge Up," March 2016. https://news.gallup.com/poll/190034/americans-concerns-water-pollution-edge.aspx.

Gallup. "Most Important Problem." Accessed September 3, 2019. https://news.gallup.com/poll/1675/Most-Important-Problem.aspx.

Gandhi, Indira. "Speech at the United Nations Conference on the Human Environment." Stockholm, June 14, 1972.

Garrett, Theodore L. "Federal Liability for Spills of Oil and Hazardous Substances under the Clean Water Act." *Natural Resources Lawyer* 12, no. 4 (1979): 693–719.

Gerard, David, and Lester B. Lave. "Implementing Technology-Forcing Policies: The 1970 Clean Air Act Amendments and the Introduction of Advanced Automotive Emissions Controls in the United States." *Technological Forecasting and Social Change* 72, no. 7 (September 1, 2005): 761–78. https://doi.org/10.1016/j.techfore.2004.08.003.

Gillete, Robert. "Suggests Wearing Hats, Sunscreen, Instead of Saving Ozone Layer: Hodel Proposal Irks Environmentalists." *Los Angeles Times*, May 30, 1987. https://perma.cc/K9KC-KA49.

Gilmer, Ellen M. "D.C. Circuit Largely Upholds Obama Ozone Standards." *E&E News*, August 23, 2019. https://www.eenews.net/stories/1061043675.

Gilmer, Ellen M., and Steven Lee. "Some EPA Enforcement Stats Stronger While Others Lag in 2019." *Bloomberg Law: Environment and Energy Report*, February 13, 2020. https://news.bloomberglaw.com/environment-and-energy/epa-civil-enforcement-drops-other-metrics-up-in-2019?context=article-related.

Glicksman, Robert L., and Matthew R. Batzel. "Science, Politics, Law, and the Arc of the Clean Water Act: The Role of Assumptions in the Adoption of a Pollution Control Landmark." *Washington University Journal of Law & Policy* 32 (2010).

Glicksman, Robert L., and Christopher H. Schroeder. "EPA and the Courts: Twenty Years of Law and Politics." *Law and Contemporary Problems* 54, no. 4 (1991): 249–309.

Goffman, Joseph. Interview by Jody Freeman, July 2, 2019.

———. Email to Jody Freeman, November 7, 2019.

Golden, Marissa Martino. "Who Controls the Bureaucracy? The Case of Agenda Setting." Washington, DC, 2003.

Goldstein, Bernard D. "EPA as a Public Health Agency." *Regulatory Toxicology and Pharmacology* 8, no. 3 (1988): 328–34.

———. "Flowback." *The Environmental Forum* 33, no. 1 (2016): 25–29.

———. "MTBE: A Poster Child for Exposure Assessment as Central to Effective TSCA Reform." *Journal of Exposure Science and Environmental Epidemiology* 20, no. 3 (2010).

Goldstein, Bernard D., Jill Kriesky, and Barbara Pavliakova. "Missing from the Table: Role of the Environmental Public Health Community in Governmental Advisory Commissions Related to Marcellus Shale Drilling." *Environmental Health Perspectives* 120, no. 4 (April 2012).

Goodnough, Abby. "When the Water Turned Brown." *New York Times*, January 23, 2016.

Goodwin, Pamela, Keith Williams, and Melissa Clarke. "Insight: EPA Moves Toward Setting Drinking Water PFAS Health Standard." *Bloomberg Law Environment & Energy Report*, April 9, 2020. https://news.bloomberglaw.com/environment-and-energy/insight-epa-moves-toward-setting-drinking-water-pfas-health-standard.

"GOP Climate Treaty Critics Step Up Oversight of Administration Strategy." *Inside EPA*, March 6, 1998.

Gore, Al. *Earth in the Balance: Ecology and the Human Spirit*. Boston: Houghton Mifflin, 1992.

Goshko, John M. "Baker Urges Steps on Global Warming." *Washington Post*, January 31, 1989. https://perma.cc/G4JU-MQ7G.

Graham, John D. *Bush on the Home Front: Domestic Policy Triumphs and Setbacks*. Bloomington, IN: Indiana University Press, 2010. https://muse.jhu.edu/book/330.

———. "The Evolving Regulatory Role of the U.S. Office of Management and Budget." *Review of Environmental Economics and Policy* 1, no. 2 (Summer 2007): 171–91.

———. *Obama on the Home Front: Domestic Policy Triumphs and Setbacks*. Bloomington, IN: Indiana University Press, 2016. http://www.iupress.indiana.edu/isbn/9780253021038.

———. "Saving Lives through Administrative Law and Economics." *University of Pennsylvania Law Review* 157, no. 2 (December 1, 2008): 395.

Belton, Keith B., and John D. Graham. "Trump's Deregulation Record: Is It Working?" *Administrative Law Review* 71, (2019): 803-80.

Graham, John D., and Cory R. Liu. "Regulatory and Quasi-Regulatory Activity Without OMB and Cost-Benefit Review." *Harvard Journal of Law and Public Policy* 37, no. 2 (January 2014): 425–45.

Graham, John D., and Paul R. Noe. "A Paradigm Shift in the Cost-Benefit State." *The Regulatory Review*, April 26, 2016.

Graham, John D., and Jonathan B. Wiener. *Risk vs Risk: Tradeoffs in Protecting Health and the Environment*. Cambridge, MA: Harvard University Press, 1997.

Gray, C. Boyden. "EPA's Use of Co-Benefits." *Engage* 16, no. 2 (2015): 31–33.

Gray, George M., Laury Saligman, and John D. Graham. "The Demise of Lead in Gasoline." In *The Greening of Industry: A Risk Management Approach*, edited by John D. Graham and Jennifer Kassalow Hartwell. Boston: Harvard University Press, 1997. https://www.hup.harvard.edu/catalog.php?isbn=9780674363274.

Gray, Wayne B., and Ronald J. Shadbegian. "Multimedia Pollution Regulation and Environmental Performance: EPA's Cluster Rule." Washington, DC: Resources for the Future, 2015. https://www.rff.org/publications/working-papers/multimedia-pollution-regulation-and-environmental-performance-epas-cluster-rule/.

Greenhouse, Steven. "Clinton Backs Off Plan for New Tax on Heat in Fuels." *New York Times*, June 9, 1993. https://perma.cc/HR76-8KG7.

Greenstone, Michael, and Justin Gallagher. "Does Hazardous Waste Matter? Evidence from the Housing Market and the Superfund Program." *The Quarterly Journal of Economics* 123, no. 3 (2008): 951–1003.

Greenwood, Mark A. "TSCA Reform: Building a Program That Can Work." *Environmental Law Review* 39 (January 2009).

Grossmann, Matthew. "Environmental Advocacy in Washington: A Comparison with Other Interest Groups." *Environmental Politics* 15, no. 4 (2006): 628–38.

Gulley, Robert L., and William L. Rosbe. "The Hazardous and Solid Waste Amendments of 1984: A Dramatic Overhaul of the Way America Manages Its Hazardous Wastes." *Environmental Law Reporter* 14, no. 12 (December 1984): 10458–67.

Gurian, Patrick, and Joel A. Tarr. "The First Federal Drinking Water Quality Standards and Their Evolution: A History From 1914 to 1974." In *Improving Regulation: Cases in Environment, Health, and Safety*, edited by Paul S. Fischbeck and R. Scott Farrow. Washington, DC: Resources for the Future, 2001.

Guzy, Gary. Interview by Jody Freeman, March 20, 2019.

Gwinn, Maureen R., Daniel A. Axelrad, Tina Bahadori, David Bussard, Wayne E. Cascio, Kacee Deener, David Dix, Russell S. Thomas, Robert J. Kavlock, and Thomas A. Burke. "Chemical Risk Assessment: Traditional vs Public Health Perspectives." *American Journal of Public Health* 107, no. 7 (July 2017). doi: 10.2105/AJPH.2017.303771.

Haagen-Smit, A. J., and M. M. Fox. "Photochemical Ozone Formation with Hydrocarbons and Automobile Exhaust." *Air Repair* 4, no. 3 (November 1954): 105–36. https://doi.org/10.1080/00966665.1954.10467649.

Hackett, Steven. "Pollution-Controlling Innovation in Oligopolistic Industries: Some Comparisons between Patent Races and Research Joint Ventures." *Journal of Environmental Economics and Management* 29, no. 3 (1995): 339–56. https://doi.org/10.1006/jeem.1995.1051.

Hahn, Robert W. "United States Environmental Policy: Past, Present, and Future." *Natural Resources Journal* 34, no. 2 (1994).

Hahn, Robert W., and Jason K. Burnett. "A Costly Benefit: Economic Analysis Does Not Support EPA's New Arsenic Rule." *Regulation* 24, no. 3 (Fall 2001). https://ssrn.com/abstract=291806 or http://dx.doi.org/10.2139/ssrn.291806.

Hahn, Robert W., Jason K. Burnett, Yee-Ho I. Chan, Elizabeth A. Mader, and Petrea R. Moyle. "Assessing Regulatory Impact Analyses: The Failure of Agencies to Comply With Executive Order 12,866." *Harvard Journal of Law and Public Policy* 23, no. 3 (Summer 2000): 859–89.

Hahn, Robert W., and Patrick M. Dudley. "How Well Does the U.S. Government Do Benefit-Cost Analysis?" *Review of Environmental Economics and Policy* 1, no. 2 (Summer 2007): 192–211.

Hahn, Robert W., and Gordon L. Hester. "Marketable Permits: Lessons for Theory and Practice." *Ecology Law Quarterly* 16 (1989): 368–76.

———. "Where Did All the Markets Go? An Analysis of EPA's Emissions Trading Program." *Yale Journal on Regulation* 6, no. 1 (1989): 109–53.

Haley, Nikki. Communication to Secretary-General of the United Nations, August 4, 2017. https://perma.cc/RZC8-3RBF.

Hamilton, James T. *Regulation Through Revelation: The Origin, Politics, and Impacts of the Toxics Release Inventory Program*. New York: Cambridge University Press, 2005.

Hamilton, James T., and W. Kip Viscusi. *Calculating Risks? The Spatial and Political Dimensions of Hazardous Waste Policy*. Cambridge, MA: MIT Press, 1999.

———. "How Costly Is 'Clean'? An Analysis of the Benefits and Costs of Superfund Site Remediations." *Journal of Policy Analysis and Management* 18, no. 1 (1999): 2–27.

Hammit, James K. "Stratospheric Ozone Depletion and Global Climate Change." In *The Reality of Precaution: Comparing Risk Regulation in the US and Europe*, edited by Jonathan B. Wiener, Michael D. Rogers, James K. Hammit, and Peter H. Sand, 159–76. London: Routledge, 2011.

Hammit, James K., and Kimberly M. Thompson. "Protecting the Ozone Layer." In *The Greening of Industry: A Risk Management Approach*, edited by John D. Graham and Jennifer Kassalow Hartwell. Cambridge, MA: Harvard University Press, 1997.

Hanlon, Jim, Mike Cook, Mike Quigley, and Bob Wayland. "Water Quality: A Half Century of Progress." Washington, DC: EPA Alumni Association, April 2020.

Hanna-Attisha, Mona, Jenny LaChance, Richard Casey Sadler, and Allison Champney Schnepp. "Elevated Blood Lead Levels in Children Associated with the Flint Drinking Water Crisis: A Spatial Analysis of Risk and Public Health Response." *American Journal of Public Health* 106, no. 2 (2016): 283–90.

Harrington, Winston. "Grading Estimates of the Benefits and Costs of Federal Regulation." Washington, DC: Resources for the Future, 2006.

Harrington, Winston, Richard D. Morgenstern, and Peter Nelson. "On the Accuracy of Regulatory Cost Estimates." *Journal of Policy Analysis and Management* 19, no. 2 (Spring 2000): 297–322.

Harris, John F., and Ellen Nakashima. "Gore's Greenness Fades." *Washington Post*, February 28, 2000. https://perma.cc/2MS9-BEFV.

Harrison, Jill Lindsey. *From the Inside Out: The Fight for Environmental Justice within Government Agencies*. Cambridge, MA: MIT Press, 2019.

Harvard Law School Environmental & Energy Law Program. "EPA Mission Tracker," n.d. https://perma.cc/GHW6-F9ZY.

———. "Regulatory Rollback Tracker," n.d. https://perma.cc/E27V-SP7R.

Hassler, Gregory L., and Karen O'Connor. "Woodsy Witchdoctors versus Judicial Guerrillas: The Role and Impact of Competing Interest Groups in Environmental Litigation." *Boston College Environmental Affairs Law Review* 13 (1986): 487–520.

Hayes, Jared, and David Andrews. "'Forever Chemicals' in Over 500 NJ Water Systems and Sources – More Than 1,000 Contaminated Sites Nationwide." *Environmental Working Group News*, November 5, 2019. https://www.ewg.org/news-and-analysis/2019/10/forever-chemicals-almost-200-nj-water-systems-and-sources-more-1000.

Health Effects Institute. "Diesel Exhaust." healtheffects.org. Accessed May 28, 2019. https://www.healtheffects.org/publications/air-pollution/diesel-exhaust/content.

Hecht, Alan D., and Dennis Tirpak. "Framework Agreement on Climate Change: A Scientific and Policy History." *Climatic Change* 29 (1995): 371–402.

Heinzerling, Lisa. "Climate Change in the Supreme Court." *Environmental Law* 38 (2008).

———. "Cost-Nothing Analysis: Environmental Economics in the Age of Trump." *Colorado Natural Resources, Energy & Environmental Law Review* 30, no. 2 (2019).

———. "Inside EPA: A Former Insider's Reflections on the Relationship between the Obama EPA and the Obama White House." *Pace Environmental Law Review* 31 (2014): 325–69.

———. "Who Will Run the EPA?" *Yale Journal on Regulation* 30 (2012).

Heinzerling, Lisa, and Frank Ackerman. *Priceless: On Knowing the Price of Everything and the Value of Nothing*. New York: New Press, 2005.

Hetherington, Marc J. "Putting Polarization in Perspective." *British Journal of Political Science* 39, no. 2 (2009): 413–48.

Hickman Jr., H. Lanier. "Activities of the Office of Solid Waste Management Programs: Fiscal Year 1975." Annual Report. Washington, DC: EPA OSWER, October 1975.

Hill, Seth, and Chris Tausanovitch. "Southern Realignment, Party Sorting, and the Polarization of American Primary Electorates, 1958-2012." *Public Choice* 176, no. 1 (2018): 107–32.

"History: California Air Resources Board." Accessed April 13, 2020. https://ww2.arb.ca.gov/about/history.

Hoffman, John S. "Assessing the Risks of Trace Gases That Can Modify the Stratosphere." Washington, DC: EPA OAR, 1987.

Hoffman, John S., Dale Keyes, and James G. Titus. "Projecting Future Sea Level Rise: Methodology, Estimates to the Year 2100, and Research Needs." Washington, DC: EPA OP, 1983.

Hogue, Cheryl. "EPA Scrubs Science Panels on Air Pollution." *Chemical & Engineering News*, October 20, 2018. https://cen.acs.org/environment/pollution/EPA-scrubs-science-panels-air/96/i42.

———. "US EPA's Science Advisers Split on Tightening Air Pollution Limit." *Chemical & Engineering News*, November 10, 2019. https://cen.acs.org/environment/pollution/US-EPAs-science-advisers-split/97/i44.

Holmstead, Jeffrey. Interview by Jody Freeman, April 23, 2019.

Hopkins, Daniel J. *The Increasingly United States: How and Why American Political Behavior Nationalized*. Chicago: University of Chicago Press, 2018.

Horinko, Marianne L., Cathryn Courtin, James Berlow, Susan Bromm, and Alan Farmer. "Waste Management: A Half Century of Progress." Washington, DC: EPA Alumni Association, April 2020.

Houck, Oliver A. "The Regulation of Toxic Pollutants under the Clean Water Act." *Environmental Law Reporter* 21 (1991).

"How California's Worst Oil Spill Turned Beaches Black and the Nation Green." *Morning Edition*. Washington, DC: National Public Radio, January 28, 2019. https://www.npr.org/2019/01/28/688219307/how-californias-worst-oil-spill-turned-beaches-black-and-the-nation-green.

Howlett, Michael P., and M. Ramesh. *Studying Public Policy: Policy Cycles and Policy Subsystems*. Oxford: Oxford University Press, 1995.

Independent Particulate Matter Review Panel. Letter to Andrew Wheeler. "Advice on EPA's Policy Assessment for the Review of the National Ambient Air Quality Standards for Particulate Matter," October 22, 2019. https://ucs-documents.s3.amazonaws.com/science-and-democracy/IPMRP-FINAL-LETTER-ON-DRAFT-PA-191022.pdf.

Institute for Policy Integrity. "Roundup: Trump-Era Agency Policy in the Courts." New York University School of Law, April 20, 2020. https://policyintegrity.org/trump-court-roundup.

International Energy Agency. "Global EV Outlook 2018." iea.org, May 2018. https://www.iea.org/reports/global-ev-outlook-2018.

"Interview with Christine Todd Whitman." *Frontline Politics*, April 24, 2007.

Johnson, Ann E., Deborah McCullough, and Rufus Isaacs. "Spotted Lanternfly: A Colorful Cause for Concern." MSU Extension: Invasive Species, May 7, 2019.

Johnson, Lyndon B. "Special Message to the Congress on Conservation and Restoration of Natural Beauty, February 8, 1965." In *Public Papers of the Presidents of the United States: Lyndon B. Johnson, 1965*, Vol. I. Washington, DC: Government Printing Office, 1966.

Johnson, Stephen L. Letter to Arnold Schwarzenegger. "California's Request for a Clean Air Act Preemption Waiver," December 19, 2007. https://perma.cc/2VRU-3W9U.

Johnson, Stephen M. "Sue and Settle: Demonizing the Environmental Citizen Suit." *Seattle University Law Review* 37, no. 891 (2014). https://ssrn.com/abstract=2478866.

Jones, Charisse. "Activists Use Research to Win Pollution Battle." *USA Today*, December 6, 2006.

Jones, Charles O. "Speculative Augmentation in Federal Air Pollution Policy-Making." *Journal of Politics* 36, no. 2 (1974): 438–64.

Jordan, Grant, Frank R. Baumgartner, John D. McCarthy, Shaun Bevan, and Jamie Greenan. "Tracking Interest Group Populations in the US and UK." In *The Scale of Interest Organization in Democratic Politics: Data and Research Methods*, edited by Darren Halpin and Grant Jordan. London: Palgrave MacMillan, 2012.

Joselow, Maxine. "EPA, Calif. Plan for Trucks: 'Cooler Heads Are Prevailing.'" *E&E News*, January 30, 2020. https://www.eenews.net/stories/1062210673.

———. "Trump's Car Rule Would Cause More Pollution Deaths." *E&E News*, April 2, 2020. https://www.eenews.net/stories/1062763069.

Kagan, Elena. "Presidential Administration." *Harvard Law Review* 114, no. 8 (2001): 2245–2385.

Kahn, Matthew E. "Environmental Disasters as Risk Regulation Catalysts? The Role of Bhopal, Chernobyl, Exxon Valdez, Love Canal, and Three Mile Island in Shaping U.S. Environmental Law." *Journal of Risk and Uncertainty* 35, no. 1 (2007): 17–43.

Kargman, Steven T. "OMB Intervention in Agency Rulemaking: The Case for Broadened Record Review." *Yale Law Journal* 95, no. 8 (1986).

Karmel, Philip E. "Interstate Transport and Regional Implementation Plans." In *The Clean Air Act Handbook*, edited by Julie R. Domike and Alec C. Zacaroli, 4th ed. Chicago: American Bar Association, 2011.

Kasperson, Roger E., Ortwin Renn, Paul Slovic, Halina S. Brown, Jacque Emel, Robert Goble, Jeanne X. Kasperson, and Samuel Ratick. "The Social Amplification of Risk: A Conceptual Framework." *Risk Analysis* 8, no. 2 (June 1988): 177–87.

Kavlock, Robert J., Tina Bahadori, Tara S. Barton-Maclaren, Maureen R. Gwinn, Mike Rasenberg, and Russell S. Thomas. "Accelerating the Pace of Chemical Risk Assessment." *Chemical Research in Toxicology* 31, no. 5 (March 2018). https://doi.org/10.1021/acs.chemrestox.7b00339.

Keiser, David A., Catherine L. Kling, and Joseph S. Shapiro. "The Low But Uncertain Measured Benefits of US Water Quality Policy." *Proceedings of the National Academy of Sciences* 116, no. 12 (2019): 5262–69.

Keiser, David A., and Joseph S. Shapiro. "Consequences of the Clean Water Act and the Demand for Water Quality." *The Quarterly Journal of Economics* 134, no. 1 (2019): 349–96.

Kennedy, Merrit. "Lead-Laced Water in Flint: A Step-By-Step Look at the Makings of a Crisis." npr.org, April 20, 2016. https://www.npr.org/sections/thetwo-way/2016/04/20/465545378/lead-laced-water-in-flint-a-step-by-step-look-at-the-makings-of-a-crisis.

Kenworthy, E. W. "Ruckelshaus: Center Lane on Pollution." *New York Times*, April 12, 1973.

———. "Senate, House Override Veto of Clean-Water Bill." *New York Times*, October 18, 1972.

———. "U.S. Agency Bars Delay on Cutting Auto Pollutants." *The New York Times*, May 13, 1972. https://www.nytimes.com/1972/05/13/archives/us-agency-bars-delay-on-cutting-auto-pollutants-ruckelshaus.html.

Keohane, Nathaniel O., Richard L. Revesz, and Robert N. Stavins. "The Choice of Regulatory Instruments in Environmental Policy." *Harvard Environmental Law Review* 22 (1998): 313–67.

Kerr, Suzi, and Richard G. Newell. "Policy-Induced Technology Adoption: Evidence from the U.S. Lead Phasedown." *Journal of Industrial Economics* 51, no. 3 (2003): 317–43.

Kerwin, Cornelius. *Rulemaking: How Government Agencies Write Law and Make Policy*. Washington, DC: CQ Press, 2003.

Killman, Curtis. "Oklahoma Attorney General Scott Pruitt Sues EPA—Again." *Tulsa World*, July 9, 2015. https://www.tulsaworld.com/news/local/crime-and-courts/oklahoma-attorney-general-scott-pruitt-sues-epa-again/article_c603ba08-dd62-5b0a-ad3e-e4b8d0e2d977.html.

Kilpatrick, Caroll. "Nixon Selects Environmental Administrator." *Washington Post*, November 7, 1970.

Kimm, Victor, Joseph Cotruvo, and Arden Calvert. "Drinking Water: A Half Century of Progress." Washington, DC: EPA Alumni Association, April 2020.

Kingdon, John W. *Agendas, Alternatives and Public Policies*. 3rd ed. London: Longman Classics, 2003.

Konisky, David M. "Environmental Justice Delayed: Failed Promises, but Some Hope for the Future." *Environment: Science and Policy for Sustainable Development* 58, no. 2 (2016).

———, ed. *Failed Promises: Evaluating the Federal Government's Response to Environmental Justice*. Cambridge, MA: MIT Press, 2015.

———. "Inequities in Enforcement? Environmental Justice and Government Performance." *Journal of Policy Analysis and Management* 28, no. 1 (2009): 102–21.

Konisky, David M., and Christopher Reenock. "Regulatory Enforcement, Riskscapes, and Environmental Justice." *Policy Studies Journal* 46, no. 1 (2018): 7–36.

Konisky, David M., and Tyler S. Schario. "Examining Environmental Justice in Facility–Level Regulatory Enforcement." *Social Science Quarterly* 91, no. 3 (2010): 835–55.

Konisky, David M., and Manuel P. Teodoro. "When Governments Regulate Governments." *American Journal of Political Science* 60, no. 3 (July 2016): 559–74.

Konisky, David M., and Neal D. Woods. "Environmental Federalism and the Trump Presidency: A Preliminary Assessment." *Publius: The Journal of Federalism* 48, no. 3 (2018): 345–71.

———. "Environmental Policy, Federalism, and the Obama Presidency." *Publius: The Journal of Federalism* 46, no. 3 (2016).

———. "Measuring State Environmental Policy." *Review of Policy Research* 29, no. 4 (2012).

Kopits, Elizabeth, Al McGartland, Cynthia Morgan, Carl Pasurka, Ronald J. Shadbegian, Nathalie B. Simon, David Simpson, and Ann Wolverton. "Retrospective Cost Analyses of EPA Regulations: A Case Study Approach." *Journal of Benefit-Cost Analysis* 5, no. 2 (2014): 173–93.

Kraft, Michael E., and Scott R. Furlong. *Public Policy: Politics, Analysis, and Alternatives*. 4th ed. Washington, DC: CQ Press, 2013.

Kraft, Michael E., and Norman J. Vig. "Environmental Policy in the Reagan Presidency." *Political Science Quarterly* 99, no. 3 (1984): 415–39.

Krupnick, Alan, and Richard D. Morgenstern. "The Future of Benefit-Cost Analyses of the Clean Air Act." *Annual Review of Public Health* 23 (2002): 427–48. https://doi.org/10.1146/annurev.publhealth.23.100901.140516.

Kundis Craig, Robin. *The Clean Water Act and the Constitution: Legal Structure and the Public's Right to a Clean and Healthy Environment*. Washington, DC: Environmental Law Institute, 2004.

Kuran, Timur, and Cass R. Sunstein. "Availability Cascades and Risk Regulation." *Stanford Law Review* 51 (April 1999): 683–768.

Landy, Mark K., Marc J. Roberts, and Stephen R. Thomas. *The Environmental Protection Agency: Asking the Wrong Questions*. New York: Oxford University Press, 1994.

Lasswell, Harold D. "The Policy Orientation." In *The Policy Sciences*, edited by Daniel Lerner and Harold D. Lasswell. Palo Alto, CA: Stanford University Press, 1950.

———. *Politics: Who Gets What, When and How*. New York: Meridian Books, 1958.

Layzer, Judith A. *Open for Business: Conservatives' Opposition to Environmental Regulation*. Cambridge, MA: MIT Press, 2012.

Lazar, Emery C., R. Testani, and A. B. Giles. "The Potential for National Health and Environmental Damage from Industrial Residue Disposal." In *Proceedings of the National Conference on Disposal of Residues on Land*. Washington, DC: EPA, 1976.

Lazarus, Richard J. *The Making of Environmental Law*. Chicago: University of Chicago Press, 2004.

———. *The Rule of Five: Making Climate History at the Supreme Court*. Cambridge, MA: Belknap Press, 2020.

League of Conservation Voters. "2017 National Environmental Scorecard: First Session of the 115th Congress." LCV.org, February 27, 2018. http://scorecard.lcv.org/sites/scorecard.lcv.org/files/LCV_Scorecard-2017-Full.pdf.

Leahy, Stephen. "Without the Ozone Treaty You'd Get Sunburned in 5 Minutes." *National Geographic*, September 25, 2017. https://perma.cc/D8YP-SX8E.

Leary, Warren E. "Appeals Court Strikes Down Major Parts of Federal Asbestos Ban." *New York Times*, October 22, 1991.

Lee, Frances. *Beyond Ideology: Politics, Principles, and Partisanship in the U.S. Senate*. Chicago: University of Chicago Press, 2009.

Lee, Jaegul, Francisco Veloso, David Hounshell, and Edward Rubin. "Forcing Technological Change: A Case of Automobile Emissions Control Technology Development in the US." *Technovation*, April 2010, 249–64. https://doi.org/10.1016/j.technovation.2009.12.003.

Lelkes, Yphtach. "Mass Polarization: Manifestations and Measurements." *Public Opinion Quarterly* 80 (2016): 392–410.

Levendusky, Matthew C. "Clearer Cues, More Consistent Voters: A Benefit of Elite Polarization." *Political Behavior* 32, no. 1 (2010): 111–31.

Levin, Michael H. "Lessons from the Birth of Emissions Trading." *BioCycle*, May 2016. https://www.biocycle.net/2016/05/04/lessons-birth-emissions-trading/.

Lewandrowski, Jan, Jeffrey Rosenfeld, Diana Pape, Tommy Hendrickson, Kirsten Jaglo, and Katrin Moffroid. "The Greenhouse Gas Benefits of Corn Ethanol: Assessing Recent Evidence." *Biofuels* 11, no. 3 (March 25, 2019): 361–75. https://doi.org/10.1080/17597269.2018.1546488.

Li, Zhengyan, David M. Konisky, and Nikolaos Zirogiannis. "Racial, Ethnic, and Income Disparities in Air Pollution: A Study of Excess Emissions in Texas." *PLOS ONE* 14, no. 8 (2019).

Light, Paul. *The President's Agenda*. Baltimore, MD: Johns Hopkins University Press, 1999.

Lipsky, Seth. "The Automakers Are Given Delay in Exhaust Rules, But Major Battles Loom." *Wall Street Journal*, April 12, 1973.

Lipton, Eric, and Coral Davenport. "Scott Pruitt, Trump's EPA Pick, Backed Industry Donors over Regulators." *New York Times*, January 14, 2017. https://www.nytimes.com/2017/01/14/us/scott-pruitt-trump-epa-pick.html.

Litfin, Karen T. *Ozone Discourses: Science and Politics in Global Environmental Cooperation*. New York: Columbia University Press, 1994.

Lizza, Ryan. "As the World Burns." *The New Yorker*, October 11, 2010. https://perma.cc/79D4-AQMN.

Lochhead, Jamie. *Ozone Hole: How We Saved the Planet*. Documentary. PBS, 2019.

Lowrance, Sylvia K. *F006 Recycling*. Official memorandum. Washington, DC: EPA OLEM, 1989. https://rcrapublic.epa.gov/files/11426.pdf.

Lundquist, Andrew. Interview by Jody Freeman, April 29, 2019.

Marcus, Alfred. "Environmental Protection Agency." In *The Politics of Regulation*, edited by James Q. Wilson, 1st ed. New York: Basic Books, 1980.

Markell, David. "An Overview of TSCA, Its History and Key Underlying Assumptions, and Its Place in Environmental Regulation." *Washington University Journal of Law and Policy* 32 (January 2010).

Martineau, Robert J., and Ben Snowden. "Hazardous Air Pollutants." In *The Clean Air Act Handbook*, edited by Julie R. Domike and Alec C. Zacaroli, 3rd ed., 739. American Bar Association, 2011.

Maxwell, James, and Forrest Briscoe. "There's Money in the Air: The CFC Ban and DuPont's Regulatory Strategy." *Business Strategy and the Environment* 6, no. 5 (January 1, 1997): 276–86.

May, James R. "Now More Than Ever: Trends in Environmental Citizen Suits at 30." *Widener Law Review* 10, no. 1 (2003).

Mayer, Frederick. "The Story of Risk." In *Policy Shock: Recalibrating Risk and Regulation after Oil Spills, Nuclear Accidents, and Financial Crises*, edited by Edward J. Balleisen, Lori S. Bennear, Kimberly D. Krawiec, and Jonathan B. Wiener. Cambridge: Cambridge University Press, 2017.

Mazur, Allan. *A Hazardous Inquiry: The Rashomon Effect at Love Canal*. Cambridge, MA: Harvard University Press, 1998.

Mazurek, Janice. "Government-Sponsored Voluntary Programs for Firms: An Initial Survey." In *New Tools for Environmental Protection: Education, Information, and Voluntary Measures*, edited by Thomas Dietz and Paul Stern. Washington, DC: National Research Council, 2002.

———. "The Use of Voluntary Agreements in the United States: An Initial Survey." Paris: OECD ENV/EPOC/GEEI, 1998.

McCarthy, Gina. Interview by Jody Freeman, June 18, 2019.

McCarthy, Gina, and William K. Reilly. "Pa. Efforts to Curb Chesapeake Pollution Have Stalled, Leaving the Bay at Risk." *Philadelphia Inquirer*, September 3, 2019, sec. Opinion.

McCarty, Nolan, Keith T. Poole, and Howard Rosenthal. *Polarized America: The Dance of Ideology and Unequal Riches*. Cambridge, MA: MIT Press, 2006.

McCarty, Nolan, and Rose Razaghian. "Advice and Consent: Senate Responses to Executive Branch Nominations 1885-1996." *American Journal of Political Science* 43, no. 4 (October 1999): 1122–43.

McCoy, Caitlin, and Joseph Goffman. "EPA's House of Cards, The Affordable Clean Energy Rule." *Harvard Law School Environmental & Energy Law Program*, October 22, 2019. https://perma.cc/6RTP-ARKU.

McCubbins, Mathew D., Roger G. Noll, and Barry R. Weingast. "Administrative Procedures as Instruments of Political Control." *Journal of Law, Economics, and Organization* 3 (1987): 243–77.

———. "Structure and Process, Politics and Policy: Administrative Arrangements and the Political Control of Agencies." *Virginia Law Review* 75 (1989): 431–82.

McCubbins, Mathew D., and Thomas Schwartz. "Congressional Oversight Overlooked: Police Patrols and Fire Alarms." *American Journal of Political Science* 28, no. 1 (1984): 165–79.

McDonald, Yolanda J., and Nicole E. Jones. "Drinking Water Violations and Environmental Justice in the United States, 2011–2015." *American Journal of Public Health* 108, no. 10 (2018): 1401–7.

McGarity, Thomas O. "On the Prospect of 'Daubertizing' Judicial Review of Risk Assessment." *Law and Contemporary Problems* 66, no. 4 (Fall 2003): 155–226.

———. "Radical Technology-Forcing in Environmental Regulation." *Loyola of Los Angeles Law Review* 27, no. 3 (April 1, 1994): 943.

McGartland, Al. "Thirty Years of Economics at the Environmental Protection Agency." *Agricultural and Resource Economics Review* 42, no. 3 (2013): 436–52.

McGee Crotty, Patricia. "The New Federalism Game: Primacy Implementation of Environmental Policy." *Publius: The Journal of Federalism* 17, no. 2 (1987).

McGee, Patrick. "How VW's Cheating on Emissions Was Exposed." *Financial Times*, January 11, 2017.

McGinty, Kathleen. Interview by Jody Freeman, June 10, 2019.

McGrory Klyza, Christopher, and David J. Sousa. *American Environmental Policy: Beyond Gridlock*. Cambridge, MA: MIT Press, 2013.

McInnis, Daniel F. "Ozone Layers and Oligopoly Profits." In *Environmental Politics: Public Costs, Private Rewards*, edited by Michael S. Greve and Fred L. Smith, Jr. New York: Praeger, 1992.

McVean, Courtney, and Justin R. Pidot. "Environmental Settlements and Administrative Law." *Harvard Environmental Law Review* 191 (2015): 192–239.

Melnick, R. Shep. *Regulation and the Courts: The Case of the Clean Air Act*. Washington DC: Brookings Institution Press, 1983.

Mendelson, Joe. Interview by Jody Freeman, November 21, 2019.

Mendelson, Nina A., and Jonathan B. Wiener. "Responding to Agency Avoidance of OIRA." *Harvard Journal of Law and Public Policy* 37 (2014): 447–521.

Meyer, Robinson. "'We Knew They Had Cooked the Books.'" *The Atlantic*, February 12, 2020. https://www.theatlantic.com/science/archive/2020/02/an-inside-account-of-trumps-fuel-economy-debacle/606346/.

Miles, Christian. "The Comprehensive Environmental Response, Compensation and Liability Act of 1980," 2014.

Minkel, J. R. "Pinching Out Sulfur." *Scientific American*, February 1, 2006. https://doi.org/10.1038/scientificamerican0206-25b.

Miranda, Marie Lynn, Sharon E. Edwards, Martha H. Keating, and Christopher J. Paul. "Making the Environmental Justice Grade: The Relative Burden of Air Pollution Exposure in the United States." *International Journal of Environmental Research and Public Health* 8, no. 6 (2011): 1755–71.

Miravete, Eugenio J., María J. Moral, and Jeff Thurk. "Fuel Taxation, Emissions Policy, and Competitive Advantage in the Diffusion of European Diesel Automobiles." *The RAND Journal of Economics* 49, no. 3 (2018): 504–40. https://doi.org/10.1111/1756-2171.12243.

Mississippi River/Gulf of Mexico Watershed Nutrient Task Force. "Gulf Hypoxia Action Plan 2008." Washington, DC: EPA, 2008.

Mitchell, John N. "Cyanide Pollution." Washington, DC: DOJ, December 9, 1970.

Mitchell, Robert Cameron, Angela G. Mertig, and Riley E. Dunlap. "Twenty Years of Environmental Mobilization: Trends among National Environmental Organizations." *Society and Natural Resources* 4, no. 3 (1991): 219–34.

Mohai, Paul, David Pellow, and J. Timmons Roberts. "Environmental Justice." *Annual Review of Environment and Resources* 34 (2009): 405–30.

Molina, Mario J., and F. Sherwood Rowland. "A Stratospheric Sink for Chlorofluoromethanes: Chlorine Atom-Catalyzed Destruction of Ozone." *Nature* 249, no. 5460 (1974): 810–12.

Molotsky, Irvin. "EPA Plans to Curb Use of Toxaphene, a Pesticide." *New York Times*, October 17, 1982.

Mondt, J. Robert. *Cleaner Cars: The History and Technology of Emission Control since the 1960s*. Warrendale, PA: Society of Automotive Engineers, 2000.

Morgenstern, Richard D., ed. *Economic Analyses at EPA: Assessing Regulatory Impact*. Washington, DC: Resources for the Future, 1997.

———. "Retrospective Analysis of U.S. Federal Environmental Regulation." *Journal of Benefit-Cost Analysis* 9, no. 2 (2018): 285–304.

———. Email to Jody Freeman, December 5, 2019.

Morgenstern, Richard D., and Mark K. Landy. "Economic Analyses: Benefits, Costs, Implications." In *Economic Analyses at EPA: Assessing Regulatory Impact*, edited by Richard D. Morgenstern. Washington, DC: Resources for the Future, 1997.

Morgenstern, Richard D., and William A. Pizer. *Reality Check: The Nature and Performance of Environmental Programs in the United States, Europe, and Japan*. Washington, DC: Resources for the Future, 2007.

Morris, John C. "Dirty Water, Clean Water: Infrastructure Funding and State Discretion in Southern States." In *Speaking Green with a Southern Accent: Environmental Management and Innovation in the South*, edited by Gerald Andrews Emison and John C. Morris. Lanham, MD: Lexington Books, 2010.

Morris, Robert D. *The Blue Death: Disease, Disaster, and the Water We Drink*. New York: Harper Collins, 2007.

Morrisette, Peter M. "The Evolution of Policy Responses to Stratospheric Ozone Depletion." *Natural Resources Journal* 29, no. 3 (1989): 793–820.

Morrison, Alan. "OMB Interference with Agency Rulemaking: The Wrong Way to Write a Regulation." *Harvard Law Review* 99 (1986).

"Mr. Ruckelshaus as Caesar." *The New York Times*, July 16, 1983, sec. Opinion. https://www.nytimes.com/1983/07/16/opinion/mr-ruckelshaus-as-caesar.html.

Mufson, Steven. "Vintage US Coal-Fired Power Plants Now an 'Aging Fleet of Clunkers'." *Washington Post*, June 13, 2014. https://perma.cc/BM59-98AD.

Mulvey, Kathy, and Seth Shulman. "The Climate Deception Dossiers." Cambridge, MA: Union of Concerned Scientists, June 29, 2015.

Nash, Jonathan Remy. "Framing Effect and Regulatory Choice." *Notre Dame Law Review* 82 (2006): 313–72.

Nathan, Richard P. *The Administrative Presidency*. Hoboken, NJ: John Wiley & Sons, 1983.

National Academies of Sciences, Engineering, and Medicine. *Preparing for Future Products of Biotechnology*. Washington, DC: National Academies Press, 2017.

———. *A Review of the Environmental Protection Agency's Science to Achieve Results Research Program*. Washington, DC: National Academies Press, 2017. https://doi.org/10.17226/24757.

National Academy of Public Administration. "Environmental Justice in EPA Permitting: Reducing Pollution in High-Risk Communities Is Integral to the Agency's Missions." Washington, DC: NAPA, December 2001.

National Atmospheric and Oceanic Administration. "Gulf of Mexico 'Dead Zone' Is the Largest Ever Measured." NOAA.gov, August 2, 2017. https://www.noaa.gov/media-release/gulf-of-mexico-dead-zone-is-largest-ever-measured.

National Center on Education and the Economy. "Who We Are." ncee.org, n.d. http://ncee.org/who-we-are/.

National Energy Policy Development Group. "Reliable, Affordable, and Environmentally Sound Energy for America's Future." Washington, DC: Government Printing Office, May 2001. https://perma.cc/M64V-UBMV.

National Highway Traffic Safety Administration, and United States Environmental Protection Agency. "Final Regulatory Impact Analysis: The Safer Affordable Fuel-Efficient (SAFE) Vehicles Rule for Model Year 2021 – 2026 Passenger Cars and Light Trucks." Washington, DC: NHTSA, EPA, March 2020.

National Research Council. *Arsenic in Drinking Water*. Washington, DC: National Academies Press, 1999. https://doi.org/10.17226/6444.

———. *Assessing Risks to Endangered and Threatened Species from Pesticides*. Washington, DC: National Academies Press, 2013.

———. *Carbon Dioxide and Climate: A Scientific Assessment*. Washington, DC: National Academies Press, 1979.

———. *Changing Climate: Report of the Carbon Dioxide Assessment Committee*. Washington, DC: National Academies Press, 1983.

———. *Cost, Effectiveness, and Deployment of Fuel Economy Technologies for Light-Duty Vehicles*, 2015. https://doi.org/10.17226/21744.

———. *Environmental Impact of Stratospheric Flight*. Washington, DC: National Academy of Sciences, 1975.

———. *Genetically Modified Pest-Protected Plants: Science and Regulation*. Washington, DC: National Academies Press, 1990.

———. *Halocarbons: Effects on Stratospheric Ozone*. Washington, DC: National Academy of Sciences, 1976.

———. *Pesticides in the Diets of Infants and Children*. Washington, DC: National Academies Press, 1993.

———. *Renewable Fuel Standard: Potential Economic and Environmental Effects of U.S. Biofuel Policy*. Washington, DC: National Academies Press, 2011. https://doi.org/10.17226/13105.

———. *Reopening Public Facilities After a Biological Attack.* Washington DC: National Academies Press, 2005. https://www.nap.edu/read/11324/chapter/6.

———. *Report by the Committee on Motor Vehicle Emissions*. Washington, DC: National Academies Press, 1973. https://doi.org/10.17226/11096.

———. *Rethinking the Ozone Problem in Urban and Regional Air Pollution*. Washington, DC: National Academies Press, 1992. https://doi.org/10.17226/1889.

———. *Review of the 21st Century Truck Partnership, Second Report*. Washington, DC: National Academies Press, 2011. https://doi.org/10.17226/13288.

———. *Risk Assessment in the Federal Government: Managing the Process*. Washington, DC: National Academies Press, 1983. https://doi.org/10.17226/366.

———. *Semi-Annual Report by the Committee on Motor Vehicle Emissions, Division of Engineering*. Washington, DC: National Academy of Sciences, 1972.

———. *State and Federal Standards for Mobile-Source Emissions*. Washington, DC: National Academies Press, 2006. https://doi.org/10.17226/11586.

———. *Strengthening Science at the U.S. Environmental Protection Agency: Research-Management and Peer-Review Practice*. Washington, DC: National Academies Press, 2000. https://doi.org/10.17226/9882.

———. *Sustainability and the U.S. EPA*. Washington, DC: National Academies Press, 2011. https://doi.org/10.17226/13152.

———. *The Measure of STAR: Review of the U.S. Environmental Protection Agency's Science To Achieve Results (STAR) Research Grants Program*. Washington, DC: National Academies Press, 2003. https://doi.org/10.17226/10701.

———. *Toxicity Testing in the 21st Century: A Vision and a Strategy*. Washington, DC: National Academies Press, 2007. https://doi.org/10.17226/11970.

National Research Council, Committee on Scientific Tools and Approaches for Sustainability. *Sustainability Concepts in Decision-Making: Tools and Approaches for the US Environmental Protection Agency*. Washington, DC: National Academies Press, 2014. https://doi.org/10.17226/18949.

Newell, Richard G., and Kristian Rodgers. "Leaded Gasoline in the United States: The Breakthrough of Permit Trading." In *Choosing Environmental Policies: Comparing Instruments and Outcomes in the United States and Europe*, edited by Winston Harrington, Richard D. Morgenstern, and Thomas Sterner. Washington, DC: Resources for the Future, 2004.

Nichols, Albert L. "Lead in Gasoline." In *Economic Analyses at EPA: Assessing Regulatory Impact*, edited by Richard D. Morgenstern. Washington, DC: Resources for the Future, 1997.

Nichols, Mary. Interview by Jody Freeman, March 15, 2019.

Nixon, Richard M. "Special Message to the Congress About Reorganization Plans to Establish the Environmental Protection Agency and the National Oceanic and Atmospheric Administration." *The American Presidency Project*. July 9, 1970. https://www.presidency.ucsb.edu/node/240055.

———. "Special Message to the Congress on Environmental Quality." *The American Presidency Project*, February 10, 1970. http://www.presidency.ucsb.edu/ws/?pid=2757.

———. "Statement About the National Environmental Policy Act of 1969." *The American Presidency Project*, n.d. https://www.presidency.ucsb.edu/node/239921.

Nolette, Paul. *Federalism on Trial: State Attorneys General and National Policymaking in Contemporary America*. Lawrence, KS: University of Kansas Press, 2015.

Nordhaus, Robert R. "Modernizing the Clean Air Act: Is There Life After 40?" *Energy Law Journal* 33, no. 2 (2012).

Nownes, Anthony J. *Interest Groups in American Politics: Pressure and Power*. New York: Routledge, 2012.

Oates, Wallace E., and Paul R. Portney. "The Political Economy of Environmental Policy." In *Handbook of Environmental Economics, Vol. I*, edited by Karl Goran Mäler and Jeffrey R. Vincent, 1st ed. Amsterdam: Elsevier, 2003.

Obama Administration Finalizes Historic 54.5 MPG Fuel Efficiency Standards. Washington, DC: White House Office of the Press Secretary, 2012.

Obama, Barack H. "Inaugural Presidential Address." Washington, DC, January 21, 2009.

———. "Second Inaugural Presidential Address." Washington, DC, January 21, 2013.

———. Speech After Final Primaries. St. Paul, MN, June 3, 2008.

———. "The State of the Union Address by the President of the United States." Washington, DC, February 12, 2013.

Oberstar, James L. "The Clean Water Act: 30 Years of Success in Peril." Washington, DC: US Congress, House, Committee on Transportation and Infrastructure, October 18, 2002.

O'Dell, John. "Auto Industry Teams with Clean-Air Groups to Cut Sulphur in Diesel." *Los Angeles Times*, June 26, 2000.

Oge, Margo T. *Driving the Future: Combating Climate Change with Cleaner, Smarter Cars*. New York: Arcade Publishing, 2015. https://www.skyhorsepublishing.com/arcade-publishing/9781628725490/driving-the-future.

———. Interview by Jody Freeman, November 20, 2019.

Olson, Mancur. *The Logic of Collective Action: Public Goods and the Theory of Groups*. 2nd ed. Cambridge, MA: Harvard University Press, 1971.

Oppenheimer, Michael. "To Delay Global Warming." *New York Times*, November 9, 1983, sec. opinion.

———. Interview by Jody Freeman, June 20, 2019.

Oreskes, Naomi, and Erik M. Conway. *Merchants of Doubt: How a Handful of Scientists Obscured the Truth on Issues from Tobacco Smoke to Global Warming*. New York: Bloomsbury Publishing, 2011.

Organisation for Economic Cooperation and Development. *OECD Regulatory Policy Outlook 2018*. Paris: OECD Publishing, 2018. https://doi.org/10.1787/9789264303072-en.

———. "Phasing Lead Out of Gasoline, An Examination of Policy Approaches in Different Countries." Paris: United Nations, 1999. https://www.oecd.org/env/ehs/risk-management/1937036.pdf.

Pahl, Dale. "EPA's Program for Establishing Standards of Performance for New Stationary Sources of Air Pollution." *Journal of the Air Pollution Control Association* 33, no. 5 (May 1, 1983): 468–82. https://doi.org/10.1080/00022470.1983.10465594.

Parson, Edward A. *Protecting the Ozone Layer: Science and Strategy*. New York: Oxford University Press, 2003.

Pashigian, B. Peter. "Environmental Regulation: Whose Self-Interests Are Being Protected?" *Economic Inquiry* 23, no. 4 (October 1985): 551–84.

Patton, Dorothy E., and Robert J. Huggett. "The Risk Assessment Paradigm as a Blueprint for Environmental Research." *Human and Ecological Risk Assessment: An International Journal* 9, no. 5 (2003): 1337–48. https://doi.org/10.1080/10807030390240364.

PBS.org. "New York Third Water Tunnel," 2001. http://www.pbs.org/wgbh/buildingbig/wonder/structure/ny_third_water.html.

Pearson, John K. *Improving Air Quality: Progress and Challenges for the Auto Industry*. Warrendale, PA: Society of Automotive Engineers, 2001.

Pedersen, William F. "Formal Records and Informal Rulemaking." *Yale Law Journal* 85, no. 1 (1975): 38–89.

———. "Regulation and Information Disclosure: Parallel Universes and Beyond." *Harvard Environmental Law Review* 25, no. 151 (2001).

———. "Why the Clean Air Act Works Badly." *University of Pennsylvania Law Review* 129, no. 5 (1981). https://scholarship.law.upenn.edu/penn_law_review/vol129/iss5/12.

Pedersen, William F., and David Schoenbrod. "The Overwhelming Case for Clean Air Act Reform." *Environmental Law Reporter* 43, no. 10971 (2013).

Percival, Robert V. "The Bounds of Consent: Consent Decrees, Settlements and Federal Environmental Policy Making." *University of Chicago Legal Forum*, 1987. http://chicagounbound.uchicago.edu/uclf/vol1987/iss1/13.

———. "The Clean Water Act and the Demise of the Federal Common Law of Interstate Nuisance." *Alabama Law Review* 55 (2004).

———. "Environmental Legislation and the Problem of Collective Action." *Duke Environmental Law and Policy Forum* 9 (1998): 9–28.

Percival, Robert V., Alan S. Miller, Christopher H. Schroeder, and James P. Leape. *Environmental Regulation: Law, Science and Policy*. Boston: Little, Brown, and Company, 1992.

Peschek, Joseph G. *Policy-Planning Organizations: Elite Agendas and America's Rightward Turn*. Philadelphia: Temple University Press, 1987.

Pianin, Eric, and David Hilzenrath. "Hill Agrees to Raise Gas Tax 4.3 Cents." *Washington Post*, July 30, 1993. https://perma.cc/HA5M-ZZAU.

Pildes, Richard H., and Cass R. Sunstein. "Reinventing the Regulatory State." *University of Chicago Law Review* 62, no. 1 (1995).

Plumer, Brad, and Coral Davenport. "Science Under Attack: How Trump Is Sidelining Researchers and Their Work." *New York Times*, December 28, 2019. https://www.nytimes.com/2019/12/28/climate/trump-administration-war-on-science.html.

Pomerance, Rafe. Interview by Jody Freeman, March 12, 2019.

Poole, Keith T., and Howard Rosenthal. *Congress: A Political-Economic History of Roll Call Voting*. New York: Oxford University Press, 1997.

Poole, Robert. *Earthrise: How Man First Saw the Earth*. New Haven, CT: Yale University Press, 2010.

Pope, C. Arden, Michael J. Thun, Mohan M. Namboodiri, Douglas W. Dockery, John S. Evans, Frank E. Speizer, and Clark W. Heath, Jr. "Particulate Air Pollution as a Predictor of Mortality in a Prospective Study of U.S. Adults." *American Journal of Respiratory and Critical Care Medicine* 151, no. 3 (March 1995): 669–74. https://doi.org/10.1164/ajrccm/151.3_Pt_1.669.

Pope, James Gray. "Republican Moments: The Role of Direct Popular Power in the American Constitutional Order." *University of Pennsylvania Law Review* 139 (1990): 287–368.

Popovich, Nadja, Livia Albeck-Ripka, and Kendra Pierre-Louis. "95 Environmental Rules Being Rolled Back Under Trump." *New York Times*, December 21, 2019. https://www.nytimes.com/interactive/2019/climate/trump-environment-rollbacks.html.

Posner, Richard A. "Theories of Economic Regulation." *Bell Journal of Economics and Management Science* 5 (1974).

Potoski, Matthew. "Designing Bureaucratic Responsiveness: Administrative Procedures and Agency Choice in State Environmental Policy." *State Policy and Politics Quarterly* 2, no. 1 (2002): 1–23.

Powell, Mark R. "The 1983-1984 Suspensions of EDB Under FIFRA and the 1989 Asbestos Ban and Phase-out Rule Under TSCA: Two Case Studies in EPA's Use of Science." Revised edition. Washington, DC: Resources for the Future, March 1997.

"President Bush Discusses Global Climate Change." Washington, DC: Office of the White House Press Secretary, June 11, 2001. https://perma.cc/TC7Q-YFTX.

President's Advisory Council on Executive Reorganization. Memo to Richard M. Nixon. "Re: Federal Organization for Environmental Protection," April 29, 1970.

———. "Memoranda from April 1969 to November 1970," n.d. https://www.nixonlibrary.gov/finding-aids/presidents-advisory-council-executive-organization-white-house-central-files-staff.

President's Council of Advisors on Science and Technology. "Report to the President: Science and Technology to Ensure the Safety of the Nation's Drinking Water," December 2016. https://obamawhitehouse.archives.gov/sites/default/files/pcast_drinking_water_final_executive_summary_final.pdf.

President's Science Advisory Committee. "Restoring the Quality of Our Environment: Report of the Panel on Environmental Pollution." Washington, DC: Government Printing Office, November 1965.

Press, Frank. "Memo to the President: Release of Fossil CO2 and the Possibility of a Catastrophic Climate Change," July 7, 1977.

Priest, Dana. "Competitiveness Council under Scrutiny." *Washington Post*, November 26, 1991.

Prior, Marcus. *Post-Broadcast Democracy: How Media Choice Increases Inequality in Political Involvement and Polarizes Elections*. New York: Cambridge University Press, 2007.

Probst, Katherine N., and David M. Konisky. *Superfund's Future: What Will It Cost?* Washington, DC: Resources for the Future, 2001.

Provost, Colin, and Brian J. Gerber. "Political Control and Policy-Making Uncertainty in Executive Orders: The Implementation of Environmental Justice Policy." *Journal of Public Policy* 39, no. 2 (June 2019).

Puko, Timothy, and Ben Foldy. "Justice Department Launches Antitrust Probe into Four Auto Makers." *Wall Street Journal*, September 6, 2019. https://perma.cc/8CQ9-QK2V.

Pullen Fedinick, Kristi, Mae Wu, Mekela Panditharatne, and Erik D. Olson. "Threats on Tap: Widespread Violations Highlight Need for Investment in Water Infrastructure and Protections." Washington, DC: NRDC, 2017. https://www.nrdc.org/sites/default/files/threats-on-tap-water-infrastructure-protections-report.pdf.

Quarles, John. *Cleaning Up America: In Insider's View of the Environmental Protection Agency*. Boston: Houghton Mifflin, 1976.

Quast, Sylvia. "Regulation of Wetlands: Section 404." In *Clean Water Handbook*, edited by Mark A. Ryan, 3rd ed. Chicago: American Bar Association, 2011.

Rabe, Barry G. "Leveraged Federalism and the Clean Air Act." In *Lessons from the Clean Air Act: Building Durability and Adaptability into US Climate and Energy Policy*, edited by Ann Carlson and Dallas Burtraw, 113–58. Cambridge: Cambridge University Press, 2019. https://doi.org/10.1017/9781108377195.004.

Race, Joseph. *Chlorination of Water*. 1st ed. New York: John Wiley & Sons, 1918.

Rahm, Dianne. *Climate Change Policy in the United States: The Science, the Politics and Prospects for Change*. Jefferson, NC: McFarland, 2009.

Rasmussen, Sara, and Richard D. Morgenstern. "Municipal Landfill Management." In *Economic Analyses at EPA: Assessing Regulatory Impact*. Washington, DC: Resources for the Future, 1997.

Reagan, Ronald. "First Inaugural Address, January 20, 1981." ReaganFoundation.org. Accessed September 3, 2019. https://www.reaganfoundation.org/media/128614/inaguration.pdf.

Reeder, John E. "Moving Forward: Future Directions for EPA and Environmental Protection." Washington, DC: American University School of Public Affairs, Center for Environmental Policy, December 2019.

Reilly, Sean. "Trump's Soot Proposal Bucks Advice of EPA Career Staff." *E&E News*, April 14, 2020. https://www.eenews.net/stories/1062872411.

———. "Wheeler's Science Advisory Board Revamp Plan Sparks Concerns." *E&E News*, December 10, 2019. https://www.eenews.net/greenwire/2019/12/10/stories/1061775673.

Reilly, William K. "Memorandum to All EPA Employees: Reflections on the Earth Day Summit." Washington, DC: EPA, July 15, 1992.

———. Panel Chief on the Gulf Spill: Complacency Led to Disaster. Interview by John McQuaid, January 27, 2011. https://e360.yale.edu/features/panel_chief_on_the_gulf_spill_complacency_led_to_disaster.

———. Interview by Jody Freeman, March 14, 2019.

Reinstein, Robert, and Stephanie Kinney. Interview by Charles Stuart Kennedy, October 5, 2010. https://perma.cc/6P7K-X8J7.

Repetto, Robert, ed. *Punctuated Equilibrium and the Dynamics of US Environmental Policy*. New Haven, CT: Yale University Press, 2006.

"Replacing All Lead Water Pipes Could Cost $30 Billion." *Water Tech Online*, March 11, 2016. https://www.watertechonline.com/home/article/15549954/replacing-all-lead-water-pipes-could-cost-30-billion.

Resh, William G. *Rethinking the Administrative Presidency*. Baltimore, MD: Johns Hopkins University Press, 2015.

Revesz, Richard L. "Environmental Regulation, Ideology and the D.C. Circuit." *Virginia Law Review* 83, no. 8 (1997).

———. "The Race to the Bottom and Federal Environmental Regulation: A Response to Critics." *Minnesota Law Review* 82 (1997).

———. "Rehabilitating Interstate Competition: Rethinking the 'Race-to-the-Bottom' Rationale for Federal Environmental Regulation." *New York University Law Review* 67 (January 1, 1992): 1210–54.

Revesz, Richard L., and Jack Lienke. *Struggling for Air: Power Plants and the "War on Coal."* New York: Oxford University Press, 2016.

Revesz, Richard L., and Michael A. Livermore. "A Truly Green Economics." *Forbes*, December 2, 2008. https://www.forbes.com/2008/12/02/environment-supreme-court-oped-cx_rr_ml_1202reveszlivermore.html#6a1918ec71f5.

———. *Retaking Rationality: How Cost-Benefit Analysis Can Better Protect the Environment and Our Health*. Oxford: Oxford University Press, 2008.

Revesz, Richard L., Michael A. Livermore, Caroline Cecot, and Jayni Foley Hein. *Environmental Law and Policy*. 4th ed. St. Paul, MN: Foundation Press/LEG/West Academic, 2019.

Revkin, Andrew C. "Bush Aide Softened Greenhouse Gas Links to Global Warming." *New York Times*, June 8, 2005. https://perma.cc/AF3F-K4BT.

———. "On Global Warming, McCain and Obama Agree: Urgent Action Is Needed." *New York Times*, October 19, 2008. https://perma.cc/67W2-D9N8.

Revkin, Andrew C., and Katherine Q. Seeyle. "Report by EPA Leaves out Data on Climate Change." *New York Times*, June 19, 2003. https://perma.cc/5EEA-XATK.

Reyes, Jessica Wolpaw. "Environmental Policy as Social Policy? The Impact of Childhood Lead Exposure on Crime." *The B.E. Journal of Economic Analysis & Policy* 7, no. 1 (2007).

Ribaudo, Marc O., and Jessica Gottlieb. "Non-Point Trading—Can It Work?" *Journal of the American Water Resources Association* 47, no. 1 (2011): 5–14.

Rice, Doyle. "LA Languishes in Same Spot as Most Polluted US City." *USA Today*, April 25, 2019.

Rich, Nathaniel. "Losing Earth: The Decade We Almost Stopped Climate Change." *New York Times Magazine*, August 1, 2018. https://perma.cc/6URT-VSPP.

Rieland, Randy. "The Blame Obama Game." *Grist*, July 27, 2010. https://perma.cc/4TRU-7SMM.

Ringquist, Evan J. "Assessing Evidence of Environmental Inequities: A Meta-Analysis." *Journal of Policy Analysis and Management* 24, no. 2 (2005): 223–47.

———. "Policy Influence and Policy Responsiveness in State Pollution Control." *Policy Studies Journal* 22, no. 1 (1994): 25–43.

Robert, David. "Why Did the Climate Bill Fail." *Grist*, July 27, 2010. https://perma.cc/8FW7-P8YL.

Rodriguez-Mozaz, Sara, and Howard S. Weinberg. "Meeting Report: Pharmaceuticals in Water—An Interdisciplinary Approach to a Public Health Challenge." *Environmental Health Perspectives* 118, no. 7 (2010).

Romano, Lois. "Rita Lavelle, Dumped." *Washington Post*, March 5, 1983.

Rombout, Peter J. A., Paul J. Lioy, and Bernard D. Goldstein. "Rationale for an Eight-Hour Ozone Standard." *Journal of Air Pollution Control Association* 36, no. 8 (1986): 913–17.

Ross, David P. "Memo: Updating the Environmental Protection Agency's (EPA) Water Quality Trading Policy to Promote Market-Based Mechanisms for Improving Water Quality." Washington, DC: EPA, February 6, 2019.

Royden, Amy. "U.S. Climate Change Policy Under President Clinton: A Look Back." *Golden Gate University Law Review* 32, no. 4 (2002).

Ruckelshaus, William D. "The City Must Be the Teacher of Man." Presented at the Annual Congress of Cities, Atlanta, GA, December 10, 1970.

———. "Decision of the Administrator Re: Applications for Suspension of 1975 Motor Vehicle Exhaust Emission Standards." Washington, DC: EPA, May 12, 1972.

———. "Decision of the Administrator Re: Applications for Suspension of 1975 Motor Vehicle Exhaust Emission Standards." Washington, DC: EPA, April 11, 1973.

———. "Environmental Regulation: The Early Days at EPA." *EPA Journal*, March 1988. https://archive.epa.gov/epa/aboutepa/environmental-regulation-early-days-epa.html.

———. Interview by Jody Freeman, May 2, 2019.

———. "Risk in a Free Society," speech at Princeton University February 18, 1984, reprinted in *Environmental Law Reporter*, https://elr.info/sites/default/files/articles/14.10190.htm.

———. "Stopping the Pendulum." *Environmental Toxicology and Chemistry* 15, no. 3 (1996). https://doi.org/10.1002/etc.5620150301.

———. "Transportation and Environmental Protection." *Traffic Quarterly* 27 (January 4, 1973): 173–81.

Russakoff, Dale. "EPA Chief Is Assailed at Hearing." *Washington Post*, February 16, 1983.

Ryan, Mark A. "Clean Water Act Citizen Suits: What the Numbers Tell Us." *Natural Resources & Environment* 32 (Fall 2017).

Salpukas, Agis. "Detroit Unhappy with EPA Action." *New York Times*, April 11, 1973.

Sargis, Joe. "Rita Lavelle, a Former EPA Official Convicted of Perjury." *UPI*, September 4, 1985.

Saunders Davenport, Deborah. *Global Environmental Negotiations and US Interests*. New York: Palgrave MacMillan, 2006.

Scheberle, Denise. "Environmental Federalism and the Role of State and Local Governments." In *The Oxford Handbook of U.S. Environmental Policy*, edited by Michael E. Kraft and Sheldon Kamieniecki. Oxford: Oxford University Press, 2012.

Schierow, Linda-Jo. "The Toxic Substances Control Act (TSCA): Implementation and New Challenges." Washington, DC: CRS, July 28, 2009.

Schmalensee, Richard. "Comment on the Environmental Protection Agency (EPA) Proposed Rule: Increasing Consistency and Transparency in Considering Costs and Benefits in Rulemaking Process," August 23, 2018. https://www.regulations.gov/document?D=EPA-HQ-OA-2018-0107-1756.

Schmalensee, Richard, and Robert N. Stavins. "Lessons Learned from Three Decades of Experience with Cap and Trade." *Review of Environmental Economics and Policy* 11, no. 1 (Winter 2017): 59–79. https://doi.org/10.1093/reep/rew017.

Schneider, Keith. "The Earth Summit; White House Snubs US Envoy's Plea to Sign Rio Treaty." *New York Times*, June 5, 1992. https://perma.cc/PY45-XSLP.

Schroeder, Christopher H. "Rational Choice Versus Republican Moment Explanations for Environmental Laws 1969–71." *Duke Environmental Law & Policy Forum* 9, no. 29 (1998).

Schuck, Peter H. "Against (And For) Madison: An Essay in Praise of Factions." *Yale Law & Policy Review* 15 (1997): 553–97.

Schwege, Henry. *Environmental Protection Agency and State Hazardous Waste Management Programs*. Statement before the Subcommittee on Oversight and Investigations, House Committee on Interstate and Foreign Commerce. Washington, DC: GAO, 1979.

Searchinger, Tim, Ralph Heimlich, Richard Houghton, Fengxia Dong, Amani Elobeid, Jacinto Fabiosa, Simla Tokgoz, Dermot Hayes, and Tun-Hsiang Yu. "Use of

U.S. Croplands for Biofuels Increases Greenhouse Gases Through Emissions from Land-Use Change." *Science* 319, no. 5867 (February 29, 2008): 1238–40. https://doi.org/10.1126/science.1151861.

Segal, Jeffrey A., and Harold J. Spaeth. *The Supreme Court and the Attitudinal Model Revisited*. Cambridge: Cambridge University Press, 2002.

Seidel, Stephen. Interview by Jody Freeman, April 3, 2019.

———. Email to Jody Freeman, November 11, 2019.

Seidel, Stephen, and Dale Keyes. "Can We Delay A Greenhouse Warming?: The Effectiveness and Feasibility of Options to Slow a Build-up of Carbon Dioxide in the Atmosphere." Washington, DC: EPA OP, 1983.

Sewall, Bradford, and Robin M. Whyatt. "Intolerable Risk: Pesticides in Our Children's Food." New York: Natural Resources Defense Council, February 27, 1989.

Shabecoff, Philip. "EPA Won't Ban Use of Chemical on Apples." *New York Times*, January 23, 1986.

———. "Global Warming Has Begun, Expert Tells Senate." *New York Times*, June 24, 1988. https://perma.cc/4GEX-3C8G.

———. "Haste on Global Warming Trend Opposed." *New York Times*, October 21, 1983. https://perma.cc/K6B7-KK6E.

———. "President Names Toxic Waste Chief to Head the EPA." *New York Times*, November 30, 1984. https://perma.cc/RB6N-LBH2.

———. "Report Says Agency Focuses on Lesser Problems." *New York Times*, February 19, 1987.

———. "US Environmental Agency Making Deep Staffing Cuts." *New York Times*, January 3, 1982.

Shanley, Robert A. *Presidential Influence and Environmental Policy*. Westport, CT: Greenwood Press, 1992.

Shaw, David. "Alar Panic Shows Power of Media to Trigger Fear." *Los Angeles Times*, September 12, 1994.

Shepard, Robert. "Vice President George Bush, Taking a New Campaign Issue." *UPI*, September 1, 1988.

Shiffman, John, and John Sullivan. "An Eroding Mission at EPA." *Philadelphia Inquirer*, December 2, 2008. https://perma.cc/Y2ZM-TLU8.

Shipan, Charles, and Megan L. Shannon. "Delaying Justice(s): A Duration Analysis of Supreme Court Confirmations." *American Journal of Political Science* 47, no. 4 (2003): 654–68.

Shor, Boris, and Nolan McCarty. "The Ideological Mapping of American Legislatures." *American Political Science Review* 105, no. 3 (2011): 530–51.

Shultz, George P. "Official Memorandum: Agency Regulations, Standards, and Guidelines Pertaining to Environmental Quality, Consumer Protection, and Occupational and Public Health and Safety." Washington, DC: OMB, October 5, 1971. https://thecre.com/ombpapers/QualityofLife1.htm.

Sinclair, Barbara. *Unorthodox Lawmaking: New Legislative Processes in the U.S. Congress*. 3rd ed. Washington, DC: CQ Press, 2007.

Skocpol, Theda. "Naming the Problem: What It Will Take to Counter Extremism and Engage Americans in the Fight against Global Warming." Harvard University, 2013.

Slovic, Paul. "'If I Look at the Mass I Will Never Act': Psychic Numbing and Genocide." *Judgment and Decision Making* 2, no. 2 (2007): 79–95.

Small, Deborah A., George Loewenstein, and Paul Slovic. "Sympathy and Callousness: The Impact of Deliberative Thought on Donations to Identifiable and Statistical Victims." *Organizational Behavior and Human Decision Processes* 102 (2007): 143–53.

"Smelter Putting Arsenic in the Air Is Set to Close." *The New York Times*, June 30, 1984, sec. U.S.

Smith, David. "1975 GM Cars May Have Catalytic Converters." *Washington Post*, May 25, 1973.

Snider, Annie. "Clean Water Act: Vetoes by Eisenhower and Nixon Presaged Today's Partisan Divide." *E&E News*, October 18, 2012. https://www.eenews.net/stories/1059971457.

———. "Vetoes by Eisenhower, Nixon Presaged Today's Partisan Divide." *E&E News*, October 18, 2012.

Snyder Bennear, Lori, and Sheila M. Olmstead. "The Impacts of the 'Right to Know': Information Disclosure and the Violation of Drinking Water Standards." *Journal of Environmental Economics and Land Management*, 2008. http://dx.doi.org/10.2139/ssrn.939590.

Solomon, Susan, Rolando R. Garcia, F. Sherwood Rowland, and D. J. Wuebbles. "On the Depletion of Antarctic Ozone." *Nature* 321 (June 1986): 755–58.

Specter, Michael. *Denialism: How Irrational Thinking Hinders Scientific Progress, Harms the Planet, and Threatens Our Lives*. London: Penguin Books, 2009.

Spector, Phillip L. "Regulation of Pesticides by the Environmental Protection Agency." *Ecology Law Quarterly* 5 (1976).

Speth, Gus. Interview by Jody Freeman, March 19, 2019.

———. Email to Jody Freeman, November 9, 2019.

Stackelberg, Katherine von, Jonathan Buonocore, Prakash V. Bhave, and Joel A. Schwartz. "Public Health Impacts of Secondary Particulate Formation from Aromatic Hydrocarbons in Gasoline." *Environmental Health* 12, no. 1 (2013): 19. https://doi.org/10.1186/1476-069X-12-19.

Steinzor, Rena I., and William F. Piermattei. "Reinventing Environmental Regulation via the Government Performance and Results Act: Where's the Money?" *Environmental Law Reporter* 28, no. 10 (October 1998).

Stewart, Richard B., and James E. Krier. *Environmental Law and Policy: Readings, Materials and Notes*. 2nd ed. Indianapolis, IN: Bobbs-Merrill, 1978.

Stoffer, Harry. "GM Fought Safety, Emissions Rules, but Then Invented Ways to Comply." *Automotive News*, September 14, 2008. https://www.autonews.com/article/20080914/OEM/309149832/gm-fought-safety-emissions-rules-but-then-invented-ways-to-comply.

Stolark, Jessie. "A Brief History of Octane in Gasoline: From Lead to Ethanol." Environmental and Energy Study Institute, March 30, 2016. https://www.eesi.org/papers/view/fact-sheet-a-brief-history-of-octane.

Stone, Deborah A. "Causal Stories and the Formation of Policy Agendas." *Political Science Quarterly* 104 (1989): 281–300.

Stout, David. "EPA Chief Whitman Resigns." *New York Times*, May 21, 2003. https://perma.cc/32A8-P9BW.

Stradling, David, and Richard Stradling. "Perceptions of the Burning River: Deindustrialization and Cleveland's Cuyahoga River." *Environmental History* 13 (2008): 515–35.

Sullivan, Daniel M., and Alan Krupnick. "Using Satellite Data to Fill the Gaps in the US Air Pollution Monitoring Network." Working paper. Washington, DC: Resources for the Future, 2018.

Sullivan, John L., R. E. Baker, B. A. Boyer, R. H. Hammerle, T. E. Kenney, L. Muniz, and Timothy J. Wallington. "CO2 Emission Benefit of Diesel (versus Gasoline) Powered Vehicles." *Environmental Science & Technology* 38, no. 12 (2004): 3217–23. https://doi.org/10.1021/es034928d.

Sunstein, Cass R. "The Arithmetic of Arsenic." *Georgetown Law Journal* 90 (2001). https://pdfs.semanticscholar.org/5ca2/433d817159185403e841d1201be800f29616.pdf.

———. "The Office of Information and Regulatory Affairs: Myths and Realities." *Harvard Law Review* 126 (2013).

Support for President's Copenhagen Announcement Receives Immediate Support. Washington, DC: White House Office of the Press Secretary, 2009. https://perma.cc/63SX-DSWS.

Suskind, Ron. *The Price of Loyalty: George W. Bush, the White House, and the Education of Paul O'Neill*. New York: Simon & Schuster, 2004.

Sussman, Robert. Email to Jody Freeman, May 5, 2019.

Switzer, David, and Manuel P. Teodoro. "Class, Race, Ethnicity, and Justice in Safe Drinking Water Compliance." *Social Science Quarterly* 99, no. 2 (2018): 524–35.

Symons, Jeremy. "How Bush and Co. Obscure the Science." *Washington Post*, July 13, 2003. https://perma.cc/K36X-JLNS.

Tabuchi, Hiroko, and Neal E. Boudette. "Automakers Sought Looser Rules. Now They Hope to Stop Trump From Going Too Far." *New York Times*, May 9, 2018. https://www.nytimes.com/2018/05/09/climate/automakers-fuel-economy-trump.html.

Tarlock, A. Dan. "Putting Rivers Back in the Landscape: The Revival of Watershed Management in the United States." *Hastings Environmental Law Journal* 6, no. 2 (2000).

Tewksbury, David. "The Seeds of Audience Fragmentation: Specialization in the Use of Online News Sites." *Journal of Broadcasting & Electronic Media* 49, no. 3 (2005): 332–48.

"The Big Cleanup: The Environmental Crisis '72." *Newsweek*, June 12, 1972.

"The Cities: The Price of Optimism." *Time*, August 1, 1969.

"The Halliburton Loophole." *New York Times*, November 2, 2009. https://www.nytimes.com/2009/11/03/opinion/03tue3.html.

The President's Climate Action Plan. Washington, DC: Executive Office of the President, 2013. https://perma.cc/JH8K-583F.

Thomas, Howard. "Some Non-Essential Aerosol Propellant Uses Finally Banned." *Natural Resources Journal* 19, no. 1 (1979): 217–20.

Thomas, Lee. "Global Challenges at EPA." *EPA Journal* 12, no. 10 (1986).

———. Interview by Jody Freeman, March 28, 2019.

Tirpak, Dennis. Interview by Jody Freeman, March 12, 2019.

Tobin, Mitch. "6 Things I Learned by Studying Public Opinion on Water." Waterpolls.org, March 24, 2017. https://waterpolls.org/public-opinion-on-water/.

Toman, Michael A., Richard D. Morgenstern, and John W. Anderson. "The Economics of 'When' Flexibility in the Design of Greenhouse Gas Abatement Policies." Washington, DC: Resources for the Future, 1999. https://perma.cc/6A9G-3SC3.

Transportation Research Board, and National Research Council. *Overcoming Barriers to Deployment of Plug-in Electric Vehicles*. Washington, DC: The National Academies Press, 2015. https://doi.org/10.17226/21725.

Trudeau, Gary. *Morale at EPA, Doonesbury*. January 28, 1982. Cartoon.

Tugend, Alina. "Teflon Is Great for Politicians, But Is It Safe for Regular People." *New York Times*, October 14, 2006. https://www.nytimes.com/2006/10/14/business/teflon-is-great-for-politicians-but-is-it-safe-for-regular-people.html.

Tyson, Ben. "An Empirical Analysis of Sue-and-Settle in Environmental Litigation." *Virginia Law Review* 100 (2014): 1545–1601.

Umshler, Sue E. "When Arsenic Is Safer in Your Cup of Tea Than in Your Local Water Treatment Plant." *Natural Resources Journal* 39, no. 3 (Summer 1999).

Ungeheuer, Friedel. "A Stockholm Notebook." *Time*, June 26, 1972.

Union of Concerned Scientists. *Scientific Integrity in Policymaking: An Investigation into the Bush Administration's Misuse of Science*. Cambridge, MA: UCS, 2004.

United Nations. *Globally Harmonized System of Classification and Labelling of Chemicals (GHS)*. 2nd revised. Geneva: UN, 2007.

———. "Rio Declaration on Environment and Development." In *Report of the United Nations Conference on Environment and Development, Rio de Janeiro, June 3-14, 1992*. New York: UN, 1992.

United Nations Environment Programme. "Report of the Twenty-Eighth Meeting of the Parties to the Montreal Protocol on Substances That Deplete the Ozone Layer." Geneva: UNEP, November 15, 2016.

United States Centers for Disease Control. "Zika Virus: Potential Range in the US." CDC.gov, n.d. Accessed April 29, 2020.

United States Commission on Civil Rights. "Not in My Backyard: Executive Order 12,898 and Title VI as Tools for Achieving Environmental Justice." Washington, DC: USCCR, October 2003. https://www.usccr.gov/pubs/envjust/ej0104.pdf.

United States Congressional Research Service. "Ethylene Dibromide (EDB)." Washington, DC: CRS, January 31, 1985. everycrsreport.com.

———. "The Information Quality Act: OMB's Guidance and Initial Implementation." Washington, DC: CRS, August 19, 2004. https://fas.org/sgp/crs/RL32532.pdf.

———. "US Environmental Protection Agency FY2019 Appropriations." Washington, DC: CRS, March 28, 2019.

United States Council on Environmental Quality. "Toxic Substances." Washington, DC: CEQ, April 1971.

United States Department of Justice. "Attorney General Loretta E. Lynch Delivers Remarks at Press Conference Announcing Settlement with BP to Resolve Civil

Claims Over Deepwater Horizon Oil Spill." October 5, 2015. https://www.justice.gov/opa/speech/attorney-general-loretta-e-lynch-delivers-remarks-press-conference-announcing-settlement.

United States Energy Information Administration. "The US Leads Global Petroleum and Natural Gas Production with Record Growth in 2018." EIA.gov, August 20, 2019. https://www.eia.gov/todayinenergy/detail.php?id=40973.

United States Environmental Protection Agency. "Alvin L. Alm: Oral History Interview." EPA 202-K-94-005. EPA.gov, 1993. https://archive.epa.gov/epa/aboutepa/alvin-l-alm-oral-history-interview.html.

———. "Chesapeake Bay Total Maximum Daily Load for Nitrogen, Phosphorus and Sediment." Washington, DC: EPA, December 29, 2010. https://www.epa.gov/sites/production/files/2014-12/documents/cbay_final_tmdl_exec_sum_section_1_through_3_final_0.pdf.

———. "Definition of 'Waters of the United States': Rule Status and Litigation Update." EPA.gov, December 23, 2019. https://www.epa.gov/wotus-rule/definition-waters-united-states-rule-status-and-litigation-update.

———. "Douglas M. Costle: Oral History Interview." EPA 202-K-01-002. EPA.gov, August 1996. https://archive.epa.gov/epa/aboutepa/douglas-m-costle-oral-history-interview.html.

———. "EPA and 3M Announce Phase Out of PFOS." EPA.gov, May 16, 2000. https://yosemite.epa.gov/opa/admpress.nsf/0/33aa946e6cb11f35852568e1005246b4?opendocument.

———. "EPA and Army Deliver on President Trump's Promise to Issue the Navigable Waters Protection Rule—A New Definition of WOTUS." EPA.gov, January 23, 2020.

———. "EPA Bans General Use of DDT." *EPA*. June 14, 1972.

———. "EPA Takes Another Step to Advance President Trump's America First Strategy, Proposes Repeal of 'Clean Power Plan.'" EPA.gov, October 10, 2017.

———. "Identifying and Assessing Technical Bases for Stack Height for the EPA Regulatory Analysis." Preliminary Report. Washington, DC: EPA, September 1979.

———. "New Law to Control Hazardous Wastes, End Open Dumping, Promote Conservation of Resources." EPA.gov, December 13, 1976. https://archive.epa.gov/epa/aboutepa/new-law-control-hazardous-wastes-end-open-dumping-promote-conservation-resources.html.

———. "Questions and Answers about the BP Oil Spill in the Gulf Coast." EPA.gov, February 20, 2016. https://archive.epa.gov/emergency/bpspill/web/html/qanda.html#role.

———. "Report on Hazardous Waste Damage Inventory." Washington, DC: EPA, September 5, 1975.

———. "Russell E. Train: Oral History Interview." EPA 202-K-93-001. EPA.gov, May 5, 1992. https://archive.epa.gov/epa/aboutepa/russell-e-train-oral-history-interview.html.

———. "State Activities in Solid Waste Management: Reports to the Federal-State Solid Waste Management Conference, October 9-11, 1973, Kansas City, Missouri."

Washington, DC: EPA, 1974. https://nepis.epa.gov/Exe/ZyPDF.cgi/9101SOU0.PDF?Dockey=9101SOU0.PDF.

———. "Strategies to Achieve Full Lead Service Line Replacement." Washington, DC: EPA, October 2019.

———. "Summary of the Oil Pollution Act." EPA.gov, February 13, 2020. https://www.epa.gov/laws-regulations/summary-oil-pollution-act.

———. "Train Sees New Toxic Substances Law as 'Preventive Medicine.'" EPA.gov, October 21, 1976. www.epa.gov/history/topics/tsca/03.htm.

———. "William D. Ruckelshaus: Oral History Interview." EPA 202-K-92-0003. EPA.gov, January 1993. https://archive.epa.gov/epa/aboutepa/william-d-ruckelshaus-oral-history-interview.html.

———. "William K. Reilly: Oral History Interview." EPA 202-K-95-002. EPA.gov, September 1995.

United States Environmental Protection Agency, and Douglas M. Costle. "Statement on Hazardous Waste Management." Washington, DC: EPA, October 12, 1979.

United States Environmental Protection Agency, Office of Air and Radiation. "About the National Vehicle and Fuel Emissions Laboratory (NVFEL)." EPA.gov, August 7, 2019. https://perma.cc/26VQ-VJXM.

———. "Acid Rain Program 2004 Progress Report." EPA OAR, October 2005. https://www.epa.gov/sites/production/files/2015-08/documents/2004report.pdf.

———. "Final Technical Support Document: Nonconformance Penalties for 2004 Highway Heavy Duty Diesel Engines." Washington, DC: EPA OAR, August 2002.

———. "Mid-Term of Greenhouse Gas Emissions Standards for Model Year 2022-2025 Light-Duty Vehicles." Washington, DC: EPA OAR, April 2018.

———. "Nonattainment Areas for Criteria Pollutants (Green Book)." Collections and Lists. EPA.gov, April 14, 2016. https://www.epa.gov/green-book.

———. "Our Nation's Air: Status and Trends Through 2018." EPA.gov. Accessed April 21, 2020. https://gispub.epa.gov/air/trendsreport/2019/#welcome.

———. "Power Sector Programs Progress Report." Washington, DC: EPA OAR, 2018. https://www3.epa.gov/airmarkets/progress/reports/.

———. "Regulatory Impact Analyses for the Particulate Matter and Ozone National Ambient Air Quality Standards and Proposed Regional Haze Rule." Research Triangle Park, NC: EPA OAR, 1997.

———. "Regulatory Impact Analysis: Protection of Stratospheric Ozone." Washington, DC: EPA OAR, 1987.

———. "Risk and Technology Review of the National Emissions Standards for Hazardous Air Pollutants." Collections and Lists. EPA, December 15, 2016. https://www.epa.gov/stationary-sources-air-pollution/risk-and-technology-review-national-emissions-standards-hazardous.

———. "Summary Nonattainment Area Population Exposure Report (Green Book)." EPA.gov, March 31, 2020. https://www3.epa.gov/airquality/greenbook/popexp.html.

———. "The Benefits and Costs of the Clean Air Act, 1970 to 1990." Reports and Assessments. Washington, DC: EPA OAR, October 1, 1997. https://www.epa.gov/environmental-economics/benefits-and-costs-clean-air-act-1970-1990-1997.

———. "The Benefits and Costs of the Clean Air Act, 1990 to 2010." Reports and Assessments. Washington DC: EPA OAR, November 1999. https://www.epa.gov/clean-air-act-overview/benefits-and-costs-clean-air-act-1990-2010-first-prospective-study.

———. "The Benefits and Costs of the Clean Air Act from 1990 to 2020." Reports and Assessments. Washington DC: EPA OAR, April 2011. https://www.epa.gov/clean-air-act-overview/benefits-and-costs-clean-air-act-1990-2020-report-documents-and-graphics.

———. "US DOT and EPA Put Safety and American Families First with Final Rule on Fuel Economy Standards." EPA.gov, March 31, 2020.

———. "White Paper for Streamlined Development of Part 70 Permit Applications." Washington, DC: EPA OAR, July 10, 1995. https://www.epa.gov/title-v-operating-permits/white-paper-streamlined-development-part-70-permit-applications.

United States Environmental Protection Agency, Office of Chemical Safety and Pollution Prevention. "Basic Information on PFAS." EPA.gov. Accessed March 16, 2020. https://www.epa.gov/pfas/basic-information-pfas.

———. "Chemical Hazard Data Availability Study: What Do We Really Know about the Safety of High Production Volume Chemicals?" Washington, DC: EPA OCSPP, April 1998.

———. "Cleaner Technologies Substitutes Assessment: A Methodology and Resources Guide." Washington, DC: EPA OCSPP, 1996.

———. "Current and Previously Registered Section 3 Plant-Incorporated Protectant (PIP) Registrations." EPA.gov, October 24, 2018. https://www.epa.gov/ingredients-used-pesticide-products/current-and-previously-registered-section-3-plant-incorporated.

———. "EPA Actions to Protect the Public from Exposure to Asbestos." EPA.gov, n.d. Accessed April 8, 2020.

———. "EPA Releases First Major Update to Chemicals List in 40 Years." EPA.gov, 2019.

———. "Fact Sheet: 2010/2015 PFOA Stewardship Program." EPA.gov. Accessed April 8, 2020. https://www.epa.gov/assessing-and-managing-chemicals-under-tsca/fact-sheet-20102015-pfoa-stewardship-program#what.

———. "Registration Review Process." EPA.gov. Accessed April 30, 2020. https://www.epa.gov/pesticide-reevaluation/registration-review-process.

———. "Re-Registration and Other Review Programs Predating Pesticide Registration Review." EPA.gov. Accessed April 30, 2020. https://www.epa.gov/pesticide-reevaluation/re-registration-and-other-review-programs-predating-pesticide-registration.

———. "Statistics for the New Chemicals Review Program under TSCA." EPA.gov, n.d. Accessed April 30, 2020.

———. "TSCA Chemical Substance Inventory." EPA.gov, n.d. Accessed March 15, 2020.

United States Environmental Protection Agency, Office of Inspector General. "EPA Needs to Consistently Implement the Intent of the Executive Order on Environmental Justice." Washington, DC: EPA OIG, March 1, 2004.

———. "Management Alert: Drinking Water Contamination in Flint, Michigan, Demonstrates a Need to Clarify EPA Authority to Issue Emergency Orders to Protect Public Health." Washington, DC: EPA OIG, October 20, 2016.
———. "Management Weaknesses Delayed Response to Flint Water Crisis." Washington, DC: EPA OIG, July 19, 2018.
———. "Report: Efforts to Manage Backlog of Water Discharge Permits Need to Be Accompanied by Greater Program Integration." Washington, DC: EPA OIG, June 13, 2005.
United States Environmental Protection Agency, Office of International and Tribal Affairs. "Minamata Convention on Mercury." EPA.gov, March 11, 2019.
United States Environmental Protection Agency, Office of Land and Emergency Management. "Advancing Sustainable Materials Management: 2015 Fact Sheet." Washington, DC: EPA OLEM, July 2018. https://www.epa.gov/sites/production/files/2018-07/documents/2015_smm_msw_factsheet_07242018_fnl_508_002.pdf.
———. "Authorization Status of All Resource Conservation and Recovery Act (RCRA) and Hazardous and Solid Waste Amendments (HWSA) Rules." EPA.gov, March 31, 2019. https://www.epa.gov/rcra/authorization-status-all-resource-conservation-and-recovery-act-rcra-and-hazardous-and-solid.
———. "Interim Recommendations for Addressing Groundwater Contaminated with PFOA and PFOS." EPA.gov, December 19, 2019.
———. "Measuring Progress at Resource Conservation and Recovery Act (RCRA) Corrective Action Facilities." Overviews and Factsheets. EPA.gov, April 18, 2016. https://www.epa.gov/hw/measuring-progress-resource-conservation-and-recovery-act-rcra-corrective-action-facilities.
———. "Population Surrounding 1,836 Superfund Remedial Sites." EPA.gov, October 2017.
———. "Quantity of RCRA Hazardous Waste Generated and Managed." In *Report on the Environment: Hazardous Waste*. Washington, DC: EPA OLEM, 2019. https://cfpub.epa.gov/roe/indicator.cfm?i=54.
———. "RCRA Online." Collections and Lists. EPA.gov. Accessed April 17, 2020. https://www.epa.gov/rcra.
———. "RCRA's Critical Mission & the Path Forward." Washington, DC: EPA OLEM, June 2014.
———. "Resource Conservation and Recovery Act (RCRA) Orientation Manual." Washington, DC: EPA OLEM, October 2014. https://www.epa.gov/hwgenerators/resource-conservation-and-recovery-act-rcra-orientation-manual.
———. "Superfund: National Priorities List (NPL)." EPA.gov. Accessed February 7, 2020. https://www.epa.gov/superfund/superfund-national-priorities-list-npl.
———. "Superfund Remedial Annual Accomplishments." EPA.gov, July 9, 2019.
———. "UST Program Facts: Data About the Underground Storage Tank (UST) Program." EPA.gov, December 2019. https://www.epa.gov/sites/production/files/2017-11/documents/ust-program-facts.pdf.
United States Environmental Protection Agency, Office of Policy. "Economic Incentives: Options for Environmental Protection." Washington, DC: EPA OP, March 1991.

———. "Environmental Equity: Reducing Risks for All Communities, Volumes 1 & 2." Washington, DC: EPA OP, 1992.

———. "Environmental Investments: The Cost of a Clean Environment." Washington, DC: EPA OP, November 1990. https://www.epa.gov/sites/production/files/2017-09/documents/ee-0294b_all.pdf.

———. "EPA's Use of Benefit-Cost Analysis:1981-1986." Washington, DC: EPA OP, 2018.

———. "Guidelines for Preparing Economic Analyses." Washington, DC: EPA OP, May 2014. https://www.epa.gov/sites/production/files/2017-08/documents/ee-0568-50.pdf.

———. "Policy Options for Stabilizing Global Climate: Report to Congress." Washington, DC: EPA OP, 1990.

———. "The Potential Effects of Global Climate Change on the United States: Report to Congress." Washington, DC: EPA OP, 1989.

———. "Unfinished Business: A Comparative Assessment of Environmental Problems." Overview Report. Washington, DC: EPA OP, February 1987. https://nepis.epa.gov/Exe/ZyPDF.cgi/2001635G.PDF?Dockey=2001635G.PDF.

United States Environmental Protection Agency, Office of Research and Development. "Biofuels and the Environment: The Second Triennial Report to Congress." Washington, DC: EPA ORD, June 29, 2018. https://cfpub.epa.gov/si/si_public_record_report.cfm?Lab=IO&dirEntryId=341491.

———. "CHESS Briefing." Washington, DC: EPA ORD, November 20, 1979.

———. "Exposure Assessment Tools by Tiers and Types—Aggregate and Cumulative." EPA.gov, n.d. Accessed April 8, 2020.

———. "Hydraulic Fracturing for Oil and Gas: Impacts from the Hydraulic Fracturing Water Cycle on Drinking Water Resources in the United States." Washington, DC: EPA ORD, 2016.

———. "Ozone (O3) Standards: Integrated Science Assessments from Review Completed in 2015." EPA.gov. Accessed March 10, 2020. https://www.epa.gov/naaqs/ozone-o3-standards-integrated-science-assessments-review-completed-2015.

———. "Strengthening Transparency in Regulatory Science." EPA.gov. Accessed April 29, 2020. https://www.epa.gov/osa/strengthening-transparency-regulatory-science.

United States Environmental Protection Agency, Office of Solid Waste and Emergency Response. "Criteria for Solid Waste Disposal Facilities: A Guide for Owners/Operators." Solid Waste Management. Washington, DC: EPA OSWER, March 1993.

———. "Green Lights Program: The First Year." Washington, DC: EPA OSWER, 1992.

———. "Guide for Industrial Waste Management." Washington, DC: EPA OSWER, February 2003. https://www.epa.gov/sites/production/files/2016-03/documents/industrial-waste-guide.pdf.

———. "History of Superfund." Washington, DC: EPA OSWER, November 1990.

———. "Introducing…The Green Lights Program." Washington, DC: EPA OSWER, December 1993.

———. "Report to Congress: Disposal of Hazardous Wastes." Solid Waste Management. Washington, DC: EPA OSWER, June 30, 1973. https://nepis.epa.gov/Exe/ZyPDF.cgi/10003IEJ.PDF?Dockey=10003IEJ.PDF.

———. "Report to Congress: Solid Waste Disposal in the United States." Solid Waste Management. Washington, DC: EPA OSWER, October 1988.

———. "The Solid Waste Dilemma: An Agenda for Action." Final Report. EPA OSWER, February 1989. https://nepis.epa.gov/Exe/ZyPDF.cgi/10001990.PDF?Dockey=10001990.PDF.

———. "Underground Storage Tank Program: 25 Years of Protecting Our Land and Water." Washington, DC: EPA OSWER, March 2009. https://www.epa.gov/sites/production/files/2014-03/documents/25annrpt-screen.pdf.

United States Environmental Protection Agency, Office of Solid Waste and Emergency Response, and Ralph J. Black. "State Activities in Solid Waste Management, 1974." Solid Waste Management. Washington, DC: EPA OSWER, June 1975. https://nepis.EPA.gov/EPA/html/DLwait.htm?url=/Exe/ZyPDF.cgi/2000Z9UH.PDF?Dockey=2000Z9UH.PDF.

United States Environmental Protection Agency, Office of the Administrator. "1996 Environmental Justice Implementation Plan." Washington, DC: EPA AO, 1996.

———. "The EPA's Environmental Justice Strategy." Washington, DC: EPA AO, 1995.

———. "Plan EJ 2014." Washington, DC: EPA AO, September 2011.

United States Environmental Protection Agency, Office of the Chief Financial Officer. "EPA's Budget and Spending." EPA.gov, n.d. https://www.epa.gov/planandbudget/budget.

———. "FY2018 EPA Budget in Brief." Washington, DC: EPA OCFO, May 2017.

———. "FY2019 EPA Budget in Brief." Washington, DC: EPA OCFO, February 2018. https://www.epa.gov/sites/production/files/2018-02/documents/fy-2019-epa-bib.pdf.

United States Environmental Protection Agency, Office of Transportation and Air Quality. "Final Determination on the Appropriateness of the Model Year 2022-2025 Light-Duty Vehicle Greenhouse Gas Emissions Standards under the Midterm Evaluation." Washington, DC: EPA OTAQ, January 2017.

———. "Renewable Fuel Standard Program (RFS2) Regulatory Impact Analysis." Washington, DC: EPA OTAQ, February 2010. https://www.epa.gov/renewable-fuel-standard-program/renewable-fuel-standard-rfs2-final-rule-additional-resources.

United States Environmental Protection Agency, Office of Water. "Addressing Nutrient Pollution in the Chesapeake Bay." EPA.gov, July 18, 2019. https://www.epa.gov/nutrient-policy-data/addressing-nutrient-pollution-chesapeake-bay.

———. "Analyze Trends: Drinking Water Dashboard." EPA.gov. Accessed March 16, 2020. https://echo.epa.gov/trends/comparative-maps-dashboards/drinking-water-dashboard?yearview=CY&view=activity&criteria=basic&state=National.

———. "Drinking Water Infrastructure Needs Survey and Assessment: Sixth Report to Congress." Washington, DC: EPA OW, March 2018. https://www.epa.gov/dwsrf/epas-6th-drinking-water-infrastructure-needs-survey-and-assessment.

———. "Economic Analysis for the Final Section 316(b) Existing Facilities Rule." Washington, DC: EPA OW, 2014.

———. "EPA Announces Proposed Decision to Regulate PFOA and PFOS in Drinking Water." EPA.gov, February 20, 2020.

———. "Handbook of Procedures: Construction Grant Program for Municipal Treatment Works." Washington, DC: EPA OW, 1984.

———. "Industrial Effluent Guidelines." EPA.gov, April 17, 2020. https://www.epa.gov/eg/industrial-effluent-guidelines.

———. "Interim Clean Water Act Settlement Penalty Policy." Washington, DC: EPA OW, 1985.

———. "A National Evaluation of the Clean Water Act Section 319 Program." Washington, DC: EPA OW, November 2011.

———. "National Primary Drinking Water Regulations." EPA.gov. Accessed February 7, 2020. https://www.epa.gov/ground-water-and-drinking-water/national-primary-drinking-water-regulations#Radionuclides.

———. "National Rivers and Streams Assessment 2008-2009." Washington, DC: EPA OW, March 2016.

———. "NPDES Permits Around the Nation." EPA.gov, December 30, 2019. https://www.epa.gov/npdes-permits.

———. "NPDES State Program Information." EPA.gov, December 2, 2019. https://www.epa.gov/npdes/npdes-state-program-information.

———. "Overview of National Estuary Program." EPA.gov, October 26, 2018. https://www.epa.gov/nep/overview-national-estuary-program.

———. "Providing Safe Drinking Water in America: National Public Water Systems Compliance Report." EPA.gov. Accessed April 9, 2020. https://www.epa.gov/compliance/providing-safe-drinking-water-america-national-public-water-systems-compliance-report.

———. "Surface Water Treatment Rules." EPA.gov. Accessed March 16, 2020. https://www.epa.gov/dwreginfo/surface-water-treatment-rules.

———. "Water Quality Assessment and TMDL Information." EPA.gov. Accessed March 16, 2020. https://ofmpub.epa.gov/waters10/attains_index.home.

———. "Water Quality Trading Policy." Washington, DC: EPA OW, January 13, 2003.

———. "Water Quality Trading Toolkit for Permit Writers." Washington, DC: EPA OW, August 2007.

United States Environmental Protection Agency, Science Advisory Board. "Commentary on the Proposed Rule Defining the Scope of Waters Federally Regulated Under the Clean Water Act." Washington, DC: EPA SAB, February 27, 2020.

———. "Reducing Risk: Setting Priorities and Strategies for Environmental Protection." Washington, DC: EPA SAB, 1990.

———. "Review of EPA's Assessment of the Risks of Stratospheric Modification." Washington, DC: EPA SAB, March 1987.

———. "Science Advisory Board (SAB) Consideration of the Scientific and Technical Basis of the EPA's Proposed Rule Titled The Safer Affordable Fuel-Efficient

(SAFE) Vehicles Rule 2021-2026 Passenger Cars and Light Trucks." Washington, DC: EPA SAB, February 27, 2020.
United States General Accounting Office. "Chemical Regulation: Approaches in the United States, Canada, and the European Union." Washington, DC: GAO, 2005.
———. "Chemical Regulation: Options Exist to Improve EPA's Ability to Assess Health Risks and Manage Its Chemical Review Program." Washington, DC: GAO, June 2005.
———. "Chemical Regulation: Options for Enhancing the Effectiveness of the Toxic Substances Control Act." Washington, DC: GAO, 2009.
———. "EPA's Preliminary Estimates of Future Hazardous Waste Cleanup Costs Are Uncertain." Washington, DC: GAO, May 1984.
———. "EPA's Progress in Implementing the Superfund Program." Washington, DC: GAO, June 2, 1982. https://www.gao.gov/assets/140/137792.pdf.
———. "Financial Audit: EPA's Financial Statements for Fiscal Years 1988 and 1987." Report to Congress. Washington, DC: GAO, 1990.
———. "Pesticides: EPA's Formidable Task to Assess and Regulate Their Risks." Washington, DC: GAO, April 18, 1986.
———. "Pesticides: Thirty Years Since Silent Spring-Many Long-Standing Concerns Remain." Washington, DC: GAO, 1992.
———. "Rulemaking: OMB's Role in Reviews of Agencies' Draft Rules and the Transparency of Those Reviews." Washington, DC: GAO, 2003.
———. "Rulemaking: OMB's Role in Reviews of Agencies' Draft Rules and the Transparency of Those Reviews." Washington, DC: GAO, 2003.
———. "Solid Waste Disposal Practices: Open Dumps Not Identified, States Face Funding Problems: Report to the Honorable Albert Gore, Jr., House of Representatives." Washington, DC: GAO, July 23, 1981. https://www.gao.gov/assets/140/134279.pdf.
———. "Solid Waste: State and Federal Efforts to Manage Nonhazardous Waste." Washington, DC: GAO, March 6, 1995. https://www.gao.gov/products/153652.
———. "Toxic Substances Control Act: Preliminary Observations on Legislative Changes to Make TSCA More Effective." Washington, DC: GAO, July 1994.
———. "Toxic Substances Control Act: Preliminary Observations on Legislative Changes to Make TSCA More Effective." Washington, DC: GAO, July 1994.
United States Government Accountability Office. "Air Emissions and Electricity Generation at U.S. Power Plants." Washington, DC: GAO, April 18, 2012.
———. "Clean Water Act: Changes Needed If Key EPA Program Is to Help Fulfill the Nation's Water Quality Goals." Washington, DC: GAO, January 13, 2014.
———. "Environmental Litigation: Impact of Deadline Suits on EPA's Rulemaking Is Limited." Washington, DC: GAO, December 15, 2014. https://www.gao.gov/products/GAO-15-34.
———. "Environmental Litigation: Impact of Deadline Suits on EPA's Rulemaking Is Limited." Washington, DC: GAO, December 15, 2014. https://www.gao.gov/products/GAO-15-34.
———. "EPA Advisory Committees: Improvements Needed for the Member Appointment Process." Washington, DC: GAO, July 2019. https://www.gao.gov/assets/710/700171.pdf.

———. "EPA Advisory Committees: Improvements Needed for the Member Appointment Process." Washington, DC: GAO, July 8, 2019.

———. "EPA Should Devote More Attention to Environmental Justice When Developing Clean Air Rules." Washington, DC: GAO, July 2005.

———. "Global Warming: Information on the Results of Four of EPA's Voluntary Climate Change Programs." Washington, DC: GAO, 1997.

———. "Hazardous Waste Cleanup: Numbers of Contaminated Federal Sites, Estimated Costs, and EPA's Oversight Role." Washington, DC: GAO, 2015. https://www.gao.gov/assets/680/672464.pdf.

———. "Nonpoint Source Pollution: Greater Oversight and Additional Data Needed for Key EPA Water Program." Washington, DC: GAO, July 2, 2012.

———. "Superfund: Funding and Reported Costs of Enforcement and Administration Activities." Washington, DC: GAO, July 2008.

United States Interagency Working Group on Social Cost of Greenhouse Gases. "Addendum to the Technical Support Document for the Social Cost of Carbon: Application of the Methodology to Estimate the Social Cost of Methane and the Social Cost of Nitrous Oxide." Washington, DC: Government Printing Office, August 2016. https://www.epa.gov/sites/production/files/2016-12/documents/addendum_to_sc-ghg_tsd_august_2016.pdf.

United States Office of Management and Budget. "2017 Draft Report to Congress on the Benefits and Costs of Federal Regulations and Agency Compliance with the Unfunded Mandates Reform Act." Washington, DC: OMB, 2017. https://www.whitehouse.gov/wp-content/uploads/2017/12/draft_2017_cost_benefit_report.pdf.

———. "Chapter I: The Role of Economic Analysis in Regulatory Reform." In *Report to Congress on the Costs and Benefits of Federal Regulation*. Washington, DC: OMB, 1997. https://obamawhitehouse.archives.gov/omb/inforeg_chap1.

———. "Circular A-4." Washington, DC: OMB, September 17, 2003. https://obamawhitehouse.archives.gov/omb/circulars_a004_a-4/.

United States Office of Technology Assessment. "Superfund Strategy." Washington, DC: OTA, April 1985.

———. "Technologies and Management Strategies for Hazardous Waste Control." Washington, DC: US Government Printing Office, March 1983. https://govinfo.library.unt.edu/ota/Ota_4/DATA/1983/8323.PDF.

University of Maryland Center for Environmental Science. "Overall Chesapeake Bay Health Improving for the First Time." UMCES.edu, June 15, 2018. https://www.umces.edu/news/overall-chesapeake-bay-health-improving-first-time.

University of Michigan. "The Dirty Dozen." Accessed February 7, 2020. https://michignanintheworld.history.lsa.umich.edu/environmentalism/exhibits/show/main_exhibit/earthday/environmental-action-moving-fo/the-dirty-dozen.

"Use of Scrubbers With Coal Boilers Pushed by Carter." *The New York Times*, May 31, 1977. https://www.nytimes.com/1977/05/31/archives/use-of-scrubbers-with-coal-boilers-pushed-by-carter.html.

Vajjhala, Shalini P., Sarah Szambelan, and Amanda Van Epp. "Integrating EJ into Federal Policies and Programs: Examining the Role of Regulatory Impact Analyses and Environmental Impact Statements." Washington, DC: Resources for the Future, 2008.

Vig, Norman J. "Presidential Leadership and the Environment: From Reagan and Bush to Clinton." In *Environmental Policy in the 1990s*, edited by Norman J. Vig and Michael E. Kraft, 2nd ed. Washington, DC: CQ Press, 1994.

Vogel, David. *California Greenin': How the Golden State Became an Environmental Leader*. Princeton, NJ: Princeton University Press, 2018. https://press.princeton.edu/books/hardcover/9780691179551/california-greenin.

———. *The Politics of Precaution: Regulating Health, Safety, and Environmental Risks in Europe and the United States*. Princeton, NJ: Princeton University Press, 2012. https://press.princeton.edu/books/hardcover/9780691124162/the-politics-of-precaution.

Voyles, Travis A. "Clearing Up Perceived Problems with the Sue-and-Settle Issue in Environmental Litigation." *Journal of Land Use & Environmental Law* 31 (2016): 287–312.

Walker, Jack L. "Setting the Agenda in the U.S. Senate: A Theory of Problem Selection." *British Journal of Political Science* 7 (1977): 423–45.

Walsh, Michael P. "Automobile Emissions." In *The Reality of Precaution: Comparing Risk Regulation in the United States and Europe*, edited by Jonathan B. Wiener, Michael D. Rogers, James K. Hammit, and Peter H. Sand. Washington, DC: Resources for the Future Press, 2011.

Wang, Yan, Itai Kloog, Brent A. Coull, Anna Kosheleva, Antonella Zanobetti, and Joel D. Schwartz. "Estimating Causal Effects of Long-Term PM2.5 Exposure on Mortality in New Jersey." *Environmental Health Perspectives* 124, no. 8 (2016): 1182–88.

Wargo, John. *Our Children's Toxic Legacy: How Science and Law Fail to Protect Us from Pesticide*. New Haven, CT: Yale University Press, 1996.

Wasserman, Lee. "Four Ways to Kill a Climate Bill." *New York Times*, July 25, 2010. https://perma.cc/HZ5K-Y64M.

Waterman, Richard W. "The Administrative Presidency, Unilateral Power, and the Unitary Executive Theory." *Presidential Studies Quarterly* 39, no. 1 (2009): 5–9.

Wayland, Susan, and Penelope Fenner-Crisp. "Reducing Pesticide Risks: A Half Century of Progress." Washington, DC: EPA Alumni Association, March 1, 2016.

Weingast, Barry, and Mark Moran. "Bureaucratic Discretion or Congressional Control?" *Journal of Political Economy* 91 (1983): 765–800.

Weisman, Steven R. "President Names Ruckelshaus Head of Troubled EPA." *New York Times*, March 22, 1983.

Weisskopf, Michael. "Auto-Pollution Debate Has Ring of the Past." *Washington Post*, March 26, 1990. https://www.washingtonpost.com/archive/politics/1990/03/26/auto-pollution-debate-has-ring-of-the-past/d1650ba3-2896-44fa-ac1b-4e28aca78674/.

———. "Bush Was Aloof in Warming Debate." *Washington Post*, October 31, 1992. https://perma.cc/H483-UPA7.

Whitaker, John C. *Striking a Balance: Environment and Natural Resources Policy in the Nixon-Ford Years*. Washington, DC: American Enterprise Institute for Public Policy Research, 1977.

Whitford, Andrew B. "The Structures of Interest Coalitions: Evidence from Environmental Litigation." *Business and Politics* 5, no. 1 (2003): 45–64.

Whitman, Christine Todd. "Address at the G8 Environmental Ministerial Meeting with Representatives of International Non-Governmental Organizations." Trieste, Italy, March 2, 2001. https://perma.cc/E83S-H59A.

———. *It's My Party Too: The Battle for the Heart of the GOP and America.* London: Penguin Books, 2006.

———. "Memorandum to the President of the United States on G-8 Meeting in Trieste," March 6, 2001. https://perma.cc/YCX3-32PQ.

"Whole Earth Conference." *Time*, May 22, 1972.

"Why Detroit Failed to Sway EPA." *Business Week*, May 20, 1972.

Wiener, Jonathan B. "On the Political Economy of Global Environmental Regulation." *Georgetown Law Journal* 87 (1999): 749–94.

———. "Protecting the Global Environment." In *Risk vs. Risk: Tradeoffs in Protecting Health and the Environment*, edited by John D. Graham and Jonathan B. Wiener. Cambridge, MA: Harvard University Press, 1997.

Wiener, Jonathan B., and Daniel L. Ribeiro. "Environmental Regulation Going Retro: Learning Foresight from Hindsight." *Journal of Land Use & Environmental Law* 32 (2016): 1–72.

Wiener, Jonathan B., and Barak D. Richman. "Mechanism Choice." In *Public Choice and Public Law*, edited by Daniel Farber and Anne Joseph O'Connell. Northampton, MA: Edward Elgar Publishing, 2010.

Williams, Dennis C. "The Guardian: EPA's Formative Years, 1970-1973." Washington, DC: EPA, 1993.

Williams, Douglas. "Catalytic Converter Suit Pits Toyota Against GM." *Washington Post*, December 4, 1977.

Wilson, James Q. "The Politics of Regulation." In *The Politics of Regulation*, edited by James Q. Wilson, 1st ed. New York: Basic Books, 1980.

Wilson, James Q., and John DiIulio, eds. *American Government: Institutions and Policies*. 11th ed. Boston: Houghton Mifflin, 2008.

Wilson, Woodrow. "The Study of Administration." *Political Science Quarterly* 2 (June 1887): 197–222.

Wittenberg, Ariel. "Democrats Vow to Battle Trump's WOTUS Rule." *E&E News*, January 24, 2020. https://www.eenews.net/eedaily/stories/1062161147.

———. "Did a Burning River Really Fuel Landmark Law's Passage?" *E&E News*, June 18, 2019.

———. "Trump's WOTUS: Clear as Mud, Scientists Say." *E&E News*, February 18, 2019. https://www.eenews.net/stories/1060121251.

———. "What Does 'Waters of the US' Mean? We Asked the Authors." *E&E News*, June 29, 2017. https://www.eenews.net/stories/1060056818.

Wood, Chris, Collin O'Mara, and Dale Hall. "Trump Weakens the Nation's Clean Water Efforts." *New York Times*, February 10, 2020. https://www.nytimes.com/2020/02/10/opinion/clean-water-act-trump.html.

Woods, Neal D. "Primacy Implementation of Environmental Policy in the US States." *Publius: The Journal of Federalism* 36, no. 2 (2005): 259–76.

World Health Organization. "Ambient Air Pollution: Health Impacts." WHO.int. Accessed April 14, 2020. http://www.who.int/airpollution/ambient/health-impacts/en/.

Yan, Holly. "The EPA Says Glyphosate, the Main Ingredient in Roundup, Doesn't Cause Cancer. Others Aren't So Sure." CNN.com, May 3, 2019.

Yandle, Bruce. "Bootleggers and Baptists in the Market for Regulation." In *The Political Economy of Government Regulation*, edited by Jason F. Shogren. Boston: Kluwer Academic Publisher, 1989.

Yardley, William. "John Hoffman, a Force in Energy Efficiency, Dies at 62." *New York Times*, October 16, 2012. https://perma.cc/HFR3-6LSR.

Zeger, Scott L., Francesca Dominici, Aidan McDermott, and Jonathan M. Samet. "Mortality in the Medicare Population and Chronic Exposure to Fine Particulate Air Pollution in Urban Centers (2000–2005)." *Environmental Health Perspectives* 116, no. 12 (2008): 1614–19.

Zoi, Cathy. Interview by Jody Freeman, September 30, 2019.

Index

About the Authors

A. James Barnes is the former Dean of the Paul O'Neill School of Public and Environmental Affairs at Indiana University where he teaches environmental law in the O'Neill School and in the Maurer School of Law. In 1970, he worked with William Ruckelshaus in the establishment of the EPA and served as Chief of Staff, later returning to the agency as its General Counsel (1983–1985) and Deputy Administrator (1985–1988).

Jonathan Z. Cannon, is Blaine T. Phillips Distinguished Professor of Environmental Law and director of the University of Virginia School of Law's Programs in Communities and the Environment (PLACE). He joined the faculty in 1998 from the EPA, where he served as General Counsel (1995–1998) and Assistant Administrator for Administration and Resources Management (1992–1995). Prior to his work with the EPA, he was in the private practice of environmental law.

Penelope A. Fenner-Crisp, in her twenty-two-year career at the EPA, served as Senior Science Advisor to the Director of the Office of Pesticide Programs (OPP), Director of the Health and Environmental Review Division (HERD) of OPPT, Acting Deputy Director and Deputy Director for OPP, Director of the Health Effects Division (HED) in OPP, Special Assistant to the Assistant Administrator for OPPT, Senior Toxicologist in the Health Effects Branch of the Office of Drinking Water (ODW), and as Manager of the Health Advisory Program for ODW. She also participated as an Expert on WHO IPCS working groups, served as the lead US Delegate to the OECD's Endocrine Disruptor Testing and Assessment (EDTA) workgroup, the EDTA's Mammalian Validation subgroup, and the Expert Consultation on Acute Toxicity.

Jody Freeman is the Archibald Cox Professor of Law at Harvard Law School and founding director of the Harvard Law School Environmental Law and Policy Program. She is a nationally renowned scholar of administrative law and environmental law, and a member of the American Academy of Arts and Sciences and the Council on Foreign Relations. She formerly served as Counselor for Energy and Climate Change in the White House from 2009 to 2010.

Bernard D. Goldstein is Dean Emeritus of the University of Pittsburgh Graduate School of Public Health. He served as Assistant Administrator for Research and Development of the EPA from 1983–1985. He has been president of the Society for Risk Analysis, and has chaired the NIH Toxicology Study Section, the EPA's Clean Air Scientific Advisory Committee, the National Board of Public Health Examiners, and the Research Committee of the Health Effects Institute.

John D. Graham is Dean Emeritus of the Paul H. O'Neill School of Public and Environmental Affairs at Indiana University. He is a specialist in risk analysis who worked closely with the EPA during his time as Administrator of the Office of Information and Regulatory Affairs (OMB) in the George W. Bush administration from 2001–2006. He was the founding director of the Center for Risk Analysis, Harvard School of Public Health (1985–2001). In 2020, Dr. Graham became chair of the EPA Science Advisory Board.

David M. Konisky is Professor at the Paul H. O'Neill School of Public and Environmental Affairs at Indiana University, where he is also a faculty affiliate at the Center for Research on Race and Ethnicity in Society, the Environmental Resilience Institute, and the Department of Political Science. His research focuses on US environmental and energy policy, with particular emphasis on regulation, federalism and state politics, public opinion, and environmental justice.

Gene Lucero chaired Latham & Watkins' global Environment, Land & Resources department before retiring in 2011 after twenty years at the firm. From 1982–1988, he served as the Director of the Office of Waste Programs Enforcement, shaping many EPA regulations and policies concerning environmental liability and directing federal enforcement of a number of laws, including the Resource Conservation and Recovery Act (RCRA); the Comprehensive Environmental Response, Compensation and Liability Act (CERCLA); the Emergency Planning and Community Right-to-Know Act (EPCRA); and the Underground Storage Tanks law. He testified regularly before Congress about federal and state environmental enforcement and played a key role in the congressional reauthorization of RCRA and Superfund.

Richard D. Morgenstern is a Senior Fellow at Resources for the Future (RFF) and a former senior executive at the EPA (1982–1995), where he directed the Agency's Policy Office for more than a decade and acted in various presidential appointee positions, including Deputy Administrator. He also served in both the US Department of State and the Congressional Budget Office.

Megan Mullin is an associate professor of environmental politics in the Nicholas School of the Environment at Duke University. She has secondary appointments in the Department of Political Science and the Sanford School of Public Policy. She is a scholar of American political institutions and behavior, focusing on environmental politics.

William F. Pedersen practices environmental and administrative law with an emphasis on air and water pollution control and control of greenhouse gasses. He served from 1972–1985 as EPA Deputy General Counsel and Associate General Counsel for Air—the government's chief Clean Air Act lawyer. He wrote the administrative procedures for issuing air, water, and solid waste permits that are still in use, and helped develop the early stages of EPA's market-based approaches to pollution control.

James E. Salzman is the Donald Bren Distinguished Professor of Environmental Law with joint appointments at the UCLA School of Law and at the Bren School of the Environment at UC Santa Barbara. In nine books and more than ninety articles and book chapters, his broad ranging scholarship has addressed topics spanning drinking water, trade and environment conflicts, policy instrument design, and the legal and institutional issues in creating markets for ecosystem services. He serves on the EPA's National Drinking Water Advisory Council.

Jonathan B. Wiener is the Perkins Professor of Law, Professor of Public Policy and Environmental Policy at Duke University, where he co-directs the Center on Risk. From 1989–1994, he served at the US Department of Justice and then at the White House Council of Economic Advisers (CEA), where he helped negotiate the UN Framework Convention on Climate Change (FCCC) (1992) and helped draft Executive Order 12,866 on regulatory review (1993). He was co-chair of the World Congress on Risk held in Sydney in 2012, after serving as President of the international Society for Risk Analysis (SRA) in 2008. He is also a University Fellow of Resources for the Future (RFF).

Marcia E. Williams is a Senior Vice President at Nathan Advisors. She was a charter member of EPA and formerly served in various senior EPA positions, including Director of the Office of Solid Waste and Deputy Assistant Administrator of the Office of Pesticides and Toxic Substances. She played a significant role in the development, implementation, and enforcement of federal regulatory programs. Since leaving EPA in 1988, she has provided expert consulting and has testified in a wide range of litigation, including insurance coverage cases, contract disputes, CERCLA cost recovery actions, toxic tort cases, federal and state civil and criminal enforcement matters, and NAFTA cases.

Terry F. Yosie is the former President and CEO of the World Environment Center (WEC). From 1978–1988, he served on the EPA's Science Advisory Board, acting as Director from 1981–1988. In this role, he advised EPA administrators and the US Congress on the scientific basis of public health and environmental decisions, and instituted policies and procedures to improve the technical basis for EPA-wide policy decisions. He has been a member of numerous scientific committees of the National Research Council/National Academy of Sciences, and has served in senior executive positions in the private sector, advised the UN Environment on global environmental issues, and is a frequent commentator on environmental sustainability issues. He is a monthly columnist at GreenBiz.com.